Practical XML for the W

Dave Addey

Chris Auld

Jon James

Oli Gauti Gudmundsson

Allan Kent

Jeff Rafter

Alex Shiell

Paul Spencer

Inigo Surguy

Published by glasshaus Ltd,
Arden House,
1102 Warwick Road,
Acocks Green,
Birmingham,
B27 6BH, UK

Printed in the United States
ISBN 1-904151-08-6

Practical XML for the Web

Acknowledgement of Election Markup Language Terms

Some example messages and schemas in Chapter 1 use the Election Markup Language (EML). These are published under the following terms:

glasshaus

web professional to web professional

Trademark Acknowledgements

Credits

Authors
Dave Addey
Chris Auld
Oli Gauti Gudmundsson
Jon James
Allan Kent
Jeff Rafter
Alex Shiell
Paul Spencer
Inigo Surguy

Technical Reviewers
Mike Brittain
Dave Browett
Mark Horner
Victoria Hudgson
Jon James
Will Kelly
Allan Kent
Chris Kenyeres
Dennis Kessler
Shefali Kulkarni
Mike McKay
Jeff Rafter
David Schultz
Michael Walston
Stephen Williams

Indexer
Bill Johncocks

Proofreader
Agnes Wiggers

Commissioning Editor
Amanda Kay

Lead Technical Editor
Chris Mills

Technical Editors
Amanda Kay
Matt Machell
Daniel Walker
Mark Waterhouse
Alessandro Ansa

Managing Editor
Liz Toy

Publisher
Viv Emery

Project Manager
Sophie Edwards

Production Coordinators
Rachel Taylor
Pip Wonson

Cover
Dawn Chellingworth

Brand Visionary
Bruce Lawson

Cover Image

We chose this image because it represents XML in two ways:

The image as a whole illustrates the theme of universal communication through the ages, from an ancient cave painting, through Alexander Graham Bell inventing the telephone, right up to communication to the far reaches of the universe. Universal communication is something of great value to humanity, and is also one of the main things that makes XML great, as its ubiquitous nature allows data to be easily passed across pretty much any platform and language combination you like!

The central device of the picture is a variation on a plaque, designed by Dr Carl Sagan and Dr Frank Drake and drawn by Linda Salzman Sagan, which was attached to the side of the Pioneer Space Probe. Using the dimensions of a hydrogen atom as a base measurement, it describes the position of the sun against local pulsars, the position of the Earth relative to the sun, and the relative sizes of human beings against the space probe itself (see http://spaceprojects.arc.nasa.gov/Space_Projects/pioneer/PN10&11.html for more information on the Pioneer 10 and 11 twin spacecraft)

This example of self-defining data seems to us to be a perfect symbol to represent XML.

The cover image for this book was created by Don Synstelien of http://www.synfonts.com, *co-author of the glasshaus book, "Usability: The Site Speaks For Itself". You can find more of Don's illustration work online at* http://www.synstelien.com.

About the Authors

Dave Addey

Dave has spent the last six years building and implementing XML-based web systems for major US and UK organisations. He is the founder and director of agant.com, a UK-based content management and intranet consultancy. He has had more experience of content management than is probably advisable, from designing and building bespoke systems to purchasing and implementing major commercial products.

To Alyson, for everything.

Chris Auld

Chris Auld is Chief Architect at New Zealand-based software firm eMedia. Chris divides his time between architecting large systems, building mobile applications, and running around like a headless chicken evangelizing all that is "new" and "only just released". Chris is a Microsoft platform specialist and a self-professed XML geek – he even has the car number plate to prove it! Chris is a graduate of Otago University in Law and Information Science.

In his "spare" time, he collects University Degrees and DJs Dark Progressive House music, and partakes in silly ritualistic adventure sport activities such as kitesurfing, whitewater kayaking and mountain biking.

I would like to thank: my Mum and Dad for getting me to where I am and for supporting me in where I am going; my darling girlfriend for enduring my late nights in front of the computer screen. I also need to thank the glasshaus crew for their encouragement and support, despite my being on the other side of the world with 12 hours time difference.

Oli Gauti Gudmundsson

Oli is 24 years old, and made in Iceland. He is the Chief Software Architect at VYRE (http://www.vyre.com), and manages the design and development of VYRE's content management systems. He co-authored Professional XSL and Professional XML 2nd edition from Wrox Press, and has written many articles on server-side Java.

Special thanx to Edda the Animator, Benjamin Bathnail, Haraldur Gumjarn, and Kalmar Kalamarez, for making life so much funnier!

Jon James

Jon has spent the past 5 years working with many different types of web technology in many different situations, and has therefore worked with XML in a large variety of projects. When not using the computer for work, he can be found in front of it writing music.

Allan Kent

Allan has been programming seriously for the last 9 years and other than a single blemish when he achieved a diploma in Cobol programming, is entirely self-taught. He runs his own company, where they try to make a living out of making a lot of noise and playing Quake. When that doesn't work they make a lot of noise while doing development and design for an advertising agency. Allan lives in Cape Town, South Africa, with his girlfriend, and four cats.

Jeff Rafter

Jeff Rafter currently resides in Iowa City, where he is studying Creative Writing at the University of Iowa. He has worked for the past six years in the computer industry and is always eager to explore emerging technologies. In his free time, Jeff composes sonnets, plays chess in parks, and skateboards.

I thank God for his love and grace in all things. I would also like to thank my beautiful wife Ali, who is the embodiment of that love in countless ways. She has graciously encouraged me to pursue my dreams at any cost. I would also like to express my gratitude to the editors and reviewers who worked tirelessly throughout the process of completing this book.

Alex Shiell

Alex is an independent IT consultant specialising in e-commerce and Internet technologies, and is particularly interested in the application of these technologies in the public sector. He currently provides his services to a government organization in Scotland, to build and maintain a large extranet application used by companies all over the country. Other than that, he does small ASP sites for charities and other small organisations – whatever he can fit in to his spare time.

My main area of expertise is in the Microsoft arena, and I have been an enthusiastic fan of XML since its conception. This is my first attempt at writing. I have been based in Edinburgh, Scotland, for the last 10 years, although I grew up in various countries around the world and intend to continue traveling around many more countries over the course of my life.

I would like to thank Amanda Kay for getting me involved in the project.

Paul Spencer

Paul runs his own business providing XML consultancy and training to both the public and private sectors in the UK and Europe. He advises the Office of the e-Envoy and other Government departments in the UK and overseas on strategy and policies for the use of XML. He wrote the Schemas for the OASIS Election Markup Language featured in this book, and contributed to the development of the Government Gateway. When not working, he is either sailing, or lying by the pool in the south of France.

Inigo Surguy

Inigo spent five years creating server- and client-side XML-based web systems for major international companies, as UK head of R & D for a major Java/XML content management system vendor. These days, Inigo works as a consultant with a particular interest in knowledge management, usability, and web services. Many of the techniques described in the chapters he contributed to are used on his personal web site, http://www.surguy.net.

Thanks go to Michelle of course, and to Ben and Tim for helping me to debug my code and test it on obscure browsers.

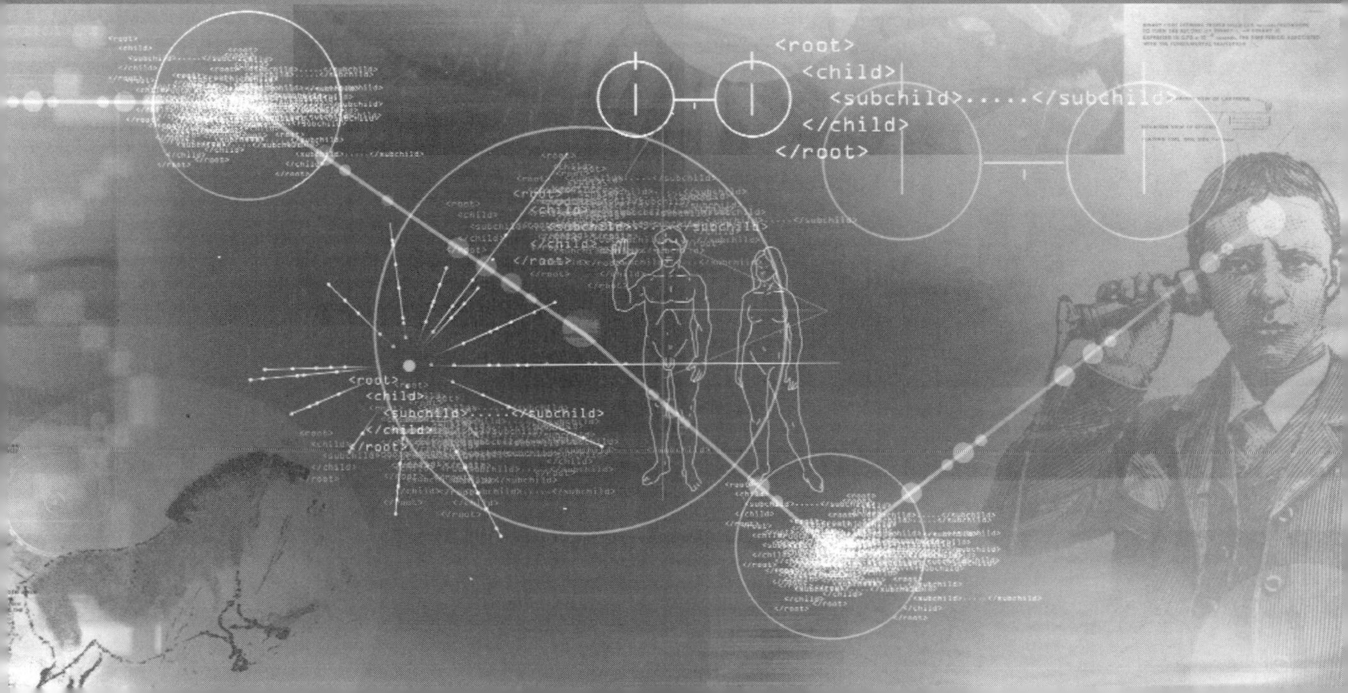
<root>
<child>
<subchild>.....</subchild>
</child>
</root>

Table of Contents

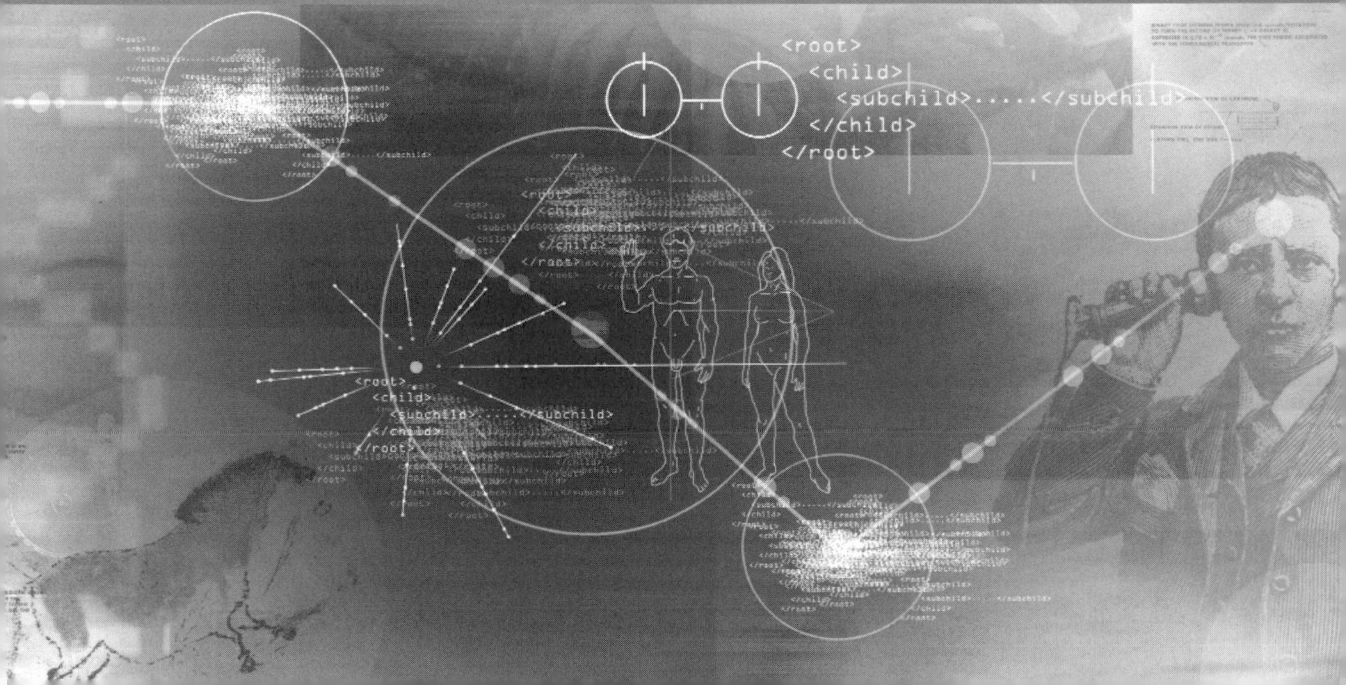
<root>
<child>
<subchild>.....</subchild>
</child>
</root>

Introduction

XML, the **Extensible Markup Language**, is a rapidly maturing technology with many selling points: it's **platform neutral**, it enables **data exchange**, it's **simple**, and it allows **separation of content from presentation**, allowing you to write much more efficient web pages that are quicker to load, and easier to maintain.

These statements may sound like hype, but this is all achievable using today's browsers and XML tools. The point of this book isn't to endlessly praise XML though!

Unlike many XML books out there, this one doesn't dwell endlessly on theory and as-yet-unsupported language specifications. Instead, we give you just enough theory to set the scene, before going on to show you how you can make great use of XML in your web development. Its focus is on the practical, all theory being backed up by techniques that are actually used on the Web today.

The latest browser versions (in this book we focus on Internet Explorer 5+, Netscape 6+/Mozilla, and Opera 6+) have good levels of intrinsic XML support, as do the latest versions of many of the server-side scripting languages (we'll cover ASP, JSP, and PHP), and the databases that are used for storing data for dynamic web sites (such as SQL Server and MySQL).

After reading this book you will be able to effectively use:

- **Extensible Stylesheet Language Transformations** (**XSLT**) to transform XML, not only into differently structured XML pages, but also into different markup languages for different purposes.
- **Cascading Style Sheets** (**CSS**) to style XML/XHTML data for display in a browser.
- **JavaScript** for further manipulation of XML (for example, via the XML DOM).
- Server-side scripting languages to generate XML.

We cover both client-side and server-side XML processing in detail, as well as going over exactly what XML support is available in the three major browsers mentioned above.

Who's This Book for?

This book is for web professionals of all levels who want to know how XML can be put to great practical use in their work **today**. It assumes some basic knowledge of HTML, but it takes you through the basic theory of XML, assuming no prior knowledge. Some knowledge of JavaScript and server-side languages would be advantageous, but ample references are provided to help you along the way.

What Do I Need To Begin?

To create simple XML documents, all you need is a basic text editor but, as discussed in *Chapter 2*, there are other tools that may make editing XML easier.

To view your XML-based pages, you'll need one of the most recent browsers. Most browsers come with a component that understands and can process XML (called a parser) so no extra software is needed. Be warned though that Opera does not at present have the added functionality of an XSLT processor built in.

Also, to work with server-side XML, as we discuss in detail in *Chapters 8 to 11*, you'll need one or more server-side environments (ASP, for example). Instructions for installing these environments are included in the relevant places in these chapters, or in readme files included with the code download for this book (see *Web Support*, below).

Support and Feedback

Although we aim for perfection, the sad fact of book publication is that a few errors will slip through. We would like to apologize for any errors that have reached this book despite our efforts. If you spot an error, please let us know about it using the e-mail address `support@glasshaus.com`. If it's something that will help other readers, then we'll put it up on the errata page at *http://www.glasshaus.com*.

This e-mail address can also be used to access our support network. If you have trouble running any of the code in this book, or have a related question that you feel the book didn't answer, please mail your problem to the above address quoting the title of the book, the last 4 digits of its ISBN, and the relevant chapter and page number.

Web Support

You'll want to go and visit our web site, at *http://www.glasshaus.com*. It features a freely downloadable compressed version of the full code for this book, in both `.zip` and `.sit` formats. You can also find details of all our other published books, author interviews, and more.

1

- XML history
- How XML differs from HTML
- Brief introduction to the most important technologies surrounding XML

Author: Paul Spencer

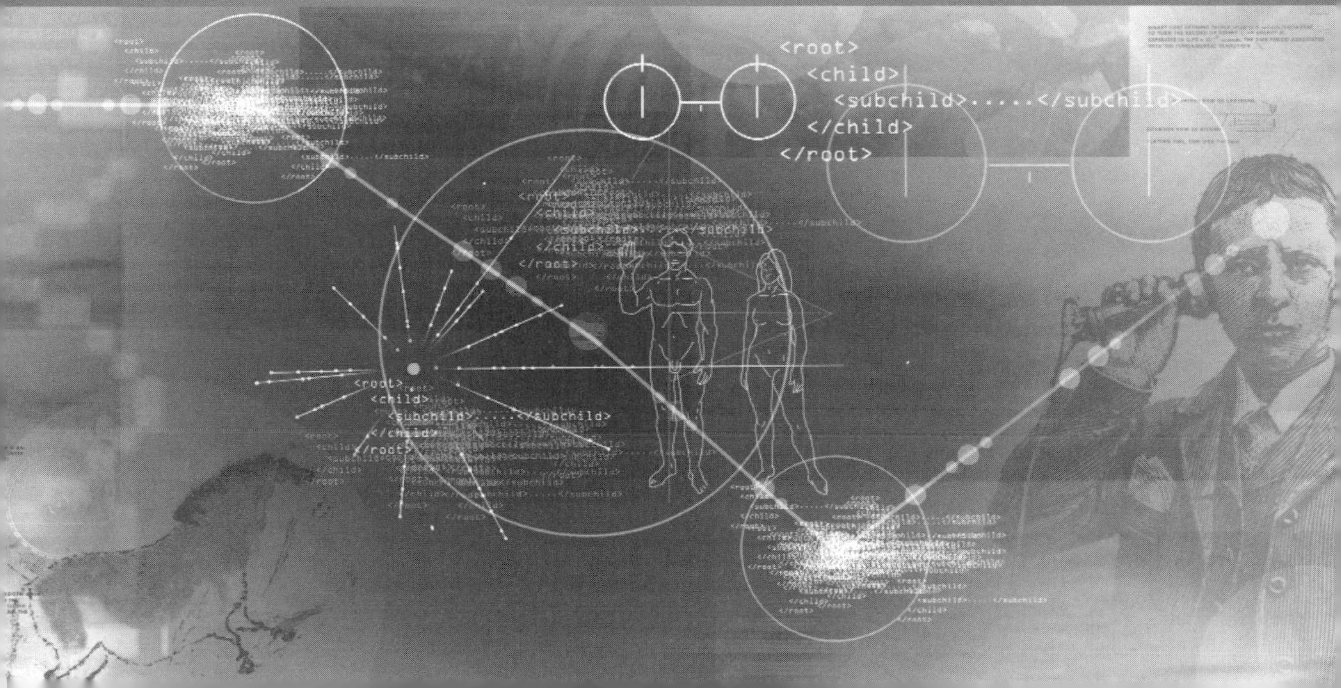

Introduction to XML

This chapter is aimed at providing a quick refresher to those of you who already have some familiarity with some of the basic concepts of XML. Readers who are completely new to XML, should probably treat this as a quick 'taster' to the world of XML: don't be intimidated by the wealth of information we will be covering here, since each topic we look at in this chapter will be explained much more thoroughly in the chapters that follow.

OK, so you've been using HTML for years and it has been good enough up to now, so why should you begin using XML too? It's just another markup language, surely?

My response would be to ask "are you really only using HTML, or are you also using JavaScript, JSP, ASP, PHP, or Flash?". Perhaps HTML is not the answer to everything after all? As time has moved on, the Web has moved beyond the original concepts of HTML and acquired more advanced technologies and facilities for new uses.

At first, much of this new technology was involved with control of presentation, where the originator of the material wanted to control how it is displayed rather than leaving that to the browser. Now it is more about using the Web to transfer structured material rather than simple text and graphics documents. This could be for entry into a database, a direct application-to-application transfer such as submitting a tax return from tax preparation software directly into a Government taxation system, or just providing a separation of content from display information. This is where XML comes in.

In this chapter, we will look at what XML is and why it is a useful addition to your repertoire of skills. In brief, we will cover the following topics:

- The history of XML.
- XML syntax, and how it differs from that of HTML.
- How XML is processed in a web application.
- How to define your own XML language.

- How XML can be displayed.
- How links can be defined in XML.

By the time you finish this chapter, you will have a good understanding of what XML is, and, hopefully, a thirst to get on and use it properly on your own web sites. We will show you exactly how to do this in later chapters.

In this chapter, we will just look at the aspects of XML that will be of use to you when developing real-world web applications in today's world.

Where Did XML Come From?

The roots of XML can be traced back to two parents: the first is a markup technology called the **Standard Generalized Markup Language** (**SGML**); the other is the World Wide Web, of course.

We all know about the World Wide Web, but what's SGML? At a simple level, it is a syntax for defining languages that can be used for marking up documents – HTML itself is based on SGML (it is what is known as an **application** of SGML – the best known, perhaps. Others can be found in complex document management applications, particularly in the automotive, aerospace, and publishing industries). As a language for defining languages, SGML is known as a **metalanguage**. It uses angle brackets, elements and attributes, but does not define specific tag names or attribute names in the way that HTML does.

So if there is already a markup metalanguage and a display-orientated markup language, what problem was XML designed to solve? Well, although SGML has been around in its current form since 1986, its main shortcoming is that it is very complex, making it difficult to learn. XML is a simplified version of SGML, which tries to overcome this problem.

HTML, too, is a simplified markup language, but as we mentioned before, it is display-orientated, so it isn't able to serve many of the purposes markup language was invented for – for example, the content of the HTML is locked into its presentational structure, so it is not easily transferable between different formats and languages (the advantages of XML over HTML will become more apparent throughout the course of this chapter, and the rest of the book).

So, XML was created in 1998 as a subset of SGML – a cross-platform markup language for the Web that allows you to define your own markup languages (known as **XML Vocabularies**). Since then, much has changed in the XML world – although SGML came from the world of documents and XML was designed for that same world, it soon became clear that XML could also be used for transferring structured data around the Web in a more ambitious way. Increasingly, XML specifications are being applied to this area, as we will see in this book.

Another thing to note is that in 1999 **Extensible Hypertext Markup Language** (**XHTML**) was created, which is basically the HTML 4.0 standard redefined as an XML vocabulary. XHTML has many advantages over HTML, such as stricter syntax rules to force developers to write more efficient, standards-compliant web pages. We will be meeting XHTML in later chapters.

The Aims of XML

The **World Wide Web Consortium** (**W3C**) XML recommendation (*http://www.w3.org/TR/REC-xml*) itself says that "Its goal is to enable generic SGML to be served, received, and processed on the Web in the way that is now possible with HTML". This has led to XML being referred to as "SGML for the Web".

Although you can use XML quite happily without understanding its history and original aims, I have found over the years that having this knowledge has helped me use XML better. It could also be argued that a failure to understand the original driving forces behind XML has led to some less than ideal specifications emerging. If you are interested in the controversies surrounding XML-related specifications, and want your views heard as new specifications are developed, I recommend subscribing to the *xml-dev* mailing list at *http://lists.xml.org/ob/adm.pl.*

The original aims of XML are explained concisely in the recommendation itself (*http://www.w3.org/TR/REC-xml#sec-origin-goals*):

- XML shall be usable over the Internet in a straightforward manner.
- XML shall support a wide variety of applications.
- XML shall be compatible with SGML.
- It shall be easy to write programs which process XML documents.
- The number of optional features in XML is to be kept to the absolute minimum, ideally zero.
- XML documents should be human-readable and reasonably clear.
- The XML design should be quickly preparable.
- The design of XML shall be formal and concise.
- XML documents shall be easy to create.
- Terseness in XML markup is of minimal importance.

There are a few things worth noting. By saying "it shall be easy to write programs which process XML documents", the aim was both to open up the market for XML processors (parsers) by keeping them simple to develop, and to enable the use of XML on small, cheap, portable devices such as mobile phones and PDAs. An XML parser is a piece of software that works through an XML document, identifying the elements and their contents, together with any attributes, and providing us with the ability to read, write, and change an existing document, or create a new one from scratch.

By keeping documents human-readable, applications can be built and debugged more easily. This, and the use of Unicode to define characters, also eases compatibility problems. Of course, the downside is that XML documents become longer than they would be using optimized binary constructions, a point acknowledged by the last statement in the list: "terseness in XML markup is of minimal importance". So terseness was not a design goal – a point that you might take issue with when using a modem to download an XML document. As a text format, however, XML compresses well, and there are various initiatives aimed at minimizing the bandwidth requirements in using XML.

XML Syntax

Now we know where XML came from and why, let's see what it looks like. Something like this will be familiar to you:

```
<p>the quick brown fox jumps over the lazy dog</p>
```

That looks like HTML doesn't it? Yes, but it is XML as well – it could also be part of an XHTML document, which, as we have learned above, is an XML vocabulary. One benefit of XML and HTML both having derived from SGML is that the syntaxes are similar. The main differences are:

- In HTML, the element and attribute names are fixed, in XML they are not. For example, the following would not be acceptable in an HTML document, but there is nothing to stop you defining an XML vocabulary to contain such elements:

```
<cd title="Metallica" artist="Metallica">
  <track number="1"> Enter Sandman </track>
  <track number="2"> Sad But True </track>
  ...
</cd>
```

- HTML element and attribute names are not case-sensitive, whereas those in XML are – for example, in HTML `<BODY>` and `<body>` are equivalent. In XML however, they would be different elements.
- In HTML, there are a lot of shortcuts that can be taken, and often are taken, to save the code writer time. Historically, this markup shorthand was deemed acceptable, and browsers were coded to reflect that, dramatically increasing the size of the browser programs. For example, it is common in HTML to open a paragraph with a `<p>` tag, then not close it again (`</p>`) when you reach the end. This approach, however, is not allowed in XML.
- In HTML, attribute values are often accepted without being enclosed in quotation marks, whereas in XML this is always mandatory. Also, in HTML, there are some attributes that don't need to be given a value (that is, when you just want to go with the default value of the attribute). In XML, attributes must always have a value. For example, `<td nowrap>` is fine in HTML, but in XML, we would have to write something like `<td nowrap="true">`.
- In HTML, you can get away with elements not being properly nested; in XML, they must be. We'll see more of this in the *Nesting of Elements* section.

> Documents that meet the rules of the XML Recommendation are described as "well-formed".

Now let's really get going, by looking at a complete XML document.

An XML Document

Complete pieces of XML are referred to as **documents**. This is the same whether the XML is a marking up of a piece of text, a request for information from a remote server, or any other data. Documents are composed of **markup** and **character data**.

Here is a simple XML document that uses some of the most commonly employed constructs in XML (you can find this document in the file `XMLSample1.xml`, in the code download for this chapter, available from *http://www.glasshaus.com.*) We will examine these constructs in detail first, and then expand the example to look at some others:

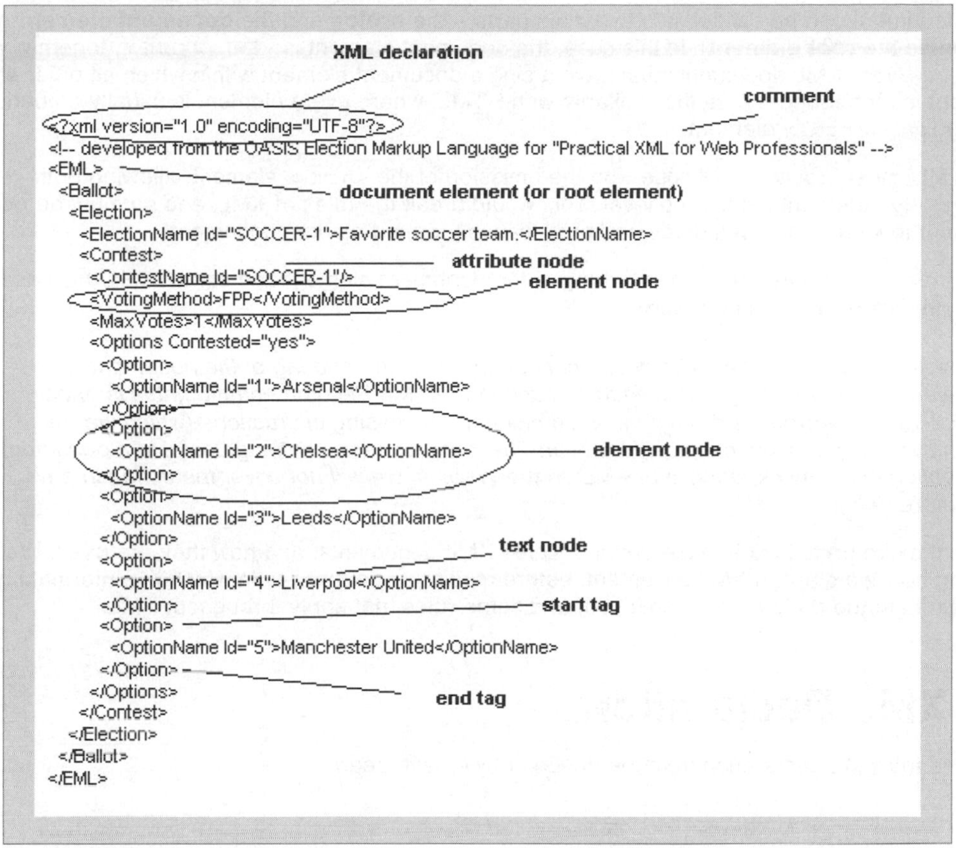


```xml
<?xml version="1.0" encoding="UTF-8"?>
<!-- developed from the OASIS Election Markup Language for "Practical XML for Web Professionals" -->
<EML>
 <Ballot>
  <Election>
   <ElectionName Id="SOCCER-1">Favorite soccer team.</ElectionName>
   <Contest>
    <ContestName Id="SOCCER-1"/>
    <VotingMethod>FPP</VotingMethod>
    <MaxVotes>1</MaxVotes>
    <Options Contested="yes">
     <Option>
      <OptionName Id="1">Arsenal</OptionName>
     </Option>
     <Option>
      <OptionName Id="2">Chelsea</OptionName>
     </Option>
     <Option>
      <OptionName Id="3">Leeds</OptionName>
     </Option>
     <Option>
      <OptionName Id="4">Liverpool</OptionName>
     </Option>
     <Option>
      <OptionName Id="5">Manchester United</OptionName>
     </Option>
    </Options>
   </Contest>
  </Election>
 </Ballot>
</EML>
```

In general, the character data comprises the text between a start tag and an end tag, and everything else is markup.

> More precisely, markup includes "start-tags, end-tags, empty-element tags, entity references, character references, comments, CDATA section delimiters, document type declarations, and processing instructions". Everything else is character data.

We can immediately see that the document above contains information on some kind of vote, in this case, a ballot "paper" for a vote to find the favorite soccer team of some electorate (perhaps users of a sports web site). This document is based on the **Election Markup Language** (**EML**) – an XML vocabulary developed by the Organization for the Advancement of Structured Information Standards (**OASIS**, see *http://www.oasis-open.org/committees/election/* for more on EML). EML will form the basis for many of the examples in this chapter. It has its own fixed elements, just like HTML does, and, similarly, they both have a fixed structure. For example, an `<Option>` element can only be used as a child of an `<Options>` element, in the same way that `<tr>` must be a child of `<table>` in HTML.

The document can be divided into two main parts – the **prolog** and the **document element** (also known as the **root element**). In this case, the document element is `<EML></EML>`, together with all its content. Every XML document must have a single document element within which all other element content is embedded – note the similarity with HTML, where every element is usually embedded within the `<html></html>` element.

In HTML, most browsers will cope with the omission of the `<html>` element, allowing both `<head>` and `<body>` elements at the top level. This would break the rules of XML, and so must be avoided if we want to keep to the standards and produce well-formed markup documents.

The prolog is the part before the start tag of the document element and contains, in this case, the **XML declaration** and a **comment**.

> *Note that there can also be document content after the end tag of the document element. Although not referred to as such in the XML Recommendation, this is often called the* ***epilog****, and can contain comments, processing instructions (which we will meet later) and white space. However, I have never seen anything useful in a document epilog in all my experience of XML on the Web, so we will not cover the epilog in any more detail.*

We will move on to look in more detail at some XML documents, and how they are used. We'll start by seeing how we start an XML document, before moving on to the way in which the information contained in the document is conveyed, and some rules that apply throughout XML.

The XML Declaration

Here is the XML declaration from the document we have seen:

```
<?xml version="1.0" encoding="UTF-8"?>
```

Several things identify this as the XML declaration. The first is the syntax of `<?xml` at the start and `?>` at the end. The second is that this is the first line of the document. Nothing (not even white space) can precede the XML declaration.

> If you want to be an XML guru, make sure to correct people who say that the XML declaration is a special processing instruction. Although the syntax looks similar, the two are treated in totally different ways.
>
> While you are at it, also remember that the correct written expansion of XML is "Extensible Markup Language", not "eXtensible Markup Language".

The XML declaration may contain up to three other pieces of information (the one we are dealing with here uses just the first two):

- The version of XML in use, which will always have the value "1.0" until (and unless) a new version of XML is released.
- The character encoding.

- A standalone attribute with a value of yes or no. This indicates to an XML processor whether it needs to look at an external file to resolve entity references. Entities effectively allow substitution of common pieces of text or markup, as we will see in the "copyright" example in a few pages.

> XML supports the Unicode character set to enable multi-language support. Unicode provides support for 2^{31} characters. It already includes every character you are likely to need, plus rather a lot you will never see. UTF-8 is a way of encoding Unicode characters so that the ASCII characters use the same codes as they do in ASCII. This obviously provides good compatibility with older systems. Other encodings are also available. If no encoding is specified in the XML declaration, UTF-8 or UTF-16 is assumed. See *http://www.unicode.org*.

Inclusion of the XML declaration is optional, but recommended. Each of the attributes is also optional.

CDATA Section

We will shortly see a couple of ways to get round the problem of characters that are not allowed in XML –*Character References* and *Entity References*. There is a third way – the **CDATA Section**. By placing text within a CDATA section, we can instruct the parser not to process the text. This has two effects: any entity or character references will not be resolved, and any reserved characters will be allowed. Really, these two effects go together – it is because we are not resolving references that we can allow the characters that would otherwise be disallowed. So we have a way of representing text with restricted characters in XML:

```
<Vendor><!CDATA[ Ben & Jerry's ]]</Vendor>
```

The CDATA section is opened with the string <!CDATA[and closed with]]. Clearly, the string "]]" cannot occur within a CDATA section. In this instance, as we'll see later, the problematic characters are the ampersand & and the apostrophe '.

In this example, the usual way to encode the text would be with a character reference or an entity reference. There are two common uses for CDATA sections in XML: for embedding code such as ECMAScript, and for containing automatically generated content that is known not to require any parser processing. For example, an application that reads data from a database and marks it up in XML might embed all data content in CDATA sections to avoid the need to explicitly process the reserved characters.

Conveying Information in XML

Two types of node are mainly used to carry information – **elements** and **attributes**. These have the same meanings as in HTML, and are generally used in much the same way. Consider the following HTML:

```
<p style="font-weight:bold">Liverpool</p>
```

In this case, we have the data that is being conveyed (Liverpool), with two additional pieces of information. The information is wrapped in a <p> element, which tells the HTML processor to display the information in a separate paragraph, and the style attribute provides additional information about the display – in this case, it tells the processor to embolden the text.

In the XML example we saw above, we have:

```
<OptionName Id="4">Liverpool</OptionName>
```

As before, the information is contained within an element, but this time the element name provides us with information about what this means, while the attribute again provides some qualifying information. Two very common uses of this technique are to convey formatting information and to indicate the use of a specific format or encoding. For example, we could convey a date as:

```
<Date Format="mmddyyyy">06081955</Date>
```

or indicate use of an **ISO** date format by using:

```
<Date Code="ISO8601">1955-06-08</Date>
```

In HTML, although the semantics of the language (that is, the vocabulary of element and attribute names and their meanings) are fully specified, there are no fixed rules in the syntax that state when to use an element and when an attribute. For example, the following HTML will give an equivalent output to the HTML we saw above:

```
<p><b>Liverpool</b></p>
```

The same is true in XML. Although it has become something of a convention to carry the main data items in element values and qualifying information in attribute values, there is no rule to say you must. This would be perfectly acceptable XML:

```
<Option Id="4" Name="Liverpool"></Option>
```

as would this:

```
<Option>
  <Id>4</Id>
  <Name>Liverpool</Name>
</Option>
```

Some XML Rules

A few things are common throughout XML, so it's worth knowing them before we reach the detail of the different XML constructs. We have already looked at some basic XML syntax rules above; now let's explore some more rules:

Names

Elements, attributes, and some other constructs in XML have names. A name is made up of a starting character followed by a number of name characters. The starting character must be a letter (upper- or lower-case), underscore, or colon. The colon is used as a delimiter for namespaces, which we will meet later in this chapter and should not be used otherwise anywhere in a name.

The characters following the start character can be drawn from a wider range, comprising any letter, digit, combining character, extender, period, dash, or underscore. The definitions of "letter", "combining character" and "extender" are provided in the recommendation. However, if you restrict your name characters to the letters of the Roman alphabet (upper- and lower-case), digits, and the approved punctuation (avoiding the colon), you will have no problems.

The best thing to do is to adopt a naming convention and stick to it. For example, the UK Government uses **upper camel case** for all element and attribute names. This means that words are concatenated and each starts with an upper-case character – in the ballot example above, for example, `OptionName`. Others use upper camel case for element names and lower camel case (all but the first word of a name start with an upper-case character) for attribute names. Unfortunately, there is no universal convention for this. Some people (particularly those coming from an EDI background) use all upper-case characters, so `OptionName` becomes `OPTIONNAME`. I would not recommend this convention – its ugliness might be a matter of taste, but it is clear that the lack of separation between words makes it more difficult to read.

Reserved Characters

Certain characters have special meanings in XML and so cannot be used in other circumstances. For example, the "less than" character (<) indicates the start of a tag, and so cannot be used within the character content of an XML document. We will see later how to include reserved characters, if needed. The list of reserved characters and words is small, and fairly easy to remember. They are:

> The character < cannot appear within character content.
>
> The character & cannot appear within character content except as the first character of an entity reference or character reference (explained later in this chapter).
>
> The character string `xml` (in any combination of upper- and lower-case) cannot occur at the start of a name except when referring to reserved names in the XML language itself, such as `xml-stylesheet`.

Common XML Constructs

In this section, we will look at those XML constructs that you will see and use most often. These are:

- Elements and attributes, both of which are used to convey information in the document.
- Comments, which are used to annotate XML documents.
- Processing instructions, which pass information to an application that is processing the XML.
- Character references, which are mainly used to encode characters that cannot be represented graphically.
- Entity references, which are used to encode reserved characters and any other character strings defined by the developer.

Elements

As we have seen, elements are structures with several different parts. In general, an element may have a start tag, an end tag, and content. The content might be text, or more elements (or both), and the start tag can contain attributes. Elements can contain other XML node types, such as comments.

There is another tag type, in addition to opening and closing tags – the empty element tag. Remember this example from earlier:

```
<Option Id="4" Name="Liverpool"></Option>
```

In this case, the element has no textual content – all the information is carried in the attributes. This is known as an **empty element**, and can use a shortened syntax:

```
<Option Id="4" Name="Liverpool"/>
```

All we do is put a forward slash before the closing angle bracket of the tag.

This syntax also exists in HTML, although you will rarely see it. Some HTML elements, such as the line break `<br>` and horizontal rule `<hr>` meet the requirements of an empty element by not requiring any text content – in fact, they should be written `<hr/>` and `<br/>`, if we want to follow the XML rules. Unfortunately, some older browsers will not understand this syntax, although they will often understand HTML elements coded in XML (perhaps as XHTML) if a space is added to produce `<hr />` and `<br />`.

The reason why you should use the empty element syntax is that it saves on file size, and improves legibility, if the element name itself conveys the information required, or the information is carried in attributes.

The empty element is one of the four types of element content. The others are **character data**, where the element contains only text, **element content**, where it contains only other elements (which may themselves contain text) and **mixed content**, where it contains both elements and text. The following example contains all four element types (see `elements.xml` in the download). It also contains a comment, which looks just like an HTML comment:

```
<?xml version="1.0" encoding="UTF-8"?>
<Elements>
  <Mixed>This element contains both text and elements
    <Element>
      <!-- This element has element content -->
      <CharacterData>This element has text content</CharacterData >
    </Element>
  </Mixed>
  <!-- The next element is empty -->
  <Empty/>
</Elements>
```

Note that the presence of the comments does not alter the element type. This is also true of other XML constructs, such as Processing Instructions, that can be embedded within an element. See later in this section for more on these constructs.

In general, a **textual document** (usually one intended for display) will contain elements with mixed content, while in a **data document** (such as a tax return, which will be read directly into a computer system) each element will contain only character data or element content. This makes it easier to process and extract data from these documents, for example to populate a database.

Nesting of Elements

As we mentioned above, XML elements must be properly nested so that each is fully inside another element (apart from the document root element, which forms the highest level of the element structure). The following file is available as `NotNested.htm` in the support material:

```
<html>
  This is <b>bold, now I am adding <i>italic, taking away the </b>bold and then the
</i>italic.
</html>
```

This will display fine in most HTML browsers, but try saving the same file with an `.xml` extension (see `NotNested.xml`: the file has no XML declaration, but it will still be parsed OK). This time, if you open the file up in a browser with XML support, such as Internet Explorer, you will see something like the following screenshot:

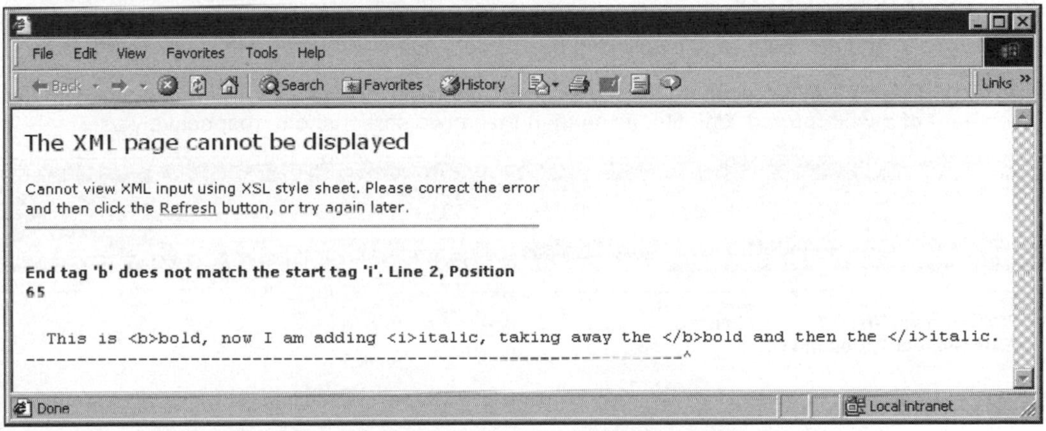

Why has it not been treated as HTML? After all, the document element is `<html>`. Simply because the file extension has indicated that this is XML, so the browser treats it like an XML file (in which an `<html>` element might mean anything), therefore chokes when it finds that the document is not well-formed. To make the file well-formed, the nesting needs to be corrected (`nested.xml`):

```
<?xml version="1.0"?>
<html>
  This is <b>bold, now I am adding <i>italic, taking away the </i></b><i>bold
  and then the </i>italic.
</html>
```

Apart from adding an XML declaration, the change we have made is to close the `<i>` element before closing the `<b>` element, then reopen it. Opening this file in IE6 gives this result:

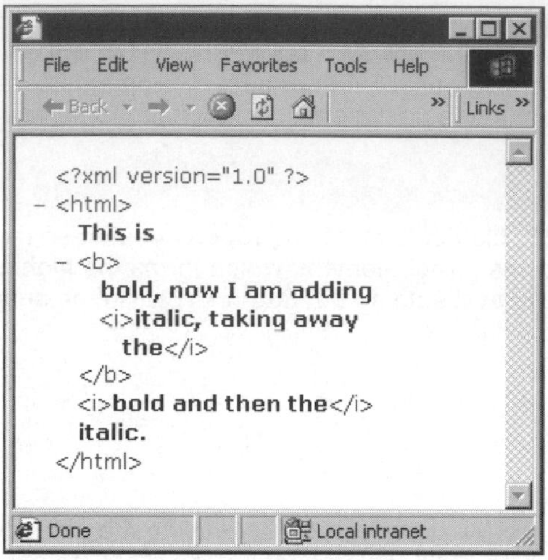

Note the way that IE has displayed this – the latest browsers understand the syntax of XML, but they do not know the meaning we want to assign to the tags. IE uses a default stylesheet (we will look at stylesheets later in this chapter and cover them in more depth later in the book) to display the XML in a **tree structure.** This indents the elements according to their nesting and also allows element content to be hidden in an interactive way by clicking on the negative (–) sign.

Netscape 6 gives a similar result on the file with the elements incorrectly nested, but just displays the text content of a well-formed XML file, as seen in these two screenshots, respectively:

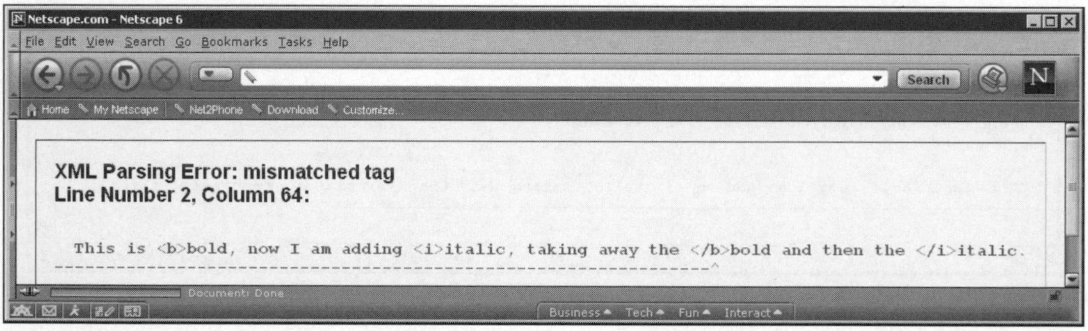

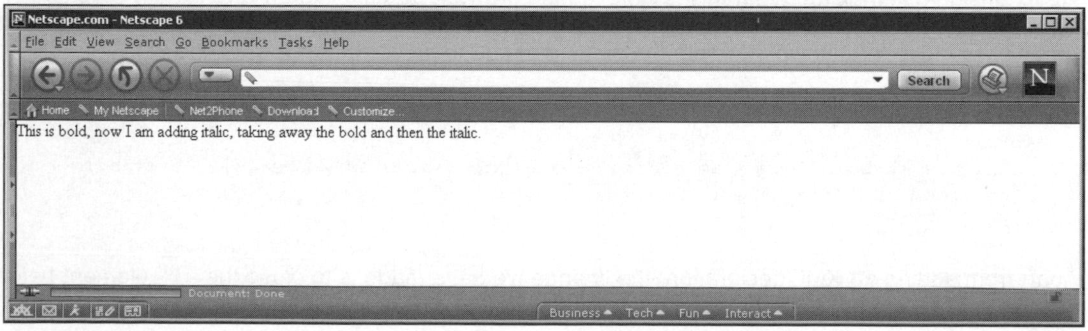

Opening an XML file in one of these browsers is a quick and easy way to identify badly-formed XML documents.

Here is a summary of the rules relating to elements:

> Element content is enclosed within start and end tags, or else the information is contained within attributes, or the element name, if we are dealing with empty elements.
>
> The tag names must obey certain naming rules; these are stricter for the first character of the name.
>
> Elements must be properly nested.

Attributes

The second way of carrying information using XML is to use attributes. An attribute has two parts – a **name** and a **value**. An example we have already seen is the `Id` attribute in the EML ballot message:

```
<OptionName Id="4">Liverpool</OptionName>
```

In this case, the attribute name is `Id` and its value is 4. The name must obey the naming rules outlined earlier, and the value must be quoted using either single or double quotes (Unicode characters 0x22 or 0x27). Note that a well-formedness error is commonly caused when you cut and paste information into an XML document from a word processor that uses "smart quotes".

I suggested earlier that attributes are usually employed to provide additional information about an element, but whether to use an element or an attribute to represent a piece of information is up to the author of the document. There is one instance when an attribute is often best, and that is when you do not know in advance the type of entity you are dealing with. For example, in the Election Markup Language, there is an XML document sent as a message from a prospective candidate to the election organizer that is used to nominate candidates for an election. In many cases, there will be some form of scrutiny to indicate whether the candidate is eligible. The following could be used to indicate whether the candidate is old enough and has paid the required fee:

```
<Fee>Cheque in the post</Fee>
<DateOfBirth>8 June 1955</DateOfBirth>
```

Unfortunately, we do not know what eligibility requirements exist throughout the world at the time of writing the EML specification. We also do not want a new requirement in, say, Missouri to force us to change a specification that is being used in New Zealand. It's better to use a more general element like this:

```
<ScrutinyRequirement Type="fee">Cheque in the post</ScrutinyRequirement>
<ScrutinyRequirement Type="dateofbirth">8 June 1955</ScrutinyRequirement>
```

The language specification (the vocabulary used in the markup) can now be fixed, and new scrutiny requirements added at a later stage. So we have added flexibility, but we will see when we look at schemas that we have limited the degree of automated checking by moving the scrutiny requirement types out of the EML language specification and into the data.

Here is a summary of the rules relating to attributes:

> An attribute comprises a name/value pair.
>
> The attribute value must be enclosed in single or double quotes.
>
> Attribute names obey the same rules as element names.

Comments

We have already seen a few XML comments, and it won't be a surprise by now to learn that they look like HTML comments:

```
<!-- this is a comment.
It starts with an angle bracket, an exclamation mark, and two dashes
and ends with two dashes and an angle bracket -->
```

There are just a couple of rules to note, as shown below:

> A comment may not contain two dashes in a row.
>
> An XML processor is not obliged to pass comments to an application (although most do). You should therefore restrict comments to information intended for human readers of the XML document itself.

Processing Instructions

I have already hinted at the existence of **Processing Instructions** (**PIs**). PIs are not processed by the XML processor, but are passed on to the application unchanged. They can therefore be used when the application that will process the XML document is known at the time the document is created. A PI is delimited by angle brackets and question marks, and has two parts – a name and a text string. For example:

```
<?xml-stylesheet type="text/xsl" href="stylesheet.xsl"?>
```

As with other names, a PI name beginning with `xml` (in any combination of case) is reserved for use in XML specifications, so you should not use it in your applications – in this case, it indicates a reference to an XSL stylesheet, so it is OK.

In the example above, the PI name is `xml-stylesheet` and the text string is `type="text/xsl" href="stylesheet.xsl"`. Although this looks like two attributes, this is not the way it is treated.

If a document contains the PI shown above, and the application is an XSL stylesheet processor, the XSL processor will use it to retrieve the stylesheet with which to display the document. Other applications can also use PIs. For example, an application might embed SQL statements in PIs and populate the XML document dynamically before saving it or sending it as a message to another application.

Character References

There are certain circumstances where it is not possible to include a literal character in an XML document. It might be a character that is not allowed as a graphic character, or simply a character not on the keyboard that the document author is using. These characters can be encoded numerically, either in decimal or hex – for example, the copyright symbol © can be encoded as `©` or `©`. The fact that the reference starts with `&#` and ends with a semicolon indicates that this is a character reference. The number between is the Unicode code for the character required. If the code is in hex, then it is prefixed with the character `x`. The text "Ben & Jerry's" can be represented as:

```
<Vendor>Ben &#x26; Jerry's</Vendor>
```

or:

```
<Vendor>Ben &#38; Jerry's</Vendor>
```

This is also one way of encoding reserved characters, although there is a better way – the entity reference, which we will look at now.

Entity References

Entity references allow access to predefined string literals, which may include single characters such as < or `&`. Some entity references are built into the XML language, whereas the creator of the XML vocabulary can define others. These are the built-in entity references:

Entity Reference	Meaning
`<`	<
`&`	&
`>`	>
`'`	'
`"`	"

The first two of these *must* be used when referring to these characters. The others are included for convenience. For example, if an attribute value is embedded within single quotes, then any apostrophe used within the value must use the `'` entity reference. However, if double quotes were used, this would not be necessary. It is never necessary to use the `>` entity reference – it is just included for symmetry. So we have two more alternative ways of encoding the text "Ben & Jerry's" in XML:

```
<Vendor>Ben &amp; Jerry's</Vendor>
```

or:

```
<Vendor>Ben &amp; Jerry&apos;s</Vendor>
```

As well as these built-in references, it is possible to define our own – for example, we could define the reference `&copyright;` to mean *Copyright 2002 glasshaus Limited*. Then every time we want to include this text, we can use the reference, and if we want to update all examples of the text, we just have to change one entity definition. For more on defining your own references, see later in the chapter, in *The Document Type Definition* section.

XML Namespaces

One point that we have been stressing is that XML allows us to define our own vocabularies of element and attribute names. This is great, but there is a potential problem just waiting to be uncovered. What happens when we want to use more than one vocabulary in the same document, and the same element is used in both vocabularies, but for different meanings? Perhaps we want to produce a furniture catalog as a structured document with some embedded XHTML information. Something like this:

```
<?xml version="1.0" encoding="UTF-8"?>
<catalog>
  <table>
    <size>
      <length>2.0</length>
      <width>0.9</width>
      <height>1.2</height>
    </size>
    <description>
      <table>
        <tr>
          <td>This is a lovely table</td>
          <td>And this is a picture of it</td>
        </tr>
      </table>
    </description>
  </table>
</catalog>
```

This shows an immediate problem – two elements called `table` with different meanings. To get around this, we need to show that parts of this document belong to two different vocabularies – we can do this with **namespaces**. As you can see below, we can qualify each element name with a **prefix**, to indicate which vocabulary they belong to:

```
<?xml version="1.0" encoding="UTF-8"?>
<cat:catalog>
  <cat:table>
    <cat:size>
      <cat:length>2.0</cat:length>
      <cat:width>0.9</cat:width>
      <cat:height>1.2</cat:height>
    </cat:size>
    <cat:description>
      <xhtml:table>
        <xhtml:tr>
          <xhtml:td>This is a lovely table</xhtml:td>
```

```
            <xhtml:td>And this is a picture of it</xhtml:td>
          </xhtml:tr>
        </xhtml:table>
      </cat:description>
    </cat:table>
  </cat:catalog>
```

We haven't solved the problem just yet, however. What we need to do now is associate the prefix with something that will identify the XHTML elements as unequivocally XHTML, and the catalog elements as part of that vocabulary. We do this using URIs. You might be familiar with the term URI (Uniform Resource Identifier), but if not, you will certainly know of URLs (Uniform Resource Locators). The URL is one type of URI, the other is the Uniform Resource Name or URN. These were an attempt to provide location-independent identifiers such as `urn:oasis:names:tc:evs:schema:eml`, but have not caught on to the extent that perhaps they should have done. In the first case in the markup above, the URI is defined by the W3C since it controls the XHTML standard. The `cat` prefix however is under our control so we can use any URI under our control.

Adding Namespaces to Our Documents

The URIs are added to the document in this way: we define these namespaces in a document by adding them as attributes of any node which contains elements belonging to those namespaces. This is frequently done at the document element, since it is an ancestor of all other element nodes. For example, in the above document, we would change the opening element to this:

```
<cat:catalog xmlns:cat="http://www.glasshaus.com/ns/furniture"
             xmlns:xhtml="http://www.w3.org/1999/xhtml">
```

We can now use these prefixes within our document. Note the syntax of the namespace declaration. The attribute name is the text string `xmlns` followed by a colon and the prefix to be used within the document.

> The important part is the URI. It does not matter what prefix we use within our document as long as it is associated with the correct URI.
>
> The URI is only used as a unique label. It does not matter what (if anything) is located at that URI. The W3C puts information about the namespace at the namespace URI for those namespaces it controls, but many other URIs do not point to any document.
>
> Many processors, for example XML Schema processors, XHTML processors, and XSL stylesheet processors use the URI to indicate that they must process certain parts of the document. You must therefore use the correct URI for these applications.

Default Namespaces

In many cases, a substantial part of our document belongs to one vocabulary. We can make this easier to deal with by defining this vocabulary with a **default** namespace. To define a default namespace, we use the `xmlns` keyword, but do not define a prefix. To make the catalog namespace the default for the previous document, we would define it like this:

```
<catalog xmlns="http://www.glasshaus.com/ns/furniture"
         xmlns:xhtml="http://www.w3.org/1999/xhtml">
```

Since it is the default namespace for the <catalog> element and all its descendants, we no longer prefix the names of the elements belonging to the catalog vocabulary.

Note also that we can define a default at any point in the document – subsequent defaults will apply to the element containing the namespace declaration and all its descendants, overriding any defaults defined earlier on. We can therefore do the same for the XHTML namespace, as seen below – only the XHTML elements (those within and including <table>) will follow this default. Our final version of the document therefore looks like this:

```
<?xml version="1.0" encoding="UTF-8"?>
<catalog xmlns="http://www.glasshaus.com/ns/furniture" >
  <table>
    <size>
      <length>2.0</length>
      <width>0.9</width>
      <height>1.2</height>
    </size>
    <description>
      <table xmlns="http://www.w3.org/1999/xhtml">
        <tr>
          <td>This is a lovely table</td>
          <td>And this is a picture of it</td>
        </tr>
      </table>
    </description>
  </table>
</catalog>
```

A final point on namespaces is their use with attributes. Within XML, by default an attribute belongs in the same namespace as its containing element. So unless we are using an attribute that is defined in a different namespace from its containing element, we do not need to qualify it.

Defining XML Languages

We have already met two examples of XML vocabularies – the Extensible Hypertext Markup Language (XHTML) and the Election Markup Language (EML). In this section, we will look briefly at how we can define our own languages. By defining our language in a formal way, we not only indicate to others how their XML documents should be constructed, but we can also ask our XML processor to check that documents conform to the language. This checking is known in the XML world as **validation** and is a standard feature of most parsers. These are known as **validating parsers**.

Before doing this, I would like to stress that we do not have to create formal language definitions to use XML. As long as our XML is well-formed, the validation checking is optional. For example, I might create a set of links to display on my web site. I will probably display these in a table, but rather than code up the table manually, I will represent them in XML and create the final display using a stylesheet:

```
<?xml version="1.0" encoding="UTF-8"?>
<Links>
  <Link>
    <URL>http://www.w3.org/TR/REC-xml</URL>
    <Description>
      The XML Specification itself.
    </Description>
  </Link>
  <Link>
    <URL>http://www.w3.org/TR/xmlschema-0/</URL>
    <Description>
      The XML Schema specification. The link is to the Primer.
    </Description>
  </Link>
  <Link>
    <URL>http://www.w3.org/TR/DOM-Level-2-Core/</URL>
    <Description>
      The XML Document Object Model. This is the Level 2 Core specification.
    </Description>
  </Link>
  <Link>
    <URL>http://www.w3.org/TR/xslt/</URL>
    <Description>
      The Extensible Stylesheet Language Transformations.
    </Description>
  </Link>
  <Link>
    <URL>http://www.w3.org/TR/</URL>
    <Description>
      The index to all W3C specifications.
    </Description>
  </Link>
</Links>
```

I know exactly how I have marked this up, and I have confidence in my data, so I can use this without any formal definition or validation. It is, however, said that 60% of the code in many applications is checking the validity of source data. If you are processing XML that you have not defined yourself, using an XML parser to carry out this validation for you can save a lot of programming effort. We have already seen that XML can be used to send a tax return to a Government revenue service. By validating the incoming XML document, the service can use the XML parser to ensure that all the required data is present and in the correct format before sending it to the application. The application will then just have to check that any business rules are met, store the information and calculate the tax due. Of course, validating your own XML documents is also a quick and easy way of checking your own work.

We define our languages using a **schema**. This is just a formal description that can be read by some sort of validation tool. There are two schema languages that are commonly used, and others that are less common. We will look at the common ones – the Document Type Definition (DTD) and XML Schema. Both of these are defined and controlled by the W3C. In fact the DTD is part of the XML Recommendation itself. We will use the example of the EML ballot we saw earlier – refresh your memory by looking at the document again:

```
<EML>
  <Ballot>
    <Election>
      <ElectionName Id="SOCCER-1">Favorite soccer team.</ElectionName>
      <Contest>
        <ContestName Id="SOCCER-1"/>
        <VotingMethod>FPP</VotingMethod>
        <MaxVotes>1</MaxVotes>
        <Options Contested="yes">
          <Option>
            <OptionName Id="1">Arsenal</OptionName>
          </Option>
          <Option>
            <OptionName Id="2">Chelsea</OptionName>
          </Option>
          <Option>
            <OptionName Id="3">Leeds</OptionName>
          </Option>
          <Option>
            <OptionName Id="4">Liverpool</OptionName>
          </Option>
          <Option>
            <OptionName Id="5">Manchester United</OptionName>
          </Option>
        </Options>
      </Contest>
    </Election>
  </Ballot>
</EML>
```

The Document Type Definition

A **Document Type Definition** (or **DTD**) can be used to describe the structure of a document. A validating parser will check that an XML document with an associated DTD is well-formed, and will also check that it has a structure complying with that DTD. If it does not, the parser will report an error. An XML document complying with a DTD is referred to as a **document instance** of that DTD.

In this book, we will not cover all aspects of DTDs, but we will describe enough to allow you to understand most DTDs that you will meet. Here is a DTD that successfully defines our EML document (that is, our document is an instance of this DTD):

```
<?xml version="1.0" encoding="UTF-8"?>
<!ELEMENT Ballot (Election)>
<!ELEMENT Contest (ContestName, VotingMethod, MaxVotes, Options)>
<!ELEMENT ContestName (#PCDATA)>
<!ATTLIST ContestName
  Id CDATA #REQUIRED
>
<!ELEMENT EML (Ballot)>
<!ELEMENT Election (ElectionName, Contest)>
<!ELEMENT ElectionName (#PCDATA)>
<!ATTLIST ElectionName
  Id CDATA #REQUIRED
>
<!ELEMENT MaxVotes (#PCDATA)>
<!ELEMENT Option (OptionName)>
```

```
<!ELEMENT OptionName (#PCDATA)>
<!ATTLIST OptionName
  Id CDATA #REQUIRED
>
<!ELEMENT Options (Option+)>
<!ATTLIST Options
  Contested CDATA #IMPLIED
>
<!ELEMENT VotingMethod (#PCDATA)>
```

This DTD shows two types of declaration, the **element type declaration** and the **attribute list declaration**. There are two further declaration types not shown in this example – the **entity declaration** (used to define entities, like those we saw earlier), and the **notation declaration**. We will look at the former of these two later, but not the latter, which is used to indicate non-XML content such as binary image files and is relatively specialized in its use.

Element Type Declaration

This declaration tells us the constraints on an element's content. For example, can the element `Option` contain another element called `KitchenSink`?

The simplest element type declaration defines the content as being **Parsed Character Data** or **PCDATA**. This means that the element's content is text, and that this text will be processed by the XML parser, for example to resolve character references and entity references. Here is an example from above:

```
<!ELEMENT MaxVotes (#PCDATA)>
```

We can also define an element to have element content:

```
<!ELEMENT Election (ElectionName, Contest)>
```

In this case, the `Election` element has a sequence of two other elements: `ElectionName` and `Contest` – they must appear in the order they are written in the DTD (this is the significance of the comma), and both must occur once. We could make the `ElectionName` optional and allow multiple contests as follows:

```
<!ELEMENT Election (ElectionName?, Contest+)>
```

The characters used to make changes like this are:

Symbol	Meaning
,	Strict order
?	Optional
+	One or more
*	Zero or more
|	Select one of a group
()	Group

Attribute List Declaration

Where an element can have attributes, we use the attribute list declaration. Here is an example from the ballot:

```
<!ELEMENT Options (Option+)>
<!ATTLIST Options
  Contested CDATA #IMPLIED
>
```

Here, the element type declaration indicates that the element `<Options>` must have one or more `<Option>` elements. It may also have an attribute `Contested` containing character data (`CDATA`). The keyword `#IMPLIED` indicates that this is optional. It could also be `#REQURIED` or `#FIXED`. `#REQUIRED` should be obvious – the attribute has to be present. If it were `#FIXED`, only a single value would be allowed. If the attribute were missing from the document, the fixed value would be inserted by a validating parser. If it were included, any value other than the fixed value would be an error. This is how we would say that the election must be contested:

```
<!ATTLIST Options
  Contested CDATA #FIXED "yes"
>
```

There is actually a better way of specifying this attribute. The values are, in practice, restricted to `yes` and `no`. We can indicate this in the DTD:

```
<!ATTLIST Options
  Contested (yes|no) "yes"
>
```

In this case, we have only allowed a choice of two values, and have provided a default of `yes`. If no value is specified, the parser will insert this default. There is no need to specify a default. We could have just used:

```
<!ATTLIST Options
  Contested (yes|no)
>
```

These are the simple forms of the attribute list declaration. There are alternatives to the `CDATA` keyword for more complex situations.

Entity Declaration

Earlier, we met entity references. We saw how to use the built-in entity types and indicated that we could define our own. At the time, we did not describe how to do this, but shall do it now using an entity declaration. The example we used before was to use the entity reference `&copyright;` to mean *Copyright 2002 glasshaus Limited*. This is how we would define this in a DTD:

```
<!ENTITY copyright "Copyright 2002 glasshaus limited">
```

This is a simple internal entity declaration. We can, however, also reference external resources. Perhaps you have used master documents in a product like Microsoft Word to define a large document made up of several smaller documents. We can achieve something similar with entity declarations. For a book, we might create a master document:

```
<book>
  <content>
    &tableOfContents;
    &chapter1;
    &chapter2;
    &chapter3;
       .
       .
    &appendixA;
       .
       .
    &index;
  <content>
</book>
```

This document is pulling in its content from several individual documents, which would all need entity declarations to identify them. For example, the `tableOfContents` entity might be defined like this:

```
<!ENTITY tableOfContents SYSTEM "file:///C:chapters/contents/TOC.xml">
```

Internal and External Subsets

We have been looking at the content of a DTD, but not how it is associated with a document instance. There are two options for doing this, known as the **external** and **internal** subsets. The external subset is a DTD contained within an external file, referenced from the XML instance like so:

```
<?xml version="1.0" encoding="UTF-8"?>
<!DOCTYPE EML SYSTEM "ballot.dtd">
<EML>
  ...
</DTD>
```

The new line we have added above to reference the DTD is called a Document Type Declaration.

If, instead, we wanted to add the DTD as an internal subset, we would embed the complete DTD within the document type declaration, like so:

```
<?xml version="1.0" encoding="UTF-8"?>
<!DOCTYPE EML [
<!ELEMENT Ballot (Election)>
<!ELEMENT Contest (ContestName, VotingMethod, MaxVotes, Options)>
<!ELEMENT ContestName (#PCDATA)>
<!ATTLIST ContestName
  Id CDATA #REQUIRED
>
<!ELEMENT EML (Ballot)>
<!ELEMENT Election (ElectionName, Contest)>
<!ELEMENT ElectionName (#PCDATA)>
<!ATTLIST ElectionName
  Id CDATA #REQUIRED
>
<!ELEMENT MaxVotes (#PCDATA)>
```

```
<!ELEMENT Option (OptionName)>
<!ELEMENT OptionName (#PCDATA)>
<!ATTLIST OptionName
  Id CDATA #REQUIRED
>
<!ELEMENT Options (Option+)>
<!ATTLIST Options
  Contested CDATA #IMPLIED
>
<!ELEMENT VotingMethod (#PCDATA)>
]>

<EML>
  ...
</EML>
```

It is possible to have both, in which case the internal subset takes precedence if there is a conflict between definitions. More often than not, you will see just the external subset used in XML applications. This has the advantage that a single copy of the DTD can be held locally and used to validate many documents, rather than requiring every document to include a copy of the DTD, so increasing its size. Also, of course, you might want to know that the version of the DTD being used is the one you want, so maintaining this control is important. In some cases, you might be making minor alterations to a publicly available DTD. In this case, you can use the internal subset to override a few definitions. You should do this with care, however, as your document may no longer be able to be processed by applications expecting documents to meet the constraints of the external subset only.

There are also circumstances when you might use just the internal subset. The most common is if you are creating a one-off document and want to indicate its structure to others. You might also do this if you are not validating against the DTD, but just using it to define a few useful entities.

Earlier, we mentioned the `standalone` attribute in the XML declaration as something that indicates to a parser whether it needs to look externally to resolve entity references. If we have no entity declarations, or they are in the internal subset of the DTD, we can have a `standalone` value of `yes`. If entity declarations are in the external subset, the value of `standalone` should be `no`. Non-validating parsers, however, might not resolve these external references. In practice, most commercial parsers will validate documents against a DTD and so will also fetch externally defined entity declarations.

Now let's look at the other commonly used XML validation language – XML Schema.

XML Schema

The W3C XML Schema Recommendation (see the Primer at *http://www.w3.org/TR/xmlschema-0/*) shares many similarities with the DTD. XML Schema defines the structure of a document, a validating parser will validate a document against it, and the XML document is again referred to as an instance. There are also many differences, however.

Firstly, a disadvantage of XML Schema is that there is no equivalent of the DTD's entity declaration in this language. There is a way around this – when using an XML Schema, it is simple to also use a DTD, possibly as an internal subset in the instance document, which only contains entity declarations. A parser will resolve these entities, and then validate the document against the XML Schema. We will look at an example later.

XML Schema is substantially more powerful than DTDs. Whilst DTDs have a document-orientated background, XML Schema comes from a more data-orientated background. Thus, as well as defining document structure, XML Schema introduces concepts such as data typing and inheritance. The downside is that with this additional power, comes additional complexity.

One important aspect of XML Schema is that a schema processor validates a document an element at a time. If different elements belong to different namespaces, they might be validated against different schemas. It is therefore possible to talk about the validity of each element. A document is considered to be valid if each element within the document is valid against its appropriate schema. A side effect of this is that XML Schema does not provide a way of specifying which is the document element of an XML document. Thus, as long as the document element and all its content are valid, the document will be valid. It is up to an application to know that the document element is the one expected.

One Approach to Structuring an XML Schema

Let's start looking at our EML ballot by considering just the `<Options>` element. Here is a schema that describes this element:

```
<?xml version="1.0" encoding="utf-8"?>
<xsd:schema xmlns:xsd="http://www.w3.org/2001/XMLSchema">
  <xsd:element name="Options">
    <xsd:complexType>
      <xsd:sequence>
        <xsd:element name="Option" maxOccurs="unbounded">
          <xsd:complexType>
            <xsd:sequence>
              <xsd:element name="OptionName">
                <xsd:complexType>
                  <xsd:simpleContent>
                    <xsd:extension base="xsd:string">
                      <xsd:attribute name="Id" type="xsd:NMTOKEN" use="required"/>
                    </xsd:extension>
                  </xsd:simpleContent>
                </xsd:complexType>
              </xsd:element>
            </xsd:sequence>
            <xsd:attribute name="ID" type="xsd:string" use="optional"/>
          </xsd:complexType>
        </xsd:element>
      </xsd:sequence>
      <xsd:attribute name="Contested" use="optional">
        <xsd:simpleType>
          <xsd:restriction base="xsd:string">
            <xsd:enumeration value="no"/>
            <xsd:enumeration value="yes"/>
          </xsd:restriction>
        </xsd:simpleType>
      </xsd:attribute>
    </xsd:complexType>
  </xsd:element>
</xsd:schema>
```

This schema shows a few immediate differences from a DTD. The most obvious is that it is tag-based. This allows simple programmatic creation or modification of a schema using standard XML tools. The XML Schema also shows data-typing (for example `type="xsd:string"`) and inheritance (using `xsd:restriction`). Let's walk through this XML Schema.

It starts with an XML declaration, since it is an XML document. It follows this with the `<xsd:schema>` element, in which the XML Schema namespace is declared. You will usually see this associated with the prefix `xsd` or `xs`. It is possible to make this the default namespace for the document, but there are disadvantages in this that are outside the scope of this book. See the XML Schema best practice document at *http://www.xfront.com/BestPracticesHomepage.html* for more information on this and other aspects of using XML Schema.

The first element we define is `<Options>`. This is the only element defined as a child of the `<xsd:schema>` element, and so is the only element with **global scope**. This means that this element definition is available for use elsewhere within the XML Schema and can be the document element of a valid instance. In a moment, we will change this schema document to give other elements global scope. This is the start of the `<Options>` definition:

```
<xsd:element name="Options">
  <xsd:complexType>
    <xsd:sequence>
```

Here, we have declared the element as being of a **complex data type**. This means that the element can contain other elements or attributes. The alternative is the **simple data type**, which we will be meeting soon. `<Options>` is defined as a sequence of elements, although it contains only one (`<Option>`). We could also define this as a choice of elements using `<xsd:choice>`, or that it must contain all of a set of elements in any order using `<xsd:all>`. `<Options>` also contains a single attribute (`Contested`). Let's look at the attribute first:

```
<xsd:attribute name="Contested" use="optional">
  <xsd:simpleType>
    <xsd:restriction base="xsd:string">
      <xsd:enumeration value="no"/>
      <xsd:enumeration value="yes"/>
    </xsd:restriction>
  </xsd:simpleType>
</xsd:attribute>
```

Compare this to the DTD definition:

```
<!ATTLIST Options
  Contested CDATA #IMPLIED
>
```

For a start, it is a **lot** longer, but it also allows us to add constraints on the attribute value that were not present in the DTD. Firstly, we make the attribute `optional` with the `use` attribute, which is the equivalent of the `#IMPLIED` of the DTD. Then we define it as a `simpleType`. This means that it cannot have element or attribute content of its own. This is, anyway, a restriction of XML – only elements can contain other elements or attributes. The data type of `Contested` is derived by restriction from a built-in data type `<xsd:string>`. This is a Unicode character string. In this case, our restriction is to allow only two enumerated values: `yes` or `no`. There are many other restrictions that can be used, depending on the base data type from which we are deriving our new type. For example, strings can have maximum lengths or patterns applied and numeric data types can have maximum and minimum values.

Let's now look at the <Option> element:

```
<xsd:element name="Option" maxOccurs="unbounded">
  <xsd:complexType>
    <xsd:sequence>
      <xsd:element name="OptionName">
        <xsd:complexType>
          <xsd:simpleContent>
            <xsd:extension base="xsd:string">
              <xsd:attribute name="Id" type="xsd:NMTOKEN" use="required"/>
            </xsd:extension>
          </xsd:simpleContent>
        </xsd:complexType>
      </xsd:element>
    </xsd:sequence>
    <xsd:attribute name="ID" type="xsd:string" use="optional"/>
  </xsd:complexType>
</xsd:element>
```

In the first line, we are saying that we can have an unlimited number of <Option> elements within the <Options> element, decreed by the maxOccurs attribute being set to "unbounded". This could also be a numeric value or be omitted. We could also have specified a minOccurs if there were a minimum number of options allowed. minOccurs defaults to the value 1, so by omitting it, we are saying that there must at least one option. maxOccurs defaults to the higher of the value 1 or the value of minOccurs. Thus, when we look at the line:

```
<xsd:element name="OptionName">
```

we know that an Option must have exactly one <OptionName>. <OptionName> is again defined as a complex data type as it has an attribute. Because it cannot have child elements it is known as a complex type with **simple content**. This is an example of an <OptionName> element:

```
<OptionName Id="1">Arsenal</OptionName>
```

Apart from the attribute, which is declared as required, the element has a string value. We have defined the Id as an NMTOKEN (name token), which is a string with a character set restricted to those characters used in XML names.

Finally, in this definition of <Option>, we have an optional Id attribute. This is of the <xsd:string> data type.

The Ballot Using Global Elements

In the example above, we only declared a single element (<Options>) as a child of the <xsd:schema> element, so only this is available globally. When we are creating a complete vocabulary such as EML, however, we will want to reuse other elements. We can therefore declare these globally as well. In this case, we make <Option> a global element, as it is likely to be used elsewhere in the language:

```
<?xml version="1.0" encoding="utf-8"?>
<xsd:schema xmlns:xsd="http://www.w3.org/2001/XMLSchema">
  <xsd:element name="Options">
    <xsd:complexType>
      <xsd:sequence>
        <xsd:element ref="Option" maxOccurs="unbounded"/>
      </xsd:sequence>
      <xsd:attribute name="Contested" use="optional">
        <xsd:simpleType>
          <xsd:restriction base="xsd:string">
            <xsd:enumeration value="no"/>
            <xsd:enumeration value="yes"/>
          </xsd:restriction>
        </xsd:simpleType>
      </xsd:attribute>
    </xsd:complexType>
  </xsd:element>
  <xsd:element name="Option">
    <xsd:complexType>
      <xsd:sequence>
        <xsd:element name="OptionName">
          <xsd:complexType>
            <xsd:simpleContent>
              <xsd:extension base="xsd:string">
                <xsd:attribute name="Id" type="xsd:NMTOKEN" use="required"/>
              </xsd:extension>
            </xsd:simpleContent>
          </xsd:complexType>
        </xsd:element>
      </xsd:sequence>
      <xsd:attribute name="ID" type="xsd:string" use="optional"/>
    </xsd:complexType>
  </xsd:element>
</xsd:schema>
```

The changes are relatively small. Instead of the declaration of `<Option>` being embedded in the declaration of `<Options>`, it has been brought outside as a child of `<xsd:schema>`. Any other definition can now access this, which is done using the `ref` keyword as in this example. This is very useful if the same element will appear in more than one place in the schema. We saw earlier, however, that XML Schema has no concept of the document element of an instance document. The previous version of this schema only had a single global definition – `<Options>`. We now have a second global definition – `<Option>` – so a document with this as the document element will be passed by a validating parser using this version of the schema.

Defining Data Types

So far, we have only used the built-in data types of XML Schema, but we can also define our own. In this case, there seems to be scope to define two useful data types. We could have several elements or attributes that can only have a value of `yes` or `no`, so we could define a data type for this:

```
<xsd:simpleType name="YesNoType">
  <xsd:restriction base="xsd:string">
    <xsd:enumeration value="no"/>
    <xsd:enumeration value="yes"/>
  </xsd:restriction>
</xsd:simpleType>
```

Before, this type was embedded within the declaration of the `Contested` attribute, and so had no name. This is known as an **anonymous** type. Now, we want to make it available to other element or attribute definitions, so it needs a name. Other than that, the declaration has not changed.

The second useful data type is for a name with an `Id` attribute. This could be pulled out from the `OptionName` and declared like this:

```
<xsd:complexType name="NameType">
  <xsd:simpleContent>
    <xsd:extension base="xsd:string">
      <xsd:attribute name="Id" type="xsd:NMTOKEN" use="required"/>
    </xsd:extension>
  </xsd:simpleContent>
</xsd:complexType>
```

We can then access these types just like the built-in data types:

```
<xsd:element name="Options">
  <xsd:complexType>
    <xsd:sequence>
      <xsd:element ref="Option" maxOccurs="unbounded"/>
    </xsd:sequence>
    <xsd:attribute name="Contested" type="YesNoType" use="optional"/>
  </xsd:complexType>
</xsd:element>
<xsd:element name="Option">
  <xsd:complexType>
    <xsd:sequence>
      <xsd:element name="OptionName" type="NameType"/>
    </xsd:sequence>
    <xsd:attribute name="ID" type="xsd:string" use="optional"/>
  </xsd:complexType>
</xsd:element>
```

So now we have seen three models for schemas: embedding everything within a single element, defining elements as global, and defining named data types. In general, when creating a schema to define a specific document, the embedded (anonymous) definitions work well and do not make "private" declarations available to others. With a language such as EML, however, where several documents may be defined based on the language, global definitions become essential.

So when to use a data type and when to use an element? If you always want an element to be referenced by the same name, then define it as an element. Where there is a chance that elements with different names might be of the same structure, define a data type. Take something simple like an address. We could define an `<Address>` element and reuse this. In EML we have an electoral address, which is what gives someone the right to vote in a particular area, and a correspondence address. So we define a global `AddressStructure` data type and use this as the data type for `<ElectoralAddress>` and `<MailingAddress>` elements.

Schemas and Namespaces

We have only given an introduction to XML Schema here. Covering it in detail would take a complete book (see, for instance, **Mohr, S. et al, Professional XML Schemas, Wrox Press, 2001**, ISBN: *1861005-47-4*). One important topic is the relationship between schemas and namespaces. When defining a schema, it is possible to define the namespace within which an instance document must reside. This is done using the `targetNamespace` attribute of the `<xsd:schema>` element. If we do this, then any reference to these elements within the schema must also use this namespace. It avoids complications if this is defined as the default namespace of the XML Schema. So our top-level element could change to:

```
<xsd:schema
  targetNamespace="urn:oasis:names:tc:evs:schema:eml"
  xmlns="urn:oasis:names:tc:evs:schema:eml"
  xmlns:xsd="http://www.w3.org/2001/XMLSchema"
  elementFormDefault="qualified"
  attributeFormDefault="unqualified">
```

In this we have also set `elementFormDefault` to `"qualified"`. This ensures that nested elements within the instance document must use the EML namespace. By setting `attributeFormDefault` to `"unqualified"`, we ensure that attributes defined in EML are treated as belonging to the namespace of their containing element, which is the default for XML. We would only change this if we were to use the EML attributes attached to non-EML elements.

Earlier, we declared some useful data types – `NameType` and `YesNoType`. These were declared within our ballot Schema. In practice, a language such as EML has multiple schemas, so we would like these definitions to be available to all of them. To do this, we can use the equivalent of the "include" files from programming languages. All we do is create a new schema document with just the definitions we want to reuse and use an `<xsd:include>` statement in the ballot schema to include it there. If we call the new document `emlcore.xsd`, we include it in the ballot schema like so:

```
<?xml version="1.0" encoding="utf-8"?>
<xsd:schema
  targetNamespace="urn:oasis:names:tc:evs:schema:eml"
  xmlns="urn:oasis:names:tc:evs:schema:eml"
  xmlns:xsd="http://www.w3.org/2001/XMLSchema"
  elementFormDefault="qualified"
  attributeFormDefault="unqualified">
  <xsd:include href="emlcore.xsd"/>
  <xsd:element name="Options">
    .
    .
    .
```

The included schema is sometimes referred to as an **architectural** schema, as its aim is to provide building blocks for the **document** schemas against which documents will be validated. If we also want to reference schemas that have a different `targetNamespace` from our schema, we can import these schemas, complete with their namespaces. This is beyond the scope of this introduction, but the XML Schemas book mentioned above covers this in detail.

Assigning a Schema to a Document

Once we have created a schema, we will need to reference it from within an instance document if we want our XML parser to validate the document. We do this with the attribute `schemaLocation` (or `noNamespaceSchemaLocation` if our schema has no target namespace). Since we have just introduced a target namespace, let us use this. Of course, these keywords have some meaning, and they are not part of the XML Recommendation, so they will be part of some other namespace. In fact, they are part of a W3C-controlled namespace known as the **XML Schema Instance** namespace. The conventional prefix used to refer to this is `xsi`. We therefore have to declare this namespace from within our instance, as well as the namespace for EML (which we will make our default). If we completed the ballot schema (remember, we have only written the schema fragment for the `<Options>` element), we would change the document element of our instance to the following:

```
<EML
  xmlns="urn:oasis:names:tc:evs:schema:eml"
  xmlns:xsi="http://www.w3.org/2001/XMLSchema-instance"
  xsi:schemaLocation="urn:oasis:names:tc:evs:schema:eml ballot.xsd">

  ...

</EML>
```

Note the syntax of the `xsi:schemaLocation` attribute. The value of this comprises a namespace URI followed by a URI that is the physical location of the XML Schema. In this case, this is a local reference, but it could be a fully qualified URI to find the schema document on the Internet. In fact, the value of `xsi:schemaLocation` can be any number of pairs of URIs, the first URI of each pair being a namespace and the second the location of the associated XML Schema. This allows several XML Schema documents to be associated with one instance. For example, the furniture catalog we produced earlier could be validated against both a catalog schema and the XHTML schema. The XML Schema to be used for each element is indicated by the namespace in which the element belongs.

Schemas and Entity Declarations

We saw earlier how we can use entity references and how we define the substitutions using entity declarations in the DTD. What happens if we are validating using an XML Schema rather than a DTD? XML Schema does not provide facilities for defining entities in the same way as a DTD, so the solution is to use both. There is no reason why you should not have both an XML Schema and a DTD referenced in your document, using the XML Schema for validation and the DTD just for entity declarations. The following example defines the entity `copyright` within the EML ballot:

```
<?xml version="1.0" encoding="UTF-8"?>
<!DOCTYPE EML [
<!ENTITY copyright "Copyright 2002 OASIS">
]>

<EML
  xmlns="urn:oasis:names:tc:evs:schema:eml"
  xmlns:xsi="http://www.w3.org/2001/XMLSchema-instance"
  xsi:schemaLocation="urn:oasis:names:tc:evs:schema:eml ballot.xsd">

  ....

</EML>
```

Defining Other Constraints

In many cases, there will be constraints required on a document that cannot be represented in either a DTD or an XML Schema. For example, a tax system will have rules such as "if the value of `Sex` is `male`, then there must not be a `MaternityPay` element". In many cases, these are hard-coded as business rules, but there are alternatives to this approach.

The DTD and XML Schema are both examples of **closed** schema languages. That is, they forbid anything that the schema does not explicitly allow. Although XML Schema allows a certain amount of extensibility, it is still a fundamentally closed language. There are other schema languages that are **open**, allowing any content that the schema does not explicitly forbid. Because they are open, they can be used either as an alternative to the two languages considered above, or as a supplement, with the processing of the supplementary schema occurring after the processing of the closed schema. This allows additional constraints to be tested independently of the main schema definition. Examples of these languages are Schematron (*http://www.ascc.net/xml/resource/schematron/schematron.html*) and RELAX NG (*http://www.oasis-open.org/committees/relax-ng/*), both of which will allow testing of constraints involving multiple XML nodes.

Summary of DTDs and Schemas

We have seen how DTDs and other forms of schema (in this case the W3C XML Schema language) can be used to constrain the markup used within a document. The DTD also allows the declaration of entities, while XML Schema allows constraints to be applied to data types as well as structure. Here are some of the key points:

- The DTD and XML Schema both allow the structure of an XML document to be defined such that it can be checked with a validating parser.
- The DTD also allows the definition of entities.
- XML Schema additionally allows data types to be assigned to character data.
- XML Schema supports the definition of custom data types.
- XML Schema supports the derivation of one data type from another.
- XML Schema has good support for namespaces, while the DTD does not.
- XML Schema allows modular development using `<xsd:include>` and `<xsd:import>`.
- XML Schema uses XML markup syntax and so schemas can be created and modified using standard XML processing tools.
- The DTD uses a far more concise syntax than XML Schema.
- In general, the DTD is good for text-based documents if good namespace support is not required. XML Schema can handle both text- and data-based documents well.
- There are other schema languages than those described here, with differing levels of support. Some of these allow inter-node constraints to be defined.

XML Schema is much newer than the DTD specification, and so has addressed some of the weaknesses of the DTD. It is more suitable than the DTD for describing data-orientated XML documents and has other strengths shown previously that make it the schema language of choice for many people for any schema. Some people with text-based applications stay with the DTD because it is more concise.

Some XML Languages

Now that you have seen how to define an XML language using a DTD or schema, I will ask you to pause for a moment. There are already many – far too many – languages defined using XML. Many of these compete with one another, and so some will grow and some die through a process of natural selection (otherwise known as marketing!). Before defining your own language, why not look to see what is out there already – there may well already be a language that will suit your needs.

We have already met a few of these XML languages such as the Election Markup Language and XML Schema, and we will meet several more in this book. The table below shows a few to consider.

XML Language	Applicability
XBRL (Extensible Business Reporting Language)	Business reporting
MDDL (Market Data Definition Language)	Stock market information
Legal XML	Legal document management
HR-XML (Human Resources XML)	Human Resource Management
NewsML	News feeds
ebXML (Electronic Business XML)	E-commerce
OAGIS (Open Applications Group Integration Specification)	Human Resource Management
	Finance e-commerce
	Purchasing
	Logistics
BPML (Business Process Modeling Language)	Logistics
EML (Election Mark up Language)	E-Voting
SMIL (Synchronized Multimedia Integration Language)	Multi-media
MathML	Marking up mathematical formulae
Chemical Markup Language	Describing chemical structures
SVG (Scalable Vector Graphics)	A vector graphics language

I have not given URLs for all of these – a web search will find them easily enough, and will be easier to type in as well. Now it's time to look at how XML documents are actually processed.

The XML Processing Model

The XML recommendation makes certain assumptions about the way in which an XML document will be processed. Rather than an application just treating the document as a piece of text, the model indicates the use of an **XML processor** that passes the content and structure of the document to an **application**. You will usually hear the XML processor referred to as an **XML parser** since it is parsing the XML document and passing on the information. The following diagram shows the model assumed:

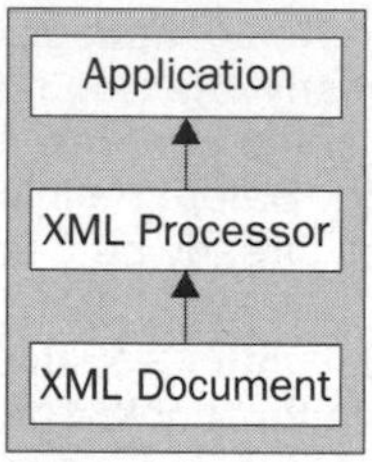

In general, you will use a standard XML processor such as Microsoft's MSXML, Apache's Xerces, or the Oracle XML parser and write an application to use the parser you choose. Some XML parsers are also available as pre-packaged software. The most common examples of these are the XSLT (Extensible Stylesheet Language Transformations – more about this language in *Chapters 5 and 6*) processors used to display XML in a web browser. Note that MSXML contains both an XML parser and an XSLT processor, and so should be considered as both an XML processor and an application.

Types of XML Processor

There are two basic categories of XML processor – **tree-based** and **event-based**. Many XML processors, including later versions of Microsoft's MSXML, support both models. You will often hear tree-based parsers referred to as **DOM-based** parsers, while the event-based parsers are referred to as **SAX** parsers. Both of these are named after the specifications they support.

The **DOM** (**Document Object Model**) is a W3C recommendation and provides an application programming interface (API) to an XML document. An application can use this API to manipulate the document, reading information, adding new nodes (elements, attributes, processing instructions, etc.) and moving and altering those that are already there.

SAX, or the **Simple API for XML**, was developed by an ad hoc team brought together through the *xml-dev* mailing list (see *http://lists.xml.org/archives/xml-dev/*). Although it does not have official standing, it is well supported by both large and small software companies. A SAX-based parser reads an XML document sequentially, firing off events as it reaches important parts of the document, such as the start or end of an element.

DOM-based Parsing

The XML representation of a ballot can be represented as a tree structure:

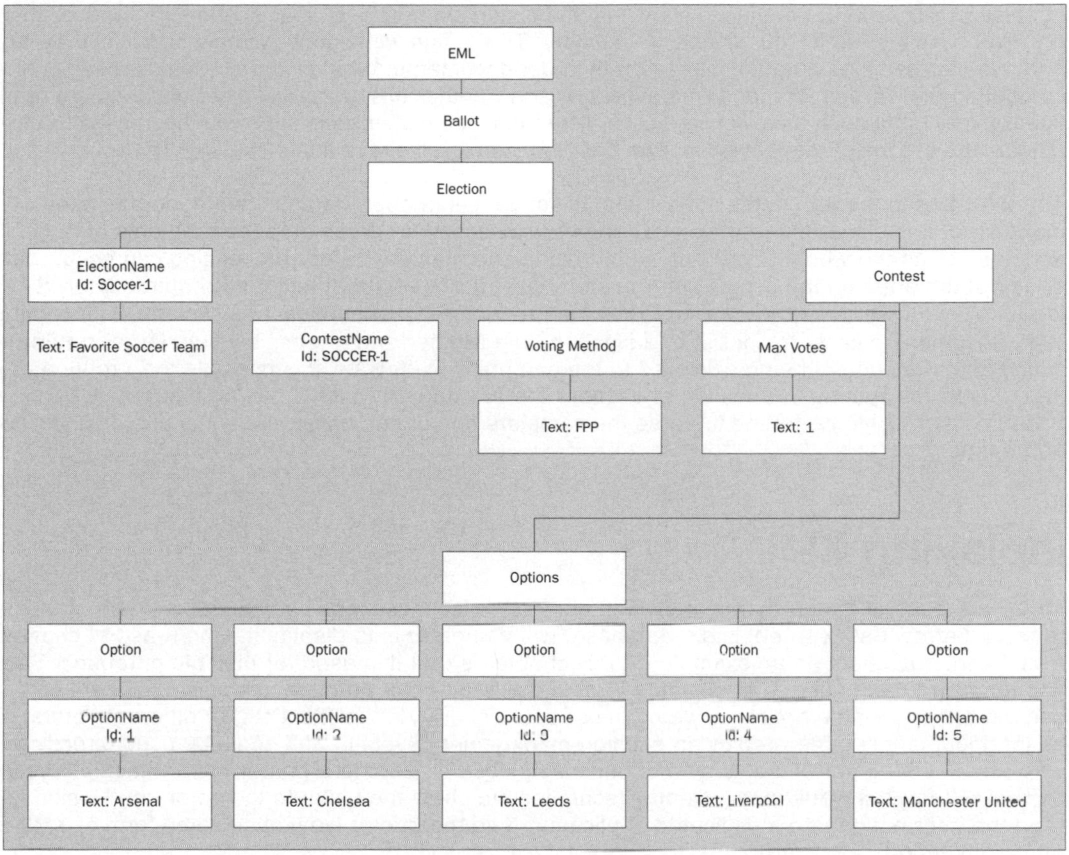

This tree structure introduces the concepts of **parent**, **child**, **sibling**, **ancestor**, and **descendant**, just as in a family tree. Thus `<ElectionName>` and `<Contest>` are children of `<Election>` and siblings of each other, while both these elements and all those below them are descendants of `<Election>`. The DOM allows access to these elements, their values, and all other parts of the XML document from either a programming language or from a scripting language such as ECMAScript.

SAX Parsing

A SAX-based parser presents a document as a string of events, where the programmer has to write handlers for each event. These handlers are bits of code that do something suitable when the occurrence of an event triggers them. Whilst this makes it suitable for use with languages with good event-handling properties like C++ or Java, it is less suitable for use with the scripting languages usually employed on the Web, so it is not covered here.

Why Have Two Parsing Models?

Each of these models has its advantages. DOM-based parsing provides full read-write access to an XML document, and easy access to any nodes within the document. It can also validate a document against a DTD or XML Schema to show that the document meets its specification. To achieve this, however, it reads the full document into memory. This is fine with small documents, but can be slow and use excessive amounts of memory with larger documents. What is large? This depends on the computing power, memory, and time available, and whether this is a single-user environment or multi-user environment such as a web server. In general, most systems will cope with documents up to megabytes or tens of megabytes in size, but care is needed above this.

The SAX-based model, on the other hand, is sequential in operation. Once a node has been processed, it is discarded and the next node processed. This eliminates the problems of large documents, as the whole document is not loaded into memory before processing can occur, but does put the onus on the programmer to store any information that might be required later. SAX is ideal, for example, for an intermediate routing product in a communications system. An incoming XML document is likely to consist of a small routing **header** and a (possibly very large) **payload**, which is the document being delivered to the end point. With SAX, it is possible for a routing device just to read the routing information and ignore the payload, in which it has no interest. A DOM-based parser would be forced to parse the complete document, using additional processing power and memory.

Displaying XML

There are several things we might do with our XML once it reaches its destination. One of these is to read the raw data content into a database, while another is to display it. One reason I chose the EML ballot document as an example for this chapter is that it is used for multiple purposes. The document we have used is a simplified form of the original. In practice, a single document can contain either a single ballot (as we have used) or several different ballots for different voters. The ballot document is generated by an election management system, and could be used directly by a web-based voting portal, some type of dedicated kiosk, or sent to a printer to print multiple ballot papers. The portal would use a display technology to show the ballot to the voter, the kiosk might read the information into a dedicated application, and the printer would use some form of XML to print conversion.

In this section, we are interested in the display technologies, so we will use the web portal example. We will use this section purely to introduce these technologies – they are described in much more detail later in the book.

XML and CSS

No doubt you have used Cascading Style Sheets with HTML. The good news is that they work in exactly the same way with XML. All you need to do is assign a style to an element name just as you would with HTML. The main difference is the way in which the stylesheet is associated with the document. In XML, this is done using a processing instruction placed immediately after the XML declaration:

```
<?xml-stylesheet type="text/css" href="style.css"?>
```

With HTML, you are used to all the text that you want to display being in character data. With XML, that might not be the case. For example, in the ballot message, we had the list of soccer teams for which you could vote, but the only indication that these were the candidates in an election was the element name `<Option>`. CSS does not let you add text to describe this when rendering the document. This is fine for mainly textual documents, such as technical reports, but less useful with data-centric products like our ballot. Even the ability to display data in a different order from that in the document is limited.

The CSS model of styling is known as a **push model**, since the data is generally displayed in the order that it is present in the source document. When displaying XML, we generally need far more flexibility to allow data to be displayed in any order and to add data when the document is rendered, even though that data may not have been in the source document. XSL gives us that flexibility.

XSL

The Extensible Stylesheet Language is divided into two parts – XSL Transformations (XSLT) and XSL Formatting Objects (XSL-FO). The former transforms the source XML document into some other form (such as HTML), and the latter applies styling. The model used is shown in the diagram.

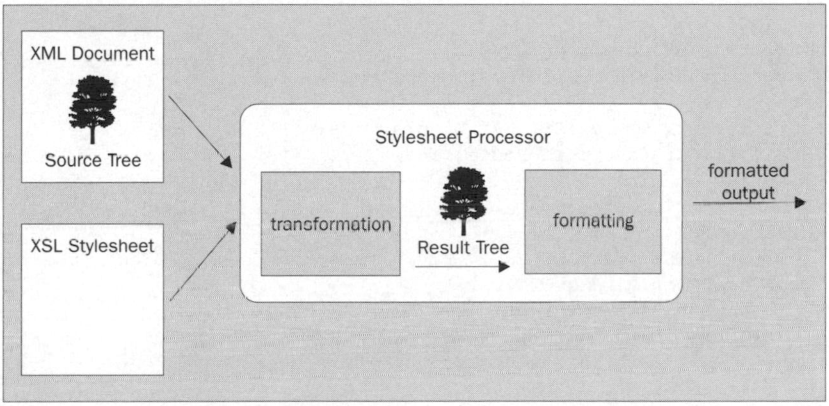

In practice, it is usual on the Web to use the transformation stage to produce HTML or XHTML (perhaps with embedded CSS) and not to use the XSL formatting stage.

Let's start with the terminology. Once it is read into memory, for example by accessing a URL or reading it from a disk, the XML document is known as the **source tree**. Nodes in the source tree (**source nodes**) are transformed using **templates** in the stylesheet to produce **result nodes**, which together form a **result tree**. The result tree will be well-formed XML (although we will see that it can be converted to produce output relevant to a particular context – known as **serialization**). This result tree can then be formatted using XSL-FO to produce a formatted output, although, as mentioned earlier, the result tree is likely to be serialized as HTML or XHTML. We will therefore only look at XSLT.

What XSLT Does For Us

We will be looking at XSLT in detail later in the book, in *Chapters 5* and *6*. Our aim here is just to walk through an example to see the power of the language. As in most web-based situations, we will use XSLT to convert an XML document into an HTML document styled with CSS. Note that in this case we are not using CSS to style the XML, but to style the HTML produced from it by applying an XSLT stylesheet.

We saw earlier that CSS styles its source document using a push model, where the structure of the output is defined by the structure of the input. XSLT allows both a push model and a **pull** model, where the structure of the output is defined by the structure of the stylesheet. In this case, we have a little of each, where the source document defines the display order of its major parts, but the stylesheet contains the main structuring information, pulling the data from the XML document as it requires it.

Transforming the Ballot

In this section, we are going to leap straight into XSLT by taking a stylesheet and explaining how it works.

XML is capable of separating content from style. The example stylesheet we're about to look at was designed to handle many different types of ballot. For that reason, EML allows some control over display style to be included in the XML message. There are two ways of doing this. The first is to allow HTML to be embedded in the message for display-orientated information. The second is the use of a `DisplayOrder` attribute. This allows the creator of the XML to control where, for example, the information on how to vote should be displayed. Here is a ballot message much as it was created as part of the EML testing process:

```
<?xml version="1.0" encoding="UTF-8"?>
<EML xmlns="urn:oasis:names:tc:evs:schema:eml">
  <Ballots>
    <ElectionEventName Id="SOCCER" DisplayOrder="1">
      Vote For Your Favourite Soccer Team
    </ElectionEventName>
    <Ballot>
      <Election>
        <ElectionName Id="SOCCER-1">Favorite soccer team.</ElectionName>
        <Description DisplayOrder="2">
          <Message Format="html">
            <html xmlns="http://www.w3.org/TR/REC-html40">
              <p>Please select your favourite soccer team.</p>
            </html>
          </Message>
          <Message Format="text">
            Please select your favourite soccer team
          </Message>
        </Description>
        <Contest DisplayOrder="3">
          <ContestName Id="SOCCER-1"/>
          <VotingMethod>FPP</VotingMethod>
          <MaxVotes>1</MaxVotes>
          <Options Contested="yes">
            <Option>
              <OptionName Id="1">Arsenal</OptionName>
            </Option>
            <Option>
              <OptionName Id="2">Chelsea</OptionName>
            </Option>
            <Option>
              <OptionName Id="3">Leeds</OptionName>
```

```
            </Option>
            <Option>
              <OptionName Id="4">Liverpool</OptionName>
            </Option>
            <Option>
              <OptionName Id="5">Manchester United</OptionName>
            </Option>
          </Options>
        </Contest>
      </Election>
    </Ballot>
  </Ballots>
</EML>
```

This is by far the simplest and smallest of the test ballots, with only three `DisplayOrder` attributes used to position the election event name at the top of the screen, followed by the description and then the options available. The description has been provided in two formats – HTML for display in a browser and text for printing. The HTML description uses the HTML 4.0 namespace to differentiate it from the remainder of the message. This is how the end result will look:

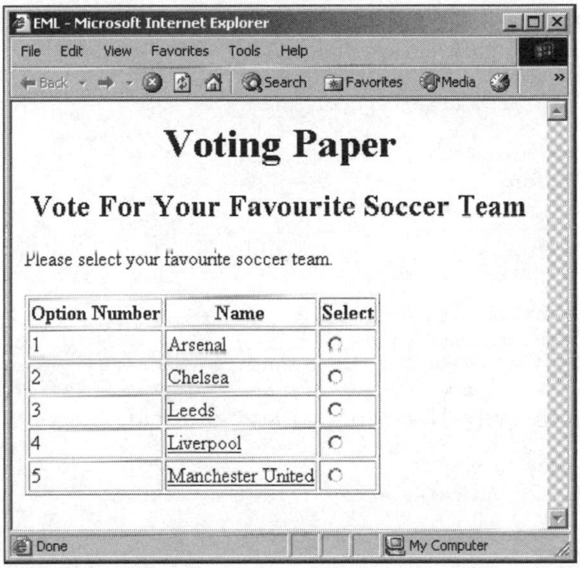

This is not a very sophisticated rendition – adding some CSS styling would help, but it serves to show that a lot appears on the display that is not in the original XML. For example, we have the heading *Voting Paper* as well as a table and some radio buttons.

This is the HTML that was produced using the stylesheet:

```
<html xmlns:html="http://www.w3.org/TR/REC-html40"
      xmlns:eml="urn:oasis:names:tc:evs:schema:eml">
<head>
<META http-equiv="Content-Type" content="text/html; charset=UTF-16">
<title>EML</title><script language="JavaScript">
  function display(strId, strTitle, strStylesheet)
```

```
  {
    var newWindow = window.open('','newWin',
                    'width=500,height=400,scrollbars=yes,top=100,left=100');
    var strOut = document.all(strId).innerHTML;
    newWindow.document.write('<html><head><title>');
    newWindow.document.write(strTitle);
    newWindow.document.write('</title>');
    newWindow.document.write('<link rel="stylesheet" type="text/css" href="');
    newWindow.document.write(strStylesheet);
    newWindow.document.write('"/></head><body>');
    newWindow.document.write(strOut);
    newWindow.document.write("</body></html>");
  }
    </script></head>
<body>
<h1 style="text-align:center">Voting Paper</h1>
<h2 style="text-align:center">
   Vote For Your Favourite Soccer Team
  </h2>
<p xmlns:auto-ns1="urn:oasis:names:tc:evs:schema:eml"
   xmlns:xsi="http://www.w3.org/2001/XMLSchema-instance"
   xmlns="http://www.w3.org/TR/REC-html40">
  Please select your favourite soccer team.</p>
<table border="1">
<tr>
<th>Option Number</th>
<th>Name</th>
<th>Select</th>
</tr>
<tr>
<td style="align:center">1</td>
<td title=""><a href="
      javascript:display('IDAQBQJB','What is the favourite soccer team.','');
     ">Arsenal</a><div style="display:none" id="IDAQBQJB">
       Name: <span style="font-weight:bold">Arsenal</span></div>
</td>
<td style="align:center">
  <input type="radio" name="ASOCCER-1" id="1" value="1">
</td>
</tr>
<tr>
<td style="align:center">2</td>
<td title=""><a href="
      javascript:display('IDAUBQJB','What is the favourite soccer team.','');
     ">Chelsea</a><div style="display:none" id="IDAUBQJB">
       Name: <span style="font-weight:bold">Chelsea</span></div>
</td>
<td style="align:center">
  <input type="radio" name="ASOCCER-1" id="2" value="2">
</td>
</tr>
<tr>
<td style="align:center">3</td>
```

```
<td title=""><a href="
      javascript:display('IDAYBQJB','What is the favourite soccer team.','');
     ">Leeds</a><div style="display:none" id="IDAYBQJB">
       Name: <span style="font-weight:bold">Leeds</span></div>
</td>
<td style="align:center">
  <input type="radio" name="ASOCCER-1" id="3" value="3">
</td>
</tr>
<tr>
<td style="align:center">4</td>
<td title=""><a href="
      javascript:display('IDA2BQJB','What is the favourite soccer team.','');
     ">Liverpool</a><div style="display:none" id="IDA2BQJB">
       Name: <span style="font-weight:bold">Liverpool</span></div>
</td>
<td style="align:center">
  <input type="radio" name="ASOCCER-1" id="4" value="4">
</td>
</tr>
<tr>
<td style="align:center">5</td>
<td title=""><a href="
      javascript:display('IDAACQJB','What is the favourite soccer team.','');
     ">Manchester United</a><div style="display:none" id="IDAACQJB">
       Name: <span style="font-weight:bold">Manchester United</span></div>
</td>
<td style="align:center">
  <input type="radio" name="ASOCCER-1" id="5" value="5">
</td>
</tr>
</table>
</body>
</html>
```

Let's have a look at how it was produced.

The Stylesheet

It is conventional to use an `xsl` prefix to denote the XSLT namespace, so we shall declare that in the document element of our stylesheet. We will be accessing EML elements in our source tree, so we also require that namespace to be declared. We are also required to declare the version of XSLT that we are using, so this is the document element of our stylesheet:

```
<xsl:stylesheet
  version="1.0"
  xmlns:xsl="http://www.w3.org/1999/XSL/Transform"
  xmlns:eml="urn:oasis:names:tc:evs:schema:eml">
```

Next, we will declare our output type to be HTML. Remember that I said earlier that the result tree was well-formed XML but that it can be serialized to something different? This is the way that is done. If we have an output type of `xml`, we will get well-formed XML with entity references where required, empty elements like `<br />` and so on. By declaring our output type as `html`, the stylesheet processor will create more conventional HTML, for example converting any `<br />` element in our stylesheet to `<br>`.

```
<xsl:output method="html"/>
```

The final alternative output type is `text`, which will convert entity references back to their character strings. This is useful, for example, to convert XML into a comma-delimited file for import to a spreadsheet.

Next, we will look at our first template:

```
<xsl:template match="/">
  <html>
    <head>
      <title>EML</title>
    </head>
    <body>
      <xsl:apply-templates select="eml:EML"/>
    </body>
  </html>
</xsl:template>
```

The first line tells us what nodes in the source tree we are matching with this template. In this case, it is the **root node**, denoted by the slash (`/`). Note that the root node is not the same as the root element – it is a level higher in the document, and has the root element as a child. This allows the stylesheet access to information in the prolog and epilog as well as information in element content.

The purpose of the template is to copy the literal text contained within it from the source tree to the result tree, while executing any XSLT commands (that is, elements in the XSLT namespace) that it meets on the way. The result of processing this template is to produce the following output:

```
  <html>
    <head>
      <title>EML</title>
    </head>
    <body>
      <!-- the result of processing the eml:EML element will go here -->
    </body>
  </html>
```

We therefore have the structure of an HTML document, and an instruction to the XSLT processor to execute another template. When it does this, it will replace the comment I have put in the code above with the result gleaned from processing the `<eml:EML>` element.

In fact, I have simplified this template. This is the actual one used:

```
<xsl:template match="/">
  <html>
    <head>
      <title>EML</title>
      <xsl:if test=".//eml:Stylesheet[@Type='text/css']">
        <link rel="stylesheet" type="text/css"
              href="{.//eml:Stylesheet[@Type='text/css']}"/>
      </xsl:if>
      <script language="JavaScript"><![CDATA[
      function display(strId, strTitle, strStylesheet)
```

```
    {
      var newWindow = window.open('','newWin',
                       'width=500,height=400,scrollbars=yes,top=100,left=100');
      var strOut = document.all(strId).innerHTML;
      newWindow.document.write('<html><head><title>');
      newWindow.document.write(strTitle);
      newWindow.document.write('</title>');
      newWindow.document.write('<link rel="stylesheet" type="text/css" href="');
      newWindow.document.write(strStylesheet);
      newWindow.document.write('"/></head><body>');
      newWindow.document.write(strOut);
      newWindow.document.write("</body></html>");
    }
    ]]></script>
  </head>
  <body>
    <xsl:apply-templates select="eml:EML"/>
  </body>
</html>
</xsl:template>
```

There are two additions here. The first is a conditional statement to reference a CSS stylesheet in the output HTML if there was one identified in the input, contained in the `<xsl:if>` element. The second is to add some ECMAScript to the output, contained within the `<script>` element. Note how the script is contained in a `CDATA` section so that the XML parser does not attempt to process it.

Let's look at the conditional instruction in more detail:

```
<xsl:if test=".//eml:Stylesheet[@Type='text/css']">
  <link rel="stylesheet" type="text/css"
        href="{.//eml:Stylesheet[@Type='text/css']}"/>
</xsl:if>
```

This contains an **XPath expression** (`.//eml:Stylesheet[@Type='text/css']`). XPath is used to identify nodes in an XML document. In this case, we are looking for a descendant of the root node whose name is `eml:Stylesheet`, and that has an attribute named `Type` with a value `text/css`. The dot at the start of the expression indicates that the rest of the expression is looking for nodes relative to our current context. The context in this case is the node for which we are applying templates, that is, the root node. The double slash indicates any descendant of the context element (whereas a single slash would just indicate a child of the context element – not grandchildren), the `@` sign indicates an attribute, and the square brackets indicate a test. XPath is an essential part of XSLT, and we will look at it in much more detail later in the book.

Let's move swiftly on to the template for the `<EML>` element:

```
<xsl:template match="eml:EML">
  <h1 style="text-align:center">Voting Paper</h1>
  <xsl:apply-templates select=".//*[@DisplayOrder]">
    <xsl:sort select="./@DisplayOrder" data-type="number"/>
  </xsl:apply-templates>
</xsl:template>
```

Again, we start with some literal text that will be passed unchanged, and interpreted by the browser as HTML (the second line). We then have another instruction to apply templates. This time, we are selecting all descendant elements (the asterisk indicates all elements) that have a `DisplayOrder` attribute. This time, we have an `xsl:sort` instruction to control the order in which these elements are processed. In this case, we will process them in ascending display order. The `data-type` value of `number` indicates that this is a numeric sort rather than alphabetical, so 2 will come before 10.

So our output tree now looks like this:

```
<html>
  <head>
    <title>EML</title>
  </head>
  <body>
    <h1 style="text-align:center">Voting Paper</h1>
    <!-- the result of processing the elements with
         DisplayOrder atributes will go here -->
  </body>
</html>
```

Here is the remainder of the stylesheet.:

```
<xsl:template match="eml:ElectionEventName">
  <h2 style="text-align:center">
    <xsl:value-of select="."/>
  </h2>
</xsl:template>
<xsl:template match="/eml:Messages">
  <xsl:apply-templates/>
</xsl:template>
<xsl:template match="eml:ContestName">
  <h3 style="text-align:center">
    <xsl:value-of select="."/>
  </h3>
</xsl:template>
<xsl:template match="eml:OptionName">
  <xsl:text>Name: </xsl:text>
  <span style="font-weight:bold">
    <xsl:value-of select="."/>
  </span>
</xsl:template>
<xsl:template match="eml:Message[@Format='html']">
  <!--  <xsl:copy-of select="html:html/*"/> -->
  <xsl:copy-of select="html:html/*"/>
</xsl:template>
<xsl:template match="eml:ElectionName">
  <h3 style="align:center">
    <xsl:value-of select="."/>
  </h3>
</xsl:template>
<xsl:template match="eml:Contest">
  <table border="1">
    <tr>
      <th>Option Number</th>
      <th>Name</th>
      <th>
```

```
        <xsl:choose>
          <xsl:when test="eml:VotingMethod='STV'">Order of Preference</xsl:when>
          <xsl:when test="eml:VotingMethod='FPP'">Select</xsl:when>
        </xsl:choose>
      </th>
    </tr>
    <xsl:for-each select="eml:Options/eml:Option">
      <tr>
        <td style="align:center">
          <xsl:value-of select="eml:OptionName/@Id"/>
        </td>
        <td title="{eml:Affiliation}">
          <xsl:variable name="strTitle" select="/.//eml:ElectionName"/>
          <xsl:variable name="strStylesheet"
                select="/.//eml:Display/eml:Stylesheet[@Type='text/css']"/>
          <xsl:variable name="strId" select="generate-id(eml:OptionName)"/>
          <a>
            <xsl:attribute name="href">
            javascript:display('<xsl:value-of select="$strId"/>',
                               '<xsl:value-of select="$strTitle"/>',
                               '<xsl:value-of select="$strStylesheet"/>');
          </xsl:attribute>
            <xsl:value-of select="eml:OptionName"/>
          </a>
          <div style="display:none" id="{generate-id(eml:OptionName)}">
            <xsl:apply-templates select="eml:OptionName"/>
            <xsl:apply-templates
                     select="eml:Description/eml:Message[@Format='html']"/>
          </div>
        </td>
        <td style="align:center">
          <!-- put in a drop-down box with the number of different options
               if should give order of preference, otherwise put a tick box. -->
          <xsl:variable name="intOptions" select="../../eml:MaxVotes"/>
          <xsl:variable name="strOption" select="eml:OptionName/@Id"/>
          <xsl:if test="$intOptions > 1">
            <select id="{$strOption}" style="width=100%">
              <xsl:for-each select="../eml:Option">
                <option value="{position()}">
                  <xsl:value-of select="position()"/>
                </option>
              </xsl:for-each>
            </select>
          </xsl:if>
          <xsl:if test="$intOptions = 1">
            <input type="radio" name="A{../../eml:ContestName/@Id}"
                   id="{$strOption}" value="{$strOption}"/>
          </xsl:if>
        </td>
      </tr>
    </xsl:for-each>
  </table>
</xsl:template>
xsl:stylesheet>
```

The meaning of much of this is clear from the examples we have looked at. There are some new XSLT constructs such as the use of variables and `xsl:choose`. Come back and have a look at this in detail once you have completed the XSLT chapters.

XSLT Summary

We have had a quick look through XSLT here to see what it can do – below are some key points to remember:

> Whilst CSS styles the XML as it finds it (a push model), XSLT can be used to transform the output into any well-formed XML that can then be serialized as XML, HTML, or text.
>
> XSLT can produce an output that has information in a different order to the input.
>
> XSLT can add text and markup (such as headings) to the output.
>
> XSLT is template-based, making it mainly a declarative language.
>
> XSLT makes extensive use of XPath to locate nodes in the source tree.

Linking with XML

When HTML first hit the streets, many SGML experts held the view that the hyperlinking was too simple to be useful. How wrong they were! It was this very simplicity that has led to the success of the World Wide Web.

This is not to say that the linking in HTML is perfect, and the linking in XML has been designed to improve on HTML, while keeping much of the simplicity. The two W3C recommendations involved are **XLink** (see *http://www.w3.org/TR/xlink/*) and **XPointer** (see *http://www.w3.org/TR/xptr/*). The former specifies the linking syntax and behavior and how to describe links between documents, while the latter defines a syntax for defining parts of documents to which a link might apply, much like an HTML **fragment identifier** (as in *http://www.domain.com/page.html#fragment-identifier*). Currently, there is very limited tool support for XLink and XPointer, although that is not to say that they should be ignored. If you are using XSLT to display XML documents in HTML, you just need a template to handle your links. I therefore use XLinks wherever I am specifying a link in an XML document.

There are two types of link that can be used: **simple** and **extended**. We will look at each in turn.

Simple Links

A simple link connects a single source to a single target, much like an HTML link:

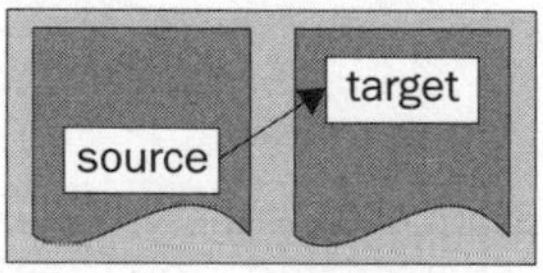

A Simple Link Example

Here is an example of a simple link:

```
<my:element xmlns:xlink="http://www.w3.org/1999/xlink"
  xlink:type="simple"
  xlink:href="soccer1.xml"
  xlink:role="http://www.example.com/ballot"
  xlink:title="Soccer Ballot"
  xlink:show="replace"
  xlink:actuate="onRequest">
  <!-- some content for my:element -->
</my:element>
```

The first three lines of this example are self-explanatory – we have an element in our own namespace (using `my` as a prefix) that contains a simple link using the XLink namespace with a target of `soccer1.xml`. The optional `role` must be a URI reference, the information at the URI being used to describe the role of the link. The optional `title` is intended to be human-readable. Whether this is displayed in some way is up to the implementation. The optional `show` attribute is used to describe the action when the link is traversed. In HTML, we might have:

```
<a href="soccer1.htm">
```

This would indicate that the new document would replace the current one. This is the action of `xlink:show="replace"`. An alternative is `xlink:show="new"`, which is intended to bring up the new resource in a separate presentation context. This could be a new window, much like the HTML:

```
<a href="soccer1.htm" target="_blank">
```

The other alternative values for `show` are `embed`, `other`, and `none`:

- The action of `embed` is similar to embedding an image in HTML – the target resource will replace the link definition in the source.
- `other` leaves the action up to the implementation, which is expected to look for other information in the link to determine its behavior.
- Lastly, `none` also leaves behavior up to the implementation, but with no hints in the link.

Finally, we have the `activate` attribute. In this example, we are going to await some user action before activating the link. This could be clicking on some blue underlined text, but could equally well be some other action. The other possible values are `onLoad`, `other`, and `none`. The value `onLoad` will cause the link to be followed immediately after the source resource is loaded. This could be used with `xlink:show="embed"` to create a display from a set of linked source documents. The values `other` and `none` have the same meanings as before.

So we can see that an XLink simple link is similar to an HTML link, but has some additional abilities. The extended link takes this much further.

Extended Links

There is currrently only limited browser support for the `Xlink` at the time of writing – and that support is restricted to the Netscape 6 browsers, as we will see in *Chapter 4*, so we will just give you a taste so that you know what is possible. You can research the subject further if you wish; *Professional XML 2nd Edition* (mentioned earlier) is a good starting point.

Extended links provide three other benefits:

- They allow more than two resources to be linked.
- They separate the direction of the link from the definition of the resources being linked.
- They allow links to be defined **out-of-line**. This means that the link does not need to be contained within any of the resources being linked.

Let's look at the benefits of each.

Linking More Than Two Resources

How often have you created a list of links in HTML that are effectively from a single point to multiple destinations? Here are a couple of examples when it is useful to be able to link to multiple destinations.

The first is a web site for cocktails. Any cocktail recipe might contain references to separate pages for the individual drinks that make up the cocktail. What if I am looking at the description of tequila, decide this takes my fancy and I want to know which cocktails contain tequila? Here my link from tequila will go to multiple destinations. In HTML we would use several links. In XML, we can use a single extended link. Of course, like XML itself, XLink does not define presentation, so it is up to us how we display these links. We could produce multiple HTML links using an XSLT stylesheet, but we could equally easily produce a drop-down list of links.

Consider this scenario instead. You are developing a travel web site. In this, the user can conduct a search for a vacation package, then follow links to any of the packages that match their requirement. The user of the site will follow several links, then might do another search, and follow others. This could go on for a while, and then they might want to go back to have another look at a vacation viewed earlier. The browser's history display might help here, but how much better to make this part of your application! All you need to do is build an extended link in memory, adding a resource every time a new vacation is viewed. This can then be presented back as a drop-down list available at any time.

Out-of-Line Linking

With HTML links and XML simple links, the definition of the link was positioned at the source point of the link. With an extended link on the other hand, the source and destination are both defined in the link itself. The link can therefore be removed from the source document. Why would you want to do that? It immediately gives you the power to add links from documents for which you do not have write permission. You can effectively build your own web of links for other people's documents. Very useful for academics and numerous others building information resources. It also makes links easier to update since they are all in a single location.

Separation of the Direction of the Link from the Resource Definitions

In an extended link, `<xlink:locator>` elements are used to define the resources participating in the links, then `<xlink:arc>` elements are used to define the connections. This allows links to be traversed in both directions, rather than having the fixed source and target of the simple link. Going back to our cocktail web site, we can now define our links so that we can follow them either way. If we are looking at a cocktail, we can follow the link to find out information about the individual ingredient included in a cocktail. If we are looking at the ingredients, we can follow the link to the cocktails that include this ingredient. All we need to do is build a "link database" containing a list of all the linked resources and the definitions of a set of arcs to be followed.

XPointer

So far, the resources we have been using have been complete documents. However, we may want our source or destination to be a point within a document or a part of a document. XPointer helps us achieve this.

This would be a typical link with a fragment identifier in HTML:

```
<a href="soccer1.htm#electiondescription">
```

The effect of clicking on this link would be to load the document and position the pointer at an element that has an attribute `name="electiondescription"`. Here is a similar XML link using XPointer:

```
<xlink:simple xmlns:xlink="http://www.w3.org/1999/xlink"
  xlink:href="soccer1.xml#xpointer(EML/Ballots/Ballot/Election/Description)"
  xlink:role="http://www.example.com/ballot"
  xlink:title="Soccer Ballot"
  xlink:show="replace"
  xlink:actuate="onRequest"/>
```

There are two major differences between the HTML link and the XPointer link. The first is that the XPointer syntax uses XPath, just as we saw with XSLT earlier. The second is that we have not had to add anything to the target document (an HTML document requires a `name` attribute). This is, of course, essential when using out-of-line extended links to link to documents that we cannot alter.

Another benefit of XPointer is that we can specify a range rather than a single point. This obviously reduces the amount of data being downloaded when viewing a small part of a large document. A further benefit is that, combined with `xlink:show="embed"`, we can embed a specified part of one document within another. In fact, we can create documents from fragments of others without needing to alter any of our source documents.

Linking with XML Summary

XLink and XPointer combine to give powerful linking facilities. Here, we have just scratched the surface.

Here are some of the main benefits compared to HTML linking:

In HTML, a link has an implied behavior – go to the end point when the user clicks on the link. In XML, there are several built-in behaviors, and others can be specified.

In HTML, a link has a single source and a single destination. An XML link can have multiple destinations.

In HTML, a link is always from the anchor (`<A>`) element to a destination. XML links can be bi-directional.

In HTML, a link is embedded at the source point of a document. In XML it can be separate from either end point of the link.

In HTML, a fragment identifier requires an attribute to be added to the destination. In XML, an XPath expression can be used instead.

In HTML a fragment identifier refers to a single point. In XML, it can refer to a portion of a document.

Some XML Tools

I am frequently asked what tools I use for XML development. There are now so many around that it is impossible for one person to compare them all, but I will give a short description of a few here. One important point is that XML Schema is complex and that tool support is mixed. I have yet to find any development tool that accurately and reliably finds every possible error in an XML schema. I therefore tend to check new schemas against two or three tools to be on the safe side. The accuracy of XML Schema development tools is improving all the time, so I hope this will become unnecessary soon.

In general, development tools for XML fall into several categories:

- Extensions to existing programmers' IDEs
- XML-specific IDEs
- Individual tools

Tools such as Visual Studio .NET (see *http://msdn.microsoft.com/vstudio/* for more details) fall into the first category. They have good XML support, but perhaps not to the level of specialization of XML-specific IDEs. If you already have a good IDE, see how well it supports XML – it might be good enough for you. Meanwhile, you can always download a trial version of one of the XML-specific tools and see if that would benefit you.

The dedicated XML IDEs tend to cover similar ground and differ in the depth of their support and their user interfaces. Most of these tools will have an XML editor, tools for creating DTDs and XML Schemas, and support for XSLT development. There are several such tools available, and it is perhaps unfair to pick any out in particular. The three I come across most often are Altova's XML Spy (*http://www.xmlspy.com/*), Tibco's Turbo XML (*http://www.tibco.com/solutions/products/extensibility/turbo_xml.jsp*), and Excelon's Stylus Studio (*http://www.exln.com/products/stylusstudio/*). Don't treat this as a complete set by any means – ask your friends and colleagues what they prefer to use.

The market in "best of breed" individual tools has been changing recently. While some of the tools have been absorbed into IDEs, new categories are coming along. Later in the book, we will be talking about tools for creating XHTML. Here I will just mention tools in a couple of categories – editors for text-based documents and repository tools for schemas. I don't often need tools in the former category, but have found that SoftQuad's XMetal (*http://www.softquad.com/products/xmetal/*) has met the few requirements I have had, while the latter category is a fairly new area in XML tools.

At the enterprise level, just creating lots of schemas and storing them as files does not work for long. Some kind of managed repository is required. Tools here are improving all the time, but two worth a mention are CorteXML from Barbadosoft (*http://www.barbadosoft.com/Products/corteXML.htm*) and XML Canon from Tibco (*http://www.tibco.com/solutions/products/extensibility/xml_canon.jsp*).

This section has just given a brief flavor of the tools available – there are many more that you might find out about from colleagues, web sites, newsgroups, or mailing lists such as *xml-dev* mentioned earlier.

Summary

In this chapter, we have described the XML syntax in some detail, and scratched the surface of several related specifications, with the purpose of giving you an introduction to XML, and a crash course in its use. In particular, we have seen:

- Several examples of how XML can benefit us on the Web.
- How DTDs allow us to specify XML languages by constraining the structure of the document.
- How XML Schema goes further by allowing specification of data types and providing additional features such as inheritance.
- How namespaces in XML allow us to use multiple vocabularies in a single document.
- How XSLT allows us to render our documents in different ways for different purposes.
- How XLink and XPointer provide far more powerful linking than the simple HTML hyperlinks.

In the next chapter we will move on to look at more of the web-specific XML vocabularies.

2

- XHTML: the next step from HTML
- SVG and MathML
- Other web vocabularies

Author: Jeff Rafter

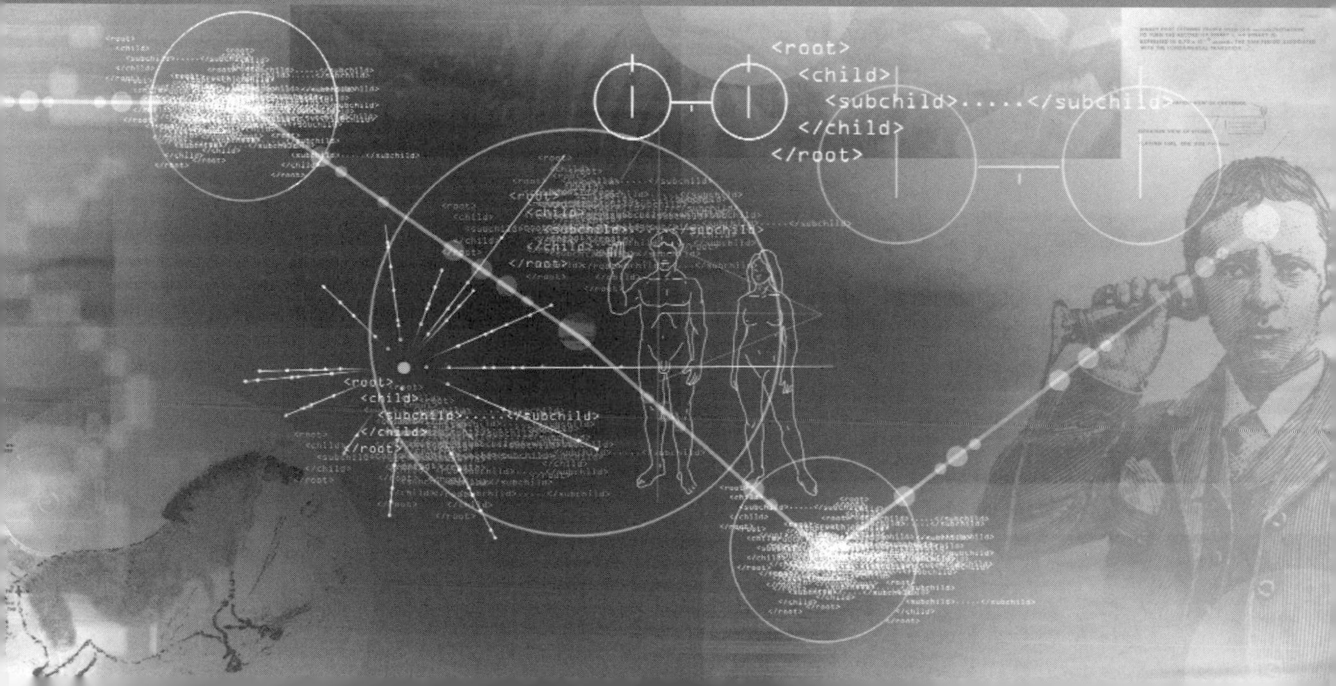

Web Vocabularies

The number of XML vocabularies has risen dramatically in the past few years. XML has been used to store database information, interchange data between companies, and even represent programming models. First and foremost, however, XML was designed for use on the World Wide Web.

As we saw in the last chapter, many XML vocabularies are used on the Web. Although any XML document can be viewed in some form on the Web, some have been designed specifically with the Web in mind. In this chapter we will focus on the vocabularies that are currently supported by web browsers and other devices, including:

- XHTML
- MathML
- Scalable Vector Graphics (SVG)
- Other important Web Vocabularies

XHTML

The most popular web vocabulary is XHTML, which was introduced in *Chapter 1*. You have probably read articles or seen presentations about the importance of XHTML and how it will solve all of your problems. In the future you may be able to order a pizza using XHTML, but you can't right now. That's right – it won't make coffee either. That said, XHTML *is* ready for use today. It is supported by the vast majority of web browsers, and new browsers and devices are being written which support only XHTML.

Basically, XHTML is HTML viewed through an XML lens. This makes XHTML a great web vocabulary: it takes the most widely used format on the web, HTML, and allows you to extend it to other vocabularies using the power of XML. If you know HTML you've already done most of the work, XHTML 1.0 is nothing other than HTML 4.01 in XML syntax.

XHTML is an XML-compliant version of HTML.

You may be thinking, "If I know HTML, then why should I read this chapter?" Well, in the next section we will see some of the benefits of using XHTML. These benefits include the **separation of presentation markup from content**, the ability to use **XML-specific tools and technologies**, and the creation of **modular documents**. Later in the chapter we will see how other vocabularies can be merged into XHTML.

What's New in XHTML

Although XML and HTML come from a common language, there are important differences in syntax and design goals. There are several rules you can follow that will ensure that your XHTML pages display properly in older browsers. In this section, we will cover some of those simple rules as well as look at some of the advantages of XHTML.

"Presentation" and "Content"

The separation of content from presentation is, perhaps, the single most important guiding force in web development today. Nearly all decisions that have been made in the creation of the web specifications are in some way related to this fundamental principle.

Content is the basic data and structure that make up a document. Within XHTML this consists of headings, paragraphs, tables, and several other document structures. **Presentation** determines how a document will look. Presentation includes fonts, colors, borders, and other visual information.

Why is it so important to separate the two aspects? The control of presentation can be very difficult – especially if you plan to support a wide audience. The presentation will have to be different for virtually every device that will render an HTML document. Some devices (such as screen readers and voice browsers) will never even *display* a document, but will instead read the document aloud to the end user.

Separating presentation from content has three major benefits:

- Accessibility
- Targeted presentation using stylesheets
- Improved processing

Let's look at each of these in more detail.

Accessibility

Over the past four years, the W3C has worked on making HTML, and now XHTML, more accessible to people with disabilities. Often these improvements are intended to make XHTML documents easier to understand by people with visual impairments. Screen readers and voice browsers literally read text aloud in addition to, or instead of, displaying it. Some screen readers are specially designed to read XHTML. Documents that follow the rules specified in the XHTML vocabulary often require little or no change to be used by a screen reader.

Many HTML designers have made web pages that misuse elements and attributes to get the page to "look right" in certain browsers. This can make it impossible for screen readers and other accessibility software to do their job. Using `<table>` elements to get graphics or sidebars to appear in the right position may seem like a good idea at first, but turning away potential customers who can no longer understand your site is a big risk. In addition to the loss of a potential customer, many countries have legislation requiring web sites to be accessible to people with disabilities. For example, in the United States, Section 508 of the Usability Act requires federal agency web sites be accessible to people with disabilities.

> *For more information, go to* http://www.usability.gov/accessibility/.

By separating the visual elements from the actual content of your page, you instantly make it much more accessible. Screen readers and other text-based browsers, such as Lynx for Unix and Linux, can easily interpret the flow of the document. Ultimately this means that users of your site will have a better experience.

> There are many screen readers available for various operating systems, however not all of them are free. If you would like to hear your web site, simply download and install a screen reader or voice browser and open your document. Home Page Reader from IBM simultaneously displays and reads a web page. You can download a trial at *http://www-3.ibm.com/able/hpr.html*. Simply Web 2000 also works with Internet Explorer. This free voice browser can be downloaded at *http://www.econointl.com/sw/*.

The World Wide Web Consortium has started a task force for accessibility requirements called the Web Accessibility Initiative (WAI). To learn more go to *http://www.w3.org/WAI/*.

> *For a complete guide to accessibility issues check out* Constructing Accessible Web Sites *(Jim Thatcher et al, glasshaus, ISBN 1904151000).*

Targeted Presentation

Of course, you will still want to control the colors and fonts of your web site for those browsers that use them. This presentation information can now be stored in a separate **stylesheet** document, which describes the visual appearance of a document. Stylesheets can be used for XHTML documents as well as other XML documents.

In addition to meeting accessibility needs, the separation of content from presentation allows you to produce different looks depending upon the browser accessing your site. For example, many or all of the documents in a web site often share one stylesheet. This means that you can easily create different stylesheets for different browsers. This also allows you to make changes to the display of your entire web site just by changing the stylesheet.

There are several different kinds of stylesheets, but the most popular are Cascading StyleSheets (CSS) and the XML Stylesheet Language (XSL). We will look at each of these concepts in detail in Chapters 4to 6.

Improved Processing

Accessibility and targeted presentation were important concerns in HTML even before XHTML was introduced. XHTML, however, directly addresses the need for an improved processing model. Because the rules for XML are so strict, processing XHTML documents can be very easy – already small utilities have popped up all over the Internet that allow you to perform special tasks on XHTML documents. For example, you can create specialized XSLT stylesheets, such as this one, *http://www.jenitennison.com/xslt/utilities/markup.html,* that highlights words and phrases, or that extract all of the links from a given XHTML page.

The rules for old HTML are quite complex, and often web designers make mistakes when creating their pages. Browsers have developed enough sophistication to cope with bad HTML (such as no closing tag for a paragraph) and still display the web page. Because of this, the Internet is littered with malformed documents that still display well on browsers. To make matters worse, as well as displaying the same elements (for example tables) in different ways, browser makers started adding proprietary extensions to their browsers. Ultimately this led to incompatible browsers and lack of compliance with the HTML specification. Writing utilities to deal with these problems is very difficult and programs that do so are often very large. For example, the installation for Netscape's 2.0 browser was 3.1 megabytes, and the installation for version 6.2 is 25.8 megabytes.

However, browser makers and tool vendors are instructed to discard XHTML documents that have not been authored correctly (those that don't use valid, well-formed XHTML). This means that they don't need to be able to cope with malformed documents, and so writing such tools and browsers is easier. Mobile web providers already have tools that can take properly authored documents and display them on cell phones and PDAs. Typically these devices use **WML** (another XML-based language for WAP-enabled phones), or small "profiles" of XHTML, such as **XHTML Basic**. XHTML Basic only includes basic markup and text, and was created using XHTML's modularization framework, which we'll look at more closely later in the chapter.

Document Types (DTDs)

In any web vocabulary you need to have a definition, or grammar, of the valid elements and attributes. Just as for HTML 4.0, XHTML 1.0 has three kinds of documents you could choose to write:

- Strict
- Transitional
- Frameset

The most recent XHTML specification, XHTML 1.1, has only one document type to choose from – XHTML 1.1.

Each of the four documents types above has a slightly different set of allowable elements and required elements. Therefore, choosing the right type of document should be the first step in building your XHTML page. Let's look at each of these document types in more detail.

In the examples in this chapter, we will create pages for an imaginary web site called "digital-poetics". We will keep the examples extremely simple so that we can focus on the XHTML.

Transitional XHTML Documents

The Transitional document type is probably the most popular for web professionals moving to XHTML, because it supports the deprecated elements not allowed in the strict DTD. If you are not ready to remove all of the presentation elements and attributes from your documents, then you should use this DTD. Let's look at an example of some transitional markup:

```
<?xml version="1.0" encoding="UTF-8"?>
<!DOCTYPE html PUBLIC "-//W3C//DTD XHTML 1.0 Transitional//EN"
  "http://www.w3.org/TR/xhtml1/DTD/xhtml1-transitional.dtd">
<html xmlns="http://www.w3.org/1999/xhtml">
  <head>
    <title>digital-poetics</title>
  </head>
  <body bgcolor="#F0F0C0">
    <h1 align="center">
      <font face="courier" color="gray">
        digital-poetics<br />
      </font>
      <font face="arial">
        <i>collections of verse on the web</i>
      </font>
    </h1>
    <hr width="100%" />
    <h2 align="center">
      <img src="flower-white100.gif"
        alt="A beautiful pink flower" border="2px"/><br />
      Torches
    </h2>
    <p align="center">
      <font color="#A09030">
        Then when the wind whirls the world with pollen,<br />
        You'll find us back behind the autumn trees<br />
        Us small scavengers, waving the fallen<br />
        Branches for fun, like torches lit with leaves.<br />
      </font>
    </p>
    <hr width="100%" />
    <p align="center">
      XHTML 1.0 Transitional Document
    </p>
  </body>
</html>
```

Notice how our document begins with an **XML declaration**:

```
<?xml version="1.0" encoding="UTF-8"?>
```

The XML declaration is not required in an XHTML document, but it is recommended that you include it.

Immediately following the XML declaration, we have a **DOCTYPE declaration** that tells the web browser exactly what kind of document we are writing. We will look at XML declarations and DOCTYPEs more closely later in the chapter.

Note that while the markup is well-formed XML, it still contains presentational information – in particular, <font> elements.

If we open the file containing this markup (poetics-transitional.html) in a web browser, we should see something like the following screenshot:

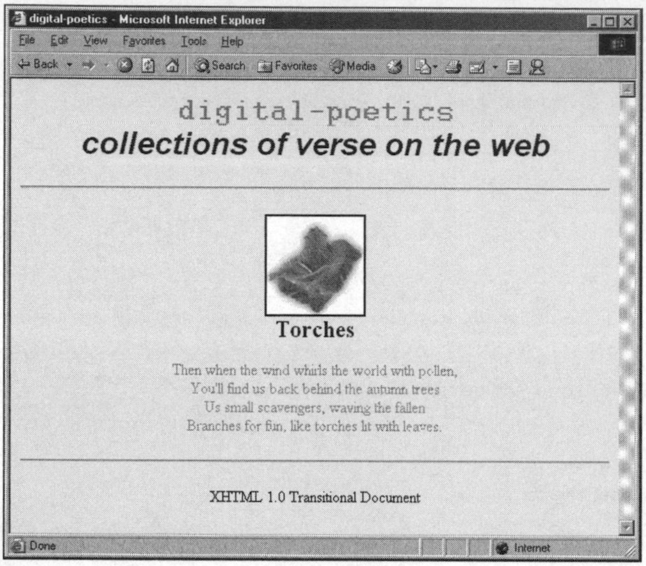

The XHTML transitional DTD can be useful if you need to support older browsers such as Netscape 3.2 or Internet Explorer 3, which require presentational markup since their support of stylesheets is poor. Otherwise, you should try to use the strict or XHTML 1.1 document types.

Strict XHTML Documents

In Strict XHTML documents, you should work with only the basic document structure, such as headings (<h1>, <h2>, <h3>, <h4>, <h5>), paragraphs <p>, and other document elements. All of the presentational elements and attributes, such as <font> and bgcolor, have been removed from the DTD. In more recent versions of XHTML, beginning with version 1.1, the W3C has completely removed presentational markup from the specification. Instead you should always utilize stylesheets to control how your document will appear in various browsers.

Let's look at a sample Strict document:

```
<?xml version="1.0" encoding="UTF-8"?>
<!DOCTYPE html PUBLIC "-//W3C//DTD XHTML 1.0 Strict//EN"
  "http://www.w3.org/TR/xhtml1/DTD/xhtml1-strict.dtd">
<html xmlns="http://www.w3.org/1999/xhtml">
  <head>
    <title>digital-poetics</title>
  </head>
  <body>
    <h1>
      digital-poetics<br />
      <i>collections of verse on the web</i>
```

```
    </h1>
    <h2>
      <img src="flower-white100.gif" alt="A beautiful pink flower"/><br />
      Torches
    </h2>
    <p>
      Then when the wind whirls the world with pollen,<br />
      You'll find us back behind the autumn trees<br />
      Us small scavengers, waving the fallen<br />
      Branches for fun, like torches lit with leaves.<br />
    </p>
    <p class="Footer">
      XHTML 1.0 Strict Document
    </p>
  </body>
</html>
```

As you can see, our strict document is much shorter. We have removed the presentational markup completely. Unfortunately, in contrast to our last example, this means that viewing the above markup (`poetics-strict.html`) in your web browser is likely to produce the following effect:

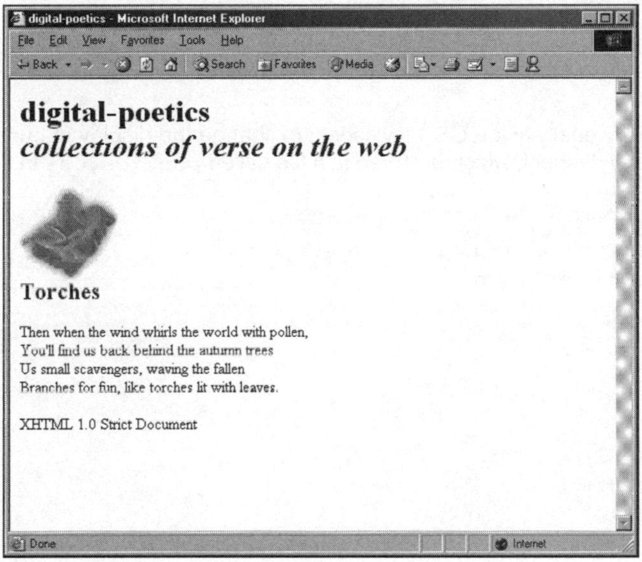

This may appear a little plain because we have removed all of the presentation elements and attributes that appeared in our first example (the file below appears in the code download for this book as `poetics-strict-style.html`):

```
<?xml version="1.0" encoding="UTF-8"?>
<!DOCTYPE html PUBLIC "-//W3C//DTD XHTML 1.0 Strict//EN"
  "http://www.w3.org/TR/xhtml1/DTD/xhtml1-strict.dtd">
<html xmlns="http://www.w3.org/1999/xhtml">
  <head>
    <title>digital-poetics</title>
```

```
    <link rel="stylesheet" type="text/css" media="screen"
      href="poetics.css" />
  </head>
  <body>
    <h1>
      digital-poetics<br />
      <i>collections of verse on the web</i>
    </h1>
    <h2>
      <img src="flower-white100.gif" alt="A beautiful pink flower"/><br />
      Torches
    </h2>
    <p>
      Then when the wind whirls the world with pollen,<br />
      You'll find us back behind the autumn trees<br />
      Us small scavengers, waving the fallen<br />
      Branches for fun, like torches lit with leaves.<br />
    </p>
    <p class="Footer">
      XHTML 1.0 Strict Document (with stylesheet)
    </p>
  </body>
</html>
```

However, we could very easily add a CSS stylesheet to change the display of our document. The following code is a very simple stylesheet, which is stored in a file called `poetics.css` in the code download:

```
/*
   This stylesheet will change the colors and fonts
   of any document which uses it
*/
body {
 background: #F0F0C0;
}
h1 {
 color: gray;
 font-family: courier;
 text-align: center;
 border-bottom:1px solid black;
}
i {
 font-family: arial;
 color: black;
}
h2 {
 text-align: center;
}
img {
 border:2px solid black;
}
p {
 color:#A09030;
```

```
  text-align: center;
 }
 .Footer {
  border-top:1px solid black;
  color:black;
  text-align: center;
 }
```

You may already be familiar with CSS, but if not, don't worry – we will look at CSS in more depth in *Chapter 4*. For now, let's look at our document in our browser again, this time with the CSS applied to it:

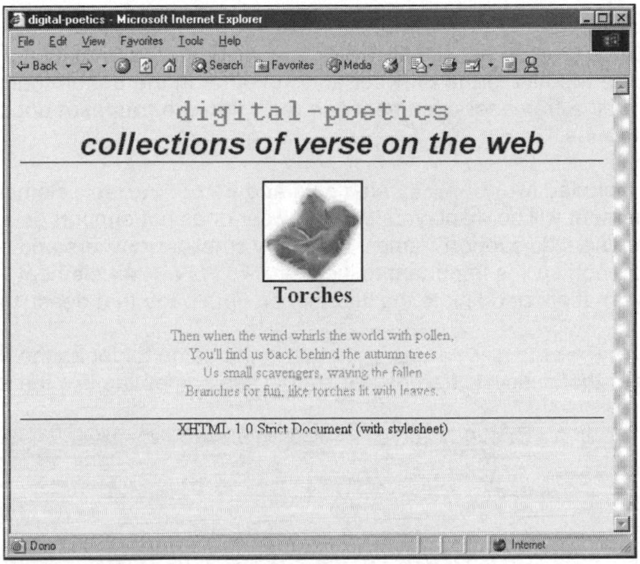

As you will see when you try it out, the stylesheet tells the browser to make the background for the `<body>` section light green (`#F0F0C0`), the text for the `<h1>` content gray in a courier font, and the text for the `<p>` section brown (`#A09030`).

Frameset XHTML Documents

XHTML allows you to write a third kind of document, called a frameset document. Frameset documents are used when you want to create a web page that utilizes frames, allowing you to display multiple pages in a single window. This technique can be helpful when you want to have the two pages next to each other, but controlled independently. Often it's used to create navigation frames at the left or top of the document. The main frame can then scroll without moving the navigation bar.

Let's look at an example frameset document:

```
<?xml version="1.0" encoding="UTF-8"?>
<!DOCTYPE html PUBLIC "-//W3C//DTD XHTML 1.0 Frameset//EN"
  "http://www.w3.org/TR/xhtml1/DTD/xhtml1-frameset.dtd">
<html xmlns="http://www.w3.org/1999/xhtml">
```

```
    <head>
      <title>digital-poetics</title>
    </head>
    <frameset rows="50%,50%" cols="1">
      <frame src="poetics-transitional.html"/>
      <frame src="poetics-strict.html"/>
      <noframes>
        <body>
          <h1>digital-poetics</h1>
          <p>Sorry, your browser does not support frames</p>
        </body>
      </noframes>
    </frameset>
  </html>
```

In this example we have created an XHTML page that includes our transitional and strict documents and displays one in the top half of the browser and the other in the bottom half. Mixing document types is allowed. In fact, a frameset document can refer to more frameset documents, allowing you to have frames within frames.

Notice that we have included two `<frame>` elements and a `<noframes>` element within our frameset. The `<noframes>` element will be displayed if the browser does not support documents with frames. Most of the major browsers do support frames, but many smaller browsers and adaptive technologies like screen readers do not, so it is important to include a `<noframes>` element – ideally this should contain the same information, or a link to the information on a page that doesn't use frames.

Save this document as (`poetics-frameset.html`) in the same folder as the first two documents we looked at. In a browser that supports frames, we should see something like the following screenshot:

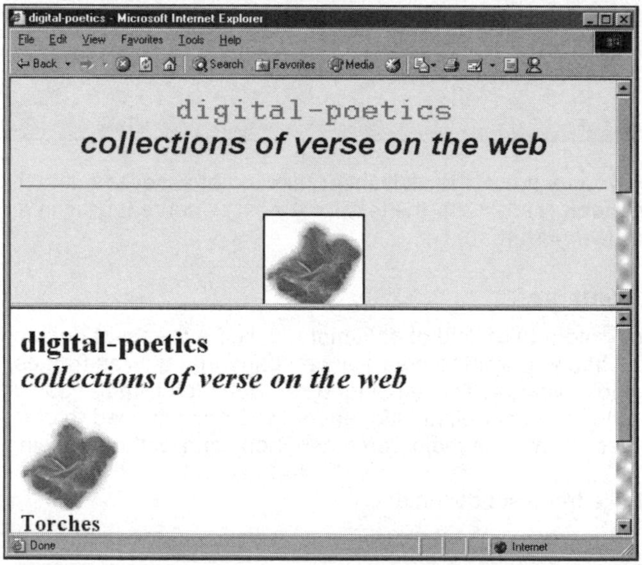

Browsers that do not support frames, such as those embedded in portable devices, would simply display the message "*Sorry, your browser does not support frames*".

XHTML 1.1 Documents

XHTML version 1.1 is a modular version of the XHTML 1.0 Strict document type – as we'll discuss below. Because it is based on the strict document type, there are no presentation elements or attributes allowed within the vocabulary. This means that all of your presentational information such as fonts and colors must be specified using a stylesheet. Frames, which are often presentational, have been moved to a separate "module" that is not enabled by default.

As I just said, the new version of XHTML is **modular**. This means that each part of an XHTML document has been divided into separate modules that can be added or removed. Later in the chapter we will look at mixing web vocabularies using different XHTML 1.1 modules.

For now, let's look at a simple XHTML 1.1 document:

```
<?xml version="1.0" encoding="UTF-8"?>
<!DOCTYPE html PUBLIC "-//W3C//DTD XHTML 1.1//EN"
  "http://www.w3.org/TR/xhtml11/DTD/xhtml11.dtd">
<html xmlns="http://www.w3.org/1999/xhtml">
  <head>
    <title>digital-poetics</title>
  </head>
  <body>
    <h1>
      digital-poetics<br />
      <i>collections of verse on the web</i>
    </h1>
    <h2>
      <img src="flower-white100.gif" alt="A beautiful pink flower"/><br />
      Torches
    </h2>
    <p>
      Then when the wind whirls the world with pollen,<br />
      You'll find us back behind the autumn trees<br />
      Us small scavengers, waving the fallen<br />
      Branches for fun, like torches lit with leaves.<br />
    </p>
    <p class="Footer">
      XHTML 1.1 Document
    </p>
  </body>
</html>
```

As you can see, the XHTML 1.0 Strict and XHTML 1.1 documents are almost exactly the same. The only major difference is the DOCTYPE declaration that is used to specify which DTD we are using as our document vocabulary. Although most of the internal reorganization is invisible to us, the modular structure is much easier for web browsers to understand. Viewing the document (`poetics-xhtml11.html`) in a browser will give us the following results:

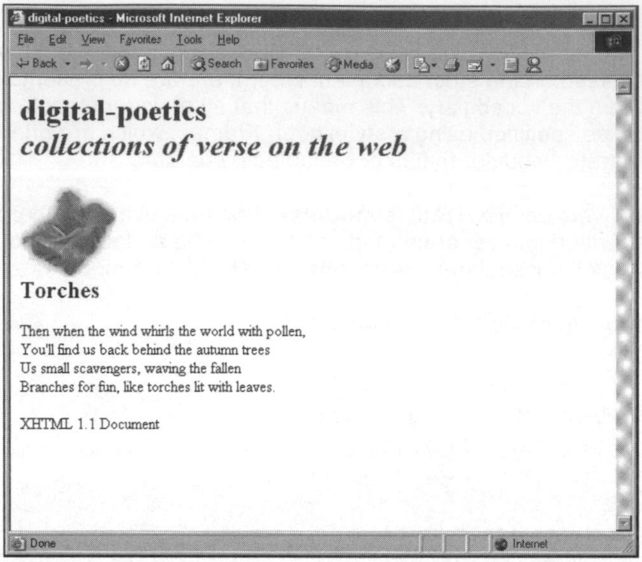

Just as we have done with our Strict document, we could easily add stylesheet information to change the display of our XHTML 1.1 document. The process is exactly the same.

Well-Formed and Valid

Within all four of these XHTML document types you need to be concerned with being well-formed and valid. In fact, you need to pay attention to these two concepts in any web vocabulary.

As we learned in the last chapter, an XML document must be **well-formed** in order that an XML parser can read it. This means making sure that the "<" and ">" are in the right places and that all of the elements are complete. A document is **valid** if it uses the correct elements and attributes for a given vocabulary or grammar. In XHTML, the elements and attributes are specified within one of the four DTDs we referred to above.

You may be asking yourself, "Why should I care about validity?" That is a great question that every web developer should be asking. If you have become accustomed to developing invalid HTML documents to get them to display correctly, then validity may seem difficult at first. Despite this, validation will guarantee that your web site is interoperable with virtually any XML application.

One of the goals of XHTML is that it should be accessible to small devices with minimal processing power. This means eliminating the need for code that checks for invalid document mistakes and accepts them: if your page isn't written correctly, these devices will not display it correctly (or at all, in some cases).

Utilizing XML and XHTML tools can ease the burden of making your site valid. Additionally, by adopting a few simple habits, creating valid web pages will become a simple task.

Support for XHTML

Of course, some of the visitors to your web site won't have the newest browser. In fact many of them will have considerably older browsers that may have problems displaying your XHTML documents. By following a few simple guidelines, you can be sure that your documents will appear correctly in old browsers as well as new. Let's begin by looking at a list of changes from HTML to XHTML:

- Case Sensitivity.
- Attribute Values.
- Empty Elements.
- Character Encoding.
- Names and IDs.
- Specifying Language.

Let's look at each of these items in more detail.

Case Sensitivity

Unlike HTML, XHTML is case-sensitive. This means that all of your elements and attributes must be in the right case in order to be considered valid. In order to make it easier for developers, the XHTML specification makes all element and attribute names lowercase. Of course the text within the element and attribute values is not case-sensitive.

Let's look at some examples. In HTML the element names generally used uppercase, but were not limited. So any of the following was allowable:

```
<HTML>
<Html>
<html>
```

In XHTML, however, the only allowable element is:

```
<html>
```

Likewise, we must specify attributes using lowercase names. In HTML any of the following were allowable:

```
<BODY ONCLICK="doSomething();">
<body OnClick="doSomething();">
<body onClick="doSomething();">
```

In XHTML, however, the element and attribute names must be lowercase:

```
<body onclick="doSomething();">
```

Notice how we have changed `onClick` to `onclick`, but we have not modified the case of our attribute value, `doSomething();`. Of course, because HTML is not concerned with case sensitivity, all of our elements and attributes should work correctly in older browsers.

> *Why is XHTML case-sensitive? Because XML is case-sensitive. Case sensitivity is a major step in internationalization efforts. Although it is easy to convert uppercase English characters to lowercase ones, or lowercase characters to uppercase, it is not so easy in other languages. Often there are no equivalent uppercase or lowercase characters, and some case mapping depends on region. In order to allow the specification to use other languages and character sets, case sensitivity was needed.*

Attribute Values

In addition to using the proper character case for attributes, we also need to make sure that our attributes and attribute values are written correctly so that our document is well-formed. In some versions of HTML attribute values could be written without quotation marks. For example, the following is legal in HTML:

```
<TD colspan=4>
```

Moreover, HTML accepts the practice of "attribute minimization" in which you can write an attribute's name without specifying a value to set it to default:

```
<OPTION selected>
```

Neither of these attribute values are acceptable in XHTML. Instead, all attributes must have a value (even if it is blank) that is enclosed in matching quotation marks:

```
<td colspan="4">
```

```
<option selected="selected" />
```

In our `<td>` element we added quotation marks around the attribute value `4`. In our `<option>` element the attribute value was minimized in the HTML, so we added a value in quotation marks. In the corrected version, we used `selected` as the value for our attribute.

Empty Elements

As we have already seen, in XHTML we have to follow a few extra rules in order to make sure that our XHTML document is well-formed. As we saw in *Chapter 1*, this includes making sure that our elements are properly nested and making sure that each of our elements has opening and closing tags. This applies to empty elements as well. When an element has no character content between its opening and closing tags, it is said to be an **empty element**.

In HTML empty elements would appear like this:

```
<IMG SRC="flower-white100.gif" alt=" A beautiful pink flower">
```

In XHTML empty elements can either appear with an immediate opening and closing tag:

```
<img src="flower-white100.gif" alt=" A beautiful pink flower"></img>
```

or in the short form:

```
<img src="flower-white100.gif" alt=" A beautiful pink flower"/>
```

In the short form, notice that we have added a "`/`" just before the final ">". This tells the XML or XHTML parser that this element is empty. Although both of these are legal XHTML, some older browsers have problems trying to read opening and closing tags for elements that are empty. Because of this, it is much better to use the short form when adding empty elements.

It is also good practice to add a space before the "/" in empty elements. Again, it is not required, but doing so allows your page to work with older browsers that do not understand the "/". For example:

```
<br />
```

is better than:

```
<br/>
```

Character Encoding

Specifying the document encoding is very important, and in some cases required to get your document to display correctly on different browsers. An **encoding** is a table that defines a numeric value for each character. Often these character values are used in incompatible ways. Almost all browsers and computers support the ASCII encoding, which contains 128 of the most commonly used characters. These characters are guaranteed to be compatible across different platforms.

If you are using characters with values higher than 128, you are required to specify the character set so that the browser knows what character to display for a given value. When validating our XHTML pages using the W3C online Validator, not specifying what encoding our documents were using would have resulted in a warning message.

Within XHTML, there are several ways that you can specify the character set that your document is using:

- Using the XML Declaration
- Using the <meta> element
- External means

It is possible to use any of these methods alone or in combination with the others. Using all of the methods ensures that the browser will be informed of your document's encoding – even if it does not support that encoding. However, including the encoding declaration may confuse some older browsers. Let's look at each of the methods more closely.

Specifying the encoding using the XML Declaration is very easy. In fact, this is how we specified the encoding in all of our earlier examples:

```
<?xml version="1.0" encoding="UTF-8"?>
```

UTF-8 is a Unicode character set that supports the first 128 ASCII characters as well as additional characters. If your document utilizes only the simple ASCII characters you can label it as UTF-8 as we have done in our examples. Often, though, your document will use characters, that are outside this range. European characters, such as "ê" and "æ" are not found in the basic ASCII character set. The numeric values for "ê" and "æ" vary depending on the specified encoding. If you label your document with an encoding and it is not encoded correctly, you will receive an error.

On an English version of Windows, your default encoding is compatible with ISO-8859-1. This encoding is widely supported (though not required). Because of this, simply changing the encoding declaration to ISO-8859-1 will allow European characters to display correctly.

Encoding rules are often complex. XML is required to support the encodings UTF-8 and UTF-16 by default. UTF-16 is a much larger character set that includes many Chinese and Japanese characters, among others. In order to have numeric values for all of the characters, it uses two or more bytes for each character (instead of one byte as in UTF-8 and ASCII). Because of this, working in simple text editors that do not support various encodings can be difficult. For more information about different encodings, go to http://www.unicode.org/.

In newer browsers, using the XML declaration is a great way to specify your document's character set. Unfortunately some older browsers have trouble using the declaration and may ignore it altogether. Worse, some browsers display the encoding declaration as if it were text in your document.

Here is a list of browsers that will display the encoding as text:

- Netscape Navigator version 3.04 and earlier
- Internet Explorer 3.0 and earlier
- HotJava version 3.0 and earlier

Bear in mind though, that even if the browser does not display the encoding as text, it does not mean that it is interpreting the XML declaration correctly. Because of this, it is not always advisable to include an XML declaration in your XHTML page (although the XHTML specification does recommend doing so). Whether or not you include an XML declaration, it is important that you specify your encoding using one or both of the other methods (using a `<meta>` tag, or by external means).

In order to specify an encoding using a `<meta>` tag, you need to add the new element to the `<head>` section of your XHTML document.

```
<?xml version="1.0" encoding="UTF-8"?>
<!DOCTYPE html PUBLIC "-//W3C//DTD XHTML 1.1//EN"
  "http://www.w3.org/TR/xhtml11/DTD/xhtml11.dtd">
<html xmlns="http://www.w3.org/1999/xhtml">
  <head>
    <title>digital-poetics</title>
    <meta http-equiv="Content-Type"
          content="text/html; charset=UTF-8" />
  </head>
  <body>
    <h1>
      digital-poetics<br />
      <i>collections of verse on the web</i>
    </h1>
```

Adding the `<meta>` tag with the `http-equiv` attribute set to `Content-Type` tells the browser what type of content this document contains. In the above example, we have specified `text/html` as our document type and `ISO-8859-1` as our encoding. If a document contains both the XML declaration and the `<meta>` element, the encoding value in the XML declaration will be used. In browsers that do not support the XML declaration, however, only the `<meta>` value will be considered.

In most cases the best way to specify the encoding is to do it on the web server using the HTTP header Content-Type. This can be done using ASP, JSP, or other server-side technologies. Of course, it is not always an option, and often varies depending on the software or hardware you are using on the server, but this is by far the most reliable way to specify the encoding.

> How important is specifying the encoding of your document? Very. Apart from possible display problems in browsers, there is a potential security risk. In February 2000, CERT, part of the Carnegie Mellon Software Engineering Institute, released a security advisory that recommended specifying the document encoding at the server level to protect from malicious users. For more information, see *http://www.cert.org/advisories/CA-2000-02.html.*

Names and IDs

In HTML, the `name` attribute was used to identify the element within the document. As the specification matured, the `id` attribute was added to replace the older `name` attribute. In HTML 4 and XHTML 1.0 you can use the `name` attribute, the `id` attribute, or both. For example, the anchor element, `<a>` could use `name` or `id` to identify the anchor in the document:

```
<a name="Section1" />
<a id="Section1" />
<a name="Section1" id="Section1" />
```

In XHTML 1.1, however, the W3C has removed the `name` attribute from the `<a>` and `<map>` elements. Only the `id` attribute is permitted:

```
<a id="Section1" />
```

Again, older browsers expect the `name` attribute to be used with anchors. Because of this XHTML 1.1 pages will not work in some older browsers. Some of these include:

- Netscape Navigator version 4.79 and earlier.
- Internet Explorer 4.0 and earlier
- HotJava version 3.0 and earlier.

So, if you create XHTML 1.1 pages that use document anchors, you risk losing browser compatibility. Of course in some cases this is OK, but for web sites that are designed to reach a wide audience it may force you to use XHTML 1.0 documents instead.

Specifying Language

HTML 4.0 and XHTML 1.0 allow you to specify the language used in documents, or even in specific elements, using the `lang` attribute. Web browsers could use this information to display elements in language-specific ways. For example, hyphenation may change depending on the language that is in use. Additionally, screen readers may read the text using different voices, depending on the language code specified.

In XHTML 1.1 the `lang` attribute was removed and replaced with `xml:lang`. `xml:lang` is a special XML attribute that can be used in many web vocabularies – not just XHTML. This makes XHTML much more compatible with other XML applications. Currently the use of `lang` and `xml:lang` by web browsers is minimal. Because of this, there are few compatibility problems with older web browsers.

XHTML Tools

Many of the tool vendors that support HTML have also written tools that support XHTML. There are three kinds of tools that you can use to edit your XHTML documents:

- Simple text editors
- XML Editors
- XHTML Editors

Each of these tools offers different benefits. Some of them are written to specifically check a document for being well-formed and valid. Let's look at each kind of tool in more detail and see some examples of each.

Text Editors

Because XHTML is a text-based format, you can use very simple editors to work with the document markup. Tools such as Notepad on Windows or Vim on Linux are used every day to create web documents. Of course these editors know nothing about XHTML or XML, so they have very few features to assist you in authoring the document. Also, they do not have built-in capabilities to check that your document is well-formed or valid.

Although they have significant limitations, simple editors are often very useful because they can open and work with documents very quickly. Larger editors often have longer application startup times. Additionally simple text editors are often free and can be used on any number of machines. The most useful text editors can display line numbers, which are invaluable for tracking down parser errors.

XML Editors

Many editors designed to work with XML documents have been released over the past few years. These editors offer many advantages over simple text-based editors. Although they may not be written specifically for XHTML, they can still offer "tag completion" (automatically completing an element that you open with the relevant closing tag) and show what elements or attributes are allowable at given points within the document.

Additionally, XML editors allow you to work with many different web vocabularies. Most XML editors also allow you to check that your document is well-formed and valid based on its DTD or XML Schema. They usually offer syntax highlighting so that you can quickly see the structure of your document.

The most popular XML editors in use today are:

- XML Spy – *http://www.xmlspy.com/*
- Topologi Collaborative Markup Editor – *http://www.topologi.com/*
- Turbo XML – *http://www.tibco.com/solutions/products/extensibility/turbo_xml.jsp*
- oXygen – *http://www.oxygenxml.com/index.html*
- XMetal – *http://www.softquad.com/products/xmetal/*

- XMLwriter– *http://www.xmlwriter.net/*
- XML Origin – *http://www.xmlorigin.com/*

XHTML Editors

Editors that are written to support XHTML give you the most features. Often these tools come with XHTML document templates and can warn you about potential display problems. Most importantly, many XHTML editors allow you to design XHTML visually without needing to see the markup at all. This can be very useful when designing complex, visually intense, web sites. You should nevertheless make sure that your tool is creating well-formed and valid markup for the document that you are designing.

- Macromedia Dreamweaver MX – *http://www.macromedia.com/software/dreamweaver/*
- Frontpage – *http://www.microsoft.com/frontpage/*
- HotMetal – *http://www.softquad.com/products/hotmetal/*
- HTML-Kit – *http://www.chami.com/html-kit/*
- Mozquito – *http://www.mozquito.org/*
- Amaya – *http://www.w3.org/Amaya/*
- Homesite – *http://www.macromedia.com/software/homesite/*
- BBEdit – *http://www.barebones.com/*
- TopStyle – *http://www.bradsoft.com/topstyle/*

If you already have one of these editors, check and see if your version supports XHTML; many editors have only recently added XHTML support.

Online Validators

In addition to the tools we have already mentioned, there are several web sites that offer free validation services. You can use these web sites to check that your document is well-formed and valid against specific versions of the HTML specification, including XHTML. The most popular online validators are:

- *http://validator.w3.org/*
- *http://www.htmlhelp.com/tools/validator/*
- *http://www.searchengineworld.com/validator/*

Let's try to validate our XHTML documents from earlier in this chapter using the W3C online validator at *http://validator.w3.org/*.

When you first open the W3C Validator you're given a form that allows you to validate a document stored at a specific URI. This means that the document must be stored somewhere on the Internet so that it's accessible to the W3C Validator.

However, we have not yet published our newly created documents to the Web. Fortunately, the W3C Validator also allows you to upload documents for validation; simply click on the "*upload files*" link or go to *http://validator.w3.org/file-upload.html*:

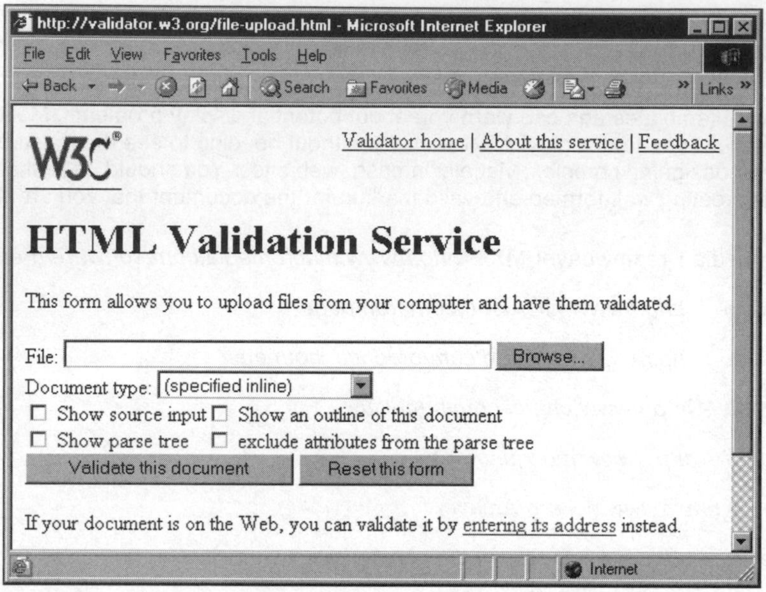

Click the *Browse* button and locate the document `poetics-transitional.html` that we created earlier in the chapter. Once you have found the document click the "*Validate this document*" button. After validating you should see a page that says "No errors found!*" If you received an error message, fix the error and try to validate your document again. When fixing multiple errors, it is usually easier to start by fixing the first error and revalidating. Often a single error in a document will cause multiple errors later in the document.

Let's modify our `poetics-transitional.html` document and add an `<unknown>` element so that we can see what the validator will do when we receive an error:

```
<head>
  <title>digital-poetics</title>
</head>
<body bgcolor="#F0F0C0">
  <unknown />
  <h1 align="center">
    <font face="courier" color="gray">
      digital-poetics<br />
    </font>
    <font face="arial">
      <i>collections of verse on the web</i>
    </font>
  </h1>
```

Save the document as `poetics-transitional-error.html` and try validating the new document. You should receive a page that contains the following error:

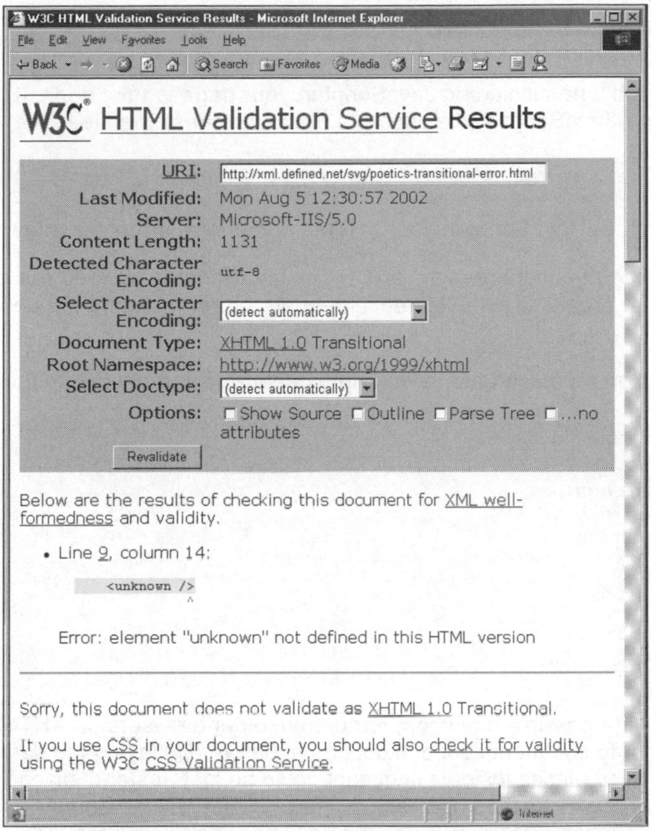

In addition to errors, the W3C Validator may also return warnings. Often these warnings refer to possible character encoding problems or possible DOCTYPE problems. The validator will usually offer suggestions for fixing your page. Try validating the rest of the XHTML documents created in this chapter. Once your document validates, you can display the W3C XHTML logo on your web page, indicating that you have produced a compliant web site.

Problems Validating Your Web Site

As we already have seen in this chapter, validating your web site should be a priority. Unfortunately web professionals use several practices that will need to change first. We'll now look at some practical tips that will help you accomplish your development, while making sure that your site is still valid. Remember that many of these tips will be helpful when using other web vocabularies as well.

Some common problems include:

- Including JavaScript in your page
- Embedding advertising information
- Unsupported elements and attributes

Including JavaScript in Your Page

The best rule of thumb when including JavaScript in your page is this: don't. It is a much better solution to move your JavaScript into a separate file and refer to the file in the <script> element.

```
<script type="text/javascript" src="poetics.js" />
```

If you do need to include JavaScript in your XHTML document, there are a few rules to follow.

For example, including the characters "<" and ">" in JavaScript is allowed (as less than and greater than operators), but it breaks the XHTML document structure, meaning the document is no longer well-formed.

In the past, web designers placed the JavaScript code in a comment inside the <script> element:

```
<script type="text/javascript"><!--
  function maxnumber(a, b) {
    if (a > b) then
      return a;
    if (a < b) then
      return b;
    if (a = b) then
      return a;
  }
--></script>
```

This worked well to hide possible document errors from older browsers. In XHTML, though, servers and browsers can freely strip comments out of a document before displaying the data. This means that the JavaScript code that you placed inside a comment could be lost. Instead, place your JavaScript code within a `<![CDATA[...]]>` section. Remember, that "<" and ">" can appear within a `<![CDATA[...]]>` section without affecting the document being well-formed:

```
<script type="text/javascript"><![CDATA[
  function maxnumber(a, b) {
    if (a > b) then
      return a;
    if (a < b) then
      return b;
    if (a = b) then
      return a;
  }
]]></script>
```

Older browsers understand CDATA sections, with the exception of Netscape Navigator version 3 and earlier. It will raise an error when it attempts to display a page that contains a CDATA section.

Embedding Advertising Information

Many web sites have advertising information displayed on their pages. Often these advertisements are not supplied in the latest version of XHTML. If this is the case for your site, you don't want to tell an advertiser that you can't do business with them because of their format. At the same time, however, you want your web site to be valid so that it works correctly in all browsers and devices. You have a dilemma.

Fortunately there are a couple of ways around this problem. The first step is to ask your advertiser if they can provide the data in another format. If this is not possible, the next option is to downgrade the version of XHTML you are using. If the advertiser supports XHTML 1.0 Transitional, then it is sometimes easiest to use XHTML 1.0 Transitional as well, rather than sticking to XHTML 1.1 or XHTML 1.0 Strict.

Perhaps the best solution is to add the advertiser information to the page using client-side JavaScript. This ensures that the data will display in the browser, while at the same time ensuring that your base page is a valid document. This means that your page will display in web browsers that support the advertiser's format as well as browsers that do not.

In *Chapter 7*, we will learn some advanced JavaScript techniques that can be used in situations just like this one.

Unsupported Elements and Attributes

You may want to add something in your XHTML page that is not valid. This is understandable, since there are many elements and attributes that you may well have grown accustomed to using over the years. There are three basic categories for unsupported elements and attributes:

- Elements or attributes that existed in earlier versions of HTML
- Elements or attributes that are specific to one browser
- New elements or attributes you want to merge into your XHTML page

The first two categories commonly occur when you are trying to design your web site for a specific browser (or a specific set of browsers) or when you are trying to port an older web site to XHTML. It is important to note that using unsupported elements is not good practice because it will ultimately limit your audience. Nevertheless, it is still possible to add this kind of information in several ways. As we noted in the previous section, it is possible to modify your document using JavaScript. Just as we did with the invalid advertiser content, we can add the element and attribute values using client-side JavaScript after the page has been loaded.

Another possibility, although more complex, is to return different pages to the user depending on their browser. By maintaining templates on the web server, you can quickly transform your web page to support various browsers using XSLT. We will look at an example of this type of system in the server-side chapters later in the book.

XHTML Modularization

The primary goal of XML was to create a simple markup language that could be extended very easily. XHTML 1.1 was created to simplify the process of extending the XHTML definition. This allows you to quickly add any vocabulary to XHTML through a process called **modularization**. Of course, the more complex the vocabulary, the more complex the modularization will become.

Although XHTML Modularization is complex, you can still enjoy the benefits. Many modularizations have already been created for the most popular web vocabularies. In fact, the W3C has released an initial draft of a modularization supporting the MathML and Scalable Vector Graphics (SVG) vocabularies. These two vocabularies are commonly embedded within XHTML and vice versa.

For more information, see http://www.w3.org/TR/XHTMLplusMathMLplusSVG/.

In addition to extending the XHTML specification, many developers have needed to limit it. As we have already mentioned, mobile phone developers have created a "profile" of XHTML that only uses the most basic modules. The profile, called XHTML Basic, is available at *http://www.w3.org/TR/xhtml-basic/.*

Using these new document types is very similar to using the other document types we have seen in this chapter. Of course, you have to follow the new rules of the document type and declare the type of document you are creating in the DOCTYPE. The DOCTYPE declaration for XHTML plus MathML plus SVG is:

```
<!DOCTYPE html PUBLIC
    "-//W3C//DTD XHTML 1.1 plus MathML 2.0 plus SVG 1.1//EN"
    "http://www.w3.org/2002/04/xhtml-math-svg/xhtml-math-svg.dtd">
```

The DOCTYPE declaration for XHTML Basic is:

```
<!DOCTYPE html PUBLIC "-//W3C//DTD XHTML Basic 1.0//EN"
  "http://www.w3.org/TR/xhtml-basic/xhtml-basic10.dtd">
```

We have seen the basics of XHTML, so let's look at some of the other popular web vocabularies. We will start with MathML and SVG as they are two common formats.

MathML

The Math Markup Language, or MathML, is a popular web vocabulary used to describe scientific and mathematical data. Just as we saw with XHTML, MathML is an XML vocabulary that must follow the rules of XML: it must be well-formed and valid, and is case-sensitive.

Support for MathML is not widespread in the most popular browsers, thought Mozilla 1.0 does support it. A full listing of implementations is available on the MathML home page at *http://www.w3.org/Math/.* Version 2.0 of the MathML recommendation is available at *http://www.w3.org/TR/MathML2/.*

As the MathML group was developing the specification, they realized that they actually had two distinct goals. They needed to be able to construct a vocabulary that could represent how mathematic equations were displayed, as well as represent the meaning of a mathematic equation. Because of this they divided MathML into two parts:

- Presentation
- Content

Let's look at an example of each of these.

MathML Presentation Markup

The presentational markup allows you fine-grained control of the display of your mathematic formulae. To begin with, the formula is divided into vertical rows using `<mrow>` elements. This basic element is used as a wrapper throughout the presentation section. Rows may contain other rows, which may contain other rows, and so on. Within the `<mrow>` elements you usually have a combination of `<mn>`, mathematical numbers, `<mi>`, mathematical identifiers, and `<mo>`, mathematical operators. Let's look at an example:

```
<?xml version="1.0" encoding="ISO-8859-1"?>
<!DOCTYPE math PUBLIC "-//W3C//DTD MathML 2.0//EN"
         "http://www.w3.org/TR/MathML2/dtd/mathml2.dtd">
<math xmlns="http://www.w3.org/1998/Math/MathML">
 <mrow>
   <mn>10</mn>
   <mo>+</mo>
   <msup>
     <mfenced>
       <mrow>
         <mi>x</mi>
         <mo>*</mo>
         <mi>y</mi>
       </mrow>
     </mfenced>
     <mn>4</mn>
   </msup>
 </mrow>
</math>
```

In the above document we begin a standard MathML document by adding our DOCTYPE for MathML and beginning with the `<math>` element. Notice that we have declared a default namespace for the MathML vocabulary. Immediately following this we have specified a `<mrow>` element, which represents the horizontal row of our equation.

Our row begins by adding the number 10 to an `<msup>` section, or a mathematical superscript section. This section allows us to display exponents. We will use this to apply the exponent 4 to an `<mfenced>` element. The `<mfenced>` element functions exactly as parentheses would in a mathematical equation. Within our parentheses we could have multiple rows to our equation. Here, however, we have only one row within our parentheses. In it we multiply the identifier `x` by the identifier `y`. If we save our document as `math-present.xml` and open it in a MathML-capable browser such as Mozilla 1.0, we would see it rendered as follows:

$$10+(x*y)^4$$

If, however, you attempt to view the document in a browser that does not support MathML such as Opera 6.01, you should see the following:

10 + x * y 4

Notice that it did not insert the parentheses for our "fenced" section. Also, the exponent was not raised. Essentially, it has ignored all of the elements and simply displayed the text of the XML document.

MathML Content Markup

The MathML content markup allows you to be very explicit about order of operations and primary equation representation. While the presentational markup consisted of about 30 elements, the content markup has more than 120 elements. Content MathML documents begin exactly as Presentational MathML documents. They also contain `<mrow>` elements to separate the lines of the equation. However, the Content MathML elements do not use `<mo>` for operators. Instead, they use the `<apply>` element and a large number of specific operator and function elements. Let's look at an example:

```
<?xml version="1.0" encoding="ISO-8859-1"?>
<!DOCTYPE math PUBLIC "-//W3C//DTD MathML 2.0//EN"
         "http://www.w3.org/TR/MathML2/dtd/mathml2.dtd">
<math xmlns="http://www.w3.org/1998/Math/MathML">
 <mrow>
   <apply>
     <plus/>
     <ci>10</ci>
     <apply>
       <power/>
       <apply>
         <times/>
         <ci>x</ci>
         <ci>y</ci>
       </apply>
       <cn>4</cn>
     </apply>
   </apply>
 </mrow>
</math>
```

Notice that all of our `<mi>` and `<mn>` elements became `<ci>` and `<cn>` elements? Also notice that we have completely removed the `<mfenced>` element. Again, the `<mfenced>` which represented parentheses in an equation, is often syntactic, whereas in the Content markup we can be explicit about the order of calculations using `<apply>`.

In our above example, all of our operators use **postfix notation**. In postfix notation you indicate the operation, followed by the two operands. Some MathML functions use postfix notation and some do not. For a complete listing, go to *http://www.w3.org/TR/MathML2/appendixf.html*.

If we attempted to view this document in our web browser it would display incorrectly. This is because this document is not supposed to be viewed, but rather is for a MathML engine that would process and possibly perform the calculation. Most web browsers would simply ignore all of the elements and only display the text, as we saw in our earlier Opera example.

Scalable Vector Graphics

Scalable Vector Graphics, or SVG, was intended to allow designers to represent extremely complex two-dimensional graphics in a relatively easy way. Just as MathML gave us a detailed model to represent mathematical equations, SVG allows us to display graphics with a high level of detail and accuracy. Again, because it is an XML vocabulary it must follow the rules of XML.

Although SVG is a fairly new language, it already has wide acceptance and support. There are many viewers and editors designed specifically for SVG. The Mozilla Browser and the X-Smiles Browser both support SVG directly. For other browsers, you need to use plugins like Adobe's SVG Viewer to view SVG documents on the Web.

> You can download the Adobe SVG viewer plugin by going to Adobe's web site, at *http://www.adobe.com/svg/*.

The SVG specification can be broken down into three basic parts.

- Vector Graphic Shapes
- Images
- Text

Let's look at each of these in more detail.

Vector Graphic Shapes

Vector Graphics allow you to describe a graphic using commands rather than raster data. For instance, you could represent a box graphic using a series of line or fill commands, instead of storing it as a Bitmap or PNG file. This means that you do not need to store the raster information that represents all of the pixels in the graphic. Because vector graphics store only the commands to reproduce the graphic, they are often much smaller than their raster-based counterparts.

In SVG, vector graphics can be represented using basic shape commands or by specifying a list of points called a **path**. You can also group objects, and make complex objects out of simpler ones. Let's look at a SVG document that contains a basic shape:

```
<?xml version="1.0"?>
<!DOCTYPE svg PUBLIC "-//W3C//DTD SVG 20010904//EN"
        "http://www.w3.org/TR/2001/REC-SVG-20010904/DTD/svg10.dtd">
<svg width="12cm" height="4cm" viewBox="0 0 1200 400"
     xmlns="http://www.w3.org/2000/svg">
  <desc>A simple rectangle with a red border</desc>
  <rect x="10"
        y="10"
        width="200"
        height="200"
        fill="none"
        stroke="red"
        stroke-width="10"/>
</svg>
```

If we save this file as `rectangle1.svg` and open it in an SVG viewer we should see the following:

In addition to creating basic shapes, we can also add complex fill patterns and other effects. As we have said, SVG allows you extremely advanced graphic control. Let's add some options to our shape.

```
<?xml version="1.0"?>
<!DOCTYPE svg PUBLIC "-//W3C//DTD SVG 20010904//EN"
        "http://www.w3.org/TR/2001/REC-SVG-20010904/DTD/svg10.dtd">
<svg width="12cm" height="4cm" viewBox="0 0 1200 400"
```

```
    xmlns="http://www.w3.org/2000/svg">
  <desc>A simple rectangle with a red border and a gradient fill</desc>
  <g>
    <defs>
      <linearGradient id="RedGradient" gradientUnits="objectBoundingBox">
        <stop offset="0%" stop-color="#F00" />
        <stop offset="100%" stop-color="#FFF" />
      </linearGradient>
    </defs>
    <rect x="10"
          y="10"
          width="200"
          height="200"
          fill="url(#RedGradient)"
          stroke="red"
          stroke-width="10"/>
  </g>
</svg>
```

If we save this file as `rectangle2.svg` and open it in our SVG viewer we should see the following:

In this example we have created a linear gradient within our graphic object defined in the `<g>` element. We named this gradient `RedGradient`. Then, within our rectangle we specified that the fill attribute should use our local `RedGradient`.

Images

Often you will need to include non-vector-based graphics in your SVG. This might be an image of a person or landscape, or any other graphical data that isn't suited for vector-based representation, such as hand-drawn art or rendered three dimensional objects. Including images in SVG is very simple. Let's create a new SVG document that contains an image.

```
<?xml version="1.0"?>
<!DOCTYPE svg PUBLIC "-//W3C//DTD SVG 20010904//EN"
          "http://www.w3.org/TR/2001/REC-SVG-20010904/DTD/svg10.dtd">
<svg width="12cm" height="4cm" viewBox="0 0 400 400"
     xmlns="http://www.w3.org/2000/svg">
  <desc>This SVG document contains puppy.jpg</desc>
  <image x="0"
         y="0"
         width="400px"
         height="400px"
         xlink:href="puppy.jpg">
    <title>My puppy</title>
  </image>
</svg>
```

If we save this file as `puppy.svg` and open it in our SVG viewer we should see the following:

Again, we could control how our image will be displayed by changing some of its properties in our SVG document. It is important that we realize the image is not converted to a vector graphic – it maintains its original format and is drawn to the SVG display.

Text

In addition to basic shapes and images, SVG documents can represent text. Of course, as we have already seen, there are many options available to change the display of the text. Let's try creating an SVG document with some text. This time we will create some text that has a color gradient outline.

```
<?xml version="1.0"?>
<!DOCTYPE svg PUBLIC "-//W3C//DTD SVG 20010904//EN"
      "http://www.w3.org/TR/2001/REC-SVG-20010904/DTD/svg10.dtd">
<svg width="20cm" height="4cm" viewBox="0 0 400 400"
    xmlns="http://www.w3.org/2000/svg">
  <desc>This SVG document contains rainbow text</desc>
  <g>
    <defs>
      <linearGradient id="RedBlueGradient"
                gradientUnits="objectBoundingBox">
        <stop offset="0%" stop-color="#F00" />
        <stop offset="100%" stop-color="#00F" />
      </linearGradient>
    </defs>
    <text x="-600"
          y="200"
          font-size="128"
          fill="white"
          stroke="url(#RedBlueGradient)"
          stroke-width="5">
      SVG makes images scalable!
    </text>
  </g>
</svg>
```

If we save this file as `text1.svg` and open it in an SVG viewer, we should see something like the following (you will need to try it yourself to fully appreciate the color gradient):

SVG makes images scalable!

Of course, this is only the very beginning of what you can do with SVG. Let's move on to a more complex example that uses these skills.

Putting It Together

Some people believe that SVG will soon replace Flash on the Web – the rush of vendors to support SVG somewhat legitimizes this claim. In this example we will create an animated introduction page for our imaginary digital-poetics web site.

```
<?xml version="1.0" encoding="UTF-8"?>
<!DOCTYPE svg PUBLIC "-//W3C//DTD SVG 20010904//EN"
  "http://www.w3.org/TR/2001/REC-SVG-20010904/DTD/svg10.dtd">
<svg width="7in" height="3.5in" viewBox="0 0 1000 500"
  xmlns="http://www.w3.org/2000/svg">
  <desc>digital-poetics introduction</desc>
```

As we have seen before, we begin with our XML declaration and DOCTYPE declaration for SVG. We start our SVG document with an `<svg>` element and a `<desc>` that has our document's description.

```
  <image x="650" y="100" width="250" height="250"
    xlink:href="flower-white250.gif"/>
```

Here we have created an image that will appear as part of our background. The next section of the SVG document is where we introduce our first bit of animation:

```
  <rect width="300" height="100" fill="rgb(200,200,200)"
    fill-opacity="0.25">
    <animate attributeName="y" attributeType="XML" from="500" to="-100"
      dur="4s" repeatCount="indefinite" fill="freeze" />
  </rect>
```

We have created a `<rect>` object as we have done before and colored it medium gray. This time however, we have changed the `fill-opacity`. The fill-opacity accepts values between 0 (completely transparent) and 1 (completely opaque). We have also added an `<animate>` element. In it we specify that we will modify the `y` attribute from the value `500` to the value `-100`. We also specify that we want the animation to last for 4 seconds (`dur`), that we want it to repeat indefinitely, and that we don't want the fill method to change during the animation. In order to make this effect more interesting, we will add six more moving `<rect>` objects that cross one another:

```
  <rect width="300" height="400" fill="rgb(200,200,200)" fill-opacity="0.5">
    <animate attributeName="y" attributeType="XML" from="600" to="-400"
      dur="14s" repeatCount="indefinite" fill="freeze" />
  </rect>
  <rect width="300" height="14" fill="rgb(200,200,200)" fill-opacity="0.25">
    <animate attributeName="y" attributeType="XML" from="600" to="-40"
      dur="3s" repeatCount="indefinite" fill="freeze" />
```

```
</rect>
<rect width="300" height="4" fill="rgb(200,200,200)" fill-opacity="0.75">
  <animate attributeName="y" attributeType="XML" from="500" to="-4"
    dur="2s" repeatCount="indefinite" fill="freeze" />
</rect>
<rect width="300" height="300" fill="rgb(200,200,200)"
  fill-opacity="0.75">
  <animate attributeName="y" attributeType="XML" from="-300" to="500"
    dur="8s" repeatCount="indefinite" fill="freeze" />
</rect>
<rect width="300" height="14" fill="rgb(200,200,200)" fill-opacity="0.75">
  <animate attributeName="y" attributeType="XML" from="-90" to="510"
    dur="3s" repeatCount="indefinite" fill="freeze" />
</rect>
<rect width="300" height="4" fill="rgb(200,200,200)" fill-opacity="0.75">
  <animate attributeName="y" attributeType="XML" from="-100" to="500"
    dur="2s" repeatCount="indefinite" fill="freeze" />
</rect>
```

Next we will add a little author text and a couple of vertical separators:

```
<!-- Default text -->
<text x="295" y="461" text-anchor="end">Scalable Vector Graphics</text>
<text x="295" y="473" text-anchor="end">by digital-poetics</text>
<!-- Separator -->
<line x1="300" y1="0" x2="300" y2="500" stroke-width="1" stroke="gray"/>
<line x1="302" y1="0" x2="302" y2="500" stroke-width="2" stroke="gray"/>
```

Notice that our text has the attribute `text-anchor` set to `end`. This is the equivalent of aligning your text to the right. If the SVG viewer you are using has right-to-left reading enabled, however, the SVG will align the text to the left. In either case it aligns it to the "end" of the text area.

Even with this small amount of code, our SVG document is quite exciting – but let's add a few more effects. Of course, we need our web site title somewhere on the page, so let's do that next. We'll animate it too. We will make it fly in from the right side of the screen quickly and then slow down for the end of the animation.

```
<text x="1000" y="200" font-size="32" font-style="italic"
  font-weight="bold" font-family="courier" fill="gray">
  <animate attributeName="x" attributeType="XML"
          begin="2s" dur="0.5s" fill="freeze" from="1000" to="350" />
  <animate attributeName="x" attributeType="XML"
          begin="2.5s" dur="0.5s" fill="freeze" from="350" to="340" />
  digital-poetics
</text>
```

To do the two-stage animation we have used two `<animate>` elements. We have added `begin` attributes to indicate the starting time of each animation.

Let's add a horizontal line that is also animated from the right side of the screen:

```
<line x1="1000" y1="202" x2="1600" y2="202" stroke-width="1"
  stroke="gray">
  <animate attributeName="x1" attributeType="XML"
          begin="2s" dur="0.5s" fill="freeze" from="1000" to="340" />
</line>
```

Next we will add another piece of text that enters just after our digital-poetics text:

```
<text x="1000" y="224" font-size="24" font-style="italic"
  font-weight="bold" fill="white" stroke="gray">
  <animate attributeName="x" attributeType="XML"
          begin="2.5s" dur="0.5s" fill="freeze" from="1000" to="370" />
  - collections of verse -
</text>
```

Finally, we need to add a link that will allow the users to reach the rest of our web site. This time we will use a graphic object `<g>` that is made up of a `<rect>` and a `<text>` element:

```
<a xlink:href="http://www.glasshaus.com/">
  <g fill-opacity="0.3" stroke-opacity="0.3">
    <rect x="900" y="450" width="80" height="24" stroke="rgb(200,200,200)"
      fill="rgb(100,100,100)"/>
    <text x="907" y="467" fill="rgb(100,100,100)"
      font-style="italic">ENTER >>></text>
  </g>
</a>
```

This completes our SVG page. Let's save it as `poetics.svg` and see how it looks (obviously it will be moving in your browser!):

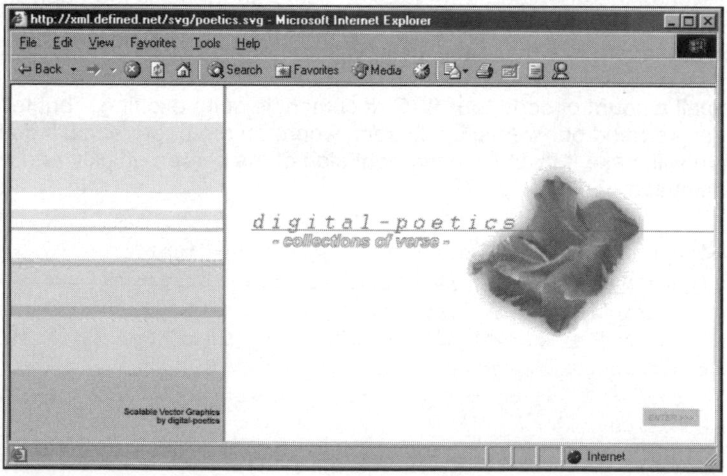

Of course, you can continue to add new effects. For more information about SVG, a great starting point is *http://www.w3.org/Graphics/SVG/*. From there, you can find links to SVG tools and the SVG specification.

It is important to remember that even though this SVG introduction is graphically rich it doesn't necessarily mean that this is inaccessible to people with disabilities. As we've seen, SVG documents have the `<desc>` element which holds an accessible textual description of the document. However, we must make sure that we provide alternatives for users who cannot view our introduction because they are using an older browser or don't have the plugin installed.

Other Web Vocabularies

We have had a brief introduction to three of the most popular web vocabularies, XHTML, MathML, and SVG. This is, however, only the tip of the iceberg: new vocabularies are being written everyday. We will list some additional web vocabularies and give a brief description of what they can be used for.

- RSS and News Feeds
- XForms
- VoiceXML
- Database output formats

RSS and News Feeds

The **RDF Site Summary** vocabulary, or RSS, is commonly used in news feeds. News feeds are streams of information that commonly contain business news or current events. For example, the Associated Press and United Press make international stories available via RSS. You can find news feeds for each of them at *http://www.newsisfree.com/syndicate.php*. Even TV listings are available in RSS.

The RSS specification fluctuated during its early development, but the 1.0 version has matured and is now widely used. We will look at a more complex example of RSS in *Chapter 10*. For more information about RSS, go to *http://groups.yahoo.com/group/rss-dev/files/specification.html*.

XForms

XForms is a specification designed to replace HTML forms in web browsers. However, currently the support for XForms is not widespread. The Mozilla 1.0 Browser and the X-Smiles Browser offer limited support. The specification is still under development; additional support should be available once it becomes a recommendation. For more information about XForms, go to *http://www.w3.org/MarkUp/Forms/*.

VoiceXML

VoiceXML was designed to represent aural communications on the web. This includes support for voice-synthesizing software, digitized audio, and command and response conversations among others. The format for VoiceXML is surprisingly easy to understand:

```
<?xml version="1.0"?>
<vxml version="2.0" xmlns="http://www.w3.org/2001/vxml">
  <form>
    <field name="gender">
      <prompt>Are you female or male?</prompt>
      <grammar src="gender.grxml" type="application/srgs+xml"/>
    </field>
    <block>
      <submit next="gender.asp"/>
    </block>
  </form>
</vxml>
```

Using grammar documents to specify the expected responses to a user's input, you can quickly create verbal forms to interact with users. For more information about VoiceXML, check out Early Adopter VoiceXML (Paul Houle et al, Wrox Press, ISBN: 1861005628), or go to *http://www.w3.org/Voice/*.

Database Output Formats

Although database formats are not explicitly web vocabularies, you may encounter them in your development. Some popular formats include:

- Microsoft Access
- Microsoft SQL Server
- Oracle XML DB
- IBM Informix
- IBM DB2
- Sybase

Each of these formats differ, but there are stylesheets available that can handle the conversion from one type of database to another. Most of these databases have the ability to export their data directly as XML. Additionally, there are tools that can extract the information from the database and format it as XML. We'll see examples of using XML and databases in the server-side chapters of this book. For more information on XML and databases check out *Professional XML Databases* (Kevin Williams et al., Wrox Press, ISBN 1861003587).

Summary

In this chapter we were introduced to several new web vocabularies. We focused on XHTML as it is the primary vocabulary in use on the Web today, but also discussed SVG and MathML, along with some other, less well-known vocabularies.

In the following chapters we will learn how to use these standard vocabularies of XML, together with those you create yourself, in a browser with CSS stylesheets, XSLT, and JavaScript.

3

- Introduction to client-side XML
- XML support in the major browsers
- Choosing between client- and server-side XML processing

Author: Chris Auld

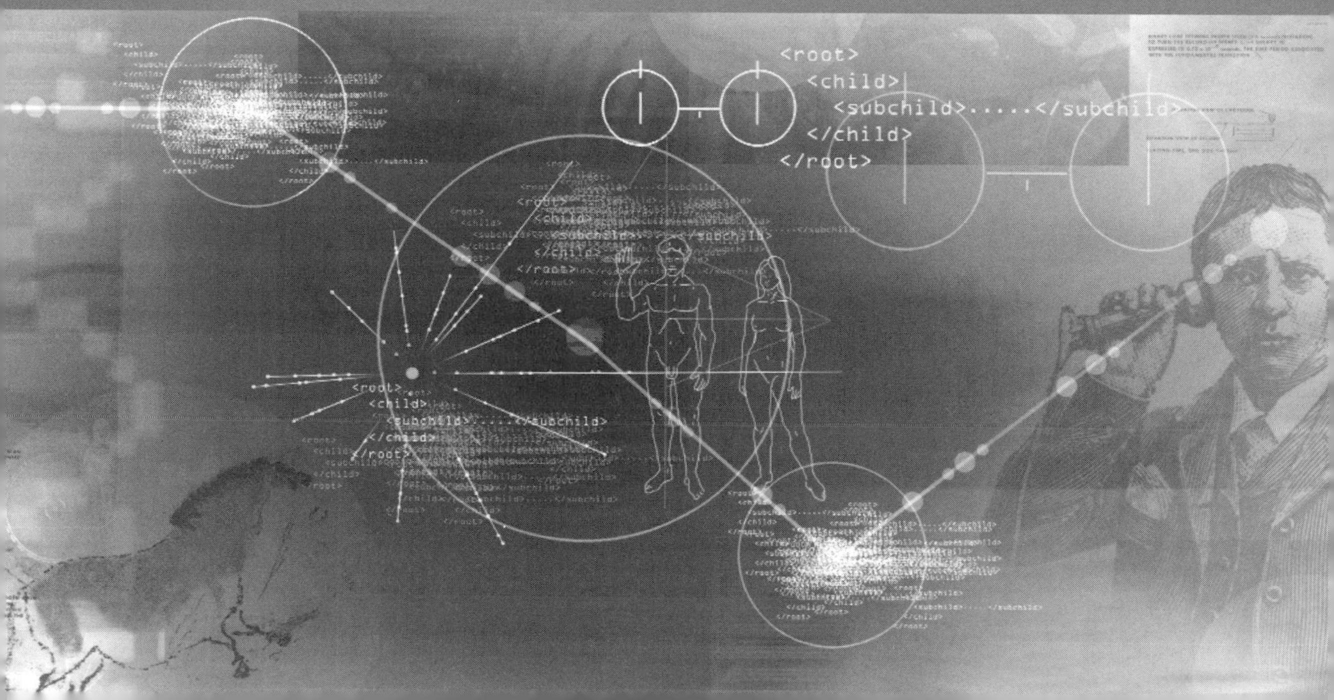

Client-side XML – Browser Support for XML

Having looked at XML in broad terms in *Chapters 1* and *2*, it is time to get our hands dirty – the next four chapters deal with XML on the client-side (in the browser). The support for XML in the major browsers has come on by leaps and bounds, even in the last twelve months. As is to be expected, support across the various browsers is by no means uniform. Fortunately though, the early adopters have for the most part followed the W3C standards in their implementation and as a result, as the other vendors catch up, we should see an increasing level of cross-compatibility.

In this chapter we will take an overview of the various ways of using XML in the browser. We will look at what levels of XML support are available in each browser and also at some of their proprietary features which make extensive use of XML.

Why Use Client-Side XML?

Let's look at why you might use XML in the browser. Like most uses of client-side programming, the goal with client-side XML is to provide a better user experience. Client-side XML comes with a similar set of caveats as JavaScript – the most notable being a lack of universal browser support.

The key advantage of using XML on the client is that we can use it to reduce the amount of data we have to transfer back and forth between client and server. This means two things for the end user – the first is an increase in the speed of their browsing experience (they no longer have to, say, download a complete HTML page on each request). The second is that we can download XML to the client as a background or asynchronous task – therefore, in some situations we can build web-based applications where there is no perceivable download lag for the user as they interact with the page.

Another advantage of using XML in the browser is that we can pass more of the responsibility for processing the page to the client. By doing this we reduce the load on our web servers and consequently provide a better experience to more users on the same server hardware. The most common way to do this is to use a stylesheet to build an XML document in the browser. *Chapters 4-6* deal with using (CSS and XSLT) stylesheets and XML together.

As you have seen in the previous chapters, XML is a language for marking up data. When using XML on the client-side we are likely to be using our marked-up data in one of two ways:

- Rendering a single XML document into XHTML with XSLT, then adding style to the XHTML with CSS (or simply rendering the XML with CSS).
- Manipulating one or more XML documents in the browser using the DOM, XSLT, and Scripting Languages such as JavaScript and VBScript.

The motivations for these two approaches tend to be somewhat different.

The first approach allows us to separate the content, the layout, and the style of our web sites. The diagram below shows this, illustrating what part each component plays in getting our XML content into an elegant representation, which we can browse:

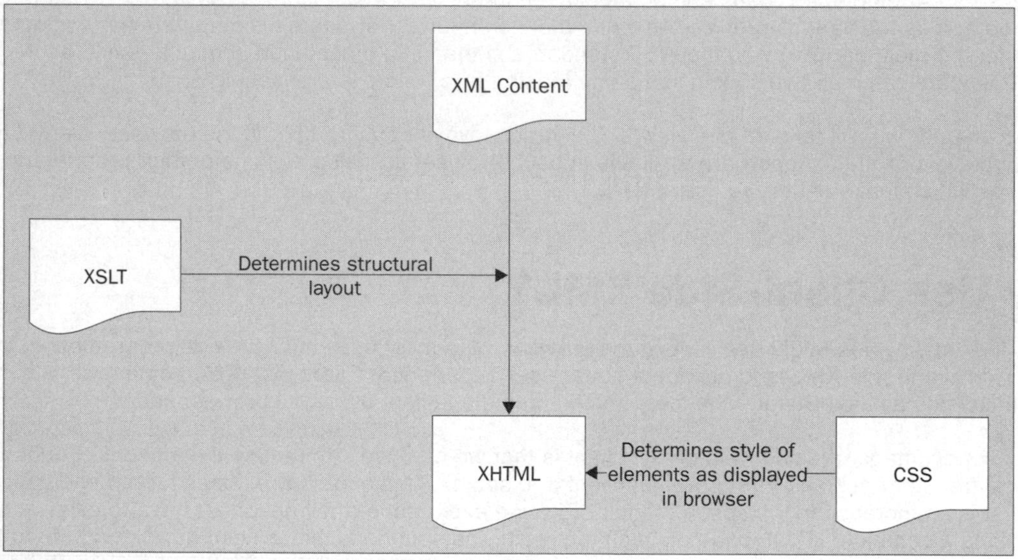

It is possible to add style directly into the XHTML during the XSLT transformation; however, the approach outlined here allows a much higher level of reuse across your site or enterprise. At e-Media Ltd (*http://www.marketeer.co.nz/*), we use the following approach in our core Marketeer e-commerce architecture:

- Server-side code is used to generate XML content dynamically.
- This content is then transformed on either the server- or client-side using XSLT.
- Finally, once in the browser, a CSS stylesheet is applied to the XHTML final document.

This approach gives us an enormous amount of flexibility over the final 'look and feel' of the site – we can change either the layout of the page, the style of the elements on that page, or both, at any time (even on the fly).

The second approach involves using XML as a data bearer for your client-side code. Think about when you have needed to deal with large amounts of data in client-side code in the past. You might have used arrays, or even delimited strings, to hold your data in a form accessible to your code. The resulting solution was probably somewhat inelegant, and prone to producing script errors. XML allows us to get rid of all of those ugly multidimensional JavaScript arrays and instead, work with data in an elegant hierarchical structure. We can also retrieve new XML data from the server without having to refresh the current page in the browser. By using JavaScript we can take our XML client-side and generate dynamic HTML content.

For example, we could take an XML document containing data about the navigational structure of our site and use it to build dynamic menus. By storing the data in XML on the client-side we can reuse the data for multiple views without having to reload the page from the server – we are effectively using the XML document stored in the browser's memory as our very own client-side data cache.

The following diagram shows an example of how we might use this ability to load and cache XML on the client for a simple example we will be looking at in greatly detail, shortly. When the user loads the page it is built using a server-side ASP script (Step 1). The ASP page inserts some XML data as a data island into the HTML page – we will look at data islands a little later in the chapter (Step 2). The HTML page and embedded XML data are then returned to the browser (Step 3). Once the HTML page is loaded in the web browser we can access the XML in the data island using JavaScript and use it to build a menu – we will look at programming with XML data in the browser when we get to *Chapter 7* (Step 4). At the same time we can load an XSLT stylesheet down to the client in the background (Step 5). In this example, the user can then choose a city from the menu we just built (Step 6), and based on their choice we will return the XML data for the properties in that city (Step 7). Finally we can use the XSLT we downloaded earlier to turn the properties XML into XHTML and then display it to the user.

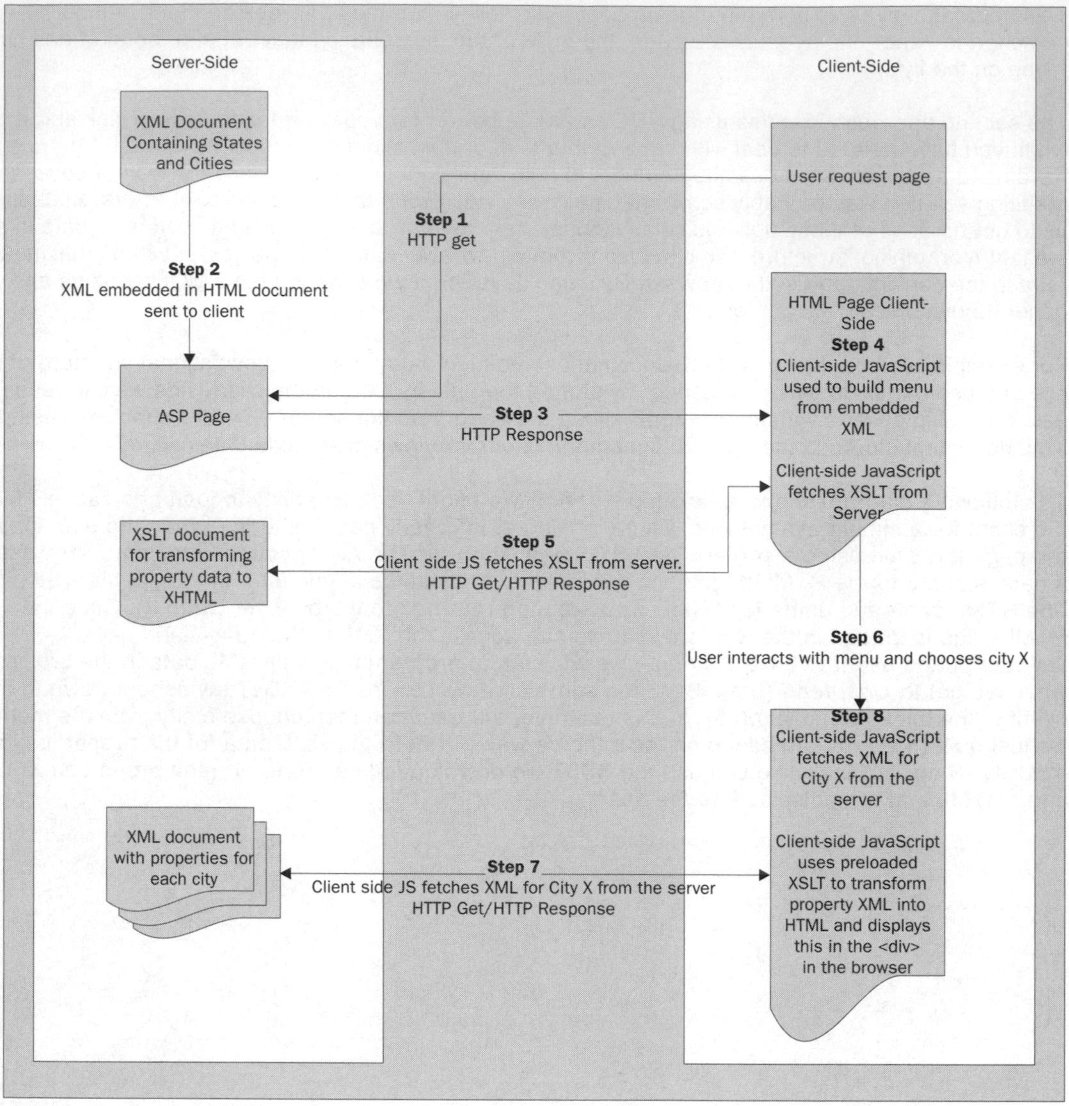

XML Support in Major Browsers

In the following sections we will examine the XML support in the current versions of the major web browsers:

- Microsoft Internet Explorer 6
- Netscape 6 and Mozilla
- Opera 6

We will look at how each browser handles raw XML, which XML parser the browser uses, and how it exposes XML to JavaScript code, before moving on to say a few words about XML support in Flash, and showing you how to decide when to use client-side XML, and when to use server-side XML.

There are three other key technologies we will look at for browser support:

- W3C Document Object Model
- XML Schema Definition
- Extensible Stylesheet Language Transformations

We will now make a few points about each of these, before moving on to the browser sections.

W3C Document Object Model (DOM)

A **Document Object Model** (**DOM**) is used to represent a document as a series of objects. You may well have dealt with a DOM implementation before – if you have written much client-side script code you would have used the HTML DOM to access certain elements in the HTML document.

You have probably also had to deal with the ugly side of the HTML DOM – cross-browser incompatibility. It may surprise you but in the very early days (Netscape 3 and IE 3), the DOM support across browsers, while not standardized, was roughly similar. It wasn't until the release of DHTML in the version 4 browsers that the DOM implementations took divergent paths. Fortunately, the days of having to write a different function for each different browser are passing into history. The W3C has set out a standardized specification for the DOM, drawing up a set of specifications for different levels (1-3) of DOM support. The higher the level, the larger the feature set supported. The W3C also refers to the early Netscape 3 and IE 3 DOMs as level 0.

DOM Level 1 defines architecture as shown in the following diagram:

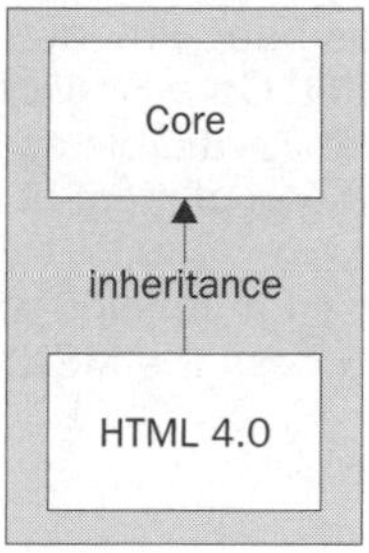

The HTML DOM extends some of the functionality from the Core, and when we start working with the XML DOM directly I'm sure you will be familiar with some of the object model from your HTML experience. The reason that the HTML DOM is required to be an extension like this, is to maintain and standardize backwards compatibility with the earlier DOM implementations without introducing functionality that would be inapplicable when dealing with XML; this makes some sense as we saw in *Chapter 2* – XHTML is just a particular specialized dialect of XML.

The W3C DOM is an interface specification, independent of any platform and/or programming language. While it has, strictly speaking, a much wider scope than XML, the specification and most of the implementations so far are designed to deal with XML and HTML documents.

As we saw in *Chapter 1*, the DOM treats data as a tree of nodes, each node having properties and methods. The advantage of the DOM is that, once you have learned how to use it, you can carry that knowledge across to whichever platform you happen to work on. So, for example, different code samples that use different vendors' XML DOM implementations should be broadly interchangeable, even though the actual libraries that the DOM is interfacing against are quite different.

More discussion of the DOM and details on how to manipulate it will be covered in *Chapter 7*. More information can also be found at the W3C DOM home page: *http://www.w3c.org/dom/*.

W3C XML Schema Definition

While XML is said to be a 'self describing' data language, it is often necessary to be able to describe the data structure that a particular document must conform to. This is where XML Schema comes into play. While XML itself has a document definition mechanism, the Document Type Definition (DTD), this was seen as being insufficient to describe the potentially complex data structures that an XML document might contain. XML Schema is aimed at filling this niche. The XML Schema dialect allows you to define complex relationships and types for an XML document.

Extensible Stylesheet Language: Transformations

As we saw in *Chapter 1*, XSLT is yet another XML dialect. XSLT is used to express a set of rules by which one XML document is transformed into another. XSLT will be explained in more detail in *Chapters 5* and *6*.

Microsoft Internet Explorer

Microsoft can take some pride in their approach to XML in Internet Explorer. They have been quick to implement new XML standards as they have emerged and have managed to avoid the temptation to 'embrace and extend' too many proprietary features into IE. IE's support for ActiveX objects is probably one of the key reasons that it has been the foremost browser in terms of XML support; it is able to take advantage of the Microsoft XML Core Services (MSXML), formally known as the Microsoft XML parser. The MSXML library of controls (available as a DLL) is now in version 4.0, service pack 1, and provides a fairly complete implementation of most of the major W3C XML standards.

Internet Explorer actually uses MSXML itself to manipulate XML internally. MSXML goes beyond this however; it is possible for developers to access the MSXML objects from any of the scripting languages running in the browser.

The MSXML Parser

As noted above, the Microsoft parser provides rich support of the major W3C XML standards. IE ships with MSXML (it has done since IE 4) although at the time of writing this is not yet true for MSXML 4.0. Not surprisingly, there is potential for compatibility problems between the different versions. These problems will be discussed later on in this chapter and will also be addressed in *Chapters 4* through *7* where they arise. However, in general, the more recent versions of IE, and thus of MSXML, provide a broad level of standards compliance. Specifically, they provide support for the DOM, XML Schema, and XSLT, as detailed opposite. MSXML also supports a number of other proprietary and non-W3C standards, such as SAX (as described in *Chapter 1*).

For more details on MSXML, visit *http://www.microsoft.com/xml/* and browse to the MSXML SDK documentation. To download the latest version (MSXML 4.0, Service Pack 1), go to *http://msdn.microsoft.com/downloads/default.asp?url=/downloads/sample.asp?url=/msdn-files/027/001/766/msdncompositedoc.xml.*

Now we'll take a brief look at the support offered by MSXML for the "key technologies" we mentioned earlier:

W3C Document Object Model (DOM)

Microsoft has supported DOM level 1 since MSXML version 2.0. Version 1.0 supported a Microsoft derivative of the DOM, which is very similar to, but not fully compliant with the W3C DOM Level 1.

W3C XML Schema Definition (XSD)

MSXML began to support the W3C XML Schema Definition standard (XSD) recommendation from version 4. MSXML 3 supported a schema variation called XML Data Reduced Schemas (XDR). You may still see XDR schemas in use in some applications, but this version is likely to be deprecated at some point in the future – your best options would be to either:

- Use a DTD instead of a Schema if you need backward compatibility.
- Update your application to use the XSD standard.

Microsoft has produced a conversion tool available to convert XDR to XSD Schemas – find it at *http://msdn.microsoft.com/downloads/sample.asp?url=/msdn-files/027/001/539/msdncompositedoc.xml.*

XSLT

One of the downsides of Microsoft's enthusiastic approach to XML uptake is that they got ahead of themselves a couple of times. We saw above that this was the case with Schemas, and XSLT is similarly affected – there is a different version called XSLT-WD, which is the W3C working draft version, supported by IE 5 and 5.5 (the proper version to use currently is XSLT 1.0, with the newest IE versions support). *Chapter 5* will discuss the differences between the two syntaxes and how to deal with any problems that may arise as a result.

MSXML Versions

As we've discussed, although IE 4+ comes with a version of MSXML, the MSXML component can also be downloaded separately for use with the browser. It is also sometimes combined with other software – it may be updated to a later version if the user installs other software that relies on it. One of the disadvantages of MSXML being a separate component like this is that it is no longer possible to determine which version of MSXML is on a user's machine by simply looking at the browser version.

The following table shows the versions of MSXML that shipped with the various versions of Internet Explorer – you can use this table to determine the baseline compatibility for each browser version. Do bear in mind that there is a possibility that the user will have installed a more recent version of the parser and, as such, it is best to 'sniff' the MSXML version explicitly rather than simply 'sniffing' the browser.

Internet Explorer version	MSXML version
4.0	1.0
4.01 SP1	2.0
5.0	2.0a
5.0a	2.0a
5.0b	2.0b
5.01	2.5a
5.01 SP1	2.5 SP1
5.5	2.5 SP1
6	3

As mentioned above, there are no IE versions to date that ship with MSXML 4.0.

There are some issues that arise with these different versions, particularly with XSLT support. *Chapter 5* will look at these XSLT issues, while *Chapter 7* will discuss how to determine the installed parser when using MSXML, via JavaScript.

Viewing Raw XML in Internet Explorer

Internet Explorer handles raw XML very elegantly, though in a slightly unusual way.

In *Chapter 1* we saw that an XML document can contain processing instructions to specify a stylesheet to be applied to that document. When IE loads an XML document, it will initially look for and follow any processing instructions in that document. If there are no processing instructions in the XML document, IE will infer its default processing instruction to apply its default XSLT stylesheet.

Let's take a look at how IE handles raw XML by using a very simple example. We will use a simple XML file (`cities.xml`) to experiment with:

```
<?xml version="1.0" encoding="UTF-8"?>
<cities>
  <city state="CA">San Diego</city>
  <city state="WA">Seattle</city>
</cities>
```

Open this XML document with IE. It will be displayed in a nice DHTML tree view, with + and - signs which can be clicked to open and close branches of the tree. It appears like this because when we load an XML document into IE without a processing instruction, the browser uses the default stylesheet resource that is included with MSXML:

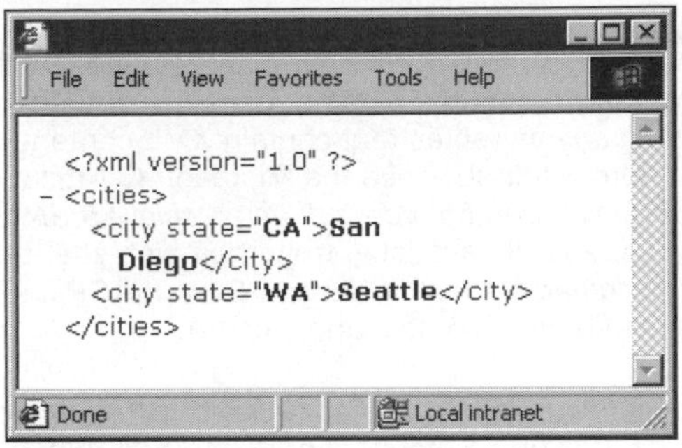

> If you want to see the raw source of the XML file you can simply choose *View Source* from the *View* menu. It is important to note that it is not possible to actually view the resulting XHTML source after the XSLT transform has been applied. To do this you will need to either use a tool such XML Spy or the Microsoft XSLT command line tool. You can download the XSLT command-line tool from:
>
> *http://msdn.microsoft.com/library/default.asp?url=/library/en-us/dnxslgen/html/msxsl.asp*

We can see the default MSXML stylesheet for ourselves by entering something like the following address into the browser: *res://msxml3.dll/defaultss.xsl* (I say "something like" because what you enter depends on what version of MSXML you are using – the address here is correct if you are using MSXML 3 – if you were using MSXML 2, you would enter *res://msxml2.dll/defaultss.xsl*). The stylesheet looks like this:

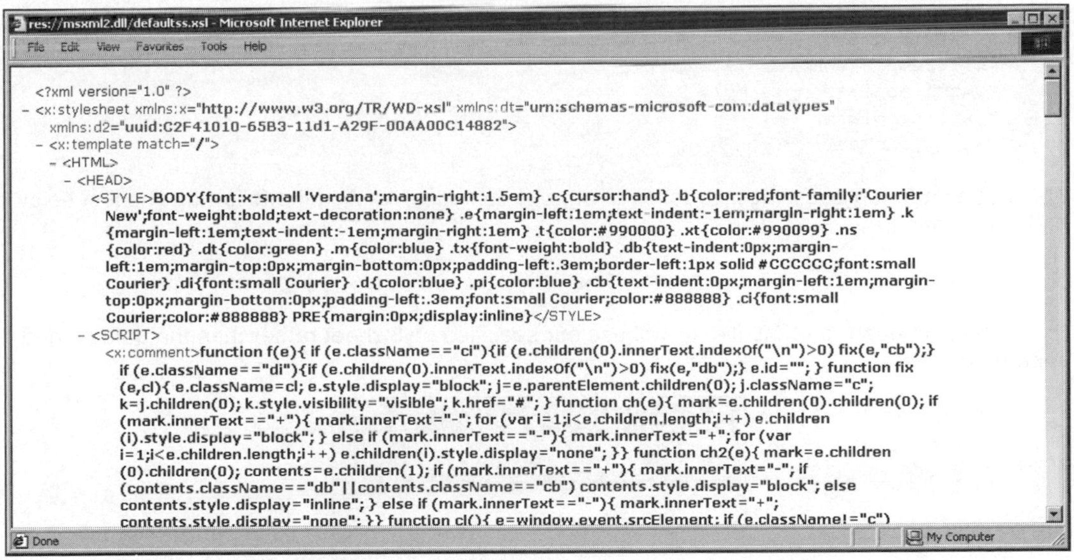

It doesn't make for easy reading but it is a very handy stylesheet to use in your own applications, particularly if you want to perform the transform on the server side or if you want to alter the behavior of the stylesheet in some way. My company, eMedia, uses the default stylesheet on our internal ASP error pages for tidily outputting any variables that contain XML content. It is not possible to save the `defaultss.xsl` document from within IE – see the Microsoft Q Article q282127 for details on why this is the case (*http://support.microsoft.com/default.aspx?scid=kb;EN-US;q282127*). Microsoft does however make the `defaultss.xsl` file available from their web site, at *http://msdn.microsoft.com/msdnmag/issues/1100/code/BeyondASP.exe* (this is a self-extracting compressed file containing the file, and some sample code).

> *There is a naming convention that you may come across that relates to the extension that an XSLT file is given. It is by no means a hard and fast rule, but sometimes an extension of `.xsl` is used to refer to a document in the XML-WD dialect, whereas an extension of `.xslt` is used to refer to a document in the W3C standard. We haven't been using this convention in the book because we feel it is too confusing, and the XSL-WD is being phased out anyway.*
>
> *All of the examples included with this chapter use the W3C standard and therefore if you are using MSXML you should make sure you have at least version 3 installed.*
>
> *Remember that the only true determinant of the dialect is the namespace declaration in the stylesheet itself. You will learn more about the different stylesheet dialects and the issues associated with them in* Chapter 5.

The way that IE handles our raw XML file is actually a little unusual. As we will see later in this chapter, most of the other browsers handle XML in the same way that they handle unknown tags in HTML – they simply output the contents of the elements, but not the attributes, to the browser window. Indeed, this approach is specified as the default behavior in the XSLT specification. To make IE apply this default processing approach we need to use a stylesheet. Let's use `default_behavior.xsl`, seen here:

```
<?xml version="1.0" encoding="UTF-8"?>
<xsl:stylesheet version="1.0" xmlns:xsl="http://www.w3.org/1999/XSL/Transform">
  <xsl:template match="*">
    <xsl:apply-templates/>
  </xsl:template>
</xsl:stylesheet>
```

We need to add a processing instruction to our `cities.xml` file. Add the following line just below the XML declaration:

```
<?xml-stylesheet type="text/xsl" href="default_behavior.xsl"?>
```

Now, when we open the XML file, IE will use our specified stylesheet rather than the default, and it will appear like this:

In *Chapters 5* and *6* we will explore XSLT stylesheets further, writing our own XSLT stylesheets to display XML content as XHTML in the browser.

Content Type Determination

In determining whether a document is an XML document, IE takes into account a number of parameters.

When the file is being loaded from the local file system, it will look first at the file extension to see if it is a known type. Failing this, it will look for an `<?xml?>` declaration at the top of the file.

When the file is coming from a remote server via HTTP or FTP, the browser first looks to the MIME content type sent by the server. Then, as above, it will look for an `<?xml?>` declaration.

> Note that, where IE is treating the document as XML based on looking at the declaration, it will still display the appropriate MIME type in the document properties box.

Once the browser has determined that the file is XML, it will parse the document and check it for well-formedness – if the document is not well formed it will throw an error; for example, if we changed our code to the following:

```
<?xml version="1.0"?>
<cities>
  <city state="CA">San Diego</city>
  <city state="WA">Seattle</city>
  <unclosed_element>
</cities>
```

Also note that IE will not validate the document against a schema or DTD, even if one is specified in the document.

Proprietary Functionality in Internet Explorer

Internet Explorer also includes a number of proprietary features that take advantage of XML, which we will outline below. We will discuss some of these features in detail in *Chapter 7*; also, for more information on how to take advantage of these advanced features see the Microsoft XML developers' site at *http://www.microsoft.com/xml/*.

XML Data Islands

As we saw in the first section of this chapter, it is very useful to be able to manipulate XML on the client-side using JavaScript. IE includes proprietary functionality to allow us to easily load XML into script-accessible variables when the page is initially loaded. Microsoft calls this functionality **XML Data Islands** – literally they are 'islands' of data contained within a sea of HTML. By using XML Data Islands we do not have to go through the rigmarole of loading XML into DOM objects ourselves – IE will do this for us automatically.

As you can see in the sample file `xml_islands.html`, included in the code download for this chapter, XML data islands are created by using the proprietary `<xml>` DHTML element. They can be created either inline:

```
<xml id="xmlisland">
  <cities>
    <city state="CA">San Diego</city>
    <city state="WA">Seattle</city>
  </cities>
</xml>
```

or by reference to a URL:

```
<xml id="xmlisland" src="cities.xml"/>
```

We can then access the data from JavaScript by using the XML DOM we discussed earlier. In this case we are using JavaScript to assign the XML `DOMDocument` objects stored in our data islands to a local variable:

```
<a href="javascript:alert(document.all.xmlisland.XMLDocument.xml);">Display Data
  Island 1
</a> <br />
<a href="javascript:alert(document.all.xmlisland2.XMLDocument.xml);">Display Data
  Island 2
</a>
```

When you run `xmlislands.html` in a browser, and click on one of the links, you will see something like this:

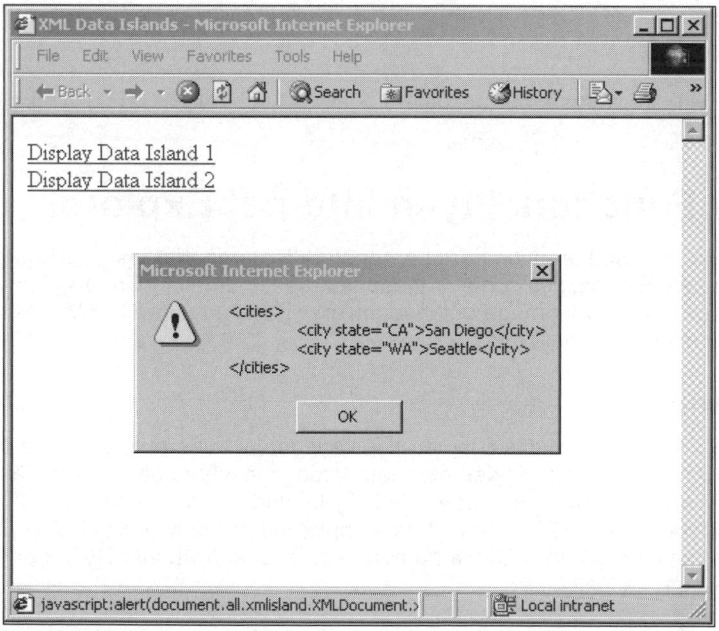

In *Chapter 7* we will look at actually using this object to traverse the XML data tree and make use of that data:

> Note that you may come across some early examples of XML data islands that use the `<script>` HTML element with attribute `language="xml"`. This syntax has been officially deprecated by Microsoft and your mileage will vary significantly if you try to make use of this syntax – particularly when creating file reference type data islands. This can result in the entire HTML page failing to render in recent versions of IE.

XML Data Binding

Internet Explorer also allows us to bind our XML data islands to various DHTML elements. Once the data has been bound to those elements it can be viewed or even updated, with the changes reflected in the actual data that is stored in the `DOMDocument` object in our data island.

While this functionality is IE-specific, it is ideal for intranet situations where you have tight control of the browser platform used. It allows the web browser to be used to deliver applications in a similar fashion to traditional GUI applications such as those written in Visual Basic.

We will discuss Data Binding in more detail in *Chapter 7*.

XMLHTTP Object

This object, included with MSXML since version 1 in its client version, is used to request data over HTTP. Since version 3 it has also been available as a version optimized for server use. We will see the client version in use in *Chapter 7*. The XMLHTTP object makes retrieving data from the server using our JavaScript code trivial:

```
var oXMLHTTP = new ActiveXObject("Microsoft.XMLHTTP");
oXMLHTTP.Open ("GET", "http://www.microsoft.com/", false );
oXMLHTTP.SetRequestHeader ("Content-type", "text/html");
oXMLHTTP.Send();
alert(oXMLHTTP.responsetext);
```

See the sample file `xmlhttp.html` to see this feature in action.

Netscape Navigator and Mozilla

After going through a number of somewhat rocky years, the Netscape browser has been 'reborn' with version 6, which is based around the open source Mozilla browser platform. The XML functionality discussed in this section should apply to all browsers that are based around the Mozilla platform. We will discuss the older versions of Netscape shortly, but for the purposes of this section I will refer to the browser engine by the more generic "Mozilla" moniker.

Mozilla uses XML extensively, even in areas of the browser that we, as web professionals, don't have to deal with. We can only scratch the surface of Mozilla XML functionality in this book, but if you want to dig into the depths of the Mozilla platform you should check out the Mozilla web site *http://www.mozilla.org*.

The Expat Parser

In a similar fashion to IE, almost all of the Mozilla XML functionality is based around a core XML parser – in Mozilla's case, this is called 'Expat'. Expat was originally developed by one of the founding fathers of XML and SGML, James Clark. It is tightly integrated with the Mozilla engine and, as such, all Mozilla versions will ship with this parser. Expat 1.2 is available separately from *http://www.jclark.com/xml/expat.html*, where you will also find more information on the parser.

DOM Support

Mozilla provides support for the W3C HTML and XML DOMs, up to Level 2. Unlike IE, the DOM support in Mozilla is built into the browser. We can therefore work very easily with a DOM representation of an XML document using JavaScript. Remember that the DOM is a standardized interface. This means that once we have created our DOM object(s), which are slightly different between IE and Mozilla, we should be able to use the same code to manipulate them. We will look at a cross-browser DOM object creation function in *Chapter 7*, when we talk about dealing with XML in client-side code.

W3C XML Schema Definition

Expat is a non-validating parser – therefore, Mozilla does not support validation using XSD, nor does it support validation using DTDs.

XSLT Support

Mozilla ships with a separate XSLT module based around the TransforMiiX engine. This means that Mozilla is able to perform XSLT transforms in the browser in the same way that we saw IE could. The use of the Mozilla XSLT functionality is covered further in *Chapter 5*. Unlike MSXML, which is a bolt-on component for IE, TransforMiiX forms an integral part of Mozilla and is therefore compiled with the application itself.

Viewing Raw XML in Mozilla

Unlike Internet Explorer, Mozilla takes the expected approach to handling raw XML files. Looking once again at our original `cities.xml` sample document, we can see that Mozilla displays the contents of the XML elements as follows:

In order to see the XML as tagged data as we did in IE, we need to view the document source. Mozilla will then display a syntax-colored version of the XML file.

```
Mozilla                                              _ □ ✕
<?xml version="1.0"?>
<cities>
        <city state="CA">San Diego</city>
        <city state="WA">Seattle</city>
</cities>
```

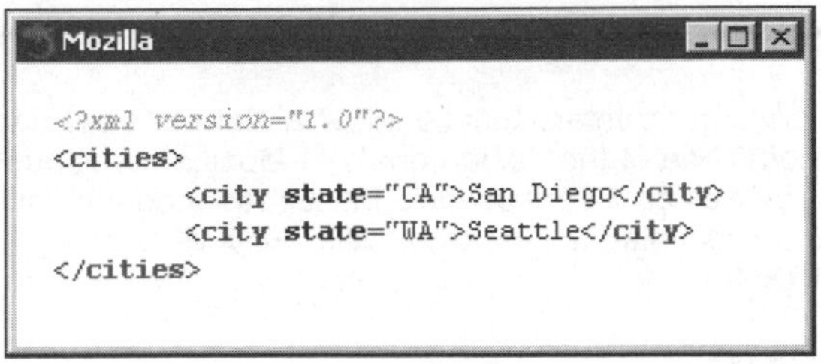

Content Type Determination

Mozilla is far more particular than IE in determining what is and isn't XML. Whether the file is coming from the file system or from a server, Mozilla will try and use the MIME type to determine content type. On platforms that support MIME types in the file system it will make the determination on that basis. On platforms with no native MIME support, such as Windows, it will use the file extension. Unlike IE, Mozilla will not look at the content of the file in making the determination; unknown file types will be treated as `text/plain` even though they may contain XML content. You can see what type Mozilla has determined by viewing the page info (press *Ctrl-I*). Mozilla will check all XML documents that it loads for being well-formed and, as we saw with IE, it will display an error in the browser (something like the image below). Mozilla will not however validate the document against an XML Schema or DTD even if one is specified in the document.

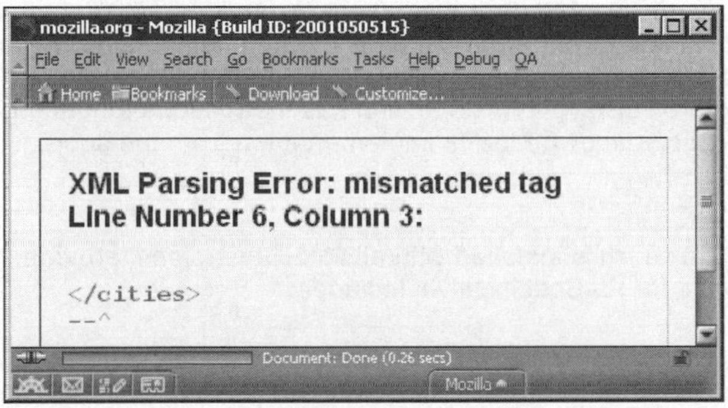

When generating server-side XML for display in Mozilla you need to be particularly careful to avoid white space at the top of the document. If the `<?xml?>` declaration is not on the first line of the resulting document, Mozilla will throw a rather cryptic parse error like the one below. This is the correct behavior – it's just that Internet Explorer is a little more lackadaisical about enforcing it.

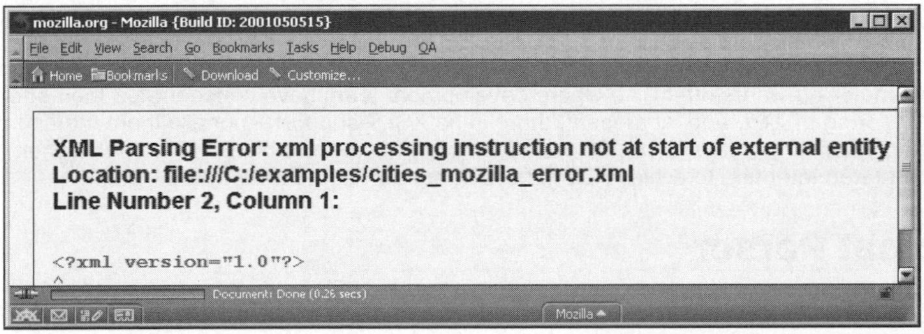

Proprietary Functionality in Mozilla

Mozilla doesn't so much have "proprietary functionality" as it has "early adoption of W3C recommendations", this being one of the design goals of Mozilla. It includes native support for MathML, RDF, and SVG, as well as a very useful XML Extras modules (see below). The most significant pieces of XML functionality unique to Mozilla are XML Binding Language (XBL) and XML User Interface Language (XUL).

XML Binding Language

XBL is a Mozilla originated technology submitted as a note to the W3C. It provides similar functionality to IE XML Data Binding, combined with IE DHTML Behaviors. We recommend that you take a look at this excellent tutorial from the Netscape Developer site for more information – *http://devedge.netscape.com/viewsource/2001/xbl/*.

XUL: XML User Interface Language

XUL allows developers and users to completely customize the user interface of Mozilla. This is done using a special XUL dialect, into which is embedded some custom scripting code. XUL is beyond the scope of this book, but a great introduction to it can be found at *http://www.mozilla.org/xpfe/xptoolkit/xulintro.html*.

Native Scalable Vector Graphics (SVG) Support

We briefly saw some examples of SVG in *Chapter 2*. Ostensibly, Mozilla supports SVG out of the box, but the release version does not ship with the SVG module due to licensing issues. For details on how to download the 'unofficial' version, which includes SVG support, see *http://www.mozilla.org/projects/svg/*. This site also has instructions for setting build flags for those of you who prefer to compile your own Mozilla implementation from the source.

XML Extras

The XML Extras module, which is installed with all Mozilla versions, provides functionality similar to that which we saw above for IE. Specifically it includes:

- A SOAP Client
- An XMLHTTP Request object almost identical in use to the XMLHTTP object in MSXML
- XML Loading and Saving Objects, which are, respectively, an XML Parser and XML Serializer.

Opera 6

Opera has supported XML since version 4, but it does not yet have the same level of support that the other two major browsers offer. The Opera development team have concentrated their efforts on CSS-based rendering of XML and, at present, there is no XSLT support – nor are there stated intentions to implement XSLT in the near future. Opera does not have any notable DOM support either, though there is a stated intention to achieve DOM Level 2 support in the near future.

The Expat Parser

Like Mozilla, Opera also makes use of the Expat open source parser.

Viewing Raw XML in Opera

Opera treats XML in a similar fashion to the way we saw previously in Mozilla:

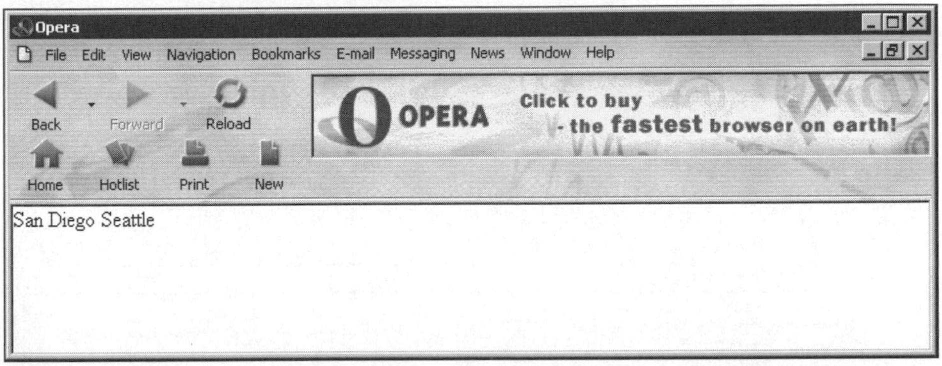

As noted above Opera does not support XSLT and will simply ignore processing instructions for XSLT stylesheets. Opera does support CSS1 and CSS2 for the styling of XML – we will see how to use CSS to render our XML in *Chapter 4*.

Content Type Determination

The Opera specification document states that Opera will use Content-Type followed by file extension (`.xml`) in determining whether a file is in fact XML content. Opera also follows the example set by IE in that it will look at the first line of the file for an `<?xml?>` declaration.

As we have seen with the other browsers above, Opera will throw a parser error if we try and load an XML document that is not well-formed.

Note that the error message is not as complete as in the two browsers above, although Opera is able to display the part of the XML file that was successfully parsed prior to reaching the error point.

Proprietary Functionality in Opera

Given its limited core XML functionality and the recent moves by the Opera development team towards a more standards-based approach, it is not surprising that there is limited proprietary functionality in Opera.

Native Wireless Markup Language (WML) Support

WML is yet another vocabulary of XML, this time for marking up documents to be displayed in mobile phone-based browsers. Opera has provided basic WML support since version 5 of the browser. In version 6, Opera supports nearly all of the WML 1.2 elements. The WML display reflects the importance of CSS in Opera – it is implemented as a custom CSS document:

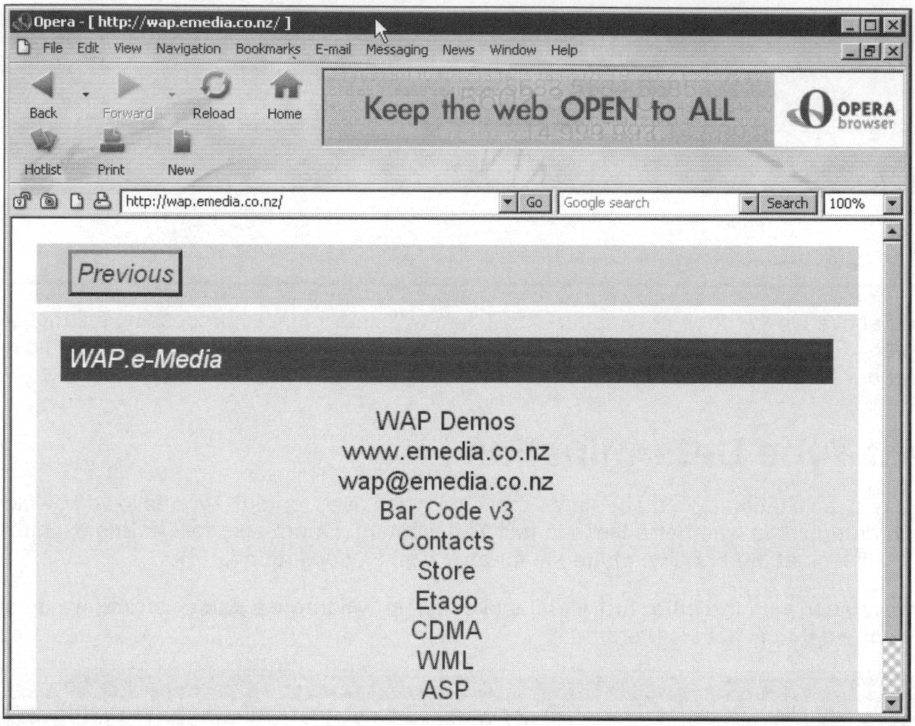

As you can see, the output is simple enough. Opera supports WBMP (Wireless Bitmap images) as well as the usual GIF graphic formats supported by more recent mobile handsets. If you don't like the way that Opera displays the WML, you can rewrite the CSS document to match your tastes – in fact, in Opera you can use CSS to customize a large number of UI features in the browser. This functionality is very useful in the testing phases of writing WML pages.

Macromedia Flash

While not strictly a browser, Macromedia Flash is another web application client that many of us use. From version 5, Flash has been able to load and deal with XML in a tree-like structure. Flash has an internal XML DOM object that is similar to, but not fully compliant with, the W3C DOM. This book will not deal with Flash explicitly in any great detail, although in *Chapter 10* we will use XML to build a scrolling news ticker as a Flash movie, passed using JSP.

For detailed information on Flash, go to *http://www.macromedia.com*, or to the Friends of ED Flash site at *http://www.friendsofed.com/flash/index.htm*, where you will find Flash books to suit all levels of experience.

A good example of XML and Flash combined in an operational site can be found at *http://www.ticketdirect.co.nz*. This site uses Flash movies to draw seating plans for sports venues. The ticket pricing and availability are loaded into the Flash movie using XML. The seating plan picker looks like this:

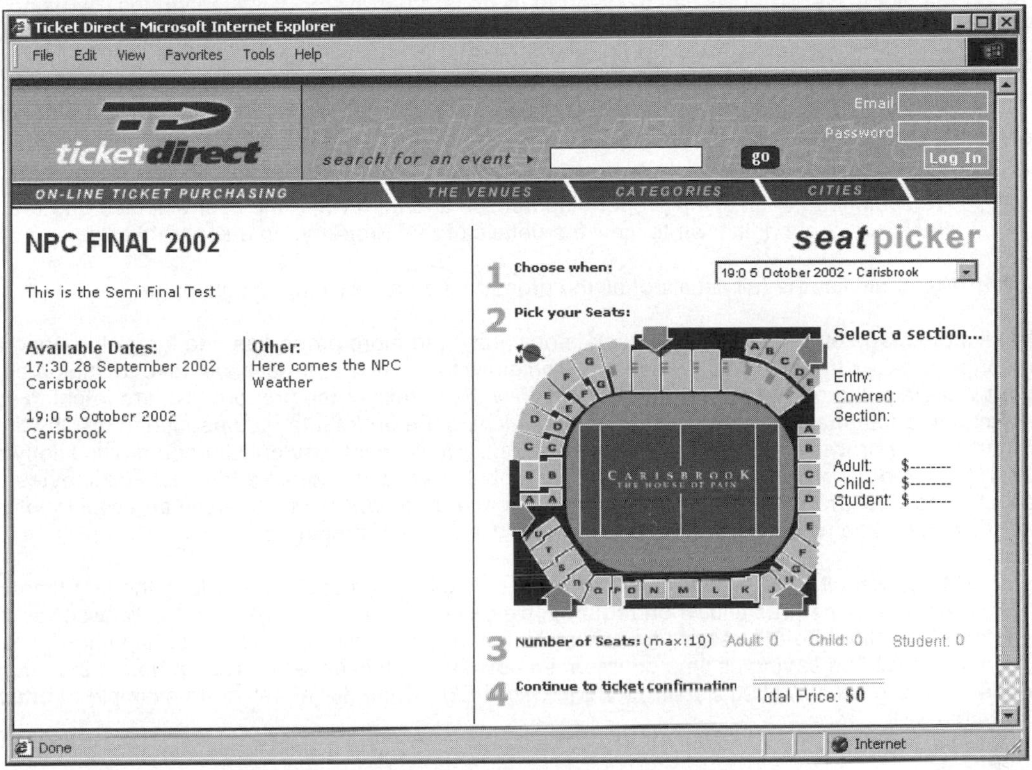

Choosing Between Client and Server

A key decision to make when designing any browser-based application that makes use of XML, will be to determine whether to employ XML on the client, the server, or both: using XML allows us to easily deal with data on both the server- and client-side of the system.

In this chapter we have looked at a number of different clients that can deal with XML. We will examine the practicalities of client-side XML processing in great detail in *Chapters 4* to *7*, and later in the book (in *Chapters 8-11*) we will see ways of generating the XML on the server side.

So don't worry if we seem like we are jumping ahead of ourselves in this section – we will cover it all in good time. This section is dedicated to examining the connection between client and server in XML-based applications. We will look at some possible approaches for using XML in our web applications and discuss the pros and cons of each – when should we take advantage of all this browser-based XML support we have learned about above?

Client-Side XML Usage

At the start of this chapter we discussed the relative merits of using XML in the browser. XML allows us to deal with data easily on the client-side. In the past, if we wanted to use JavaScript to deal with data on the client, we generally had to resort to using large arrays or delimited strings. By using XML we can now deal with data in a rich format directly on the client; we don't need to make a trip back to the server every time we need new data. Where might this be important?

Say we want to display a list of properties for sale on a web site. Traditionally there were a couple of approaches we might take:

- We could load a list of the property addresses and then when the user selected one of these, we could drill down to view the details of that property, on a separate page.

- We could list the full details of all the properties on a very large single page.

The disadvantage of the second approach is obvious – the more properties, the larger the page and the longer it takes to download. To see the problem with the first approach we have to think a bit more about what is going on. When we drill down to view the details of the property, we are fetching some information about that property but we are also fetching the entire interface needed to display that property in the browser. So, while the actual information we want may only be one or two kilobytes, the HTML interface required to display it nicely probably accounts for an additional 20 kilobytes. If we can somehow separate the content (2Kb) from the interface (20Kb) we can save an awful lot of traffic, and thus save time when we need to drill down to the different properies.

Using XML on the client-side allows us to do this – we can download the interface the first time we load the page and then, as and when required, we can download the content to the browser as XML, transform this XML into the desired format, style it as required, and insert this content into our cached interface. As well as saving us time on interface downlaods, this saves on round trips to the server. See later, in the section titled *Serving XML to Client-Side Code*, for a real-world example of effective client-side XML usage.

Server-Side XML Usage

Of course, the fabulous solution outlined above has its flaws – it relies on the application writer being able to guarantee that the client's browser has the necesssary XML support to run the application. As you have seen in this chapter, the support for XML among the two or three major browsers is by no means uniform. If you can specify that your site will target only IE and Mozilla version 6 browsers and above, then you can build cross-platform XML applications, but these browsers are still in the early stages of uptake. Therefore, such an application may only be wisely used in an intranet environment – think about your target audience, and the kind of XML functionality you will be utilizing.

The solution might be to do your XML processing on the server instead – this way, you can take advantage of the rich data structure XML provides without having to specify a browser type. This method has its downside, in that it will result in more load being placed on (and more round trips to) the server, but unless you are dealing with a particularly data-intensive application, this is not likely to overshadow the advantages of the server-side approach. Look at the next two sections for more detail on using XML on the server (of course, we also look at this topic in way more detail in *Chapters 8-11*, along with technology-specific implementations).

In the next few sections we will look at three broad approaches to using XML in our applications:

- Using XML on the server-side only and sending HTML to the client
- Determining whether the client supports XML, then performing the transform either on the client (if it does) or the server (if it doesn't).
- Sending HTML to the browser and then using either script code or some other browser-side object such as a Flash movie to request XML from the server.

XML as Part of a Dynamic Web Page

I am sure that most of you are familiar with the idea of dynamic web pages, using a server-side scripting language such as ASP, PHP, or JSP. Traditionally, data presentation on this kind of page involves querying a relational database such as SQL Server, MySQL, or Oracle, and then outputting the results to the browser as HTML.

Unfortunately, while the relational model is great for a lot of situations, it doesn't cope so well with outputting data from two or more related tables; generally it requires multiple SQL queries. XML is ideal for dealing with this sort of data, which can usually be well-modeled as a tree-type hierarchy. By storing our data as XML, or by extracting our data from the database in XML format, we can take advantage of the easier data management offered by XML in our server-side code. We can retrieve two or more tables-worth of XML data from the database using a single query and then manipulate this data in a number of ways, either using the DOM or XSLT to generate HTML to send to the client.

The resulting output will be plain HTML and, as such, we can serve it up on most common browser platforms without too much difficulty. For a real example of a web application using server-side XML in this manner, see *Chapter 11* of this book.

Applications that Choose Client- or Server-Side XML Processing

XML in conjunction with XSLT and CSS (see *Chapters 4* to *6*) makes for a very sophisticated toolkit for generating dynamic interfaces for applications. In this kind of situation, we generate XML instead of HTML in our server-side code. We then transform the XML with XSLT on either the server- or client-side, depending on what browser we are serving content to, then apply CSS to this XML to display it in the browser.

This architecture is based around the idea that the XSLT transformations can occur either on the client- or the server-side, based on the type of browser making the request – we sniff the browser in stage two, seen below, and do the transformation on client or server, depending on whether the browser we have identified has the necessary XML support or not.

The following diagram shows the workflow we use to generate a page using this approach:

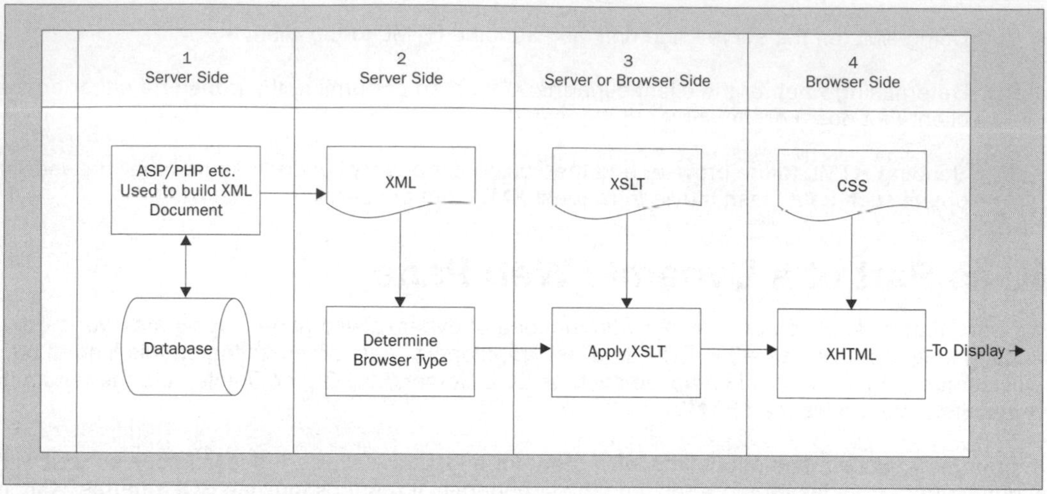

It probably looks a bit daunting so I will talk you through each of the stages.

1: Server-side XML Generation

Stage one is much like building a normal dynamic web page, except that instead of generating HTML we generate XML. This XML can take whatever structure is appropriate for our application.

2: Choosing Our Transformation

At stage two we first sniff out what browser we are serving content to, and as a result, determine whether the transformations are to be done on the server or the client, and which XSLT stylesheet(s) we need to apply to the XML. We can do this based on a number of criteria including:

- The browser that is being used.
- The IP address that the user is browsing from.
- The URL of the site that is being browsed.

We do it like this because we want to do the transformation on the client wherever possible, as this will reduce the processing load on our server.

It is important to be careful here though. If the XSLT is picking just a small amount of content out of a very large XML document, then the overhead of sending the XML to the browser may outweigh the savings and it may make more sense to simply transform on the server and send the HTML. Another way around this problem is to transform on both server and client. The server-side transform picks out the important elements and sends these as XML to the client. The client then performs another transform to generate the final display code.

3: Transforming our XML with XSLT

At stage three the stylesheet is then applied, either on the server or on the client, by passing the XML to the client with the correct XML processing instruction. The result of the transformation is an XHTML document that probably contains either a CSS processing instruction, or, the usual HTML CSS references.

4: Styling our XHTML with CSS

At stage four the browser applies any CSS styles that have been specified and the result is displayed to the user.

At the start of this chapter I mentioned the Marketeer e-Commerce architecture that we have developed at e-Media. We chose to take this approach because it offers a number of major advantages to traditional HTML-based dynamic web pages:

- Firstly it allows us to rigidly separate the data, the layout, and the style of our pages with these being handled by XML, XSLT, and CSS respectively.

- Secondly it allows us to target a very large number of different platforms with the same server-side script code. If we need to target a new platform, say, a mobile phone browser, all that we need to do is write a new XSLT stylesheet to describe how our applications' data should be presented to that device.

- Thirdly, it allows us to really think outside the box and use our web applications for things that would not have been possible without XML. For example, we could apply a stylesheet, which turned our application-specific XML into a format suitable for sharing with business partners. They could then write a system at their end, which 'browsed' our XML, and interacted with our e-Commerce system, without us having to change our core codebase.

But this server-side XSLT approach is not a panacea to be applied to everything. It comes with its drawbacks:

The most obvious drawback is that it involves a significant degree of extra processing to perform the transforms on the server-side. At e-Media our estimates are that it requires between 30% and 50% more processing than a straight HTML approach would need. This means that even where some of the XSLT processing is being done in compatible browsers, those requests that do their XSLT transforms on the server-side will probably counteract any performance gains.

Saying this though, we feel that the additional hardware needed is cheap enough to justify the extra benefits allowed by this system. By using separate stylesheets to describe how the interface should be laid out we create a large degree of separation between the content and the layout of the page. With this separation comes a better degree of manageability, and the ability to easily target a wide range of clients, as noted above. It would also be easy to break this sort of system out to a number of tiers in a server farm environment.

In terms of implementing this sort of architecture, there are two broad options. The first is to build your own framework in the server-side tool of your choice. The second, and most likely option is to use a ready-made tool. These tools usually include functionality to detect browsers and efficiently apply XSLT transforms.

The main toolkits are all available for download free of charge:

- AxKit for Apache. *http://www.axkit.org/*.

- Cocoon for Apache. *http://xml.apache.org/cocoon/*.

- IBM XML Enabler *http://www.alphaworks.ibm.com/tech/xmlenabler*.

- XSLISAPI for Microsoft IIS.
  http://msdn.microsoft.com/Downloads/webtechnology/xml/xslisapi.asp

To see this approach in operation and for a more detailed description of the architecture see *http://www.marketeer.co.nz/*.

Serving XML to Client-Side Code

This is where client-side XML comes into its own – the most advanced and most platform-specific approach to serving up XML data to the browser is to actually deal with the XML as data in code on the client-side. This approach allows us to build pages that can display dynamic properties without having to make a round trip to the server for additional processing. We have seen earlier in this chapter that there are a few ways for us to make XML data available to our client-side code. These include:

- Loading XML into a DOM variable using the browser's proprietary DOM load method.
- The XML HTTP Request objects in IE and Netscape – though the first option is probably more appropriate for XML data than HTML data.
- XML-aware client-side development tools such as Flash.
- XML data islands

The key advantage of this kind of approach over server-side XML processing is that it reduces the number of round trips to the server. By doing so we make possible interfaces that would have been too slow under traditional HTML-only development models. However, as we have seen above, browser support for these kinds of features is by no means universal yet, so they are probably best used in intranet-type situations, where it is fairly easy to control the browser platform that your web applications will be used on.

The exception to this rule is Macromedia Flash, which is improving in its XML support very quickly. Because of the near ubiquitous nature of the Flash plugin (Macromedia claims 97% coverage with Flash 5+), and its unique cross-browser and cross-platform support, it is more than appropriate for use on the wider Internet. As I mentioned earlier in the chapter, a good example of this is the seat booking application at *http://www.ticketdirect.co.nz/*.

By using XML we can load a very rich dataset into the Flash movie. This allows us to show the pricing for each section of the stand, along with the entry gate. The sequence of events when this page loads is something like the following:

1. The browser fetches the HTML Page.
2. The browser loads the Flash movie, passing in some parameters from the HTML page.
3. The Flash movie loads the XML from a remote server. The XML is generated from a relational database on the fly, based on parameters passed to the ASP page by the Flash movie.
4. The Flash movie loads the XML into a set of variables and then uses these variables to calculate pricing when the user chooses a section of the ground to buy tickets in.

Without XML we would have had to make a call back to the server each time a new section was chosen – this would have made the application impractically slow. This is a great example of the kind of situation where client-side XML processing has a major advantage over server-side processing.

Summary

In this chapter we have primarily looked at what support for XML is available in the current versions of the major browsers. We have looked at the core methods of using XML in the browser, including some of the advanced functionality offered by Netscape and Internet Explorer. We have also looked at three different approaches to using XML in our web applications. In the next few chapters we will flesh out our knowledge of how to actually implement the features that we have looked at in this chapter.

We will examine these topics in greater depth in the following chapters:

- *Chapter 4* will look at applying style to XML documents using Cascading Style Sheets.
- *Chapters 5* and *6* will look in detail at XSLT, which, as we have seen, allows us to restructure XML documents, and even transform them into other languages, for example HTML or WML.
- In Chapter 7 we will tie our new-found XSLT skills together with the XML DOM and JavaScript to dynamically retrieve and render XML content on the client.

4

- A brief look at using CSS to style XHTML
- Using CSS to style XML
- CSS support in the major browsers

Author: Jon James

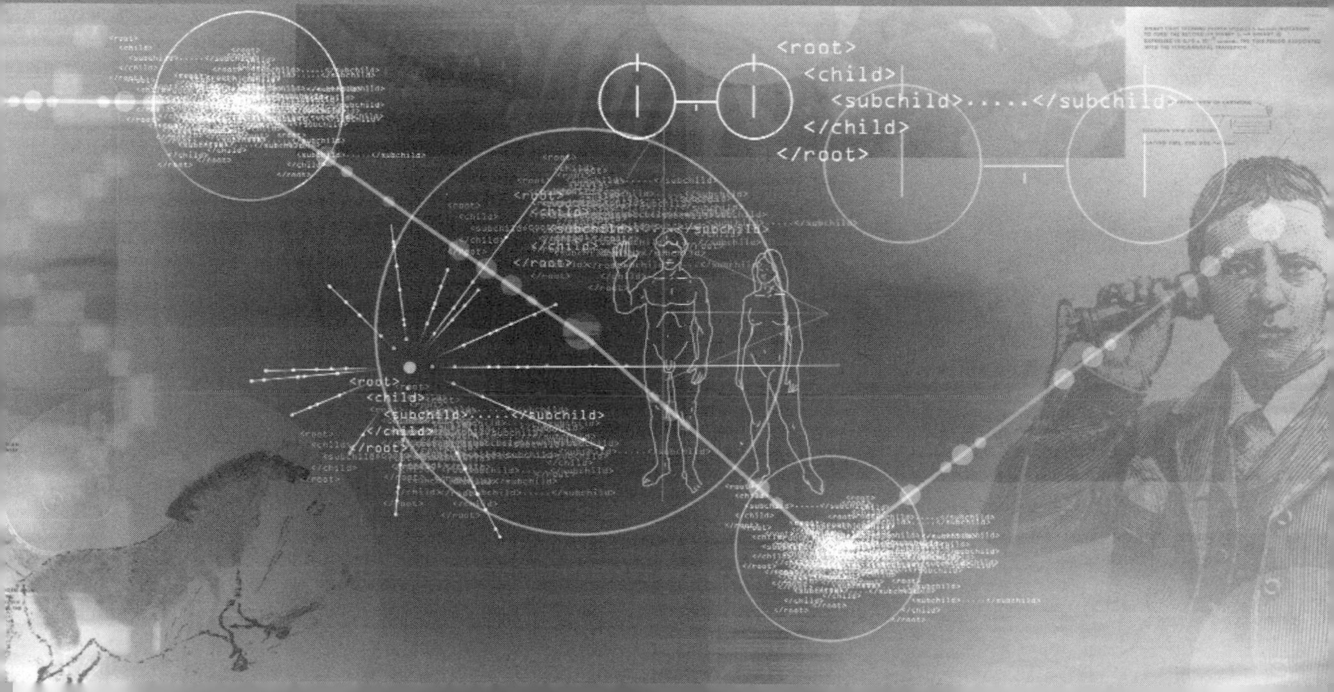

Displaying XML Using CSS

You are probably familiar with CSS (Cascading Style Sheets) after using it to style HTML pages. As such, it is a very helpful tool for separating the **contents** of an HTML page from how it appears to the reader, and for allowing us to update styles across many pages using a single stylesheet.

By way of a reminder (or an introduction if you are not too familiar with CSS) we'll start by spending just a couple of pages having a look at how to style an XHTML document with CSS. This will make sure we are clear about the terms defined by CSS, and will remind us about what we can do with CSS. We will be putting as much of the style rules for our pages into CSS as possible, including table size and positioning.

Having seen a simple XHTML example, we will go on to look at styling with other vocabularies of XML. When it comes to using CSS with XML there are some important things we need to be aware of; in particular the limitations of what we can display from an XML document using CSS, and how it can be presented. Therefore, we will be looking at the main aspects of displaying our XML documents, seeing what we can and cannot do, and looking at ways in which we can overcome the hurdles we are likely to face when working with CSS and XML.

After all, with XHTML, the browser is intrinsically aware of the meaning of some of the elements and will display them accordingly. For example a browser will know that when it comes across a `<table>` tag it must start to render a table, whereas in generic XML a `<table>` tag could just as likely relate to a piece of furniture – there is no predefined idea of how this should be displayed. As we shall see, this makes styling XML documents a lot more interesting than styling XHTML documents. We will also look at issues such as adding links, adding content before or after elements, and displaying attribute content.

Much of what we will be looking at is only just starting to be supported in the version 6 browsers, so it will push your experience of what is possible with CSS, and also whet your appetite for what will be possible in the near future.

In all, this chapter will cover:

- A quick summary of how CSS works with XHTML.
- Styling XML documents with CSS.
- Using CSS selectors with XML.
- The CSS Box Model and the positioning schemes.
- Laying out tabular XML data with CSS.
- Linking between XML documents.
- Adding images to XML documents.
- Adding text to our documents from the stylesheet.
- Using attribute values in our documents.
- A summary of where we are at in terms of CSS support with version 6 browsers.

The examples in this chapter have been tested with the latest browser versions at the time of writing, on both Windows and Mac. On PC, these were IE 6, Netscape 6.2, and Opera 6. On Mac, the latest available versions were IE 5, Netscape 6.2, and Opera 5. Unless otherwise stated, when referring to Netscape 6, it is specifically Netscape 6.2. In cases where an example is indicated as ***not*** *working in one of these versions, it did not work in any of the previous versions of that browser on that operating system, either.*

So, let's start off with a quick recap of what CSS is and how it does its job.

Introduction to CSS

CSS allows us to add style rules to elements of a document, indicating how the content of those elements should be rendered. Stylesheets have existed since the early days of printing, when a printer would be given instructions on font family and size of font to use when printing a document. When designers use elements such as `<font>` or `<i>` in HTML or XHTML to indicate the style of text wanted, or when they use tables to control layout, then the content can easily get lost in the middle of style or presentation rules. By separating out the content from the stylesheet, and using a stylesheet to indicate how a document can be visually presented, we get the following benefits:

- We can alter the appearance of multiple pages from one stylesheet rather than changing each individual page.
- We can use different stylesheets with the same document to offer different views (perhaps a larger text view for the visually impaired).
- The content is simpler to author and read because you do not have to include all the styles for each element.

- The download of pages is faster because the stylesheet only needs to be downloaded once (and cached), and it contains all style rules, as opposed to their being included in every page.

CSS is based upon **rules** that govern how the content of an element or set of elements should be displayed. Here is an example of a CSS rule.

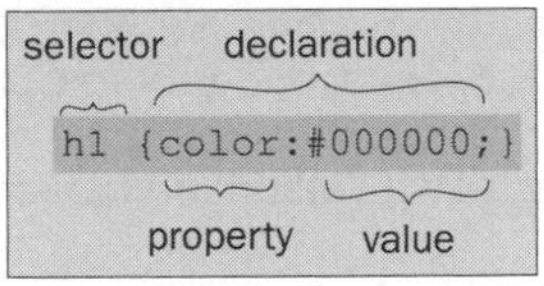

The **rule** is split into two parts, the **selector** and the **declaration**.

The selector indicates which element or elements the declaration applies to (you can have a comma-separated list of several elements). The declaration sets out how the element(s) should be styled. In this case, all `<h1>` elements have been specified, but selectors can be more sophisticated, as we will see later.

The declaration has two components: a **property** and a **value**, which are separated by a colon. The property is the property of the selected element(s) we want to affect. For example, here we are setting the `color` property (for foreground color alone: there is a separate property for `background-color`). Its value is a specification for this property, in this case the hex code for black: `#000000`. The rule ends with a semicolon.

While it is not necessary to add a semicolon at the end of a single declaration, a declaration can consist of several property-value pairs, and each property-value pair within a rule must be separated with a semicolon. Therefore, it is good practice to start adding them from the beginning, in case you want to add another later. Should you forget to add the semicolon any further property-value pairs will be ignored.

Note that, once you have declared a rule, the rule will apply to all child elements of the element to which it was applied, so if you set a rule specifying the `color` on the `<body>` element to be black, all its children will be black (`<p>`, `<h1>`, `<h2>`, `<h3>` elements, etc. with the exception of links which the browser will often override, unless you provide a rule for the `<a>` element). This is one reason why CSS stylesheets are known as **cascading** stylesheets, because the rules flow down the tree, the other reason being that you can use rules from several stylesheets by importing one into another or importing multiple stylesheets into the same XHTML file.

In the next example, you can see a rule that applies to several elements. We have separated their names in the selector with commas and we're specifying several properties for these elements, separated by semicolons. All the properties are kept between the curly braces:

```
h1, h2, h3 {color:#000000;
            background-color:#FFFFFF;
            font-family:verdana, arial, sans-serif;
            font-weight:bold;}
```

If you want the `<h3>` element to be in italic as well, then you can just add the following rule.

```
h3 { font-style:italic }
```

This saves repeating all the other property-value pairs, which the `<h3>` element has in common with the `<h1>` and `<h2>` elements. The more specific a rule is within a stylesheet the greater precedence it has in the cascade, so if we added a `font-weight:normal` declaration in the rule for `<h3>`, it would override the `bold` declaration before it. The order in which rules appear within the stylesheet does not matter, however.

At the time of writing, there were two versions of CSS: CSS1 and CSS2. The features of CSS1 are mostly supported by IE 6, Netscape 6, and Opera 6 on Windows, and by IE 5, Netscape 6 and Opera 5 on Mac. Support for CSS2 is more patchy, as we shall see in this chapter, despite being made a W3C recommendation in May 1998.

Here is a list of the properties of a document you can change in CSS2:

FONT	**BORDER**	**PADDING**	**TABLE**
font	border	padding	border-collapse
font-family	border-bottom	padding-bottom	border-spacing
font-size	border-bottom-color	padding-left	caption-side
font-size-adjust	border-bottom-style	padding-right	empty-cells
font-stretch	border-bottom-width	padding-top	table-layout
font-style	border-color		
font-variant	border-left	**DIMENSIONS**	**LIST and MARKER**
font-weight	border-left-color	height	list-style
	border-left-style	line-height	list-style-image
TEXT	border-left-width	max-height	list-style-position
color	border-right	max-width	list-style-type
direction	border-right-color	min-height	marker-offset
letter-spacing	border-right-style	min-width	
text-align	border-right-width	width	**GENERATED CONTENT**
text-decoration	border-style		content
text-indent	border-top	**POSITIONING**	counter-increment
text-shadow	border-top-color	bottom	counter-reset
text-transform	border-top-style	clip	quotes

TEXT	**BORDER**	**POSITIONING**	**CLASSIFICATION**
unicode-bidi	border-top-width	left	
white-space	border-width	overflow	clear
word-spacing		right	cursor
		top	display
BACKGROUND	**MARGIN**	vertical-align	float
background	margin	z-index	position
background-attachment	margin-bottom		visibility
background-color	margin-left	**OUTLINES**	
background-image	margin-right	outline	
background-position	margin-top	outline-color	
background-repeat		outline-style	
		outline-width	

Styling an XHTML Document with CSS

As we saw in *Chapter 2*, XHTML is the reformulation of HTML using XML syntax. Version 1.1 was the first version of XHTML that was modularized, which meant new Internet-enabled devices (from phones to fridges) either support whole modules of XHTML (such as the **tables** module or **forms** module) at a time or they do not, making it easier to create sites for these new devices. We saw the differences in writing XHTML back in *Chapter 2*, so let's quickly look at how to write a CSS stylesheet to work with it.

This is the page that we will be creating:

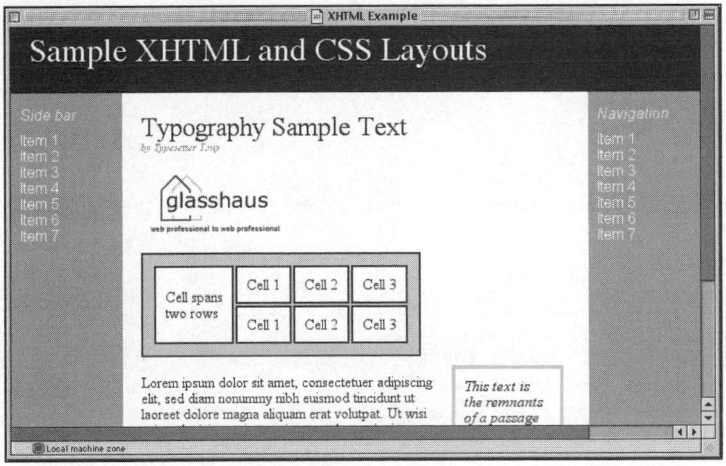

Without the stylesheet, the document would look something like this:

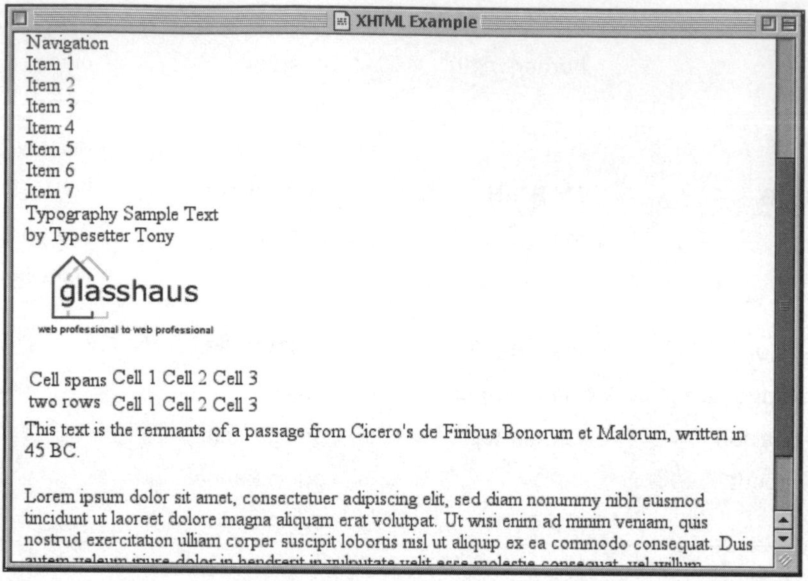

Unsurprisingly, the process of writing a CSS stylesheet for an XHTML document is very similar to how we write one for HTML. One thing that you will notice, however, is that we are removing almost all styling from the XHTML, and relying solely on CSS for all styling rules – we are using CSS for positioning of content, header, and navigation, as opposed to tables or frames.

We are using an external stylesheet, linked to the XHTML document using the `<link>` element (as with using CSS with HTML, you can include the style rules within the document inside a `<style>` element within the `<head>` element, or on an element with a `style` attribute, but the use of a separate stylesheet means that changes to the one document will be reflected across all pages and save bandwidth). Here is the file (`eg0.html`):

```
<!DOCTYPE html PUBLIC "-//W3C//DTD XHTML 1.0 Transitional//EN"
                    "DTD/xhtml1-transitional.dtd">

<html xmlns = "http://www.w3.org/1999/xhtml">
<head>
  <title>XHTML Example</title>
  <link rel="Stylesheet" href="eg0.css" type="text/css" media="screen" />
</head>

<body>
  <div class="header">Sample XHTML and CSS Layouts</div>
  <div class="contents">
    <div class="sideBarHead">Side bar</div>
      <div class="item">Item 1</div><div class="item">Item 2</div>
      <div class="item">Item 3</div><div class="item">Item 4</div>
      <div class="item">Item 5</div><div class="item">Item 6</div>
  </div>
```

```
    <div class="navigation">
      <div class="sideBarHead">Navigation</div>
        <div class="item">Item 1</div><div class="item">Item 2</div>
        <div class="item">Item 3</div><div class="item">Item 4</div>
        <div class="item">Item 5</div><div class="item">Item 6</div>
    </div>

    <div class="page">
      <div class="title">Typography Sample Text</div>
      <div class="credit">by Typesetter Tony</div>
    <img src="logo.gif" alt="GlassHaus Logo" width="165" height="75" /><br /><br />

    <table>
      <tr><td rowspan="2">Cell spans<br />two rows</td>
         <td>Cell 1</td><td>Cell 2</td><td>Cell 3</td></tr>
      <tr><td>Cell 1</td><td>Cell 2</td><td>Cell 3</td></tr>
    </table>

    <div class="pullQuote">This text is the remnants of a passage from Cicero's de
      Finibus Bonorum et Malorum, written in 45 BC. </div>
      <p>Lorem ipsum dolor sit amet, consectetuer adipiscing elit, sed diam nonummy
      nibh euismod tincidunt ut laoreet dolore magna aliquam erat volutpat. Ut wisi
      enim ad minim veniam, quis nostrud exercitation ulliam corper suscipit
      lobortis nisl ut aliquip ex ea commodo consequat. Duis autem veleum iriure
      dolor in hendrerit in vulputate velit esse molestie consequat, vel willum
      lunombro dolore eu feugiat nulla facilisis at vero eros et accumsan et iusto
      odio dignissim qui blandit praesent luptatum zzril delenit augue duis dolore
      te feugait nulla facilisi. </p>
    <div>

  </body>
  </html>
```

Here you can see the stylesheet for this document, `eg0.css` (this is just a text document like an HTML/XHTML page saved with the `.css` extension – although some tools, such as Dreamweaver, offer a CSS authoring tool in the application). If you are not familiar with the absolute positioning we are using in this example, don't worry – we will cover it in depth in the XML section later in this chapter.

```
  body {
    color:#000000;
    background-color:#FFFFFF;}

  .header {
    position:absolute;
    top:0px;  bottom:auto;  left:0px;  z-index:100;
    width:100%;  height:60px;
    padding-top:10px;  padding-left:20px;
    font-size:26pt;  font-family:times, timesnewroman, serif;
    color:#FFFFFF;  background-color:#000000;}

  .contents, .navigation {
    width:100px;  height:500px;
    font-size:14pt;  font-family:arial, helvetica, sans-serif;
```

```
    color:#FFFFFF;  background-color:#999999;
    padding:10px;}

  .contents {
    position:absolute;
    left:0px;  top:60px;}

  .navigation {
    position:absolute;
    right:0px;  top:60px;
    padding-left:10px;}

  .sideBarHead {
    font-size:12pt;  font-style:italic;
    padding-top:15px;  padding-bottom:10px;}

  .item {font-size:12pt;}

  .page {
    width:auto;
    background-color:#FFFFFF;
    padding-top:75px;  padding-left:10px;  padding-right:10px;  padding-bottom:10px;
    margin-left:120px;  margin-right:120px;}

  .title {font-size:22pt;}

  .credit {
    font-size:8pt;  font-style:italic;
    color:#999999;
    padding-bottom:15px;}

  table, td {
    padding:10px;
    border-style:solid;  border-width:2px;}

  table {background-color:#CCCCCC;}
  td {background-color:#FFFFFF;}

  .pullQuote {
    float:right;
    width:20%;
    background-color:#FFFFFF;
    font-style:italic;
    border-style:solid;  border-width:4px;  border-color:#CCCCCC;
    padding:10px;  margin:10px:}

  p {padding-bottom:20px;}
```

As you can see, the process is very similar to that of writing stylesheets for HTML documents. There are a few things we should note before moving on, however.

Firstly, it is important to understand that while XHTML is HTML reformulated in XML syntax, there is a difference between this and other XML vocabularies. The difference is that the browser already knows what to do with certain elements; it knows that a `<table>` element requires it to render a table, it knows the `rowspan` attribute on a table cell indicates how many rows that cell should span, and so on. So, the browser already knows a lot about this vocabulary. When we come to other XML vocabularies we do not have the same advantages. This means that we have to be a lot more careful about how we author our stylesheets.

Of course, as with any rule, there are some other exceptions: languages such as SVG, CML, or XUL, and all languages used to present information written in an XML vocabulary. The difference with these languages is that you will need a plugin or particular browser to view them; the language they use and how they are interpreted is not as widespread or standard in browsers as HTML is.

Even though we have used absolute positioning for the header and the side bars, we have included a table where there might be tabular content. Using absolute positioning for layout is preferable to using tables because it separates the content of the document from the layout rules (making the content easier to work with and more reusable). A table should still be used for presenting tabular data, however.

The next thing we should note about this example is that we still add in a few formatting or presentation rules into the XHTML. We specify the size of images (because they are required attributes, and when there are several on a page it will be able to continue rendering the page correctly even if the image has not yet loaded). We use the `rowspan` attribute on the table cell that spans two rows. As you will see later, there are other ways to position elements using CSS, but for some things we will still be relying on tables for layout for a while to come yet, both in supporting older browsers and for complex layouts that even version 6 browsers have difficulty with.

Finally, we should note that the images appear and links work in this example. This is one big difference between XML and XHTML, which we will look at in detail later, as including images and links is a problem in XML with version 6 browsers. For now, it is sufficient to say that a browser that is presented with a different vocabulary of XML from XHTML will not assume that the `<table>` or `<a>` elements mean what they do in XHTML – I'm sure you could imagine possible alternative uses for both.

Styling XML Documents with CSS

Having looked at XHTML (an application of XML that was designed for presentation purposes, and which browsers understand) let's see what happens when we look at a vocabulary that the browser has no idea about.

We could be faced with some custom XML that we want to render in our browser created from a database, we might want to incorporate an RSS feed (Rich Site Summary, an XML description of site content) from a news site that gives us its headlines in XML, or we could be dealing with a vocabulary and message that is specific to one of our trading partners... Wherever it comes from, it is unlikely that a browser will understand it and be able to present it without help. That's where CSS can come in.

Because our XML elements do not have any implicit means of presentation, we need to address the following issues:

- How to link to the stylesheet from the XML document.
- How to control layout without the use of tables.
- How to present tabular data in XML.
- How to link between XML documents.
- How to display images in our XML documents.

Other issues we need to address are:

- The extent to which we can re-order the content so that elements are presented in a different sequence to the one in which they appear in the original XML document.
- How we can add content that is not in the XML document, such as headers for what an element's content refers to (in the XML file this will be described by the element's name).
- How we can display attribute content, since many XML files contain important data we may wish to view as attribute values.

Let's start by seeing how we attach the stylesheet so that we can see some examples of rendering XML with CSS in the browser.

Attaching the Stylesheet

When working with XML vocabularies other than XHTML, we have to use a standalone stylesheet – we cannot include the rules inside the document. We link a stylesheet to an XML document using a processing instruction, like so:

```
<?xml-stylesheet type="text/css" href="eg01.css"?>
```

We use an XML processing instruction to attach the stylesheet because the `<link>` element was specific to XHTML – it could mean anything to the browser if it appeared in another XML vocabulary. The attributes the processing instruction requires are as follows:

- `href` indicates the location of the stylesheet – its value is `CDATA`.
- `type` indicates the MIME type of the stylesheet, in our case `text/css`. If the user agent does not understand the type (for example, a non CSS-aware mobile phone) it will not need to download it.

The processing instruction can also take the following optional attributes:

- `title` is the name of the stylesheet – you can give it any title you like, and its value is `CDATA`.
- `media` indicates the intended media the stylesheet is for viewing on. Values include the most common which is `screen` (primarily color computer screens), as well as `aural`, `braille`, `handheld`, and `tv`.
- `charset` indicates the character set used.
- `alternate` indicates whether the stylesheet is the preferred stylesheet. It can take the values `yes` or `no`; if not supplied the default is `no`.

You can include multiple CSS stylesheets by adding further processing instructions for each of the stylesheets you want to use with the document. You can also add processing instructions to include a different sort of stylesheet: XSLT. This will be covered in *Chapter 5 and 6*.

Selectors

Before we continue, we should briefly talk about selectors in CSS – the portion of the CSS rule that indicates which elements the rule should apply to. From your work with CSS and HTML you may be familiar with the following selectors:

Selector Type	Example	Description
Universal	`*`	A wildcard, which matches all element types in the document.
Type	`myElement, page, paragraph`	Matches all element types specified in the comma-delimited list. In this case, it matches all `<myElement>`, `<page>`, and `<paragraph>` elements.
Class	`.myClass`	Matches elements with a `class` attribute whose value is the name after the dot or period (in this case, elements with attribute `class="myClass"`). Note that this only works with HTML and XHTML, not XML.
ID	`#myID`	Matches an element with an `id` attribute whose value is the name after the hash or pound sign (in this case elements with attribute `id="myID"`). This is of limited use with XML.
Descendent	`myElement1 myElement2`	Matches an element type which is a descendent of another. In this case it matches `<myElement2>` elements that are contained in `<myElement1>` elements.
Child	`parent > child`	Matches an element type which is a direct child of another. In this case it matches `<child>` elements that are direct children of `<parent>` elements.
Adjacent sibling	`sibling1 + sibling2`	Matches an element type which is the next sibling of another. Here it matches `<sibling2>` elements that have the same parent as a `<sibling1>` element but appear immediately after the `<sibling1>` element.

There are also a series of selectors called **attribute selectors.** We'll take a look at these later in the chapter in a section called *Using Attributes in Selectors*.

Note that the Class selector only works for HTML or XHTML documents, because the browser already knows the meaning of the `class` attribute for these vocabularies. Even if your XML contained a `class` attribute, the browser would not associate it with the Class selector.

Similarly, the ID selector only works with attributes of ID type. While the browser will understand this for HTML and XHTML elements, for other XML vocabularies it would need to know that an `id` attribute was of type ID, and this would require a DTD or schema that specified this. Since the browser is not forced to validate with a DTD or schema, even if one is specified for the XML document, you cannot rely on it knowing when an attribute is of type ID.

Layout of XML with CSS

The most obvious difference when laying out XML examples is that, even if we are able to control the vocabulary, we cannot use tables to lay out our XML, which can make things more difficult. The vast majority of HTML and XHTML web sites use tables for formatting complex layouts.

Recently there are an increasing number of sites that use CSS to control layout, rather than tables. HTML and XHTML sites that use CSS for layout usually rely on `<div>` *and* `<span>` *elements with* `id` *and* `class` *attributes that associate the particular purpose of that* `<div>` *or* `<span>` *with a style. However, they remain a small percentage compared with those that still rely on tables. The principles of using CSS to lay out HTML sites are similar to those we will see for use with XML.*

As we have seen, when working with XML the browser does not associate any meanings with elements such as `<table>`. Therefore we need to control all of our layout rules using CSS.

One of the great things about CSS is that it is very easy to start writing CSS stylesheets. You don't need a great understanding of how it works to get results: attach style to elements and off you go. However, when we start working with XML, in particular positioning and layout, it is important to understand how CSS is used to render a page. CSS operates on something known as **the box model**, so we'll first have a look at what this model is. Then we can look at how it is implemented when we come to lay out pages using this model.

Understanding the Box Model

When displaying a document, CSS treats each element in the document as a **rectangular box**. Each box is made up of four components: **content** surrounded by **padding**, a **border**, and **margins**.

For each box, its margins are transparent, borders can have styles (solid, dashed), and backgrounds apply to the area inside the border, which includes padding and content. The padding is the area between the border and the content.

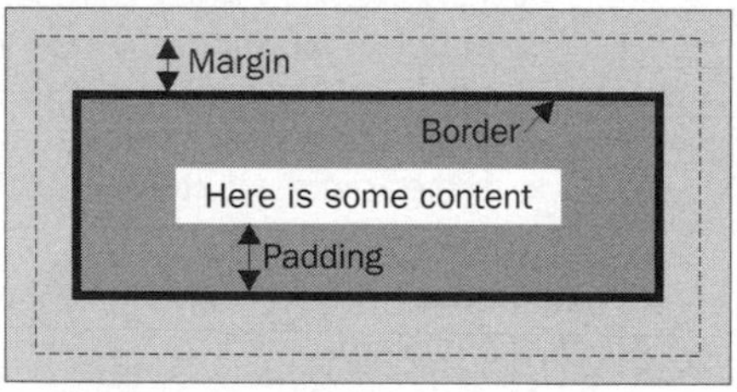

The default width for margins, borders, and paddings is zero. However, the width can be specified using CSS, in fact different widths can be given for each side of the box. For example you might have a wider border on the top and more padding to the right.

If you specify a `width` and `height` for a box, you are actually setting the width and height of the content area. However, note that some versions of Internet Explorer actually read `width` and `height` values as measuring the height and width of the content plus padding plus border.

Each box can contain other boxes, corresponding to elements that are nested inside of it.

There are two types of boxes in CSS, **block** and **inline**. In HTML, block boxes are created by elements such as `<p>`, `<div>`, or `<table>`, while inline boxes are created by tags such as `<b>`, `<em>`, and `<span>`, as well as content such as text and images. Block boxes deal with a block of content (it is like having a carriage return before and after their content), while the contents of inline boxes can flow together, without the carriage returns.

Some elements in HTML such as lists and tables have other types of box, but the browser treats them as a block or inline box when it comes to positioning, so we will not go into that here.

When styling XML with CSS the browser does not know which elements should be displayed as a block and which as inline, so we need to specify it as a property of the element. To do this we use the `display` property, which takes a value of either `block` or `inline`. As we shall see, the way in which we lay out our document, and the style of a parent box can affect these (for example, an absolutely positioned element is always treated as a block-level element).

For example, look at the following paragraph:

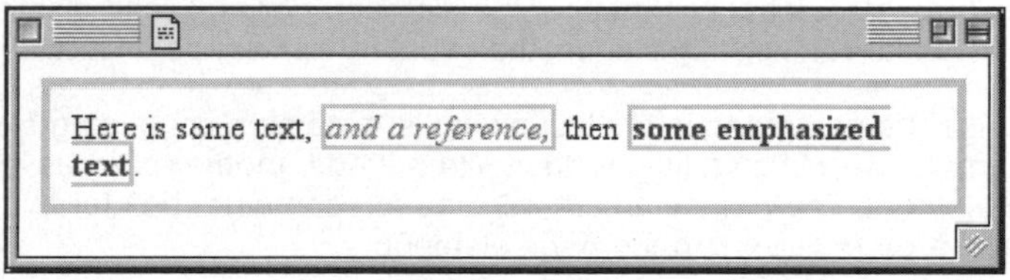

If this was written in HTML or XHTML, the code might look something like this:

```
<p>Here is some text, <em>and a reference</em>, then <strong>some emphasized
text</strong>.</p>
```

The browser would know that a paragraph should be displayed as a block, and the italicized and emboldened text should be displayed inline, flowing within the text of the rest of the paragraph. However, this document was actually created using the following XML (`eg01.xml`):

```
<paragraph>Here is some text, <reference>and a reference,</reference> then
  <important>some emphasized text</important>.
</paragraph>
```

Therefore, in order to display it correctly, we have to set the `display` property for each element (`eg01.css`):

```
paragraph {
  display:block;
  padding-top:10px;
  border:solid;
  border-width:4px;
  border-color:#CCCCCC;
  padding: 10px;}

reference {
  display:inline;
  font-style:italic;
```

```
  color:#CC3333;
  border:solid;
  border-width:2px;
  border-color:#CCCCCC;}

important {
  display:inline;
  font-weight:bold;
  color:#990000;
  border:solid;
  border-width:2px;
  border-color:#CCCCCC;}
```

As you can see, we have also set a border so that you can see where each box (be it an inline or block-level box) starts and ends.

As well as `block` and `inline`, we could also set the `display` property to `none`, to prevent a box being created. The browser will act as if neither the element, nor any child elements, exist (even if those children have declared `display` values, their content will not be displayed).

A block-level box, like the paragraph in the last example, acts as a containing block for boxes within it. So, in the next example, we will go a little further. We will add another block-level box representing the content of a `page` element. The `page` element will create a container box for two paragraph elements. We have also added a `pageNumber` to the `page` element:

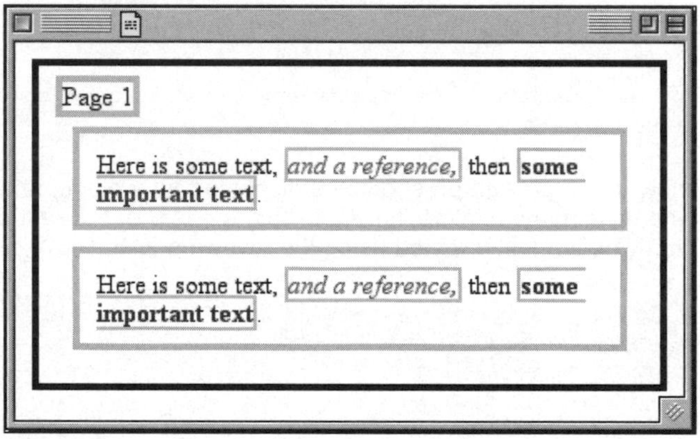

Here is the new XML for this example (`eg02.xml`):

```
<page>
  <pageNumber>Page 1</pageNumber>
  <paragraph>Here is some text, <reference>and a reference,</reference> then
    <important>some important text</important>.
  </paragraph>

  <paragraph>Here is some text, <reference>and a reference,</reference> then
   <important>some important text</important>.
  </paragraph>

</page>
```

And here are the two new styles we have added to the stylesheet (eg02.css):

```
page {
  display:block;
  border:solid;
  border-width:4px;
  border-color:#000000;
  padding: 10px;
  margin:10px;}

pageNumber {
  display:inline;
  border:solid;
  border-width:4px;
  border-color:#CCCCCC;}
```

One interesting thing about how CSS works is that, to simplify positioning, block boxes only contain all inline boxes or all block boxes. So, while the pageNumber element has its display property set to inline, it behaves like a block box because an **anonymous** block box is created around it (the anonymous block box is just a container for the inline element so that it gets treated as a block box – we cannot access it to set rules for it).

Positioning in CSS

As we mentioned when starting this section, we need to understand the box model so that we can see how to lay out element content using CSS. Knowing that each element is displayed as a box, the process of layout becomes a case of deciding what type of box we want an element to be in (inline or block), and where we want to position that element on the page.

CSS2 has three types of positioning: **normal**, **float** and **absolute**. So, let's see how we can use these to position the boxes that correspond to each element.

Normal Flow

Normal flow is the default type of positioning. In this scheme **block boxes** flow from the **top to the bottom** of the page starting at the top of their containing block, while **inline boxes** flow horizontally from **left to right**.

To see how this works, we have added a document element to the XML, and repeated the page we saw in the last example so that there are two pages in the document (the files for this example are eg03.xml and eg03.css):

You can see that the document contains two pages, the second beneath the first, and the paragraphs flow from top to bottom within the pages. Meanwhile, the `reference` and `important` elements (which are inline) flow with the normal text from left to right.

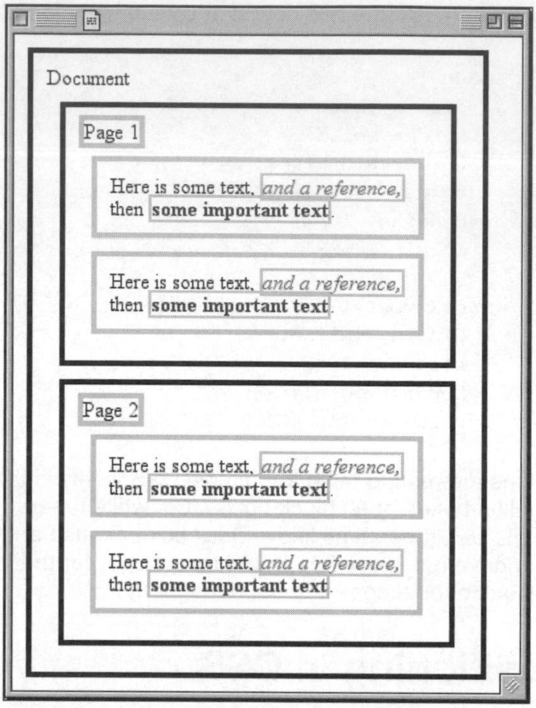

Inline boxes are wrapped as needed, moving down to a new line when the available width is exceeded.

Furthermore, vertical margins of boxes collapse in the normal flow. So, instead of adding the bottom margin of a block box to the top margin of the following block box to create the distance between their respective borders, only the larger of the two values is used.

Horizontal margins, however, are never collapsed.

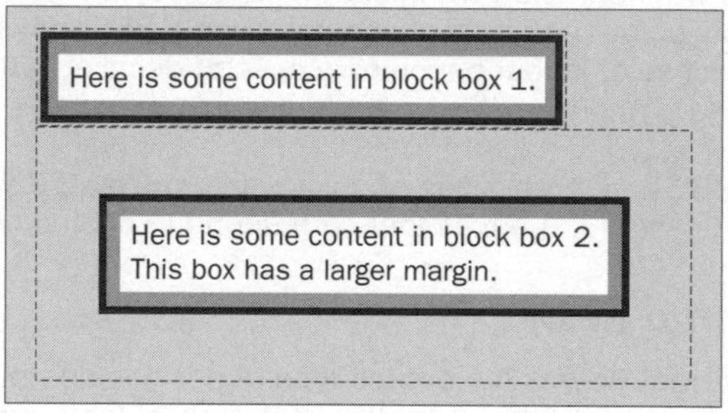

Relative Positioning

Another form of positioning under the "normal" banner is relative positioning. This renders the page according to normal flow, but then offsets the box by a given amount. One example of where this is particularly useful, and which demonstrates this nicely, is in creating subscript or superscript text. Here we have added a footnote to the reference:

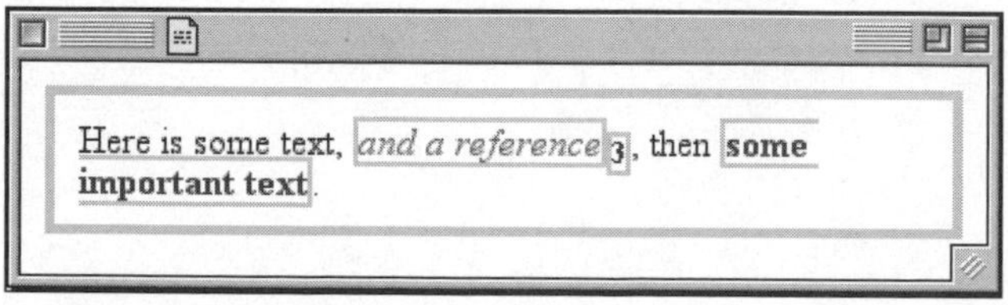

You indicate that a box should be relatively positioned using the `position` property with a value of `relative`. Then you can use `left`, `right`, `top`, and `bottom` properties to specify offset values. Here is the style rule for the `footnote` element we have added (`eg04.css`):

```
footnote {
  position:relative;
  top:3px;
  font-size:9pt;
  display:inline;
  font-weight:bold;
  color:#990000;
  border:solid;
  border-width:2px;
  border-color:#CCCCCC;}
```

Note that the `top` offset is specified to push the box down.

You should only specify a left or right offset and a top or bottom offset. If you specify both one must be the absolute negative of the other (for example `top:3px; bottom:-3px;`*). Otherwise the right or bottom offset will be ignored.*

Relative Positioning and Overlapping Boxes

When you are using relative positioning you can end up with some boxes overlapping others. Because you are offsetting a box relative to normal flow, if the offset is large enough one box will end up on top of another. This may create an effect you are looking for, however there are a couple of pitfalls you should be aware of:

- Unless you set a background for a box (either a `background-color` or `image`), it will, by default, be transparent, so when overlapping of text occurs, you would get an unreadable mess.
- The CSS specification does not say which element should appear on top when relatively positioned elements overlap each other, therefore there can be differences between browsers.

In the following example, the `important` element has been given a `relative` position 45 pixels in from the right-hand side of where it would have been under normal flow. We have also set `background-color` properties for both the `reference` and `important` elements (`eg05.css`).

```
important {
  position:relative;
  background-color:#FFFFFF;
  right:45px;
  display:inline;
  font-weight:bold;
  color:#990000;
  border:solid;
  border-width:2px;
  border-color:#CCCCCC;}
```

In IE and Netscape the relatively positioned element will appear at the front. Here is the result in IE 5 on a Mac:

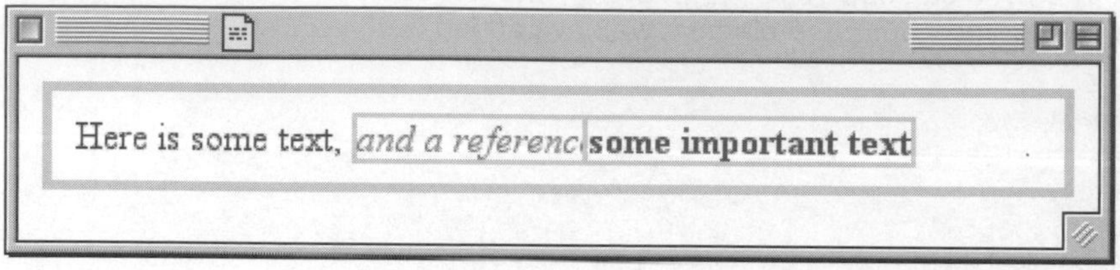

Opera, on the other hand, uses the order in which the elements appear in the document to determine which one appears on top:

The later the element, the nearer to the top it appears. As you can see, Opera also creates a jumble of text despite having the `background-color` property set.

The offsets used in relative positioning will also be ignored if they conflict with a `width` or `height` setting for a block-level box.

Floating

The second type of positioning creates a box that floats, allowing other content to flow around it. A box that is floated will not have its vertical margins collapsed above or below it, like block boxes in normal flow can, but will be aligned with the top of the containing box. Horizontally, however, it is shifted as far to the left or right of the containing box as is possible within that block's padding.

To indicate that an element's content should appear within a floating box, you set the `float` property and give it a value of either `left` or `right`. Note that floated boxes are treated as block boxes even if defined as inline.

You should also set a `width` property too, indicating the width of the containing box that the floating box should take up. If you do not set a `width` property, the floating box will automatically take up 100% of the width of the containing box, without anything flowing around it, just like a non-floated block-level element.

In the following example, we have a `<pullQuote>` element. We have set this to be a floating box, taking up 20% of the width of its container, and aligned to the right.

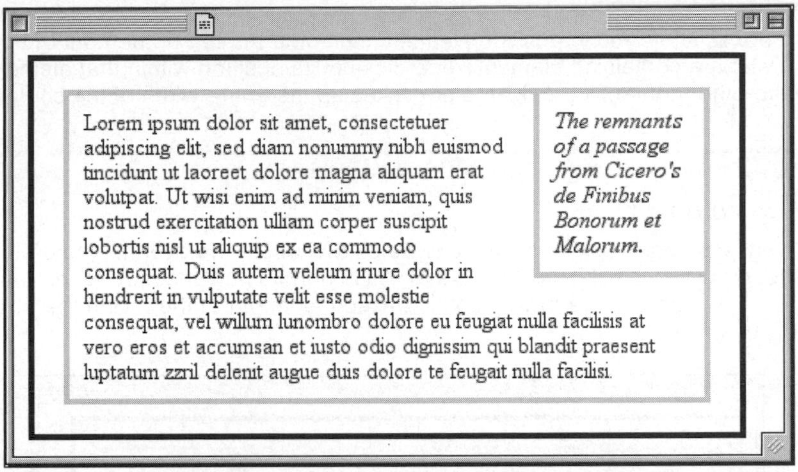

Here is the XML for this example (`eg06.xml`):

```
<page>
  <pullQuote>
    The remnants of a passage from Cicero's de Finibus Bonorum et Malorum.
  </pullQuote>
  <paragraph>Lorem ipsum dolor sit amet, consectetuer adipiscing elit, sed diam
   nonummy nibh euismod tincidunt ut laoreet dolore magna aliquam erat volutpat. Ut
   wisi enim ad minim veniam, quis nostrud exercitation ulliam corper suscipit
   lobortis nisl ut aliquip ex ea commodo consequat. Duis autem veleum iriure dolor
   in hendrerit in vulputate velit esse molestie consequat, vel willum lunombro
   dolore eu feugiat nulla facilisis at vero eros et accumsan et iusto odio
   dignissim qui blandit praesent luptatum zzril delenit augue duis dolore te
   feugait nulla facilisi.
  </paragraph>
</page>
```

The new style we have added for the `<pullQuote>` element looks like this (`eg06.css`):

```
pullQuote {
  float:right;
  width:20%;
  font-style:italic;
  border-style:solid;
  border-width:4px;
  border-color:#CCCCCC;
  padding:10px;
  margin:10px:}
```

One interesting thing to point out here is that it does not matter whether the `<pullQuote>` element appears before or after the `<paragraph>` element – it will still be in the same place. This has important implications for the ability to present the contents of an XML document in a different sequence to the one it follows in the XML source.

> Floated boxes allow you to position element content to the left or the right of other content within a containing element, regardless of its position within that element, or above the other content if the floated box takes up the entire width of the containing box.

Overlapping Floated Boxes

As with relatively positioned boxes, we have to be careful about the overlapping of floated boxes too! A floated box can overlap block-level boxes that are in normal flow mode. Here we have added another `paragraph` element. We have also increased the length of the text in the `pullQuote` for the purpose of this example.

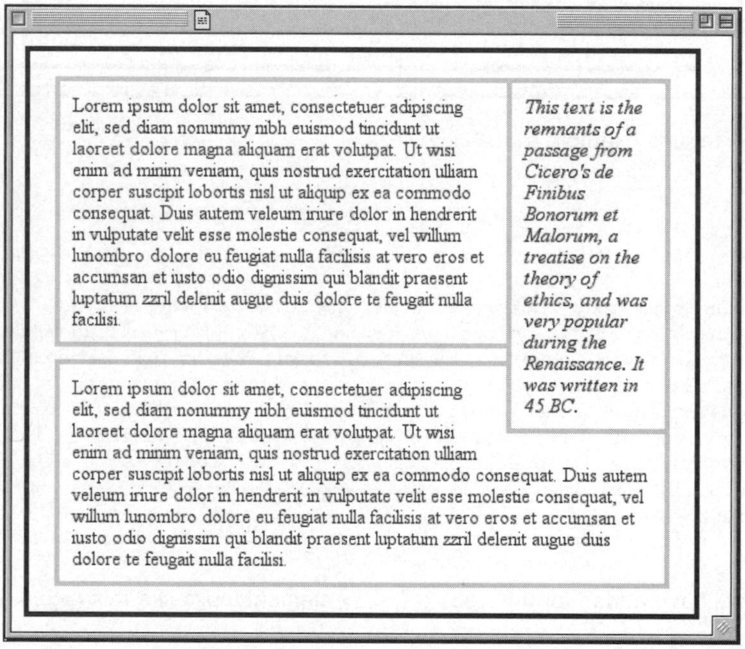

This will still happen if we add another layer of nesting in the XML. This time we put the first `paragraph` in a `<subsection>` element, and then add the second `<paragraph>` as a sibling of `<subsection>`. Here is the structure of the XML file (`eg07.xml` and `eg07b.xml`):

```
<page>
  <subsection>
    <pullQuote>...</pullQuote>
    <paragraph>...</paragraph>
  </subsection>
  <paragraph>...</paragraph>
</page>
```

Despite the second `<paragraph>` element being outside the `<subsection>` element, its content is still wrapping around the floated box:

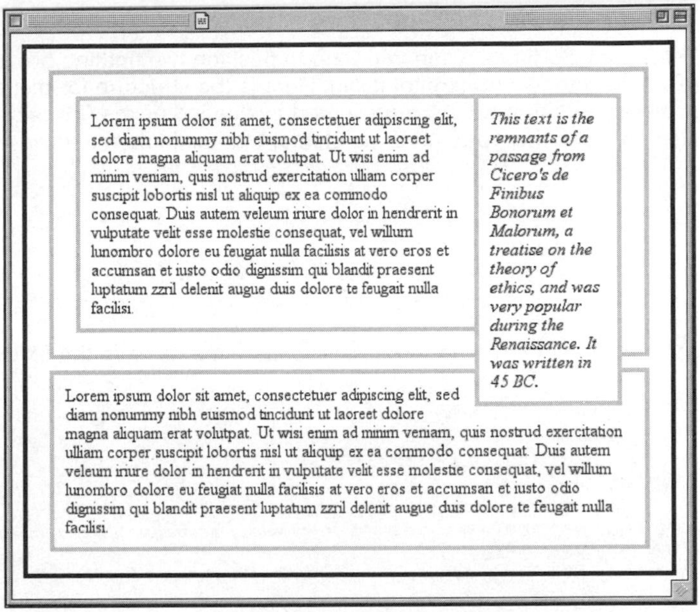

We can fix this, so that it is does not wrap around it using the `clear` property on the second paragraph. We have to be able to distinguish it from the other paragraph in order to do so – in this case we have changed the name of the second paragraph element to `<paragraph2>` (`eg07b.css`):

```
paragraph2 {
  clear:right;}
```

The `clear` property indicates which side(s) of an element's box must not be adjacent to an earlier floating box. It can take the values `left`, `right`, `both`, `none`, or `inherit`:

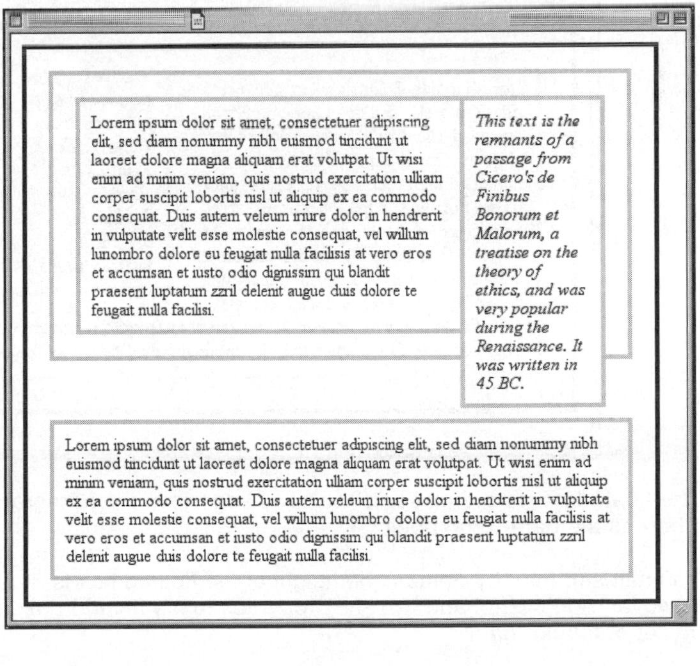

Multiple Floats Side by Side

There may be times when you want to position two floating boxes next to each other. Let's look at an example with two horizontal floats. Here is the structure for this example: we have a page containing two elements that will be represented by floating boxes (`<history>` and `<pullQuote>`). The page also contains the `<paragraph>` element that is in normal flow (`eg08.xml`):

```
<page>
  <history>...</history>
  <pullQuote>...</pullQuote>
  <paragraph>...</paragraph>
</page>
```

Both the `<history>` and `<pullQuote>` elements have the following style (`eg08.css`):

```
pullQuote, history {
  float:right;
  background-color:#FFFFFF;
  width:20%;
  font-style:italic;
  border-style:solid;
  border-width:4px;
  border-color:#CCCCCC;
  padding:10px;}
```

Here is the result: the floating boxes aligned in the opposite order to which they appear in the XML document: `<pullQuote>` and then `<history>`. Remember that they are both aligned from the right, so that is why the box representing the `<history>` element is further right than the `<pullQuote>`. Note that, if we wanted them to appear the other way around, we would have to alter the XML source.

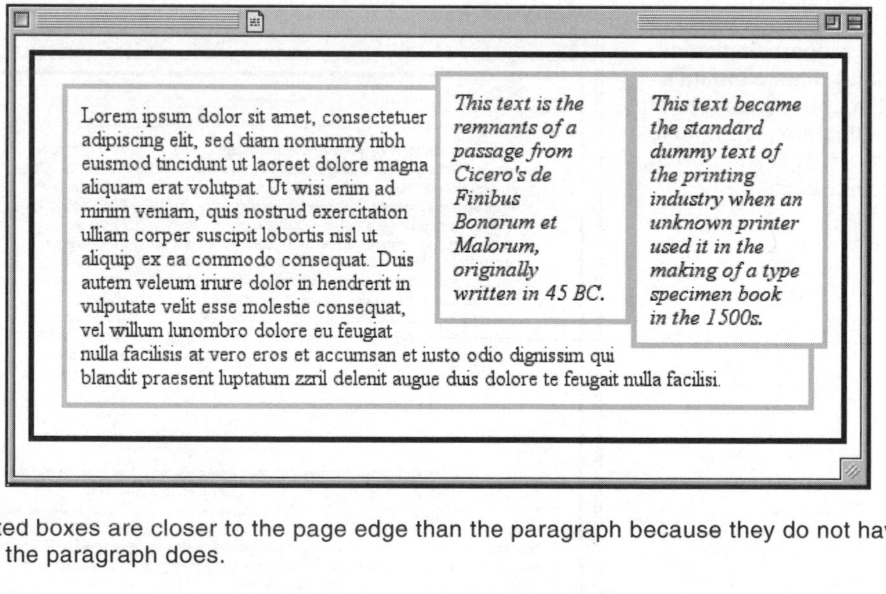

The floated boxes are closer to the page edge than the paragraph because they do not have a margin, whereas the paragraph does.

You can see that, by default, the height of the floated box is determined by its content. You can, however, add `width` and `height` properties to the floated box, as we will see when we come to the layout of tabular data.

If there were not enough space for both of the floated elements next to each other, the one that appears later on in the XML document would be placed beneath the first one to appear in the document. A similar effect can occur on a single floated element if there is not enough space for it within the context of the document.

Absolute Positioning

The third method of positioning is **absolute positioning**, which is set by giving the `position` property a value of `absolute`. Absolutely positioned elements are completely removed from the normal flow. They are always treated as block-level elements, and are positioned within their containing block using offset values for the properties `left`, `top`, `right`, and `bottom`.

This is where we can run into some difficulties with different browsers, so let's take a closer look. We will create a block-level element called `<facingPages>`. Inside this element we will have a `<pageLeft>` and a `<pageRight>` next to each other. Each page will contain one `<paragraph>` element to start with (`eg09.xml`).

```
<facingPages>
  <pageLeft>
    <paragraph>...</paragraph>
  </pageLeft>
  <pageRight>
    <paragraph>...</paragraph>
  </pageRight>
</facingPages>
```

Here are the styles we are applying to these elements:

```
facingPages {
  display:block;
  width:90%;
  border:solid;
  border-width:4px;
  border-color:#000000;
  padding: 10px;
  margin:10px;}

pageLeft {
  position:absolute;
  top:10px;
  right:auto;
  bottom:auto;
  left:10px;
  width:40%;
  border:solid;
  border-width:4px;
  border-color:#000000;
  padding: 10px;
  margin:10px;}

pageRight {
```

```
    position:absolute;
    top:10px;
    right:10px;
    bottom:auto;
    left:auto;
    width:40%;
    width:40%;
    border:solid;
    border-width:4px;
    border-color:#000000;
    padding: 10px;
    margin:10px;}

  paragraph {
    display:block;
    padding-top:10px;
    border:solid;
    border-width:4px;
    border-color:#CCCCCC;
    padding: 10px;
    margin:10px:}
```

The results in Netscape 6 are as you would hope:

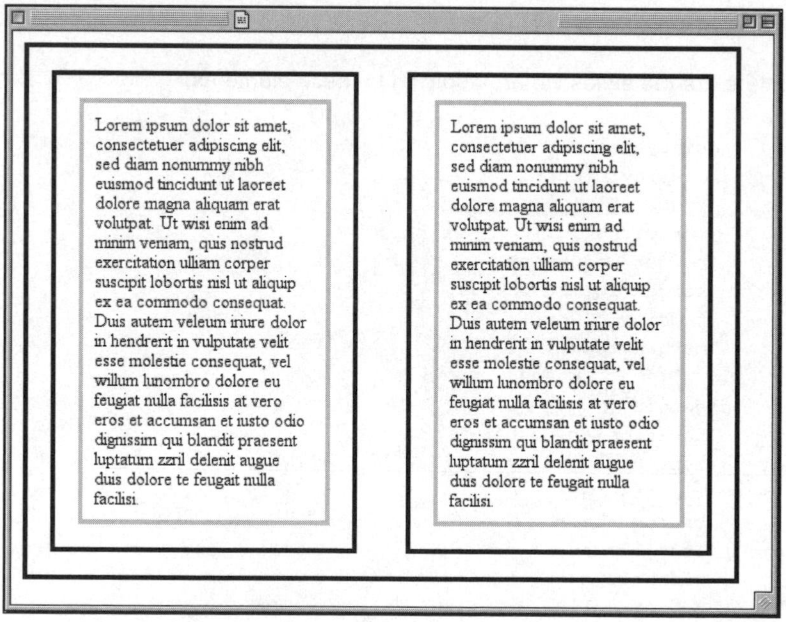

IE 6 and Opera 6, however, show signs of the problems we are about to face, because they do not support the `right` property (nor do they support `bottom`), therefore we would have to use `top` and `left` to position the right-hand page as well.

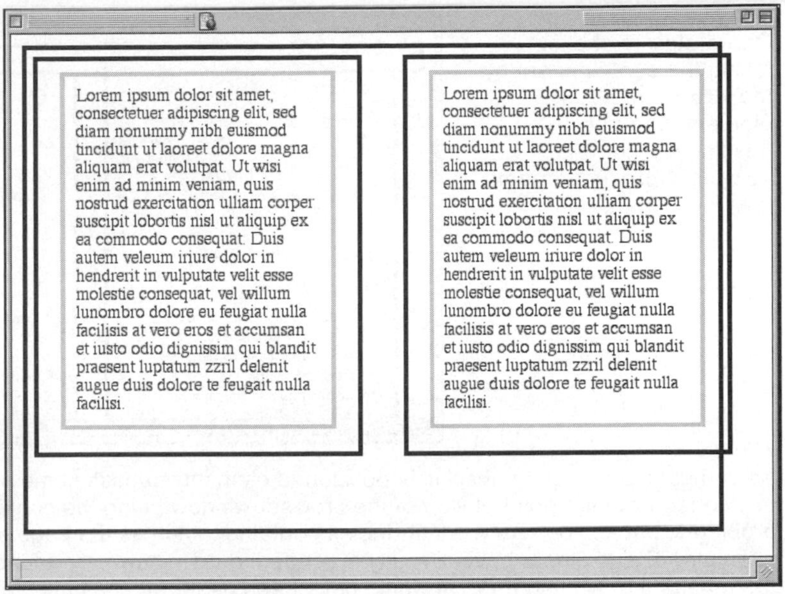

While this might not worry you too much, things get worse when we introduce the `<pullQuote>` back into the page and use absolute positioning for it rather than a floated box.

Netscape 6 can handle what is going on. This is what we wanted – note that the contents of the `<paragraph>` element are not flowing around the content of the `<pullQuote>` element because the `<pullQuote>` is absolutely positioned, not in a floating box:

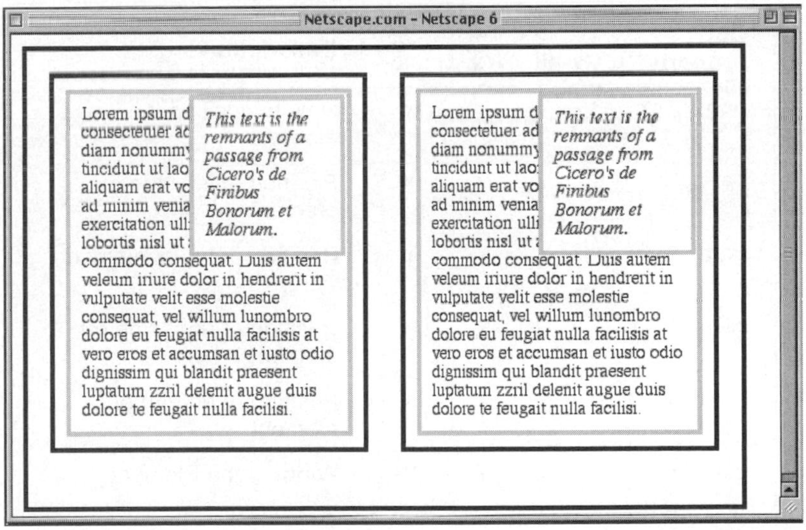

However, poor IE and Opera start to choke, losing the container set by the `<facingPages>` element, and not positioning the `<paragraph>` underneath the `<pullQuote>`:

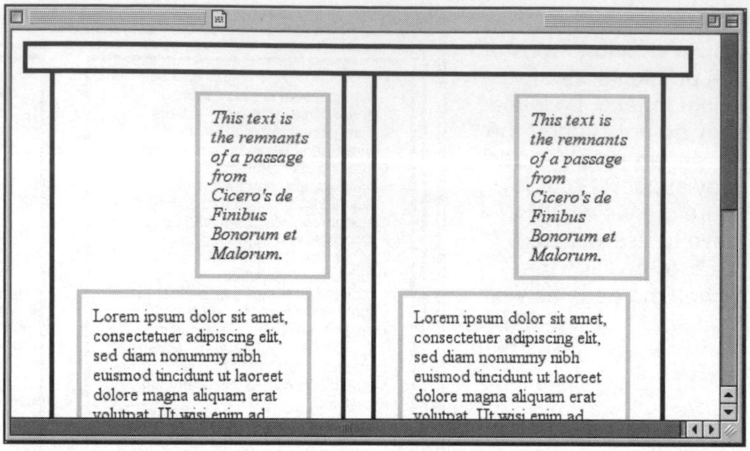

As you can see, nesting absolutely positioned elements causes some problems. If the boxes are positioned from the point of view of the browser window being the containing box, there are no problems, but as soon as you introduce a container, such as the page or `<facingpages>` in our example, IE and Opera have difficulty in rendering them correctly. Indeed, while Netscape produces the results that we told it to, we would have been better off combining a floated `<pullQuote>` within the containing box to prevent overlap.

Here is a summary of which browsers support which properties for absolute positioning:

CSS Property	IE 6	NS6	Op6	Description	Allowed Values
`position`	Y	Y	Y	How to position the element	static, relative, absolute,fixed
`left`	Y	Y	Y	Position of left side of element	a length, a percentage, auto, inherit
`top`	Y	Y	Y	Position of top of element	a length, a percentage, auto, inherit
`right`	N	Y	N	Position of right side of element	a length, a percentage, auto, inherit
`bottom`	N	Y	N	Position of bottom of element	a length, a percentage, auto, inherit
`width`	Y	Y	Y	Width of the Element	a length, a percentage, auto, inherit
`height`	Y	Y	Y	Height of the Element	a length, a percentage, auto, inherit

The data given here is for the Windows version. The same results are true for IE5, Netscape 6, and Opera 5 on a Mac.

Fixed Positioning

Fixed positioning is a special subset of absolute positioning, where the containing block is always the viewport of the browser window. A fixed element will not move when a web page is scrolled like the other elements do.

> Netscape 6.1+, and Opera 6 support fixed positioning. IE 5 Mac also supports fixed positioning. IE 6 Windows and Netscape 6 only support fixed backgrounds (via the background-attachment property) which produces a similar effect, but only for images.

Let's look at an example of fixed positioning (`eg10.xml`):

```
<document>
  <title>...</title>
  <page>
    <pullQuote>...</pullQuote>
    <paragraph>...</paragraph>
  </page>
</document>
```

Here you can see that the content of the title (which is styled as fixed using the style property `position: fixed`) is remaining fixed within the viewport while other content moves. Note that the floated box will appear on top. (This example will not work in IE 6 or earlier on Windows, but will work in IE 5 Mac.)

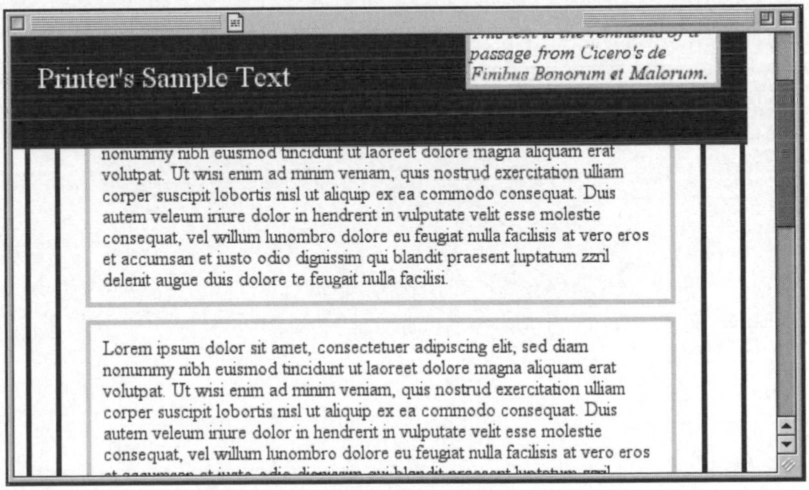

Overlapping in Absolutely Positioned Elements

Absolutely positioned elements may overlap non-positioned elements and each other. When this happens, by default they will appear in the same order in which they occur in the document, the first elements lying underneath the later ones – this is the **stacking context**. However, you can control positioning explicitly with the **`z-index`** property.

The `z-index` property is given a value to indicate the order in which it should appear: the higher the `z-index` an element has, the nearer the "top" it will appear.

In the previous example, because the `<pullQuote>` element appeared after the `<title>` element it was visible over the top of the `<title>` element. By giving a `z-index` property with a value of 1 or more to the `<title>`, however, we can make it appear as if it is on top of the `<pullQuote>`, which will now scroll under it (this is illustrated in `eg11.xml` and `eg11.css` in the code download).

Let's see another example, using multiple pages, here is the structure of the XML (`eg12.xml`):

```
<document>
  <page1><paragraph>...</paragraph></page1>
  <page2><paragraph>...</paragraph></page2>
  <page3><paragraph>...</paragraph></page3>
</document>
```

And here is the CSS (`eg12.css`). We have a common set of declarations for the pages in one rule, and then separate additional rules for each of the separate pages, giving each one a different `z-index`. `<page1>` has a `z-index` value of `300`, `<page2>` has a `z-index` of `200`, and `<page1>` has a `z-index` of `100`; this will mean that they are displayed in the opposite order to that in which they appear in the document. They are also positioned `5%` in from the top and right-hand side of their `document` container for `<page1>`, `10%` for `<page2>`, and `15%` for `<page3>` (see `eg12.css`):

```
page1, page2, page3 {
  display:block;
  width:90%;
  background-color:#FFFFFF;
  border:solid;
  border-width:4px;
  border-color:#000000;
  padding:10px;
  margin:10px;}

page1 {
  z-index:300;
  position:absolute;
  width:70%;
  left:5%;
  top:5%;
  right:auto;
  bottom:auto;}

page2 {
  z-index:200;
  position:absolute;
  width:70%;
  left:10%;
  top:10%;
  right:auto;
  bottom:auto;}

page3 {
  z-index:100;
  position:absolute;
  width:70%;
  left:15%;
  top:15%;
  right:auto;
  bottom:auto;}
```

Here is the result in Netscape 6, as we would hope it should be:

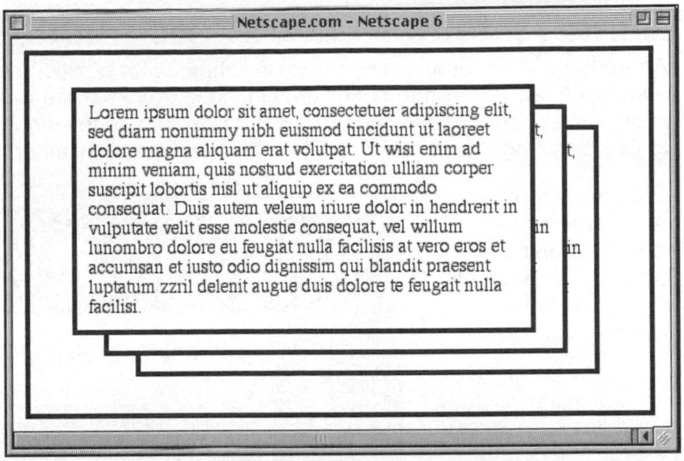

IE 5 on Mac has a problem with the positioning from the top, but the `z-index` is working.

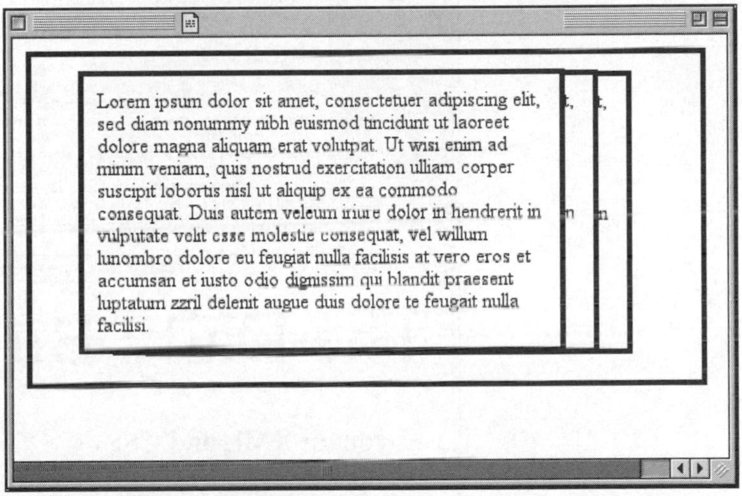

IE 6 on Windows, however, chokes in the same way that Opera does with this example. Here's what happens in Opera for Mac: while it orders and places the pages correctly, there's a problem with the containing element again.

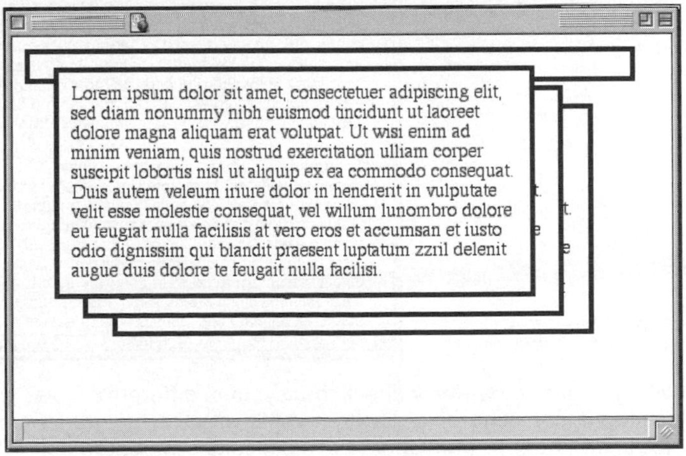

Pulling Together Layout Techniques

As we have seen, then, there are three schemes for positioning elements: normal flow, floated boxes, and absolutely positioned boxes. Within those groups there were two subgroups: we can use relative positioning to change the positioning of a box relative to its normal flow, and we can use fixed positioning to fix a box's position according to the browser window (rather than the containing element).

With these tools we can create some rather sophisticated layouts. For example `eg15.xml` with `eg15.css`...

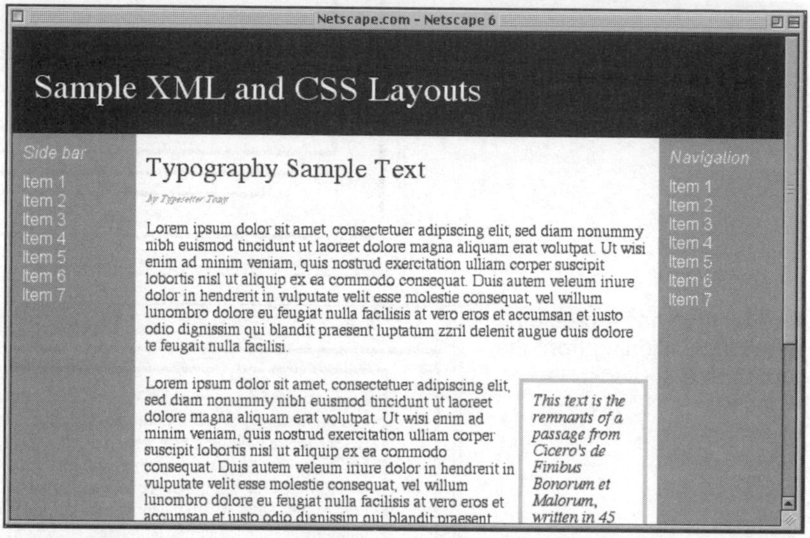

... and `eg16.xml` with `eg16.css`.

We do need to carefully check the layout in different browsers, however, as there are some problems we have met, regarding display of XML with CSS – indeed the above examples look best in Netscape 6.2+, and both IE and Opera have difficulties with them.

This is all very well for laying out pages that contain blocks of text. However, we will often be dealing with tabular data in XML, and there we are heading into interesting territory. Let's go on to look at that, as it deserves special attention.

Laying Out Tabular Data

The instant problem we face when coming to look at tabular data in XML is that we do not have the table elements that we had in HTML. But, as we have seen, we have a well-developed box model for positioning. So, how do we deal with tables?

> You cannot use absolute positioning for tables if you do not know how many rows and columns of data there are.

Here is our sample XML document, which as you can see uses element names we will be able to relate to from HTML (eg16.xml):

```
<document>
  <table>
    <tableRow>
      <tableCell>Cell 1</tableCell>
      <tableCell>Cell 2</tableCell>
      <tableCell>Cell 3</tableCell>
    </tableRow>
    <tableRow>
      <tableCell>Cell 4</tableCell>
      <tableCell>Cell 5</tableCell>
      <tableCell>Cell 6</tableCell>
    </tableRow>
   </table>
   <tableCaption>Table caption</tableCaption>
</document>
```

With this first example of laying out tables, we will be using some special values for the `display` property specifically designed for laying out tabular data. These values are:

- `display: table;` to indicate an element's content represents a table
- `display: table-row;` to indicate an element's content represents a table row
- `display: table-cell;` to indicate an element's content represents a table cell
- `display: table-caption;` to indicate an element's content represents a table caption

Their use is pretty obvious – just like the corresponding HTML meanings for `<table>`, `<tr>`, `<td>`, and `<caption>`. Here is the stylesheet we'll be using (`eg17.css`):

```
document {
  color:#000000;
  display:block;
  background-color:#FFFFFF;
  border:solid;
  border-width:2px;
  padding:10px;
  margin:10px;}

table {
  display:table;
  background-color:#CCCCCC;
  border:solid;
  border-color:#000000;
  border-width:2px;
  padding:30px;}

tableRow {
  display:table-row;}

tableCell {
  display:table-cell;
  background-color:#FFFFFF;
  border:solid;
  border-color:#000000;
  border-width:2px;
  padding:10px;}

tableCaption {
  display: table-caption;}
```

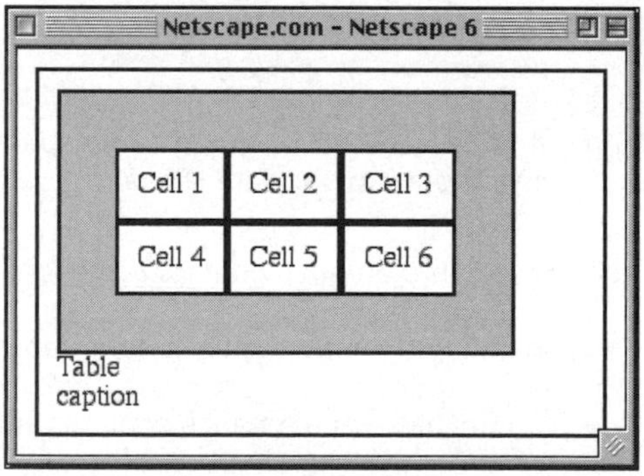

Note that you can't give a `table-row` margins, padding, borders, or background color as it works like a group for the cells it contains. A `table-cell` will not respond to margins, although you can set its `background-color` and `padding` properties.

Obviously, we are limited by this example requiring that we have an XML structure that allows us to attach the CSS properties in the way we have here.

The CSS table properties do not work in IE 5 Mac or IE 6 on Windows, or any of their previous versions, in either case.

Tables Using Floats

Let's look at an alternative way of laying out tabular data: using floats. In this example we use an XML structure where the "cell" elements for each "column" have different names. This is not strictly necessary here (though we do use it to specify a different margin for the first column cells), but may well be the case with the source XML you are supplied with. For example, in an XML document that specifies personnel information, each table row may consist of elements such as `<name>`, `<address>`, and `<phonenumber>`. Here is the structure we are using (`eg18.xml`):

```
<document>
  <table>
    <tableRow>
      <tableCellLeft>Cell 1</tableCellLeft>
      <tableCellMiddle>Cell 2</tableCellMiddle>
      <tableCellRight>Cell 3</tableCellRight><spacer />
    </tableRow>

    <tableRow>
      <tableCellLeft>Cell 4</tableCellLeft>
      <tableCellMiddle>Cell 5</tableCellMiddle>
      <tableCellRight>Cell 6</tableCellRight><spacer />
    </tableRow>
  </table>
</document>
```

The `<spacer>` element after the last cell in each row is only needed for IE 5, otherwise the alignment of each row indents from the previous one. Other browsers do not need it.

Here is the stylesheet (`eg18.css`):

```
document {
  color:#000000;
  display:block;
  background-color:#FFFFFF;
  border:solid;
  border-width:2px;
  padding:10px;
  margin:10px;}

table {
  display:block;
  background-color:#FFFFFF;
  border:solid;
  border-color:#000000;
  border-width:2px;
  padding:10px;}

tableRow {
```

```
    display:block;
    width:80%;
    height:40px;
    background-color:#CCCCCC;
    border:solid;
    border-color:#000000;
    border-width:2px;
    padding:10px;
    margin:10px;}

  tableCellLeft {
    float:left;
    width:25%;
    background-color:#FFFFFF;
    border:solid;
    border-color:#000000;
    border-width:2px;
    padding:10px;}

  tableCellMiddle, tableCellRight {
    float:left;
    width:25%;
    background-color:#FFFFFF;
    border:solid;
    border-color:#000000;
    border-width:2px;
    padding:10px;
    margin-left:10px;}

  tableCaption {
    float:right;
    }

  spacer{clear:both;}
```

Note that if you employ shading in rows you have to set the height of the row so that the cells fit within in, as we have done here. Otherwise, you will see an offset where the cell is larger than the row.

Here you can see the result:

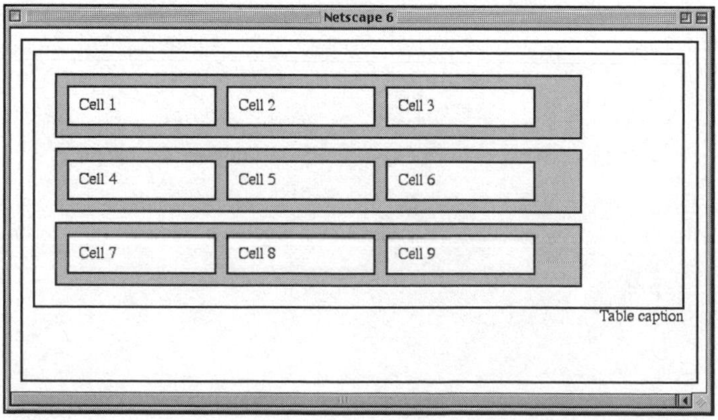

A disadvantage of this method is that you need to know the number of columns in the table in order to ensure that you can set the widths correctly for each row and cell – if they arent set correctly, you may run into problems such as cells wrapping across multiple rows.

Table Row Spans

When dealing with cells that span rows of tables, the first of the two methods we just looked at, using CSS table properties for elements, does not help us out as there is no equivalent to the `rowspan` or `colspan` attributes that we know from HTML. The answer therefore is to use the second method we just looked at, and add in another float.

This now requires that the XML has a different element name for each cell within the repeating section, as you can see here, and that each separate entry also needs to be marked off with a containing element, as so (`eg19.xml`):

```
<document>
  <table>
    <entry>
      <rowSpanCell>Row span cell</rowSpanCell>
      <tableRow1>
        <tableCellLeft>Cell 1</tableCellLeft>
        <tableCellMiddle>Cell 2</tableCellMiddle>
        <tableCellRight>Cell 3</tableCellRight><spacer />
      </tableRow1>
      <tableRow2>
        <tableCellLeft>Cell 4</tableCellLeft>
        <tableCellMiddle>Cell 5</tableCellMiddle>
        <tableCellRight>Cell 6</tableCellRight><spacer />
      </tableRow2>
    </entry>
    <entry>
      <rowSpanCell>Row span cell</rowSpanCell>
      <tableRow1>
        <tableCellLeft>Cell 1</tableCellLeft>
        <tableCellMiddle>Cell 2</tableCellMiddle>
        <tableCellRight>Cell 3</tableCellRight><spacer />
      </tableRow1>
      <tableRow2>
        <tableCellLeft>Cell 4</tableCellLeft>
        <tableCellMiddle>Cell 5</tableCellMiddle>
        <tableCellRight>Cell 6</tableCellRight><spacer />
      </tableRow2>
    </entry>
  </table>
</document>
```

Of course, this might not fit in with the structure of the XML that you are using but it is the nearest we can get to such a layout. As you can tell from the screenshot here, we have given the cell that spans the row a `float` property with a value of `left`, and this time we are using a `float` property with a value of `right` for the cells. Again this will come out slightly distorted on IE 5 on a Mac or Windows.

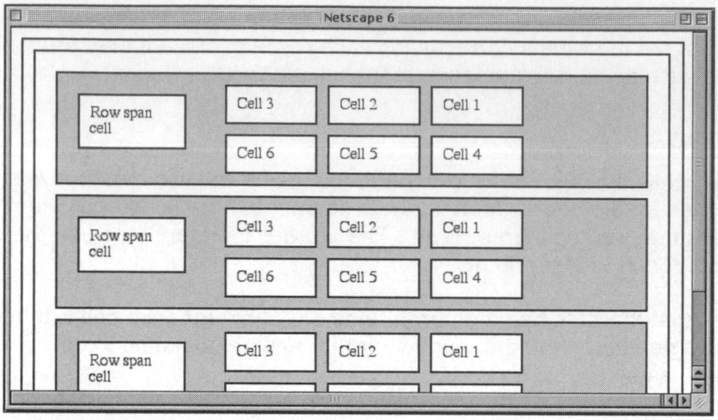

> The use of the `float` property with a value of `right` is helpful in displaying the cells in an order different from the original document.

Linking Between XML Documents Displayed Using CSS

This simplicity of creating hyperlinks in HTML documents was undoubtedly one of the reasons for the success of the Web, with the ability to jump from one page to another via a simple link. When we come to dealing with XML, however, as with so many of the issues in this chapter, there is no equivalent of the `<a>` (anchor) element in the XML specification. If we are going to display our XML pages with CSS we need a way of indicating that an element should be a link. The CSS recommendations do not enable us to do this, although Opera does support a proprietary extension to CSS that allows you to define a link, which we shall look at shortly.

The concept of linking is not covered in the XML recommendation itself. We must turn to a different W3C Recommendation, **XLink**. You can see this recommendation at *http://www.w3.org/TR/xlink*. Support for XLink in browsers, however, is far from standard. Netscape 6 was the first browser to support a limited subset of XLink (similar to that of `<a>` links and `<img>` tags in HTML). IE 6 and Opera 5/6 do not support it at all.

> *XLink is a powerful linking technology that goes far beyond HTML linking. It allows users to specify multiple destinations in a single link, add links in more than one direction, and even define links in a separate link document/database in the same way that CSS allows you to define styles separately from the content. We do not have space to cover XLink in full here, if you want to learn more check out:* **Professional XML 2nd Edition**, *Birbeck et al, Wrox Press, 2001, ISBN 1861005059.*

The ability to link between XML documents is vital if we are to use CSS to display our XML documents in browsers. So, while we cannot demonstrate linking in IE, let's see what can be achieved in Netscape 6 and Opera 5.

XLink in Netscape

The support for XLink in Netscape 6 is fairly basic, although it is enough to replicate what you can do in HTML, and a clear advance on other version 6 browsers. In Netscape 6 you can use XLink to embed a link into the document which can:

- Replace the current document with the new document (just like a normal link in HTML)
- Open the new document in a new window (like having `target="_new"` in HTML)
- Open a link automatically when a page loads. (Using this technique you can replace the current content of a page that is loading, or open it in a new window – kind of like an `onload` event in JavaScript triggering a new page.)

We can use any element as a link element in XML – we just add attributes to it that belong to the XLink namespace to indicate that the element should be treated as a link. Here you can see the namespace declaration we will be using with the namespace for the XLink recommendation:

```
xmlns:xlink="http://www.w3.org/1999/xlink"
```

This namespace needs to be added into our XML document that contains the links, preferably as an attribute to the root element so that we can use the attributes that belong to XLink on any element we wish to act as a link. In our examples we will be using an element called `<link>` to act as a link. We will then style this appropriately using CSS to indicate that it is a link (for example, underlining it or changing its color).

Here are the attributes that we will be using on our `<link>` element:

- `xlink:type` which is used to indicate whether the link is a **simple** or **extended** link. Netscape 6 only supports simple links, so we give it a value of `simple`. Simple links are just like those we are familiar with using in HTML: they link from one document to another. The document we are linking to will be given as the value of the `href` attribute.
- `xlink:href` indicating the target of the link. Its value is a URI.
- `xlink:title` allow us to provide a human-readable title for the link – this is like the popup text that appears when links in HTML are given a `title` attribute.
- `xlink:show` indicates whether the target document should appear in a new window, should be embedded in the current page at this point (only works for images in Netscape 6), or should replace the content of this window, the values being `new`, `embed`, and `current`, respectively.
- `xlink:actuate` allows us to specify when the link should be activated. We can specify one of two values: `onRequest` will wait for the user to activate the link, `onLoad` will activate it when the page loads.

Because we can use these attributes on any element, we must prefix them with the `xlink:` prefix we declared to associate them with the XLink namespace. By default, any attribute in XML is assumed to belong to the same namespace as the element that carries it, unless otherwise indicated by a namespace prefix.

So, let's look at some examples. This link will open the document in the current window. Note how we have defined the XLink namespace in the root element so we can use it throughout the document, and that the XLink attributes on our `<link>` element have the namespace prefix `xlink` (`eg20.xml`):

```
<document xmlns:xlink="http://www.w3.org/1999/xlink">
  <page>
    <title>Linking With XLink</title>
    <paragraph>This
      <link xlink:type="simple"
        xlink:show="replace"
        xlink:actuate="onRequest"
        xlink:title="Open eg20c.xml to open in this window"
        xlink:href="eg20c.xml">link
      </link>
      will <important>replace</important> this page with a new page.
    </paragraph>
  </page>
</document>
```

In HTML, the equivalent would be:

```
<a href="eg20c.xml" title="Open eg20c.xml in this window" href="eg30c.xml" />
```

The following link will open a new window with the document specified in the `href` attribute when this page loads:

```
<link xlink:type="simple"
            xlink:show="new"
            xlink:actuate="onLoad"
            xlink:title="eg20f.xml loading eg20g in a new window as it opens"
            xlink:href="eg20f.xml" />
```

To indicate a link, there is just a simple CSS rule changing the `color` property:

```
link {
  color:#FF0000;}
```

Here is the example of the different types of links:

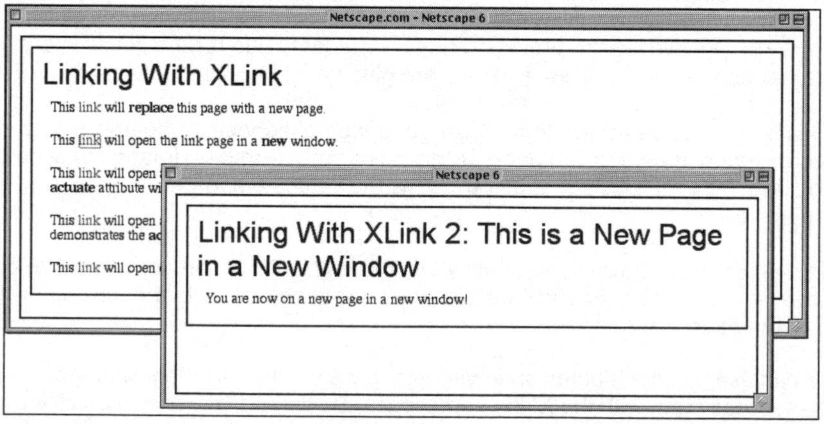

While the support for XLink in Netscape 6 is limited, it is definitely more advanced than in other browsers.

CSS Links in Opera

Opera offers a couple of proprietary CSS properties that allow you to use an element in XML as a link. You can either use the element content or one of the attribute values of the element for the link.

The two extensions are both prefixed with a dash, to indicate that they are extensions to the CSS specification, and are:

- `-set-link-source` to indicate the document that you want to link to. The value can either be the name of the element whose content is to be used for the link address, or `attr(attributeName)` where the attribute whose value is to be used is given in the parentheses.
- `-use-link-source` to indicate that the information of the current element should be used. It takes the value, `current`. Opera also supports a value of `next` for this attribute, but this is more for use with WAP.

Here is an example of both of these. The first `<link>` element uses the `href` attribute, while the second `<link2>` element uses the element content for the link (`eg21.xml`):

```
<paragraph>This
  <link href="eg21b.xml">link</link>
  will <important>replace</important> this page with a new page.
</paragraph>

<paragraph>This is the same link, this time using element content rather than
           an attribute for the link, it
  <link2>eg21b.xml</link2>
  will <important>replace</important> this page with a new page.
</paragraph>
```

Here are the rules that we are using with these two link elements (`eg21.css`):

```
link {
  -set-link-source:attr(href);
  -use-link-source:current;
  color:#FF0000;}

link2 {
  -set-link-source:link2;
  -use-link-source:current;
  color:#FF0000;}
```

Here is the source page and the page that replaces it:

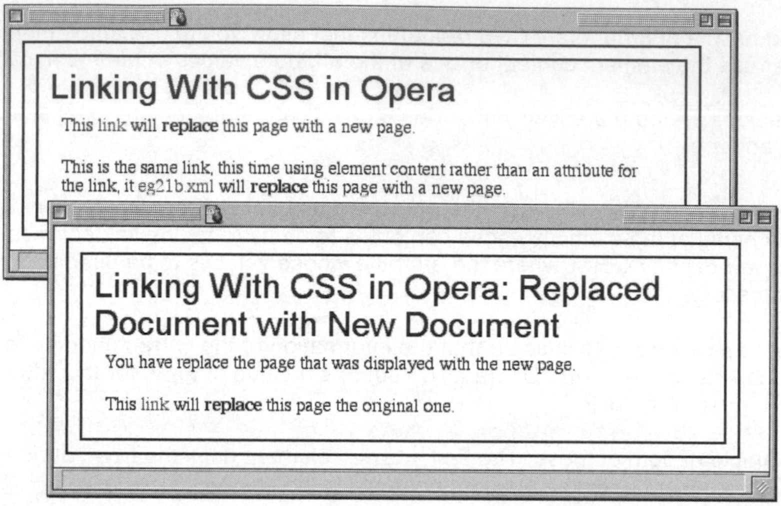

> For future-proofing your XML documents, if you were to use this technique with Opera, it would be a good idea to use full XLink syntax for your links. That way, while the browser will only use the `xlink:href` attribute, the source XML will be ready for when Opera does support XLink, and will only require a couple of lines to be deleted from your stylesheets when that time comes.

Forcing Links Using the HTML Namespace

One other trick that you can use is to embed HTML syntax into your XML documents using the HTML namespace, so that the browser will pick up the meaning of the HTML elements and render them appropriately. This technique works in Opera 5, Netscape 6, and IE 6 on Windows, but does not work in IE 5 Mac (it displays the link as if it will follow it, but doesn't actually work (`eg22.xml`).

```
<document xmlns:html="http://www.w3.org/TR/REC-html40">
  <page>
    <paragraph>The <html:a href="http://www.glasshaus.com">link</html:a>
    will <important>replace</important> this page with a new page.
    </paragraph>
  </page>
</document>
```

While this is a handy way of mixing HTML with XML on Netscape, Opera, and IE (Windows version), it is not the ideal approach, especially where there are alternative solutions.

Images in XML Documents

Having just seen how to create links in our documents, it is an easy step to look at adding images into them. In HTML, images are incorporated via a link to an image file which is embedded in place of the `<img>` element.

To achieve the same thing in XML, we could use the HTML hack we just saw when creating links with the HTML namespace. The alternative is to use the `background-image` property in CSS as we will see in a moment.

> *In a later section on "Adding to Examples" we will see another workaround for adding images to our XML documents.*

Image Links in Netscape 6 and Opera

While you can display simple links in Netscape 6 using XLink, you cannot currently use the `xlink:show` attribute with a value of `embed` to embed images into your document. (The file `eg23.xml` has been written to test this method of showing images, but it did not work on any version 6 browser at the time of writing.)

If you use `xlink:show = "replace"`, you can replace a document with an image on its own, or open the image in a new window. Similarly, in Opera we have the added CSS rules that allow us to define links to an image that replaces the current page. However, neither of these is very helpful as they do not allow us to display images directly in the document.

Using background-image To Add an Image

With clever use of CSS, we can create an XML structure similar to what follows, where we give each image a separate element name, then we use the `background` or `background-image` properties in the CSS stylesheet to display the image. This technique works in Netscape 6, IE 5, and Opera 5 (`eg24.xml`).

```
<document>
  <page>
    <image1 />
    <title>Adding an Image in XML</title>
    <paragraph>Here we have added the Glasshaus logo to the top of the
               document.</paragraph>
  </page>
</document>
```

We have set a size for the block so that the image does not repeat if a larger box is displayed (`eg24.css`).

```
image1 {
  display:block;
  margin:10px;
  width:615px;
  height:76px;
  background-image:url(header.jpg)}

title {
  display:block;
  font-size:24pt;}
```

Here is the result:

On the plus side, this technique works with IE 5+, Netscape 6, and Opera 5. The drawback of this approach is, obviously, you need to have a separate element and a separate rule in the stylesheet for each image you use.

An Aside On CSS2 Attribute Selectors

As we'll see shortly, CSS2 introduced the ability to select which elements a style would apply to, based on attributes and even their values. Unfortunately, at the time of writing, only Netscape 6 and Opera offer limited support for the attribute selectors, not including selecting them by their value.

Ideally, we would be able to use the attribute selectors in CSS2, with the following syntax in the XML:

```
<image xlink:type="simple"
          xlink:show="embed"
          xlink:actuate="onLoad"
          xlink:title="Glasshaus Header"
          xlink:href="header.jpg" />
```

and with the following CSS2 selector syntax:

```
image[xlink:href="header.jpg"] {
  display:block;
  margin:10px;
  width:615px;
  height:76px;
  background-image:url(header.jpg)}
```

This way, the link would work when XLink is better supported. However, this type of selector is not available in Netscape 6, IE 6, or Opera 5.

Adding To Examples

The examples we have looked at so far deal with displaying the content of an XML file. There are times, however, when we might need to add some other form of content, such as some text to describe what the element's content is or refers to. CSS2 introduced **pseudo-elements** that allow us to do exactly this.

- `:before` to insert content before an element.
- `:after` to insert some content after an element.

This means that we are able to add text, images, and sounds before any element in our source document.

There are also two pseudo-elements that allow us to add different effects to the first line or first letter of some text. These are:

- `:first-line` adds special styles to the first line of the text in a selector.
- `:first-letter` adds special styles to the first letter of the selector.

The syntax for all pseudo-elements is:

```
selector:psuedo-element {property: value;}
```

Let's look at each of these. We have four paragraphs with some text in each – they are called `<paragraph1>`, `<paragraph2>`, `<paragraph3>`, and `<paragraph4>`, and we will associate different pseudo-elements with each.

In the first paragraph, we will make the first letter larger, italic, and bold. So that it displays properly, we have positioned it using a float which works in Netscape 6, IE 5, and Opera 5 (`eg26.css`).

```
paragraph1:first-letter {
  float:left;
  font-size:24pt;
  font-style:italic;
  font-weight:bold;
  padding-right:4px;}
```

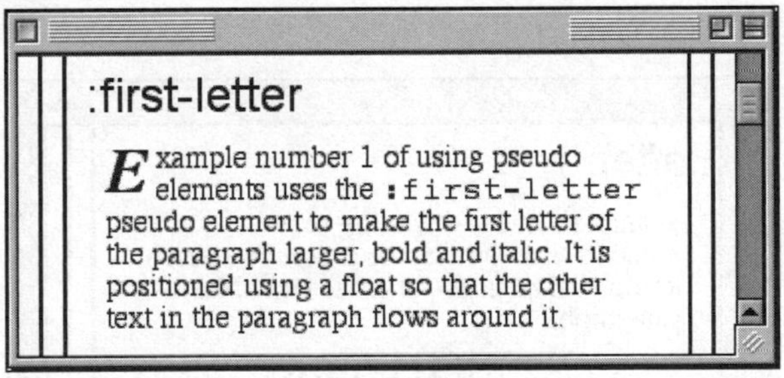

In the second paragraph, we have made the whole of the first line uppercase (this works in Netscape 6, IE 5, Opera 5):

```
paragraph2:first-line {
  text-transform:uppercase;
  font-weight:bold;}
```

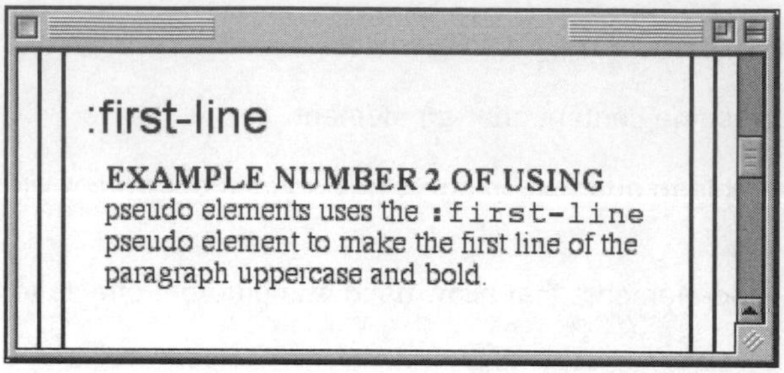

In the third paragraph, we have inserted some text before the paragraph. The text we want to add is put in quotes as the value of the `content` property (this works in Netscape 6, IE 5 Mac, but not IE 5.5 on Windows, or Opera 5):

```
paragraph3:before {
  font-weight:bold;
  content:"paragraph3 contents: "; }
```

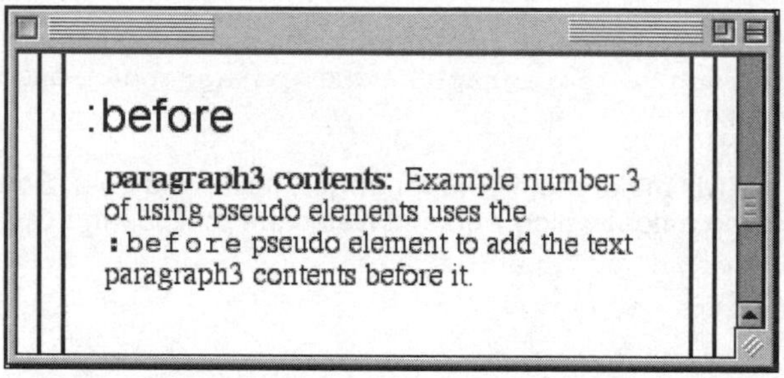

In the fourth paragraph, we have added an image at the end of the paragraph, using `url(`*`location of image`*`)` as the value of the content property (this only works in Netscape 6):

```
paragraph4:after {
  content: url(logo.gif);}
```

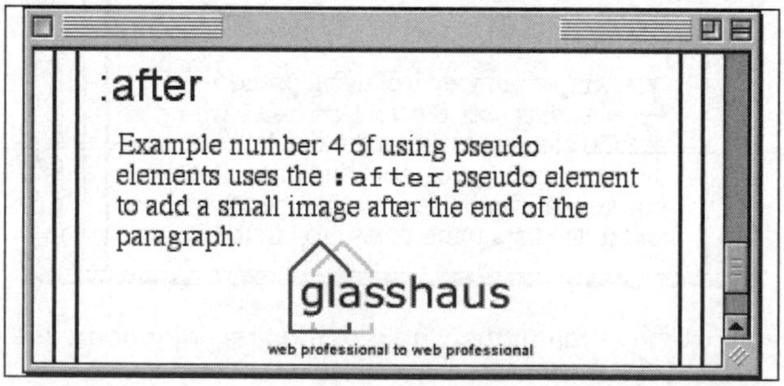

There are also three dynamic pseudo-classes in CSS2, namely `:hover`, `:active`, and `:focus`. These are used to change the appearance of a link when a user hovers over it, when the link is active, and when it gains focus. However, when working with XLink in Netscape 6 (the only browser to support XLink), these pseudo-classes had no effect upon the link.

Working with Attribute Content

So far, all of the examples we have been working with have relied on element names for selectors and have only displayed element content. So, what happens when it comes to attributes? In this section we will look at two topics, first the supported features of using attributes in selectors, and secondly using attribute values in documents.

Using Attributes in Selectors

CSS2 introduced the ability to use attributes and their values in conjunction with element names as the selector for a CSS rule.

- myElement[myAttribute] matches when <myElement> carries an attribute called myAttribute
- myElement[myAttribute=myValue] matches when <myElement> carries an attribute called myAttribute whose value is myValue
- myElement[myAttribute~="myValue"] matches when <myElement> carries an attribute called myAttribute whose value is a space-separated list of words one of which is exactly the same as myValue
- myElement[myAttribute|="myValue"] matches when <myElement> carries an attribute called myAttribute whose value begins with myValue

As mentioned earlier, support for this is limited in browsers. To see an example of how these are supposed to work, take the following XML structure. Note how each <paragraph> has a different value for the style attribute (eg27.xml):

```
<paragraph style="normal">Here is some text in a paragraph whose <code>style</code>
attribute has a value of <code>normal</code>.</paragraph>

<paragraph style="summary">Here is some text in a paragraph whose
<code>style</code> attribute has a value of <code>summary</code>.</paragraph>

<paragraph style="code foreground">Here is some text in a paragraph whose
<code>style</code> attribute has a value of <code>code
foreground</code>.</paragraph>

<paragraph style="code background">Here is some text in a paragraph whose
<code>style</code> attribute has a value of <code>code
background</code>.</paragraph>
```

Here are the different ways of matching these attributes and attribute values in the order we introduced them (eg27.css):

```
paragraph[style] {
  font-size:12pt;
  color:#0000FF;}

paragraph[style="summary"] {
  font-style:italic;
  padding:40px;}
```

```
paragraph[style~="code foreground"] {
  font-family:courier, couriernew, serif;
  font-weight:bold;
  background-color:#CCCCCC; }

paragraph[style|="background"] {
  font-family:courier, couriernew, serif;
  font-weight:bold;
  background-color:#FFFFFF;
  border-style:solid;
  border-color:#000000;
  border-width:2px; }
```

Unfortunately, Netscape 6 only supports the first two attribute selectors, while IE 6 and Opera fail to support any of them. Here are the first two working in Netscape 6. Note that the styles specified using the first style rule above are applied to each element, since they all have `style` attributes.

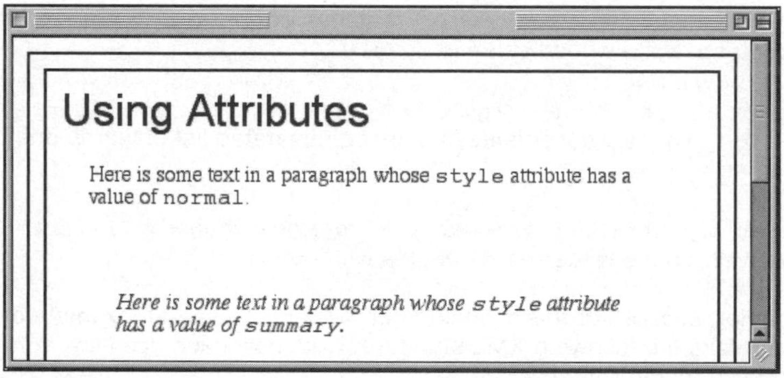

When supported, attribute selectors will prove a powerful tool for allowing us to give a style to an element based on the presence of an attribute or its value. Remember the table examples we saw earlier in the chapter? They might be an example of where we could find the additional information required to lay out the table, with attributes holding values that differentiate between intended cells in a structure. Attribute selectors will also give us a way to associate images with a `background-image` property.

Using Attribute Values in Documents

All of the examples so far have displayed element content on the screen. Very often, when working with XML, however, we will want to be able to work with attribute content. However, we are very limited in the way in which we can display attribute values. CSS rules govern how the content of an element or set of elements should be displayed. Did you get the important word there? The element's **content**. Indeed, the only way of displaying attribute values is using a trick with the `:before` or `:after` pseudo-elements.

As we saw when we looked at pseudo-elements in the *Adding to Examples* section, these elements allow us to add text or an image before or after an element. The `:before` and `:after` pseudo-elements also allow us to add the content of an attribute using the `content` property, with a value of `attr(`*`attributeName`*`)` where *`attributeName`* is the name of the attribute whose content we want to add before or after the element.

For example, take the following XML, with the `keyWords` and `xref` attributes on the `<paragraph>` element (`eg28.xml`):

```
<paragraph
   keyWords="displaying, attribute, content, XML, CSS"
   xref="CSS2 Section 12.2">

   This example demonstrates how we can use the <code>:before</code> and
   <code>:after</code> pseudo classes to add attribute content to a document.
</paragraph>
```

We can use the `:before` and `:after` pseudo-elements to add in what we are displaying and the content of the attributes, like so (`eg28.css`):

```
paragraph {
  display:block;
  background-color:#FFFFFF;
  font-family:times, timesnewroman, serif;
  padding:20px;}

paragraph:before {
  display:block;
  background-color#CCCCCC;
  font-weight:bold;
  color:#0000FF;
  content:"Cross reference:" attr(xref);}

paragraph:after {
  font-style:italic;
  color:#0000FF;
  content:"Key words: " attr(keyWords);}
```

This only works in Netscape 6 and Opera 5, but here is the result:

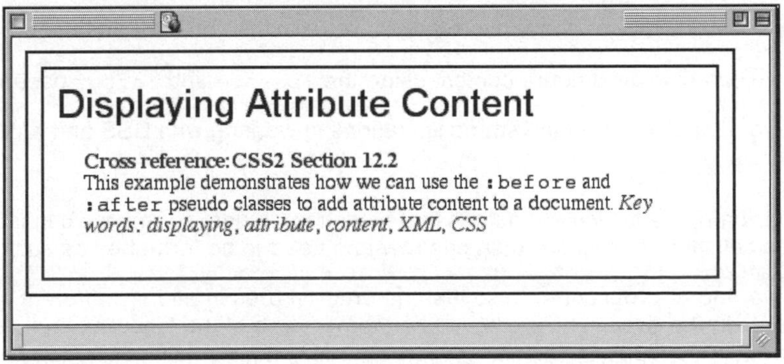

As you can imagine this is very helpful for displaying content, although we are somewhat limited with this approach in two ways:

- Firstly, in how much formatting control we have over the attribute values. While we have been able to display the added text in either a block or inline box, or change the `color`, `font-style`, and `font-weight` properties, we are not able to use the text in something like a table.
- Secondly, we can only present the content of two attributes, as we can only use one `:before` and one `:after` pseudo-element with each element. If we try to use more, then the last rules in the stylesheet for that pseudo-element take preference over earlier ones.

> While CSS is capable of rendering XML documents it is very limited in its ability to display attribute content.

Summary

In this chapter, we have seen a lot about how to display XML in the browser directly using CSS. Because an XML document is just focused on containing structured data and includes no display information, we need to use CSS to specify exactly how each element should be displayed on the screen. This requires more work than using CSS with (X)HTML, which already contains a lot of information that the browsers use to display the data, and sometimes (such as the case of rendering tabular data) relies on the structure of the XML document. This means that we had to learn:

- How to use element type selectors without `class` or `id` attributes
- How CSS uses the box model to lay out element content using three positioning schemes: normal flow, floated boxes, and absolute positioning
- How we can use CSS table, table-row, and table-cell properties to lay out tabular data
- How we can use floated boxes to create more complex table layouts
- How we can link between documents using XLink in Netscape 6 and CSS extensions in Opera 5
- How we can coerce an image into our XML documents using the `background` or `background-image` properties of CSS
- How we can add images and text to our examples with the `:before` and `:after` pseudo-classes
- How we can display attribute content using the `:before` and `:after` pseudo-classes

Despite learning all this, we still face strong limitations in working with CSS and XML directly in the browser. Particularly:

- Tabular data needs element names that fit with our model so that we can identify rows, as well as cells that span more than one row and need to be formatted as such.
- If we want to re-order content, so that the order of presentation is different from the order of elements in the document, we have to either use one of the following techniques:
  - Absolute positioning, which requires that we know exactly how much data/how many elements we will be displaying.
  - Floated boxes which can re-order boxes from left to right within the screen's width.

- Linking via XLink is only supported in Netscape 6, although this limitation can be circumvented using the `html` namespace and `<a>` tags in IE and Opera, or via proprietary extensions in Opera.

- In order to display images we need to have a different element name or different attribute name for each image.

- We can only display the values of two attributes per element.

- Browser support is mixed and unstable.

All in all, it seems fair to conclude that CSS is capable of presenting XML content when stored in elements. As such it is suitable for things like layout of documents. When it comes to data and tables, however, things can get a lot more complicated. Furthermore, the support for linking and images is rather disappointing and does not make for a good user experience. It is hard not to point the finger at one certain browser manufacturer, as the level of support in Netscape 6 is acceptable to produce usable documents with XML and CSS alone, but IE has very weak support for CSS2.

For IE users and older browser versions, it looks like we will still be heavily relying on HTML or XHTML and CSS.

In the next chapters you will see an alternative to using XML and CSS for display: that of transforming the XML into another language, such as HTML or XHTML, using XSLT. This allows for dynamic manipulation of the data on the client. You will also see examples of using XSLT on the server in later chapters of the book, so that you can deliver HTML or XHTML to browsers without them having to understand XSLT. However, when dealing with these transformations, remember that using CSS with your HTML or XHTML documents offers a lot better separation of content from style, easier updating of pages, and prevents the style rules having to be downloaded many times. Indeed you will now have a better understanding of how you can employ CSS, whether it is with XML, XHTML, or good old HTML.

Additional Reading

Cascading Style Sheets: Separating Content from Presentation, *Briggs et al, glasshaus, ISBN: 1-904151-04-3.*

W3C CSS2 Recommendation:
http://www.w3.org/tr/css2/

W3C XLink Recommendation:
http://www.w3.org/TR/xlink

Some useful CSS sites:

- *http://www.devguru.com/Technologies/css/quickref/css_index.html*
  (a useful CSS reference)

- *http://css.nu/*
  (in particular their bugs and workarounds page: *http://css.nu/pointers/bugs-nn.html*)

- *http://glish.com/css/*

- *http://www.meyerweb.com/eric/css/edge/*

5

- Introduction to XSLT
- Using XSLT to transform XML on the client
- XPath

Author: Dave Addey and Inigo Surguy

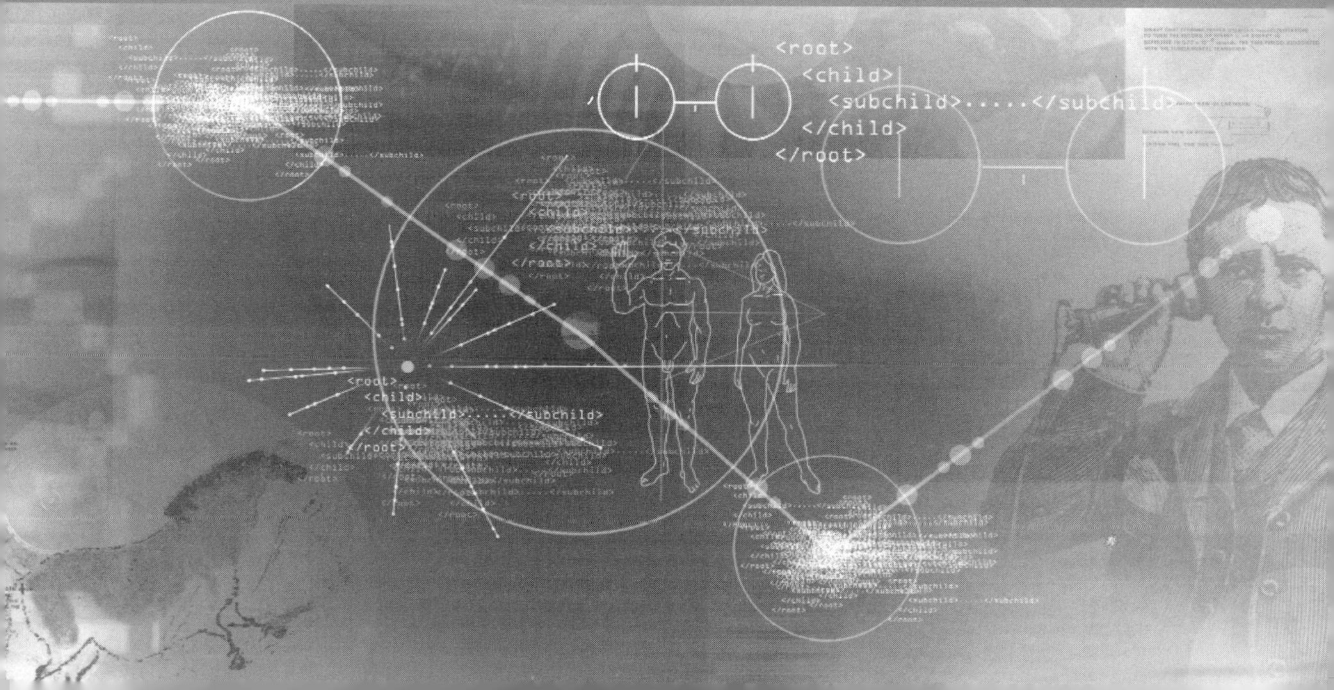

Introduction to XSLT

In this chapter and the next, we're going to introduce the use of **XSLT** – **Extensible Stylesheet Language Transformations** – to format and display XML documents. In this chapter we'll give you an overview of XSLT, and how to use it in the client's browser with some real-world examples of transformations. *Chapter 6* will then develop this knowledge with some more complex examples of XSLT in action. You will then learn about using XSLT to transform XML on the server in *Chapters 8 to 11*.

An extreme example of XSLT can be found at *http://people.w3.org/maxf/ChessGML/* (you'll need the SVG plug-in from *http://www.adobe.com/*). Here, an XML representation of a chess game (stored as ChessGML, a standard XML vocabulary for representing chess games in XML) is converted into an SVG animation using XSLT. SVG is an XML-based standard for describing images and animations, and the XSLT stylesheet used by this site converts a simple ChessGML game into a fully-animated representation of the game being played move by move.

So what is XSLT? Essentially, it is a way of transforming XML documents into other documents (often other XML documents). When it comes down to it, XHTML web pages are just XML documents, so we can use XSLT to transform an XML document into a styled XHTML web page, and display it in a browser.

We have already seen how XML can be displayed using CSS. XSLT goes one stage further by giving you complete flexibility to change the layout of your content. Furthermore, it allows you to define rules that not only alter the design, but can also add, change, and remove elements of the content, if appropriate. So if you want to exclude some content from a page based on your XML, XSLT can automatically strip out this content for you. Conversely, XSLT can add in content or generate new content based on the existing XML document, such as headers and footers. You can go further still with XSLT, and convert your content into alternative formats such as RTF (Rich Text Format) documents and CSV (Comma Separated Value) files for Word and Excel.

Although XSLT is very powerful, CSS is often better for simple tasks. We're certainly not suggesting that, having just read the CSS chapter, you throw all of your CSS knowledge away and use XSLT instead. It is often best to use a combination of CSS and XSLT to achieve the look we want.

We will be focusing on the most practically useful aspects of XSLT, and by the end, you should not only have an understanding of how to use XSLT, but more importantly recognize why XSLT is useful and know where to use it.

Server-side versus Client-side

There are two approaches to applying XSLT to your XML content. You can perform these XSLT transformations server-side on your web server, and serve up the resulting HTML web page to a browser. *Chapters 8-11* of this book will cover **server-side** XSLT transformation in detail.

The other way to use XSLT is to send a source XML document and an XSLT stylesheet to a browser, and ask the browser to apply the XSLT transformation for you. Here we will learn which browsers support this **client-side** application of XSLT, see what benefits it gives, and see some examples of client-side XSLT in action.

Browser Support for XSLT

Given the inconsistencies between HTML support in the different browsers, it should come as no surprise that they offer varying support for XSLT as well. The good news is that through careful use of XSLT it is possible to achieve support by more than 95% of the browsers on the market while still providing readable content for the rest.

There are only two different XSLT specifications to worry about. The recent browsers with XSLT support (Internet Explorer 6, Netscape 6+, and Mozilla) all support the XSLT 1.0 standard – the specification for this is available online at *http://www.w3c.org/TR/xslt*. Unfortunately Internet Explorer, in versions 5 and 5.5, as well as PocketEI, support an earlier form of the XSLT standard – the XSL Working Draft (see *http://www.w3.org/TR/1998/WD-xsl-19981216*, although only the transformations section of this specification is implemented). We'll see how to support both soon.

The picture is muddied further because the older IE browsers can be updated to use more recent XSLT processors. In practice only a tiny fraction of users, mostly developers, will have updated, and they will have almost certainly have upgraded their actual browsers by now.

Throughout the rest of the book, to make things less confusing we'll be referring to the XSL Working Draft implemented by IE 5.0 and IE 5.5 as **XSL-WD**, and the full version of XSLT 1.0 supported by IE 6, Netscape 6+, and Mozilla as **XSLT 1.0**. XSLT 1.0 is also the version of XSLT implemented by the server-side XSLT processors described later in this book.

Browser	XSLT version	XSLT processor
Internet Explorer 5	XSL-WD	MSXML 2.0
Internet Explorer 5.5	XSL-WD	MSXML 2.0
Internet Explorer 6.0	XSLT 1.0 or XSL-WD	MSXML 3.0
Internet Explorer 5.0, 5.1, 5.2 for Mac	XSL-WD	MSXML 2.0
Netscape 6+	XSLT 1.0	TransforMiiX
Mozilla	XSLT 1.0	TransforMiiX
Opera	No support	-

For the most part, XSL-WD is a subset of the functionality available in XSLT. For a list of the exact differences between XSL-WD and XSLT, see the table at the end of the chapter, as well as *http://www.zvon.org/xxl/XSLTreference/Output/index.html*. Most browsers on mobile devices do not support XSLT, with the exception of the Pocket PC, which supports XSL-WD.

The examples in this chapter will work across all of IE 5+, Netscape 6+, and Mozilla, with only very slight changes for XSL-WD browsers. *Chapter 6* will introduce some of the features of XSLT 1.0, and also some of the Microsoft-specific extensions.

As explained in *Chapter 3*, even if the client doesn't support the level of XSLT that you would like to use, you can still get many of the benefits of XSLT by using server-side script to do browser version sniffing, and then styling on the server for older clients and sending XML/XSLT to the browser for newer clients. The same XSLT 1.0 stylesheet can be used server-side and client-side.

Example 1: Saving Bandwidth by Using XSLT for Headers and Footers

Let's start by taking a normal web page, and seeing how we can use XSLT to add some standard content to the page. In this example, we'll add a header and footer to a simple page of XHTML.

All of the examples in this chapter can be downloaded from the glasshaus web site at *http://www.glasshaus.com*. The downloadable versions have additional comments so you don't need to keep referring back to the book as you read them.

The benefits of doing this in XSLT are as follows:

- We only need to store one copy of the header and footer code to cover every page on the site, making it easy to change them globally without editing every single page.
- Users only need to download the header and footer XSLT code once, even though they are used on every page in the site. This can give bandwidth savings, which is important if your service provider charges by the megabyte, or if you are supporting modem users.
- Server processing is reduced as all the work is being done on the client.

How else could we do it? We could manually add the header and footer to every web page, but this would result in a site maintenance nightmare, especially for a large site. The other alternatives are as follows:

- By using **Server-Side Includes** (**SSI**) to include standard header and footer content on every page.
- By using a scripting language (such as ASP, PHP, or JSP) to generate web pages with the header and footer included.

Although these methods share the first advantage of only storing one copy of the header and footer, they do not reduce the bandwidth or server load.

Take it From the Top

Here's our starting XHTML page, `dinosaur.html`. It's nice and simple, not very pretty, but functional (don't worry: we'll beautify it later):

```
<html lang="en">
<head>
  <title>A simple HTML page</title>
  <style type="text/css">
    body { font-family: Verdana, Times, Serif; }
  </style>
</head>
<body>

  <h1>My big list of dinosaurs</h1>

  <h2>Brontosaurus</h2>
  A Brontosaurus is big and scary.
  <ul>
    <li><b>Weight:</b> 200 tons</li>
    <li><b>Length:</b> 90 m</li>
    <li><b>Color:</b> Blue</li>
  </ul>

  <h2>Tyrannosaurus Rex</h2>
  A Tyrannosaurus Rex would eat you.
  <ul>
    <li><b>Weight:</b> 50 tons</li>
    <li><b>Length:</b> 20 m</li>
    <li><b>Color:</b> Red</li>
  </ul>

  <h2>Stegosaurus</h2>
  A Stegosaurus has lots of spiny plates.
  <ul>
    <li><b>Weight:</b> 25 tons</li>
    <li><b>Length:</b> 20 m</li>
    <li><b>Color:</b> Green</li>
  </ul>

</body>
</html>
```

And here's that code in action:

(Well, we did say it wasn't that exciting.)

Let's spice up our page by adding a header and footer. We could of course just add some extra header and footer XHTML into our page and do things the old-fashioned way, but that wouldn't give us the benefits we describe above. Instead, we'll add an extra line to the top of `dinosaur.html`, and save the resulting code as `dinosaur_1.xml`:

```
<?xml-stylesheet type="text/xsl" href="headerfooter_1.xsl" ?>

<html lang="en">
<head>
  ...
```

This new line performs one very important task: referencing our first XSLT stylesheet file, `headerfooter_1.xsl`. The rest of our XHTML stays the same.

During this chapter, we will encounter slight differences between how various browsers deal with stylesheets. In a minute, we'll learn a useful trick to specify different stylesheets for different browsers, but for now we'll keep things simple and just specify `headerfooter_1.xsl`.

You may have spotted that our new page has an `.xml` extension rather than `.html`. There's a reason for this. In order to start using XSLT to transform our page, we need to be sure that the page is well-formed XML, rather than just any old HTML we've chucked together. Our new page is in fact XHTML, as introduced in *Chapter 2* – we therefore give it the `.xml` extension.

An Aside on XHTML Namespaces

If you're familiar with XHTML, you may have realized that the page above is not strictly conforming to XHTML. It is lacking an `xmlns` attribute in the `<html>` root element, and there is no DOCTYPE declaration at the beginning of the document.

An XSLT stylesheet will normally act on elements in the default namespace. If the `xmlns` attribute was present in the source document, then all of the document elements would be in the XHTML namespace. This means that the template match in the stylesheet for the `<body>` element would have no effect – it would be looking in the wrong namespace for the match.

In order to make the match correct, we need to tell the stylesheet about the XHTML namespace. Just as in the source document, we do this with an `xmlns` attribute, giving the URI for the XHTML namespace. The amended `xsl:stylesheet` element would look like this:

```
<xsl:stylesheet version="1.0" xmlns:xsl="http://www.w3.org/1999/XSL/Transform"
                              xmlns:html="http://www.w3.org/1999/xhtml">
```

Having done this, we can now refer to the `body` element as `html:body`, thus:

```
<xsl:template match="html:body">
```

The reason for leaving this out of the example is to keep it simple – and most of the time, it's enough to use the default namespace.

Creating Your First XSLT Stylesheet

Here's our first XSLT stylesheet, `headerfooter_1.xsl`:

```
<xsl:stylesheet version="1.0" xmlns:xsl="http://www.w3.org/1999/XSL/Transform">

  <xsl:template match="/">
    <xsl:apply-templates />
  </xsl:template>

  <xsl:template match="node()|@*">
    <xsl:copy>
      <xsl:apply-templates select="node()|@*"/>
    </xsl:copy>
  </xsl:template>

  <xsl:template match="body">
    <body>
      <table style="border: solid thin black">
        <tr>
          <td><a href="mammoth.html">Visit the Mammoth zone!</a> - </td>
          <td><a href="play.html">Play Pteranodon Poker</a></td>
        </tr>
      </table>

    <xsl:apply-templates />

    <hr/>
      Copyright 2002 DinosaurOrg.
    </body>
```

```
    </xsl:template>

</xsl:stylesheet>
```

If you are using IE 5 or IE 5.5, you should replace the second line of code in the stylesheet (ignoring all comment lines) with:

```
<xsl:stylesheet xmlns:xsl="http://www.w3.org/TR/WD-xsl">
```

This file is already present in the code download as `headerfooter_ie5_1.xsl`. Save your stylesheet in the same folder as `dinosaur_1.xml`, and then view `dinosaur_1.xml` in a browser:

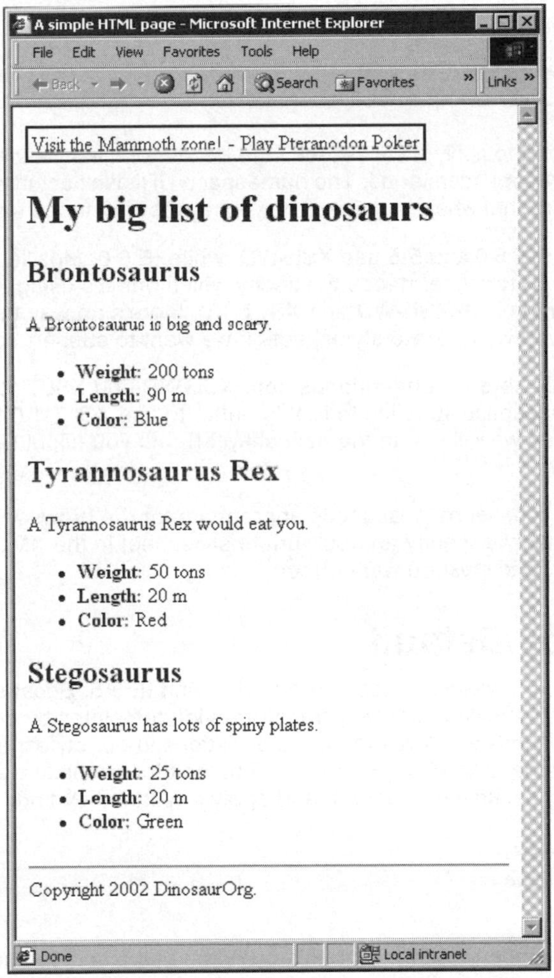

As if by magic, exciting links to the Mammoth Zone and Pteranodon Poker appear at the top of our page, together with a copyright message in the footer. But how?

About the Stylesheet

Starting from the top of our stylesheet:

```
<xsl:stylesheet version="1.0" xmlns:xsl="http://www.w3.org/1999/XSL/Transform">
```

specifies two properties of the stylesheet:

- The version of XSLT that the stylesheet conforms to
- The XML namespace for any tags in the stylesheet that begin with "`xsl:`"

> Note that the equivalent in XSL-WD (for IE 5 and 5.5) would be:
>
> ```
> <xsl:stylesheet xmlns:xsl="http://www.w3.org/TR/WD-xsl">
> ```

A browser will only attempt to apply a stylesheet if the header of the stylesheet declares that it uses a namespace that the browser understands. The namespace URL isn't actually loaded by your browser – it's just a check to ensure that when you say `xsl`, you're referring to the same thing as the browser.

As we described earlier, IE 5.0 and 5.5 use XSL-WD, while IE 6.0, Mozilla, and Netscape 6+ use XSLT 1.0. Therefore, our stylesheet needs to specify which one it's using. Even though the templates that we're using will work in both XSL-WD and XSLT 1.0, there's no way to tell a browser this – instead, we need to have two separate stylesheets if we want to support both situations.

IE 6.0 is a slight anomaly here – it understands both XSL-WD and XSLT 1.0, and chooses which one to use based on the namespace supplied to it. It is better to use XSLT 1.0 if developing for IE 6 (it has a lot more functionality as we will see in the next chapter), but you might have to use XSL-WD for backwards compatibility.

For the moment, use whichever namespace is appropriate for the browser you're using. In a moment, we'll see how to automatically specify an appropriate stylesheet in the XML. Note that our stylesheet is itself an XML document, and must be well-formed.

Transforming by Default

The next three lines of our stylesheet also relate to IE 5 and IE 5.5. Because these browsers use XSL-WD rather than XSLT 1.0, they do not apply transformation templates by default. To put it another way, we could define all kinds of interesting transformations in our stylesheets, and IE 5 and 5.5 would happily ignore them. We need to tell IE 5 and IE 5.5 to look for template transformations, starting at the very root of our XML document structure, and apply any that they find:

```
<xsl:template match="/">
  <xsl:apply-templates />
</xsl:template>
```

Browsers that correctly support XSLT 1.0 do this by default as a built-in rule, and so adding this code into our stylesheet ensures that both types of browser perform XSLT transformations by default. You'll see these three lines of code at the start of all stylesheets in this chapter to ensure compatibility with IE 5 and IE 5.5. For more information on this and other built-in rules in XSLT 1.0, see *http://www.w3.org/TR/xslt#built-in-rule*.

You Too Can Transform Your <body>

Now we've made sure that transformations will actually happen, we begin defining the transformations themselves. Further down the stylesheet are some lines that perform a template transformation on the `<body>` element of `dinosaur_1.xml`:

```
<xsl:template match="body">
  <body>
    <table style="border: solid thin black">
      <tr>
        <td><a href="mammoth.html">Visit the Mammoth zone!</a> - </td>
        <td><a href="play.html">Play Pteranodon Poker</a></td>
      </tr>
    </table>

    <xsl:apply-templates />

    <hr/>
    Copyright 2002 DinosaurOrg.
  </body>
</xsl:template>
```

The first line of this section tells the XSLT processor to search through the XML document until it finds the opening tag of a `<body>` element, and then perform a transformation on the contents of this `<body>` element (everything from `<body>` to `</body>`). It's called `xsl:template` because its content defines a template for how to transform a `<body>` element.

The next seven lines are the start of this `<body>` element template. These lines of HTML are added in to the transformed page **before** the content of the original `<body>` element. The template does not do anything with the matched `<body>` tag itself, and so we insert a `<body>` tag ourselves in the template.

The start of `dinosaur_1.xml` is transformed from

```
<body>

  ...
```

to

```
<body>
  <table style="border: solid thin black">
    <tr>
    <td><a href="mammoth.html">Visit the Mammoth zone!</a> - </td>
    <td><a href="play.html">Play Pteranodon Poker</a></td>
    </tr>
  </table>

  ...
```

Our header is successfully added!

Transformation Without Change

The stylesheet has added some code to the beginning of the translated <body> element, but hasn't yet done anything with the original contents of the <body> element. That's the job of the next line, <xsl:apply-templates />. This line says "Work through all of the contents of the <body> element, and perform any other transformations you need to on any tags you find". In our next example, we'll create some more template transformations for some other elements, but for now we don't want to change anything else at all. We want the rest of the <body> element contents to be passed through unchanged.

Even though we want the content to remain unchanged, we still need to specify a transformation for the other tags in our page – <html>, <head>, <title>, <style>, <b>, <h1>, <h2>, <ul> and <li>. If we don't specify a transformation for these tags, they will be ignored, leaving us with a mass of unformatted text and no tags at all. This isn't nice. We use the **Identity Transformation** to pass these tags through unchanged.

The Identity Transformation is specified in those curious few lines right in the middle of headerfooter_1.xsl:

```
<xsl:template match="node()|@*">
  <xsl:copy>
    <xsl:apply-templates select="node()|@*"/>
  </xsl:copy>
</xsl:template>
```

The Identity Transformation is a transformation that leaves everything just the way it found it. It matches every part of our source XML document for which we haven't given a specific rule, and passes it through unchanged – let's look at how this works now.

How Does the Identity Transformation Work?

Very often when writing a stylesheet, we find that we only want to make small changes to the input document. If this is the case, then it's easiest to pass through almost everything unchanged, and just match the few elements that need alteration.

We do this using the Identity Transformation introduced above:

```
<xsl:template match="node()|@*">
  <xsl:copy>
    <xsl:apply-templates select="node()|@*" />
  </xsl:copy>
</xsl:template>
```

This template matches both node() (any node in the input document) and @* (any attribute), so it matches everything. When it matches, it uses <xsl:copy> to create an identical copy of the item it has matched, and then uses <xsl:apply-templates> to process the contents of the item if there are any.

If this was the only template in a stylesheet, it would produce an output document functionally the same as the input one. The identity transformation isn't appropriate when the output document needs to be considerably different from the input document.

Normally, as we have done in *Example 1* above, we would use the identity template alongside others that add, remove, or alter a few nodes. These other templates, such as the template matching `<body>` that we defined above, will be used rather than the identity template for the nodes that they match. Each element or attribute in the source XML document can only be matched by one template (as we'll see later in this chapter, the most specific template available is used in XSLT 1.0); this is why we had to specifically copy the `<body>` element to our output document rather than relying on the identity template to do it for us.

Adding the Footer

Lastly, we want to add some footer text after the unchanged `<body>` element contents. This is performed by the end section of our `<body>` element template:

```
    <hr/>
    Copyright 2002 DinosaurOrg.
    </body>
  </xsl:template>
```

After the body content has been passed through unchanged, these lines add some footer HTML to the page and then close the `<body>` tag. We then close our body `<xsl:template>` element, to tell the XSLT processor we have finished dealing with the `<body>` element.

Finally, the last line of `headerfooter_1.xsl` tidies up the stylesheet with the line `</xsl:stylesheet>`. We're done!

Specifying Stylesheets for Different Browsers

We've already seen that you need to specify a different XSL namespace in your stylesheet depending on whether you're targeting XSLT 1.0 in the recent browsers (IE 6 and Netscape 6) or XSL-WD in IE 5.0 or IE 5.5. This might seem a major obstacle to supporting multiple browsers, since you need to change the source XML document to reference a different stylesheet depending on the browser.

In fact, the situation isn't too bad. It's possible to make sure each browser gets an appropriate stylesheet using the `alternate` attribute.

As with CSS, it is possible to provide both one main, and several alternative stylesheets with which to render a page. The main stylesheet is specified in the `<?xml-stylesheet ... ?>` reference with `alternate="no"`, and each of the alternative stylesheets is specified with `alternate="yes"`. Fortunately, there is varying support for this in the different browsers, which we can exploit to provide them with different stylesheets.

Rather than the `<?xml-stylesheet ... ?>` reference we used in *Example 1* above, we can instead use:

```
<?xml-stylesheet type="text/xsl" href="stylesheet_ie5.xsl" alternate="yes" ?>
<?xml-stylesheet type="text/xsl" href="stylesheet_ie6.xsl" alternate="no" ?>
<?xml-stylesheet type="text/xsl" href="stylesheet_ns6.xsl" alternate="yes" ?>
```

This gives us different stylesheets for the different browsers because:

- IE 5 and IE 5.5 don't understand the `alternate` attribute, and will act on the first stylesheet found.
- IE 6 does understand the `alternate` attribute, and will use the stylesheet that has `alternate="no"`.
- Netscape 6 doesn't understand the `alternate` attribute, and will act on the last stylesheet found.

The former two items can be trusted to work in future. The latter is a bug in Netscape that may be fixed in future, but for the moment we can exploit it to provide a different stylesheet for Netscape 6 and 7 to the one we provide for the various versions of IE.

Typically, rather than the example above, it's more useful to use:

```
<?xml-stylesheet type="text/xsl" href="stylesheet_ie5.xsl" alternate="yes" ?>
<?xml-stylesheet type="text/xsl" href="stylesheet_v6.xsl" alternate="no" ?>
```

because it's rare that you'll want to use a different stylesheet for the two version 6 browsers.

In this chapter, we'll continue to just reference one stylesheet in our XML for simplicity. When working through these examples, use the correct `<xsl:stylesheet ... >` tag in your XSLT stylesheets for whichever browser you use.

For browsers that support XSLT 1.0, this is:

```
<xsl:stylesheet version="1.0" xmlns:xsl="http://www.w3.org/1999/XSL/Transform">
```

or, for XSL-WD:

```
<xsl:stylesheet xmlns:xsl="http://www.w3.org/TR/WD-xsl">
```

This does mean that in some cases, you'll have a lot of code shared between the XSL-WD and the XSLT 1.0 stylesheets. The best way of avoiding this is with server-side code to include the common templates in both files – using SSI, ASP, JSP, or whatever. This does still retain the benefits of client-sdie XSLT, but makes maintenance easier.

Example 2: Creating a Table of Contents with XSLT

In this example, we'll create a table of contents as a list of links to our dinosaurs using XSLT, without changing the source XHTML page. This is an example of generating new content automatically from existing content – and it's useful for creating navigation, cross-references, summaries, and so on.

The benefits of doing this in XSLT are:

- The table of contents will automatically update when the list of dinosaurs changes. This wouldn't have been the case if we'd just used static HTML.
- The table of contents can easily be generated from existing XHTML. If we were generating such an index with a scripting language like ASP, we'd probably want to do this in a more complex way by pulling the information out of a database or separate data file instead.

- We gain even more bandwidth savings than in the last example. With our header and footer example above, the header and footer data was only downloaded once. This time, the HTML for the table of contents isn't downloaded at all. Instead, the browser only needs to download the rules to create the table.

- As in the previous example, no server-side processing is required to generate the table of contents, reducing load on the server.

How else could we do it?

- By using a server-side scripting language (such as ASP, PHP, or JSP) to generate the list of contents from a data source or by parsing the existing HTML

- By using JavaScript to manipulate the DOM client-side, and using `document.write` to create HTML

Create a new copy of `dinosaur_1.xml`, and call it `dinosaur_2.xml` (or find it in the code download for this chapter). Change the first line of `dinosaur_2.xml` to reference a new stylesheet:

```
<?xml-stylesheet type="text/xsl" href="contents_2.xsl" ?>
```

and create `contents_2.xsl` in the same folder, using the code below (replacing the first line as described above, if necessary):

```
<xsl:stylesheet version="1.0" xmlns:xsl="http://www.w3.org/1999/XSL/Transform">

  <xsl:template match="/">
    <xsl:apply-templates />
  </xsl:template>

  <xsl:template match="node()|@*">
    <xsl:copy>
      <xsl:apply-templates select="node()|@*"/>
    </xsl:copy>
  </xsl:template>

  <xsl:template match="body">
    <body>
      <table style="border: solid thin black">
        <tr>
          <td><a href="mammoth.html">Visit the Mammoth zone!</a> - </td>
          <td><a href="play.html">Play Pteranodon Poker</a></td>
        </tr>
      </table>

      <h2>Quick reference</h2>
      <ul>
        <xsl:for-each select="h2">
          <li>
            <a>
              <xsl:attribute name="href">
                #<xsl:value-of select="text()"/>
              </xsl:attribute>
              <xsl:value-of select="text()"/>
            </a>
          </li>
        </xsl:for-each>
      </ul>
```

```
      <xsl:apply-templates />

      <hr />
      Copyright 2002 DinosaurOrg.
    </body>
  </xsl:template>

  <xsl:template match="h2">
    <a>
      <xsl:attribute name="name"><xsl:value-of select="text()"/></xsl:attribute>
      <h2><xsl:apply-templates/></h2>
    </a>
  </xsl:template>

</xsl:stylesheet>
```

Here's how `dinosaur_2.xml` should look in a browser:

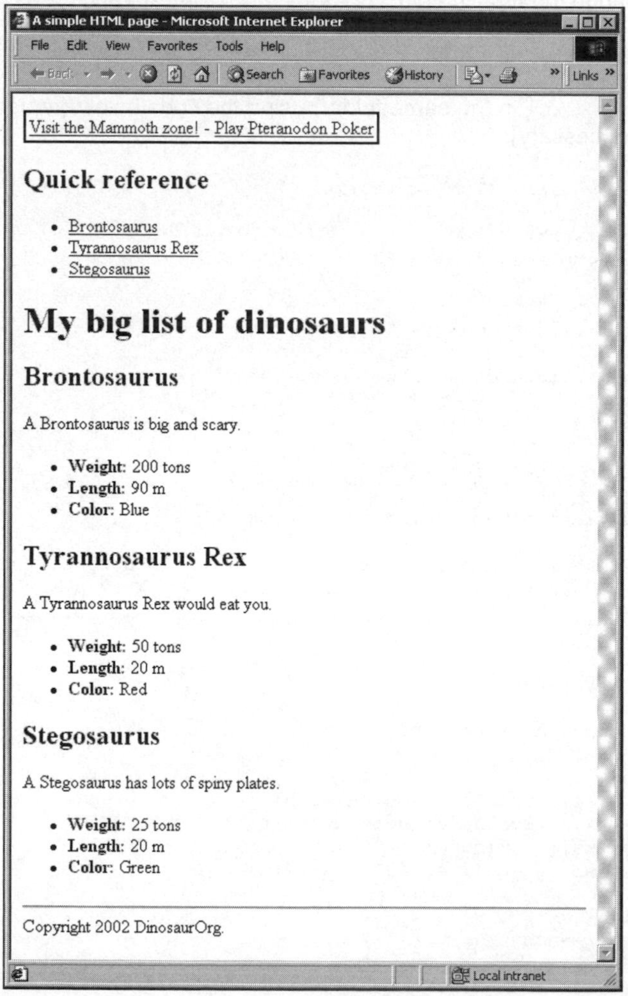

Hunting for Dinosaurs with <xsl:for-each>

The first few lines of `contents_2.xsl` are the same as in our previous example – defining the version and namespace, making sure IE 5 and IE 5.5 perform transformations, defining the Identity Transformation, finding the `<body>` tag, and inserting the header links. We then add some more content to the header, using the following section of the stylesheet:

```
<h2>Quick reference</h2>
<ul>
  <xsl:for-each select="h2">
    <li>
      <a>
        <xsl:attribute name="href">
          #<xsl:value-of select="text()"/>
        </xsl:attribute>
        <xsl:value-of select="text()"/>
      </a>
    </li>
  </xsl:for-each>
</ul>
```

The first two lines of this section give a header and begin the list for our TOC, and the last line closes it. The interesting bit comes in the middle. Here, we set up a loop to find all `<h2>` tags in the `<body>` element content, and create a list of anchor links based on the contents of these `<h2>` tags. Because all of our dinosaur names in the page are nicely wrapped in `<h2>` elements (for example, `<h2>Tyrannosaurus Rex</h2>`), this becomes a list of links to our dinosaurs.

For each `<h2>` in the body of the page, we first output an `<li>` tag. We then create an `<a>` tag, use `xsl:attribute` to add an attribute called '`href`', and set this attribute to be a hash symbol followed by the content of the `<h2>` tag. We then close the `href` attribute. We use the text content of the `<h2>` tag again to output the dinosaur name as visible text for the link, and finish off with an `</a>` tag to close the link. Finally, we close our `<li>` element, and end the `for-each` loop with `</xsl:for-each>`, giving (for example):

```
<li><a href="#Tyrannosaurus Rex">Tyrannosaurus Rex</a></li>
```

For `dinosaur_2.xml`, the complete block of navigation created by this code looks like this:

```
<h2>Quick reference</h2>
<ul>
  <li><a href="#Brontosaurus">Brontosaurus</a></li>
  <li><a href="#Tyrannosaurus Rex">Tyrannosaurus Rex</a></li>
  <li><a href="#Stegosaurus">Stegosaurus</a></li>
</ul>
```

Let's add a pterodactyl to `dinosaur_2.xml`:

```
<h2>Pterodactyl</h2>
A Pterodactyl can fly round at high speeds.
<ul>
  <li><b>Weight:</b> 0.05 tons</li>
  <li><b>Length:</b> 2 m</li>
  <li><b>Color:</b> Gray</li>
</ul>
```

Reload `dinosaur_2.xml`, and the Pterodactyl will be added to the contents list without the need for us to change the stylesheet.

Now that we have created a list of links, we need to add some `<a name="xxxx">` tags to our dinosaurs further down the page to give the links somewhere to link to. The stylesheet above contains a new template to transform the `<h2>` element:

```
<xsl:template match="h2">
  <a>
    <xsl:attribute name="name"><xsl:value-of select="text()"/></xsl:attribute>
    <h2><xsl:apply-templates/></h2>
  </a>
</xsl:template>
```

When we call `<xsl:apply-templates />` in the middle of the `<body>` template, any `<h2>` tags within the body content will be transformed using this new template, rather than the Identity Transformation. `<h2>` tags are transformed from:

```
<h2>Tyrannosaurus Rex</h2>
```

...to:

```
<a name="Tyrannosaurus Rex"><h2>Tyrannosaurus Rex</h2></a>
```

So, we've seen how to generate new content from an existing XHTML document. This is a good technique to use when you have existing HTML that has a regular format, and want to add information and change formatting without completely altering your source documents.

> Which template will be applied?
>
> There is a reason for the ordering of templates we have used in the examples above. This is because of a difference between how the XSLT 1.0 standard and XSL-WD prioritize templates, if several could match the same node.
>
> In XSLT 1.0, `<xslt:template>` has a `priority` attribute that allows you to specify which template will be applied if there are several that match a node. A higher priority indicates that the template will be applied preferentially.
>
> If no priority is specified, then the order in which templates are applied is quite complicated. The full process is described in section 5.5 of the XSLT specification (*http://www.w3.org/TR/xslt#conflict*), but the essence of it is that, of all the templates that could match an element, the most specific is always used. In *Example 2*, the identity template will match every node, including the `<body>` element, but because we specifically look for `<body>`, that rule will apply. If we were just targeting XSLT 1.0-compatible browsers, we could put the templates in any order, and rely on these rules to apply the correct templates.
>
> This is not true of XSL-WD in IE 5.0 and IE 5.5. In these browsers, the matching template that is listed last in the XSL file is the one that will be used. This often means that you need to re-order the templates in an XSL file intended for IE 5 to make it work the same way as in IE 6. For this reason, we have placed the Identity Transformation at the top of our stylesheets. If we put it at the bottom, it would override all other templates in IE 5.0 and IE 5.5.

Example 3: Separating Design from Content

So far, we've been basing our transformations on an XHTML document, containing layout information for our content. This is fine, but in order to gain the real benefits of XML and XSLT, we'd like to be able to remove **all** layout code from the source file, and store all design transformations within an XSLT stylesheet.

The benefits of doing this in XSLT are:

- The source XML document contains useful structured content without needing to be concerned about the layout of that content. This makes content reuse and content sharing much easier.
- Layout and design can be completely changed in the future without the need to change the underlying content.
- It is easy to produce several different versions of the same document – for example, for mobile devices, for internationalization, or for accessibility.
- The bandwidth savings are potentially even greater than in the previous examples, as **all** design and layout rules are defined and downloaded once only. XML can be automatically validated using a DTD or a schema. This ensures that XML conforms to your specific document rules, and allows you to enforce document requirements.

How else could we do it?

- By using a server-side scripting language (such as ASP, PHP, or JSP) to pull the page contents from an XML document, or some other storage mechanism such as a data file or database, and then generate HTML from this content based upon rules defined in the script.
- As we saw in *Chapter 4,* CSS can be used to style XML within the browser. However, CSS does not give the level of complete control that we get with XSLT.

Even though CSS on its own cannot do as much as XSLT, it's very powerful when used alongside XSLT. CSS is much better for applying styles to content, but cannot make the wholesale transformations that are possible with XSLT.

Moving from XHTML to Raw XML

Let's remove all design from our source XML file, and create a new file, `dinosaur_3.xml`, as shown below:

```
<?xml-stylesheet type="text/xsl" href="xml2html_3.xsl" ?>

<dinosaurs>
  <dinosaur name="Brontosaurus">
    <description>
      A Brontosaurus is big and scary.
    </description>
    <weight>200</weight>
    <length>90</length>
```

```
      <color>Blue</color>
      <discoverer>Primrose McFadden</discoverer>
    </dinosaur>

    <dinosaur name="Tyrannosaurus Rex">
      <description>
        A Tyrannosaurus Rex would eat you.
      </description>
      <weight>50</weight>
      <length>20</length>
      <color>Red</color>
      <discoverer>George Grimble</discoverer>
    </dinosaur>

    <dinosaur name="Stegosaurus">
      <description>
        A Stegosaurus has lots of spiny plates.
      </description>
      <weight>25</weight>
      <length>20</length>
      <color>Green</color>
      <discoverer>Charles Degramy</discoverer>
    </dinosaur>
  </dinosaurs>
```

dinosaur_3.xml is much simpler than our previous XHTML files, and contains all of the important information about dinosaurs without needing to concern itself at all with how this information is displayed. We've also introduced a new item for each dinosaur, namely <discoverer>.

Styling the XML with XSLT

We'll create a new stylesheet, xml2html_3.xsl, to transform our XML file. Change the first line for XSL-WD if you need to, as described above (you can find the XSL-WD-friendly version in the code download too, as xml2html_ie5_3.xsl).

```
<xsl:stylesheet version="1.0" xmlns:xsl="http://www.w3.org/1999/XSL/Transform">

  <xsl:template match="/">
    <xsl:apply-templates />
  </xsl:template>

  <xsl:template match="text()" />

  <xsl:template match="dinosaurs">
    <html>
    <head>
      <title>A simple HTML page</title>
      <style type="text/css">
        body { font-family: Verdana, Times, Serif; }
      </style>
    </head>
    <body>
```

```
      <table style="border: solid thin black">
        <tr>
          <td><a href="mammoth.html">Visit the Mammoth zone!</a> - </td>
          <td><a href="play.html">Play Pteranodon Poker</a></td>
        </tr>
      </table>

      <h1>My big list of dinosaurs</h1>

      <xsl:apply-templates />

    <hr/>
    Copyright 2002 DinosaurOrg.
    </body>
    </html>
  </xsl:template>

  <xsl:template match="dinosaur">
    <h2><xsl:value-of select="@name"/></h2>
    <xsl:value-of select="description/text()"/>
    <ul>
      <xsl:apply-templates/>
    </ul>
  </xsl:template>

  <xsl:template match="weight">
    <li><b>Weight: </b><xsl:value-of select="text()" /> tons</li>
  </xsl:template>

  <xsl:template match="length">
    <li><b>Length: </b><xsl:value-of select="text()" /> m</li>
  </xsl:template>

  <xsl:template match="color">
    <li><b>Color: </b><xsl:value-of select="text()" /></li>
  </xsl:template>

</xsl:stylesheet>
```

The beginning of this stylesheet looks remarkably like our previous example, except that rather than searching for a <body> element, we instead search for the <dinosaurs> element. Because our XML file contains no HTML at all, the stylesheet has to include the <html> and <head> elements in its transformation this time round. Likewise, the template for the <dinosaurs> element must close the <html> element at the bottom of the page.

Rather than search for an <h2> tag to find out our individual dinosaur names, this stylesheet searches for the <dinosaur> element and references its name parameter. This is much better than the previous approach of matching the <h2> tag, as you may have other <h2> tags in your document that don't refer to dinosaurs.

```
<xsl:template match="dinosaur">
  <h2><xsl:value-of select="@name"/></h2>
  <xsl:value-of select="description/text()"/>
  <ul>
    <xsl:apply-templates/>
  </ul>
</xsl:template>
```

The `@name` reference on line 2 of this section points to the value of the `name` attribute of the `<dinosaur>` tag, transforming `<dinosaur name="Tyrannosaurus Rex">` into `<h2>Tyrannosaurus Rex</h2>`. The `description/text()` reference on line 3 then points to the text contents of the `<description>` child element for our current `<dinosaur>` element. `<xsl:apply-templates />` then tells the XSLT processor to apply any templates to the contents of the `<dinosaur>` element – in this case, `<weight>`, `<length>`, and `<color>`. We have defined templates for these three tags, and so they are translated by their templates into the same HTML code as in our previous examples.

Removing Content with XSLT

You may have noticed that we haven't provided an `<xsl:template>` for our new `<discoverer>` element. Additionally, we haven't included the identity transformation in this stylesheet, so as a result our `<discoverer>` element is ignored. Don't worry, we won't forget the dinosaur discoverers completely – we'll come back to them in *Chapter 6* and make sure they get the credit they deserve.

This does show how easy it is to exclude content with XSLT – one application for this would be to strip out confidential company information when an internal document is republished on an extranet. (However, this would have to be done with server-side XSLT, not client-side, otherwise a simple *View Source* would show the hidden information.)

Our decision to exclude the identity transformation from this example is because the output of this stylesheet is very different from the source XML file. As we saw earlier, the identity transformation is useful when the output is very similar to the source and we wish to leave most things unchanged.

We have added a new template:

```
<xsl:template match="text()" />
```

XSLT has a built-in rule for text, specifying that any text in the source XML is passed through unchanged by default. In this example we don't want this to happen – we want to suppress text, and only display it when we specifically match it with `value-of` rules. If we didn't include this `text()` template, the names of our explorers (which are text nodes in the XML tree) would be passed through and displayed, even though we have not given a rule for their parent (the `<discoverer>` tag).

The resulting web page from these transformations is essentially the same as the one shown in *Example 1* earlier, only this time we started with simple, reusable XML.

XPath – We've Used It a Lot Already, Without Even Noticing

So far, we've used XPath several times without really explaining what it is. In the template above, where we use:

```
<xsl:value-of select="description/text()" />
```

...we are using an XPath statement to reference the `text` child of the `description` element that is a child of the current node. Again, in the template:

```
<xsl:template match="body">
```

...we are using XPath to reference the element identified by the name "body".

XPath is used inside the `match` and `select` attributes of many XSLT elements, to choose nodes in the input document, and to alter them. XPath consists of two parts – the path-like document navigation parts shown above, and a set of JavaScript-like functions like `substring`. These functions will only work in XSLT 1.0, so we will cover some examples of them in the next chapter.

To select attributes with XPath, we just use the attribute name with an "@" in front of it. For example, to output the `href` attribute of an `<a>` element we were currently on, we use:

```
<xsl:value-of select="@href" />
```

We can also write our XPath so that we match only elements that have a certain attribute. For example, to match only those `<dinosaur>` elements that have a `name` attribute, we'd use:

```
<xsl:template match="dinosaur[@name]" />
```

It is possible to use conditional statements within XPath as well – for example, to match only the dinosaur with name "Triceratops", we'd use:

```
<xsl:template match="dinosaur[@name='Triceratops']" />
```

Conditions can be combined with `"and"` and `"or"`, for example:

```
<xsl:template match="dinosaur[@name='Brontosaurus' or @name= 'Triceratops']" >
```

...will match the `<dinosaur>` elements with the name "Brontosaurus" or "Triceratops".

We can also match elements that have a specific parent – for example:

```
<xsl:template match="description/b" >
```

...would only match `<b>` tags that were directly inside the `<description>`, while:

```
<xsl:template match="description//b" >
```

would match `<b>` tags that were within the `description`, directly or not. For example, in the following description, the `<b>` would be matched by the `description//b` XPath, but not by `description/b`.

```
<description>A Brontosaurus is <i><b>big</b> and scary.</i></description>
```

XSL-WD doesn't support the full XPath specification, and so this is the limit of what's possible using XSL-WD inside IE 5.0 and IE 5.5. There are a lot more possibilities available using XSLT 1.0, such as accessing the parent and the siblings of the current node, and a set of functions that includes `substring`, `count`, and `contains` that we'll talk about more in *Chapter 6*.

XPath is a large subject, and we have barely touched upon it here. However, not too much of it is necessary for everyday use. We will explain more of XPath as we go through the examples below and in the next chapter. A complete XPath reference can be found at *http://www.zvon.org/xxl/XSLTreference/Output/index.html*, while the XPath specification is available at *http://www.w3.org/TR/xpath*.

Example 4: Referencing Images Using XPath

In this example, we will use XPath to reference external images for our page, and see how browsers that support XSLT 1.0 can include stylesheets within other stylesheets. To start, do the following:

- Create a copy of `dinosaur_3.xml` called (you've guessed it) `dinosaur_4.xml`, and modify it to reference a new stylesheet called `addimages_4.xsl`.
- Create `addimages_4.xsl` as a copy of our previous stylesheet, `xml2html_3.xsl`.
- In `addimages_4.xsl`, replace the existing dinosaur template with the revised one below:

```
<xsl:template match="dinosaur">
  <img align="right" width="160" height="120">
    <xsl:attribute name="src">
      <xsl:value-of select="@name"/>.jpg
    </xsl:attribute>
  </img>

  <h2><xsl:value-of select="@name"/></h2>
  <xsl:value-of select="description/text()"/>
  <ul>
    <xsl:apply-templates/>
  </ul>
</xsl:template>
```

This new template creates an `<img>` element with some predefined attributes (`align`, `width`, `height`), and adds an `src` attribute, transforming `<dinosaur name="Stegosaurus">` into `<img align="right" width="160" height="120" src="Stegosaurus.jpg">`. Note that any spaces in the `<dinosaur>` element's `name` attribute will also be in the `<img>` element's `src` attribute, and the image file names will need to reflect this.

This works specifically because we are transforming into XHTML. If we used another XML vocabulary, the browser would not understand how to put the images in. Netscape 6 supports limited use of Xlink, but it will not embed images. As we saw in *Chapter 4*, the only way around this, in a pure XML document, would be to use a different element name for each required picture, and then use the `background-image` property of CSS on named elements. None of the v6 browsers lets you differentiate between elements simply by their attribute values.

When we load `dinosaur4.xml` into a browser, now, we get the following beautified page, with images:

Including Templates within Templates

If you are using a browser that supports XSLT 1.0 (IE 6, Mozilla, Netscape 7+), you can avoid the need to copy all of the contents of your previous stylesheet as mentioned above (although Netscape 6 uses XSLT 1.0, its support for `<xsl:import>` is buggy so this technique is not useful for it). For these browsers, you can instead replace the entire contents of `addimages_4.xsl` with the following:

```
<xsl:stylesheet version="1.0" xmlns:xsl="http://www.w3.org/1999/XSL/Transform">

  <xsl:import href="xml2html_3.xsl" />

  <xsl:template match="dinosaur">
    <img align="right" width="160" height="120">
      <xsl:attribute name="src">
        <xsl:value-of select="@name"/>.jpg
      </xsl:attribute>
    </img>
```

```
        <xsl:apply-imports />

    </xsl:template>

</xsl:stylesheet>
```

In XSLT 1.0, the `<xsl:import href="xml2html_3.xsl" />` line will import all of the template matches defined in `xml2html_3.xsl`. These imported templates can then be optionally overridden in the current stylesheet. Templates defined in `addimages_4.xsl` take priority over templates matching the same thing that are found in the imported file, and so our new dinosaur template overrides the imported one and transforms the `<dinosaur>` element by adding an image as before.

If we wish, we can also apply the lower-priority imported dinosaur template. The `<xsl:apply-imports />` line within the dinosaur template does exactly this, resulting in the imported dinosaur template adding the heading and text that appeared before. Without this, we would just get an image appearing for each dinosaur with no text. This is not transforming each dinosaur twice – instead, it is as if the contents of the `dinosaur` template in the parent stylesheet is appended to the `dinosaur` template defined in the current stylesheet.

We have not overridden any of the other templates in `xml2html_3.xsl`, and so these other imported templates are applied as normal, giving the same page shown in the previous diagram.

An alternative technique, that is less powerful but will work in Netscape 6+, is the `<xsl:include>` tag. This simply includes all of the templates defined in another stylesheet file in the current one. For example:

```
    <xsl:include href="xml2html_3.xsl" />
```

This does not allow us to use `apply-imports`, nor do the imported templates have a lower priority than the ones defined in the current stylesheet.

Tools for XSLT Development

As with HTML, you'll need to check any XML/XSLT in all the browsers that you intend to use it in. It's not possible to have IE 5.0, IE 5.5, and IE 6.0 installed side by side on the same computer, so if you don't have several computers available, then it may be worth investing in VMWare's "virtual computer" software (*http://www.vmware.com*). On the other hand, low-spec computers are so cheap nowadays that it may be easier just to buy several with different versions insatalled on them.

Mozilla is a good choice of browser to develop in as well as test in. There are several resources freely available for Mozilla that make XSLT development easier:

- The **Mozilla Source Generator** (available from *http://mozilla-evangelism.bclary.com/sidebars/*) allows you to view the *generated* source of a page, rather than the *actual* source that "View Source" will show you. This is the HTML/XHTML source that has been generated from the XML via XSLT.

- The **Zvon XSLT sidebar reference** – an excellent source of XSLT documentation, available on the web from Zvon (*http://www.zvon.org/xxl/XSLTreference/Output/index.html*). This is a useful reference for any browser, and options exist to add various resources from the site to the sidebars of the major browsers.

- The **JavaScript Console** – in XSLT 1.0, there is an `<xsl:message>` element that can be used for sending debug messages. In Mozilla, these messages appear in the JavaScript console (if you have a full install of the browser). This is also very useful for debugging server-side stylesheets. The syntax is simply:

```
<xsl:template match="h1">
 <xsl:message>
  Now processing the h1 tag!
  It contains the text <xsl:value-of select="text()"/>
 </xsl:message>
</xsl:template>
```

You can use one of the standalone XSLT processors described in Part 3 of this book for development, and then transfer the stylesheet to the browser once you're happy with it. This can be a useful technique for very complicated stylesheets.

There are commercial tools to make writing XSLT easier – for example, XMLSpy (*http://www.xmlspy.com/*), Visual XSLT (*http://www.activestate.com/Products/Visual_XSLT/*), and Excelon's Stylus Studio (*http://www.exln.com/products/stylusstudio/*). An intelligent editor and stylesheet debugger can save you huge amounts of time.

The Elements of XSLT

Before we summarize what we've covered, here, let's run through the levels of implementation and support to be found for the various elements of XSLT. The following table lists the degree of implementation for each element to be found within XSLT 1.0, XSL-WD, and the Microsoft extentions to XSLT-WD. It then lists the degree of support for each that you will find in the various XSLT-enabled browsers. **XSLT 1.0 – MS extension** refers to the Microsoft-specific extensions available in IE 5.0, IE 5.5, and in IE 6.0 when it is using XSL-WD. As you can see, when it comes to support of IE 6 generally (when it is in XSLT 1.0 mode), support for XSLT 1.0 is nearly complete. The same is true of Netscape 7, and Mozilla 1.0 – in fact, all three of the most recent versions of these browsers offer similar support for XSLT 1.0.

Element	XSL-WD	XSLT 1.0	XSL-WD – MS extension	NS 6	NS 7/ Mozilla 1.0/IE 6	Notes
apply-imports		X			X	
apply-templates	X	X		X	X	
attribute	X	X		X	X	
attribute-set		X		X	X	
call-template		X		X	X	

Table continued on following page

Element	XSL-WD	XSLT 1.0	XSL-WD – MS extension	NS 6	NS 7/ Mozilla 1.0/IE 6	Notes
choose	X	X		X	X	
comment	X	X		X	X	
copy	X	X		X	X	
copy-of		X		X	X	
decimal-format		X			X	
element	X	X		X	X	
eval			X			
fallback		X			X	
for-each	X	X		X	X	
if	X	X		X	X	
if with "expr" attribute			X			
import		X		o	X	NS 6 documentation claims it does not support reduced import precedence, making it equivalent to `xsl:include`. In practice, it does not appear to work at all.
include		X		X	X	
key		X		X	X	
message		X		X	X	
namespace-alias		X			X	
number		X		o	X	"`any`" and "`lang`" attributes not supported in Netscape
otherwise	X	X		X	X	
output		X			X	
param		X		X	X	
preserve-space		X		X	X	

Element	XSL-WD	XSLT 1.0	XSL-WD – MS extension	NS 6	NS 7/ Mozilla 1.0/IE 6	Notes
`processing-instruction`	X	X		X	X	
`script`			X			XSLT 1.1 also includes the `xsl:script` element, but it is not part of XSLT 1.0 and not supported by current XSLT browsers.
`sort`		X		X	X	
`strip-space`		X		X	X	
`stylesheet`	X	X		X	X	
`template`	X	X		X	X	
`text`	X	X		o	X	NS 6 doesn't support the "`disable-output-escaping`" attribute
`value-of`	X	X		X	X	
`variable`		X		X	X	
`when`	X	X		X	X	
`when with "expr" attribute`			X			
`with-param`		X		X	X	

Summary

In this chapter, we have introduced XSLT as a way of transforming XML documents into other formats, specifically XHTML for display in a web browser. We have focused on browser-based XSLT transformation as a means of styling XML without server-side processing.

We have looked at current browser support for XSLT, and seen how it falls into two main groups: browsers that support XSLT 1.0 (IE 6, Mozilla, Netscape 6+), and those that support an earlier working draft, XSL-WD (IE 5.0, IE 5.5). We've picked up some useful tools to simplify the process of supporting both sets of browsers.

We have used XSLT to add content to an existing XHTML document, and generated new content based on existing content. Taking this a stage further, we have used XSLT to apply layout and styling to data-centric XML, separating design and content completely. We have used XSLT to selectively exclude as well as create content.

In the next chapter, we will go into more detail with some advanced XSLT examples, and suggest solutions to some of the thornier issues that arise when transforming XML documents with XSLT.

6

- Sorting data with XSLT
- Extension functions for Internet Explorer
- Using named templates to reduce code duplication
- Creating JavaScript with XSLT
- XSLT: tips and troubleshooting

Author: Dave Addey and Inigo Surguy

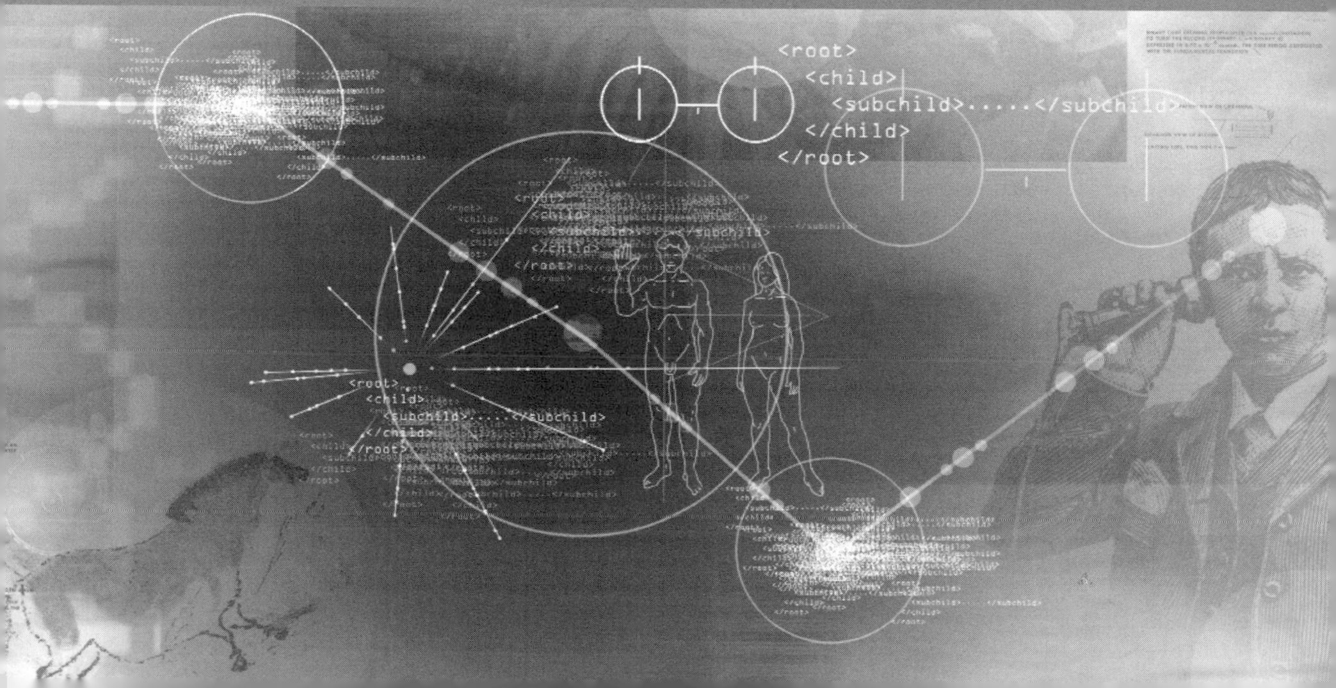

Advanced Client-Side XSLT Techniques

In *Chapter 5*, we established a good foundation in XSLT and its use on the client-side. In this chapter, we'll look in more detail at some practical applications of client-side XSLT.

We will start by using XSLT to sort XML data for display on the client. Using JavaScript, we will dynamically trigger this sorting process, and change the sort criteria from within the browser without requiring a page reload.

Later in the chapter, we will see how to extend the functionality of XSLT by creating extension functions, and we will create some practical extension functions to enable XSLT to perform regular expressions and manipulate text in more detail. We will move beyond using XSLT for simple HTML generation by creating some custom JavaScript based on an XML source document.

We will finish our introduction to client-side XSLT with some tips and troubleshooting. We'll provide practical advice and hard-learned lessons for best-practice XSLT creation, and tackle some of the more common issues of XSLT development.

Example 5: Sorting data with XSLT

In this example, we'll use XSLT to sort some XML data within a browser.

What are the benefits of doing this in XSLT?

- XSLT provides a built-in `<xsl:sort>` element, supporting different types of sorting (string and numeric being the only ones available client-side) and both ascending and descending sorting.
- When we add new elements of the same type to the XML source, they will automatically be sorted by our existing `<xsl:sort>`.
- We can add additional sorting processes with just one line of XSLT code.

How else could we do this?

- By writing custom client-side JavaScript functions to traverse the XML DOM and put appropriate elements into a JavaScript array, and then sort this array. This is not as simple as the one-line XSLT solution.
- By using a server-side technology (such as ASP, PHP, or JSP) to parse and sort the XML server-side, and generate HTML based on the outcome.

For now, the sorting criteria will be hard-coded into our XSLT files. In example 6, we'll show how the sorting criteria can be changed – once the page has loaded – by using JavaScript.

This example will only work in browsers that fully support the XSLT 1.0 specification, as it uses the `<xsl:sort>` function. As a result, it will not work in IE 5.0 or 5.5, although it will work in IE 6, Netscape 6+, and Mozilla. See the previous chapter for an explanation of support for XSLT in various browsers.

Make a copy of `dinosaur_4.xml` from the previous chapter, and call it `dinosaur_5.xml`. Change the first line to reference a new stylesheet, `sorting_5.xsl`. In addition to the three dinosaurs already defined, let's add two more dinosaurs to make sorting more interesting:

```
<?xml-stylesheet type="text/xsl" href="sorting_5.xsl" alternate="no" ?>

<dinosaurs>
  <dinosaur name="Triceratops">
    <description>
      A Triceratops has three big pointy horns.
    </description>
    <weight>30</weight>
    <length>30</length>
    <color>Green</color>
    <discoverer>Crispin Thripple</discoverer>
  </dinosaur>

  <dinosaur name="Pterodactyl">
    <description>
      A Pterodactyl can fly round at high speeds.
    </description>
    <weight>0.05</weight>
    <length>2</length>
    <color>Gray</color>
    <discoverer>Betty Welforth</discoverer>
  </dinosaur>
```

```
  <dinosaur name="Brontosaurus">

  ...

</dinosaurs>
```

In the previous chapter, we saw how to include stylesheets within other stylesheets in browsers that support XSLT 1.0. Throughout this chapter, we'll use this method to avoid having to define the HTML layout of our page in every example.

> Netscape 6.0, 6.1 and 6.2 – a warning.
>
> Netscape's support for the `<xsl:import>` element is buggy in versions 6.0, 6.1, and 6.2, but works in version 7 (and version 1.0 of Mozilla). We are, nevertheless, using `<xsl:import>` in several of the XSLT stylesheets in this chapter. It allows us to put working stylesheets into the chapter without wasting space writing out the same old code every time – so we can concentrate on explaining the new features.
>
> In the code examples downloadable from the web site, however, we don't have these same space constraints, so the examples don't use `<xsl:import>` and will work in Mozilla, Netscape 6+, and IE 6 (except where otherwise noted, of course).

We created a stylesheet in example 3 in the previous chapter that transforms dinosaur XML into HTML – it was called `xml2html_3.xsl`. Make a copy of this file, and rename it `dinosaurs.xsl`. It doesn't need modifying in any way, and we'll use it to provide HTML layout for some other examples in this chapter.

Let's create our sorting stylesheet, `sorting_5.xsl`:

```
<xsl:stylesheet version="1.0" xmlns:xsl="http://www.w3.org/1999/XSL/Transform">

  <xsl:import href="dinosaurs.xsl" />

  <xsl:template match="dinosaurs">
    <html><head><title>Sorted dinosaurs</title></head><body>
    <h1>My big (sorted) list of dinosaurs</h1>

    <xsl:apply-templates>
      <xsl:sort select="@name" order="descending" />
    </xsl:apply-templates>

    </body></html>
  </xsl:template>

  <xsl:template match="discoverer">
    <li><b>Discoverer: </b><xsl:value-of select="text()" /></li>
  </xsl:template>

</xsl:stylesheet>
```

The first thing we do in this stylesheet is to import `dinosaurs.xsl`. As in example 4 in the previous chapter, all of the imported templates will be applied unless we have specified templates with a higher-priority match for any element in our source XML. In this case, `sorting_5.xsl` specifies a transformation template that matches the `<dinosaurs>` element, and so the lower-priority `<dinosaurs>` template match in the imported stylesheet is not used.

View `dinosaur_5.xml` in a web browser, and you will note that the dinosaurs have been ordered thus: *Tyrannosaurus Rex*, *Triceratops*, *Stegosaurus*, *Pterodactyl*, *Brontosaurus*:

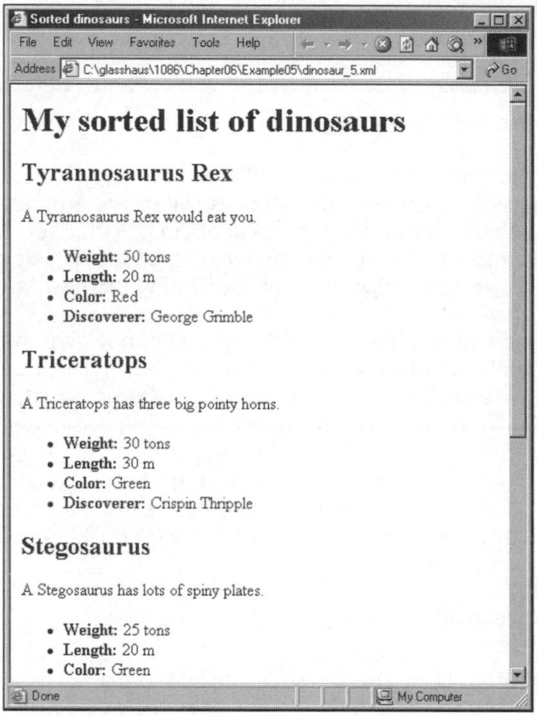

Our transformation has ordered the dinosaurs in descending alphabetical order based on their name. This ordering is performed by the line below:

```
<xsl:sort select="@name" order="descending" />
```

This tag orders the child elements of the `<dinosaurs>` tag – in this case, `<dinosaur>` elements – by their `name` attribute, in descending order. If we didn't specify a value for the `order` attribute, then the sort order would be ascending by default.

Let's look at an alternative sort process. Replace the `xsl:sort` line in `sorting_5.xsl` with the line below:

```
<xsl:sort select="discoverer/text()"/>
```

Reload `dinosaur_5.xml` in your browser, and the dinosaurs will be re-ordered, this time by the discoverer's first name – *Betty Welforth* is first, and *Primrose McFadden* is last. This time, our sort is based on the `text()` contents of the `<discoverer>` child element of the `<dinosaur>` elements –the discoverer's names.

We have chosen to define a template match for the `<discoverer>` element in `sorting_5.xsl`. As a result, the discoverer information is displayed in the browser in this example. We don't *need* to display the discoverer information for this sort to work; it just helps to show that the stylesheet is working as expected.

Sorting by first name is not very useful for library archive purposes – we'd ideally like to sort by the discoverer's surname instead. The alternative sort code below does exactly this:

```
      <xsl:sort select="substring-after(discoverer/text(), ' ')"/>
```

This sorting code correctly puts the *Stegosaurus* (*Charles Degramy*) first, and the *Pterodactyl* (*Betty Welforth*) last. It does this by sorting on everything after the first space in the text contents of the `<discoverer>` element. This has the limitation of relying on a "Forename Surname" layout for the discoverer's name – if middle names were included in the source XML, then the search would not work correctly. Similarly, if two discoverers had the same surname, this `xsl:sort` would not then take their first names into account.

It would be better to describe the discoverers' names in a more structured way, such as:

```
  <discoverer>
    <firstname>Primrose</firstname>
    <surname>McFadden</surname>
  </discoverer>
```

and then sort on the `<surname>` element, followed by a sort on the `<firstname>`:

```
  <xsl:sort select="discoverer/surname/text()"/>
  <xsl:sort select="discoverer/firstname/text()"/>
```

We do not, however, always have control over the format of the XML source to be sorted and styled.

Later in this chapter, we will look at other ways to work with substrings of element attributes and contents by using regular expressions within XSLT.

Example 6: Dynamic sorting with XSLT and JavaScript

Example 5 has one major failing – the sort criteria cannot be altered once the page is loaded. We'll now look at using some JavaScript to alter the sort conditions and trigger XSLT sorting once the page has loaded.

Why is this good?

- We can use a small amount of client-side scripting to alter the sort settings and re-perform the altered sort transformation.
- Because the transformation is client-side, re-sorting is much faster than a trip back to the server would be.

How else could we do it?

- If we have created custom JavaScript functions as described in the alternatives for example 5, these same functions could be reused to re-sort the array. As explained above, however, this requires considerably more code to traverse the XML DOM and perform the sort process.

- By using a server-side technology to parse and sort the XML server-side, as suggested for the previous example. This method does not, unfortunately, allow the sorted list to be re-sorted in the browser once the page has loaded.

The JavaScript required to do this is different for IE6 and Netscape 6+. Loading and transforming of stylesheets is handled using ActiveX objects in IE, whereas Netscape follows the DOM standard for loading stylesheets, and applies them using its own Transformiix XSLT processor. The code below is for IE6 only, but a version of this example with code for both browsers is available in the code download. In *Chapter 7*, we'll provide a JavaScript library that makes supporting both browsers simple.

For this example, we'll use a simplified layout stylesheet to make the sort process easier to see in action. Make a copy of `dinosaur_5.xml`, call it `dinosaur_6.xml`, and change the first line to reference a new stylesheet, `sortingjs_6.xsl`, based on the code below:

```
<xsl:stylesheet version="1.0" xmlns:xsl="http://www.w3.org/1999/XSL/Transform">

  <xsl:template match="dinosaurs">
    <div>
    <table>
    <thead><td>Name</td><td>Weight</td><td>Discoverer</td></thead>
    <tbody>
      <xsl:apply-templates>
        <xsl:sort select="@name" order="ascending" />
      </xsl:apply-templates>
    </tbody>
    </table>
    </div>
  </xsl:template>

  <xsl:template match="dinosaur">
    <tr>
      <td><xsl:value-of select="@name" /></td>
      <xsl:apply-templates/>
    </tr>
  </xsl:template>

  <xsl:template match="weight">
    <td><xsl:value-of select="text()" /></td>
  </xsl:template>

  <xsl:template match="discoverer">
    <td><xsl:value-of select="text()" /></td>
  </xsl:template>

  <xsl:template match="text()"></xsl:template>

</xsl:stylesheet>
```

In the stylesheet opposite, the `<dinosaurs>` template creates a simple table with appropriate column headers, and specifies a sort of the `<dinosaur>` child elements by name in ascending order. Each `<dinosaur>` is added as a row of the table, together with its `<weight>` and `<discoverer>`.

We now need some JavaScript to sort the table columns. Create a new file, `sortingjs_6.html`, with the following HTML and JavaScript:

```
<html>
<head>
<style>
  body { font-family: Verdana; }
  td { padding: 3px;  }
</style>
<script language="JavaScript">

var xmlfile = "dinosaur_6.xml";
var xslfile = "sortingjs_6.xsl";

function init() {
  xml = loadDocumentIE(xmlfile);
  xsl = loadDocumentIE(xslfile);
  doTransform();
}

function loadDocumentIE(filename) {
  var document = new ActiveXObject("MSXML.FreeThreadedDOMDocument");
  document.async = false;
  document.load(filename);
  return document;
}

function doTransform() {
  var xslTemplate = new ActiveXObject("MSXML2.XSLTemplate");
  xslTemplate.stylesheet = xsl;
  var processor = xslTemplate.createProcessor();
  processor.input = xml;
  processor.transform();
  document.getElementById("sortoutput").innerHTML = processor.output;
}

function orderBy(select, dataType) {
  xsl = loadDocumentIE(xslfile);
  var sortItem = xsl.getElementsByTagName("xsl:sort")[0];
  sortItem.setAttribute("select", select);
  sortItem.setAttribute("data-type", dataType);
  doTransform();
}

function orderByName() {
  orderBy("@name", "text");
}

function orderByWeight() {
  orderBy("weight/text()", "number");
}

function orderByDiscoverer() {
  orderBy("substring-after(discoverer/text(), ' ')", "text");
```

```
}

</script>
</head>
<body onLoad="init()">
<h1>Table of dinosaur information</h1>
<div id="sortoutput">Sort output goes here</div>
<form>
<input type="button" onClick="orderByName()" value="Order by name" />
<input type="button" onClick="orderByWeight()" value="Order by weight" />
<input type="button" onClick="orderByDiscoverer()" value="Order by discoverer" />
</form>
</body>
</html>
```

Load this HTML page into Internet Explorer 6, and you'll see some inviting buttons. Click on these buttons, and the dinosaurs will be sorted before your very eyes. But how?

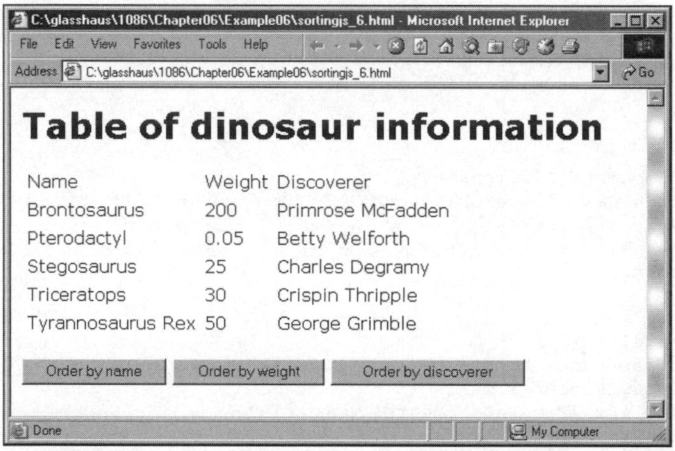

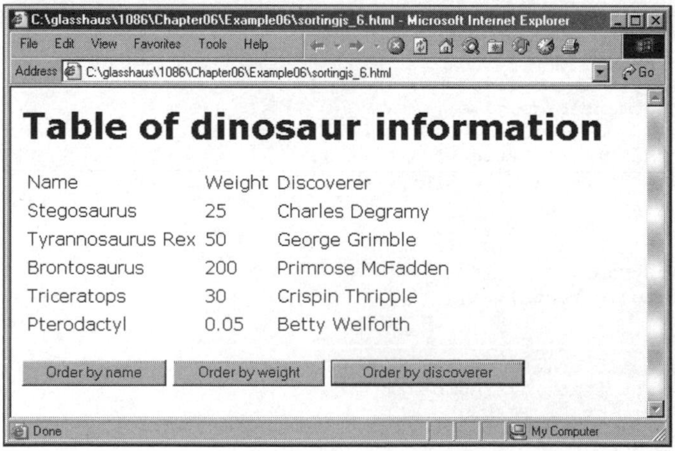

When this HTML page is loaded, the `body onLoad` event triggers the `init()` function to load the source XML file and the XSLT stylesheet, apply the stylesheet, and output the results into a `<div>` section on the page. Because we are not viewing the XML file directly in the browser, we need to load both of these files and bring them together ourselves. This is done by two functions: `loadDocumentIE()` and `doTransform()`.

The Internet Explorer mechanism for loading documents is to use an ActiveX object, as in the first line of `loadDocumentIE()`:

```
function loadDocumentIE(filename) {
  var document = new ActiveXObject("MSXML.FreeThreadedDOMDocument");
  document.async = false;
  document.load(filename);
  return document;
}
```

This function loads the file synchronously, that is, the function waits until the document has finished loading before it returns the document and processing continues. Otherwise, we would need to check that the document had finished loading before continuing.

Once both documents have loaded, `doTransform()` is called:

```
function doTransform() {
  var xslTemplate = new ActiveXObject("MSXML2.XSLTemplate");
  xslTemplate.stylesheet = xsl;
  var processor = xslTemplate.createProcessor();
  processor.input = xml;
  processor.transform();
  document.getElementById("sortoutput").innerHTML = processor.output;
}
```

This function also uses an ActiveX object, this time to create a new MSXML XSLT object (`MSXML2.XSLTemplate`). It assigns our loaded stylesheet to this XSLT object, creates an XSLT processor for the object, and passes the source XML file as input for the processor. Having done so, `doTransform()` tells the processor to perform transformations on the source XML document. Finally, the output of these transformations is displayed as the `innerHTML` contents of the `<div id="sortoutput">` tag further down the page. The output of this transformation is exactly what you would see if you viewed `dinosaur_6.xml` directly in a browser.

Note that `dinosaur_6.xml` doesn't actually need to contain an `xml-stylesheet` reference in this example, as `doTransform()` applies `sortingjs_6.xsl` to `dinosaur_6.xml` for us. We've left the stylesheet reference in the XML source file, however, as doing so makes it easier to debug the XML and XSLT files – you can always view `dinosaur_6.xml` in your browser and see how it will be styled, without needing the JavaScript functionality.

So far, we have just covered what happens when the page first loads. What about when we click on the buttons?

Each button has its own function to pass a sort criterion and a data type to the `orderBy()` function. `orderBy()` first reloads `sortingjs_6.xsl` – this is an unfortunate but necessary step due to the fact that IE makes the loaded stylesheet read-only once it has been used to apply a transformation. Reloading it makes it read/write again, so we can change its contents with JavaScript. Whether this involves another trip to the server, depends on whether or not the stylesheet is cached locally, which in turn will depend on the HTTP caching headers sent with the stylesheet.

Now we do a little manipulation of the DOM (the Document Object Model) of the stylesheet. We'll talk a lot more about this in the next chapter. It's essentially similar to using JavaScript to alter the objects in an HTML page but, instead of altering HTML, we're altering the elements in our XSLT stylesheet.

> This is a very powerful technique – it allows us to effectively alter the stylesheet on the fly and re-apply it.

We could potentially add whole new templates to the stylesheet like this, but we're just using it to alter the `sort` and `data-type` attributes of the existing `<xsl:sort>` element.

`orderBy()` uses a DOM method, `getElementsByTagName()`, to find all elements called `<xsl:sort>` within our XSLT document. We only want the first one, and so we append `[0]` to indicate this. Having found our `<xsl:sort>` element, we change its `select` attribute to match the sort criteria of the button we pressed. We also set the `data-type` of the sort to `text` or `number` as appropriate. Although a `data-type` attribute isn't specified in `sortingjs_6.xsl`, we can still set it from within our JavaScript. Having set the sort criteria, we call `doTransform()` to perform the altered transformation and update the page.

Note that when we order by weight, setting the `data-type` to `number` ensures that the weight column is ordered correctly based on the numeric value of the `<weight>` element's text contents, rather than performing an alphanumeric string sort.

There are a lot of additional features we could add to this example, and we do so in the example downloadable from the book's web site. Now, let's press on and look at another topic.

Example 7 – Extension Functions for Internet Explorer

The authors of the XSLT specification were painfully aware of the lessons of HTML. In particular, they had seen the early HTML standard fractured into competing dialects by the various browser vendors, as they added new and incompatible HTML tags to gain an advantage in the browser wars. To prevent this from happening again, they defined a standard way of extending XSLT with **extension functions** and **extension elements** that allows XSLT to overcome its limitations without breaking compatibility. In this section we explain how to create extension functions: we do not cover creating your own extension elements (and they are not supported by MSXML 3). Extension functions allow us to write our own functionality in languages outside XSLT, that are better suited to tasks like text manipulation and disk access. They are particularly useful for intranets, where you can rely on a company-standard browser.

Although most server-side processors support extension functions, only Internet Explorer supports client-side extension functions. So, the example below will only work in Internet Explorer and not the Mozilla-based browsers. We'll begin with an XSLT 1.0 example for IE 6, and then expand upon this example to show an alternative that also works in XSL-WD browsers. We've chosen to use JavaScript as the scripting language for the extension functions opposite, but we could have used VBScript.

In this example, we will create JavaScript extension functions to manipulate the text within the XML `<description>` element. We will match the dinosaur's name whenever it appears within the description, and highlight it in one of two ways. A real-world application of this is styling search results, where you will often want to highlight the search terms in the output. We are using JavaScript's regular expression support to match the dinosaur name case-insensitively, but we could use more complex regular expressions just as easily.

Although it would be possible to achieve the same results in XSLT, it would be more complicated since XSLT has no regular expression support. JavaScript's text manipulation is simple and powerful, and it is therefore a more appropriate language for the task.

Copy `dinosaur_6.xml` to `dinosaur_7.xml`, and change the first line to reference the following new file, `extensionfns_7.xsl`:

```
<xsl:stylesheet version="1.0" xmlns:xsl="http://www.w3.org/1999/XSL/Transform"
  xmlns:msxsl="urn:schemas-microsoft-com:xslt"
  xmlns:user="http://mycompany.com/mynamespace"
  extension-element-prefixes="msxsl">

  <xsl:import href="dinosaurs.xsl" />

  <msxsl:script language="JScript" implements-prefix="user">
    <![CDATA[
    function capitalizeMatchingText(fullText, name) {
      var reg = new RegExp(name, "gi");
      var splitList = fullText.split(reg);
      return splitList.join(name.toUpperCase());
    }

    function wrapMatchingText(fullText, name) {
      var reg = new RegExp(name, "gi");
      var splitList = fullText.split(reg);
      return splitList.join("<span class='dinosaurname'>"+name+"</span>");
    }
    ]]>
  </msxsl:script>

  <xsl:template match="dinosaur">
    <h2><xsl:value-of select="@name"/></h2>

    <xsl:value-of select="user:capitalizeMatchingText(
                          string(description/text()),string(@name))"/>

    <ul>
      <xsl:apply-templates/>
    </ul>
  </xsl:template>

  <xsl:template match="dinosaurs">
    <html>
```

```
    <head>
      <title>A simple HTML page</title>
      <style type="text/css">
        body { font-family: Verdana, Times, Serif; }
        .dinosaurname { color: red; }
      </style>
    </head>
    <body>
      <xsl:apply-templates />
    </body>
    </html>
  </xsl:template>

</xsl:stylesheet>
```

We'll explain how this works as we learn *More About Namespaces*.

> In Example 8, we will see how we could have avoided copying and pasting the `dinosaurs` template from `dinosaurs.xsl` by using a `named template`.

More About Namespaces

The first major change in this stylesheet is the inclusion of two new namespace declarations. We define the `msxsl` namespace to match the `urn:schemas-microsoft-com:xslt` URI. This URI is recognized by the XSLT processor in IE 6, and its presence tells the XSLT processor to make a number of extension elements available to us, including the `<msxsl:script>` extension element. We specify the `extension-element-prefixes="msxml"` attribute within `<xsl:stylesheet>`, as the `<msxsl:script>` extension element is within the `msxsl` namespace. We'll see in a moment how this element is used to define the two extension functions we will use for this example.

Rather than `msxsl:`, we could use any prefix if we wished (such as `cia:`), as long as we used it consistently and still referenced `urn:schemas-microsoft-com:xslt`. We use `msxsl:` because it is the convention for IE extension elements.

We now have `<msxsl:script>` available for our use. Note that this is a standard MSXML extension **element**, not an extension **function**. Within this extension element, we define two extension functions, `capitalizeMatchingText()` and `wrapMatchingText()`, using JavaScript. We'll define what these functions do in a moment. The `implements-prefix="user"` attribute of the `<msxsl:script>` element tells the processor that these newly defined extension functions will be prefixed by `user:` whenever we refer to them in our stylesheet.

Our second namespace declaration backs this up, defining a namespace URI for the `user:` namespace. There is nothing special about the URI for this namespace. By convention, this should be a URI referencing our company and might have a web page describing the functions available within the user namespace. Likewise, there is nothing special about the word "user" – we could use whatever we wanted to here, as long as it matches the `implements-prefix` attribute in our `<msxsl:script>` tag (see opposite), and the prefix we use when the functions are called.

Adding Extension Functions to Our Stylesheet

After importing our standard layout stylesheet (dinosaurs.xsl), we begin defining our extension functions. We do so within the <msxml:script> element mentioned above. This element has an implements-prefix attribute that specifies how these functions will be referenced in the rest of the stylesheet. Here, we've said that they will be prefixed with user:.

Our JavaScript extension functions are enclosed within a CDATA block because we are using "<" and ">" within the functions. The alternative would be escaping each one with < or >, but it is usually easier and clearer to use CDATA.

capitalizeMatchingText() is a JavaScript function that takes two text strings, and if the second appears in the first (ignoring case), replaces the second with a capitalized version of itself. For example, capitalizeMatchingText("xml is great","Xml") would return "XML is great".

wrapMatchingText() is a similar function, but rather than capitalizing, it wraps the matched text with a <span> tag. Thus, wrapMatchingText("xml is great","Xml") would return "<span class='dinosaurname'>xml</span> is great".

Although we've imported dinosaurs.xsl, we've overridden its <dinosaur> template with a new one, so we can add in calls to the newly defined functions. The key addition to our <dinosaur> template is the line shown below:

```
<xsl:value-of select="user:capitalizeMatchingText(
                    string(description/text()),string(@name))"/>
```

This line calls our new user:capitalizeMatchingText() function with two arguments: the description text, and the dinosaur name. The output of this function is passed back and added to the page by the xsl:value-of element.

Note that we use string() here to convert the text nodes (description/text() and @name) into plain text strings. Otherwise, we'd have to convert these nodes into a string in the capitalizeMatchingText() function instead.

Let's replace the line above with a call to our other new function:

```
<xsl:value-of disable-output-escaping="yes"
    select="user:wrapMatchingText(string(description/text()),string(@name))"/>
```

This line is very similar to the previous call, but this time, we set disable-output-escaping to "yes". This is because we are generating XML from the function – we are returning <span> elements – and if we did not disable output escaping, the < and > characters would be converted to < and > respectively, and we don't want this to happen.

This is one way to create new tags in the output, and although often the easiest, it should be used with caution. Chapter 7 will go into more detail about using the DOM to generate XML nodes, rather than simply creating them as text as we have done here. The advantage of a DOM approach is that the generated XML will be well-formed, as that approach adds elements to the DOM tree directly. The text-based approach used here would cause problems if we accidentally missed out a > character, for example.

Finally, the following screenshot shows what you should see:

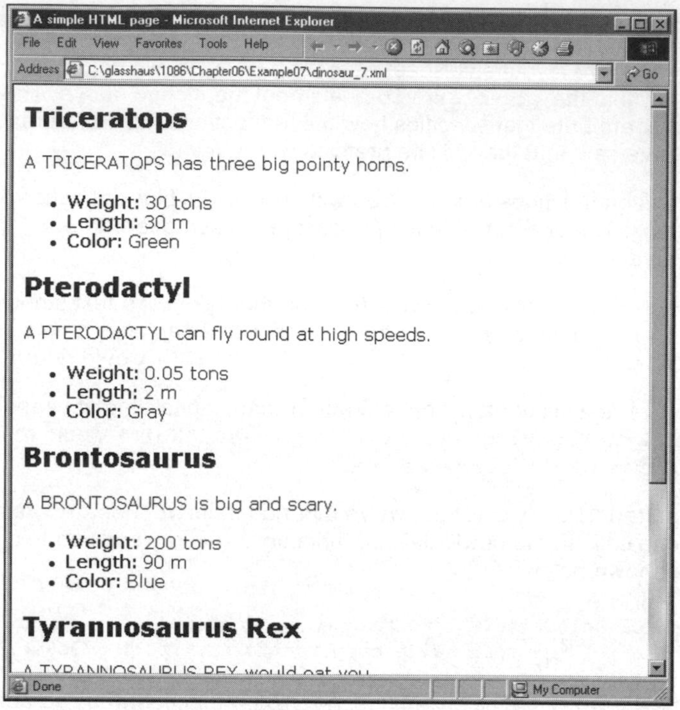

Fallback support for non-IE browsers

It would be convenient to use the same stylesheet for *all* XSLT 1.0 browsers, and provide an alternative output for those browsers that do not support extension functions. This can be done by using the `<xsl:choose>` element to check for the presence of our functions, and call different transformations accordingly.

Modify the `<dinosaur>` template as shown below:

```
<xsl:template match="dinosaur">
  <h2><xsl:value-of select="@name"/></h2>

  <xsl:choose>
    <xsl:when test="function-available('user:wrapMatchingText')">
      <xsl:value-of disable-output-escaping="yes"
       select="user:wrapMatchingText(string(description/text()),string(@name))"/>
    </xsl:when>

    <xsl:otherwise>
      <xsl:value-of select="description/text()"/>
    </xsl:otherwise>
  </xsl:choose>
```

```
    <ul>
      <xsl:apply-templates/>
    </ul>
  </xsl:template>
```

The `<xsl:choose>` block provides basic "if / else" functionality for our stylesheet. It first performs an XSLT `function-available` test for our `wrapMatchingText()` function, and if it exists, calls the function as before. If the function is not available (as it won't be when this is called in a non-IE browser), the stylesheet just outputs the text contents of the dinosaur's `<description>` element with no processing, as can be seen in the following screenshot:

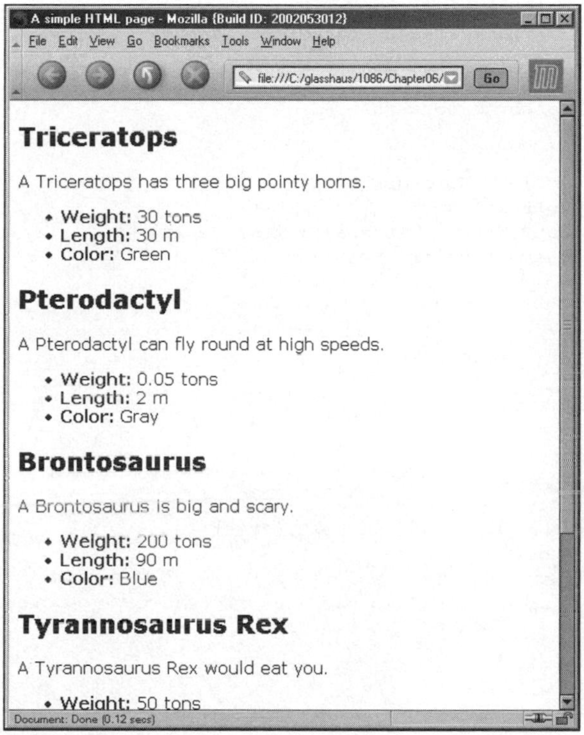

Extension Functions for XSL-WD

We need to take a slightly different approach if we want to use extension functions in XSL-WD browsers. Because IE 6 supports XSL-WD as well as XSLT 1.0 (depending on the namespace referenced in the stylesheet's `xsl:stylesheet` tag), the version below is supported by IE versions 5 and above.

For XSL-WD support, replace the contents of `extensionfns_7.xsl` with the following code:

```
<xsl:stylesheet version="1.0" xmlns:xsl="http://www.w3.org/TR/WD-xsl">

  <xsl:template match="/">
    <xsl:apply-templates />
  </xsl:template>
```

```
<xsl:template match="text()" />

<xsl:template match="weight">
  <li><b>Weight: </b><xsl:value-of select="text()" /> tons</li>
</xsl:template>

<xsl:template match="length">
  <li><b>Length: </b><xsl:value-of select="text()" /> m</li>
</xsl:template>

<xsl:template match="color">
  <li><b>Color: </b><xsl:value-of select="text()" /></li>
</xsl:template>

<xsl:template match="dinosaurs">
  <html>
  <head>
    <title>A simple HTML page</title>
    <style type="text/css">
      body { font-family: Verdana, Times, Serif; }
      .dinosaurname { color: red; }
    </style>
  </head>
  <body>
    <xsl:apply-templates />
  </body>
  </html>
</xsl:template>

<xsl:script language="JScript">
  <![CDATA[
  function wrapMatchingText(fullText, name) {
    var reg = new RegExp(name, "gi");
    var splitList = fullText.split(reg);
    return splitList.join("<span class='dinosaurname'>"+name+"</span>");
  }
  ]]>
</xsl:script>

<xsl:template match="dinosaur">
  <h2><xsl:value-of select="@name"/></h2>

  <xsl:eval no-entities="true">
    wrapMatchingText( this.selectSingleNode("description/text()").text,
                      this.selectSingleNode("@name").text )
  </xsl:eval>

  <ul>
    <xsl:apply-templates/>
  </ul>
</xsl:template>

</xsl:stylesheet>
```

There are several major differences between this and the previous IE 6 example. We cannot import stylesheets in XSL-WD, and so we have to add templates for `<weight>`, `<length>`, `<color>`, and `text()` into the stylesheet directly, as well as the standard match for `"/"` that XSL-WD requires.

We do not need to specify additional namespaces to identify our extension functions for XSL-WD. This is because XSL-WD doesn't use the mechanism for extending XSLT that we describe above. Instead, it has several Microsoft-specific extensions built in – the `<xsl:script>` and the `<xsl:eval>` tags, and any extension functions that we define go directly into the default namespace.

We've kept the revised `<dinosaurs>` template from the IE 6 version; it's been moved up the stylesheet slightly, to be near the other layout templates for ease of reading. The JavaScript function definitions have also stayed the same, but they appear in an `<xsl:script>` element, rather than the `<msxsl:script>` element from before. We only include the `wrapMatchingText` function this time (we could include the other function in the same way). Additionally, there's no need to specify an `implements-prefix` attribute for this element, as we are no longer using a separate namespace for our extension functions.

To call our extension functions, we simply place them inside an `<xsl:eval>` element. This element evaluates (runs) the functions, and knows to look inside `<xsl:script>` elements to find their definitions. It's very similar to defining JavaScript functions inside a `<script>` element in HTML – when you refer to the JavaScript functions elsewhere in your HTML, any functions that have been defined in a `<script>` block will be available to use.

The syntax used to pass XML content to the function calls is slightly different for XSL-WD, using (for example) `this.selectSingleNode("@name").text` rather than just `string(@name)`. The principles, however, are the same as before – it passes in the text value of the node rather than the node itself.

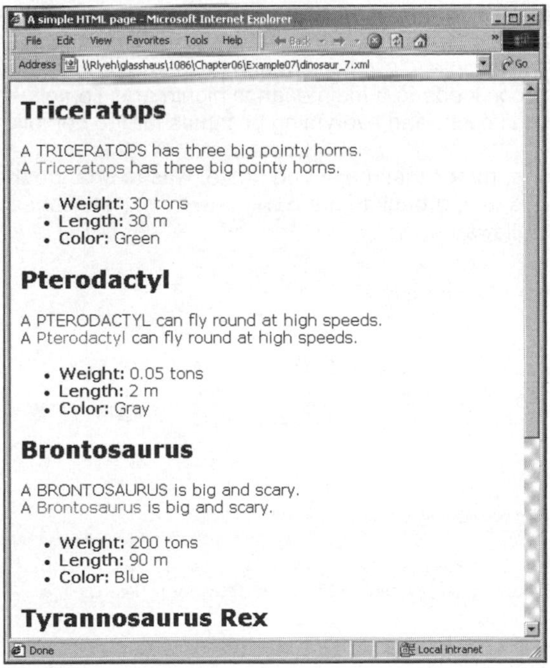

It doesn't make sense for us to provide any fallback functionality for non-IE browsers, since only IE 5+ supports XSL-WD anyway.

> **`xsl:script` – part of the XSLT standard or not?**
>
> `xsl:script` is a Microsoft extension to XSL-WD used by MSXML. It is not part of XSLT 1.0. It *is*, however, part of the forthcoming XSLT 1.1 standard. No current browsers support XSLT 1.1, and nor are they likely to for some time, so you can safely ignore the `xsl:script` tag unless you're targeting XSL-WD.

Example 8 – Reducing Code Duplication with Named Templates

In the previous example, we had to copy the whole "dinosaurs" template from our parent stylesheet `dinosaurs.xsl` just to add a single line of CSS. In this particular situation, we'd be better off referencing an external CSS file, but similar situations occur quite often in practice.

Typically, when you create a web site, you'll create a master XSLT file for the whole site, and then find that each site section requires a slightly different presentation. So, you make a stylesheet for each one that inherits from the master XSLT file.

Then, six months down the line, you have to add another section, with a different design again. This time, you realize that one of the templates in the master stylesheet isn't quite right. The temptation is to do what we've just done in example 7 – to just cut and paste the template from the master stylesheet, and edit it a bit – but this soon leads to a maintenance nightmare! Templates are duplicated all over the site, with small differences in each, and everything becomes far too complicated.

What we should have done, rather than copy and paste, was to change the master stylesheet to introduce a `named template`. Go back to the `dinosaurs.xsl` stylesheet, and change the `dinosaurs` template as follows:

```
<xsl:template match="dinosaurs">
  <html>
    <head>
      <title>A simple HTML page</title>
      <style type="text/css">
        <xsl:call-template name="css" />
      </style>
    </head>
    <body>
      <table style="border: solid thin black">
        <tr>
          <td><a href="mammoth.html">Visit the Mammoth zone!</a> - </td>
          <td><a href="play.html">Play Pteranodon Poker</a></td>
        </tr>
      </table>

      <h1>My big list of dinosaurs</h1>
```

```
        <xsl:apply-templates />

        <hr/>
        Copyright 2002 DinosaurOrg.
      </body>
    </html>
  </xsl:template>

  <xsl:template name="css">
    body { font-family: Verdana, Times, Serif; }
  </xsl:template>
```

We've added the line:

```
  <xsl:call-template name="css" />
```

and the template named `css` that it will call:

```
  <xsl:template name="css">
    body { font-family: Verdana, Times, Serif; }
  </xsl:template>
```

When the stylesheet processor reaches the `<xsl:call-template>` tag, it searches through the templates it knows about to find one with a matching name (if it doesn't find one, it will throw an error), and then acts on it. Even if the call is in a parent stylesheet, it will look at the templates in the current stylesheet first.

This makes it ideal for our purposes of reducing duplicated code. We can change the parent stylesheet as above, and all of the other stylesheets depending on it won't be broken. Then, we just add a new named template to our current stylesheet, with the content that we want to override. Thus:

```
  <xsl:template name="css">
    body { font-family: Verdana, Times, Serif; }
    .dinosaurname { color: red; }
  </xsl:template>
```

Unfortunately, with named templates there's no equivalent to `<xsl:apply-imports>`, so we can't just define the new "dinosaurname" rule and call the original template. This situation is still better than duplicating the whole `dinosaurs` template as we were doing before.

> `xsl:call-template` is one of the most powerful tools in XSLT. You can pass parameters into a template, and treat it very much like a JavaScript function with arguments. It can also be used in recursive functions that can perform complicated programming tasks.
>
> We don't go into any more details on named templates and the `xsl:call-template` here, but you can find more information on templates and XSLT programming in the *XSLT Programmer's Reference* (Wrox Press, Michael Kay, ISBN: 1861005-06-7).

Example 9 – Creating JavaScript with XSLT

So far, we've been using XSLT to create HTML layout code for our XML, and manipulating that XML in the process. In this example, we'll see how XSLT can be used to create non-HTML output – in this case, some JavaScript to request user interaction.

There are two main reasons for generating client-side JavaScript – to create dynamic behavior for the user based on XML content and, less commonly, as an alternative to extension functions to carry out some task that is difficult in pure XSLT. Here, we're doing the former.

You know the drill by now – we copy the `dinosaur.xml` file to `dinosaur_9.xml`, and it references a new stylesheet, `javascript_9.xsl`, making the following changes:

> Warning! The stylesheet below won't work as-is in Netscape or Mozilla. In a moment, we'll see why not and how to make it work.

```
<xsl:stylesheet version="1.0" xmlns:xsl="http://www.w3.org/1999/XSL/Transform">

  <xsl:param name="blank">--- Please select a dinosaur ---</xsl:param>

  <xsl:output indent="no" />

  <xsl:template match="dinosaurs">
    <html>
    <head>
    <title>Dinosaurs with JavaScript</title>
    <style>body { font-family: "Verdana", "Times", "sans-serif"; }</style>
    <script language="JavaScript">
      var dinosaursList = new Array();

      <xsl:apply-templates mode="js" />

      function displayDinosaur(name) {
        if (name!="<xsl:value-of select="$blank"/>") {
          var w = window.open("","dinosaurpopup",
                              "resizable,width=400,height=200");
          w.document.open();
          w.document.write(dinosaursList[name]);
          w.document.close();
        }
      }
    </script>
    </head>
    <body>
      <form>
        Select your dinosaur:
        <select onChange="displayDinosaur(this.options[selectedIndex].text)">
          <option><xsl:value-of select="$blank"/></option>
          <xsl:apply-templates />
        </select>
      </form>
```

```
      </body>
      </html>
    </xsl:template>

    <xsl:template match="dinosaur" mode="js">
      dinosaursList["<xsl:value-of select="@name"/>"]=
        '<xsl:apply-templates select="." mode="onelinehtml" />';
    </xsl:template>

    <xsl:template match="dinosaur" mode="onelinehtml">
      <img src="images/{@name}.jpg" align="right" width="160" height="120" />
      <h2><xsl:value-of select="@name" /></h2>
      <p><xsl:value-of select="normalize-space(description/text())"/><br />
      <xsl:text>(Copyright 2002 DinosaurOrg)</xsl:text>
      </p>
    </xsl:template>

    <xsl:template match="dinosaur">
      <option><xsl:value-of select="@name" /></option>
    </xsl:template>

  </xsl:stylesheet>
```

If you view `dinosaur_9.xml` in a browser and select a dinosaur from the list, a pop-up window will appear with details about the selected dinosaur (and an appropriate picture, if you have one). Let's study the stylesheet in more detail, and find out how the HTML and JavaScript are created.

About Parameters

We start our stylesheet with a new XSLT feature – a parameter. We have defined a parameter in this example to avoid duplicating code, as we need to use the same text (`--- Please select a dinosaur ---`) to generate an entry in an HTML select list, and to check for that entry in some JavaScript.

If we didn't use a parameter, then there would be a danger that subsequent XSLT authors might only edit one of the two instances of this text, rather than both, and the JavaScript check would break. So, we create a parameter called `blank`, and set it to be this text. We'll reference it again below.

Another reason for using parameters is that global parameters (that is, those defined at the top level of the stylesheet) can be set from outside the stylesheet, by the stylesheet processor. This is very easy in server-side XSLT, but in order to use this in client-side XSLT, we need to use JavaScript to launch the processor and set the parameters, which we'll talk about more in *Chapter 7*. The advantages of this are that it's possible to change the text produced by a stylesheet (and even its behavior) just by passing in parameters, without having to change a possibly complicated stylesheet.

White Space and Modes

The next line of the stylesheet, `<xsl:output indent="no" />`, helps us to remove excess whites pace. By default, a stylesheet's output will be indented according to the depth that elements are nested. Although this makes no difference to HTML output (as white space is largely ignored in HTML), surplus white space can cause problems when we output JavaScript code. The most common problem is newline characters in the middle of strings. Hence, we disable this by setting `indent="no"`.

We have not imported dinosaurs.xsl in this stylesheet, as we are generating predominantly JavaScript rather than HTML in this example. Instead, we have a new template for the <dinosaurs> element, and this template creates some JavaScript to set up a JavaScript array containing HTML descriptions of our dinosaurs.

Having created the dinosaursList array, we next have the line:

```
<xsl:apply-templates mode="js" />
```

This line will apply templates to all elements within the current <dinosaurs> tag as we have seen previously, but only if those templates have a matching mode specified – in this case, a mode of js. This stylesheet only contains one template that specifies a mode of js, and it defines a transformation for the <dinosaur> elements.

We generally use the mode attribute to apply several different templates to the same XML element in different circumstances. Here, for example, we're acting on the <dinosaur> element with the js mode to produce JavaScript. Later in the stylesheet, we use the onelinehtml mode to produce a single-line HTML version of the <dinosaur> element. We also have a <dinosaur> template with the default (unspecified) mode to produce a list of options.

There is no special significance to the name js, except that this name must match the mode in the template that we define below in order for that template to be applied. The js mode template adds an entry to the dinosaursList array for each <dinosaur>, with a key of the dinosaur's name. It then applies any onelinehtml mode templates (we only have one, again for <dinosaur>), creating a line of HTML about each dinosaur.

The Dinosaur onelinehtml Template

Let's have a closer look at the onelinehtml template:

```
<xsl:template match="dinosaur" mode="onelinehtml">
  <img src="images/{@name}.jpg" align="right" width="160" height="120" />
  <h2><xsl:value-of select="@name" /></h2>
  <p><xsl:value-of select="normalize-space(description/text())"/><br />
  <xsl:text>(Copyright 2002 DinosaurOrg)</xsl:text>
  </p>
</xsl:template>
```

We're using an abbreviated syntax to fill in the img src in the onelinehtml template. Inside an attribute, an expression within curly brackets is interpreted as an XPath. This is more concise and usually preferable to the <xsl:attribute> syntax we explained in *Chapter 5*, but it will only work in XSLT 1.0-compatible browsers.

Within the <p> tag, we're using the normalize-space function. This acts on a piece of text to strip leading and trailing white space characters, and converts multiple white space characters in the body to a single space. We need to do this because in our source XML document, there are new line characters between every line of the description. This isn't a problem when outputting HTML, but if we have new lines in the middle of a JavaScript string it will cause a JavaScript "unterminated string literal" error.

Another way of removing this white space would be simply to edit the dinosaur_9.xml source document, and put the whole description element on one line. This would work, but it makes the original document harder to maintain, and is best avoided.

The template ends with an <xsl:text> element wrapping our copyright text. This illustrates another source of white space problems in XSLT, and the way of dealing with it.

For XSLT stylesheets, the rule for white space is that white space appearing in between two elements with no text is ignored, but white space between an element and a piece of text is significant. So, the white space (spaces and linefeeds) between the </h2> and <p> tags in the following code:

```
<h2><xsl:value-of select="@name" /></h2>
  <p><xsl:value-of select="normalize-space(description/text())"/><br />
```

is ignored and is not passed through the transformed HTML. In the following code, however:

```
<p><xsl:value-of select="normalize-space(description/text())"/><br />
(Copyright 2002 DinosaurOrg)
```

the spaces and carriage return between the <br /> tag and the "(Copyright" text *are* significant, as they are between a tag and a piece of text.

We can use the <xsl:text> tag to wrap text in this kind of situation. The case above becomes:

```
<p><xsl:value-of select="normalize-space(description/text())"/><br />
<xsl:text>(Copyright 2002 DinosaurOrg)</xsl:text>
```

Because there are no spaces between tags and text, only between tags, there is no extra white space produced.

As a result of these measures, we can be sure that the HTML produced by our onelinehtml <dinosaur> template contains no carriage returns, and can be used in our JavaScript code without causing an error. We talk about white space again in the *Tips and Troubleshooting* section.

The result of the js and onelinehtml mode <dinosaur> templates is the following JavaScript (for example):

```
dinosaursList["Brontosaurus"] = '<img src="images/Brontosaurus.jpg" align=right
width="160" height="120" /><h2>Brontosaurus</h2><p>A Brontosaurus is big and
scary.<br />(Copyright 2002 DinosaurOrg)</p>';
```

Making it Work in Netscape and Mozilla

As we mentioned before, the stylesheet above won't work properly in Netscape or Mozilla. The reason is a subtle difference between the way that IE and Mozilla treat the output of XSLT. IE serializes its XML/XSLT output, and then re-parses it as HTML – but Mozilla/Netscape generates the HTML tree directly.

What does this mean for us? Well, in normal HTML, a `<script>` element isn't allowed to contain other elements, such as the `<img>` tags and the `<p>` tags that we're outputting from the `onelinehtml` template. This isn't a problem for IE, because it flattens the XSLT output to text, and then re-parses it as HTML. It is perfectly valid to have the text representing the `<img>` tag inside a `<script>`element, just not the tag itself.

For Mozilla/Netscape, though, it causes a problem. The `<img>` tag and the others are created directly as tags into the output – and so the `<script>`element will have tags inside it, which is not legal in HTML. These tags are silently ignored by Mozilla 1.0 and Netscape 6 and 7; so the `dinosaursList[]` array entry is created empty.

We avoid this problem by ensuring that we're not generating tags inside the `<script>` element – instead we generate the equivalent text. We do this by surrounding the tags in the template with `CDATA` sections so they are treated as text, not as tags. We also need to make sure that we're not wrapping any of the XSLT tags with `CDATA`, as they will not execute if we do.

The amended template looks like this:

```
<xsl:template match="dinosaur" mode="onelinehtml">
  <![CDATA[<img src="images/]]><xsl:value-of select="@name"/>
  <![CDATA[.jpg" align="right" width="160" height="120" /><h2>]]>
  <xsl:value-of select="@name" /><![CDATA[</h2><p>]]>
  <xsl:value-of select="normalize-space(description/text())"/>
  <![CDATA[<br />]]>
  <xsl:text>(Copyright 2002 DinosaurOrg)</xsl:text><![CDATA[</p>]]>
</xsl:template>
```

It's a lot harder to read than the original template, but it will work in both Mozilla/Netscape **and** Internet Explorer.

It can be hard to keep track of the distinction between elements and text representations of elements. On the whole, you don't need to worry too much about the difference, but if your stylesheet works fine in Internet Explorer and not in Mozilla/Netscape, then you could be encountering this problem.

Finishing Off the Page

Having added all of the dinosaurs to `dinosaursList`, we next define a JavaScript function, `displayDinosaur()`. This function features the first use of our blank parameter, and the first line of this function is transformed from:

```
if (name!="<xsl:value-of select="$blank"/>") {
```

to:

```
if (name!="--- Please select a dinosaur ---") {
```

After the JavaScript function, we output the rest of our HTML page – a select list using the blank parameter again, followed by a list of dinosaurs. The `<xsl:apply-templates />` line in this `<select>` element calls the default `<dinosaur>` template, as neither `<xsl:apply-templates />` nor the default template specify a mode (and therefore they match). The default `<dinosaur>` template outputs a suitable `<option>` element for the `<select>` form element. Our page is complete!

Now it is possible to select a dinosaur from the drop-down list on the web page that we've produced, and see it appear in a pop-up window using JavaScript:

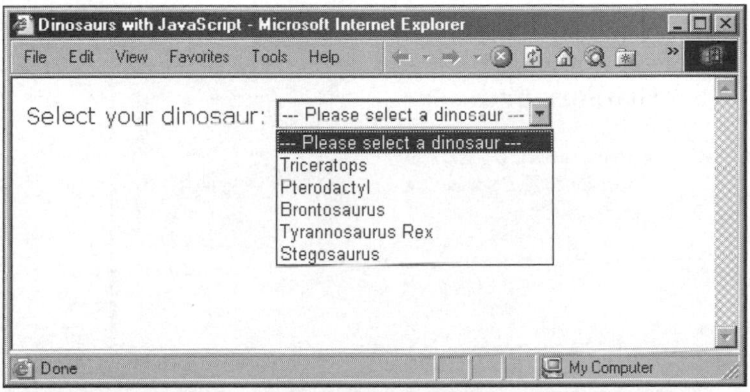

And with the necessary changes, it works in Mozilla as well:

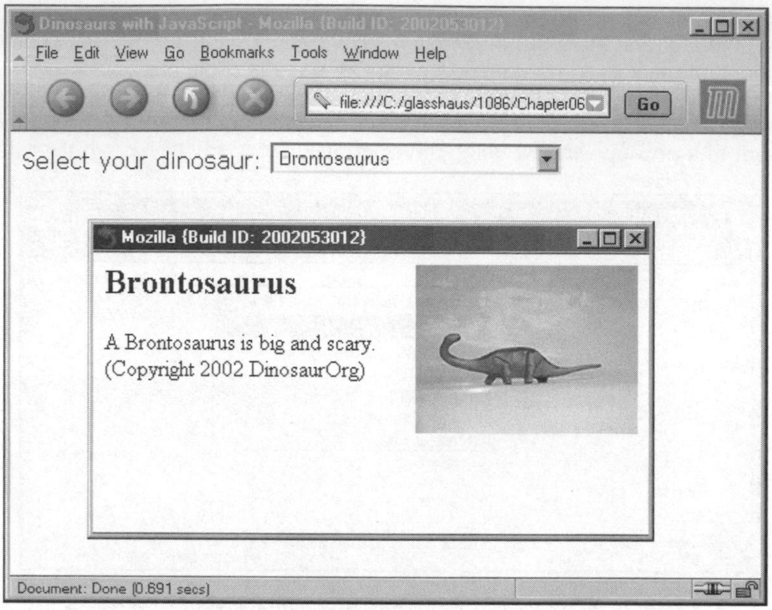

This is a fairly simple example of generated JavaScript, but it demonstrates what can be done, and shows how to overcome the problems that commonly occur. Another typical use of generated JavaScript from XSLT is to produce menus for a web site – XML is the ideal form for storing a hierarchical site map, and this can be used to produce both flat HTML navigation and dynamic JavaScript drop-down menus.

Tips and Troubleshooting

Dealing with White Space Problems

White space is one of the areas that traditionally cause most problems for new XSLT developers. As long as you're generating HTML it's not often a problem, but as soon as you're generating something like JavaScript, it is. This is particularly a problem on the server side, when generating formats such as CSV or RTF.

Usually, the problem is too much white space. This is from one of three sources:

- Output indentation
- White space in the XML source document
- White space in the stylesheet

We've already mentioned output indentation in Example 9. When using XSLT client-side, it's almost never useful to use output indentation, so get into the habit of adding.

```
<xsl:output indent="no"/>
```

to all of your stylesheets (this also has a benefit for server-side stylesheets. Because there's less white space included, the generated files are smaller).

White space in the source document can be dealt with using the `normalize-space()` function, as we've already seen in Example 9. This strips leading and trailing spaces, and compresses internal white space to a single space character. For example:

```
<xsl:value-of select="normalize-space(description/text())"/>
```

You can also use the top-level `<xsl:strip-space>` element that will strip out the white space-only nodes from the specified elements in the source document. Usually, this is a good thing, so it is often useful to add:

```
<xsl:strip-space elements="*" />
```

to your stylesheet. Its companion element, `<xsl:preserve-space>`, allows you to preserve white space that an overenthusiastic `<xsl:strip-space>` would otherwise remove. The important difference between `<xsl:strip-space>` and normalize-space is that `<xsl:strip-space>` will only act on nodes that are only white space, like "   ", not on nodes that are part text and part white space, like `"      text  "`.

Dealing with white space in the stylesheet requires an understanding of what happens when an XSLT processor generates output; it will remove all text nodes that contain only white space, unless they're within an `<xsl:text>` element. A useful technique is to use an empty `<xsl:text/>` element to split text with a mixture of white space and characters into two separate text nodes – for example:

```
<xsl:template match="dinosaur">    <xsl:text/>Name: <xsl:value-of select="@name"/>
</xsl:template>
```

If we didn't have the `<xsl:text/>` element, then there would be white space before the "`Name`" text, but instead we've split the "   `Name`:" text into two parts, one white space-only so ignored, and one with just the "`Name: `" text in.

If your problem is that white space you require is being stripped out, then you can force it to be kept by putting it inside an `<xsl:text>` element – for example:

```
<xsl:template match="/">
  <br/><xsl:text>
</xsl:text>
</xsl:template>
```

will force a new line after the `<br/>`. A slightly clearer way of doing this is to use the entity for a new line:

```
<xsl:text>&#10;</xsl:text>
```

You can read the full details of how XSLT deals with white space at *http://www.w3.org/TR/xslt#strip*.

Using HTML Entities in XSLT

In HTML, you'll be used to using entities such as é and   to represent certain characters. As explained in *Chapter 1*, however, the only entities that are defined in XML are < (<), > (>), & (&), " ("), and ' ('). This means that in XSLT you have to use the numeric form – where & represents &, for example.

One way of getting around this is to make a local copy of the standard XHTML entity declarations, and include that in your stylesheet. The syntax for that is:

```
<!DOCTYPE xsl-with-entities [
  <!ENTITY % HTMLlat1 SYSTEM "xhtml-lat1.ent">
  %HTMLlat1;
]>
```

This includes the standard XHTML latin-1 entities. Then, you can use them in your stylesheet with the normal syntax, for example À. This can be helpful if you have large chunks of existing HTML that you want to use in your XSLT with as little editing as possible.

The XHTML entity definitions are available from:

- *http://www.w3.org/TR/xhtml1/DTD/xhtml-lat1.ent* (latin-1)
- *http://www.w3.org/TR/xhtml1/DTD/xhtml-special.ent* (special characters)
- *http://www.w3.org/TR/xhtml1/DTD/xhtml-symbol.ent* (symbols definitions)

They are also included in the code examples for this book.

There is, however, a big problem with this approach – Netscape 6 and 7 and Mozilla 1.0 do not support external entities. It would be possible to define all of the entities within the stylesheet, but that would make each stylesheet prohibitively large. The best approach is to bite the bullet, and get used to the numeric values. The W3C XHTML entity files are at least a useful reference for this.

Using system-property('xsl:vendor') for Browser Checking

If you're used to programming JavaScript, you might be wondering how to do the XSLT equivalent of browser checking. In XSLT 1.0 browsers, you can use the "system-property" function:

```
<xsl:value-of select="system-property('xsl:vendor')"/>
```

Microsoft's browsers will return "Microsoft", whereas Mozilla and Netscape will return "Transformiix". There is unfortunately no way to do this in XSL-WD browsers.

This is a technique that should be used with great caution – it is almost always possible to write XSLT that works fine in both XSLT processors. We mention it because it can sometimes be useful to work around browser bugs.

My XSLT Works in Internet Explorer But Not in Netscape!

Both Internet Explorer 6, and Mozilla/Netscape, stick very closely to the XSLT 1.0 standard, but there are slight differences in interpretation. In general, Mozilla/Netscape is more accurate than Internet Explorer in its use of XSLT, but less forgiving of errors. A stylesheet that works in Mozilla/Netscape will almost invariably work in IE 6, but the reverse isn't always true.

If a stylesheet works coming from your local machine, but doesn't work in Mozilla/Netscape when you put it on a web site, then the most likely problem is that the web server is not using a "`text/xml`" mime-type for serving the XML and XSLT pages. You'll need to change the web server configuration appropriately. One way to test this is to use the *Browse Web* tool of the (free, but Windows only) *Sam Spade* application available from *http://www.samspade.org/*, and look at the Content-Type header that your page returns.

If no output appears from your stylesheet in Mozilla/Netscape even locally, then it may be that you're not generating what the browser considers to be valid HTML. In order to display HTML output, the minimum output required is:

```
<html><body>Some content</body></html>
```

If either the `<html>` or the `<body>` tag is present, but not both, then the text of the document will appear, but without any HTML markup. Without either, no text will appear.

The major source of difference between Internet Explorer and Mozilla/Netscape is the way they treat the output of XSLT. IE serializes its XML/XSLT output, and then re-parses it as HTML, but Mozilla/Netscape generates the XHTML tree directly.

We encountered this difference in Example 9. Internet Explorer allows us to generate elements inside the `<script>` element, because they are flattened to text and then re-parsed as HTML. Mozilla/Netscape, on the other hand, doesn't allow elements to be created inside the `<script>` element because that wouldn't be valid HTML, and requires that we create the text equivalent of the tags, rather than the tags themselves.

You can find more on Mozilla's XSLT support at *http://www.mozilla.org/projects/xslt/*. The differences between XML DOM support in Internet Explorer and Mozilla/Netscape will be covered in *Chapter 7*.

Build On What Others Have Done

EXSLT (*http://www.exslt.org/*) is a community initiative to provide extensions for XSLT, for example for dealing with dates, string manipulation, and mathematics. Some of them are written in pure XSLT (and so can be used in any XSLT 1.0-compatible client), some use MSXML extensions (so they can be used in IE), and some are only for use server-side.

An excellent document describing best practices in writing XSLT is *The Design of the DocBook XSL stylesheets* by Norman Walsh (*http://nwalsh.com/docs/articles/dbdesign/*). This describes the decisions he made while writing over 30 files of XSLT, containing 1000 templates, to create the stylesheets using for the DocBook technical writing XML standard.

When Your Only Tool Is a hammer, Everything Looks Like a Nail

Once you get interested in XSLT, and realize that it is a full programming language in its own right, it's very easy to get carried away and use it outside the areas at which it is best. This problem is exacerbated by most books about XSLT – they're generally only too happy to demonstrate its power by creating complex recursive templates, without asking whether it is the most appropriate technology for the task.

XSLT is at its best when transforming structured data. It's not so good for transforming the text within XML documents, and it's not good for doing calculations. There are other methods of doing these that are often simpler and more efficient.

CSS 2 is more powerful than most people give it credit for. For example, the "`text-transform`" property and the "`first-letter`" pseudo-attribute allow you to do simple text reformatting much more easily than the equivalent XSLT (and both are supported in the same browsers that support XSLT 1.0).

Don't ignore extension functions – they tie you to a specific XSLT processor, but that may not be an issue for you (especially in an intranet environment). If you can't use extension functions, you may still be able to generate client-side JavaScript code to perform calculations rather than doing it directly in the XSLT.

Also, don't neglect the role of the server. Although we've mostly talked about client-side XSLT as a replacement for doing styling on the server, server-side code has a part to play. In fact, one of the common approaches for client-side XSLT is that an XML data file is assembled by server-side code, perhaps from a database or other back-end system, and then sent down to the browser to be styled with client-side XSLT.

Summary

In this chapter, we have seen some of the more advanced features of browser-side XSLT in action. We have used XSLT to sort XML data, and dynamically changed the sorting criteria with JavaScript.

As well as looking at advanced XSLT, we have seen how to expand XSLT with extension functions in Internet Explorer to create custom transformations. As this is only possible in IE, we learned how to check for our functions' availability and perform alternative transformations for non-IE browsers.

Having expanded XSLT functionality, we saw how to reduce code duplication by using named templates to reuse code wherever possible. We saw how to use XSLT for more than just simple HTML generation by creating some custom JavaScript based on an XML source document.

Having passed on some useful tricks for XSLT development, we finished with an important piece of advice. XSLT is powerful, but should only be used where appropriate: when we require flexible manipulation and transform of structured data.

7

- Manipulating XML with the W3C XML DOM
- Browser support for the W3C XML DOM
- Manipulating XSLT using the DOM

Author: Chris Auld

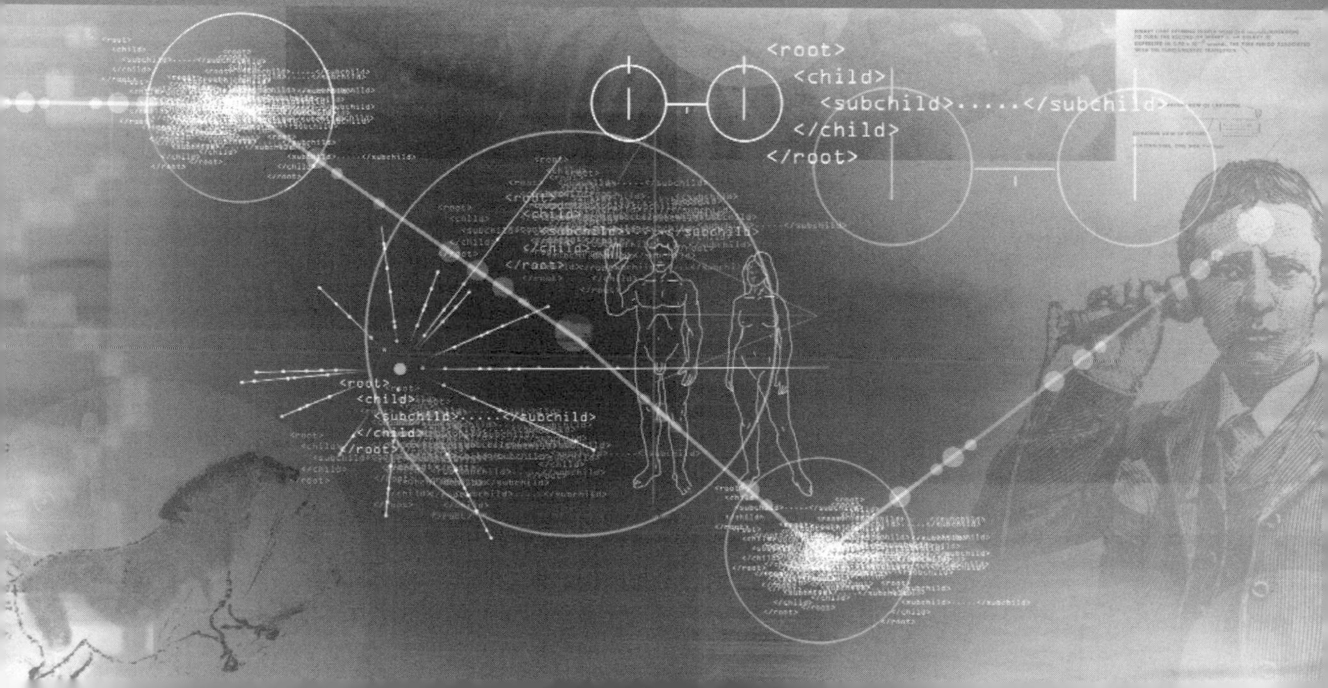

Scripting in the Browser

In the past three chapters we have looked at taking XML and rendering it into the browser using two different types of stylesheet technology. Now it is time for us to combine the knowledge that we have gained with some JavaScript to create some truly sophisticated client side dynamism using XML. This is the last of the three broad approaches to using XML that we looked at in *Chapter 3*.

In this chapter, we will take a closer look at the W3C XML Document Object Model (DOM), explaining how it can help us manipulate XML documents with ease. We'll examine some of the key DOM interfaces, before moving on to look at how Internet Explorer and Mozilla/Netscape handle the DOM.

Given the differences we'll see, we introduce a wrapper library, xDOM, for using the DOM with either browser. After we've explained how the key elements of this cross-browser XML enabler work, we'll look at using the DOM in code, through our xDOM library. We'll round off the chapter with a look at a real application of what we've seen so far.

XML in the browser gives a whole new toolbox of techniques to deal with data on the client side. We will be able to perform tasks that would have traditionally required one or more round trips back to the server for processing. By reducing the number of times we have to refresh the page from the server we will greatly increase the application's speed, as perceived by the end user.

We will be using Mozilla 1.0 and IE 6.0 for our examples. The examples will also work with earlier versions of IE, back to version 5, provided you have either MSXML 3 or 4 installed as some examples use XSLT and only these more recent versions support the current XSLT standard.

The W3C XML DOM

The W3C DOM (Document Object Model) has raised its head already several times in this book. In this chapter we will look at programming with the DOM using JavaScript in the two major browsers, Internet Explorer and Mozilla. The DOM is a standardized set of interfaces to access XML data. The DOM allows us to represent our XML document, which is really just a big long string of characters, in a more manageable form – namely a tree of objects. Once we have our XML in this form we can easily move around the tree, adding, editing, or removing bits of it as we go. The DOM interfaces can be implemented by vendors in their language or platform of choice so, in our script code, we can call the same methods on the Mozilla DOM or the MSXML DOM and get the same result.

> An interface is basically the contract that an object has with the outside world. Interfaces specify which methods or properties will be available on objects that implement those interfaces. The W3C DOM defines a set of interfaces for accessing XML programmatically. Vendors can write objects in their language or platform of choice that implement these interfaces. So for example, both the Mozilla DOM and MSXML implement the W3C DOM. They have been written by different teams of people at different companies, but they share a common set of properties and methods. This is because they both implement the same interfaces.

In both Mozilla and Internet Explorer the W3C DOM can be used in place of the browser's proprietary DOM for manipulating the HTML document loaded into the browser. *Chapter 3* looked at the relationship between the W3C DOM and the DHTML/HTML DOMs that you are probably familiar with.

The DOM represents an XML document as a tree of nodes. So, for example the following XML:

```
<?xml version="1.0"?>
<cities>
  <city state="CA">San Diego</city>
  <city state="WA">Seattle</city>
</cities>
```

can be represented in the following diagrammatic tree:

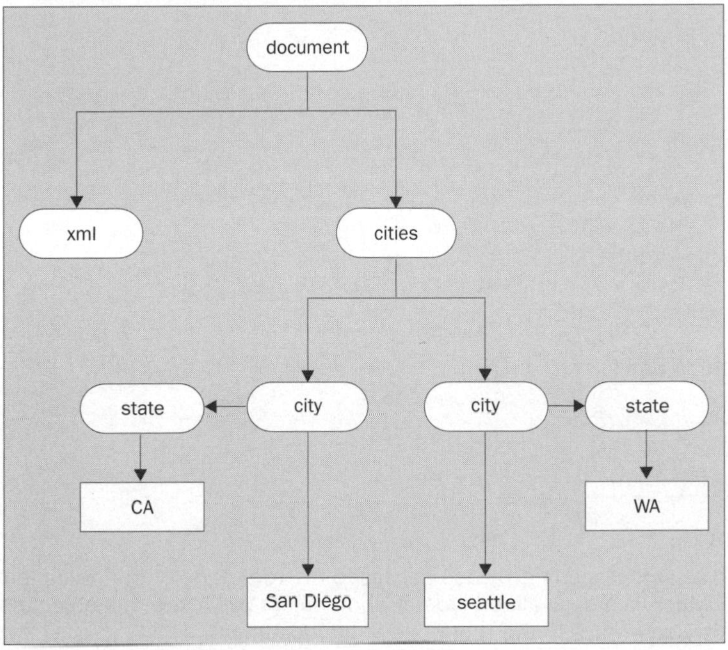

Key DOM Interfaces

This section will briefly touch on what each of the DOM objects is, and will also take a brief look at the most important properties and methods of each object. We will cover most of these in more detail when we actually look at using them in code later on in the chapter.

While the headings below strictly refer to the W3C-defined interfaces, I am going to refer to them as objects as that is how we will be thinking of them in our script code. The objects we'll be looking at are as follows:

- `Document`
- `Node`
- `NodeList`
- `NamedNodeMap`

Document

The `Document` is the parent for the rest of the object model – it represents the whole XML document as stored in memory. The `Document` object exposes the root element of the XML tree and also contains a number of factory methods. Factory methods are used to create new objects by making a method call – in the DOM we use factory methods to create new elements and attributes when adding data to the document in code. The `Document` is a bit like a gatekeeper in DOM programming; it is the one essential object that we will need whenever we are dealing with an XML document in the DOM. We will look at the following members of the `Document` interface:

- `documentElement`
- `load()`
- `loadXML()`
- `readystate`
- `onreadystatechange()`
- `getElementsByTagName()`
- `createElement()`
- `createTextNode()`
- `createAttribute()`

documentElement

The `documentElement` property provides access to the root node of the document. It returns an `Element` object, which is a specialized type of `Node` object (we'll see this object shortly), and that `Element` object is a reference to the root node of the document.

load(url)

This method loads XML from a specified URL. It is an MSXML-specific method, but we will see later on how to make the Mozilla `Document` object behave in this way also. The actual loading happens asynchronously – this means that when we call `load` the method returns immediately and then the parser loads the XML. As it is loading it will change the value of `readystate` and raise the `onreadystatechange` event. For example the following line of code uses the `load` method to load some XML from a file.

```
oXMLFromURL.load("cities.xml");
```

loadXML(xml)

This method is used to load raw XML data in a string into a `Document` object. Once again it is MSXML-specific but we will add this functionality to Mozilla later in the chapter. When called, it follows the same process as the load method in terms of asynchronously loading the XML into the `Document` object. This method is very useful where we may want to create some XML using string manipulation in JavaScript and then load it into a DOM. For example, the following line loads some very simple XML content into a DOM from a string literal.

```
oXMLFromString.loadXML('<?xml version="1.0"?><cities/>');
```

readyState

This read-only property indicates the state that the `Document` object is in as it loads XML. Once again it is an MSXML-specific property that we will add to Mozilla. We will look at how to load XML into the `Document` asynchronously a bit later on in the chapter. This property is crucial for us to know when our XML has actually completed loading. It can take the following constant values:

Constant	Value	Description
LOADING	1	The loading process has started and the data is being retrieved from the server.
LOADED	2	The data has been retrieved and now the parser is parsing the XML document; the object model is not yet available.
INTERACTIVE	3	Some data has been parsed, and the object model is available on the partial data set. The object model at this stage is read-only.
COMPLETED	4	The loading process has completed. Note that `readyState` will reach 4 whether the load was successful or not.

onreadystatechange

Another MSXML-specific member that we will add to Mozilla. This event is fired every time the `readyState` property changes.

getElementsByTagName(tagName)

This method returns a `NodeList`, which contains all those `Elements` in the document whose `nodeName` is equal to the `tagName` parameter. Note that this method will only return nodes of type `Element`. This means that for the following XML:

```
<parks>
  <park name="Yosemite" state="CA">
    <state>This park is in a state of nature.</state>
  </park>
</parks>
```

this method call will only return the `<state>` element and not the `state` attribute:

```
oParksDOM.getElementsByTagName('state');
```

createElement(tagName)

The `createElement()` method is a factory method used to create `Element` objects. There are a number of different create methods, all with a similar syntax. It is important to note that when we create a new element using this factory method it will not actually be visible as part of the DOM tree until we insert it, usually by using the `appendChild()` method of the `Node` object. So for example the following code uses the `createElement()` method to create a new element and then appends it to the `documentElement`:

```
oDocument.documentElement.appendChild(oDocument.createElement("my_element"));
```

The `createElement()` method creates an instance of the element for the specified `tagName`. The code above would create an `Element` `<my_element/>`, and append it to the root element of the document we're working with.

> When using any of these factory methods it is important to use the factory method on the DOM `Document` object that you intend to insert that node into. This is because when you create a node using a factory method it contains some references to the `Document` that created it.

createTextNode(value)

This factory method creates `Text` nodes that contain the value of the data parameter passed in. As we saw earlier in the chapter the actual value of an element or attribute is contained within a `Text` node inside that element or attribute. So, if we want to add some content to the element we created in the last code example it will look something like this:

```
oElement = oDocument.createElement("my_element");
oElement.appendChild(oDocument.createTextNode("my text content");
oDocument.documentElement.appendChild(oElement);
```

The result of this code would be XML that looks like this:

```
<my_element>my text content</my_element>
```

createAttribute(attrName)

This factory method is used to create `Attr` (`Attribute`) objects. In the same way that we saw with elements, the actual value of an attribute is stored in a text node within that attribute. We can use the same approach that we saw above, or we can take advantage of the `value` property, which allows us to directly set the value of the text node contained within that attribute. The following piece of code creates an attribute, gives it a value and inserts it into the attributes collection of an element by calling the `setNamedItem()`) method on a `NamedNodeMap` – we'll learn more about this method shortly.

```
oAttribute = oDocument.createAttribute("ID");
oAttribute.value = "the id";
oNamedNodeMap = oDocument.documentElement.attributes;
namedNodeMap.setNamedItem(oAttribute);
```

There are other factory methods for creating all of the different types of `Nodes` available in the DOM:

- `createCDATASection()`
- `createComment()`
- `createDocumentFragment()`
- `createEntityReference()`
- `createProcessingInstruction()`

We won't deal with these here, but they are described in the references for both MSXML and the Mozilla DOM.

> If you come from an IE development background you may be wondering why we need these factory methods. Why don't we just create them using `ActiveXObject()`?
>
> The reason is that by using these factory methods we can keep the actual creation of these objects platform-neutral. The only object that we should have to create directly is the `Document` object; we will deal with making the creation of this object cross-platform-compatible a bit later in the chapter.

Node

The `Node` is the fundamental building block of a DOM representation of XML data – the object that actually contains the items of data within an XML file.

The `Node` object comes in a variety of different types – they all share the common methods and properties of the `Node` object, even though some may not necessarily apply to that particular type of node. For example, some nodes may contain children while others may not – all nodes however have the `childNodes` property. The `Node` object has a very large number of properties and methods. We will cover the following main ones here:

- `attributes`
- `parentNode`
- `childNodes`
- `firstChild`
- `lastChild`
- `previousSibling`
- `nextSibling`
- `nodeName`
- `nodeType`
- `hasChildNodes()`
- `xml`
- `appendChild()`
- `removeChild()`
- `replaceChild()`
- `transformNode()`
- `transformNodeToObject()`

The following diagram shows most of the properties we will look at in diagrammatic form.

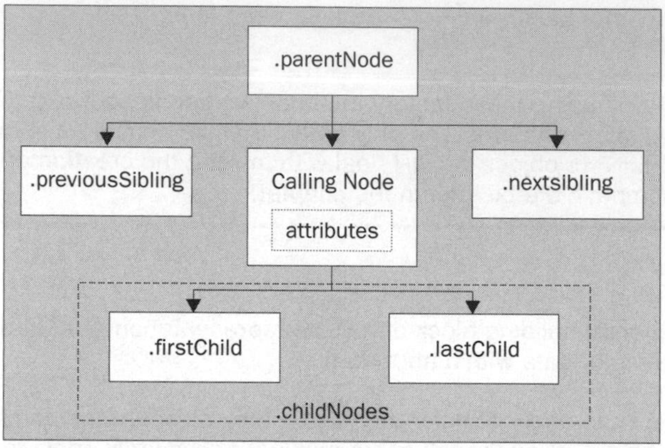

attributes

The `attributes` property returns a `NamedNodeList` (see below for details on this object) containing the attributes of a given node. This property is only applicable to `Node` types that can contain attributes, namely `Element`, `Entity`, and `Notation` – we will only deal with the first of those in this book.

parentNode

The `parentNode` property returns the parent node of the node that it is called on. Sometimes a node will not have a parent, for example if it has yet to be inserted into the tree – in this case, `parentNode` will return `Null`. In addition to this, some node types cannot have parents – namely, `Document`, `DocumentFragment`, and `Attribute`. This fact can be very useful if we want to climb up to the document object on the top of the tree from a node somewhere in the tree. We simply keep calling the `parentNode` property until it returns `Null`.

childNodes

The `childNodes` property returns a `NodeList` that contains all the children, that is the nodes one layer down in the tree, of a given element (the element for which it is the `childNodes` property). Once again only some element types can contain children. The following element types can contain children: `Attribute`, `Document`, `DocumentFragment`, `Element`, `Entity`, and `EntityReference`. The table later in this section gives a more complete rundown as to what child node types each of these elements may contain.

You may be a little surprised by the fact that the `Attribute` Node can contain other nodes. The reason for this is that the DOM treats the text content of an attribute as a child Node of the `Attribute` node. So for example the following XML:

```
<car wheels="4"/>
```

would look something like this in a DOM tree:

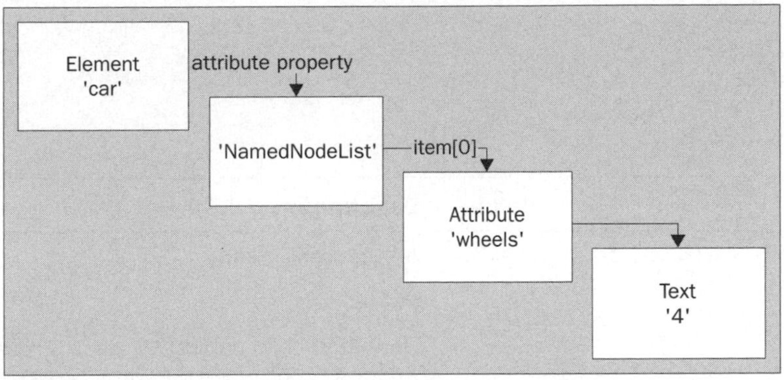

firstChild and lastChild

These two properties return the first and last nodes in the `childNodes NodeList` for the node that they are called from. As you will see below we can use `firstChild` and `nextSibling` to elegantly iterate through the `childNodes` collection.

previousSibling and nextSibling

These properties return the previous and next nodes in the document that are at the same level as the node that they are called from. Used in conjunction with the `firstChild` property these properties allow us to easily iterate through the `childNodes NodeList`.

```
for(var n = oDOMDocument.documentElement.firstChild; n != null; n = n.nextSibling){
  alert(n.nodeName)
}
```

nodeName

This property is read-only and returns the name of the node that it is called on. So for example if we had a `car` node:

```
<car wheels="4"/>
```

then the `nodeName` property would return "`car`".

nodeType

As we noted above, `Nodes` come in a number of different types, each with their own properties. Generally we shouldn't run into a situation where we don't know what type a given node is, but if we're not sure then this property will tell us. For example if we have a `NodeList` containing a variety of different node types and we want to handle each one differently, then we achieve this by looking at the `nodeType` of each node as we take it out of the `nodeList`.

Different parsers will support a different subset of node types; the following table lists those supported by most parsers with details as to which child nodes that node can contain and which nodes that node can be a child of. There are other node types though, take a look at the W3C Specification to see what they are: *http://www.w3.org/TR/1998/REC-DOM-Level-1-19981001/level-one-core.html#ID-1950641247*. The specification defines the different node types by using a series of named constants (the numbers in the brackets are the numeric value of each constant). For example:

```
//IDL as specified by W3C- Note this is NOT JavaScript.
interface Node {
  // NodeType
  const unsigned short       ELEMENT_NODE       = 1;
  }
```

Constant	Value	Description
NODE_ELEMENT	1	An Element node. <city/> Permitted child nodes: Element, Text, Comment, ProcessingInstruction, CDATASection, and EntityReference. Permitted to be a child of: Document, DocumentFragment, EntityReference, and Element nodes.
NODE_ATTRIBUTE	2	An attribute node. <city **state="WA"**/> Permitted child nodes: Text and EntityReference. Permitted to be a child of: None. An attribute is not the child of another node; the attributes of an element will not be returned in the childNodes NodeList, instead they are accessed through a node's attributes property.
NODE_TEXT	3	A text node. This node type represents the text content of another node. Permitted child nodes: None. Permitted to be a child of: Attribute, DocumentFragment, Element, and EntityReference nodes.
NODE_ENTITY_REFERENCE	5	An entity reference. & Permitted child nodes: Element, ProcessingInstruction, Comment, Text, CDATASection, and EntityReference. Permitted to be a child of: Attribute, DocumentFragment, Element, and EntityReference nodes.

Constant	Value	Description
NODE_PROCESSING _INSTRUCTION	7	A processing instruction. `<?xml-stylesheet type="text/xsl" href="a.xslt"?>` Permitted child nodes: None. Permitted to be a child of: Document, DocumentFragment, Element, and EntityReference nodes.
NODE_COMMENT (8)	8	A comment. `<!--This is a comment-->` Permitted child nodes: None. Permitted to be a child of: Document, DocumentFragment, Element, and EntityReference nodes.
NODE_DOCUMENT	9	The node type assigned to the Document object. Permitted child nodes: Element (maximum of one), ProcessingInstruction, Comment, and DocumentType. Permitted to be a child of: None.

hasChildNodes()

This method simply returns a Boolean, which indicates whether the calling node has any child nodes. This is very useful if we are recursively navigating our way down the tree. Another approach is to check if the length of the NodeList is 0 as shown below. Using hasChildNodes() is the better approach.

xml

This is not a W3C standard property, but it is so useful that it is worth mentioning here. This is a read-only property that returns the serialized contents of a node – that is the raw XML in text form. Microsoft added this property to their implementation of the Node interface. We will see later on in this chapter how to add it to the Mozilla implementation.

appendChild(newChild)

This method adds a new child to a node. We need to use one of the Node factory methods on the Document to create the child before we insert it. The inserted node will be appended to the end of the calling node's childNodes collection. So for example in the following code we create a new element node and add it as a child of the documentElement:

```
oNewNode = oDOMDocument.createElement("city");
oDOMDocument.documentElement.appendChild(oNewNode);
```

removeChild(oldChild)

The removeChild() method removes the node passed as a parameter from the calling node's childNodes collection, and then returns that removed node. So for example the following code removes the last node from the childNodes collection of oCallingNode:

```
oCallingNode = oDOMDocument.documentElement;
oOldNode = oCallingNode.removeNode(oCallingNode.lastChild);
```

replaceChild(newChild,oldChild)

This method replaces one of the calling node's children. It returns the old child in the same way as we saw with removeChild. So for example the following code creates a new node and then replaces the last child of the calling node with this new node:

```
oNewNode = objXMLDoc.createElement("city");
oRootNode = oDOMDocument.documentElement;
oOldNode = oRootNode.replaceChild(oRootNode.lastChild,oNewNode);
```

transformNode(styleSheet)

This is another MSXML-specific method. It is used for performing transformations on the calling node (using XSLT) and returns the result of the transformation as a string. The single parameter is a DOM Document containing an XSLT stylesheet. Once again we will take a look at adding this functionality to the Mozilla DOM later in the chapter. We will also look at how to use transformNode() to perform XSLT transformations from JavaScript within our web pages.

transformNodeToObject(styleSheet, OutputDOM)

This method is very similar to the previous one except that instead of returning the result as a string it fills the OutputDOM object with the result of the transformation. This is another MSXML-specific method that we will mimic in Mozilla.

NodeList

A NodeList provides support for accessing a set of nodes – as we saw above this will commonly be the set of nodes accessed using the childNodes property of another node. To access the nodes in a NodeList you will generally use the following members of the object:

- length
- item()

length

This is a read-only property that indicates the length of the NodeList, that is, the number of items (nodes) in the list.

item (index)

The item() method takes an index and returns the node at that index in the list.

Putting length and index together with a `for` loop we get something like the following:

```
for (var i=0; i < oDOMDocument.documentElement.childNodes.length; i++) {
  alert(oDOMDocument.documentElement.childNodes.item(i).nodeName);
}
```

This code iterates through the `childNodes` collection of the `documentElement` and pops up an alert box with the `nodeName` of each node in that collection. While maybe not as elegant as the example above that used `firstChild` and `nextSibling`, this is an effective way of iterating through a `NodeList`. This approach is most useful when you want to do something a little more complex than just iterate through each item. For example, if you wanted to get every second item in the `childNodes` collection, using this sort of loop would be much more effective than the one we saw earlier. All we would need to do is change `i++` to `i=i+2`.

Note that there is also a shorthand syntax for getting indexed access to the list of nodes – this involves treating the `NodeList` as if it were an array, as in the following code:

```
alert(oDOMDocument.documentElement.childNodes[i].nodeName);
```

> `NodeList` and `NamedNodeMap` (below) are live objects – that is, when you make changes to the list by, say, adding or removing nodes, those changes will be reflected immediately. You should therefore be very careful when adding or removing nodes to the list while inside a loop which is iterating through that list.
>
> For example suppose your loop has an exit condition that relies on reaching the end of the list, but while inside the loop you add more elements to the list. Your loop may never reach the termination condition because the length of the list keeps on changing.

NamedNodeMap

The `NamedNodeMap` is a slightly more advanced `Node` collection interface than the simple `NodeList`. `NamedNodeMap` allows access to nodes by their name as well as by their index. `NamedNodeMap` also provides for adding and deleting `Nodes` from the collection itself rather than having to reference another node.

`NamedNodeMap` is most commonly associated with a collection of attributes returned by the `attributes` member of a `Node`. A `NamedNodeMap` is also returned for a couple of other collections of `Nodes`, namely `entities` and `notations` members of the `DocumentType` interface – we will not discuss these here. We cannot use a `NamedNodeMap` with the `childNodes` collection, only a `NodeList`. `NamedNodeMap` has the same members as `NodeList` that we saw above; in addition it has the following key members:

- `getNamedItem()`
- `removeNamedItem()`
- `setNamedItem()`

getNamedItem(name)

This method takes a string, which is the name of the `Node` to be returned.

removeNamedItem(name)

This method takes a string, which is the name of the `Node` item to be removed. This method returns the `Node` that is removed.

setNamedItem(newNode)

This method takes a `Node` as a parameter and adds it to the end of the `NamedNodeMap`. Remember when you use this method that the `Node` that you are inserting must be of the right type – refer back to the `Node` type table earlier in the chapter if you are unsure about which nodes are allowed to go where in the tree.

Browser Support for the W3C DOM

In this section we will look at using script code (JavaScript to be precise) to work with data stored in a DOM representation on the client.

Compatibilities and Incompatibilities

Despite being ostensibly compatible, the two main implementations of the W3C DOM for client-side XML programming, MSXML and the Mozilla DOM, are still not completely compatible. These incompatibilities basically come down to the doctrine of 'embrace and extend' – this is where a developer implements a standard and then, just for good measure, adds a few of their own features. We have already seen some of the Microsoft-specific extensions to their implementation of the W3C DOM earlier in the chapter.

If we want to develop our client-side code to work on both IE and Mozilla, we really only have two options when it comes to these extensions:

- Avoid them at all costs.
- Write some sort of wrapper that will make the parser that doesn't support the extensions behave as though it does.

Given that some of the extensions (things like the `load()` method) are pretty essential to doing any useful development with XML on the client, the second option probably makes more sense. In the next section we will look at how we might put this approach into practice.

xDOM – Cross-platform XML Enabler

xDOM is a JavaScript library that I have included with this chapter that allows you to more easily write cross-browser code for client-side manipulation of the DOM.

Given that most of the differences between the two most common W3C DOM implementations (Mozilla and MSXML) are in the ancillary features, we should be able to wrap these features with some sort of platform-aware handler code to hide these differences from our day-to-day coding. The solution then (and didn't you just know I had one tucked up my sleeve?) is to use the `xDOM.js` (X Platform DOM) library that I have written and included with the code for this chapter. What this library allows us to do is write code that will work on both the Mozilla and MSXML DOM implementations. It provides a wrapper to several of the non-standard DOM features which are nevertheless essential to actually using the DOM from code. Specifically xDOM provides the following:

- A wrapper for the proprietary `load()` method implemented by both Mozilla and MSXML.
- An extension to Mozilla functionality to mimic the MSXML `loadXML()` method for loading a raw XML string.
- Extensions to Mozilla functionality to provide several events and properties related to these loading methods. Namely: `readyState`, `parseError`, and `onreadystatechange`.
- A wrapper for the Mozilla XSLT processor to allow it to be called in the same fashion as the MSXML XSLT processor is called.
- An extension to Mozilla functionality to allow the raw XML content of a DOM Node to be returned as a string. Again, this is to replicate the behavior of the `xml` property found in MSXML.

The following table summarizes the functions in `xDOM.js`:

Function Name	Description
`xDOM.createDOMDocument`	This is the main function in xDOM. We will be calling this function from our JavaScript code to create a DOM Document. The functions below should be treated as local to the xDOM library. They should not be called from code outside the xDOM library.
`_Moz_Document_loadXML(strXML)`	An implementation of `loadXML()` for the Mozilla DOM. We add a method to the Mozilla DOM to call this function.
`_Moz_Document_load(strURL)`	Replaces the Mozilla DOM `load()` method. We override the existing method on the Mozilla DOM to call this function.
`document_onload()`	A local event handler that we use to call `fireOnLoad()` when the document is loaded in Mozilla.
`fireOnLoad(oDOMDocument)`	Checks for a parser error, and changes the `readyState` if required.

Table continued on following page

Function Name	Description
`_Moz_node_transformNode(oStylesheetDOM )`	An implementation of the `transformNode()` method for the Mozilla DOM. We add a method to the Mozilla DOM to call this function.
`_Moz_node_transformNodeToObject (oStylesheetDOM,oOutputDOM)`	An implementation of the `transformNodeToObject()` method for the Mozilla DOM. We add a method to the Mozilla DOM to call this function.
`_Moz_Node_getXML()`	An implementation of the `xml` property for the Mozilla DOM. We add a property to the Mozilla DOM to call this function.
`updateReadyState(oDOMDocument, intReadyState)`	Changes the `readyState` property that we have added to the DOM and calls the `onreadystatechange()` event handler if there is one.

xDOM makes use of some fairly complex JavaScript functionality and if such things aren't quite your thing, then I suggest 'turning down the volume' for a few paragraphs as we go over it.

> The xDOM library uses the "Ultimate client-side JavaScript client sniff. Version 3.03" created by Netscape Communications. This is included in the code directory (as `browserDetect.js`) along with `xDOM.js`. As you will see later it is important to include both of these JavaScript files in order to make use of xDOM.

xDOM Walkthrough

For those of you who want to brave the details, this section will briefly walk through the `xDOM.js` file and describe what is happening at each point.

The first thing we do is declare some global variables that will be used by the various functions in the library. The only really important declaration to discuss here is this line:

```
var arrMSXMLProgIDs = ["MSXML4.DOMDocument", "MSXML3.DOMDocument",
                       "MSXML2.DOMDocument", "MSXML.DOMDocument",
                       "Microsoft.XmlDom"];
```

This creates an array of strings that contain the ProgIDs for creating the various versions of the MSXML `DOMDocument` object. We will use this later to determine which version of MSXML is installed on the machine.

Next we run some initialization code based on which browser the user is running.

Initialization – IE

For IE the initialization code consists of determining which version of MSXML the user has available on their machine by iterating through the array above:

```
//Internet Explorer initialization
if (is_ie) {
  var blnSuccess = false;

  //iterate through array of ProgIDs
  for (var i=0; i < arrMSXMLProgIDs.length && !blnSuccess; i++) {

    //Try to create the ActiveX Object at this index
    try {

      //If this fails we will leave the try and go to the catch
      var oDOMDocument = new ActiveXObject(arrMSXMLProgIDs[i]);

      //If we have not left the try then initialize the variables
      strMSXMLProgID = arrMSXMLProgIDs[i];

      //And set the success flag so that we stop looping
      blnSuccess = true

    } catch (oException) {
      //Do nothing. We just want to keep on looping.
      //We will check for a success further down.
    }
  }

  //Check there was success, set the failed flag and reason.
  if (!blnSuccess  ){
     blnFailed = true;
     strFailedReason = "No suitable MSXML library on machine."
  }
}
```

Initialization – Mozilla

The Mozilla initialization code is slightly more complicated. It makes use of a little known JavaScript feature called prototypes. **Prototypes** allow us to add methods or properties to objects at run-time – in this case we are adding methods that will mimic the way that MSXML behaves. Here are some of the prototypes that we add when we use xDOM. Note that `_Moz_Document_load` is a function that is declared a bit further down in the page:

```
//load() (Override)
//Keep the original method as we need to call it later
Document.prototype.__load__ = Document.prototype.load;

//...and add the overriding prototype
Document.prototype.load = _Moz_Document_load;
```

Here we are replacing the default load method in the Mozilla DOM with a new method, `_Moz_Document_load()`. We keep a reference to the default method by first assigning it to a prototype of a different name – we will need to call the original method from within our new method. If you are from an object oriented development background this is a bit like overriding a method and then calling that method on the super/parent class within the new method implementation.

```
Document.prototype.onreadystatechange = null;
```

With this prototype we are declaring a new event handler, and pointing it initially to a `null` value. Later, when we come to use xDOM in our own web pages we will be able to attach code to this event handler to be run when it is fired:

```
//xml (This is a read-only property so no need for a setter)
Node.prototype.__defineGetter__("xml", _Moz_Node_getXML);
```

This final prototype is a bit of a special case. It uses a slightly different syntax to allow us to declare a property Getter method. A Getter method looks like a simple property to the end user but is in fact implemented as a function. By declaring a Getter method but no Setter method we make the property read-only – this is appropriate in this case as the `xml()` method is going to give us the read-only raw XML contents of a node. The reason we are doing this is to mimic the `xml` property found in MSXML. We learned about the `xml` property earlier in this chapter when we discussed the `Node` interface.

xDOM.createDocument() Method

The `xDOM.createDOMDocument()` is the only method that we will call directly from our code. It is the method that actually creates the DOM `Document` object for us, and is fairly self-explanatory. It determines which browser is being used and creates a `DOMDocument` object using the appropriate method for that browser. The only special thing that we do is attach our own event handler to the Mozilla `load` event so that we can instead raise this event in the same way that IE would:

```
//Function to allow cross-browser creation of DOMDocument
xDOM.createDOMDocument = function() {

  var oOutDOMDocument = null;

  //determine if this is a standards-compliant browser like Mozilla
  if (is_gecko) {

    //create the DOM Document the standards way
    oOutDOMDocument = document.implementation.createDocument("", "", null);

    //add an event listener for the load event so that we can
    //handle it like IE does.
    //Parameters are the event type, the listener that we have declared
    //in the xDOM library, and useCapture which we set to false.
    //See the Mozilla Documentation for more on the addEventListener() method.
    oOutDOMDocument.addEventListener("load", document_onload, false);

  } else if (is_ie) {

    //create the DOM Document the IE way
    oOutDOMDocument = new ActiveXObject(strMSXMLProgID);

    //Enable MSXML preserveWhite space so that MSXML DOM behaves
    //like Mozilla with regard to white space nodes.
    oOutDOMDocument.preserveWhite space = true;

  }

  //return the object
  return oOutDOMDocument;
}
```

Private xDOM Library Functions

The last half of the library file consists of the implementations of the prototypes that we declared earlier. These are worth looking at if you want to know how Mozilla natively handles some of its more advanced XML features. The first method that we implement is the Mozilla version of the MSXML `loadXML()` method. This uses the `XMLParser` object that is included in the Mozilla `XMLExtras` library that ships with all Mozilla installations. We learned about the `XMLExtras` library in *Chapter 3*:

```
function _Moz_Document_loadXML(strXML) {

  //change the readystate of 'this' DOMDocument
  updateReadyState(this, 1);

  //create an XMLExtras DOMParser
  var oDOMParser = new DOMParser();

  //create new document from string
  var oDOM = oDOMParser.parseFromString(strXML, "text/xml");

  //Clear 'this' DOMDocument
    while (this.hasChildNodes())
      this.removeChild(this.lastChild);

        //Copy the nodes from the newly parsed DOMDocument to 'this' DOMDocument
        for (var i=0; i < oDOM.childNodes.length; i++) {

          //import the node
          var oImportNode = this.importNode(oDOM.childNodes[i], true);

          //append to 'this' DOMDocument
          this.appendChild(oImportNode);

        }

      //Fire the onload event manually
      fireOnLoad(this);
}
```

Note the section of this method where we copy the nodes from the newly parsed DOM. We will be looking at this sort of code in depth later in this chapter when we deal with iterating through the DOM objects in our own applications.

The `_Moz_Document_load` method is our override of the Mozilla load method. The reason that we have overridden the default method is so that we can include code for firing the MSXML equivalent events and also to support the `parseError` property:

```
//Note that load() method is still non-standard per the DOM spec
function _Moz_Document_load(strURL) {

  //Clear the parse error
  this.parseError = 0;

  //update the readyState  to Loading
```

```
    updateReadyState(this, 1);

    //Call original load method in a try catch block
    try {
      this.__load__(strURL);
    } catch (oException) {
      //set the parseError
      this.parseError = -1;
    }

    //change the readystate
    updateReadyState(this, 4);
  }
```

The `updateReadyState()` method is a little helper method declared in the xDOM library, which deals with the detail of setting the `readyState` property and firing the necessary events:

```
  //Function to change ready state and fire event handler if necessary
  function updateReadyState(oDOMDocument, intReadyState) {

    oDOMDocument.readyState = intReadyState;

  //Check that we have actually got an event handler before we raise the event

    if (oDOMDocument.onreadystatechange != null &&
                            typeof DOMDocument.onreadystatechange == "function")
      oDOMDocument.onreadystatechange();
  }
```

The two XSLT-oriented functions are very similar; the only difference being that one of them serializes the result to a string and the other simply returns the processed result as a `DOMDocument` object. These two functions allow the Mozilla `XSLTProcessor` object to be accessed in the same way that XSLT transformations can be performed in MSXML:

```
  function _Moz_node_transformNode(oStylesheetDOM) {

    //Create an XSLTProcessor Object
    var oXSLTProcessor = new XSLTProcessor();

    //Create a DOMDocument to receive output
    var oOutDOM = document.implementation.createDocument("","",null);

    //Perform the transform
    oXSLTProcessor.transformDocument( this, oStylesheetDOM, oOutDOM, null);

    //Return serialization of OutDOM
    return (new XMLSerializer()).serializeToString(oOutDOM);
  }
```

There are a few additional functions that we haven't covered in this brief walkthrough. The xDOM library is included with the sample code for this chapter. If you are feeling curious take a look through it to get a better idea of how it works.

> Given that the Mozilla implementation is more standards-compliant, you may be wondering why I decided to follow the approach of making Mozilla more like IE. My reasoning is based on the following:
>
> Firstly, because MSXML is a separate library from Internet Explorer it is not possible to use the JavaScript prototype mechanism to extend it.
>
> Secondly, love it or hate it, IE was the first out of the blocks with XML support. By replicating the behavior of IE we will more easily be able to use the large number of IE-specific examples available on the Internet in our own projects.

xDOM Caveats

There are a few important caveats to using xDOM.

The first is that we are unable to check the version of XSLT supported by the DOM `Document` we create. As you saw in *Chapter 4* there are some significant issues with running XSLT in different versions of MSXML. If you need to support these old browsers you may need to conditionally load a different XSLT document based on the version of MSXML installed. You can do this by looking at the `strMSXMLProgID` variable that is initialized when the xDOM library loads.

The xDOM library doesn't support creating the Free Threaded version of the MSXML DOM Document. This is not too much of an issue as the free threaded version is really only important when we are running code on the server-side. The 'Free Threaded' prefix indicates that the object makes use of a different threading model to interact with the operating system. This is very important when there is the potential for multiple requests to access the `DOMDocument` at the same time, as might occur in server-side applications. We will see the Free Threaded DOM Document in action in *Chapters 8* and *9*.

The xDOM does not provide a complete solution to the differences between MSXML and Mozilla. It is still going to be important to rigorously test your application in all the browser versions that you wish to target. xDOM was checked with IE 6.0 and Mozilla 1.0.

> The latest version of the xDOM library will always be available from the glasshaus web site.

Using the DOM in Code

In this section we will look at the basics of using the DOM in our code. We will do this by walking through the xDOM test harness page. This page, `test_harness.html`, contains a set of routines that show how to perform most of the simple XML-related tasks with the xDOM library. The following screen-shot shows the xDOM test harness loaded into a browser:

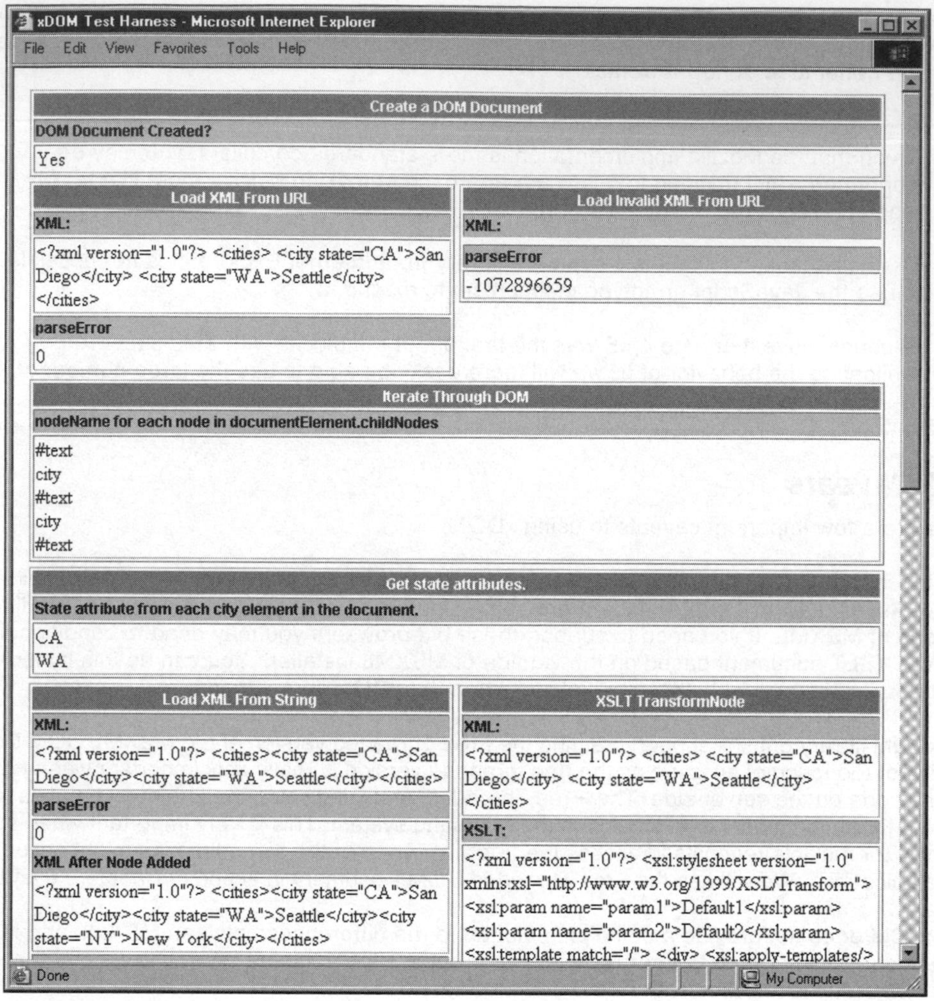

If you look at the headings in the test harness you will see the various tasks that we will be looking at:

- Creating a DOM Document
- Loading XML from a URL
- Checking that our XML is well-formed and has been loaded successfully
- Iterating through the DOM
- Iterating through elements
- Iterating through attributes

- Loading XML from a string variable.
- Adding nodes to the Document
- Removing and Replacing nodes in the Document
- Applying XSLT transformation
- Using parameters in XSLT transformations

> It is important that you remember that we are using the xDOM library to allow us to write cross-browser code. Apart from when we actually create the DOM `Document`, all of this code should work as standard with IE. In Mozilla on the other hand, the xDOM library manages several of the function calls. If you need to know how to actually do the tasks below natively in Mozilla, take a look at the xDOM library walkthrough earlier in this chapter.

Creating DOM Document Objects and Loading XML

Before we can do anything useful with our XML we need to get it out of the simple text format that it is stored in and into a useful object model – that object model is of course the W3C DOM.

Creating a DOMDocument Object

The first thing for us to do is to create a `DOMDocument` object:

```
function doCreateDOMDocument() {
  var oDOMDocument;
  var oElement;
  try {
    //Create a DOM Document
    oDOMDocument = xDOM.createDOMDocument();

    //Check that we have actually created a DOM Document object
    //by calling a method on it.
    oElement = oDOMDocument.createElement("city");
    document.getElementById("tdCreateDOMDocument").innerHTML = "Yes"
  } catch (oException) {
    document.getElementById("tdCreateDOMDocument").innerHTML = "No"
  }
}
```

The important line here is when we actually create the `DOMDocument` using the method that we have included in the xDOM library:

```
oDOMDocument = xDOM.createDOMDocument();
```

If we run this code, the value of `oDOMDocument` should be set to reference a new `DOMDocument` object. We can then check if the creation has been successful by calling a method on the `DOMDocument` object – for the moment don't worry about the specifics of this test as we will discuss the `createElement()` method a bit further on in this chapter. A successful result is indicated by the following in the browser:

Create a DOM Document
DOM Document Created?
Yes

Loading XML from a URL

Once we have created a `DOMDocument` object we load some XML into it from a URL:

```
function doLoadXMLFromURL() {
  oXMLFromURL = xDOM.createDOMDocument();

  //Bind an event handler to the onreadystatechange event
  //Event handler is defined below
  oXMLFromURL.onreadystatechange = onLoad_LoadXMLFromURL;

  //Call load. This will return immediately and then we just
  //wait for the event handler to deal with the document
  //after it is loaded.
  oXMLFromURL.load("cities.xml");
}

function onLoad_LoadXMLFromURL() {

  //Ignore the event unless the load has completed, with a readyState of 4
  if (oXMLFromURL.readyState == 4) {
    var strXML = doReplace(oXMLFromURL.xml);
    document.getElementById("tdXMLFromURLRawXML").innerHTML = strXML;
    document.getElementById("tdXMLFromURLParseError").innerHTML =
                                                oXMLFromURL.parseError;
  }
}
```

The important thing to notice with this piece of code is that the load is handled asynchronously. What this means is that the method call `load("cities.xml")` will return immediately but the XML File will actually be loaded in the background. In order for us to know when the XML document has finished loading we attach an `onreadystatechange` event handler to our `DOMDocument`.

The event handler is the second function in the code snippet above. The event will be raised every time the `readyState` property changes. We can't be sure that the document has been completely loaded until `readyState` is equal to `4` so we ignore any events raised to indicate that `readyState` has changed to something other than `4`. See the table in the *readyState* section for the possible values of `readyState`, note however that xDOM only guarantees that `readyState` will take a state of `1` or `4`. This is because Mozilla doesn't provide any information for states `2` and `3`.

Once the `readyState` has changed to `4` we are able to output the result to the browser. Note that the method call to `document.load()` returns immediately. This allows the browser to continue processing other JavaScript methods wile the XML loads in the background. The following diagram shows the flow of control when we perform an asynchronous load of an XML document:

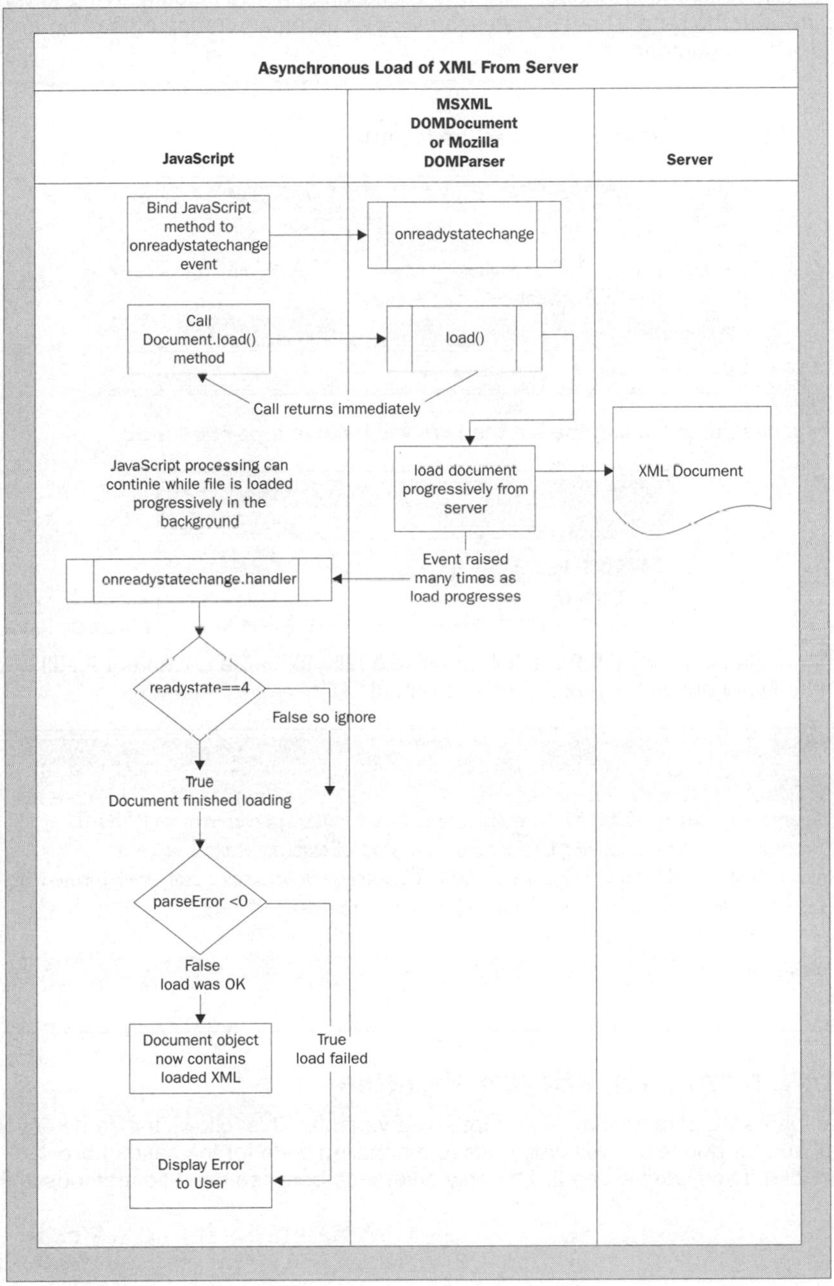

> Note that, even if we try and load an invalid XML file, the loading process will seem to complete successfully – that is, the parser will not throw an error and `readyState` will equal `4`. Because of this we need to check the `parseError` property of the `DOMDocument` to check that our load was successful prior to actually trying to do anything with the data. The test harness includes a demonstration of loading an invalid XML document.

If the file is loaded successfully we will see the following:

Load XML From URL
XML:
<?xml version="1.0"?> <cities> <city state="CA">San Diego</city> <city state="WA">Seattle</city> </cities>
parseError
0

If we are unsuccessful in loading the file then we will receive a `parseError`:

Load Invalid XML From URL
XML:
parseError
-1072896659

The error in Mozilla is slightly different. When Mozilla fails to load a document it still populates the contents of the DOM but with a `parseerror` element:

Load Invalid XML From URL
XML:
<parsererror xmlns="http://www.mozilla.org/newlayout/xml/parsererror.xml">XML Parsing Error: xml processing instruction not at start of external entity Location: file:///C:/My%20Documents/glasshaus/1086/Chapter_07/code/cities_not_well_formed.xml Line Number 1, Column 2:<sourcetext> <?xml version="1.0"?> -^</sourcetext></parsererror>
parseError
-1

Loading XML from a JavaScript Variable

We can also load XML data from a JavaScript string variable. This follows the same asynchronous load process that we saw above so I will omit the event handling code for the sake of brevity – take a look in the event handler if you want to see it. The only difference between the load methods is this line:

```
oXMLFromString.loadXML('<?xml version="1.0"?><cities><city state="CA">' +
                       'San Diego</city><city state="WA">Seattle</city></cities>');
```

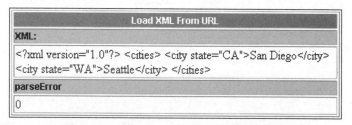

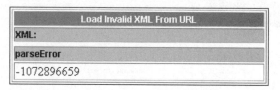

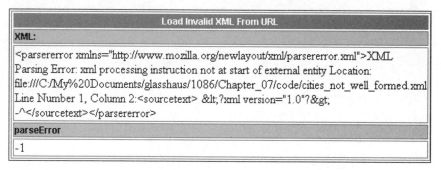

> One little gotcha here is making sure that you use different quotation marks for enclosing the XML attributes to those you use for enclosing the string. So for example here we have used double quotation marks in the XML and single quotation marks in the JavaScript – it is of course possible to escape the quotation marks instead, but it is a whole lot easier this way.

Getting Raw XML Out of the DOM

We will see how to manipulate and modify the XML data in the DOM a bit later in this chapter. One of the things that we are going to want to do at some point though is get the XML data back out of the DOM as a string. Surprisingly the W3C DOM Specification is silent on how to do this. MSXML provides a read-only property called `xml` on the `Node` interface, which will return the raw XML content of that node. This allows us to serialize all or part of the document – xDOM provides a Mozilla version of this property. There is no specific example for this property in the Test Harness, but it is used in almost all of the other test harness examples. Note that the `xml` property is on the `Node` interface and not the `Document` interface, but because the `Document` interface inherits the `Node` interface we can still access the `xml` property on our DOM Document object:

```
var strXML = oXMLFromString.xml;
```

So, in the code above we set the variable `strXML` to equal the serialized contents of the whole of the `oXMLFromString` `DOMDocument`.

Manipulating the DOM

In this section we will look at using code to move around a DOM Document and add to or edit its contents.

Basic DOM Traversal

We can iterate through the collections of the DOM in much the same way as we would most other data structures such as arrays:

```
function doIterationExample() {

  //Demonstrate iterating through the DOM by using a for loop.
  var strOutput;
  strOutput = "";

  for (var node=oXMLFromURL.documentElement.firstChild;
           node != null;
           node = node.nextSibling) {

    strOutput = strOutput + node.nodeName + "<br/>";
  }
  //Insert the result into the HTML DOM
  document.getElementById("tdIterateDOM").innerHTML = strOutput;
}
```

Note that the output contains a number of text nodes even though there is no obvious text in our XML document:

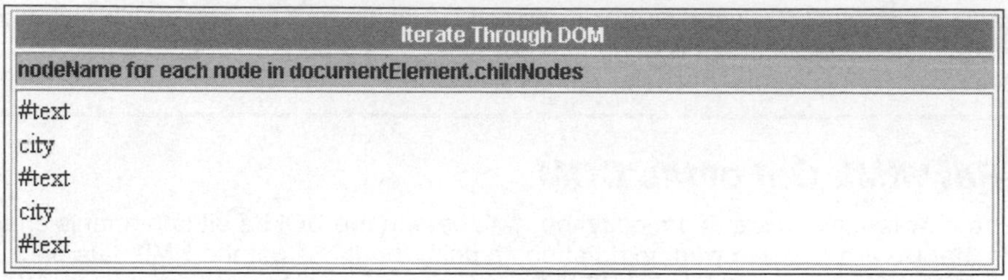

The reason for this is that the parser is sensitive to white space and treats this as text when it falls within an element. So in this case the tabs and carriage returns inside the `<cities>` element are treated as text nodes.

> Note that this is not the default behavior for the MSXML parser. We need to explicitly tell the parser to preserve the white space nodes when we create our ActiveX Object in the xDOM library:

```
//Enable MSXML preserveWhite space so that MSXML DOM behaves
//like Mozilla with regard to white space nodes
oOutDOMDocument.preserveWhite space = true;
```

> If we didn't set the parser to `preserveWhite space` then the DOM would behave differently between MSXML and Mozilla and we wouldn't be able to write cross-browser code.

Accessing Attributes

Because they can be accessed by name, attributes can be much easier to work with than nodes. Retrieving attributes is child's play. We can use code like this:

```
alert(oCityNode.attributes.getNamedItem("state").firstChild.nodeValue);
```

Note that we get the value out of the first child of the attribute node. This is the text node that contains the actual content of the attribute.

I have included an example of accessing attributes in the xDOM test harness:

```
function doGetAttributesExample() {

  //Iterate through the documents city elements.
  var strOutput;
  strOutput = "";
  var oNodeList;
```

```
    oNodeList = oXMLFromURL.documentElement.getElementsByTagName("city");

    for (var i=0; i < oNodeList.length; i++) {

      //Only try and get the attributes if we are dealing with a city node
      //Output the value of the attribute,
      //remembering that it will be in a text node within the attribute.
      strOutput = strOutput +
                  oNodeList[i].attributes.getNamedItem("state").value + "<br/>";
    }
    document.getElementById("tdAttributeDOM").innerHTML = strOutput;
  }
```

The result of this code is the following:

Get state attributes.
State attribute from each city element in the document.
CA WA

Adding Elements and Attributes

As we saw at the start of the chapter there are a number of methods for moving nodes around within the DOM. Let's take a look first at adding nodes to the DOM – there is an example of this in the xDOM test harness:

```
  //First create and add a new element
  var oElement= oXMLFromString.createElement("city");

  //Next create an attribute, set its value and add it to the attributes of oNewNode
  var oAttribute = oXMLFromString.createAttribute("state");
  oAttribute.value = "NY";
  oElement.attributes.setNamedItem(oAttribute);

  //Finally add a text node to the new city element and add it to the document
  oElement.appendChild(oXMLFromString.createTextNode("New York"));
  oXMLFromString.documentElement.appendChild(oElement);

  //Output to the HTML document
  strXML = doReplace(oXMLFromString.xml);
  document.getElementById("tdXMLFromStringNodeAdded").innerHTML = strXML
```

In this code we are adding a new `<city>` element to the XML that we saw being loaded from a string a bit earlier in the chapter. There are a number of steps in the process. First we need to create the new `<city>` element. Then we create a `state` attribute, set the attributes value to "`NY`" and then add the attribute to our new element. Finally we add a text node to our `<city>` element and add it to the `DOMDocument`.

If we take a look at the `xml` property of our `DOMDocument` after we have added the new element, you can see that indeed there is a new element, `<city state="NY">New York</city>`, at the end of the document:

XML After Node Added
<?xml version="1.0"?> <cities><city state="CA">San Diego</city><city state="WA">Seattle</city><city state="NY">New York</city></cities>

Deleting and Replacing Elements

Now let's manipulate the New York `<city>` element we created in the last example. To demonstrate removing and replacing nodes we will remove the New York `<city>` element and then use it to replace the San Diego `<city>` element.

```
//Now remove this node from the document and use it to replace the first city node
var oRootNode = oXMLFromString.documentElement
var oOldNode = oRootNode.removeChild(oRootNode.lastChild);
oRootNode.replaceChild(oOldNode,oRootNode.firstChild);

//Output to the HTML document
strXML = doReplace(oXMLFromString.xml);
document.getElementById("tdXMLFromStringNodeReplaced").innerHTML = strXML
```

We use the remove method to take the old node out of the document and place it into a temporary variable. We then use the replace method to replace the first `<city>` element, San Diego, with the `<city>` element that we just removed. Looking at the result in the browser, we can see that the San Diego `<city>` element has been replaced by the New York `<city>` element. Note also that the New York element has indeed been removed from its previous position at the end of the document.

XML After Node Removed and Replaced
<?xml version="1.0"?> <cities><city state="NY">New York</city><city state="WA">Seattle</city></cities>

XSLT Manipulation

As we saw in *Chapters 5* and *6*, XSLT is a great tool to use when we want to dynamically generate XHTML content from XML. Once again MSXML has led the way here with two methods, `transformNode()` and `transformNodeToObject()`, and so we have followed by implementing the same in xDOM. The functionality of these two methods is very similar, the only difference being the way they return their result – `transformNode()` returns the result as a string whereas `transformNodeToObject()` takes a `DOMDocument` object as a parameter and populates this before returning.

> The MSXML `transformNodeToObject()` method can also be used to send the results to an `IStream`. The `IStream` interface is a special interface used by many of the components in Microsoft component libraries to allow information to be streamed into another object easily and efficiently. Because it is Microsoft-specific this is not supported by the xDOM version, so you will need to steer clear of this feature if you want your code to remain cross-platform.

Applying Stylesheets to Documents

The test harness contains an example of using the `transformNode()` and `transformNodeToObject()` methods that we looked at earlier in the chapter:

```
function onLoad_XSLTDOM() {

  //Wait until XSLT has completed loading
  if (oXSLT.readyState == 4) {
  var strOutput;
  var oOutput = xDOM.createDOMDocument();

  //Transform node to string using XSLT
  strOutput = oXMLFromURL.transformNode(oXSLT);

  //Transform node to object using the same XSLT

  //Output the various properties into the HTML document
  oXMLFromURL.transformNodeToObject(oXSLT,oOutput);
  document.getElementById("tdTransformNodeXML").innerHTML =
                                              doReplace(oXMLFromURL.xml);;
  document.getElementById("tdTransformNodeXSLT").innerHTML = doReplace(oXSLT.xml);
  document.getElementById("tdTransformNodeResult").innerHTML = strOutput;
  document.getElementById("tdTransformNodeToObjectResult").innerHTML = oOutput.xml;
  }
}
```

Note that it is important that the variable we pass into `transformNodeToObject()` is in fact initialized. It is also important that if you want to use `transformNodeToObject()` your XSLT stylesheet must generate valid XML – the most common problem here is not having a single root node. Note that the example XSLT (`test.xslt`) uses a `<div>` tag to wrap the output of the transform.

We can see the result of our transform in the test harness:

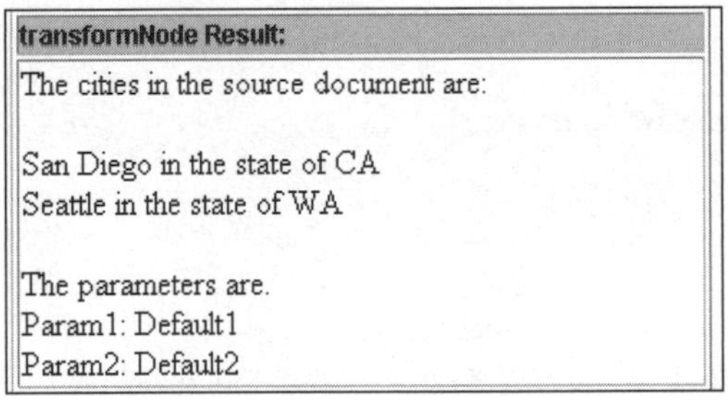

transformNode Result:
The cities in the source document are:
San Diego in the state of CA
Seattle in the state of WA
The parameters are.
Param1: Default1
Param2: Default2

> XSLT supports a special element called `output` which allows developers to set various options for the output of the resulting transformation. If you are working to create cross-browser XSLT for use in JavaScript you should be careful about how you use the element. Specifically, using `<output method="html"/>` may cause problems in Mozilla as the resulting output from Transformiix (the Mozilla parser) will contain an arbitrary namespace in the HTML elements it outputs, so you may end up with something like `<a0:br/>` for a line break element. This means that Mozilla will not display such HTML properly in the browser. It is best to simply leave the output method set to the default, which is XML.

MS Template and Processor Objects

MSXML includes two objects which can be used together to allow an XSLT stylesheet to be compiled and then used for several transformations. This functionality is most suited to a server-side environment where the same stylesheet will be run on each page request. These objects allow us to pre-compile the stylesheet to make it execute more efficiently. We won't cover these objects here but if you are interested in them take a look at the `IXSLProcessor` interface and the `IXSLTemplate` interface in the MSXML documentation. Another advantage of the MSXML `Processor` object is that it allows us to pass parameters into the stylesheet. Because it is not platform-independent we will not look at the feature here.

Cross Platform Workaround to Pass Parameters to Stylesheet

Parameterized stylesheets are very useful and it would be very nice if we could still use parameters in our cross-browser code. While there is no specific support for parameters in Mozilla there is a very simple cross-browser workaround – it also saves the overhead of creating `Template` and `Processor` objects when using MSXML alone.

The workaround relies on a single simple fact: XSLT is really just XML. Because of this, when we load the XSLT Stylesheet into a `DOMDocument` we can modify the parameters using the DOM prior to passing the stylesheet to the `transformNode()` methods. An example of this is included in the test harness:

```
//Set the parameters on the stylesheet and run it again
var arrParams = ["Example Set In Code 1", "Example Set In Code 2"];
var j = 0;

for (var i=0; i < oXSLT.documentElement.childNodes.length; i++) {
  if (oXSLT.documentElement.childNodes[i].nodeName == "xsl:param") {

    //Set value
     oXSLT.documentElement.childNodes[i].childNodes[0].nodeValue = arrParams[j];

    //Increment parameter counter j
    j++;
  }
}

strOutput = oXMLFromURL.transformNode(oXSLT);
document.getElementById("tdTransformNodeResultWithParams").innerHTML = strOutput;
```

Notice how we access and modify the parameter elements in our XSLT DOM Document. We iterate through the `childNode` collection of the `documentElement` and when we find a parameter element we replace it with a value from our array of parameter values.

You might ask why I didn't use `getElementByTagName()` here to select the parameter elements. I chose not to because the `<xsl:param>` element can also appear as the child of an `<xsl:template>` and we only want to set the value of those parameters that are children of the `<xsl:stylesheet>` element.

Looking at the resulting HTML in the test harness we can see that the parameters we have set in code are output in the resulting transform:

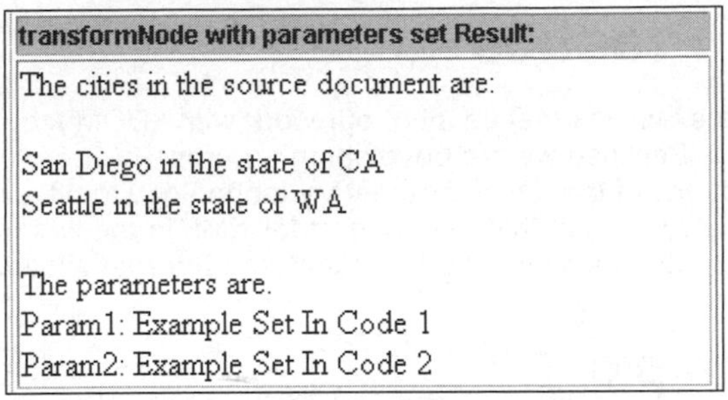

transformNode with parameters set Result:
The cities in the source document are:
San Diego in the state of CA
Seattle in the state of WA
The parameters are.
Param1: Example Set In Code 1
Param2: Example Set In Code 2

DOM Manipulation and XSLT Combined

> Note: At the time of publication there are some issues with Mozilla that prevent the `transformNode()` and `transformNodeToObject()` prototypes being bound to some `Node` objects in the tree. This means that the methods described in this section may not work in some versions of Mozilla. The current version of xDOM is always available from the glasshaus web site, and it will include any updates on this outstanding issue.

Because the `transformNode()` methods are declared on the `Node` interface we can combine the power of DOM iteration with XSLT by selecting a `Node` using the DOM and then applying the transform to just this `Node`:

```
//Now transform just part of the source tree.
strOutput = oXMLFromURL.getElementsByTagName("city")[1].transformNode(oXSLT);
document.getElementById("tdTransformNodePartOfTree").innerHTML = strOutput;
```

Observe how it has only applied the `match="city"` template to the Seattle node – this is because rather than calling the `transformNode()` method on the whole document, we called it on the second `<city>` node in the document. The transform was only applied to part of the XML tree – basically what we did was equivalent to applying the XSLT stylesheet to the following segment of the XML document:

```
<city state="WA">Seattle</city>
```

As a result the only template in our stylesheet that will match will be:

```
<xsl:template match="city">
  <xsl:value-of select="."/> in the state of <xsl:value-of select="./@state"/>
  <br/>
</xsl:template>
```

Putting it Into Practice

Let's take a look at some examples that tie all of our work with xDOM together into something that we might use in real systems. Because we are developing for cross-browser compatibility our examples cannot take advantage of any of the flashy proprietary technology in either browser. I think you will see from the examples below though that the support for XML in the two major browsers is now at a stage where we can really start using it in both intranet and Internet situations.

Real Estate Example

In the sample code that comes with this chapter is an example called `real_estate_demo.html`. This is a very simple demo – no frills or pretty pictures – but it does show many of the principles we have looked at in action. It also outlines my preferred approach to working with XML on the client-side. It places a fairly heavy emphasis on XSLT; the reason for this is that the XSLT implementations are very similar between the two browsers and therefore make it easy to get consistent cross-browser display. Trying to generate complex HTML using DOM manipulation alone is more work than it is worth. Generally, if you need to display much more than a couple of items of data plucked from an XML document, you should jump out to XSLT to build the desired HTML.

The demo application loads an XML document containing information about real estate properties. It then uses two XSLT stylesheets to dynamically display this data to the user. The first stylesheet is used to draw a link for each of the properties. Clicking the link calls a JavaScript function passing the `propertyid` of the property to be displayed. The display function then uses a parameterized XSLT stylesheet to draw the data and it is then inserted into the HTML document. The following diagram shows what is going on – it may look a bit daunting, but just start at the top right-hand corner and follow the arrows:

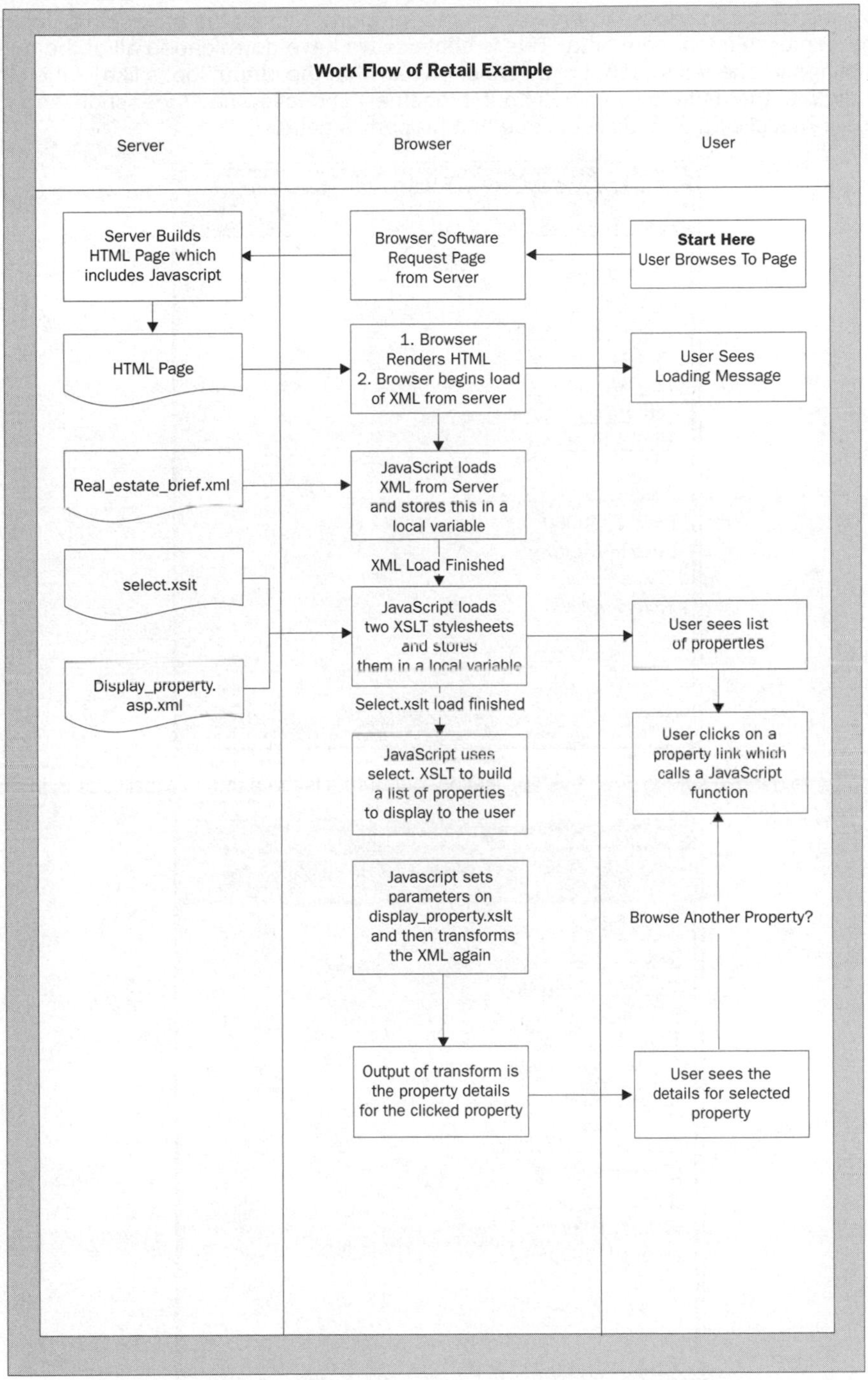
Work Flow of Retail Example
Server
Browser
User
Server Builds HTML Page which includes Javascript
Browser Software Request Page from Server
Start Here
User Browses To Page
HTML Page
1. Browser Renders HTML
2. Browser begins load of XML from server
User Sees Loading Message
Real_estate_brief.xml
JavaScript loads XML from Server and stores this in a local variable
XML Load Finished
select.xsit
Display_property.asp.xml
JavaScript loads two XSLT stylesheets and stores them in a local variable
User sees list of properties
Select.xslt load finished
JavaScript uses select. XSLT to build a list of properties to display to the user
User clicks on a property link which calls a JavaScript function
Javascript sets parameters on display_property.xslt and then transforms the XML again
Browse Another Property?
Output of transform is the property details for the clicked property
User sees the details for selected property

Notice how the user can choose to browse another property without the browser having to make a trip back to the server to fetch more data. This is because we have downloaded all of the relevant property listings in one fell swoop. Let's take a look at what the output looks like in the browser and then we'll dig into the code to see how to put it together. The following screenshots show the display after the user has click *5 Silly Street* to see that property's details:

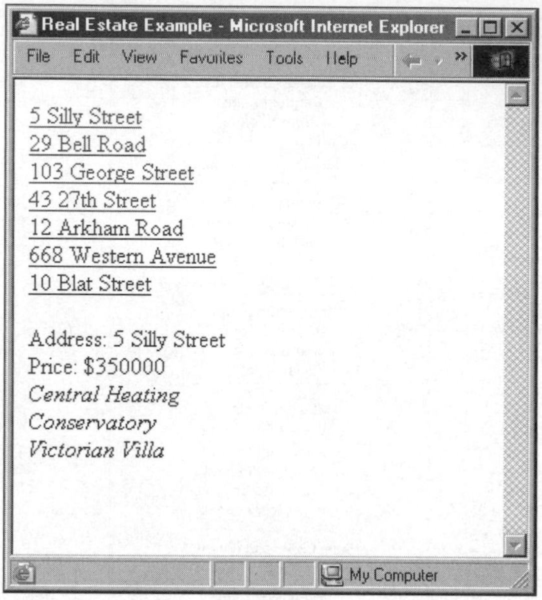

Because we have used xDOM to drive this application, our output is the same in Mozilla as in Internet Explorer:

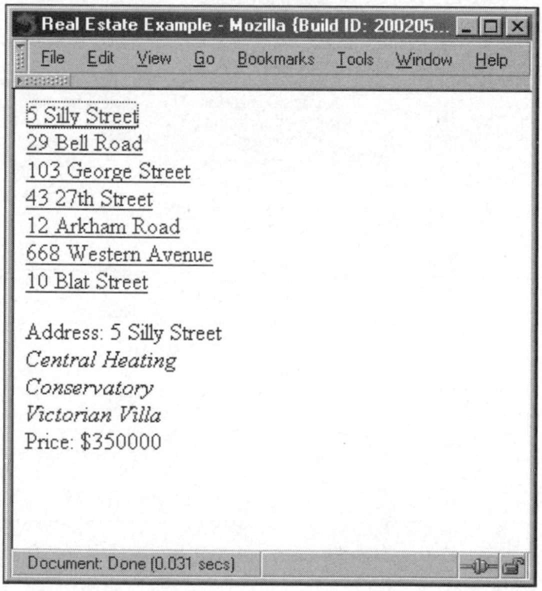

The source XML document, `real_estate.xml`, looks like this:

```
<root>
  <property property_id="9407001" seller_id="10000000" agent_id="A0001"
          address_line1="5 Silly Street" address_line2="Dunedin" address_line3=""
          suburb="Roslyn" name="Tara" type="101" zoning="R" age="35"
          floor_area="100.0" land_area=".05" construction="B" roofing="T"
          style="B" rooms="6" floors="1" govt_valuation="300000"
          asking_price="350000" date_on_market="1905-06-10T00:00:00"
          sold_flag="N">
    <property_feature feature_code="CENHT" property_id="9407/001">
      <feature feature_description="Central Heating"/>
    </property_feature>
    <property_feature feature_code="CONSV" property_id="9407/001">
      <feature feature_description="Conservatory"/>
    </property_feature>
    <property_feature feature_code="VVILL" property_id="9407/001">
      <feature feature_description="Victorian Villa"/>
    </property_feature>
  </property>
  <!--Some more property nodes omitted for clarity-->
</root>
```

In the demo application this XML is loaded from a file. It could just as easily be generated on the fly in something like ASP or PHP. The load procedure is exactly the same.

Let's walk through the stages in producing the output in the browser.

We kick everything off by using an `onload` handler in the page's `<body>` tag.

```
<body onLoad="runInit()">
```

This triggers a series of function calls and events that load the XML data, just as we saw it being loaded in the xDOM test harness:

```
function runInit() {

  //Check that xDOM has initialized properly
  if (blnFailed){
    alert(strFailedReason);
  }
  else {

    //Proceed with page
    doLoadXMLFromURL();
  }
}

function doLoadXMLFromURL() {
```

```
    oXMLFromURL = xDOM.createDOMDocument();
    oXMLFromURL.onreadystatechange = onLoad_LoadXMLFromURL;
    oXMLFromURL.load("real_estate.xml");
  }

  function onLoad_LoadXMLFromURL() {

    if (oXMLFromURL.readyState == 4) {

      //Load Initial XSLT Document to Build Drop-Down List
      oXSLT=xDOM.createDOMDocument();
      oXSLT.onreadystatechange = onLoad_XSLTDOM;
      oXSLT.load("select.xslt");

      //Load XSLT to Display Property in HTML
      oXSLTDisplay=xDOM.createDOMDocument();
      oXSLTDisplay.onreadystatechange = onLoad_XSLTDOM;
      oXSLTDisplay.load("display_property.xslt");
    }
  }
```

Note that we load two XSLT stylesheets into respective `DOMDocument` objects at this time.

The first stylesheet, `select.xslt`, is used to draw the links that drive the rest of the application:

```
<?xml version="1.0" encoding="UTF-8"?>
<xsl:stylesheet version="1.0" xmlns:xsl="http://www.w3.org/1999/XSL/Transform">
  <xsl:output method="html"/>
  <xsl:template match="/">
  <div>
    <xsl:apply-templates select="/root/property"/>
  </div>
  </xsl:template>
  <xsl:template match="property">
    <a href="javascript:showProperty({@property_id});">
      <xsl:value-of select="@address_line1"/>
    </a><br/>
  </xsl:template>
</xsl:stylesheet>
```

From your reading in *Chapters 5* and *6* you should be able to get the idea behind this stylesheet fairly quickly. The only gotcha might be the shorthand notation for `<xsl:value-of>` that I have used to insert the `property_id` attribute value into the `href` attribute on the link.

The second XSLT stylesheet is just as trivial. It is however parameterized and you will see the parameter being used in the stylesheet to select which property node we want to display. It does this by using a filter expression:

```
<?xml version="1.0" encoding="UTF-8"?>
<xsl:stylesheet version="1.0" xmlns:xsl="http://www.w3.org/1999/XSL/Transform">
  <xsl:output method="html"/>
  <xsl:param name="propertyid">0</xsl:param>
  <xsl:template match="/">
    <xsl:if test="$propertyid > 0">
      <xsl:apply-templates select="/root/property[@property_id=$propertyid]"/>
    </xsl:if>
  </xsl:template>
  <xsl:template match="property">
    Address: <xsl:value-of select="@address_line1"/><br/>
    Price: $<xsl:value-of select="@asking_price"/>
    <br/>
    <xsl:apply-templates select="./property_feature"/>
  </xsl:template>
  <xsl:template match="property_feature">
    <i><xsl:value-of select="./feature/@feature_description"/></i><br/>
  </xsl:template>
</xsl:stylesheet>
```

When the first stylesheet has been loaded by the following code, we use it to transform the source XML into the list of links. Note that this is a non-destructive process in that, after the transform is completed, we still have our original `DOMDocument` object containing the XML intact:

```
function onLoad_XSLTDOM() {
  var strOutput;
  var oOutput = xDOM.createDOMDocument();
  if (oXSLT.readyState == 4) {
    strOutput = oXMLFromURL.transformNode(oXSLT);
    document.getElementById("properties").innerHTML = strOutput;
  }
}
```

Because the XML data remains intact in the `DOMDocument` we can use it again when the user clicks one of the links. Effectively, we have cached the data in a client-side variable. When the user clicks one of the links it calls a function and passes the relevant `propertyid` to the function. This parameter is then subsequently passed into the parameterized stylesheet using the workaround method that we discussed earlier in the chapter:

```
function showProperty(intPropertyID){
  var strOutput;

  //Set the parameters on the stylesheet
  var arrParams = [intPropertyID];
  var j = 0;

  for (var i=0; i < oXSLTDisplay.documentElement.childNodes.length; i++) {
    if (oXSLTDisplay.documentElement.childNodes[i].nodeName == "xsl:param") {
```

```
            //Set value
            oXSLTDisplay.documentElement.childNodes[i].childNodes[0].nodeValue =
                                                                    arrParams[j];
            //Increment parameter counter j
            j++;
         }
      }

   //Run the stylesheet and output to the browser.
   strOutput = oXMLFromURL.transformNode(oXSLTDisplay);
   document.getElementById("displaydiv").innerHTML = strOutput;
   }
```

The result is then output to the `innerHTML` property of the appropriate `<div>` element.

> Remember that, when the user clicks the link, everything is happening client-side. The browser does not have to make a return trip to the server. This means that the whole process is lightning-fast.

You do have to be careful with this approach. Because we download all of the data to the client at the first instance, we run the risk of downloading a large amount of information that we may never actually need. The user may decide that they are happy with the first property they view and never bother to click on the other links. With a relatively small XML data set like the one we are using this is not too much of a problem but, as the amount of data increases, that upfront load time will be correspondingly longer. Not only this but, once it gets to the client-side, the user's machine will have to parse all of that XML data into a `DOMDocument` – this can potentially take quite some time, and quite a large amount of memory. In the next section we will look at how to deal with situations where we have too much data to download in a single hit.

Dealing with Large XML Documents

There may be times that the XML data for our application is too large to download in one hit. In fact in most cases it is not efficient to download all the data unless you know the user is going to view all the data. One option is to send an overview data set in XML to the client, and then load each specific item of data at run-time from the server. You are probably already used to taking a similar approach when developing web sites with dynamic server-side languages. The advantage of taking this approach with XML is that each trip to the server is for data only; we do not transfer a large amount of redundant user interface each time. The entire user interface remains cached on the client-side.

Let's take a look at modifying the real estate example from above to follow this approach. You can find the new version under the `real_estate_async` folder with the sample code for this chapter. We will use similar stylesheets and draw exactly the same page content, it's just that this time we will be getting the XML data from the server as and when it is required. Here is the diagram for the asynchronous version of the real estate example. Note how we don't load the detailed information for each property until that property is actually selected:

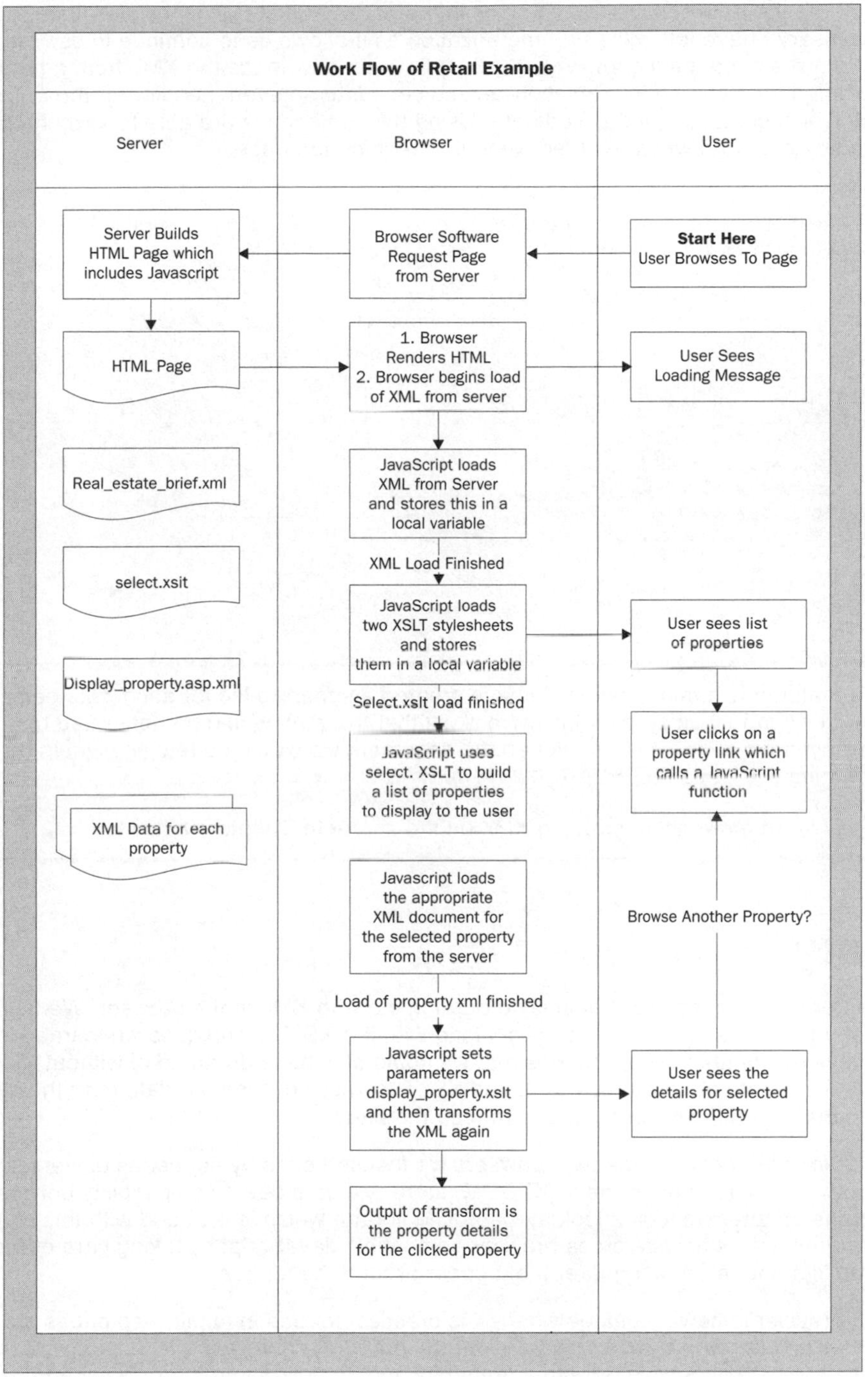
Work Flow of Retail Example
Server
Browser
User
Server Builds HTML Page which includes Javascript
Browser Software Request Page from Server
Start Here
User Browses To Page
HTML Page
1. Browser Renders HTML
2. Browser begins load of XML from server
User Sees Loading Message
Real_estate_brief.xml
JavaScript loads XML from Server and stores this in a local variable
XML Load Finished
select.xslt
JavaScript loads two XSLT stylesheets and stores them in a local variable
User sees list of properties
Display_property.asp.xml
Select.xslt load finished
JavaScript uses select. XSLT to build a list of properties to display to the user
User clicks on a property link which calls a JavaScript function
XML Data for each property
Javascript loads the appropriate XML document for the selected property from the server
Browse Another Property?
Load of property xml finished
Javascript sets parameters on display_property.xslt and then transforms the XML again
User sees the details for selected property
Output of transform is the property details for the clicked property

The core difference between the two versions in the `showProperty()` function. Although it's not strictly necessary I have left in the parameterization as it allows us to continue to use the same stylesheet. This is because the `showProperty()` function now loads the XML from a remote server. We have shifted the actual transformation-related code into an event handler for the `onLoad` of the XML DOM, which contains the detailed data. Using this method we are able to asynchronously load the required data as and when required without refreshing the page:

```
function showProperty(intPropertyID){
  oXMLDetailFromURL = xDOM.createDOMDocument();
  oXMLDetailFromURL.onreadystatechange = onLoad_XMLDetail;

  //Load the right stylesheet
  oXMLDetailFromURL.load("real_estate_" + intPropertyID + ".xml");
}

function onLoad_XMLDetail() {
  var strOutput;

  if (oXMLDetailFromURL.readyState == 4) {
    //Run the stylesheet and output to the browser.
    strOutput = oXMLDetailFromURL.transformNode(oXSLTDisplay);
    document.getElementById("displaydiv").innerHTML = strOutput;
  }

}
```

> Note that in this demonstration we have created a separate file for each XML detail item. In a production system it is more likely that the XML would be generated by using dynamic code on the server so the document we would be fetching would be something like `detailsxml.asp?id=9407003`.
>
> We will learn more about creating XML on the server in Chapters 8 to 11.

Summary

In this chapter we have looked at actually programming with XML in the browser. We have seen how to use existing HTML and JavaScript skills, along with the XSLT techniques we learned in *Chapters 5 and 6*, to develop client-side applications that we could only have dreamed of without XML. Specifically we looked at how to use XML and XSLT to easily get remote data from the server and display it in the browser without having to refresh the page.

The support for XML between the two browsers we focused on is by no means universal yet but, because both browsers support the W3C DOM, there is a core set of compatibility between them. Early on in the chapter we took a look at the xDOM library, which is included with this chapter. The xDOM library allows us to write cross-browser-compatible JavaScript by taking care of the differences between Mozilla and Internet Explorer that appear around the fringes.

XML in the browser is now at a stage where it is practical for use in public web pages as well as on the intranet. Provided we as developers are careful not to run before the technology can walk when dealing with XML, it will provide us with a great new tool to build more interactivity and bandwidth efficiency into our browser-based applications.

8

- A comparison of the XML support available from ASP, PHP, and JSP
- Basic server-side XML techniques (CD library application)

Author: Oli Gauti Gudmundsson with Alex Shiell and Allan Kent

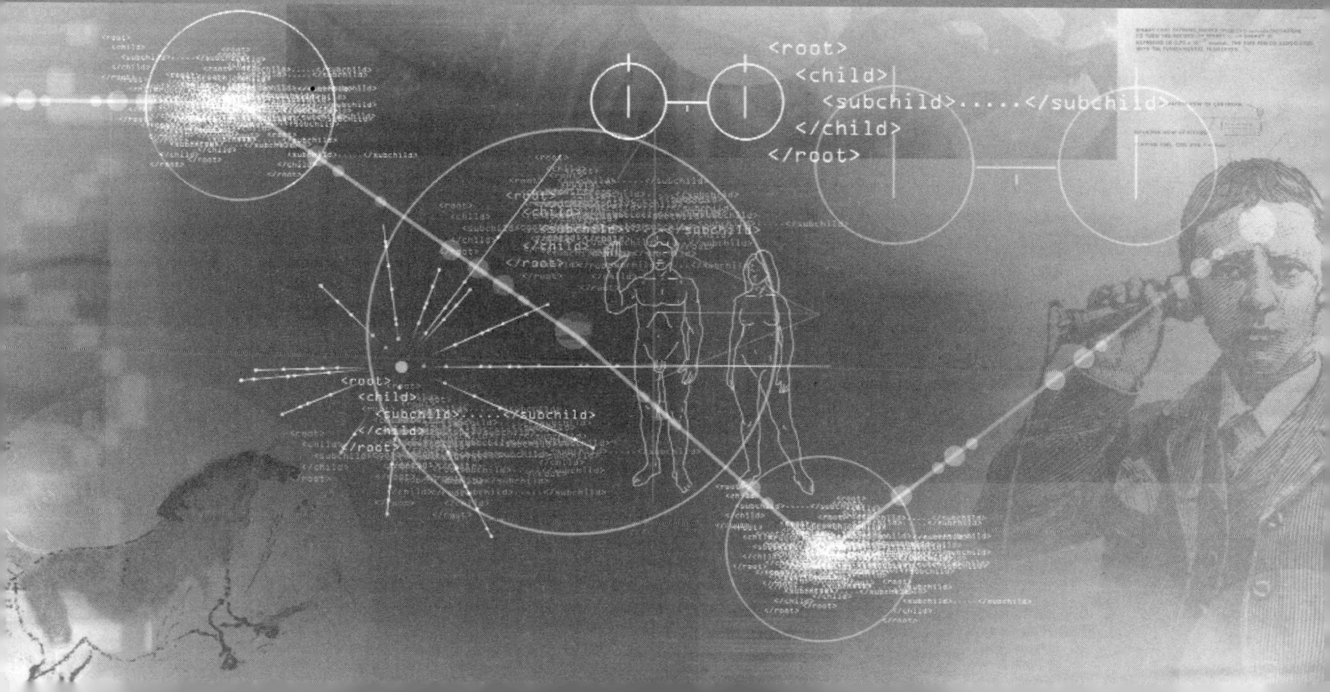

Introduction To Server-Side XML

In this chapter, and the ones to follow, we'll switch from client-side to server-side XML processing. We'll start by examining why you would want to consider server-side processing, and then we'll introduce the three main server-side languages used in web development: **ASP**, **JSP**, and **PHP**.

We'll discuss the pros and cons of each, and then go through some simple XML processing techniques with short code examples from each language. By way of a running example, we'll show you how to maintain an online list of your favorite CDs, stored in XML format. You'll learn how to add new elements to the XML document, modify existing ones, and delete unwanted items. You'll also learn how to transform the XML to HTML.

We'll go through this step-by-step, showing you the code needed in all three languages, giving you a solid overview of basic server-side XML techniques.

The chapters that follow will then show you in-depth case studies for each of these languages.

Server-Side Versus Client-Side XML Processing

By now you're probably all excited about what's possible using client-side XML processing. So why would you want to learn about server-side techniques? Trust me, you do.

Server-side XML gives you even more power. For example, since the processing is done on the server, only the results are sent to the client, so you don't have to worry about making your code cross-browser compatible. It is true that processing XML on the server-side transfers some of the load to the server, but since web servers are usually extremely powerful creatures with the ability to cache data, that is probably nothing to be worried about.

In addition, the server-side approach also greatly reduces the amount of data that flows across the network connection. If you want to display different results for different browsers, then that is easily accomplished by detecting the browser-type on the server side and using the correct stylesheet for the transformation.

The following points sum up the advantages of server-side processing:

- Systems can provide better performance and maintainability for data-driven web sites by generating and caching frequently accessed pages ahead of time on the server.
- You can have direct control over the security of your data – sensitive information can be filtered out before sending the data to the client. For example (an extreme one), if we have an XML document that contains a list of users and passwords, there is a security risk involved in sending the whole XML document to the client to be transformed there – it would be better to filter the passwords out of the server side.
- Maintaining your code becomes easier, since you don't have to modify it when new browser types or versions become available.
- By doing transformations on the server side you can greatly simplify what is sent to the client, avoiding the problem of designing functionality that works for all possible browser combinations (even mobile devices).

XML support in browsers is still limited, so if you want to dispense with browser-compatibility issues and suchlike, I would recommend that you use client-side XML processing only when developing something like closed intranets where all clients use the same browser. Your safest bet is still usually server-side processing.

Before We Continue

This chapter contains code examples using ASP, PHP, and JSP. If you wish to try running these examples on your computer, then you need to install some software before you continue.

Detailed installation instructions for each language can be found online at *http://www.glasshaus.com/*.

Server-Side Languages

The server-side market is a crowded one. Developers can choose from a variety of languages – ASP, ColdFusion, JSP, Perl, PHP, and more. With such a wealth of options out there, determining which environment best suits your needs can be bewildering.

The choice of a server-side programming language is a constant source of heated debate. The languages can all pretty much achieve the same things, but there are differences in portability, scalability, performance, and learning curve.

In this section we'll cover the three biggest players in the server-side market: ASP, PHP, and JSP. We'll give you a very brief overview of the advantages and shortcomings of each platform, and an idea of the XML support they offer.

ASP

Active Server Pages (**ASP**) is a framework that lets you combine one of a number of scripting languages (VBScript and JScript being the most popular choices) with an expandable set of software components. It's easy to learn, powerful enough for most mainstream server-side web development, and good on performance (since ASP files are compiled to native code, as opposed to JSP files, which are translated each time).

Advantages

- Professional support available (at a price).
- Extensively documented on MSDN (*msdn.microsoft.com*).
- A large number of corporate intranets are already running on Windows NT/2000 servers, and ASP is ideal for intranet applications in these circumstances.
- It's easy to learn for developers used to a Microsoft environment.
- Although it isn't totally "free", it is widely available since it runs on all PWS or IIS servers, which are packaged free with most recent Windows operating Systems.

Drawbacks

- ASP is closely linked to the Windows operating system, and Microsoft IIS web server. It is neither practical nor desirable to run a web site based on ASP on anything but a Windows-based server, so in this way, it is rather limiting.

XML Support

Extensive support for XML is provided for ASP and indeed any kind of programming on the Windows platform through **Microsoft XML Core Services 4.0** (**MSXML 4.0**), which is a full API for the parsing, validation, and processing of XML documents. Previous versions of the parser were distributed with various versions of Internet Explorer and other products, but to get the full functionality of the latest version, it needs to be downloaded.

Download the latest version (MSXML 4.0, Service Pack 1) from:
http://msdn.microsoft.com/downloads/default.asp?url=/downloads/sample.asp?url=/msdn-files/027/001/766/msdncompositedoc.xml.

Microsoft's XML parser has gone through a number of generations, the latest of which has been renamed to reflect the fact that it is far more than just an XML parser. In previous versions, Microsoft have jumped the gun a bit and provided their own functionality, such as support for their own version of XPath and their own version of XSLT. However, in version 4.0 they have fully adhered to the W3C's recommendations and come up with a fully compliant validating parser and processor.

MSXML 4.0 supports the following:

- The Document Object Model (DOM) – allows an XML document to be loaded into memory and manipulated. Nodes of the document can be read, written to, added, removed, moved, replaced etc.

- The XML Path Language (XPath) 1.0 – the querying language used to navigate XML documents. Support for the full W3C standard for XPath is provided, as well as support for Microsoft's earlier implementation. XSLT uses XPath for document navigation, as we saw in *Chapter 5*.
- Extensible Stylesheet Language Transformations (XSLT) 1.0 – the current W3C XML stylesheet language standard. Support remains for Microsoft's earlier XSL-WD implementation, though this should only be used for legacy applications (see *Chapter 5* for more on these different XSLT versions).
- The XML Schema definition language (XSD) – the current W3C standard for using XML to create XML Schemas. XML Schemas are used for the validation of XML documents, as an alternative to DTDs (we met both of these in *Chapter 1*).
- The Schema Object Model (SOM), an additional set of APIs unique to MSXML for accessing XML Schema documents programmatically.
- The Simple API for XML (SAX) – an alternative to the DOM for processing XML documents. It doesn't load the whole document into memory so its much more lenient on server resources, but it is also more limited in its functionality. We first met SAX in *Chapter 1*.
- There is also a unique API for transferring documents over HTTP, which comes in versions optimized for client or server use. This is particularly useful for facilitating communication between disparate systems.

Server Used for Examples

For the examples in this chapter, we used IIS 5.0 on Windows 2000 Professional. IIS comes with Windows 2000, and is an add-in component. The examples in this chapter will actually run with MSXML versions as old as MSXML 2.0, so if you have IE 5 or newer on your machine, you will be OK in this respect.

ASP.NET

You've probably heard of .NET – one of the latest Microsoft initiatives. Along with updates to much of its software and languages, we now find ASP.NET available to us. This extends the functionality of ASP to include all of the .NET Framework, including some expanded libraries for working with XML. However, this is rather a large area to explore, so we won't be covering it in any detail in this book.

PHP

PHP: Hypertext Preprocessor (PHP) is a server-side scripting language that can be embedded in HTML pages. It has been around for a few years now, but has undergone significant changes over that time. PHP borrows much of its syntax from Perl. When it was first created, it was intended to provide a more trimmed-down, easier-to-write, HTML-embeddable alternative to Perl, a task at which it seems to have succeeded. PHP is free, cross-platform, open source software; it integrates with all major web servers on all major operating systems.

Advantages

- It's open source and freely available from *http://www.php.net/*.

- It's cross-platform.
- It has a very active user community.
- It's seen as having a light footprint and not being processor-intensive.

Drawbacks

- It's relatively difficult to expand the language to add non-standard functionality that not handled by its built-in functions.
- PHP's extensibility is limited compared to say, Java, ASP, and COM (although new libraries pop up with every release)
- The function syntax to connect to each different brand of database is slightly different. Compare this to Java, which has a generic JDBC interface to connect to databases or ASP, which has its ADO abstraction layer.

XML Support

PHP has 4 extensions for performing XML tasks. Perhaps the most widely used of these are the XML parser functions – these use the **Expat** library, a SAX-based parser. Although it can parse XML, it does not perform any validation of the document. It supports 3 character encodings, namely US-ASCII, ISO-8859-1 and UTF-8, but does not support UTF-16. As you already know, with a SAX parser you define event handlers for XML events: as the parser works through the XML document it will call these handlers as and when events occur. The Expat library can be found at *http://www.jclark.com/xml/*.

PHP can also do DOM parsing of the XML document, but at the moment this extension is considered experimental. The extension is being overhauled for PHP 4.3.0 and the behaviour of many of the functions may change, so when using this extension it is best to avoid any non-object-oriented function (a full list of deprecated functions is available with the documentation). The extension uses the Gnome XML library, which you can find at *http://www.xmlsoft.org/*.

The PHP extension that provides XSLT support currently supports the Sablotron library. This extension has recently been rewritten in order to provide support for other libraries like Xalan and libxslt. Sablotron can be found at *http://www.gingerall.com/*.

> For our PHP examples here to work properly, you need to make sure you have the XSLT and XML DOM extensions installed. Don't worry, as they are included in the PHP package downloadable from *http://www.php.net/do_download.php?download_file=php-4.2.2-Win32.zip* (see the `InstallPHP.txt` file in the code download for more instructions on installing this properly).

Finally, PHP also contains RPC support through the XMLRPC extension, although this is also considered experimental.

Server Used for Examples

For the examples in this chapter, we used Apache 1.3.26 and PHP 4.2.2 on Windows 2000 Professional.

JSP

JavaServer Pages (JSP) are written in Java, which (unlike VBScript and PHP) is an object-oriented programming language that can be used to build enterprise-strength applications. Java is arguably the most powerful platform for server-side web development today. Portability, multithreading, extensive class libraries, object-oriented code, strong safety features, robust security measures, elegance, and extensibility are just a few of Java's advantages.

Java was designed to be platform-independent and very portable. Therefore, a web application developed in Java can be packaged as a WAR (web application archive) file and installed on any Java-enabled application server, on any platform.

The disadvantage is that Java is not very easy to learn. If you just need to get a more simple site up and working quickly, and are not serious about learning an object-oriented language, a simpler language like PHP might be a better choice. By using JavaBeans and tag libraries, however, web designers can quickly learn to create JSPs that retrieve data from a database, process XML, and carry out other powerful functions, without having to know anything about the underlying technology. You don't need to be a sophisticated Java programmer to utilize the power of JSP.

JSP files can also be a little slower than ASP or PHP because of the way they work. The first time JSPs are called, they are converted into servlets (special Java classes that produce outputs for sending over HTTP), which are stored by the JSP engine. After this, requests for the JSP files are served from the converted servlet (JSP engines also double as servlet engines). The most readily available JSP engine is Tomcat, which also serves static content at a slower rate. If you want a fast web site, get a dedicated web server such as Apache or IIS to serve the static content, while Tomcat (or another engine) serves the JSP content.

Advantages

- It's free. You can download the Tomcat application server from the Jakarta web site, and start coding in minutes (assuming you've got Java installed, which is also free).
- It's cross-platform.
- It has a very active user community.
- It's extremely powerful and scalable.

Drawbacks

- A steep learning curve.
- Third-party hosting isn't common, and can cost extra for installation.

XML Support

There is enormous XML support in Java. There are loads of parsers and XSLT and XPath processors available, and most of them are open source. To name them all would be pointless, but the following is a short overview of some of the products available (the list includes the most popular products in each category).

XML Parsers

- **Xerces**: Xerces is a high-performance, fully compliant XML parser from the Apache XML Project. It is a fully conforming XML Schema processor. It is free, and available both in sourcecode and precompiled binary (JAR file) form. For more information, visit *http://xml.apache.org/xerces2-j/index.html*.

- **XML4J**: XML Parser for Java is a validating XML parser and processor written in 100% pure Java – a library for parsing and generating XML documents, available as freeware from IBM. For more information, visit *http://www.alphaworks.ibm.com/tech/xml4j*.

- **XP**: XP is an XML 1.0 parser written in Java, fully conforming, which detects all non well-formed documents. It is currently not a validating XSLT processor, but it can parse all external entities: external DTD subsets, external parameter entities, and external general entities. For more information, visit *http://www.jclark.com/xml/xp/*.

- **MXP1**: MXPl, or Maximum Perf. Minimum Size XML Parser, is a Java-based, non-validating pull parser that implements the *Common Application Programming Interface (API) for XML Pull Parsing* (*http://www.xmlpull.org*) specification. MXP1 was designed for minimal footprint (less than 20k) and maximum speed (it claims up to 20% better performance than the nearest competitor) and is suited for fast serialization and deserialization of Simple Object Access Protocol (SOAP)-based XML objects. For more information, visit *http://www.extreme.indiana.edu/xgws/xsoap/xpp/mxp1/*.

XSLT Processors

- **Xalan**: Xalan is an XSLT processor for transforming XML documents, from the Apache XML Project. It implements the W3C Recommendations for XSL Transformations (XSLT) and the XML Path Language (XPath). It can be used from the command line, in an applet or a servlet, or as a module in other programs. For more information, visit *http://xml.apache.org/xalan-j/index.html*.

- **XT**: XT is a *fast*, free implementation of XSLT in Java. For more information, visit *http://www.blnz.com/xt/index.html*.

- **SAXON**: The SAXON package is a collection of tools for processing XML documents. It contains an XSLT processor, and Java libraries for access to the processor from Java applications. For more information, visit *http://saxon.sourceforge.net/*.

Java-Specific Document Object Models

These are frameworks that provide a more Java-centric coding approach to parsing, transforming, etc. than the DOM and SAX interfaces. They can be configured to use DOM or SAX for parsing, but provide a much more convenient API for Java programs.

- **JDOM**: JDOM is, quite simply, a Java representation of an XML document. JDOM provides a way to represent that document for easy and efficient reading, manipulation, and writing. It has a straightforward API, is lightweight, fast, and is optimized for the Java programmer. It's an alternative to DOM and SAX, although it integrates well with both of them. For more information, visit *http://www.jdom.org*.

- **dom4j**: dom4j is an easy to use, open source library for working with XML, XPath, and XSLT on the Java platform using the Java Collections Framework and with full support for DOM, SAX, JAXP, TrAX, and XSLT. dom4j is distributed under an open source, Apache-style license that does not restrict users to creation of open source products only. For more information, visit *http://www.dom4j.org*.

Other

- **Java XML Pack**: The Java XML Pack is an all-in-one download of Java technologies for XML from SUN. Java XML Pack brings together several of the key industry standards for XML – such as SAX, DOM, XSLT, SOAP, UDDI, ebXML, and WSDL – into one convenient download, thereby giving developers the technologies needed to get started with web applications and Web Services. Included in the bundle are: Java API for XML Processing (JAXP), Java Architecture for XML Binding (JAXB), Java API for XML Messaging (JAXM), Java API for XML-based RPC (JAX-RPC), and Java API for XML Registries (JAXR). For more information, visit *http://java.sun.com/xml/javaxmlpack.html*.
- **Cocoon**: Cocoon is an XML framework that allows easy integrated usage of XML and XSLT technologies for server applications, around pipelined SAX processing, with a centralized configuration system to make things simple. It is available for usage under the Apache Software License. For more information, visit *http://xml.apache.org/cocoon/index.html*.

There are also lots of utility packages available, such as XML tag libraries (XTags) for JSP from Jakarta, which give web designers with limited Java knowledge the full powers of XML processing through simple tags. For more information, visit *http://jakarta.apache.org/taglibs/doc/xtags-doc/intro.html*.

Server Used for Examples

For the examples in this chapter, we used **Tomcat 4.0.4** on Windows 2000 Professional. Tomcat is available from *http://jakarta.apache.org/builds/jakarta-tomcat-4.0/release/v4.0.4/bin/* (sourcecode is also available from *http://jakarta.apache.org/builds/jakarta-tomcat-4.0/release/v4.0.4/src/* if you want to compile Tomcat yourself).

As well as Tomcat, we also used **XTags**, nightly builds of which are available from *http://jakarta.apache.org/builds/jakarta-taglibs/nightly/projects/xtags/* (this is a work in progress), and **dom4j**, available from *http://dom4j.org/download.html*. The JAR files for these two resources are provided in the code download.

Overview

The following table summarizes these three server-side languages:

	ASP	PHP	JSP
Language	VBScript, JavaScript (amongst others)	PHP	Java
Platforms	Windows (other platforms need third-party porting software).	Any platform for which the sourcecode or binaries are available, which is most.	Any platform for which the sourcecode or binaries for a JSP/servlet engine such as Tomcat are available, which is any with Java.
Web Servers	Microsoft IIS (other servers need third party software).	Apache, IIS, Netscape, etc.	JSP files are served by a JSP/servlet engine (such as Tomcat). Any web server, including Apache, IIS, and Netscape, can be configured to send requests for JSP files to the JSP engine. Any J2EE-compliant application server should have a JSP/servlet engine.
Portability	Poor	Excellent	Excellent
Scalability	Good	Poor	Good
Component Support	COM objects	None	Java classes, JavaBeans, Enterprise JavaBeans
Learning curve	Low	Medium	High

The only major vendor for ASP is Microsoft (Sun market an opensource version of ASP called Sun ONE Active Server Pages – formerly known as Chili!Soft ASP.) We won't go into this here – see *http://wwws.sun.com/software/chilisoft/* for more details). PHP is open source, so there is no vendor to deal with. JSP is a set of standards and interfaces that can be implemented by anyone interested. Sun provides a reference implementation of a Java application server, which uses Tomcat as the JSP engine, but there is currently a variety of implementations (both commercial and open source) on the market.

Basic Techniques

Enough talk! It's time to see these server-side languages in action. We'll now go through some basic XML processing techniques, with examples from each language. This section should give you a good basic arsenal for tackling the most common XML tasks.

We'll create a simple web application for organizing our CD collection. We'll store the name of the artist, the name of the CD, and the year it was released. The list of CDs will be stored in an XML document. We need to be able to add new CDs to the list, modify existing ones, and also remove CDs from the list. We also want to display the list in HTML format, so we need to be able to transform the XML document to HTML.

The files that we'll create are the following:

`cd_list.xml`	The XML document containing the list of CDs.
`cd_list.xsl`	The XSL stylesheet that transforms the CD list to HTML.
`cd_list.(asp/php/jsp)`	The page that transforms `cd_list.xml` using `cd_list.xsl` and outputs the result.
`cd_edit.(asp/php/jsp)`	The page that allows the user to input/modify information about a specific CD.
`cd_save.(asp/php/jsp)`	The page that saves the information that was input in `cd_edit.(asp/php/jsp)`.
`cd_delete.(asp/php/jsp)`	The page that deletes a specific CD from the `cd_list.xml`.

The XML Document

The XML document that contains the CD list is very simple. Each `<cd>` element contains three elements: `<name>`, `<band>`, and `<year>`. Following is an example instance (`cd_list.xml` in the code download):

```
<?xml version="1.0" encoding="UTF-8"?>
<cd-list>
  <cd id="1">
    <name>Kid A</name>
    <band>Radiohead</band>
    <year>2000</year>
  </cd>
  <cd id="2">
    <name>OK Computer</name>
    <band>Radiohead</band>
     <year>1997</year>
  </cd>
  <cd id="3">
    <name>Felt Mountain</name>
    <band>Goldfrapp</band>
    <year>2001</year>
```

```
    </cd>
    <cd id="4">
      <name>Tourist</name>
      <band>St. Germain</band>
      <year>2000</year>
    </cd>
    <cd id="5">
      <name>The Private Press</name>
      <band>DJ Shadow</band>
      <year>2002</year>
    </cd>
    <cd id="6">
      <name>Protection</name>
      <band>Massive Attack</band>
      <year>1994</year>
    </cd>
  </cd-list>
```

Note that each `<cd>` element has a unique `id`. We'll put this `id` in the query string to send it between pages, to identify which CD we are currently working with. For those of you who don't know, the query string is the part after the "?" in the URL. We can send variables using the syntax "name=value", and separate multiple **name/value pairs** with "&". For example `http://myserver.com/mypage.html?param1=value1&param2=value2`.

Transforming the XML

Our first task is to display the list of CDs in HTML format. We need to create an XSLT stylesheet to transform the XML to HTML, and then we'll create a server-side page to carry out the transformation (that is, to apply the XSLT to the XML, and output the resulting HTML).

We just want a plain HTML table, listing the CDs ordered first by band and then by name. We also need links for modifying and deleting, and a link for adding a new CD. We want the page to look something like the following:

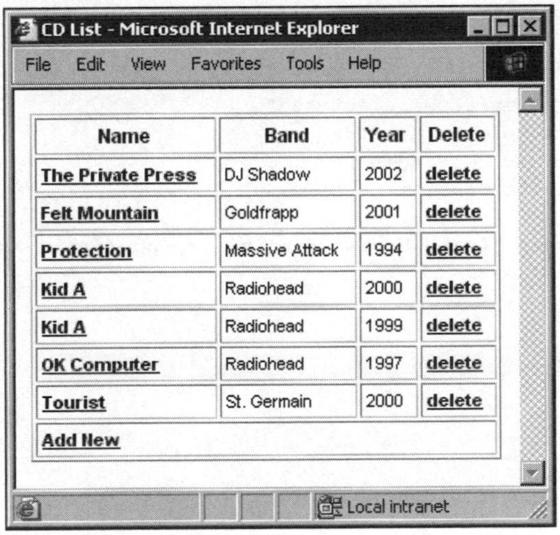

The following very simple XSLT stylesheet (`cd_list.xsl`) accomplishes this:

```
<?xml version="1.0"?>
<xsl:stylesheet version="1.0" xmlns:xsl="http://www.w3.org/1999/XSL/Transform">
<xsl:output method="html" omit-xml-declaration="yes" />

<xsl:template match="/cd-list">
  <html>
    <head>
      <title>CD List</title>
      <style>
        table {
          color: #000000;
          font-family:  Arial, Helvetica, sans-serif;
          font-size: 11px;
        }
        th {
          font-size: 12px;
          font-weight: bold;
        }
        a {
          color: #000000;
          font-weight: bold;
        }
        a:hover {
          text-decoration: underline;
        }
      </style>
    </head>
    <body>
      <table border="1" cellpadding="3" width="300">
        <tr>
          <th>Name</th>
          <th>Band</th>
          <th>Year</th>
          <th>Delete</th>
        </tr>
        <xsl:apply-templates select="cd">
          <xsl:sort select="band"/>
          <xsl:sort select="name"/>
        </xsl:apply-templates>
        <tr>
          <td colspan="4"><a href="cd_edit.(asp/php/jsp)">Add New</a></td>
        </tr>
      </table>
    </body>
  </html>
</xsl:template>

<xsl:template match="cd">
  <tr>
    <td>
```

```
      <a>
        <xsl:attribute name="href">
          cd_edit.(asp/php/jsp)?id=<xsl:value-of select="@id"/>
        </xsl:attribute>
        <xsl:value-of select="name"/>
      </a>
    </td>
    <td>
      <xsl:value-of select="band"/>
    </td>
    <td>
      <xsl:value-of select="year"/>
    </td>
    <td>
      <a>
        <xsl:attribute name="href">
          cd_delete.(asp/php/jsp)?id=<xsl:value-of select="@id"/>
        </xsl:attribute>
        delete
      </a>
    </td>
  </tr>
</xsl:template>

</xsl:stylesheet>
```

There is not much to explain here. We simply create a `<table>` that contains a row for each CD. The name of the CD is a link to `cd_edit.(asp/php/jsp)`, and the `id` of the CD is sent as a query string variable:

```
<a>
    <xsl:attribute name="href">
      cd_edit.(asp/php/jsp)?id=<xsl:value-of select="@id"/>
    </xsl:attribute>
    <xsl:value-of select="name"/>
</a>
```

The `cd_edit.(asp/php/jsp)` page is a page that contains a form to allow the user to modify the CD information. This page will be created later. In the same way, the last column of each row contains a link to `cd_delete.(asp/php/jsp)` for deleting the CD from the list. The `id` is sent as a query string variable. Finally, at the bottom of the table there is a link to `cd_edit.(asp/php/jsp)` for adding a new CD (note that no `id` is sent, since a new CD does not yet have an `id`).

> NOTE: We'll use this stylesheet almost unchanged for ASP, PHP, and JSP. The only thing that changes is the file extension in the links (`.asp`, `.php`, or `.jsp`). In the above section I've therefore included (`asp/php/jsp`) as the extension, to emphasize that the file extension depends on the server-side technology being used.

The next thing is to create the page that performs the transformation on the server side.

ASP: Transforming the XML

The following page (cd_list.asp) does the trick:

```
<%@ Language=VBScript %>
<%
  Dim oXML, oXSL

  Set oXML = CreateObject("MSXML2.DOMDocument")
  oXML.load(Server.MapPath("cd_list.xml"))

  Set oXSL = CreateObject("MSXML2.DOMDocument")
  oXSL.load(Server.MapPath("cd_list.xsl"))

  Response.write oXML.transformNode(oXSL)
%>
```

First we create an XML document object:

```
Set oXML = CreateObject("MSXML2.DOMDocument")
```

Then we load the cd_list.xml into the object:

```
oXML.load(Server.MapPath("cd_list.xml"))
```

We do the same for the cd_list.xsl document, and finally we perform the transformation and write out the result.

PHP: Transforming the XML

Performing an XSL transformation in PHP is relatively straightforward. Once you have the XSLT extension installed the following script is all it takes (cd_list.php):

```
<?php
  $xsltHnd = xslt_create();
  xslt_set_base($xsltHnd,'file://c:/xml/chapter10/');
  $html =  xslt_process($xsltHnd, 'cd_list.xml', 'cd_list.xsl');
  echo $html;
?>
```

The first line:

```
$xsltHnd = xslt_create();
```

creates a new XSLT processor. The function returns the XSLT processor resource, which we will use for all our other XSLT functions.

If you are working on a Windows machine and intend to pass external files to the XSLT functions, you will need to set the base URI so that XPath can resolve the file names. In the setup I used, the URI is as follows:

```
xslt_set_base($xsltHnd,'file://c:/xml/chapter10/');
```

With all the XML and XSL documents residing in *C:\xml\chapter10*. `xslt_set_base` takes 2 arguments – the XSLT processor resource and the URI. Once we have set that, we can then use the `xslt_process` function to perform the transformation.

```
$html =  xslt_process($xsltHnd, 'cd_list.xml', 'cd_list.xsl');
```

In our example we have passed the function the three arguments – the XSLT processor resource, the name of the XML file, and the name of the XSL stylesheet. The result of the transformation is returned and stored in the variable `$html`.

The `xslt_process` function has an additional 3 optional arguments, and it is through these that we have great versatility in the manner in which we can use the function. Let's take a look at some of the other ways in which we could have written this script:

```
<?php
  $xsltHnd = xslt_create();
  xslt_set_base($xsltHnd,'file://c:/xml/chapter10/');
  xslt_process($xsltHnd, 'cd_list.xml', 'cd_list.xsl','cd_list.html');
?>
```

In this example we are not returning the result of the transformation into a variable; instead we are specifying a file name as the fourth argument – the results will be saved in `cd_list.html`. Another way we can use the function is by having our XML and XSL stored in variables:

```
<?php
  $xsltHnd = xslt_create();
  $xml = join('',file('cd_list.xml'));
  $xsl = join('',file('cd_list.xsl'));
  $arguments = array(
      '/_xml' => $xml,
      '/_xsl' => $xsl
  );
  $html = xslt_process($xsltHnd, 'arg:/_xml', 'arg:/_xsl', NULL, $arguments);
  echo $html;
?>
```

In this example, the first thing you'll notice is that we have left out the line that sets the base URI. Since our data is going to be stored in variables we will not need to set this. The two lines:

```
$xml = join('',file('cd_list.xml'));
$xsl = join('',file('cd_list.xsl'));
```

are simply setting the variables `$xml` and `$xsl` to the contents of the XML and XSL files. The `file()` function reads a file off disk into an array, one line per element. The `join()` function joins array elements with a specified string.

We then create an associative array, called `$arguments`, containing `$xml` and `$xsl`. Since we don't want to output to a file, we make the fourth argument `NULL`. While we are talking about the arguments to the `xslt_process` function, it is worth noting that we can pass it an optional fifth argument, which is an array of parameters. These parameters can then be accessed in your XSL document with `<xsl:param name="parameter_name">`.

JSP: Transforming the XML

Here we'll use the **XTags** tag library from Jakarta, which can be downloaded freely from the Jakarta web site (*http://jakarta.apache.org*). The XTags library is a set of simple tags that give web designers access to powerful XML processing actions without any Java programming knowledge. Using this tag library, the JSP that transforms `cd_list.xml` using `cd_list.xsl` is extremely simple (`cd_list.jsp`):

```
<!doctype html public "-//w3c//dtd html 4.0 transitional//en">
<%@ taglib uri="http://jakarta.apache.org/taglibs/xtags-1.0" prefix="xtags" %>

<xtags:parse uri="cd_list.xml" id="cdList"/>
<xtags:style xsl="cd_list.xsl" document="<%= cdList %>"/>
```

The following line declares that we'll be using the XTags tag library, with the "`xtags`" prefix:

```
<%@ taglib uri="http://jakarta.apache.org/taglibs/xtags-1.0" prefix="xtags" %>
```

The next line parses the XML document specified in the `uri` attribute (an external XML document can also be specified by using the `url` attribute and supplying the full URL to the document), and the final line transforms the document using the XSL stylesheet specified in the `xsl` attribute, and prints out the result.

Adding a New CD (Writing To an XML File)

The next task is to provide support for adding a new CD to the list. We want to be able to specify all the information for the new CD that is present for the existing CD, namely year, band, and name.

For this we're going to use two pages. The first one will display a form into which the user can input information about the CD. The second page will take the information submitted from the form and insert it into the CD list.

When viewed in a browser, the page should look something like this:

The first page is, at this stage, almost identical for all the languages (apart from the extensions), and contains only HTML code. We will therefore just show it once here (`cd_edit.(asp/php/jsp)`):

```
<!doctype html public "-//w3c//dtd html 4.0 transitional//en">
  <head>
    <title>Edit CD information</title>
  </head>

  <body>
    <form method="get" action="cd_save.(asp/php/jsp)">
      <p>
        <table cellSpacing=1 cellPadding=1>
          <tr>
            <td>Name</td>
            <td><input name="name" value=""></td>
          </tr>
          <tr>
            <td>Band</td>
            <td><input name="band" value=""></td>
          </tr>
          <tr>
            <td>Year</td>
            <td><input name="year" value=""></td>
          </tr>
        </table>
      </p>
      <input type="submit" value="Submit">
      <input type="reset" value="Reset">
      <input type="button" value="Back" onclick="history.back()">
    </form>
  </body>
</html>
```

The page contains an empty form. When the user hits the *Submit* button, the form is submitted to another page (`cd_save.(asp/php/jsp)`) using the `get` method, which sends the information from the form as query string parameters.

When we add support for modifying existing CDs, we'll need to insert some scripting code into this page, and it then becomes different for each language – for now however, this is sufficient.

Now we need to create the page that inserts the new `<cd>` element into the CD list. This page needs to generate a unique `id` for the CD. For simplicity's sake this `id` will be generated by adding one to the `id` of the last CD in the list.

ASP: Adding a New CD

Here is the code for `cd_save.asp`:

```
<%@ Language=VBScript %>
<%
  Dim sXML, oXML1, oXML2, iID

  'create empty XML
  sXML = "<cd id=''><name/><band/><year/></cd>"
```

```
    'load into document object
    Set oXML1 = CreateObject("MSXML2.DOMDocument")
    oXML1.loadXML(sXML)

    'fill in node values
    oXML1.selectSingleNode("cd/name").text = Request.QueryString("name")
    oXML1.selectSingleNode("cd/band").text = Request.QueryString("band")
    oXML1.selectSingleNode("cd/year").text = Request.QueryString("year")

    'get CD List document
    Set oXML2 = CreateObject("MSXML2.DOMDocument")
    oXML2.load(Server.MapPath("cd_list.xml"))

    'get ID by getting ID of last node and adding one
    iID = Cint(oXML2.documentElement.lastChild.selectSingleNode("@id").text) + 1

    oXML1.selectSingleNode("cd/@id").text = iID

    'add new item to the list
    oXML2.documentElement.appendChild oXML1.documentElement

    'save list
    oXML2.save(Server.MapPath("cd_list.xml"))

    Set oXML1 = Nothing
    Set oXML2 = Nothing
%>

<html>
  <head>
    <title>Success</title>
  </head>
  <body>
    CD list successfully modified.<br />
    <a href="cd_list.asp">Back to CD List</a>
  </body>
</html>
```

We start by creating an empty <cd> element and loading it into an XML object. This is done in the following lines:

```
'create empty XML
sXML = "<cd id=''><name/><band/><year/></cd>"

'load into document object
Set oXML1 = CreateObject("MSXML2.DOMDocument")
oXML1.loadXML(sXML)
```

We then set the values for name, band, and year with the data from the form that is embedded in the query string. Next we load the `cd_list.xml` document, and generate the new CD `id` by adding one to the `id` of the last CD in the list. We set the `id`, add the item to the list, and finally we save the document. We display a message to the user, indicating that the CD was successfully added to the list.

Note that in order to be able to write the XML document, you'll need IIS to be set up with write permission on the folder the XML file is stored in (in this case, `cdlist`).

PHP: Adding a New CD

We'll use the DOM XML extension for this script (`cd_save.php`):

```
<?php
  $name = $_GET['name'];
  $band = $_GET['band'];
  $year = $_GET['year'];

  $xml = join('',file('cd_list.xml'));

  $dom = domxml_open_mem($xml);

  $elements = $dom->get_elements_by_tagname('cd');
  $lastElement = $elements[count($elements)-1];
  $id = $lastElement->get_attribute('id');
  $id++;
  $parent = $lastElement->parent_node();

  $childNode = $dom->create_element('cd');
  $childNode->set_attribute('id',$id);
  $hndChild = $parent->append_child($childNode);

  $tempNode = $dom->create_element('name');
  $hndNode = $hndChild->append_child($tempNode);
  $hndNode->set_content($name);
  $tempNode = $dom->create_element('band');
  $hndNode = $hndChild->append_child($tempNode);
  $hndNode->set_content($band);
  $tempNode = $dom->create_element('year');
  $hndNode = $hndChild->append_child($tempNode);
  $hndNode->set_content($year);

  $xmldata = $dom->dump_mem();

  $fp = fopen('cd_list.xml','wb');
  fwrite($fp, $xmldata);
  fclose($fp);
?>

<html>
  <head>
    <title>Success</title>
  </head>
  <body>
    CD list successfully modified.<br />
    <a href="cd_list.php">Back to CD List</a>
  </body>
</html>
```

We start off by grabbing the form details from the `$_GET` superglobal array. We then grab the contents of our XML document and store it in an array. The `domxml_open_mem` function creates a DOM object from the XML.

The line:

```
$elements = $dom->get_elements_by_tagname('cd');
```

creates an array of elements that have the tag name of "`cd`". We then grab the `id` of the last element and increment it to use later. Once we have the parent of the element we can start creating our new node:

```
$childNode = $dom->create_element('cd');
$childNode->set_attribute('id',$id);
$hndChild = $parent->append_child($childNode);
```

After we have created the element we set its `id` attribute to the `id` we worked out earlier. `set_attribute` will create the attribute if it doesn't already exist. We can then use `append_child` to append the new node we created to the end of the `<cd>` elements.

Adding the name, band, and year works in the same way, except we use `set_content` to specify the value of that tag.

JSP: Adding a New CD

Here we are going to use **dom4j** for manipulating the XML document. See the *JSP* section of the *Server-side Languages* section for more details. Here is the code for `cd_save.jsp`:

```
<%@ page import="java.io.File,
                 org.dom4j.Document,
                 org.dom4j.Element,
                 org.dom4j.io.SAXReader" %>
<%
  // get the parameters:
  int id = 0;
  String name = request.getParameter("name");
  String band = request.getParameter("band");
  String year = request.getParameter("year");

  // parse the document:
  SAXReader reader = new SAXReader();
  String path = application.getRealPath("/cd_list.xml");
  Document doc = reader.read( new File(path) );

  // we generate the id by adding 1 to the ID of the last node:
  java.util.List list = doc.selectNodes( "//cd-list/cd" );
  org.dom4j.Node lastCd = (org.dom4j.Node) list.get( list.size()-1 );
  id = Integer.parseInt( lastCd.valueOf("@id") ) + 1;

  // create the new element
  Element newCd = doc.getRootElement().addElement( "cd" )
```

```
                    .addAttribute( "id", Integer.toString(id) );

    newCd.addElement("name").addText(name);
    newCd.addElement("band").addText(band);
    newCd.addElement("year").addText(year);

    // write the file:
      java.io.FileWriter output = new java.io.FileWriter( path );
    doc.write( output );
    output.close();
%>

<html>
  <head>
    <title>Success</title>
  </head>
  <body>
    CD list successfully modified.<br />
    <a href="cd_list.jsp">Back to CD List</a>
  </body>
</html>
```

This code is almost self-explanatory. We retrieve the name, band, and year from the query string by calling the `request.getParameter()` method, then parse the `cd_list.xml` document. Note that the path to the file is retrieved by calling:

```
String path = application.getRealPath("/cd_list.xml");
```

This might return, for example, `C:\tomcat\webapps\cdlist\cd_list.xml`. We then generate the `id` for the new CD by adding one to the `id` of the last `<cd>` element. The last `<cd>` element is retrieved by these lines:

```
java.util.List list = doc.selectNodes( "//cd-list/cd" );
org.dom4j.Node lastCd = (org.dom4j.Node) list.get( list.size()-1 );
```

And then the `id` is generated:

```
id = Integer.parseInt( lastCd.valueOf("@id") ) + 1;
```

We then create the new element, and add the `id`, `name`, `band`, and `year` values to it. Finally we write the modified document to the file and print a message indicating that the action was successfully completed.

Modifying CD Information

Now we want to add support for modifying information about an existing CD in the list. This can be accomplished by modifying the two pages (`cd_edit` and `cd_save`) that we created in the last section. These pages must now check if the `id` that they receive in the query string (if they receive one) exists in the list. If so, the `cd_edit` page should display the information for that CD in the form, and the `cd_save` page should update that `<cd>` element.

ASP: Modifying CD Information

We modify `cd_edit.asp` (which earlier just contained plain HTML), so that it displays information about the CD with the `id` specified in the form. The changes are highlighted:

```
<%@ Language=VBScript %>
<%
  Dim sID, oXML, oNode, sName, sBand, sYear

  sID = Request.QueryString("id")

  If sID <> "" then
    'get CD List document
    Set oXML = CreateObject("MSXML2.DOMDocument")
    oXML.load(Server.MapPath("cd_list.xml"))

    'select desired CD node
    Set oNode = oXML.selectSingleNode("//cd[@id=" & sID & "]")

    sName = oNode.selectSingleNode("name").text
    sBand = oNode.selectSingleNode("band").text
    sYear = oNode.selectSingleNode("year").text

    Set oNode = Nothing
    Set oXML = Nothing
  End if
%>

<html>
  <head>
    <title>Edit CD information</title>
  </head>

  <body>
    <form method="get" action="cd_save.asp">
      <p>
        <table cellSpacing=1 cellPadding=1>
          <tr>
            <td>Name</td>
            <td><input name="name" value="<%=sName%>"></td>
          </tr>
          <tr>
            <td>Band</td>
            <td><input name="band" value="<%=sBand%>"></td>
          </tr>
          <tr>
            <td>Year</td>
            <td><input name="year" value="<%=sYear%>"></td>
          </tr>
        </table>
      </p>

      <input TYPE="hidden" name="id" value="<%=sID%>">
```

```
      <input type="submit" value="Submit" name="submit1">
      <input type="reset" value="Reset" name="reset1">
      <input type="button" value="Back" onclick="history.back()">
    </form>
  </body>
</html>
```

We first retrieve the `id` from the query string:

```
sID = Request.QueryString("id")
```

If the `id` is not empty, we then load the information about the CD with that `id`. We first find the correct CD:

```
  Set oNode = oXML.selectSingleNode("//cd[@id=" & sID & "]")
```

Then we load the data from that CD:

```
  sName = oNode.selectSingleNode("name").text
  sBand = oNode.selectSingleNode("band").text
  sYear = oNode.selectSingleNode("year").text
```

Finally, we display the information about the selected CD in the form, and store the `id` in a hidden field so that `cd_save.asp` knows which CD to update.

We then need to modify `cd_save.asp` so that it performs an update if it receives a non-empty `id`, and else an insert. The changes are highlighted:

```
<%@ Language=VBScript %>
<%
  Dim sID, sXML, oXML1, oXML2, iID, oNode

  sID = Request.QueryString("id")

  'get CD List document
  Set oXML2 = CreateObject("MSXML2.DOMDocument")
  oXML2.load(Server.MapPath("cd_list.xml"))

  If sID <> "" then

    'select desired CD node
    Set oNode = oXML2.selectSingleNode("//cd[@id=" & sID & "]")

    oNode.selectSingleNode("name").text = Request.QueryString("name")
    oNode.selectSingleNode("band").text = Request.QueryString("band")
    oNode.selectSingleNode("year").text = Request.QueryString("year")

  Else

    'create empty XML
    sXML = "<cd id=''><name/><band/><year/></cd>"
```

```
      'load into document object
      Set oXML1 = CreateObject("MSXML2.DOMDocument")
      oXML1.loadXML(sXML)

      'fill in node values
      oXML1.selectSingleNode("cd/name").text = Request.QueryString("name")
      oXML1.selectSingleNode("cd/band").text = Request.QueryString("band")
      oXML1.selectSingleNode("cd/year").text = Request.QueryString("year")

      'get ID by getting ID of last node and adding one
      iID = Cint(oXML2.documentElement.lastChild.selectSingleNode("@id").text) +1

      oXML1.selectSingleNode("cd/@id").text = iID

      'add new item to the list
      oXML2.documentElement.appendChild oXML1.documentElement

    End if

    'save list
    oXML2.save(Server.MapPath("cd_list.xml"))

    Set oXML1 = Nothing
    Set oXML2 = Nothing
  %>

  <html>
    <head>
      <title>Success</title>
    </head>
    <body>
      CD list successfully modified.<br />
      <a href="cd_list.asp">Back to CD List</a>
    </body>
  </html>
```

First we get the id from the query string:

```
      sID = Request.QueryString("id")
```

Then, if that id is not empty, we update the CD with the id, otherwise we insert a new CD. If the id is not empty, the desired <cd> element is selected in the following way using an XPath expression:

```
      Set oNode = oXML.selectSingleNode("//cd[@id=" & sID & "]")
```

And then the values are updated with the data from the form:

```
      oNode.selectSingleNode("name").text = Request.QueryString("name")
      oNode.selectSingleNode("band").text = Request.QueryString("band")
      oNode.selectSingleNode("year").text = Request.QueryString("year")
```

PHP: Modifying CD Information

To perform this task, we'll use `cd_edit.php`, as seen below. Here we populate the form with the CD details if it is passed a CD `id`.

```
<?php
  $id = $_GET['id'];
  if ($id) {
    $xml = join('',file('cd_list.xml'));
    $dom = domxml_open_mem($xml);
    $xpObj = xpath_new_context($dom);
    $resObj = xpath_eval($xpObj, "//cd[@id=$id]");
    $theOne = $resObj->nodeset[0];
    $nElement = $theOne->get_elements_by_tagname('name');
    $name = $nElement[0]->get_content();
    $bElement = $theOne->get_elements_by_tagname('band');
    $band = $bElement[0]->get_content();
    $yElement = $theOne->get_elements_by_tagname('year');
    $year = $yElement[0]->get_content();
  }
?>
```

```
<!doctype html public "-//w3c//dtd html 4.0 transitional//en">
<html>
  <head>
    <title>Edit CD information</title>
  </head>
  <body>
    <form method="get" action="cd_save.php">
      <p>
        <table cellSpacing=1 cellPadding=1>
          <tr>
            <td>Name</td>
            <td><input name="name" value="<?php echo $name; ?>"></td>
          </tr>
          <tr>
            <td>Band</td>
            <td><input name="band" value="<?php echo $band; ?>"></td>
          </tr>
          <tr>
            <td>Year</td>
            <td><input name="year" value="<?php echo $year; ?>"></td>
          </tr>
        </table>
      </p>
      <input type="hidden" name="id" value="<?php echo $id; ?>">
      <input type="submit" value="Submit">
      <input type="reset" value="Reset">
      <input type="button" value="Back" onclick="history.back()">
    </form>
  </body>
</html>
```

We start off by grabbing the value of `id` that is passed through in the URL. If one has been passed, then we load the XML document as a DOM object. An XPath search is used to find the node that has the `id` that the user has selected. To do this we first create a new XPath context like so:

```
$xpObj = xpath_new_context($dom);
```

and then we evaluate the XPath search string `"//cd[@id=$id]"`:

```
$resObj = xpath_eval($xpObj, "//cd[@id=$id]");
```

`xpath_eval()` returns an XPath object. One of the properties of the XPath object is `nodelist` – `nodelist` is an array of the nodes returned by the XPath search we just did. We are only expecting one, so we can grab the first one from the array:

```
$theOne = $resObj->nodeset[0];
```

We can then grab the contents of each of the elements within this node, and then output the values into the form. We must also add a new hidden input field that contains the `id` of the current record so that we know which record to update.

Our next step is to alter the `cd_save.php` script to update the existing information with the new from the form (`cd_save_2.php`):

```
<?php
  $id = $_GET['id'];
  $name = $_GET['name'];
  $band = $_GET['band'];
  $year = $_GET['year'];
  $xml = join('',file('cd_list.xml'));
  $dom = domxml_open_mem($xml);
  if ($id) {
    $xpObj = xpath_new_context($dom);
    $resObj = xpath_eval($xpObj, "//cd[@id=$id]");
    $hndChild = $resObj->nodeset[0];
    while($hndChild->has_child_nodes()) {
      $toGo = $hndChild->first_child();
      $hndChild->remove_child($toGo);
    }
    $parent = $hndChild->parent_node();
  }
  else {
    $elements = $dom->get_elements_by_tagname('cd');
    $lastElement = $elements[count($elements)-1];
    $id = $lastElement->get_attribute('id');
    $id++;
    $parent = $lastElement->parent_node();
    $childNode = $dom->create_element('cd');
    $childNode->set_attribute('id',$id);
    $hndChild = $parent->append_child($childNode);
  }
  $tempNode = $dom->create_element('name');
```

```
  $hndNode = $hndChild->append_child($tempNode);
  $hndNode->set_content($name);
  $tempNode = $dom->create_element('band');
  $hndNode = $hndChild->append_child($tempNode);
  $hndNode->set_content($band);
  $tempNode = $dom->create_element('year');
  $hndNode = $hndChild->append_child($tempNode);
  $hndNode->set_content($year);
  $xmldata = $dom->dump_mem();

  $fp = fopen('cd_list.xml','wb');
  fwrite($fp, $xmldata);

  fclose($fp);
?>

<html>
  <head>
    <title>Success</title>
  </head>
  <body>
    CD list successfully modified.<br />
    <a href="cd_list.php">Back to CD List</a>
  </body>
</html>
```

We use an XPath search to find the CD that is specified by the `id`. Since we already have some code to add elements of the band, name, and year, we'll continue to use this code. Since we don't want duplicate name, band, and year tags, we just delete the existing ones.

```
    while($hndChild->has_child_nodes()) {
      $toGo = $hndChild->first_child();
      $hndChild->remove_child($toGo);
    }
```

We then wrap the section that creates the `<cd>` element in the else part of our code and we're done.

JSP: Modifying CD Information

We modify `cd_edit.jsp`, so that it displays information about the CD with the `id` specified in the form. We do this by using the **XTags** tag library. The changes are highlighted:

```
<!doctype html public "-//w3c//dtd html 4.0 transitional//en">
<%@ taglib uri="http://jakarta.apache.org/taglibs/xtags-1.0" prefix="xtags" %>

<xtags:parse uri="cd_list.xml"/>

<html>
  <head>
    <title>Edit CD information</title>
  </head>
```

```
  <body>
    <form method="get" action="cd_save.jsp">
      <xtags:context select="/cd-list/cd[@id=$param:id]">
        <p>
          <table cellSpacing=1 cellPadding=1>
            <tr>
              <td>Name</td>
              <td><input name="name" value="<xtags:valueOf select="name"/>"></td>
            </tr>
            <tr>
              <td>Band</td>
              <td><input name="band" value="<xtags:valueOf select="band"/>"></td>
            </tr>
            <tr>

              <td>Year</td>
              <td><input name="year" value="<xtags:valueOf select="year"/>"></td>
            </tr>
          </table>
        </p>
      </xtags:context>

      <input type="hidden" name="id" value="<xtags:valueOf select="$param:id"/>">
      <input type="submit" value="Submit">
      <input type="reset" value="Reset">
      <input type="button" value="Back" onclick="history.back()">
    </form>
  </body>
</html>
```

We start by loading the tag library, and parsing the XML document. We then move to the CD with the `id` in the query string with the following tag:

```
<xtags:context select="/cd-list/cd[@id=$param:id]">
```

In XTags, the values of the query string parameters are referenced in XPath expressions as `$param:name` where `name` is the name of the parameter. For example, have a look at the following query string:

```
http://myserver.com/mypage.html?name1=value1&name2=value2
```

Here, `$param:name1` would return `value1`, and `$param:name2` would return `value2`. Therefore `$param:id` is the value of the `id` parameter.

We then display the name, band, and year information for the selected CD in the form by using the `<xtags:valueOf>` tag. This tag displays the value of the XPath expression in its `select` attribute. If no CD is found with the `id` specified then these tags will print no value, leaving the form empty.

Finally we have added a hidden variable containing the `id` that was received. This `id` will be submitted to `cd_save.jsp`, so that it will be able to know which CD is being updated.

The cd_save.jsp page must now be modified so that it checks whether it has received a valid id. If it has, then an update will be performed, but if it hasn't, then an insert will be performed. The changes are highlighted:

```
<%@ page import="java.io.File,
                 org.dom4j.Document,
                 org.dom4j.Element,
                 org.dom4j.io.SAXReader" %>
<%
  // get the parameters:
  int id = 0;
  try {
    id = Integer.parseInt( request.getParameter("id") );
  } catch ( NumberFormatException ne ) {}

  String name = request.getParameter("name");
  String band = request.getParameter("band");
  String year = request.getParameter("year");

  // parse the document:
  SAXReader reader = new SAXReader();
  String path = application.getRealPath("/cd_list.xml");
  Document doc = reader.read( new File(path) );

  if ( id == 0 ) {

    // if we have a new CD then we generate the id by
    // adding 1 to the id of the last node:
    java.util.List list = doc.selectNodes( "//cd-list/cd" );
    org.dom4j.Node lastCd = (org.dom4j.Node) list.get( list.size()-1 );
    id = Integer.parseInt( lastCd.valueOf("@id") ) + 1;

    // create the new element
    Element newCd = doc.getRootElement().addElement( "cd" )
                      .addAttribute( "id", Integer.toString(id) );

    newCd.addElement("name").addText(name);
     newCd.addElement("band").addText(band);
    newCd.addElement("year").addText(year);

  }

  else {
    // we locate the CD that we are going to modify
    Element cd = (Element)doc.selectSingleNode("//cd-list/cd[@id=" + id + "]");

    // and then we modify the values
    cd.selectSingleNode( "name" ).setText(name);
    cd.selectSingleNode( "band" ).setText(band);
    cd.selectSingleNode( "year" ).setText(year);
  }

  // write the file:
```

```
    java.io.FileWriter output = new java.io.FileWriter( path );
    doc.write( output );
    output.close();
  %>

  <html>
    <head>
      <title>Success</title>
    </head>
    <body>
      CD list successfully modified.<br />
      <a href="cd_list.jsp">Back to CD List</a>
    </body>
  </html>
```

The first change that we've made is to try to get the `id` from the query string parameter. If that is not successful, the `id` variable will remain 0.

The second change we've made is to check whether to insert or update (by checking the value of the `id` variable). If `id == 0` then we are adding a new CD (because no `id` was sent from `cd_edit.jsp`), else we are updating an existing CD. If we are performing an update, we simply select the `<cd>` element to be modified with an XPath expression:

```
// we locate the CD that we are going to modify
Element cd = (Element)doc.selectSingleNode( "//cd-list/cd[@id=" + id + "]");
```

And finally we modify the values of that element's children:

```
cd.selectSingleNode( "name" ).setText(name);
cd.selectSingleNode( "band" ).setText(band);
cd.selectSingleNode( "year" ).setText(year);
```

Deleting a CD from the List

The final task that we are going to perform is to delete a CD from the list. This simply involves removing the `<cd>` element that corresponds to the `id` specified in the query string.

ASP: Deleting a CD from the List

Here is the code for `cd_delete.asp`:

```
<%@ Language=VBScript %>
<%
  Dim sID, oXML, oNode

  sID = Request.QueryString("id")

  'get CD List document
  Set oXML = CreateObject("MSXML2.DOMDocument")
  oXML.load(Server.MapPath("cd_list.xml"))
```

```
  'select desired CD node
  Set oNode = oXML.selectSingleNode("//cd[@id=" & sID & "]")

  oXML.documentElement.removeChild oNode

  oXML.save(Server.MapPath("cd_list.xml"))

  Set oNode = Nothing
  Set oXML = Nothing
%>

<html>
  <head>
    <title>Success</title>
  </head>
  <body>
    CD successfully removed.<br />
    <a href="cd_list.asp">Back to CD List</a>
  </body>
</html>
```

We retrieve the `id` of the CD to be removed from the query string. We then parse the `cd_list.xml` document, select the desired node using an XPath expression, and remove it. Finally we save the modified document and print a message to the user, indicating that the CD was successfully removed.

PHP: Deleting a CD from the List

The code for `cd_delete.php` is as follows:

```
<?php
  $id = $_GET['id'];
  $xml = join('',file('cd_list.xml'));
  $dom = domxml_open_mem($xml);
  $xpObj = xpath_new_context($dom);
  $resObj = xpath_eval($xpObj, "//cd[@id=$id]");
  $theOne = $resObj->nodeset[0];
  $root = $dom->document_element();;
  $root->remove_child($theOne);
  $xmldata = $dom->dump_mem();
  $fp = fopen('cd_list.xml','wb');
  fwrite($fp, $xmldata);
  fclose($fp);
?>

<html>
  <head>
    <title>Success</title>
  </head>
  <body>
    CD successfully removed.<br />
    <a href="cd_list.php">Back to CD List</a>
  </body>
</html>
```

There's nothing too complex here – once we have found the specified CD using our XPath query, we remove it and write the remaining XML out to file. Note that remove_child is called from the parent node of the node you wish to remove, passing the node to be released as an argument to the function.

JSP: Deleting a CD from the List

We use the XTags tag library again to achieve this. The code for the cd_delete.jsp page is as follows:

```
<%@ taglib uri="http://jakarta.apache.org/taglibs/xtags-1.0" prefix="xtags" %>

<xtags:parse uri="cd_list.xml" id="cdList"/>
<xtags:remove select="/cd-list/cd[@id=$param:id]"/>
<%
  // write the file:
  String filePath = application.getRealPath("/cd_list.xml");
  java.io.FileWriter output = new java.io.FileWriter( filePath );
  cdList.write( output );
  output.close();
%>

<html>
  <head>
    <title>Success</title>
  </head>
  <body>
    CD successfully removed.<br />
    <a href="cd_list.jsp">Back to CD List</a>
  </body>
</html>
```

We start by importing the XTags library. Then we parse the cd_list.xml document, and remove the desired CD from it. We do this by using the following tag:

```
<xtags:remove select="/cd-list/cd[@id=$param:id]"/>
```

This tag removes the element specified with the XPath expression in the select attribute. Finally we write the modified document to file, and display a message to the user indicating a successful removal of the CD.

Note that the document was parsed into a variable with the name of cdList. The name of this variable is specified by the id attribute of the <xtags:parse> tag. We can then reference this variable directly in the Java code we use to write the file.

Summary

In this chapter we've discussed server-side XML processing, and what advantages it has over client-side processing. For example, we've seen that sending the transformed content to the client ready to display allows for server-side caching, reduces the amount of data flowing over the connection, and makes the site easier to maintain (since the server-side processing code is not dependent on the client's browser).

We've given you an overview of the major server-side languages, and shown you examples of how to perform some of the most common XML tasks in these languages.

Specifically, for ASP, JSP, and PHP we've seen:

- Advantages and drawbacks of each language, and their support for XML.
- How to transform XML into HTML, using a simple XSL stylesheet.
- How to create new elements and write them to an XML file.
- How to read information from an XML file, and modify or delete specific elements.

Note that even though we've only seen three different technologies here, the basic techniques are the same, and if you're using another scripting language (ColdFusion, for example) you should still have taken away some useful lessons from this chapter.

You should now be prepared for a more in-depth discussion of the server-side processing in the case study chapters to follow.

Further Reading

If you want more information about the platforms discussed in this chapter, check out some of these links.

ASP

- *http://msdn.microsoft.com/library/default.asp?URL=/library/psdk/iisref/aspguide.htm*
- *http://www.asptoday.com* – a daily knowledge site for professional ASP programmers
- *http://www.asp101.com* – news, code examples, forums, articles, and links
- *http://www.aspin.com/* – code examples, tutorials, and ready-to-run scripts
- *http://www.aspalliance.com* – a free resource for ASP developers, featuring samples, tutorials, and lessons from a variety of industry authors and columnists

PHP

- *http://www.php.net/*
- *http://www.phpbuilder.com* – another great resource for PHP Developers

JSP

- *http://java.sun.com/products/jsp/*
- *http://www.javaskyline.com/learnjsp.html* – an intro to JSP, with links to tutorials, articles, etc.
- *http://www.theserverside.com* – a J2EE Community with news, patterns, reviews, discussions, articles, and books
- *http://www.jguru.com/faq/JSP* – Answers to frequently asked questions about JSP
- *http://www.jsptags.com* – A JSP web site where special interest is given to JSP Tag Libraries
- *http://www.jspinsider.com* – a site with articles and links to JSP resources
- *http://www.jspin.com* – code examples, tutorials, and ready-to-run scripts

9

- Advanced ASP XML case study (camera shop)
- Using a combination of database (Access) and XML to store data
- Generating XML from a recordset
- Transforming XML using the DOM

Author: Alex Shiell

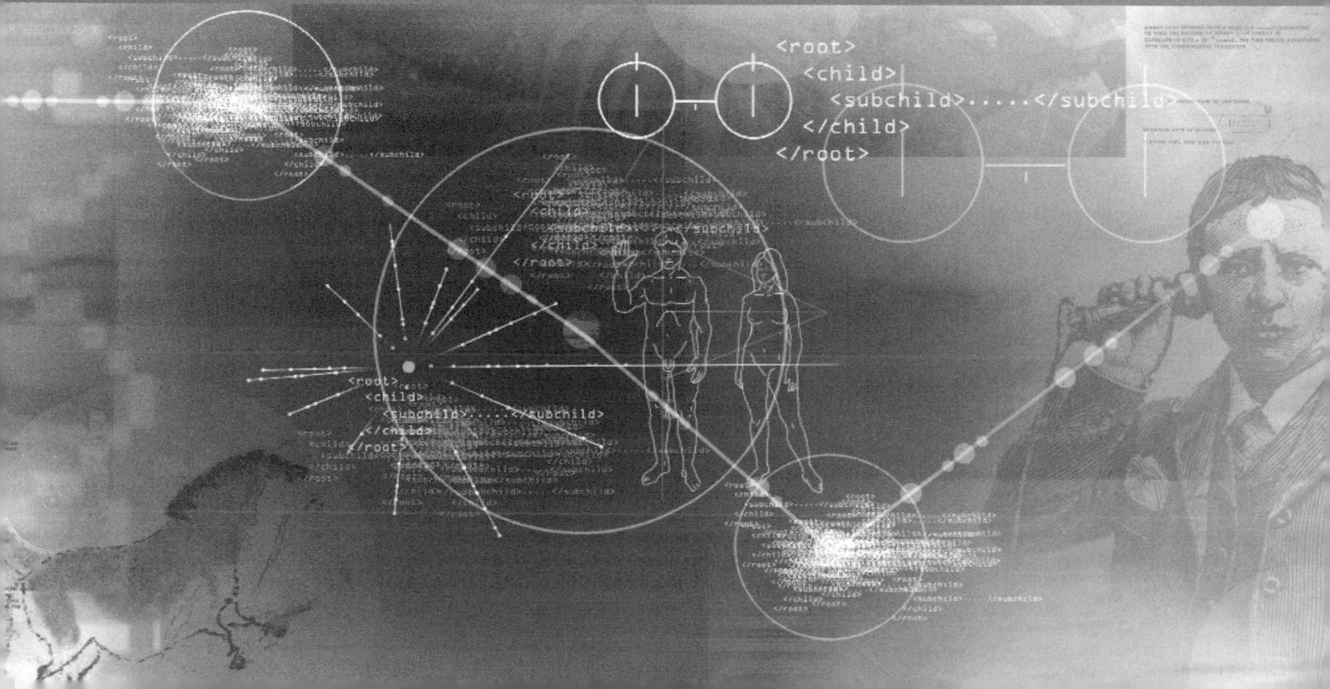

Case Study: Using ASP for an XML- and XSLT-Driven Site

As we have learned from the previous chapter, there are numerous advantages to using XML on the server. Microsoft has been very enthusiastic about XML for a number of years now, and the support for XML in ASP is extensive.

For the ASP case study I have built a shopping site, which sells digital cameras, camcorders, and associated accessories. My motivation for choosing these products was that I wanted products that had a large number of attributes associated with them, and as it happened I had a product list from a real site. I have imaginatively named it the "Photo Electronics Shop" as coming up with a catchy name was the lowest of my priorities!

This site is not intended to be a fully-fledged e-commerce site, but rather a showcase for what can be done with XML on the server. The main advantages of doing transformations on the server as opposed to the client are that it results in a fully browser-compatible site (accommodating both older browsers and other devices such as PDAs), and that the server is completely under our control. Throughout this site I've endeavored to generate straightforward HTML that can be understood by any browser. I have used a stylesheet for the formatting so, while the site may not look so pretty in older browsers that don't understand CSS, it should nevertheless be fully functional.

I have used XML techniques extensively throughout the site, which I'll be taking you through in this chapter. I'm assuming that you have a full understanding of ASP, so I will only be explaining the XML techniques. I will not be reproducing every function as I go through them, just the relevant bits. So to get the most out of this chapter you should be looking at the actual code itself, to see how the fragments I illustrate fit in with the rest.

Through the case study, you will learn about using ASP to accomplish the following XML-powered tasks:

- Creating XML data from a `Recordset`.
- Resolving IDs without joining lookup tables.
- Creating an XML template for generic page structure across a site.
- Storing a `Recordset` for future use, column sorting, and `Recordset` paging.
- Retaining frequently accessed data.

Requirements for the Code

Since the case study is written in ASP 3, you'll need to have Microsoft IIS 5, which comes as part of Windows 2000. However, if you're still using Windows NT then you just need to remove any occurrences of `server.transfer`, and replace them with `response.redirect`. We have chosen to use VBScript sa the scripting language for the ASP in this chapter.

In order to handle the XML, you'll need an XML parser. The site uses **Microsoft XML Core Services 4.0 (MSXML 4)**. MSXML 3.0 ships with Internet Explorer 6, but for this example you will need version 4.0. At the time of writing, the latest version is MSXML 4.0 Service Pack 1. When you install the package, you will find that it comes with an extremely comprehensive Help file, which covers just about everything that can be done with MSXML 4. Whilst it doesn't make easy reading, it is an invaluable reference for the XML developer.

MSXML 4 can be downloaded from the MSDN site at the following very long URL:

http://msdn.microsoft.com/downloads/default.asp?url=/downloads/sample.asp?url=/msdn-files/027/001/766/msdncompositedoc.xml

Finally, we're using an Access database – this suits our purposes here since we're focusing on the XML, not the database aspects of the site. If this were a real, live site, we would obviously want to use something more scalable than Access (like, say, SQL Server 2000).

The full code for the case study can be downloaded from the glasshaus web site at *http://www.glasshaus.com/*.

The Site

From this point on, I'll be referring to the case study as *the site*. I have laid out the components of the site in the following diagram; you may find it useful to refer back to this figure throughout this chapter:

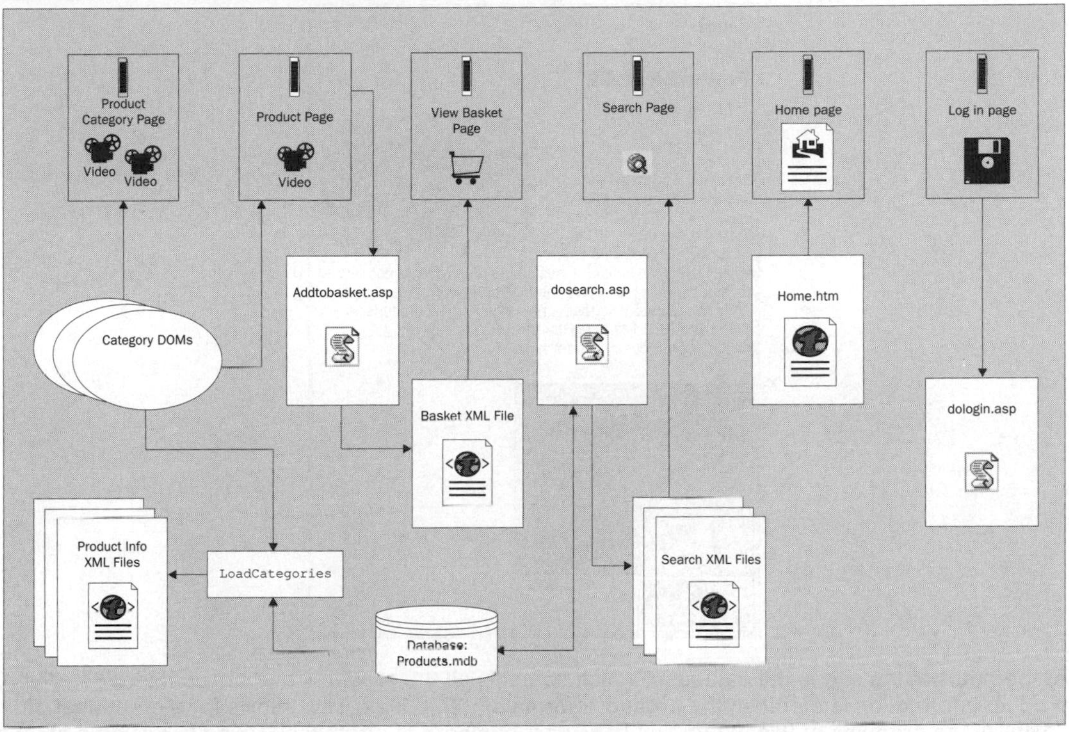

I will briefly introduce you to the features of the site, and then they will be explained in detail as we go through the case study.

The Product Pages

The products available from the site are divided into categories, which appear on the left hand side of each page. Clicking on one of these categories takes you to a page that shows a selection of products available in that category; clicking on a product takes you to the *Product* page. The *Category* and *Product* pages are shown in the following screenshots:

At the heart of the site is the database, which contains all the products and prices. More detailed product information is stored in the product information XML files. This allows for a great deal of flexibility, as products of this nature can have vast numbers of attributes. Trying to design a database to store all this information can be quite a laborious process, whereas with this approach we are free to define whatever tags we like for each different product type. Each product here can have its own XML file that can store any necessary additional information.

During the application initialization procedure, the product database is combined with the product information files to form a large XML document for each category, which remains in memory. Bear in mind that there will be a certain size of product list (say several thousand products in a category) where it would no longer be practical to do this, but at that point you should really be thinking about breaking down that category into subcategories. The *Product Category* and *Product* pages are created directly from these XML documents.

The Shopping Basket

Products can be added to the basket from either the *Product* page or the *Category* page. The shopping basket is an XML file that is saved with the user's ID as a file name. Once the basket is created, it remains on the server so it is still there when the user returns to the site. The *View Basket* page shows the contents of the basket and allows them to be modified:

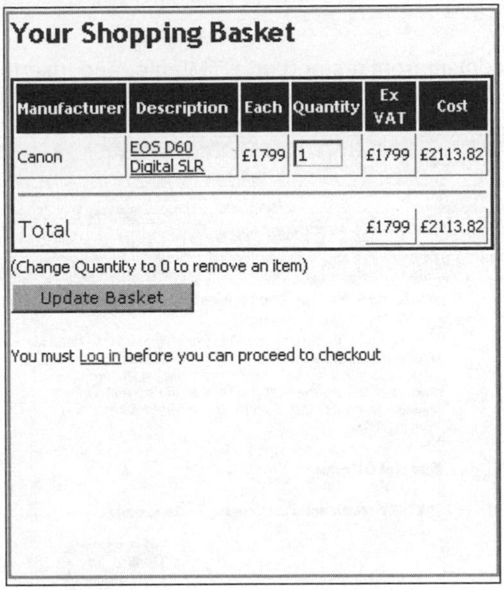

The Search Page

When a search is performed, the database is queried and an XML file is produced. This file remains on the system for the duration of the user's session, and is deleted when that session expires. Reloading the XML file can retrieve any search that is performed.

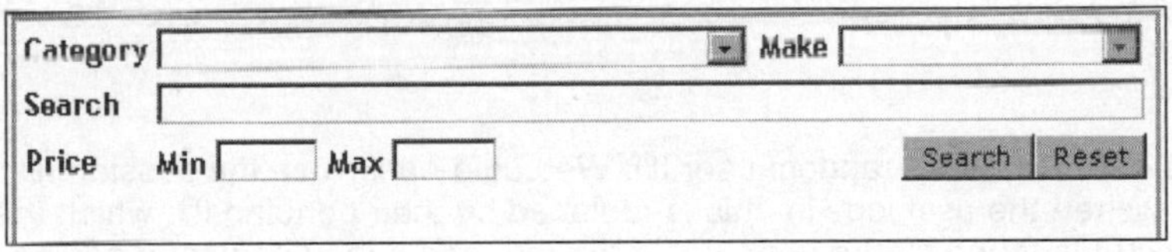

The Home Page

The home page grabs its content from a standard HTML file, and inserts it into the standard page template.

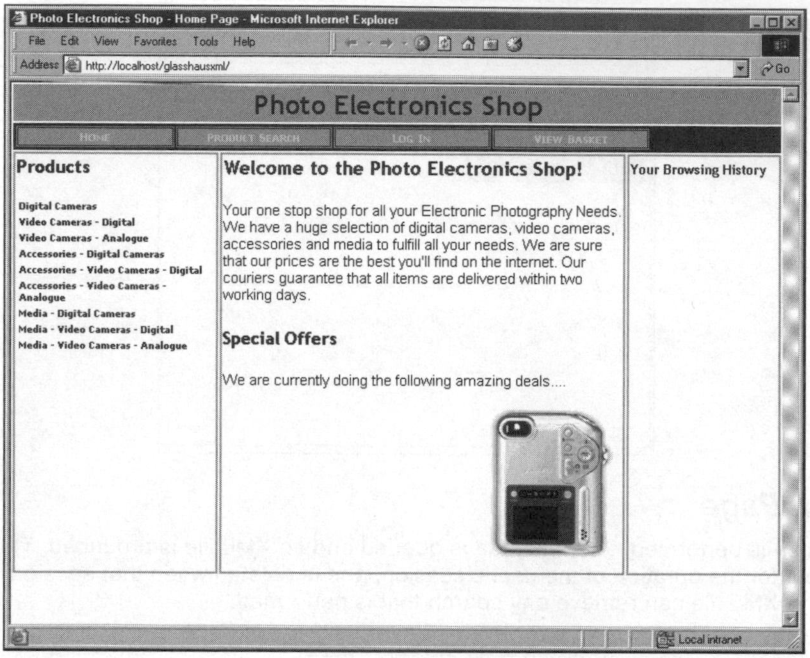

Logging in

An anonymous user is given a random user ID. We could easily use the session ID for this, but that is large and ugly. When the user logs in, this is replaced by their genuine ID, which they are allowed to choose. If a basket is found for the user, it is retrieved, and if they had been adding items before logging in it is merged with the existing basket. It is possible that prices may have changed since the user's last session, so therefore when a basket is retrieved the prices of items are updated to reflect the current prices in the database. We let the user put items in a basket before logging in so as to not put them off by forcing them to register before they're done browsing.

File Structure

The files that make up the site are arranged according to the type of file. All ASPs are in the root, the common functions are stored in include files in the `inc` directory, stylesheets in the `xsl` directory, and so on. In addition, there are directories for saving the shopping basket files (`basket`), search files (`search`), and the product information files (`info`). There are four files of common functions that are used throughout the site; `common.inc` contains the common functions specific to this site, `database.inc` contains functions for querying the database, `xml.inc` contains XML functions, and `global.inc` contains the functions that are used by `global.asa`. The Access database is stored in the `_private directory`, to prevent it from being downloaded. Obviously, if a scalable database platform (such as SQL Server 2000 or Oracle) were being used then this would not be an issue, but Access suits the needs of this case study. Besides, the study is about XML and XSLT, not databases. The directory structure is shown in the following diagram:

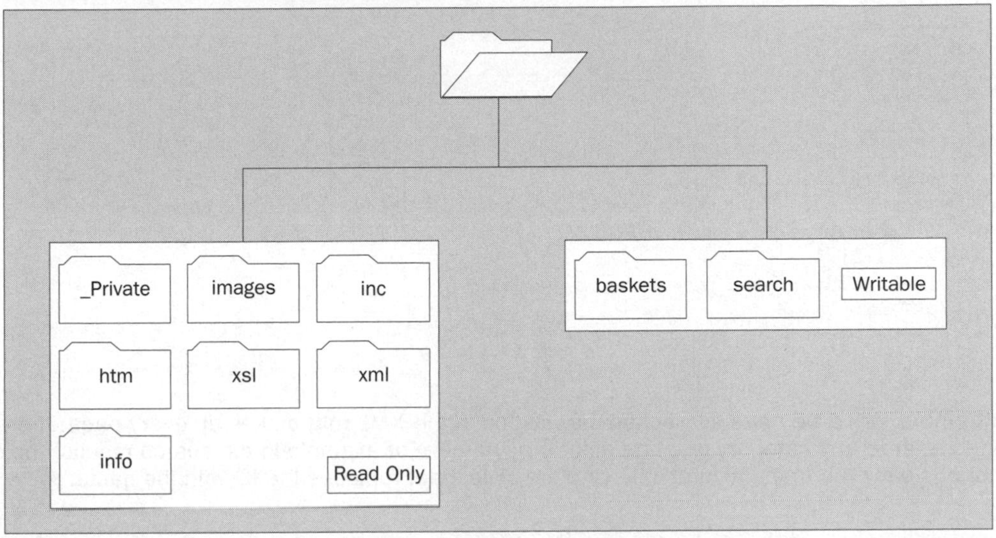

Lookups

The list of product categories appears on every page, in order to link to the category pages. Instead of hard-coding this into the common stylesheet, which would be no good as the categories may change, we need to have a section in the XML of every page that contains the category codes and descriptions so that this can just be transformed to create the category links.

Once this list is in the page it can then also be used whenever else we need to create a list of categories, like for example to create the categories drop-down in the search page. Given that we'll also need to create a drop-down of manufacturers on the search page and possibly in other places, it makes sense to hold a list of these in each page too. Just as you store drop-down entries in a lookup table in a traditional database-driven application, we'll be holding this information in a `lookups` node. This is how you would create a drop-down from the lookup, as taken from the search page stylesheet (`search.xsl`) (note how the `SELECTED` option is specified):

```
<SELECT id="ddCat" name="ddCat">
<OPTION/>
<xsl:for-each select="//lookups/categorys/category">
  <OPTION>
    <xsl:attribute name="value">
      <xsl:value-of select="category_id"/>
    </xsl:attribute>
    <xsl:if test="category_id=//SEARCH:search/SEARCH:criteria/category">
      <xsl:attribute name="SELECTED"/>
    </xsl:if>
    <xsl:value-of select="category_name"/>
  </OPTION>
</xsl:for-each>
</SELECT>
```

Furthermore, once we have this lookup information in the XML that makes up every page, there is no need to refer to any category or manufacturer by name. For example in the search results, the search just brings back the manufacturer's ID, and the stylesheet replaces the ID with the name:

```
<xsl:variable name="x" select="."/>
<xsl:value-of
select="//lookups/manufacturers/manufacturer[manufacturer_id=$x/manufacturer_id]/ma
nufacturer_name"/>
```

This is useful and efficient because it means that, when you're querying the database, you don't need to create a join with the table of manufacturer names. In this case it wouldn't make much difference, but if you work with larger and more complex databases the beauty of not having to create additional joins to replace IDs with names will soon become apparent.

Creating XML from a Recordset

The category and manufacturer lookups are obtained from the database in the application initialization procedure. This is done by querying the database and then converting the resultant `Recordset` to XML. A number of database platforms (such as Microsoft SQL Server) have the ability to return XML directly, rather than a traditional `Recordset` object. Parsing a `Recordset` and creating an XML string from it is a fairly straightforward exercise, and in any case, if you want to have complete control over your XML then you would need to write your own function. However, creating XML directly for the database is much quicker, and requires less coding.

The `rsToXML` function is in `database.inc`. It accepts two parameters, one for the name of the XML top or root element that represents a record, and one for the namespace declaration, if any. Basically all this function does is parse through the `Recordset`, create elements for each field, and encapsulate them in an element with the supplied name. The entire `Recordset` is then encapsulated in an element with the supplied name in plural.

The following code shows how each field node is created:

```
sXML = sXML & "<" & oRSInput.Fields.Item(i).Name & ">"
sField = SafeNull(oRSInput.Fields.Item(i).Value)
If Len(sField) > 0 Then
```

```
        If IsDate(sField) Then
            sValue = FormatDateTime(sField, 2)
        ElseIf IsNumeric(sField) Then
            sValue = CStr(sField)
        Else
            sValue = "<![CDATA["
            sValue = sValue & Server.HTMLEncode(sField)
            sValue = sValue & "]]>"
        End If
    Else
        sValue = ""
    End If
    sXML = sXML & sValue
    sXML = sXML & "</" & oRSInput.Fields.Item(i).Name & ">" & vbCrLf
```

First we need to ensure that the field value is not `null` or zero-length, otherwise it will cause an error when we try appending the value. Then, given that it's not `null` or zero-length, we need to look at what kind of data it contains. If it's a date, we want to convert it to a specific date format, and if it's a number, we can simply append the number. For any other type of data, we need to encapsulate the data in a `CDATA` section, and then HTML-encode it. Encapsulating the data in a `CDATA` section does in fact mean that the data does not have to be HTML-encoded to prevent errors on loading the document, as the parser will ignore any special characters within the data. It is only because this data is being produced for display on a web page that we need to HTML-encode it (`Server.HTMLEncode(sField)`).

The resultant lookup string that is produced looks like this:

```
<categorys>
<category>
  <category_id><![CDATA[C-D]]></category_id>
  <category_name><![CDATA[Digital Cameras]]></category_name>
</category>
<category>
  <category_id><![CDATA[V-D]]></category_id>
  <category_name><![CDATA[Video Cameras - Digital]]></category_name>
</category>
...
</categorys>
```

All the lookups are then concatenated into one string and encapsulated in a `<lookups>` element tag. The string is then stored in an application variable. These would be updated whenever the application restarts. As the lookups shouldn't change very often, the application can be restarted whenever the data does change.

Incorporating a Generic Page Structure

For just about any site on the Internet, it is highly desirable to achieve consistency across all pages. They should all have the same look and feel, and a number of common components such as navigation elements and the company's branding and contact details. In order to facilitate site maintainability, these common components really need to come from one central source so that when the site is redesigned, the changes take effect globally.

Every page of this site has the same structure, as shown in the following screenshot. There is a header along the top, and a horizontal menu to access the four principal pages. On the left-hand side of each page the product categories are listed, and these link to the category pages. On the right-hand side there is a section for the user's browsing history, so that they can retrieve searches and quickly go back to products they have viewed:

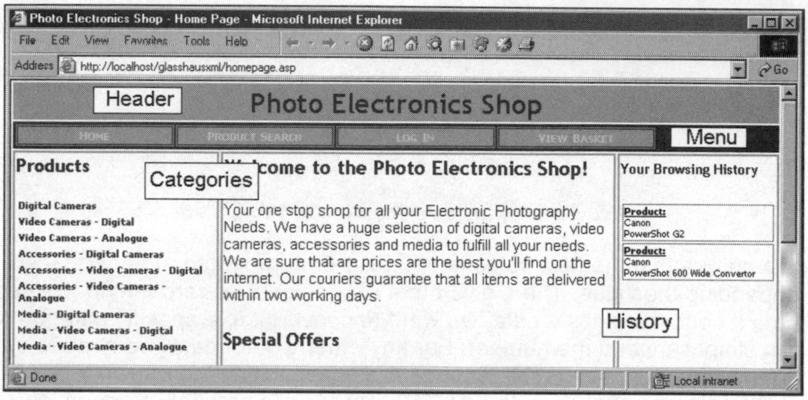

The starting point of any page in the site is the `pagetemplate.xml` file, which you'll find in the `xml` directory. It contains nodes for these common page elements, and nodes to hold some information on the user. It also contains a node into which the common lookups will be inserted. You'll see that the nodes that make up the site menu have been hard-coded into the template. This is because the menu is very simple in this case. For a more complex menu structure, you would want to store the menu XML in a separate file and insert it when you build the page.

```
<?xml version="1.0" encoding="ISO-8859-1"?>
<xmlpage title="" site="">
  <lookups/>
  <MENU:items xmlns:MENU="uri=http://glasshausxml/menu">
    <MENU:item>
      <desc>Home</desc>
      <address>homepage.asp</address>
    </MENU:item>
    <!-- other menu items here… -->
  </MENU:items>
  <HISTORY:items xmlns:HISTORY="uri=http://glasshausxml/history"/>
  <page_content/>
  <user_info>
    ...
  </user_info>
</xmlpage>
```

Notice that we're using namespaces to identify the Menu and History items as being different things.

Creating the DOMDocument Object

In order to create pages using this template, we need to first load the template into a `DOMDocument` object, and insert the page content into it. As we saw in the previous chapter, in ASP a `DOMDocument` is created like this:

```
Set oXML = CreateObject("MSXML2.DOMDocument")
```

The above line will create a basic `DOMDocument` object, as defined in the version 2.0 or 3.0 release of MSXML, depending on how MSXML 3 was installed. For our site, however, we need to explicitly specify that we want to use a version 4.0 object as we want to use the latest properties and methods. This is done by amending the Class ID with the version number, as follows:

```
Set oXML = CreateObject("MSXML2.DOMDocument.4.0")
```

The version 4.0 `DOMDocument` requires certain properties to be explicitly specified before it can be used, and furthermore any namespaces that are used in the document have to be specified in advance as well, so we make sure we do that:

```
oXML.async = False
oXML.setProperty "SelectionLanguage", "XPath"

sNameSpaces ="xmlns:MENU='uri=http://glasshausxml/menu' "
oXML.setProperty "SelectionNamespaces", sNameSpaces
```

The `DOMDocument` object, just like any other object that is suitable for scripting, uses the apartment-threading model. This makes it efficient for creating and destroying within the execution of a single script. There are times when you want a `DOMDocument` to remain in memory, either to be available to multiple users, or to retain information throughout the session (we'll be doing this later on when we come to the product category pages). For this kind of use, an apartment-threaded object is no good as it can only support a single thread – we need an object that can support multiple threads. In this case, we need to open a **free-threaded** `DOMDocument` object with an alternative Class ID:

```
Set oXML = CreateObject("MSXML2.FreeThreadedDOMDocument.4.0")
```

Note that a free-threaded `DOMDocument` uses a lot more server resources that a normal one, so it should only be used when necessary.

So, all in all, there are quite a few things to consider when creating a `DOMDocument`. Rather than explicitly specifying these things every time we need to create one, here's a function to create it, which you can find in `xml.inc`:

```
Function CreateXMLObject(bFreeThreaded)
  Dim o, sClassId, sNameSpaces

  If bFreeThreaded then
    sClassId = "MSXML2.FreeThreadedDOMDocument.4.0"
  Else
    sClassId = "MSXML2.DOMDocument.4.0"
  End if
  Set o = CreateObject(sClassId)
  o.async = False
  o.setProperty "SelectionLanguage", "XPath"

  sNameSpaces ="xmlns:MENU='uri=http://glasshausxml/menu' "
  sNameSpaces =sNameSpaces & "xmlns:HISTORY='uri=http://glasshausxml/history' "
  sNameSpaces =sNameSpaces & "xmlns:SEARCH='uri=http://glasshausxml/search' "
```

```
    sNameSpaces =sNameSpaces & "xmlns:PRODUCT='uri=http://glasshausxml/product' "
    sNameSpaces =sNameSpaces & "xmlns:BASKET='uri=http://glasshausxml/basket' "

    o.setProperty "SelectionNamespaces", sNameSpaces
    Set CreateXMLObject = o
End Function
```

Now when Microsoft brings out their version 5 parser, which will inevitably have advantages over this one, we can simply change the version number in this function rather than in every place where the `DOMDocument` is created. Notice how I've specified all the namespaces that are used throughout the site. It doesn't matter whether the document that is loaded contains these namespaces or not, but they do need to be specified just in case. For a truly generic function, you would pass in another string with the namespace definitions, but it'll keep the rest of our code cleaner if we do it this way.

Lastly, since every `DOMDocument` we create is going to have these same properties, if we want to use more than one within the same ASP it is much more efficient to create one and then clone it, rather than calling this function multiple times.

The `cloneNode` method accepts a parameter that indicates whether or not to clone all nodes that are descendants of this node. If `true`, it creates a clone of the complete tree below this node. If `false`, it clones this node and its attributes only. We just want to clone the object itself, so we set it to `false`, as in this example:

```
Set oXML = CreateXMLObject(false)
Set oXML1 = oXML.cloneNode(false)
```

Creating the DOMDocument for Any Page of the Site

So now we're ready to look at how to create the generic page `DOMDocument` and insert content into it.

Loading XML into the DOMDocument

First of all, we create a `DOMDocument` for the page, and a clone that we'll be using to temporarily store other information prior to inserting it into the page `DOMDocument`. The template XML file (`pagetemplate.xml`) is then loaded into the page `DOMDocument`, by calling the `load` method of the `DOMDocument`:

```
Set oXMLPage = CreateXMLObject(false)
Set oXMLTemp = oXMLPage.cloneNode(false)

oXMLPage.load(Server.MapPath("xml/pagetemplate.xml"))
```

The first thing we'll be using the temporary `DOMDocument` for is to load the common lookups. These are stored as an XML string in an `Application` variable. To load XML directly from a string rather than a file, the `loadXML` method is used rather than the `load` method:

```
oXMLTemp.loadXML(Application("lookupsxml"))
```

Loading XML from a string is marginally more efficient than from a file, as it saves the need to open the file and read the string from it. Provided that the file or string that was loaded exists and contains valid, well-formed XML, the `DOMDocument` will now contain a loaded document. In this instance, we know the XML that we're loading so we know it's well-formed. At other times, though, how can we be sure? We can find out by querying the `parseError` property. This contains an object with a number of properties, the most useful ones being `errorCode` and `reason`:

```
If oXMLTemp.parseError.errorCode > 0 then Response.write oXMLTemp.parseError.reason
```

Selecting, Reading, and Writing Nodes and Attributes

Once we have a loaded document in the `DOMDocument`, we need to be able to query it for information and manipulate the information with in it. The `DOMDocument` is essentially a hierarchy of node objects, and we use XPath to navigate the `DOMDocument`. Single nodes are selected by using the `selectSingleNode` method of the `DOMDocument` or a node, or alternatively a `collection` of nodes can be returned with the `selectNodes` method. A `collection` of nodes is just like any other `collection` of objects in VBScript – you can't call properties and methods on it directly, apart from the `length` and `item` properties – so you need to iterate through the `collection` and access the individual node objects.

If `oXML`, the object from which the nodes are being selected, is the `DOMDocument` object itself, then the XPath expression needs to lead to the desired node(s) from the root of the document. If `oXML` is a node, then the XPath expression is evaluated from that node.

We define the XPath query:

```
sXPath = "//path/node[@someattribute=1]"
```

If the XPath query will return a single node, or you only want the first node returned by the query, we use `selectSingleNode`, as follows:

```
Set oNode = oXML.selectSingleNode(sXPath)
```

If the XPath query returns a number of nodes, we can use `selectNodes` instead:

```
Set oNodeList = oXML.selectNodes(sXPath)
```

If we want to select the top-level element of a `DOMDocument`, we don't need to specify it explicitly as it is contained in the `documentElement` property of the `DOMDocument`.

```
Set oNode = oXML.documentElement
```

We can read or modify the value of a node by accessing its `text` property:

```
sText = oXML.selectSingleNode(sXPath).text
oXML.selectSingleNode(sXPath).text = sText
```

Attributes of elements are also nodes that can be navigated to in the same way with XPath, although there are two older methods that can be used with attributes – `getAttribute` and `setAttribute`. If an attribute does not exist already then `setAttribute` will create it, which makes it useful. If the node does exist already, then `setAttribute` will overwrite it:

```
sText = oNode.getAttribute(sName)
oNode.setAttribute sName, sText
```

Let's get back to our page template `DOMDocument`. A page needs a title and this will just be passed in by the calling ASP, and then inserted into the `title` attribute of the top-level element:

```
oXMLPage.documentElement.selectSingleNode("@title").text = sTitle
```

Replacing a Node

Earlier on we loaded the lookups into the temporary `DOMDocument`. Now we need to insert them into the page `DOMDocument`. This will be done by replacing the empty `<lookups>` node in the page `DOMDocument` with the populated one from the temporary `DOMDocument`.

To replace a node, you need to select the immediate parent node of the node you would like to replace, and then call the `replaceChild` method, into which you pass first the new node and then a pointer to the one that will be replaced:

```
oXMLPage.documentElement.replaceChild _
        oXMLTemp.selectSingleNode("//lookups"), _
        oXMLPage.selectSingleNode("//lookups")
```

In each case, we are using XPath to locate the node. The new node is physically removed from its previous location in the `DOMDocument`, although in this case that doesn't matter as we've only loaded the document in order to move the node into the page template. If we wanted the node to remain in its position in the temporary `DOMDocument`, we would pass in a clone of the node instead. The `cloneNode` method has a parameter, which specifies whether or not you want to clone the contents of the node. If it is set to `true`, then the value is cloned as well as any attributes and any nodes contained within the node. If it is set to `false`, then only the element itself is replicated:

```
oXMLPage.documentElement.replaceChild _
        oXMLTemp.selectSingleNode("//lookups").cloneNode(true), _
        oXMLPage.selectSingleNode("//lookups")
```

Note that the VBScript '_' operator has been used so that this code can be written over several lines.

The browsing history is inserted into the document in exactly the same way, the only difference being that the XML string comes from a `Session` variable rather than an `Application` variable.

Appending a Node

If rather than replacing an existing node we want to append a node as a child of an existing node, then we can use the `appendChild` method:

```
oXML.selectSingleNode(sXPath).appendChild oNode
```

Like `replaceChild`, this will remove the node from its original location so, if we want it to remain there, we pass in a clone instead.

You can find an example of this in the `AddToHistory` function (in `common.inc`), when it inserts a copy of the search or product information into the new history node:

```
oNode.appendChild oNodeToAdd.cloneNode(true)
```

The `appendChild` method will always append the node at the top of the subtree, so the newly appended node will always be the first child node. If the node needs to be inserted into a particular position, then the `insertBefore` method can be used instead. This will insert the node before the reference node that is passed in. If no reference node is passed in, then the new node will be appended after the last child node, so it will appear at the end of the list of child nodes:

```
oXML.selectSingleNode(sXPath).insertBefore oNode, oReferenceNode
```

You can also find an example of this in the `AddToHistory` function (in `common.inc`), when it inserts the new history node into the list of history items – we want the new node to appear at the top of the list:

```
oXMLHistory.selectSingleNode("//HISTORY:items").insertBefore oNode, _
           oXMLHistory.selectSingleNode("//HISTORY:items/HISTORY:item")
```

Inserting the Page Content

To insert the actual page content it first has to be loaded into a `DOMDocument` as well, and then the <page_content> node will be replaced just like the <history> and <lookups> nodes. Although this time, rather than loading an XML string, we'll be passing the `DOMDocument` in from the calling ASP for maximum flexibility. So first of all we need to see if it is an object at all, as nothing may have been passed in.

If you look at the `CreatePageXMLDOM` function (in `xml.inc`), you'll see that I've specified that the `DOMDocument` be passed in by reference. This isn't strictly necessary, as what you're actually passing is a pointer to the `DOMDocument` object in memory and, if you didn't specify `ByRef`, then you would just be creating a replica of the pointer rather than the object. I've put `ByRef` there as a reminder that the object being manipulated within the function is the same actual object in memory. In this case we do not want append the selected node itself, but rather a clone of it, as at this point we don't know what the calling ASP may want to do with the `DOMDocument` after passing it in. For example, when we come to creating the category page we do not want to remove the nodes from the category `DOMDocument` as they need to remain in memory to be used again.

Furthermore, as the `DOMDocument` comes from the calling ASP, we do not know what the `DOMDocument` is going to contain so we'd better check for a parse error. It may be that the file loaded by the calling ASP was not found, or it may not be well-formed.

And finally, for a bit of added flexibility, we can let the calling ASP pass in a node rather than a whole document. For this we need to be able to ascertain what kind of object it was that was passed in, as we'll get an error by trying to examine the `parseError` property on a node, because that is a property of the document. We can do this by looking at the `nodeType` property of the object. There are many different types of nodes (you can see the full list by looking up "nodeType" in the MSXML 4 Help file), but the ones we're interested in are `1`, which is a node element, and `9`, which is a document. There's also type `11`, which is a document fragment. A document fragment is a node that does not belong to a parent document and, if we get one of these, we can put it straight into the page `DOMDocument`:

```
If isObject(oXMLContent) then
  Select Case oXMLContent.nodeType

    Case 1
```

```
        'ELEMENT - Append a clone
          oXMLPage.selectSingleNode("//page_content").appendChild _
                                                  oXMLContent.cloneNode(true)

        Case 9
        'DOCUMENT - Check for parse error, append a clone of the document element
          If oXMLContent.parseError.errorCode = 0 then
            oXMLPage.selectSingleNode("//page_content").appendChild _
                                                  oXMLContent.documentElement.cloneNode(true)
          End if

        Case 11
        'DOCUMENT FRAGMENT - Append the node
          oXMLPage.selectSingleNode("//page_content").appendChild oXMLContent

    End Select
  End if
```

Filling in the User Info

The last thing that remains to be done is filling in the user information. In the session initialization procedure, a random user ID is allocated to the user (which is replaced by their real ID when they log in). We also collect some information about their browser such as the type and version, which will be useful later on when we need to code parts of stylesheets for specific browsers. This information is stored in session variables, the values of which are simply inserted into the nodes.

This approach is the best here, as there is not a lot of information. In a fully-fledged e-commerce application, however, you may well want to hold a lot more information on the user, in which case it would be better to build up an XML string in the session initialization procedure and insert it in the same way as the browsing history.

Transforming the DOMDocument

Now we have our page completely defined in a `DOMDocument`. This isn't much use to us yet as we need to transform the `DOMDocument` into HTML before we can send it to the browser.

As with creating an XML object, this is the sort of thing we're going to want to do all over the place, so it's best to have a function into which we can pass the `DOMDocument` so it can be transformed and written to the response stream.

Before we can transform the `DOMDocument`, we need to load the stylesheet into a separate `DOMDocument`. At this point it's useful to check for a parse error in the stylesheet, as it's so easy to miss out a quote or a slash here and there which will prevent it from working. If there is a parse error, then it is written out instead of the transformed page so that the stylesheet author can immediately find the error and correct it.

> *Incidentally another way of checking a stylesheet – or an XML file for that matter – for being well-formed is to load it into Internet Explorer 5+. Its default stylesheet will highlight any errors immediately.*

Provided there is no error, we can write the transformed document:

```
Set oXSL = CreateXMLObject(false)
oXSL.load(sXSLPath)

If oXSL.parseError then
  Response.Write "Error:" & oXSL.parseError.Reason
Else
  Response.Write oXMLInput.transformNode(oXSL)
End if
```

This is the essence of the `TransformWriteDOM` method that you'll find in `xml.inc`.

Passing Parameters into a Stylesheet

That was easy enough wasn't it? Unfortunately it's not so easy when you want to pass parameters into a stylesheet, as we'll be doing later on. In `xml.inc` you'll find a procedure called `ApplyXSLParamsWriteDOM`, into which you can pass a parameter string and the `DOMDocument` to be transformed. I don't want to go through this function in detail, as it would be beyond the scope of this book, but the crux of it is as follows:

A `DOMDocument` is created and the stylesheet is loaded. An XSL Template object (`XSLTemplate`) is then created, and the stylesheet is set to be the `DOMDocument` containing the loaded stylesheet. Then a template processor object is created, into which the parameters are appended one by one. If any parameters are left out, then they will have their default values. The template processor then transforms the `DOMDocument`, and outputs the HTML string, which is then written to the response stream.

This process is essentially what is going on under the skin when you call the `transformNode` method.

Stylesheet Structure

There is a common stylesheet (`common.xsl`) that contains the template rules for all the common page elements. Each page of the site has its own stylesheet, which includes this common stylesheet. The stylesheet of each page follows the pattern of `base.xsl`:

```
<?xml version="1.0" encoding="ISO-8859-1"?>
<xsl:stylesheet version="1.0" xmlns:xsl="http://www.w3.org/1999/XSL/Transform">
<xsl:output method="html" omit-xml-declaration="yes"/>

<xsl:template match="/">
  <xsl:apply-templates select="xmlpage"/>
</xsl:template>

<xsl:template match="page_content">

</xsl:template>

<xsl:include href="common.xsl"/>

</xsl:stylesheet>
```

First of all the `<xmlpage>` node is transformed, the rule for which is defined in `common.xsl`. This defines the page structure, as you see below. Within the rule for the `<xmlpage>` node, there is a call to apply the template of the `<page_content>` node. This takes us back to the original stylesheet, in which the template rules specific to the page are defined:

```
<xsl:template match="xmlpage">
  <html>
  <head>
  <title>Photo Electronics Shop - <xsl:value-of select="@title"/>
  <xsl:if test="//PRODUCT:products">
    - <xsl:value-of
select="//lookups/categorys/category[category_id=//PRODUCT:products/@category]/cate
gory_name"/>
  </xsl:if>
  </title>
  </head>
  <body topmargin="0" leftmargin="0">
  <link rel="stylesheet" type="text/css" href="StyleSheet.css"/>

  <table class="pagetable">
  <tr><td colspan="3" class="pagetableheader">Photo Electronics Shop</td></tr>
  <tr><td colspan="3" class="menuholder">
        <xsl:apply-templates select="MENU:items"/>
      </td>
  </tr>
  <tr>
    <td class="pagetablecell" VALIGN="TOP" WIDTH="200">
      <xsl:apply-templates select="lookups/categorys"/>
      <br/><br/><br/><br/><br/><br/><br/><br/><br/><br/>
    </td>
    <td class="pagetablecell" valign="top">
      <xsl:apply-templates select="page_content"/>
    </td>
    <td class="pagetablecell" valign="TOP" width="150">
      <xsl:apply-templates select="HISTORY:items"/>
    </td>
  </tr>
  <tr><td colspan="3" class="pagetablefooter"></td></tr>
  </table>

  </body>
  </html>
</xsl:template>
```

Creating the Page

So now we have our stylesheets and our complete `CreatePage` function, so we're ready to start creating pages on the fly. Here's the complete procedure for creating the page (from `common.inc` in the `inc` folder):

```
Sub CreatePage (sStylesheet, sTitle, sParams, bFreeThreaded, ByRef oXMLContent)

  Dim oXMLPage
  Set oXMLPage = CreatePageXMLDOM(sTitle, bFreeThreaded, oXMLContent)

  sStylesheet = Server.MapPath("xsl/" & sStylesheet & ".xsl")
```

```
    If sParams="" then
      TransformWriteDOM sStylesheet, oXMLPage
    Else
      ApplyXSLParamsWriteDOM sStylesheet, sParams, oXMLPage
    End if

    'oXMLPage.save(Server.MapPath("search") & "/temp.xml")

    Set oXMLPage = Nothing
  End Sub
```

You'll notice that I have a line commented out which saves the page to a file. This is useful for debugging purposes – if you want to see what the XML of any page looks like, uncomment that line and refresh the page, and the XML will be saved in that file.

Each page of the site can now be created by calling this function. The calling ASP has to create a `DOMDocument` or select a node for the page content, specify the stylesheet and any parameters, and also pass in the title. The free-threaded flag is there to tell the function what kind of object is being passed in – it is not possible to mix threading models, so if a free-threaded document is being passed in, then the page `DOMDocument` must also be a free-threaded `DOMDocument`.

Let's now have a look at the home page to see this function in action.

Inserting the Content of an HTML File

The home page of our site is the first thing anyone sees when they come to the site. It needs to be packed full of relevant information, and needs to change on a regular basis. Furthermore we can't have a standard pattern for the home page, as we need to cater to every whim of the site designer. So the best thing would be to let the site designer provide us with an HTML page that they've designed, and then we insert it into our template page.

The first thing we do is to load the HTML file. For this to be possible, the HTML file must adhere to the rules of being well-formed. The latest versions of the popular web page editing suites should all have the capacity to output well-formed HTML, so our designer needn't worry about that. The other thing is the popular use of ` ` for spaces – this will cause an "undefined entity" error in XML, so we need to replace this with the correct character entity which is ` `. The popular web page editing suites are unlikely to do this, so this needs to be done prior to publishing using the find and replace function of a text editor, or programmatically with a script.

First the HTML page is loaded into a `DOMDocument`:

```
Set oXMLTemp = CreateXMLObject(false)
oXMLTemp.load(Server.MapPath("htm/home.htm"))
```

Then we simply select the `BODY` node and pass it into the `createPage` function:

```
Set oXMLContent = oXMLTemp.selectSingleNode("//body")
CreatePage "homepage", "Home Page", "", false, oXMLContent
```

In the stylesheet, we can let the HTML pass straight through:

```
<xsl:template match="page_content">
  <xsl:copy-of select="*"/>
</xsl:template>
```

And we have our homepage, as in the following screenshot:

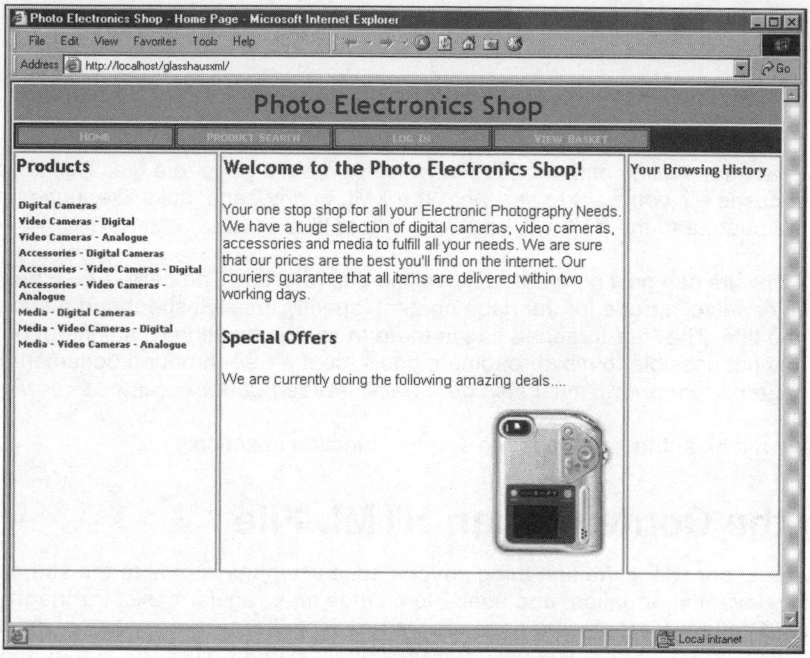

Catering for Different Browsers

While the main ethos of the design of this site was to create HTML that works well in most if not all browsers, there will always be times when you want to code for specific browsers or devices. It may be that you want to take advantage of the capabilities of the latest browsers, or it may simply be that some bits just don't look good in certain browsers.

In the session initialization procedure a function is run which examines the user agent string, and populates some session variables with the browser type and version. Unfortunately the user agent string is not comprehensive enough on quite a few browsers. Older versions of Netscape just say "Mozilla" rather than "Netscape" – and every browser contains "Mozilla" in its user agent string. Because it is ignored by many DHTML authors, Opera has to pretend to be Internet Explorer 5 in order that pages coded for IE will run, but unfortunately it doesn't behave in exactly the same way. But nevertheless, the function I have provided correctly detects IE and Netscape 6, and sets a variable to indicate DHTML-compatibility accordingly. Browser information is stored in the page template in the `<browser>` tag.

```
<browser vers="5.5" dhtml="Y">MSIE</browser>
```

In this site, there are two places in which I've coded for specific browsers. The first of these is in the *Search* page, where the text box for entering a string to search for was appearing too large in older versions of Netscape. As I've said, older versions of Netscape don't make themselves known too well, so we just provide a smaller text box if it's not IE or Netscape 6.

From `search.xsl`:

```
<input id="txtSearch" name="txtSearch">
<xsl:attribute name="SIZE">
  <xsl:choose>
  <xsl:when test="//user_info/browser='MSIE' or //user_info/browser='NS'">
    70
  </xsl:when>
  <xsl:otherwise>50</xsl:otherwise>
  </xsl:choose>
</xsl:attribute>
  <xsl:attribute name="VALUE"><xsl:value-of
                select="//SEARCH:search/SEARCH:criteria/search"/></xsl:attribute>
</input>
```

While most of the linking in the site is done with traditional hyperlinks, in the product category page we wanted users to be able to click anywhere within the cell that shows a product, to jump to the product page. Only certain browsers support a clickable `<div>`, so we have to provide a hyperlink for the other browsers.

This was a bit more complicated, because we don't want to repeat the entire cell contents twice, so we only want to write an opening `<div>` or `<a> tag` before writing the cell contents. XSLT doesn't allow you to just write an opening tag without closing it, as that would cause the stylesheet not to be well-formed. So instead we have to use stylesheet scripting to write the tag directly to the output stream.

From `catbasic.xsl`:

```
<xsl:choose>
 <xsl:when test="//user_info/browser/@dhtml='Y'">
   <xsl:value-of
           select="layoutfunctions:createOpenDiv(string(product_id))"
           disable-output-escaping="yes"/>
 </xsl:when>
 <xsl:otherwise>
   <xsl:value-of
           select="layoutfunctions:createOpenLink(string(product_id))"
           disable-output-escaping="yes"/>
 </xsl:otherwise>
</xsl:choose>
```

Note the `disable-output-escaping="yes"` attribute – this prevents the output tags from being HTML-encoded. The actual functions themselves are very simple:

```
<msxsl:script language="JScript" implements-prefix="layoutfunctions">
    <![CDATA[function createOpenLink(sProductId){
    return("<A HREF='productpage.asp?id="+sProductId+"'>");
    }
```

```
function createOpenDiv(sProductId){
  return("<DIV STYLE='width:100;height:200px;cursor:hand;' " +
         "ONCLICK=\"document.location.href='productpage.asp?id="+sProductId+"'\">");
}
</msxsl:script>
```

Similar functions are used to close the tags after the cell contents have been written. I'll be explaining stylesheet scripting in more detail later on, when we come to cover the category pages.

Site Skins

The main advantage of using XML in web development is the complete separation of style and content. What this essentially means is that if we want to change what our site looks like, we simply rewrite the stylesheets without touching any other part of the application. But why should we only do this when we want to change our site's appearance? We can do this anyway to provide our site with different façades for different purposes.

"Skins" are rapidly becoming a popular phenomenon in computer programs, especially from smaller vendors who want to make their products more appealing by offering a greater degree of customization. In this case, the customization takes the form of allowing the look and feel of the product to be changed to something else, while retaining its essential functions. *Winamp* was probably the first product to use skins, but a host of others soon followed, including Netscape, and Microsoft with their *Windows Media Player*. The truth is that there is not much merit in allowing visitors to a web site to choose what they want a site to look like; it's a gimmick really. If you turn the tables and think about it from a company's point of view, however, it suddenly becomes a very powerful tool. To be able to use the same site to sell the same products to different markets by offering your site in different guises would have many advantages.

How you approach the issue of site skins depends on how different you want the site to be. If it really needs to be completely different, you would need to provide a complete alternative set of stylesheets, and build into the transformation functions a way to determine which set of stylesheets to use. If it's just the appearance and layout you want to change, you can build this into the common stylesheet.

If you open up `common.xsl` and uncomment the line at the bottom where it imports `xmlpage.xsl` and then load the site, you'll see that it suddenly looks completely different – it transforms our site from this:

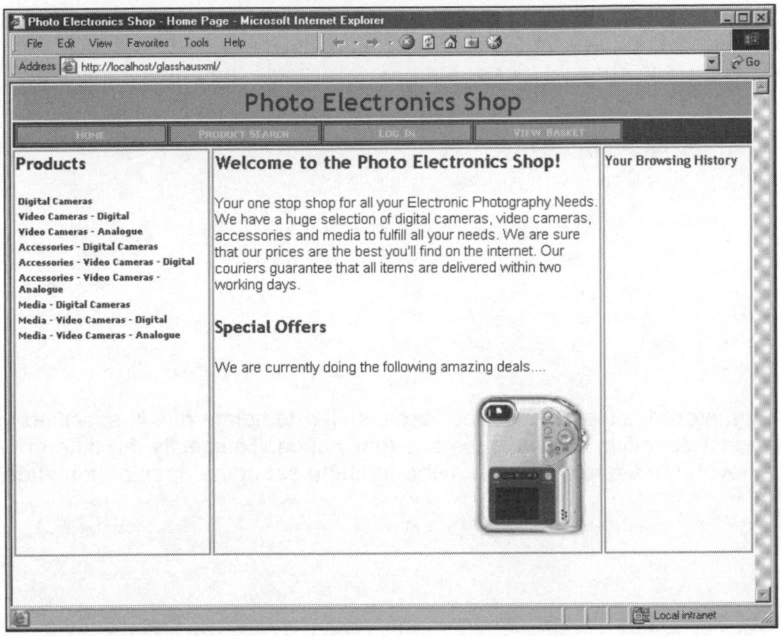

to this:

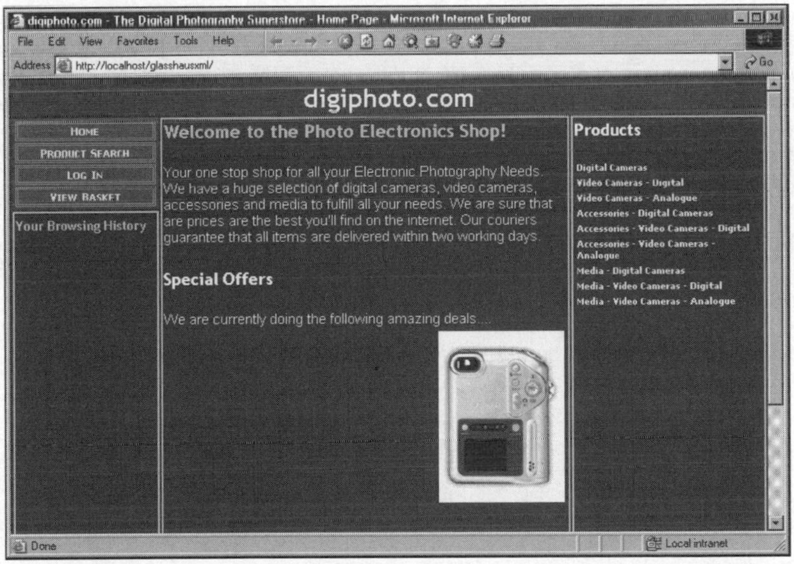

In the session initialization procedure, a session variable value is set according to which site the user is browsing, and this is then put into the `site` attribute in the page template whenever a page is created. In this site I've just hard-coded the value, but in reality you would want to look at the domain name the user was using to access the site, and set the value accordingly. (If you actually wanted to give the user the ability to change the look of the site, this value could easily be updated at run-time, and then stored with the user's details so that the look they've chosen remains.)

In order to achieve this, I've taken advantage of template modes. Template modes allow you to specify alternative template rules for the same node. In `xmlpage.xsl`, I've replaced the template rule for the `xmlpage` node with one that looks at the `site` attribute, and then applies another template rule with the mode set accordingly:

```
<xsl:template match="xmlpage">
<xsl:choose>
<xsl:when test="@site=2">
  <xsl:apply-templates select="." mode="site2"/>
</xsl:when>
<xsl:otherwise>
  <xsl:apply-templates select="." mode="site1"/>
</xsl:otherwise>
</xsl:choose>
</xsl:template>
```

This template rule overrides the original one, because if a template rule is specified more that once in a stylesheet, the last definition is always the one that's used. To specify the different modes, you simply create a new template rule with the mode attribute set in the opening template tag:

```
<xsl:template match="xmlpage" mode="site2">
...
</xsl:template>
```

The mode for site 2 is the new "skin", whereas the mode for site 1 is just a copy of the original template. The same change was made to the template rules for the menu items, and can be done with any template rules.

I've only changed the colors and marginally changed the layout, but if you have a play with it you'll see that it's possible to make a site that looks substantially different. In the real world you may want to have different information on the home page and possibly offer a different selection of products, all of which you could easily build into your application by examining the `site` session variable at strategic points.

The Search Page

To produce the blank search form, we simply create an empty page template and transform it with the `searchform.xsl` stylesheet. To create an empty page template, remember, we run the `CreatePage` function without passing in a content `DOMDocument` or node (this is why we needed to check if `oXMLContent` is in fact an object at all when creating the page). The template has the search criteria fields hard-coded, as they are not going to change unless there is a change of design. This is just a standard HTML form, which is submitted to `dosearch.asp`:

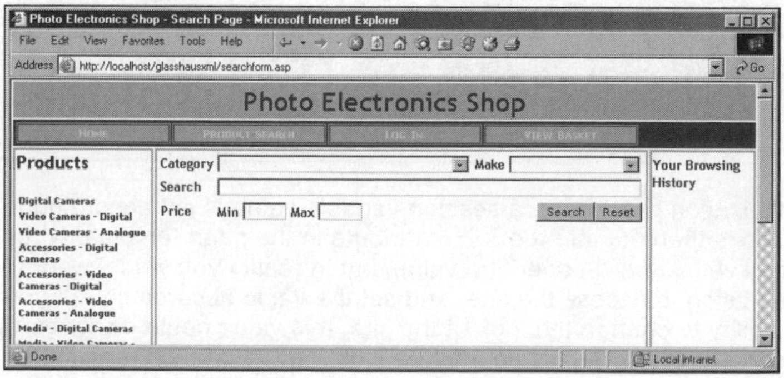

The first thing that `dosearch.asp` does is to put the criteria into variables. If none were supplied then it just redirects the user back to the blank search form (this could be done with JavaScript on the client-side, but that would rely on the browser supporting JavaScript). Next, it creates a `DOMDocument`, loads the search results template file, `search.xml`, and inserts the search criteria:

```
oXML.load(Server.MapPath("xml") & "\search.xml")

oXML.selectSingleNode("//SEARCH:criteria/category").text = sCat
oXML.selectSingleNode("//SEARCH:criteria/manufacturer").text = sMake
oXML.selectSingleNode("//SEARCH:criteria/search").text = sSearch
oXML.selectSingleNode("//SEARCH:criteria/price/@min").text = sPMin
oXML.selectSingleNode("//SEARCH:criteria/price/@max").text = sPMax
```

Once it's done that, it builds and executes the query. Provided that the query did return some records, then the `Recordset` is converted to an XML string. This is loaded into a `DOMDocument`, and then the `SEARCH:results` node in the template `DOMDocument` is replaced with the corresponding node in the freshly loaded `DOMDocument`. If no results are found, then a 'Y' is inserted into the `none` attribute of the `SEARCH:results` node – this is just a flag which will cause the "nothing found" message to appear.

At this point we could pass the search results `DOMDocument` into the `createPage` function, and transform it with the search page stylesheet. Since the server has gone to the trouble of getting this data, however, it would be a shame to throw it away just to create a page on the fly. So instead, we're going to save the XML in a file, so that the search can be retrieved again.

The search is only relevant to the user, and furthermore it's only relevant for the duration of the session, so the logical solution would be to save it with the user's session ID. The user is likely to perform a number of searches during their session, however, and we don't want to be overwriting the file every time a search is performed. Therefore we keep track of how many searches the user has performed (in a session variable), and append the number to the session ID to make up the file name. Note that the search number is only incremented when results are found, as there is little point in retrieving a search that returned no results!

```
oXML.save(Server.MapPath("search") & "\" & Session.SessionID & "_" & n & ".xml")
```

Now the search has been performed and the results have been saved to a file ... but that's not much use to the user who's sitting there waiting for the search results to come back. We still need to display the search results in the browser.

In order to do this, we're going to use the same page as the blank search form, as we essentially want to insert the criteria and results into it. If you recall, the blank search form was created by transforming a blank page template with the search stylesheet; all that we need to do this time is actually pass a populated `DOMDocument` into the `createPage` function.

First we need to tell `searchform.asp` which file to retrieve, so the search number is passed in the querystring. `searchform.asp` can now examine the querystring and load the correct results file:

```
n = Request.QueryString("searchno")

If isNumeric(n) then

   Set oXMLContent = CreateXMLObject(false)
   oXMLContent.load(Server.MapPath("search") & _
```

```
                "\" & Session.SessionID & "_" & _
                n & ".xml")
    End if
```

If the file is not found, then the content `DOMDocument` will contain a parse error, so a blank search form will be displayed. Otherwise, the criteria will be filled in and the results will be shown below them:

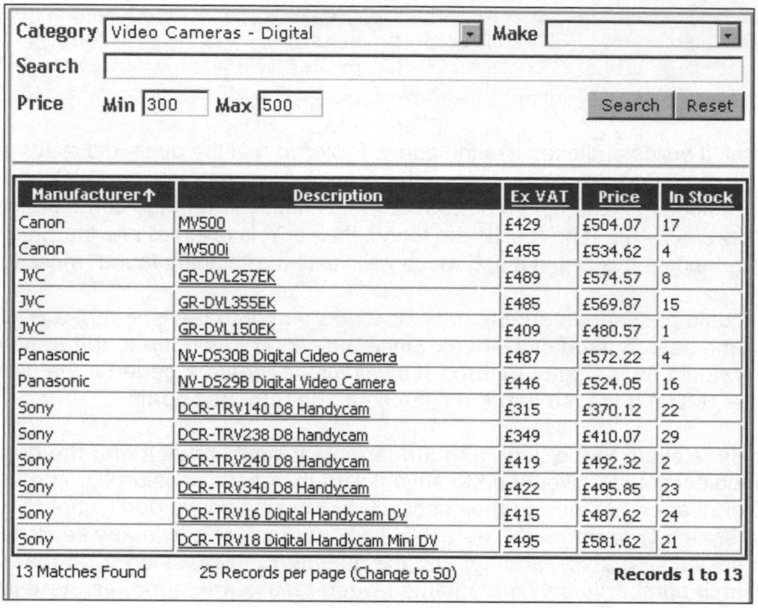

Manufacturer↑	Description	Ex VAT	Price	In Stock
Canon	MV500	£429	£504.07	17
Canon	MV500i	£455	£534.62	4
JVC	GR-DVL257EK	£489	£574.57	8
JVC	GR-DVL355EK	£485	£569.87	15
JVC	GR-DVL150EK	£409	£480.57	1
Panasonic	NV-DS30B Digital Cideo Camera	£487	£572.22	4
Panasonic	NV-DS29B Digital Video Camera	£446	£524.05	16
Sony	DCR-TRV140 D8 Handycam	£315	£370.12	22
Sony	DCR-TRV238 D8 handycam	£349	£410.07	29
Sony	DCR-TRV240 D8 Handycam	£419	£492.32	2
Sony	DCR-TRV340 D8 Handycam	£422	£495.85	23
Sony	DCR-TRV16 Digital Handycam DV	£415	£487.62	24
Sony	DCR-TRV18 Digital Handycam Mini DV	£495	£581.62	21

Later on you'll see how the search details are added to the browser history. Suffice it to say for the moment that, if the link in the browsing history is clicked on, this search is retrieved.

There is no standard way of storing and retrieving a `Recordset` using traditional ASP and database techniques, so already the power and flexibility of using XML for this sort of thing is becoming apparent. Despite this, we've hardly even begun yet!

Column Sorting

Collecting some search criteria, using them to build a query, and writing out the results is one of the first things budding ASP developers learn. Once they've got the hang of that, they tend to add links to the column headers of the results table to resubmit the query with a different `ORDER BY` clause specified – and the query is returned again, sorted by the column that was clicked.

That approach is all very well – it does work after all – but it is rather wasteful of server resources. We've already used those resources to retrieve the data in the first place, so why go to all that effort again just to bring back the same data in a different order? Apart from anything else, if the user has already had to wait quite a while for the results to come back, they're not going to be very enamored with having to wait the same length of time for the data to be sorted as they want it.

It is of course possible to use JavaScript to sort the table client-side, but we're trying to support as many browsers as possible here so that's not really an option. Instead, we're going to use the `xsl:sort` element in the stylesheet to order the XML data. Regardless of what the `ORDER BY` clause was in the query, the results will be sorted by *Manufacturer* by default:

```
<xsl:for-each select="SEARCH:result">
  <xsl:sort select="manufacturer_id" order="ascending" data-type="number"/>
    <xsl:apply-templates select="."/>
  </xsl:sort>
</xsl:for-each>
```

This will sort by manufacturer ID rather than manufacturer name, hence the specification of the data type as `number`. In order for the manufacturers to appear alphabetically, the IDs will have to correspond to alphabetical order. I've done that here, but that's not always going to be practical. If you were dealing with a large list of manufacturers that was prone to change, you should assign IDs starting with the same letter as the manufacturer name. This issue will not affect any other column, as the actual data is contained here, rather than the ID.

Hard-coding the column name like this isn't much use, as of course we are trying to allow sorting by any column. The simplest way to do this would be to have an attribute in the `SEARCH:results` tag, which tells it what to sort by. We would also need other attributes for sort direction and data type:

```
<xsl:for-each select="SEARCH:result">
  <xsl:sort select="../@sortby"
            order="string(../@sortdir)"
            data-type="string(../@sortdata)"/>
    <xsl:apply-templates select="."/>
  </xsl:sort>
</xsl:for-each>
```

This is all well and good, but how would we set the values of these attributes when clicking on a column heading? We would need to select the attributes and insert the values into the stylesheet when the search results XML file is loaded.

Stylesheet Parameters

That approach would have been fine for this case study, but it won't always be good enough. You might not want, or be able to, modify the XML that you're receiving, or there may be times when you need a lot more flexibility. There is a more professional way of doing this, and that is to pass parameters into the stylesheet.

Let's first have a look at the stylesheet. Any parameters that are to be passed into it need to be declared at the top, under the `<stylesheet>` tag.

```
<xsl:stylesheet version="1.0" xmlns:xsl="http://www.w3.org/1999/XSL/Transform"
                              xmlns:SEARCH="uri=http://glasshausxml/search">
<xsl:output method="html" omit-xml-declaration="yes"/>
<xsl:param name="sortby" select="'manufacturer_id'" />
<xsl:param name="sortdir" select="'ascending'" />
```

Note that the default values must be strings, so we need to put quotes around them. Rather than passing in the data type, we're going to determine it and store it in a variable. Only the `desc` node of the result set contains data that would need to be sorted alphabetically, so any other node needs to be sorted numerically. So we need to examine the value of the `sortby` parameter and set the variable accordingly:

```
<xsl:variable name="sortdatatype">
  <xsl:choose>
  <xsl:when test="$sortby='desc'">text</xsl:when>
  <xsl:otherwise>number</xsl:otherwise>
  </xsl:choose>
</xsl:variable>
```

And now we're ready to use these values to sort the table. The `select` attribute of the `<xsl:sort>` element requires a node to be passed to it rather than a string. The wildcard operator (`*`) selects all elements regardless of the element name, but we can restrict it by specifying that the name must be equal to the value of our parameter. Therefore the expression `*[name()=$sortby]` will evaluate the node itself. The other sorting attributes require strings to specify order and data type. For these we can just put the variables straight in, although note the brackets that specify it contains the value of the variables rather than the variables themselves:

```
<xsl:for-each select="SEARCH:result">
  <xsl:sort select="*[name()=$sortby]"
            order="{$sortdir}"
            data-type="{$sortdatatype}"/>
  <xsl:apply-templates select="."/>
</xsl:for-each>
```

Passing the Parameters into the Stylesheet

Now we need to get these parameters from the HTML form in the browser and into the stylesheet. If no parameters are supplied, then they will take their default values, as they will when the `resultset` is opened. We want to be able to sort on particular columns when they are clicked on, so we need to create links that refresh the page with the desired sort attributes appended to the querystring.

I've already shown you the `ApplyXSLParamsWriteDOM` function, which is used by the page creating function to append parameters into the stylesheet; you might want to take another look at it just now. It expects a list of parameters and values separated by a pipe character, so in the `searchform.asp` we need to get the parameters from the querystring and build the parameter string from them:

```
sSortBy = Request.QueryString("sortby")
sSortDir = Request.QueryString("sortdir")

If Len(sSortBy)>0 then
  sParams = "sortby=" & sSortBy
  If Len(sSortDir)>0 then
    sParams = sParams & "|sortdir=" & sSortDir
  End if
End if
```

This parameter string is then passed into the `CreatePage` function, which does the rest. In fact I've expanded on the above function to save the parameters in session variables, so that we don't have to worry about passing them in the querystring as well when we come to `recordset` paging. These session variables are cleared when a new search is performed.

The final thing that remains to be done is to create the links on the column headings in the stylesheet, as shown in the following screenshot:

Manufacturer	Description	Ex VAT	Price↑	In Stock
Sony	DCR-TRV140 D8 Handycam	£315	£370.12	22
Sony	DCR-TRV238 D8 handycam	£349	£410.07	29
JVC	GR-DVL150EK	£409	£480.57	1

We also want to display an arrow to show which column the table is sorted by, and the direction of the sort. Each column heading of the results table is formed as shown below. Note that the first querystring parameter in the link is still the search number, as we'll still need to select and load the file of search results. After that we supply the `sortby` parameter, and then we only need to supply the direction if it's going to be descending – which is only if the table is already being sorted by that column. The first thing to do is to store the search number in a variable, as we'll be using it in every link:

```
<xsl:variable name="searchnumber"
              select="//SEARCH:search/SEARCH:criteria/@number"/>
```

Here's the code that makes up each column header:

```
<th class="resultstableheader">
  <a class="resultstableheader">
    <xsl:attribute name="href">
      searchform.asp?searchno=<xsl:value-of select="$searchnumber"/>
      &amp;sortby=manufacturer_id
      <xsl:if test="$sortby='manufacturer_id' and $sortdir='ascending'">
        &amp;sortdir=descending
      </xsl:if>
    </xsl:attribute>
    Manufacturer</a>
  <xsl:if test="$sortby='manufacturer_id'">
    <font face="wingdings"><xsl:choose>
    <xsl:when test="$sortdir='ascending'">á</xsl:when>
    <xsl:when test="$sortdir='descending'">â</xsl:when>
    </xsl:choose></font>
  </xsl:if>
</th>
```

Finally, if this is the column being sorted on, then we want to display an arrow. We'll use the 'Wingdings' font as it's pretty much universal – an up arrow equates to 'á' and a down arrow equates to 'â' – but images can easily be substituted for these characters if you prefer.

A Small Note on Character Encoding

Including non-standard characters like this will cause a parse error when you try to load the stylesheet, unless you've specified an encoding standard that can handle them. The most popular encoding standard is probably ISO-8859-1, which can certainly handle these characters and any others that you'd be likely to come across unless you wanted to display completely exotic alphabets.

As a general rule, it's good practice to specify the encoding standard in any XML or XSL file. This is done in the XML declaration at the top of the file:

```
<?xml version="1.0" encoding="ISO-8859-1"?>
```

Recordset Paging

So now we've got our working search page, and we can sort the results by each column. Our search page is still flawed because, as we're not enforcing the use of strict criteria, it's possible for very large sets of results to be brought back. If for example you were to choose the category "Accessories – Digital Cameras", that would bring back over 300 products. Trying this out as you sit with the case study in front of you, it would probably not be such a big deal but imagine trying to download a page of that size over a slow connection.

Anybody who programs database applications will sooner or later encounter a situation like this that requires `Recordset` paging – the ability to view a certain number of records at a time. In a desktop application this isn't so difficult to achieve; you just hold your `Recordset` in memory as the user takes their time to browse through the records. In an ASP application, though, this would go against the whole ethos of good programming practice.

To preserve server resources to as great an extent as possible, you want to open your database connection, run the query, parse the `Recordset` and write the HTML, then close the `Recordset` and the connection immediately, all during the execution of one ASP script. You can't afford to keep expensive `Recordset` objects in memory while the user reads through what they have on the screen, or possibly quits the site altogether leaving the session to time out. There is no correct way of doing `Recordset` paging in ASP: it normally requires a bit of creativity. Techniques commonly used include only retrieving records between certain IDs, retrieving a whole `Recordset` and only creating the HTML for a certain number of records, or converting the `Recordset` to a two-dimensional array and keeping it in memory. All these methods have their drawbacks; the first would be fiddly to implement (plenty of scope for bugs unless you really know your data), the second is still quite expensive in server resources and, while the last is efficient, you encounter problems when you want to change the sort order.

You'll be pleased to hear that achieving this with XML and XSLT is going to be a walk in the park!

We're going to do this by passing in a parameter telling the stylesheet which record to start with. The stylesheet (`search.xsl`) will then display that record and the next 24, displaying 25 records in total. We'll give the parameter a default value of `1` as, when it's not supplied, we'll want it to start from the beginning:

```
<xsl:param name="startrecord" select="1" />
```

Once we know what record we're starting with, we only want to display a record if its position is between that record and the upper limit, which we've chosen to be 25 records:

```
<xsl:for-each select="SEARCH:result">
  <xsl:sort select="*[name()=$sortby]"
            order="{$sortdir}"
            data-type="{$sortdatatype}"/>
  <xsl:if test="(position() &gt; ($startrecord - 1))
                and (position() &lt; ($startrecord + 25))">
```

```
        <xsl:apply-templates select="."/>
      </xsl:if>
   </xsl:for-each>
```

Note that the sort element sorts all the nodes before we look at the position, so what we're examining is the position of the current node after the sort has been performed.

There is no reason to hard-code the number of records to show per page. In fact we can let the user choose and pass that in as a parameter as well. In this case I've just given them a choice of 25 or 50, but you could let them have a drop-down of different choices. If you wanted to be really clever you could pass the screen resolution back to the server when the user first enters the site, and choose an optimum number of records for that screen resolution.

Once the parameter has been specified, the value is saved in a session variable so it remains until it's changed again. It might be an idea to update the user's profile with this value as well, so when they return their preference has been kept.

In searchform.asp, we check to see if it's been supplied in the querystring, and if not it's read from the session variable. Finally we check if there's a value at all and then add it to the parameter string:

```
sRPP = Request.QueryString("rpp")

If Len(sRPP)>0 then
  Session("search_recordsperpage") = sRPP
Else
  sRPP = Session("search_recordsperpage")
End if

If Len(sRPP)>0 then
  sParams = sParams & "recordsperpage=" & sRPP & "|"
End if
```

Then this is passed to the stylesheet along with the other parameters and, if it's missing, the parameter assumes a default value of 25. The final version of the statement in search.xsl that decides whether or not to display a record now looks like this:

```
      <xsl:sort select="*[name()=$sortby]"
                order="{$sortdir}"
                data-type="{$sortdatatype}"/>
      <xsl:if test="(position() &gt; ($startrecord - 1))
                    and (position() &lt; ($startrecord + $recordsperpage))">
        <xsl:apply-templates select="."/>
```

In the following screenshot you see the information that is displayed below the recordset and links to navigate through the recordset. Creating these links is the next thing that needs to be done:

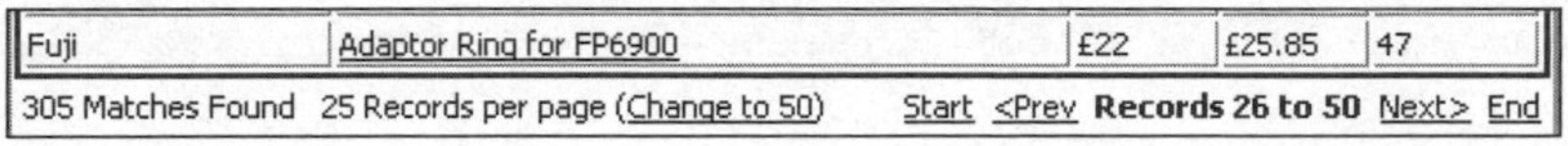

The record count is going to be needed quite a few times in this exercise, so the first thing to be done is to create a variable rather than evaluating it every time. Displaying the count is then just a matter of evaluating the variable:

```
<xsl:variable name="recordcount" select="count(SEARCH:result)"/>

... <!—other code -->

<xsl:value-of select="$recordcount"/> Matches Found
```

Next we want to display the number of records per page, and provide the link to change it. For this we'll be using another variable:

```
<xsl:variable name="rppnew">
  <xsl:choose>
  <xsl:when test="$recordsperpage = 50">25</xsl:when>
  <xsl:otherwise>50</xsl:otherwise>
  </xsl:choose>
</xsl:variable>

... <!—other code -->

xsl:value-of select="$recordsperpage"/> Records per page
(<a class="blacklink"><xsl:attribute name="href">
searchform.asp?searchno=<xsl:value-of select="$searchnumber"/>
&amp;rpp=<xsl:value-of select="$rppnew"/>
</xsl:attribute>Change to <xsl:value-of select="$rppnew"/></a>)
```

And now to the navigation links. We don't want to display the *Start* and *<Prev* links for the first set of results, so we'll only do so if the start record is greater than 1. The *Start* link is simply a link to the search form without any parameters appended to the querystring, apart from the search number of course. The *<Prev* link simply sets the start record to the current start record less the number of records per page. So if you're on the second page, you've moved forward 25 records so the start record is 26, and the *<Prev* link will take you back to record 1. In the bit that tells you which records are showing, the start record is always going to be the first one (obviously!):

```
<xsl:if test="($startrecord &gt; 1)">

  <a class="blacklink">
  <xsl:attribute name="href">
  searchform.asp?searchno=<xsl:value-of select="$searchnumber"/>
  </xsl:attribute>Start</a> 

  <a class="blacklink">
  <xsl:attribute name="href">
  searchform.asp?searchno=<xsl:value-of select="$searchnumber"/>
  &amp;startrecord=<xsl:value-of select="($startrecord - $recordsperpage)"/>
  </xsl:attribute>&lt;Prev</a> 

</xsl:if>

<B>Records <xsl:value-of select="$startrecord"/> to </B>
```

Determining what is the last record showing is moderately trickier; we have to consider whether there are more records to show or not, which is also what we have to consider when deciding whether to show the *Next>* and *End* links or not. To do this, we'll use an `<xsl:choose>` statement; when there are more to show, we'll display the start record plus the number of records per page, otherwise we'll just show the number of records. To create the *Next>* link, it's just the start record plus the number of records per page. To get to the end of the `Recordset`, we need to calculate what the start record would be on the last page. First of all we'll use the `mod` operator (this returns the remainder produced when one number is divided by another), which conveniently gives us the number of records on the last page. So we just subtract this from the record count, and then add one, as it's the first record of that set we're trying to get to:

```
<xsl:choose>
<xsl:when test="(($startrecord + $recordsperpage) &lt; $recordcount)">

  <b><xsl:value-of select="$startrecord + $recordsperpage - 1"/></B> 

  <a class="blacklink"><xsl:attribute name="href">
  searchform.asp?searchno=<xsl:value-of select="$searchnumber"/>
  &amp;startrecord=<xsl:value-of select="($startrecord + $recordsperpage)"/>
  </xsl:attribute>Next&gt;</a> 

  <a class="blacklink"><xsl:attribute name="href">
  searchform.asp?searchno=<xsl:value-of select="$searchnumber"/>
  &amp;startrecord=<xsl:value-of
              select="($recordcount - ($recordcount mod $recordsperpage) + 1)"/>
  </xsl:attribute>End</a>

</xsl:when>
<xsl:otherwise>

  <B><xsl:value-of select="$recordcount"/></B>

</xsl:otherwise>
</xsl:choose>
```

The only links that pass in the start record parameter to the stylesheet are these navigation links, so if you're halfway through browsing a `Recordset` and then decide to sort on a particular column, you get taken back to the beginning of the `Recordset`. This behavior is by design, because the entire `Recordset` is sorted which makes the current position meaningless anyway. The same applies if you decide to change the number of records shown per page.

So there you have it: some very elegant and efficient methods of column sorting and `Recordset` paging. The only time when significant server resources are used is when the search is performed in the first place. After that you can navigate and re-sort the table as much as you like, and all you're doing each time is reloading the XML file and transforming it in a slightly different way.

Removing the Search Files

We don't want all these search files cluttering up the server after the user's session has finished, so we delete them in the session termination routine. This is done by `RemoveSearchFiles`, which can be found in `global.inc`. The session termination routine won't always run, like for example when the server is rebooted, so some of these files will be left behind occasionally. It might be an idea to write a scheduled script that removes the old files as well.

There are no special XML techniques involved here, just the good old `FileSystemObject`, so I won't go through this function. It is worth noting, however, that `Server.MapPath` cannot be called in the session termination routine. So in order to be able to find our `search` folder, we need to call `Server.MapPath` in the application initialization routine, and store it in a variable.

Browsing History

Now that we're familiar with the search, let's see how the browsing history works. The user's browsing history has been referred to a number of times so far in this case study. It stores two things: links to retrieve any searches that have been performed, and links to any products that have been browsed:

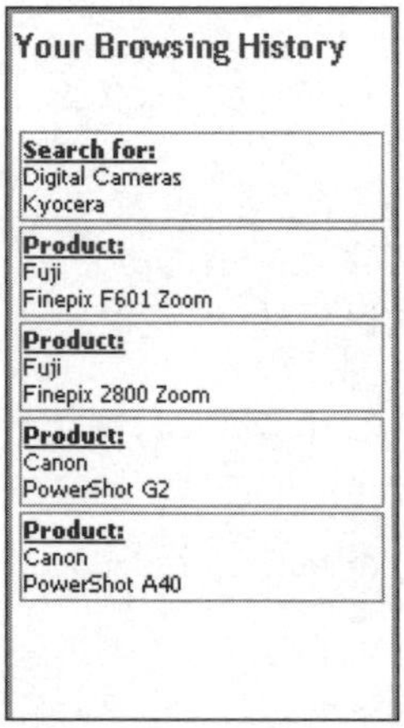

As you saw when we were discussing the creation of pages, the browsing history is held in an XML string in a session variable. If you look in `global.asa`, you'll see that this is initialized to an empty `<HISTORY:items>` node:

```
Session("history_xml") =
                "<HISTORY:items xmlns:HISTORY='uri=http://glasshausxml/history'/>"
```

When we want to add an item to the history, we load this XML string into a `DOMDocument` and append child nodes to it. You'll find the full function in `common.inc`, but here's the important bit. A node is passed into it from the calling ASP, but before we can append the node, we need to create a new history item node. This is done using the `createNode` method, which accepts three parameters, node type, node name, and namespace URI. In this case, the node type is 1, which is an element (for a full list of the possible node types, refer to the MXSML 4 Help file). A namespace URI needs to be provided if the node name has a namespace prefix:

```
Set oXMLHistory = CreateXMLObject(false)
oXMLHistory.loadXML(Session("history_xml"))
```

```
Set oNode = oXMLHistory.createNode(1, "HISTORY:item", _
                                   "uri=http://glasshausxml/history")
```

Once the node has been created, we can append a clone of the node that was passed in to the function:

```
oNode.appendChild oNodeToAdd.cloneNode(true)
```

The important thing to note is that, even though the node was created by calling a method of the `DOMDocument` object, the newly created node is not part of the loaded document; it exists as a document fragment. To make the new node part of the document hierarchy, it must be inserted into the document tree. In this case it must be appended at the top of the tree so that it appears first in the list. We'll select the first history item node as a reference node and use the `insertBefore` method:

```
oXMLHistory.selectSingleNode("//HISTORY:items").insertBefore oNode, _
                    oXMLHistory.selectSingleNode("//HISTORY:items/HISTORY:item")
```

Finally the document is extracted as an XML string and saved in the session variable:

```
Session("history_xml") = oXMLHistory.xml
```

When a search is performed, provided that results have been found, the search criteria node is selected and passed into the function to add to the history. For products it's a bit more complicated because, when we visit a product page, we don't want to save the entire product `DOMDocument` to the history, as all we need is the manufacturer and description. Furthermore, we don't want to add the product to the history every time the product page is looked at, only the first time.

In `productpage.asp` we need to load the history document first and see if the product has already been listed. To do this we attempt to select the node. In VB and VBScript, if a node does not exist, then the select method will return an empty object pointer, rather than a `null` as it does in JavaScript and other languages. So we need to check if the selected node is `Nothing`.

Then, provided it doesn't already exist, we create a new simple document that contains just the information that is needed, by building up an XML string and loading it. The root node of this new document is then passed into the `AddToHistory` function:

```
If oXMLTemp.selectSingleNode("//HISTORY:item/product[product_id=" _
                             & sProductId & "]") is Nothing then

  sXML = "<product>"
  sXML = sXML & oNode.selectSingleNode("product_id").xml
  sXML = sXML & oNode.selectSingleNode("manufacturer_id").xml
  sXML = sXML & oNode.selectSingleNode("desc").xml
  sXML = sXML & "</product>"

  oXMLTemp.loadXML(sXML)

  Set oNode = oXMLTemp.documentElement

  AddToHistory(oNode)

End if
```

Finally a quick look at the template rule for the browsing history, which you'll find in the `common.xsl` stylesheet. As we go through each history node there are two types of potential node that could be there, so we use an `<xsl:choose>` element to see what kind of element is present and display the information accordingly:

```
<xsl:for-each select="HISTORY:item">
<xsl:variable name="historynode" select="."/>
 <tr>
  <xsl:choose>
  <xsl:when test="SEARCH:criteria">
  <td class="historycell">
  ...
  </td>
  </xsl:when>
  <xsl:when test="product">
  <td class="historycell">
  ...
  </td>
  </xsl:when>
  </xsl:choose>
 </tr>
</xsl:for-each>
```

The Category and Product Pages

Clicking on the product categories on the left-hand side of each screen takes you to a page that displays a selection of products from that category. These pages can be sorted by *Price* or M*anufacturer*, and there's also a detailed view that gives you more information on each product. The standard information about a product, such as the manufacturer, price, and description is stored in the database, but the more detailed information (including specifications) comes from XML files that are specific to each product:

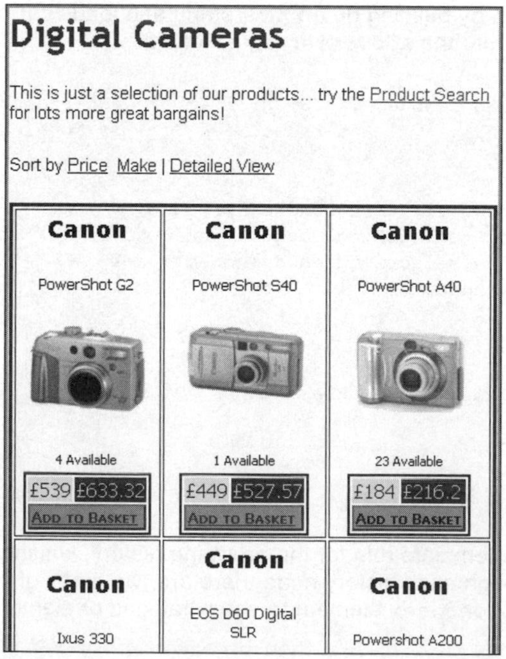

Each of these pages contains rather a lot of information, which needs to be current at any time. The traditional way to create a page like this would be to read the data from the database for each visit to the page. This would be very wasteful of server resources, as the data isn't really going to be changing that often. Another traditional way would be to run a scheduled script that queries the database and generates HTML files, which would be a more prudent way to use server resources. The drawback of this would be that the pages are completely static, and we want to be able to re-sort them and so on. Likewise, whenever any information changes, the files would need to be rewritten.

So we're going to be doing things in a more radical way. The logical way of doing this would be to treat it in the same way as the search, and create an XML file, except this time one that can be accessed by everyone. This file, however, would also need to be rewritten every time any information changes. Furthermore, some categories have a very large number of products in them, so if the XML file contained them all it would be quite hard work for the server to load and parse every time. Instead, we're going to be loading a `DOMDocument` once, and keeping it in memory with application scope for everybody to access.

When a price changes, the `DOMDocument` could be updated directly while it's in memory by a script which would select the relevant node and update the value. When the next user views a category page the new price is displayed – without any need to reload the document or rewrite any files. Bear in mind that these are large objects and therefore, your server must have enough memory to store them, although if it doesn't this will quickly become apparent during testing as the test server is likely to have less memory than the live one.

Loading the Category DOMDocument

A `DOMDocument` for each category is loaded when the application starts. This is why it takes a bit of time to load the home page when you first start the application. Once they are in memory, however, they remain there for anyone to use so subsequent visitors will get the home page as quickly as they expect.

The functions that load the categories are found in `global.inc`. When the application starts, we're already obtaining a list of categories from the database for the category lookup. The `LoadCategories` function loads the categories lookup and then calls the `LoadCategory` function for each category in the list.

Let's now go through what happens in the `LoadCategory` function. The first thing it does is to query the database for the list of products, prices, and stock levels. There is also a flag on each product record to indicate whether it should be shown on the page for that category. Next it creates a `DOMDocument` to load the `Recordset` into. In this case a free-threaded `DOMDocument` is required, as we're going to be storing the `DOMDocument` in application scope, so it has to support multiple threads. The `Recordset` is then converted to XML and loaded into the `DOMDocument`.

Inserting Detailed Product Information

The database only contains the basic essential information about each product. More detailed information is stored in XML files held in the `info` directory, with the product ID as a file name. This approach allows you to provide whatever information you like about a product, without being restricted by your database structure. Whenever one of these information files is updated, the function to load the category should be called again. If the file was being updated manually then the application would need to be restarted, whereas if it was being updated programmatically, the function to load the category that contains the product could be called directly.

Each information file follows a common structure, but in theory you could add in any tags you wanted. Of course, adding the extra information would be pointless unless it was going to be visible on screen, so any extra tags you add would need to be added to a stylesheet too. The most sensible approach would be to have a common set of tags for each product category, as products within a category are likely to have similar characteristics. As it happens, I've just created a generic XML structure that could be used by any category, but there's no reason why it would have to be:

```
<?xml version="1.0" encoding="ISO-8859-1"?>
<product_info>
<product_id>2792</product_id>
<full_desc><![CDATA[
The DiMAGE 5 gives you more than just high resolution-it offers a wealth of
features for advanced creative imaging. A sophisticated 7X zoom lens with 250mm
equivalent telephoto. High-performance SLR functions. And versatile digital
features for flexible, on-the-spot adjustments. A fusion of Minolta's finest
optical and digital technologies, the DiMAGE 5 opens up a world of creative
possibilities with fast, responsive operation. Discover the possibilities.
]]></full_desc>
<dimensions>116.5 x 112.5 x 90.5mm</dimensions>
<weight> 480g</weight>
<characteristic name="CCD Mega Pixels">3.3</characteristic>
<characteristic name="Optical Zoom"> 7.0X</characteristic>
<characteristic name="Maximum Resolution">2048x1536</characteristic>
<characteristic name="Digital Zoom">2.0X</characteristic>
<characteristic name="Lens equivalent">35.0 - 250.0mm</characteristic>
<characteristic name="LCD monitor">1.8"</characteristic>
<characteristic name="Movie Mode"> yes</characteristic>
<characteristic name="Memory">CompactFlash</characteristic>
</product_info>
```

Once the `LoadCategory` function has loaded the product information from the database, it then goes through every product node and inserts the product information from the file, if there is one:

```
For each oProduct in oXML.selectNodes("//PRODUCT:products/PRODUCT:product")

  oInfo.load(Server.MapPath("info") & "\" & _
             oProduct.selectSingleNode("product_id").text & ".xml")

  If oInfo.parseError.errorCode <> 0 then
    oInfo.loadXML("<error>" & oInfo.parseError.reason & "</error>")
  End if

  oProduct.appendChild oInfo.documentElement
Next
```

I've appended the parse error information as well just in case any file turns out not to be well-formed. In a real-life situation, however, this would not really be necessary as these product information files would be generated by a content management system rather than typed in late at night!

Finally, we put the `DOMDocument` into application scope by creating a pointer to it in the application object, giving it the category code as a name. This is stored in the string `sCategory`:

```
Set Application(sCategory) = oXML
```

The DOMDocuments for all categories are now loaded. You can view their contents by running applicationtest.asp, which writes out the entire contents of the application object.

Creating the Category Pages

The category pages are created by showcategory.asp. It requires the category ID to be passed in the querystring, and then it selects the appropriate category DOMDocument:

```
sCat = Request.QueryString("cat")
Set oCat = Application(sCat)
```

The DOMDocument is then passed directly into the createPage function, but note that we have to set the "free-threaded" argument to true, as you cannot mix threading models. This means that if the content DOMDocument is free-threaded, then the page template DOMDocument will also have to be free-threaded:

```
CreatePage sStyleSheet, "Product Category", sParams, true, oCat
```

The Category Page Stylesheets

There is a generic stylesheet, catbasic.xsl, which works for all the stylesheets. There are also other stylesheets that are specific to each category, which are used for the detailed view. I've only done one, for the *Digital Cameras* category as that's the only category I've created additional product information for, but that's enough to give you the idea. The *Category* page can be sorted by *Price* or *Make*, but I won't go through how this is done as it works in exactly the same way as the *Search* page.

I've already shown you how the stylesheet writes a <DIV> for some browsers and an anchor link for others in each product cell, back when we were discussing supporting different browsers. The only other tricky part of the stylesheet was writing the table three cells across as the product nodes were being transformed. Using traditional techniques, this is relatively easy to do: you just write a closing and an opening <TR> tag after writing every three records. In XSLT you can't just write an opening tag without a closing tag, because then the stylesheet would not be well-formed. So we need to use the same technique as we used earlier, using a script to output the tag as a string:

```
<xsl:template match="PRODUCT:product">
<xsl:value-of select="layoutfunctions:checkRow()" disable-output-escaping="yes"/>
  <td class="catcell" align="center" valign="bottom">
  ...
  </td>
<xsl:value-of select="layoutfunctions:checkRow()" disable-output-escaping="yes"/>
</xsl:template>
```

The checkRow function is called before and after every cell is written, to check whether or not to output a <tr> tag. I'll draw your attention again to the disable-output-escaping="yes" attribute. This prevents the output from being HTML-encoded, which we don't want as we're trying to write a tag, and not text for display. Note also how the function call has a namespace prefix. This is to identify the script block in which to find the function.

I'll briefly mention here how to do stylesheet scripting for MSXML4. First, you declare the msxml namespace as shown below, and then namespaces for each block of script that you're going to have. These are declared at the top of the stylesheet, along with the namespaces used in the XML document:

```
<?xml version="1.0" encoding="ISO-8859-1"?>
<xsl:stylesheet version="1.0"
                xmlns:xsl="http://www.w3.org/1999/XSL/Transform"
                xmlns:PRODUCT="uri=http://glasshausxml/product"
                xmlns:msxsl="urn:schemas-microsoft-com:xslt"
                xmlns:layoutfunctions="urn:glasshausxml:layoutfunctions">
```

Then you write your script block much like you would do in an HTML page, though note the namespace prefix. The scripting language can be JScript or VBScript. You then label your script block with the namespace you've chosen for it, in the `implements-prefix` attribute. Finally, just like you would encapsulate script in an HTML page with comment tags, you need to encapsulate your script in a `CDATA` section to prevent parse errors.

```
<msxsl:script language="JScript" implements-prefix="layoutfunctions"><![CDATA[
```

And now we're ready to look at the function. There's nothing too complicated going on here: we have a global variable that is initialized to zero, and if it's at zero the function outputs an opening `<tr>` tag. Every time the function is called, the variable is incremented by one. When it gets to six, since that would mean that three cells have been drawn because the function is called twice for each cell, a closing `<tr>` tag is output and the variable is reset to zero:

```
<msxsl:script language="JScript" implements-prefix="layoutfunctions"><![CDATA[
  var iCellCount = 0;

  function checkRow(){
    var sReturn = "";
    if(iCellCount==0) sReturn = "<TR>";
    iCellCount++;
    if(iCellCount==6){
      sReturn = "</TR>";
      iCellCount=0;
    }
    return(sReturn);
  }
]]></msxsl:script>
```

This approach works fine if the number of products in your category page is neatly divisible by three, but what if it's not? Then the last `<tr>` tag will be missing. So we need to call another function that detects this and writes the tag if necessary, before closing the table:

```
<xsl:value-of select="layoutfunctions:checkLastRow()"
              disable-output-escaping="yes"/>
</table>
```

All this function does is check if `iCellCount` is a value other than zero, and write the tag in that case:

```
function checkLastRow(){
  if(iCellCount==0) return("");
  else return("</TR>");
}
```

The Detailed View

The detailed view of the product category pages is achieved by calling a stylesheet that is specific to that category. The one that I have done is for digital cameras, and can be found in `catdetail_C-D.xsl` – the others would follow the same pattern. You'll see that it imports the basic category stylesheet, so the template rules and the scripting functions from `catbasic.xsl` are all available. The only thing that it does differently is to show you a few product characteristics. If you feel the inclination, you could develop it further to sort or filter by particular product characteristics. I've kept it simple, but the possibilities are endless.

To tell `showcategory.asp` that we want to use the detailed stylesheet, all we have to do is append a parameter to the querystring:

```
sStyleSheet = "catbasic"
If Request.QueryString("detail") = "yes" then sStyleSheet = "catdetail_" & sCat
```

I've only provided the link on the page if the category is *Digital Cameras*, but this restriction can be removed when the other detailed stylesheets are in place.

The Product Page

The product pages also take their data directly from each category's `DOMDocument`. This is why we want to load all the product data into them, rather than just the products that appear in the category pages. The following screenshot shows you what the *Product* page looks like, assuming there is an information file for it:

For products without an information file, the *Product* page looks considerably sparser; in fact you won't see anything you don't see on the *Category* page. We can assume that in a real-life scenario, the products listed on the *Category* page would be the ones for which further information is available, which is what I've done for the *Digital Cameras* category.

The product pages are created by `productpage.asp`, to which the product ID needs to be passed. The image is saved with the product ID, in the `products` subfolder of the `images` folder. Likewise the thumbnail pictures from the category page are saved in the `productthumbs` subfolder. I've not made any effort to make up for missing images, so you'll see broken image links where no picture is available, but the product name and description will appear.

Creating the Product Page

Creating the product page is a simple matter of selecting the product node from the category `DOMDocument` and passing it to the `createPage` function. But how do we know which category a product is in? The most obvious way would be to pass the category into the querystring as well, but that's going to be a bit of a pain. We want to be able to just pass the product ID in and be done with it. So we need to go back to the drawing-board; what we need is a lookup `DOMDocument`, which contains all the product IDs and the categories each product is in.

This isn't going to involve much more work, because we're already iterating through the products and categories while we're loading the categories. So now we're going to revisit the functions for loading categories.

In `LoadCategories`, we're going to create a new free-threaded `DOMDocument`, as it will be stored in the application object. Into this, we load a blank `product_ids` node, into which we're going to insert a copy of each `product_id` node with an additional attribute for the category, as we're iterating through the products:

```
Sub LoadCategories(sLookups)

  Dim oProductCats, oCats, oNode

  Set oProductCats = CreateXMLObject(true)
  oProductCats.loadXML("<product_ids/>")
```

Then in `LoadCategory`, we just need to select the product ID node from each product, append them to the new DOM, and set a new attribute with the category code. These lines are added into the loop that iterates through the products:

```
For each oProduct in oXML.selectNodes("//PRODUCT:products/PRODUCT:product")
  Set oNode = oProductCats.documentElement.appendChild( _
                         oProduct.selectSingleNode("product_id").cloneNode(true))
  oNode.setAttribute "category", sCategory
```

Finally, back in `LoadCategories`, we give the DOM application scope:

```
  For each oNode in oCats.selectNodes("//lookups/categorys/category")
    LoadCategory oNode.selectSingleNode("category_id").text, oProductCats
  Next

  Set Application("ProductCats") = oProductCats

End Sub
```

Now that we have our category lookup DOM, we can go back to the product page. If you recall, we need to select the product node from the appropriate category DOM. This may well be useful outside of the product page – in fact it is going to be used again later on – so it's done in a common function, `GetProductNode` (which can be found in `common.inc`).

The first thing that needs to be done is to get the category and for this we're going to interrogate our newly created lookup `DOMDocument`:

```
Function GetProductNode(sProductId)

  Dim oProductCats, oCat, oNode

  If sProductId="" then
    Set GetProductNode = Nothing
    Exit Function
  End if

  'Find out which category the product is in
  Set oProductCats = Application("ProductCats")
  Set oNode = oProductCats.selectSingleNode( _
                                  "//product_id[.=" & sProductId & "]/@category")
  If oNode is Nothing then
    Set GetProductNode = Nothing
    Exit Function
  End if
```

If the product does not exist, or if the product ID was not supplied, then we need to return `Nothing` as the function is meant to return an object.

Now that we've located the product in the lookup `DOMDocument`, we can select the node from the category DOM. We can be sure that if we found it in the lookup `DOMDocument` it's going to be in the category `DOMDocument`, but in any case even if it's not then it will just return `Nothing` anyway:

```
Set oCat = Application(oNode.text)
Set GetProductNode = _
          oCat.selectSingleNode("//PRODUCT:products/PRODUCT:product[product_id=" _
          & sProductId & "]")
```

In the product page, we just need to add a check to see whether the product was found or not, so we can provide a way of informing the stylesheet and knowing whether or not to add the product to the history:

```
Set oNode = GetProductNode(sProductId)

bAddtoHistory = true

If oNode is Nothing then
  Set oNode = CreateXMLObject(true)
  oNode.loadXML("<noproduct/>")
  bAddtoHistory = false
End if
```

Finally, the node can be passed into the `createPage` function, and the page is displayed. If the product was found, then it is added to the browsing history, as discussed already.

The Shopping Basket

The shopping basket is an XML file that is stored in the `baskets` directory, with the user's ID as a file name. We're quite happy for site visitors to add items to their baskets without logging onto the site; just in case they are tempted to buy anything, we don't want to put them off by forcing them to register. So when a visitor first enters the site, they are assigned a user ID that consists of "ANON" and a random number. This is used as a file name for the shopping basket until they log in, when it is replaced with their real user ID.

The empty basket is created from the `basket.xml` file. This just contains a node into which to insert the items, a blank item to use as a template, and nodes for the total cost of the basket:

```
<?xml version="1.0" encoding="ISO-8859-1"?>
<BASKET:basket xmlns:BASKET="uri=http://glasshausxml/basket">
  <BASKET:user_id/>
  <BASKET:items/>
  <BASKET:item>
    <product_id/>
    <manufacturer_id/>
    <desc/>
    <price/>
    <price_vat/>
    <quantity/>
    <total_price/>
    <total_price_vat/>
  </BASKET:item>
  <BASKET:total_price/>
  <BASKET:total_price_vat/>
</BASKET:basket>
```

Adding Items to the Basket

Items are added to the basket by passing the product ID into `addtobasket.asp`. Links for this appear on the *Product* and *Category* pages. The first thing the script has to do is see if there is an existing basket. To do this, you determine the name of the basket file, and attempt to open it. If there is a parse error, then we can assume the basket does not exist, so we load the blank one instead. If a basket file is successfully loaded, then we need to check if the item is already in the basket, in which case we increase the quantity by one. If not, then we set a flag to say that we need to add the item in the next part of the script. We also need to update the `total_price` and `total_price_vat` nodes for this item:

```
Set oItem = _
    oBasket.selectSingleNode("BASKET:basket/BASKET:items/BASKET:item[product_id=" _
    & sProductId & "]")

If oItem is Nothing then
  bAddItem = true
Else
  bAddItem = false
```

```
    iQuantity = CInt(oItem.selectSingleNode("quantity").text) + 1
    oItem.selectSingleNode("quantity").text = CStr(iQuantity)
    oItem.selectSingleNode("total_price").text = _
                        CStr(CSng(oItem.selectSingleNode("price").text)*iQuantity)
    oItem.selectSingleNode("total_price_vat").text = _
                     CStr(CSng(oItem.selectSingleNode("price_vat").text)*iQuantity)

  End if
```

Now we're ready to add the item. First we need to get the product node from the category `DOMDocument`, using the same function as we did before in the product page. If the item is not found, then there's nothing to add to the basket, so we just redirect to the *View Basket* page:

```
  If bAddItem then
    'Get the product Node from the Application DOMDocument
    Set oProductNode = GetProductNode(sProductId)
    If oProductNode is Nothing then Response.redirect "viewbasket.asp"
```

Next we create a clone of the empty basket item, and fill in the values from the product node. As this is the first time the item has been added, the quantity is one, and therefore the total price is the same as the price of an item:

```
    Set oItem = oBasket.selectSingleNode("BASKET:basket/BASKET:item").cloneNode(true)

    oItem.selectSingleNode("product_id").text = _
                        oProductNode.selectSingleNode("product_id").text
    ...
    oItem.selectSingleNode("quantity").text = "1"
    oItem.selectSingleNode("total_price").text = _
                        oProductNode.selectSingleNode("price").text
    oItem.selectSingleNode("total_price_vat").text = _
                        oProductNode.selectSingleNode("price_vat").text
```

And finally the new item node is added to the node that contains the items:

```
    oBasket.documentElement.selectSingleNode("BASKET:items").AppendChild oItem
  End if
```

The last thing that remains to be done is to calculate the total price of the basket. This is done by the `GetBasketTotals` function, which is in `common.inc`. All this function does is iterate through the items in the basket and sums the total price of each item.

View Basket

Viewing the basket is a simple matter of loading the `basket.xml` file, and passing it to the `CreatePage` function. We've already seen how to ascertain the file name from the user ID. If a basket is not found, then the empty basket template file is loaded instead. The following screenshot shows the *View Basket* page:

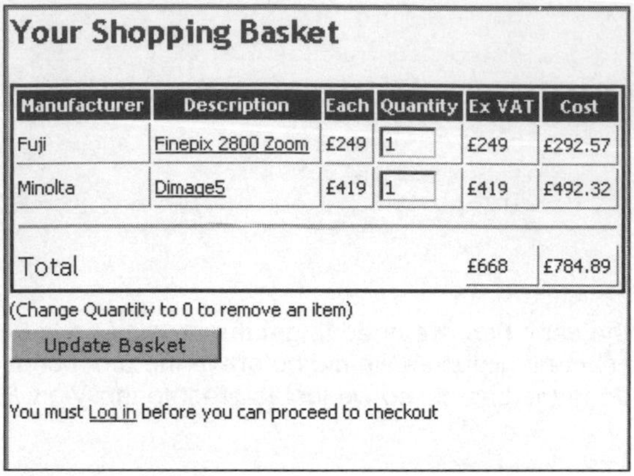

Your Shopping Basket
Manufacturer
Description
Each
Quantity
Ex VAT
Cost
Fuji
Finepix 2800 Zoom
£249
1
£249
£292.57
Minolta
Dimage5
£419
1
£419
£492.32
Total
£668
£784.89
(Change Quantity to 0 to remove an item)
Update Basket
You must Log in before you can proceed to checkout

From the *View Basket* page, the first thing we need to be able to do is change our mind about what we want to buy. The page is a standard HTML form, with fields for the quantities, so they can be changed. The name of the field contains the product ID of the item – the name of a form field element can't just be a number, which is why we need to append some text to it, as shown below in `basket.xsl`:

```
<input type="text" size="3">
  <xsl:attribute name="name">
    quantity_<xsl:value-of select="product_id"/>
  </xsl:attribute>
  <xsl:attribute name="VALUE"><xsl:value-of select="quantity"/></xsl:attribute>
</input>
```

Setting a quantity to *0* will remove as item from the basket. Sure, that's not as user-friendly as a button, but we don't want to encourage people to remove items! The form is submitted to `updatebasket.asp`. The first thing the script does is load the basket; then it iterates through the form that was submitted, and updates the quantity of each item. Looking at the key of each form field, and extracting the characters beyond character 10 will obtain the product ID. Next, we need to select the item in the basket that corresponds to that product ID:

```
For n=1 to Request.Form.Count
  sID = Mid(Request.Form.key(n),10)
  Set oItem = oBasket.selectSingleNode("//BASKET:item[product_id=" & sID & "]")
```

Next we look at the quantity that was provided. As we're keeping this site free of client-side scripting for maximum browser support, there's no validation being done before the form is submitted. So we need to check that they have supplied a number. If not we assume it's zero:

```
  If not oItem is Nothing then
    If isNumeric(Request.Form(n)) then
      iQuantity = CInt(Request.Form(n))
    Else
      iQuantity = 0
    End if
```

If the quantity is zero, then we just remove the node from the tree:

```
        If iQuantity = 0 then
          oBasket.selectSingleNode("//BASKET:items").removeChild oItem
```

Otherwise, we update the quantity and recalculate the total price of that item:

```
        Else
          oItem.selectSingleNode("quantity").text = CStr(iQuantity)
          oItem.selectSingleNode("total_price").text = _
                             CStr(CSng(oItem.selectSingleNode("price").text)*iQuantity)
          oItem.selectSingleNode("total_price_vat").text = _
                         CStr(CSng(oItem.selectSingleNode("price_vat").text)*iQuantity)
        End if
      End if
    Next
```

Finally, the `GetBasketTotals` function is called, to calculate the total price of the basket – then the file is saved.

Logging in

The other thing to do from the *View Basket* screen is proceed to the checkout and actually make the purchase when we're satisfied with the contents of our basket. We're not going to let our anonymous users do that, though; they have to log in first.

Suppose they had been to the site before, registered and been adding items to their basket, and then left the site without actually committing to the purchase. Well, they're back again today and we're hoping that this time they will buy something. For that reason we don't delete the basket when they leave the site, and the file should still be on the server when they return. When a user logs in, therefore, we want to load their existing basket. That's easily done: the *View Basket* screen loads the basket file with the user's ID anyway. It's not as simple as that though; what if they'd been adding items to their basket before logging in? We therefore need to consolidate the basket that was created in their anonymous session with the one that's already saved.

The other thing to consider is that it may have been some time since the user's last visit, so the price of the items in their basket may well have changed. When we load the saved basket we need to update the prices of any items in the basket. We also need to let the user know that their items have changed in price since they decided they might buy them. Hopefully the price will be lower and that will be enough to convince them to proceed with the purchase!

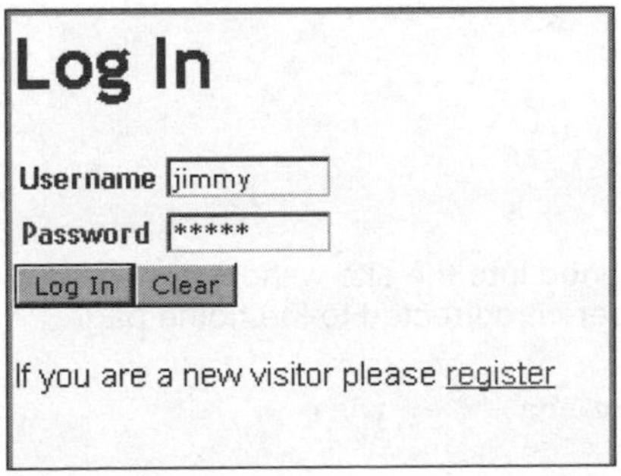

I'll have to admit here that I've cheated in the logging-in procedure. I haven't got a table of users in the database, and I haven't built a registration process. All that happens when the user logs in is that the anonymous user ID stored in the session object is replaced with the username that they type into the login screen, as shown in the previous screenshot. There would have been nothing new to show you about looking the user up in the database, so it was not worth my while coding it. But I'm sure you all know how a proper registration and logging-in procedure would work.

Let's now have a look at what happens to Jimmy's shopping basket when he logs in, which will run `dologin.asp`. The first time Jimmy came to the site, he registered and added a few items to his basket, but then left without making the purchase. In the `baskets` directory, there is now a file called `jimmy.xml`, which contains his basket. Now he's back to buy the stuff, and the first thing he does is log in. The *Log In* screen form is submitted to `dologin.asp`. The first thing it does is replace his anonymous ID with his real one. As I've already mentioned, at this point you should be going to the database and verifying his username and password. We also set a flag to indicate that the user has logged in:

```
Session("userid") = Request.Form("username")
Session("loggedin") = "Y"
```

Next we're going to call the `ConsolidateBaskets` function. This function basically does all the things that were mentioned above. The previous (anonymous) user ID is passed into the function, but only if a user was not already logged in, because we don't want to be combining a user's basket with the basket of another user. The function creates two `DOMDocument` objects, one for the user's saved basket and one for the basket created under the anonymous session. It then attempts to load each of these basket files, and sets flags according to which ones were successfully loaded:

```
'Load Basket created under anonymous session
sFileName = Server.MapPath("baskets") & "\" & sAUId & ".xml"
oAnonBasket.Load(sFileName)

If oAnonBasket.parseError.errorCode <> 0 then
  bAnonBasket = false
Else
  bAnonBasket = true
End if

'Load Basket created under username
sFileName = Server.MapPath("baskets") & "\" & sUID & ".xml"
oBasket.Load(sFileName)

If oBasket.parseError.errorCode <> 0 then
  bBasket = false
Else
  bBasket = true
End if
```

If a user had registered and logged into the site without ever having had a basket the function returns `false` at that point, and the user is redirected to the home page:

```
If not bBasket and not bAnonBasket then
  ConsolidateBaskets = false
  Exit Function
End if
```

If either saved basket exists, then the function returns `true` later on, and the user is redirected to the *View Basket* page:

```
'There are baskets, so true is returned
ConsolidateBaskets = true
```

Jimmy went straight to the *Log In* screen when he returned to the site, so he never created a basket under his anonymous session. Regardless, the `UpdateBasketPrices` function is called if a saved basket is found. This function iterates through the items in the basket, and checks the price against the price currently held in the category `DOMDocument`.

First, it gets the product node from the category `DOMDocument` using the same function as before:

```
For each oItem in _
        oXMLBasket.selectSingleNode("BASKET:basket/BASKET:items").childNodes
  Set oProductNode = GetProductNode(oItem.selectSingleNode("product_id").text)
```

If a product is not found, then that means it's no longer available, so we have to set the quantity to zero:

```
  If oProductNode is Nothing then
    'product no longer available
    oItem.selectSingleNode("quantity").text = "0"
    oItem.selectSingleNode("total_price").text = "0"
    oItem.selectSingleNode("total_price_vat").text = "0"
```

Next, it compares the prices. If they are different, the price of the item in the basket is updated and the total price is worked out again. We also need to create a new attribute, to indicate that the price has changed:

```
  Else
    If oItem.selectSingleNode("price").text <> _
                            oProductNode.selectSingleNode("price").text then
      oItem.setAttribute "pricechanged","Y"
      oItem.selectSingleNode("price").text = _
                                  oProductNode.selectSingleNode("price").text
      oItem.selectSingleNode("price_vat").text = _
                               oProductNode.selectSingleNode("price_vat").text

      iQuantity = CInt(oItem.selectSingleNode("quantity").text)
      oItem.selectSingleNode("total_price").text = _
                        iQuantity*CSng(oProductNode.selectSingleNode("price").text)
      oItem.selectSingleNode("total_price_vat").text = _
                    iQuantity*CSng(oProductNode.selectSingleNode("price_vat").text)
    End if
  End if
Next
```

Now, back in the `ConsolidateBaskets` function, the `GetBasketTotals` function is called to work out the total price, and the basket is saved. Jimmy is then redirected to the *View Basket* screen. He needs to know if the prices have changed on any items he was planning to purchase – so we'll put a check in the stylesheet for the new attribute that was added, and display the price of an item in red if it's changed:

```
<td class="resultstablecell">
  <xsl:if test="@pricechanged='Y'">
    <xsl:attribute name="STYLE">background-color:red;color:white;</xsl:attribute>
  </xsl:if>
  £<xsl:value-of select="price"/>
</td>
```

We'd also better put in a note to tell him what it means when a price appears in red, as shown in the following screenshot:

Your Shopping Basket
Manufacturer
Description
Each
Quantity
Ex VAT
Cost
Canon
PowerShot G2
£539
1
£539
£633.32
Polaroid
PDC Studio Kit
£175
0
£175
£205.62
Fuji
Finepix 2800 Zoom
£249
1
£249
£292.57
Minolta
Dimage5
£419
1
£419
£492.32
Total
£1382
£1623.83
(Change Quantity to 0 to remove an item)
Update Basket
Proceed to Checkout>>>
One or more items in your basket is no longer available
The price has changed for one or more items in your basket (marked in red)

Finally, if any item was no longer available and had its quantity set to zero, we need to draw the user's attention to this. If a product is not found in the category `DOMDocument`, then that means that the product has actually been removed from the database, and not just that it's out of stock. If the quantity has been reset to zero, we need to make sure that he doesn't then just increase the quantity again, so we make the field read-only in that case. Not all browsers support the `readonly` attribute on an input field, and we don't want to use the `disabled` attribute because then the field won't be submitted with the form. So instead we'll make sure the user can't focus on that field in order to overwrite it:

```
<xsl:if test="quantity=0">
  <xsl:attribute name="ONFOCUS">blur();</xsl:attribute>
</xsl:if>
```

So Jimmy is now happy. He can see the items he was thinking about buying, and he can see that the price has changed on one, and the other is no longer available. He can now continue shopping, or proceed to the checkout (notice how that button appears once the user has logged in?).

Our next returning site visitor, Bobby, now comes to the site. He knows exactly what he wants to buy, puts a few items in his basket and goes to the *View Basket* screen with the intention of making the purchases. He's then told he has to log in, so he types in his username and password and submits the form. Now we need to revisit the `ConsolidateBaskets` function, to see what happens for him. Bobby hadn't put any items in his basket the last time he came to the site, so he has no saved basket. All that happens in this case is that the pointer to the saved basket is directed to the basket created under the anonymous session, so it will now be saved with Bobby's username. Bobby will then be redirected to the *View Basket* screen and he'll be able to proceed with his purchase:

```
If bAnonBasket then
  If bBasket then
    ...
  Else
    Set oBasket = oAnonBasket
    oBasket.selectSingleNode("//BASKET:user_id").text = sUID
  End if
End if
```

Our next site visitor, Billy, has been to the site before, when he registered and put some items in his basket. Now he's back, and he's putting items into his basket without logging in, so they're going into an anonymous basket. Then he goes to log in so that he can proceed to the checkout. This time, both baskets exist and we need to combine the two. This is done at the stage of the procedure after his original saved basket has had its prices updated and items checked.

The function iterates through all the items in the basket created under the anonymous session, and checks if the item is in the saved basket. If it is, then we do nothing (we don't want to increase the quantity, as it's unlikely that Billy intended to buy two just because he added the item to his basket again in another session). If the item is not in the saved basket, then the item node is appended to the saved basket. The following code is what's missing from the sample above:

```
For each oNode in _
          oAnonBasket.selectSingleNode("BASKET:basket/BASKET:items").childNodes

If oBasket.selectSingleNode("BASKET:basket/BASKET:items/BASKET:item[product_id='" _
             & oNode.selectSingleNode("product_id").text & "']") is Nothing then
  oBasket.selectSingleNode("BASKET:basket/BASKET:items").appendChild oNode
End if
Next
```

Billy's basket will now be saved again, and he will be redirected to the *View Basket* screen. He can now update his basket and proceed to the checkout.

Proceed to Checkout

I've continued to cheat in the *Checkout* page. What should be happening at this point is the ASP should go back to the database and retrieve the user's address, and any previously stored card details. Instead I've just hard-coded a fictitious address in the ASP, as retrieving it from a database would not be showing you anything new.

In `checkout.asp`, the script loads the file `userdetails.xml`, which is a blank template for the user's address and payment method. I've kept things simple here, assuming one address and one credit card per customer. Of course in reality you'd want your customers to specify as many addresses and cards as they felt like. The user details `DOMDocument` is filled in with my hard-coded data, and then the *Checkout* page is created, as you see in the following screenshot:

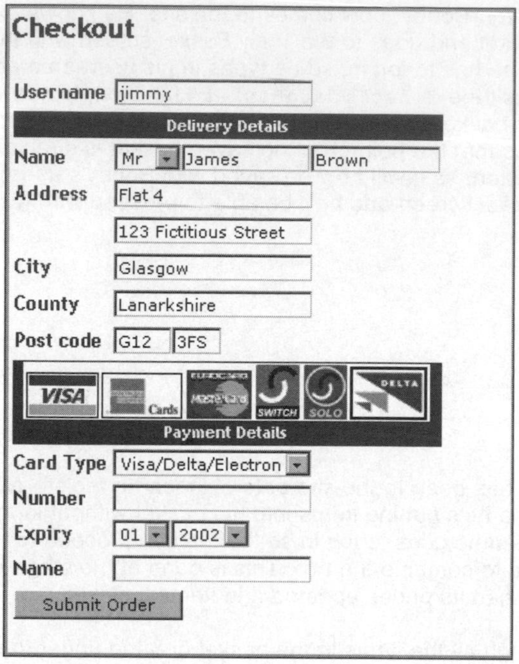

As Jimmy hasn't got this far before, the system doesn't have his card details. It does have his address from when he registered, so he doesn't need to enter that again, unless he wants to specify a different delivery address. Once he's entered his credit card details, he can submit the order.

Submitting the Order

The order is processed by `submitorder.asp`. Before this order can be processed, we must first check that all the information has been provided properly. So we must first go through the laborious process of validating the data, and if anything is wrong we have to redirect the user back to the checkout page so they can re-enter their data. There must also be a way to indicate to the user what their mistake was.

Checking the Form Input

We're going to start by loading the empty user details template file. Then, we'll go through each item in the form collection, and enter it into the appropriate node. If there is no data, or if the format of the data is wrong, then we create a new attribute `missing`, and append it to the node:

```
Set oNode = oXML.selectSingleNode("//USERDETAIL:name/forename")
If Len(Request.Form("forename"))=0 Then
  oNode.setAttribute "missing","Y"
Else
  oNode.text = Request.Form("forename")
End if
```

Sometimes we need to ensure the entry is valid – for example the credit card number must be at least 15 digits, and must contain only numeric data:

```
Set oNode = oXML.selectSingleNode("//USERDETAIL:payment_method/card_no")
If Len(Request.Form("cardno"))<15 or not IsNumeric(Request.Form("cardno")) Then
  oNode.setAttribute "missing","Y"
Else
  oNode.text = Request.Form("cardno")
End if
```

And so on until all the fields have been checked and inserted. Next we're going to temporarily save the file. We don't want to keep this file any longer than necessary as, apart from anything else, it contains credit card data, so we'll just save it with the session ID as a file name. I've chosen to stick it in the `baskets` directory, as that already has write permissions on it and the names won't conflict. The only reason the file is being saved is so that the data is still there if the user has to go back and change anything, or if they continue shopping and then come back to the *Checkout* screen again. Now we check to see if anything was wrong and, if so, redirect the user back to the *Checkout* screen:

```
If not oXML.selectSingleNode("//@missing") is nothing then _
                                              Response.Redirect "checkout.asp"
```

In this case, `checkout.asp` loads the file that was saved, rather than looking the user up in the database again (or in reality just inserting my hard-coded data). In the stylesheet we check initially if anything was missing and display an appropriate message:

```
<xsl:if test="//@missing">
<B class="smalltext">Some required information was missing or inaccurate</B>
</xsl:if>
```

Then in each individual field, we need to check whether that field was causing a problem and, if so, we'll set the background color to yellow, but also insert a `*` as a sign for browsers that don't support CSS:

```
<tr>
    <td class="criteria">
    <xsl:if test="//USERDETAIL:payment_method/card_name/@missing">
      <xsl:attribute name="STYLE">background-color:yellow;</xsl:attribute>*
    </xsl:if>
    Name
    </td>
    <td>
    <xsl:if test="//USERDETAIL:payment_method/card_name/@missing">
      <xsl:attribute name="STYLE">background-color:yellow;</xsl:attribute>
    </xsl:if>
    <input name="cardholder">
      <xsl:attribute name="VALUE">
        <xsl:value-of select="//USERDETAIL:payment_method/card_name"/>
      </xsl:attribute>
    </input>
    </td></tr>
```

Now if Jimmy tried to submit the order without entering his card details, this is what he'll see:

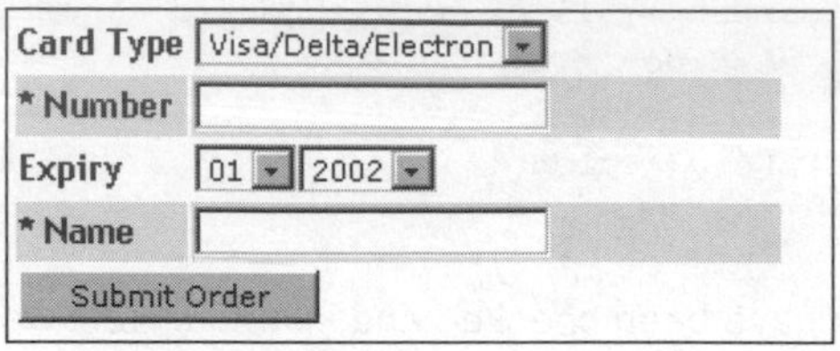

Once the information has finally been submitted correctly, the basket file is loaded and inserted into the `DOMDocument`.

Posting the Order Over HTTP

Another ASP file, `processorder.asp`, does the actual order processing. We're going to post the `DOMDocument` that contains the user information and shopping basket to this ASP over HTTP. This is done using the `ServerXMLHTTP` object. First you need to initialize a request with the `open` method, which has two compulsory parameters: the method, `POST` in this case, and the URL to send the data to. There are also optional parameters to specify an asynchronous post, and authentication information. Once the request has been initialized, it is sent using the `send` method:

```
Set oXMLHTTP = CreateObject("MSXML2.ServerXMLHTTP.4.0")

oXMLHTTP.open "POST","http://localhost/glasshausxml/processorder.asp"
oXMLHTTP.send (oXML)
```

`processorder.asp` accepts an XML document as input, processes the order and generates XML to indicate the status of the order. The first thing it does is to create two `DOMDocument` objects – one for the request being posted to it, and another to create the response. Because the data being posted to the ASP is an XML document, the request can be loaded straight into the `DOMDocument`. The response `DOMDocument` loads an XML string:

```
oXMLRequest.Load(Request)
oXMLResponse.LoadXML("<?xml version='1.0'?><xmlresponse> _
                      <status/><reason/><order_id/></xmlresponse>")
```

Now we would go through the laborious process of validating the data, authorizing the payment, and inserting the order into the database. I haven't done any of that, but I'll show you briefly what happens if something is out of order. In order to demonstrate how this works, the site will reject a credit card number that is all ones:

```
If oXMLRequest.selectSingleNode("//USERDETAIL:payment_method/card_no").text = _
                                "1111111111111111" Then
  sStatus = "F"
  oXMLResponse.selectSingleNode("xmlresponse/reason").text = _
                                "Credit Card refused by Issuing Bank"
End if
```

However, if everything goes according to plan, the status will be "S" for success, and there will be an order ID which is inserted into the `DOMDocument`. The last things the script does are update the status node and write out the XML of the `DOMDocument`.

Back in `submitorder.asp` we can now load the response XML from `processorder.asp` and create a page from it, which will show the user the order status, and the order ID or reason for failure:

```
Set oXML2 = oXMLHTTP.responseXML
CreatePage "orderstatus", "Order Status", "", false, oXML2
```

Posting from Another System

The reason why I chose to post the order XML over HTTP to `processorder.asp` was so that the system is not restricted to accepting orders from the web site only. All that the system requires to create an order is to have an XML document that contains the user details and the shopping basket posted to it. This could easily be sent to it from another system.

This is really a consumer site, so it's not that relevant here, but if you imagine for a moment that this is a site for supplying businesses with stock then it makes sense to integrate systems with your regular suppliers. After all, that was one of the main reasons behind XML: to create a simple language that allows different systems to exchange data. If another company trades with your company regularly and you trust them sufficiently, you can give them the structure of the XML document and the URL to post it to. They can then build the capability of automatically submitting orders when stocks get low into their own systems. The code they would use would be identical to that shown above.

Of course in reality, there are many things to consider. You have no control over their systems, so you would need to validate the incoming XML document with a **schema**, to ensure it is of the correct format and that all the data is what you expect. Schemas are beyond our scope here, but they would certainly be the next thing you should look into once you've got to grips with the content of this book. You would also need to examine your security setup to ensure that you were only receiving orders of this type from the trusted customers. Additionally, to submit an order the customer would need a copy of your product database in order to get the product IDs that they would need. It might be an idea to provide an alternative way of posting the order, in which the basket only contains the manufacturer and model, and the system looks up the product when it processes the order.

Summary

In this case study, I have shown you how to incorporate XML techniques throughout the site. What we've ended up with is a highly maintainable site of modular construction that makes extremely efficient use of server resources.

Amongst other things, you have seen how to create XML data from a `Recordset`, how to resolve IDs without having to join to lookup tables, and how to use an XML template to achieve a generic page structure across a site. You've also seen how to store a `Recordset` to avoid having to rerun a query, and very efficient techniques for column sorting and `Recordset` paging. You've also seen how to retain frequently accessed data in an XML document in memory, and how to retain XML data throughout a user's session. And finally, you've seen how disparate systems can exchange XML data.

By running transformations on the server, it's possible to have an application that makes full use of XML capabilities, yet can work in any browser. Furthermore, we can easily code for different browsers wherever necessary.

By storing your `Recordset` in an XML file, and using XML as an interim data storage format, it is possible to keep trips to the database to a minimum. This results in prudent use of server resources, which in turn leads to an application that performs quickly and is easily scaled to a large number of users.

This just goes to show how a thorough understanding of XML techniques and their capabilities, combined with a bit of imagination and creativity, can result in a highly structured application that performs extremely well.

10

- Advanced JSP XML case study (news ticker component)
- Passing XML for display in Flash

Author: Oli Gauti Gudmundsson

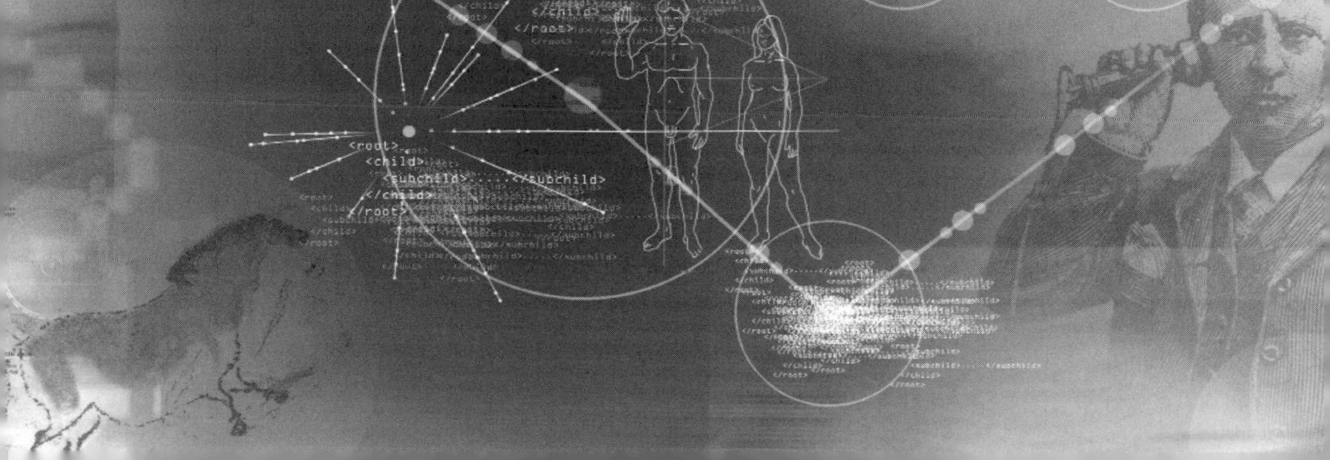

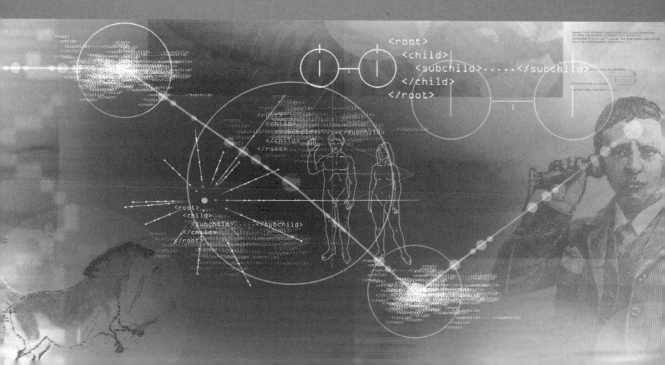

Case Study: Displaying XML Data in Flash Using JSP

In this chapter we'll take a look at a real-world example of XML processing on a server using **JavaServer Pages** (JSP), which were introduced in Chapter 10. I'll show you how to retrieve data from both a database and an online XML feed, and how to display that data using **Macromedia Flash**. I'll also show you how to transform the data to HTML using XSLT when Flash is not supported.

In this section I'll go through the requirements for the case study, and provide a brief overview of how we are going to meet those requirements. You are advised to read this section to gain a good overview of what's happening in the later, more complex sections.

The Requirements

What is it exactly that we are going to build in this chapter? Let's imagine that we have just been hired as a web developer at a newspaper. Our manager has just handed us our first assignment: we are to build a reusable, dynamic news ticker component.

The exact requirements are as follows:

- Build a news ticker component that can be reused on multiple web sites. The purpose is to display the latest news headlines on the newspaper's web site and also make them accessible to external web sites.

- The news ticker shall first display the five latest headlines from the newspaper's local database, and then the five latest headlines from the XML news site.

- The news must be the latest available from the sources in use, and new headlines must be picked up automatically.

- The news ticker will display news headlines from both the newspaper's local database, and an external XML news site. The headlines shall be links, which when clicked, will take the user to the newspaper's web site or the XML news site for the full story.

The Solution

So, how are we going to meet these requirements? We immediately decide that XML should be at the heart of our solution. I can hear you thinking "well, anything else would be nonsense since this is an XML book!". But as you're about to find out, there is more to it than that. After a few hours of intense brainstorming we come up with the following scenario:

- We will build the news ticker component in Macromedia Flash. Flash can read XML documents, and provides an easy way of animating the news headlines.

- We will define an XML format readable by the Flash news ticker.

So far so good, but we need to read data from two sources: a database, and an online XML document. Once we have the data from those sources, we need to merge it into the XML format understood by the Flash file. How on earth are we going to accomplish that? Enter JSP.

We will create a JSP that retrieves the data from the two sources, and delivers the merged set of headlines to the Flash application as an XML document.

At this point you might have a few questions:

- *How can a JSP be an XML document?*
  Well, that will become clear in the sections to follow, but essentially what we will do is set the content-type of the JSP to be XML. This will mean we're returning XML, rather than the more usual HTML.

- *Why are we merging the data from the two sources into a single XML document?*
  Firstly, we need to transform the data into the XML format understood by our Flash file (the external XML document from which we will retrieve the sports news will not be in this format, and will therefore need transformation). Secondly, it makes the Flash much more maintainable to have all the data in a single file.

- *What happens if the user does not have the Flash player installed?*
  If Flash is not supported, we'll display the news headlines statically.

Finally, we'll create a JSP that displays the full story matching a selection from the ticker (if the headline clicked was from the newspaper's database).

Before You Continue

Before we delve into the code, you'll need to install some software. What you need are the following:

- The Java Development Kit (JDK)
- Jakarta Tomcat for serving up the JSP pages
- MySQL database from which we will retrieve the news
- The MM.MySQL JDBC driver for connecting to MySQL from the JSP pages
- Macromedia Flash for editing the Flash file

Detailed installation instructions can be found with the code download at: *http://www.glasshaus.com*.

> Note: I will not spend time explaining what JDBC is or how it works, but rather just show you how to use it. This chapter focuses on the XML aspect of JSP. For more info about JSP and JDBC, refer to the *Further Reading* section at the end of this chapter.

Now with the formalities out of the way let's start our implementation of the news ticker. Before we build the Flash file we must have the XML document ready, and that is the subject of the next section.

Preparing the Data

In this section I'll show you how we prepare the XML data for the Flash file. First I'll show you the XML structure that will be understood by our Flash file, and then I'll show you how to build the XML document in JSP by retrieving and merging the data from the two sources. Finally I'll discuss caching the data.

The XML Structure

We need to define an XML structure that the Flash file can read as input. The XML document must contain the following information about each news item:

- Headline
- Category (general / sports / business / entertainment / etc.)
- Link (holds the URL to the full story)

The document structure is fairly simple. We decide to name the root element `<articles>`, and to name each article element `<article>`. All the other information is stored in direct child elements.

The following diagram shows the structure of our XML document:

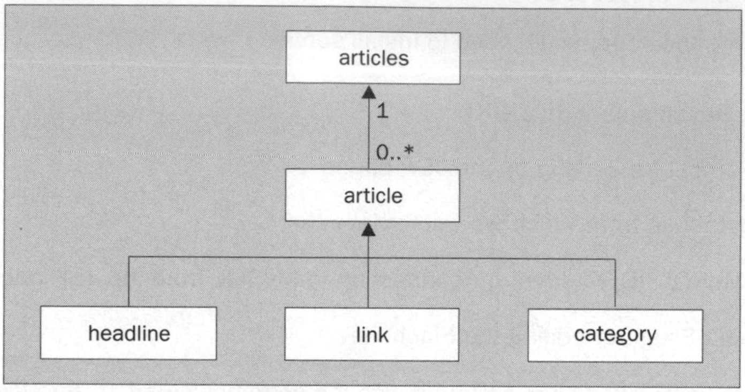

As you see from the diagram, the root element (<articles>) can have zero or more (0...*) <article> elements. Here is an outline of the XML instance:

```
<?xml version="1.0" encoding="ISO-8859-1"?>
<articles>
  <article>
    <headline>A Headline</headline>
    <category>general</category>
    <link>http://localhost:8080/news/full_story.jsp?id=123</link>
  </article>
  ...
</articles>
```

Retrieving Data from the Database

Now that we've decided on the XML structure to use, we can start building the XML document. For that we need to retrieve data from two sources. Let's start by getting the data from the newspaper's database.

Before we begin coding, we need some information about the database that we will be taking the information from. To begin with, we need to know where it is, the username and password of an authorized user, and the structures of the tables in which the data is stored, so that we can build our queries.

We contact the newspaper's database administrator, and he tells us the name of the database and where it is. We are told to use the user `'news'` with password `'papadom'`. He also tells us that there are two tables that we must use: `articles` and `categories`. He supplies us with the following information about the table structure:

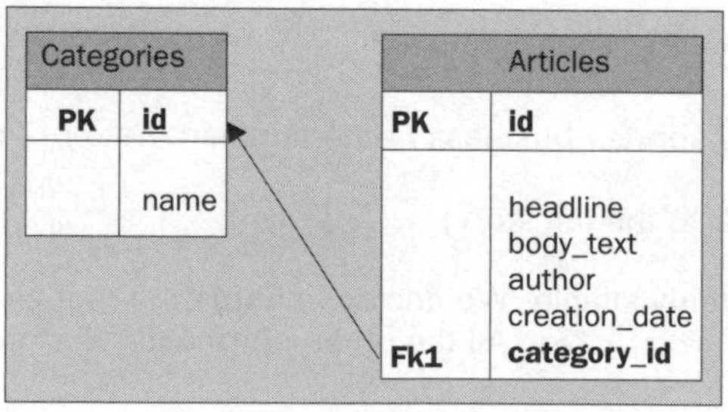

The `categories` table stores the news categories, and the `articles` table stores the news articles. Each article is linked to a specific category in the `categories` table through the `category_id` column, which references the `id` column in the `categories` table.

What we are going to do is roughly the following: we'll write a JSP that creates a connection to the database, selects the five latest news articles (that is, the five articles with the latest creation dates), creates an XML document to hold the data, and finally prints the XML. Let's go through this process step by step.

Preparations

Before we start with the code, let's look at the variables and directory structure that we'll be using in the sections to follow:

- `$CATALINA_HOME`: this is the full path for the Tomcat installation directory. For example `D:\tomcat`.
- `$NEWS_HOME`: this is the full path to the root of our news web application under Tomcat. This will be `$CATALINA_HOME/webapps/news`. We need to create this directory after installing Tomcat.

> NOTE: To keep things simple, we'll create our web application directly under Tomcat's `webapps` directory. A better way to do this would be to use a special source directory for our news application, and build a WAR (web application archive) file from that source. This WAR could then be deployed on Tomcat or any J2EE-compliant application server. For this example, though, we'll focus on the functionality, not the portability.

The following list describes the inner structure of the `$NEWS_HOME` directory:

- `$NEWS_HOME`

  This directory will contain the JSP pages.

- `$NEWS_HOME/WEB-INF`

  This directory will contain the web application deployment descriptor, `web.xml`.

- `$NEWS_HOME/WEB-INF/lib`

  This directory will contain any third-party class libraries that we will be using in our news application.

- `$NEWS_HOME/WEB-INF/classes`

  This directory would contain any classes that we would create for our news application. However, we will not be doing that in this case study. This directory will therefore be empty.

If you get lost in acronyms in this chapter, refer to the *Further Reading* section at the end of this chapter.

Connecting To the Database

The first thing to do is to establish a connection with the database. Our web application will be accessing the newspaper's database via a JDBC driver. I'll be using the `MM.MySQL` JDBC driver for MySQL (see the installation instructions for information about downloading and setting this up).

All J2EE application servers make available a **DataSource** (that is, a connection pool for JDBC connections) that applications can use to get connections to the database. The purpose of defining the data source outside of the application is to allow database-based applications to run unchanged on any J2EE server. Tomcat offers this support.

Before we start coding the JSP, let's very quickly go through how to configure the `DataSource` for our news application.

Installing the JDBC Driver

This is easy: just copy the JAR (Java Archive) driver file `mm.mysql-2.0.14-bin.jar` into the `$CATALINA_HOME/common/lib` directory.

Configuring Tomcat's Resource Factory

To declare the `DataSource`, we add the following lines to the `$CATALINA_HOME/conf/server.xml` file.

```
<Context path="/news" docBase="news" debug="0">

  <Resource name="jdbc/NewsDB" auth="Container" type="javax.sql.DataSource"/>

  <ResourceParams name="jdbc/NewsDB">
    <parameter>
      <name>user</name>
      <value>news</value>
    </parameter>

    <parameter>
      <name>password</name>
      <value>papadom</value>
    </parameter>

    <parameter>
      <name>driverClassName</name>
      <value>org.gjt.mm.mysql.Driver</value>
    </parameter>

    <parameter>
      <name>driverName</name>
      <value>jdbc:mysql://localhost/test</value>
    </parameter>
  </ResourceParams>

</Context>
```

This <Context> element should appear after the <Host> element. Here we have defined the username and password for the database connection, and also the class name of the driver and the database URL. We have named this resource jdbc/NewsDB and will use this name when specifying which resource to get connections from in the JSP.

This resource can now be used by all web applications running on this application server.

Note that the server.xml file is an XML document (obviously) used by Tomcat to set up server behavior and specify resources, like the DataSource.

Declare the Resource Requirements for Our Application

Next we must declare which resources to use in our news application. This we do by adding the following element to the web application descriptor ($NEWS_HOME/WEB-INF/web.xml):

```
<resource-ref>

  <description>
    Resource reference to a factory for java.sql.Connection
    instances that may be used for talking to a particular
    DataSource that is configured in the server.xml file.
  </description>

  <res-ref-name>jdbc/NewsDB</res-ref-name>
  <res-type>javax.sql.DataSource</res-type>
  <res-auth>Container</res-auth>

</resource-ref>
```

Here we are simply referencing the resource from server.xml, specifically the DataSource we called jdbc/NewsDB. As with the server.xml file, web.xml is used to specify resources, except in this case they are specific to the web application the file is written for.

Code the Application

Now we're finally ready to create the JSP that reads the data from the database. We create the JSP in the $NEWS_HOME directory, and call it news.jsp. Here is the first version of news.jsp:

```
<%@ page import="java.sql.Connection,
                 javax.naming.Context,
                 javax.naming.InitialContext,
                 javax.sql.DataSource" %>
<%
  Connection conn = null;
  try {

    // look up the correct DataSource:
    Context initCtx = new InitialContext();
    Context envCtx = (Context) initCtx.lookup("java:comp/env");

    DataSource ds = (DataSource) envCtx.lookup("jdbc/NewsDB");
```

```
        // get a connection:
        conn = ds.getConnection();

      } catch ( Exception e ) {
        out.println("Error occurred: " + e.getMessage());
      } finally {
        // close the connection
        if ( conn != null ) {
          conn.close();
        }
      }
    %>
```

Let's go through this code. We begin by importing the classes that we'll be using in the JSP. This is done by the `<%@ page import="..." %>` directive. In JSP, all Java code must be between `<%` and `%>`.

We start by looking up the `DataSource` that we defined earlier. We first get the environment context, and then we look up the `DataSource` in that context. Note that we look up the `DataSource` using the resource reference name (`jdbc/NewsDB`) that was declared in the web application deployment descriptor. This is matched up against the resource factory that is configured in `$CATALINA_HOME/conf/server.xml`.

Then we get the database connection from the `DataSource`:

```
conn = ds.getConnection();
```

Note that the username and password are abstracted from the application. We could therefore swap to another database without the application ever knowing about it, simply by changing the details in `server.xml`.

We catch all exceptions that might be thrown, and print the error message to the output stream. The variable `out` is defined automatically for all JSP pages. Each `String` that is printed through the `out` variable (as in `out.println("Error occurred")`) is printed to the response. In the `Finally` block, we close the database connection whether or not there has been an exception. Now we can start getting the articles from the database.

Querying the Database

The next thing to do is to get the data from the database. This we do by creating a SQL statement, and executing it. This will return a `ResultSet` containing the results of the SQL query. Let's add this to `news.jsp` (the changes are highlighted):

```
<%@ page import="java.sql.Connection,
                 java.sql.PreparedStatement,
                 java.sql.ResultSet,
                 javax.naming.Context,
                 javax.naming.InitialContext,
                 javax.sql.DataSource" %><%
  Connection conn = null;
  try {
```

```
        // look up the correct DataSource:
        Context initCtx = new InitialContext();
        Context envCtx = (Context) initCtx.lookup("java:comp/env");

        DataSource ds = (DataSource) envCtx.lookup("jdbc/NewsDB");

        // get a connection:
        conn = ds.getConnection();

        // select the five latest news articles:
        String sql = "SELECT a.id, a.headline, c.name "
                     + "FROM articles a, categories c "
                     + "WHERE a.category_id = c.id "
                     + "ORDER BY a.creation_date DESC "
                     + "LIMIT 5"
                     ;
        PreparedStatement ps = conn.prepareStatement(sql);
        ResultSet rs = ps.executeQuery();

        // scroll through the ResultSet,
        while ( rs.next() ) {
          // print the headlines
          out.println(rs.getString("headline") + "<BR>");
        }
        // close the ResultSet and the statement:
        rs.close();
        ps.close();

      } catch ( Exception e ) {
        out.println("Error occurred: " + e.getMessage());
      } finally {
        // close the connection
        if ( conn != null ) {
            conn.close();
        }
      }
%>
```

We have added two more classes to the import. These are classes for the statement, and for the `ResultSet`. We then start by creating the `String` containing SQL statement:

```
String sql = "SELECT a.id, a.headline, c.name "
             + "FROM articles a, categories c "
             + "WHERE a.category_id = c.id "
             + "ORDER BY a.creation_date DESC "
             + "LIMIT 5"
             ;
```

Here we are selecting the article `ID` and headline, and the name of the category. Since the name of the category is stored in the `categories` table, we have to join the `articles` and `categories` tables on the category ID. We ensure that we get the latest headlines first by ordering in a descending order by the creation date, and finally limit the `ResultSet` to only five records. Then we get a `PreparedStatement`, by preparing the SQL statement:

```
PreparedStatement ps = conn.prepareStatement(sql);
```

Next we execute the statement, and get a `ResultSet`:

```
ResultSet rs = ps.executeQuery();
```

We then scroll through the records in the `ResultSet`. Currently we just print the headline to the output stream.

Creating the XML document

Our next task is to create the XML document. For this task we'll be using the **JDOM** API. JDOM is a Java-based document object model that provides a way to represent an XML document for easy and efficient reading, manipulation, and writing (see the *Further Reading* section for more information). Before you continue, ensure that you have the `jdom.jar` file in your `$NEWS_HOME/WEB-INF/lib` folder.

What we need to do is the following: create the document instance, create the `<articles>` root element, and then create the `<article>` elements with the data from the database. This proves to be very simple with JDOM. Let's have a look at `news.jsp` with the changes highlighted:

```
<%@ page import="java.sql.Connection,
                 java.sql.PreparedStatement,
                 java.sql.ResultSet,
                 javax.naming.Context,
                 javax.naming.InitialContext,
                 javax.sql.DataSource,
                 org.jdom.Document,
                 org.jdom.Element" %>
<%
    Connection conn = null;

    // define the XML Document and the root element:
    Document doc = new Document();
    Element root = new Element("articles");

    try {

        // Connect to the database, initialize and execute the SQL statement
        // code missing for space


        // scroll through the ResultSet,
        // but stop after the 5 latest headlines

      String linkBase = "http://localhost:8080/news/full_story.jsp?id=";
```

```
while ( rs.next()) {

    // create an XML element for this article
    Element article = new Element("article");
    article.addContent(
      (new Element("headline")).addContent(rs.getString("headline"))
    );
    article.addContent(
      (new Element("category")).addContent(rs.getString("name"))
    );
    article.addContent(
      (new Element("link")).addContent(linkBase + rs.getString("id"))
    );

    // add the article element to the root element:
    root.addContent( article );

}

  // code finishes as before
```

We've imported two new classes: `Document` and `Element`. We create an instance of `Document`, which will hold our XML document. Then we create the root element.

```
Document doc = new Document();
Element root = new Element("articles");
```

We then define a variable called `linkBase`, which is the base of the link to the full story. We just add the ID of the article to the end of this base to form the article link.

Finally, as we loop through the `ResultSet` we create the `<article>` elements (each containing a `<headline>`, `<category>`, and `<link>` element), and add them to the root element (`<articles>`). We use the `addContent()` method of the `Element` class to add content to the element. For example, the following line adds the `<headline>` element to the current `<article>` element:

```
article.addContent((new Element("headline")).addContent(rs.getString("headline")));
```

Here we create the `<headline>` element and add to it the text from the `headline` column in the `articles` database table.

Printing the XML

We're almost done with the database part. The only thing we now need to do is to print the XML to the output stream. Before we do that, though, we must set the content type of the JSP to `text/xml`. The default content type is `text/html`, so we must change it before we output anything. This we do with the following line:

```
Connection conn = null;

// set the content type of the page to XML:
response.setContentType("text/xml");
```

```
// define the XML Document and the root element:
Document doc = new Document();
Element root = new Element("articles");
```

The JSP is now disguised as an XML document, because when it is called it will return the XML document it has generated. The `response` variable is an instance of the `javax.servlet.http.HttpServletResponse` class, and is made available automatically to all JSP pages (along with a `request` variable among others).

Now we can print the XML to the JSP output stream. JDOM has a class called `XMLOutputter` that is specially designed for this purpose. First we import this class:

```
<%@ page import="java.sql.Connection,
                java.sql.PreparedStatement,
                java.sql.ResultSet,
                javax.naming.Context,
                javax.naming.InitialContext,
                javax.sql.DataSource,
                org.jdom.Document,
                org.jdom.Element,
                org.jdom.output.XMLOutputter" %>
```

Then, we use it to output the XML:

```
      // close the ResultSet and the statement:
      rs.close();
      ps.close();

      // output the XML
      doc.setRootElement( root );
      XMLOutputter outputter = new XMLOutputter();
      outputter.setEncoding("ISO-8859-1");
      outputter.output( doc, out );

    } catch ( Exception e ) {
      out.println("<error>" + e.getMessage() + "</error>");
    } finally {
      // close the connection
      if ( conn != null ) {
          conn.close();
      }
    }
%>
```

Note that we've modified our error-handling code to print the error message within `<error>` tags. We had to do this since the JSP is now an XML document, and otherwise it would not be well-formed.

We set the root element (which now has all the `<article>` elements), create an instance of the `XMLOutputter`, set the encoding, and finally output the XML. If you try pointing your browser to the URL *http://localhost:8080/news/news.jsp* (assuming that you have Tomcat running on port 8080 on your machine), you should see something like the following screenshot (assuming you're using Internet Explorer):

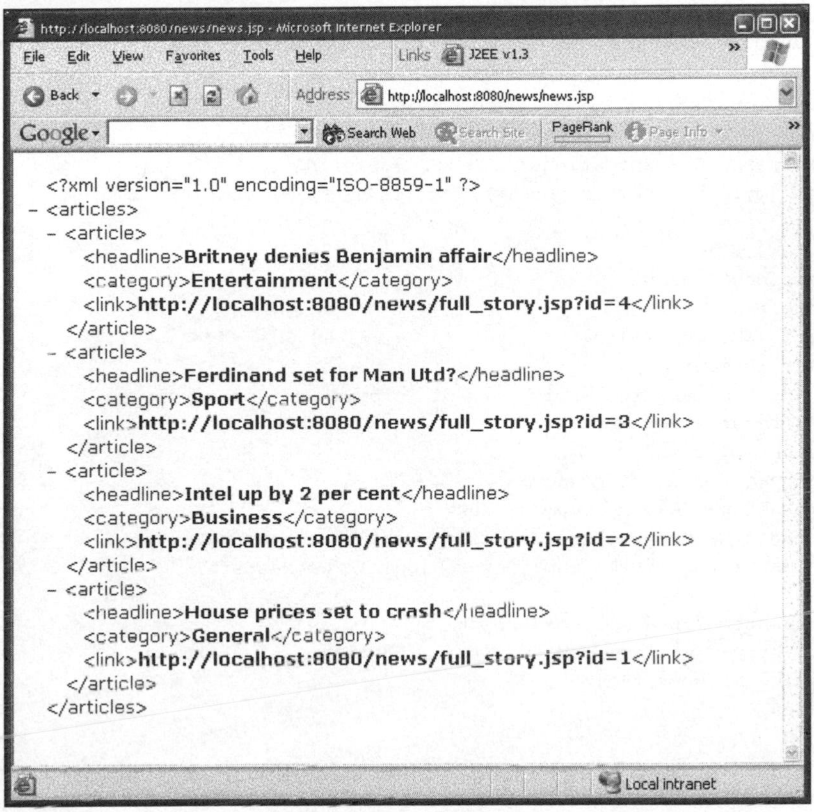

Retrieving Data from the Online XML Document

Now that we have all the data from the database ready we can move on to the next task, which is getting the data from the XML web site. We'll be using a news feed from *XML.com*, which can be retrieved from *http://www.xml.com/xml/news.rss.*

What we have to do is the following: using the same JSP as before (`news.jsp`) we'll create a connection to the online XML feed and parse it, retrieve the five latest news headlines, and add them to the end of our XML document. First, though, let's examine the structure of the online XML document.

The Structure of the XML Document

The XML feed that we'll be using is in the **RSS** (**Rich Site Summary**) format mentioned in Chapter 2. This is a lightweight XML format designed for sharing headlines and other web content. Think of it as a distributable "What's New" for your site. Originally developed by Netscape to fill channels for Netcenter, RSS has evolved into a popular means of sharing content between sites (including the BBC, CNET, CNN, Disney, and more). See the *Further Reading* section at the end of this chapter for more information. An example XML instance document (formatted to fit the page) is shown below:

```
<?xml version="1.0" encoding="iso-8859-1"?>
<!DOCTYPE rss PUBLIC
  "-//Netscape Communications//DTD RSS 0.91//EN"
  "http://my.netscape.com/publish/formats/rss-0.91.dtd"
>

<rss version="0.91">
  <channel>
    <title>XML.com</title>
    <description>
       XML.com features a rich mix of information and services
       for the XML community.
    </description>
    <language>en-us</language>
    <link>http://www.xml.com/</link>
    <managingEditor>edd@xml.com (Edd Dumbill)</managingEditor>
    <webMaster>peter@xml.com (Peter Wiggin)</webMaster>
  <image>
    <link>http://www.xml.com/</link>
    <url>http://www.xml.com/universal/images/xml_tiny.gif</url>
    <title>XML.com</title>
  </image>

    <item>
      <title>A Realist's SMIL Manifesto, Part II</title>
      <link>http://www.xml.com/pub/a/2002/07/17/smil.html</link>
      <description>In the second part of his overview of SMIL 2.0,
                   Fabio Arciniegas shows how SMIL can be used to
                   implement common narrative strategies: condensation,
                   synecdoche and spatial montage.
      </description>
    </item>
    <item>
      <title>Implementing XPath for Wireless Devices, Part II</title>
      <link>http://www.xml.com/pub/a/2002/07/17/wirelessxpath2.html</link>
      <description>In the second of a two-part series, we explore the
                   implementation of XPath on wireless devices using
                   the WAP family of standards.
      </description>
```

```
      </item>



   </channel>
</rss>
```

The first part of the document is of no interest to us. It's the <item> elements we're after. We'll have to parse the document, and get the five first <item> elements. We will map the values from this document to our XML document in the following way:

RSS	Our document
/rss/channel/item/title	/articles/article/headline
/rss/channel/item/link	/articles/article/link

We'll set the category to "XML" for all the headlines retrieved from this RSS feed.

Parsing the Remote Document

Next, we import two new classes into news.jsp, SAXBuilder and URL:

```
<%@ page import="java.sql.Connection,
                 java.sql.PreparedStatement,
                 java.sql.ResultSet,
                 java.net.URL,
                 javax.naming.Context,
                 javax.naming.InitialContext,
                 javax.sql.DataSource,
                 org.jdom.Document,
                 org.jdom.Element,
                 org.jdom.input.SAXBuilder,
                 org.jdom.output.XMLOutputter" %>
```

We'll use the URL class to represent the URL to the online XML feed. The SAXBuilder class uses that URL to locate the XML, and then loads and parses the document.

Loading and parsing the remote document with the SAXBuilder class is very simple. We simply create an instance of the URL class, supplying the location of the remote document, and then pass the URL instance to the SAXBuilder:

```
      // close the ResultSet and the statement:
    rs.close();
    ps.close();

    // parse the remote XML document:
    SAXBuilder sb = new SAXBuilder();
    URL url = new URL("http://www.xml.com/xml/news.rss");
```

```
        Document remoteDoc = sb.build( url );

        // output the XML
        doc.setRootElement( root );
        XMLOutputter outputter = new XMLOutputter();
        outputter.setEncoding("ISO-8859-1");
        outputter.output( doc, out );
```

When testing this script, always make sure that the news feed is active. If the suggested news feed is not active you can use another, or a local copy simply by changing the `URL("")` section of the code.

Adding the News Headlines

The remote document has now been parsed and built into memory. The next thing to do is to get the first five `<item>` elements, and copy the data from them to new `<article>` elements. Before we do that we need to import two more classes:

```
<%@ page import="java.sql.Connection,
                 java.sql.PreparedStatement,
                 java.sql.ResultSet,
                 java.net.URL,
                 java.util.Iterator,
                 java.util.List,
                 javax.naming.Context,
                 javax.naming.InitialContext,
                 javax.sql.DataSource,
                 org.jdom.Document,
                 org.jdom.Element,
                 org.jdom.input.SAXBuilder,
                 org.jdom.output.XMLOutputter" %>
```

We'll use the `List` and `Iterator` classes for scrolling through lists of elements. Now we can copy the data from the `<item>` elements:

```
        // close the ResultSet and the statement:
        rs.close();
        ps.close();

        // parse the remote XML document:
        SAXBuilder sb = new SAXBuilder();
        URL url = new URL("http://www.xml.com/xml/news.rss");
        Document remoteDoc = sb.build( url );

        // get the first five <item> elements, and add them to our root element:
        Element remoteRoot = remoteDoc.getRootElement();
        List items = remoteRoot.getChild("channel").getChildren("item");
        Iterator it = items.iterator();
        int counter = 0;
        while ( counter < 5 && it.hasNext() ) {
```

```
        Element item = (Element) it.next();
        Element article = new Element("article");
        article.addContent(
            (new Element("headline")).addContent(item.getChildText("title"))
          );
        // the category for the XML news is 'XML':
        article.addContent( (new Element("category")).addContent("XML") );
        article.addContent(
            (new Element("link")).addContent(item.getChildText("link"))
          );

        // add the article element to the root element:
        root.addContent( article );

        // increase the counter
        counter++;
      }

      // output the XML
      doc.setRootElement( root );
      XMLOutputter outputter = new XMLOutputter();
      outputter.setEncoding("ISO-8859-1");
      outputter.output( doc, out );
```

We first get the root element, and retrieve the list of `<item>` elements:

```
      Element remoteRoot = remoteDoc.getRootElement();
      List items = remoteRoot.getChild("channel").getChildren("item");
```

We then iterate through the first five items in the list. For each item, we create an `<article>` element and copy the data to it. The data from the item's `<title>` element goes to the article's `<headline>` element, the `<link>` element is a straight transfer, and since there is no category information about the `<item>` elements, we put them into the "`XML`" category. We then add each new `<article>` element to the `<articles>` root element.

That's it; the XML document is now ready to be processed by Flash. Before we continue, however, here is a quick discussion about caching.

Caching the Data

The newspaper's writers only update the news database every hour, and a longer time passes between updates to the XML news feed. However, every time that a request is made for `news.jsp`, a database connection is created, and data is fetched over the Internet. We are therefore spending most of our processing time fetching data that we've already retrieved. Under heavy load, this easily could turn our system and database performance into something unacceptably slow. We therefore decide to cache our XML document.

> NOTE: The caching strategy that we'll use here is very simple, and might not be suitable for larger systems. The point of this section is to convince you to consider caching your data, not to show you the ultimate caching strategy.

Our strategy is very simple: We'll cache the XML to a static file. When a request comes in, we perform the following checks:

- If the cache file does not exist, or the cache is out of date, we cache the document and print it.
- Otherwise, we forward the request to the static cache file, thereby avoiding building the file, and saving processing power.

> NOTE: For this to work, the user running Tomcat must have write privileges to the `$NEWS_HOME` folder.

We import two classes, `File` and `FileOutputStream`, for the file handling. To determine whether to cache the document, we check if the cache file (`xml_cache.xml`) exists, and, if it exists, we check when the file was last modified to determine if an hour has passed since the last modification. If the file does not exist, or it is out of date, then we create and cache the document; otherwise we forward the request to the cached file.

Below is `news.jsp` with the cache addition:

```
<%@ page import="java.io.File,
                 java.io.FileOutputStream,
                 java.sql.Connection,
                 java.sql.PreparedStatement,
                 java.sql.ResultSet,
                 java.net.URL,
                 java.util.Iterator,
                 java.util.List,
                 javax.naming.Context,
                 javax.naming.InitialContext,
                 javax.sql.DataSource,
                 org.jdom.Document,
                 org.jdom.Element,
                 org.jdom.input.SAXBuilder,
                 org.jdom.output.XMLOutputter" %>

<%  Connection conn = null;

    // set the content type of the page to XML:
    response.setContentType("text/xml");

    try {

      // cache interval set to 1 hour ( in milliseconds ):
      long CACHE_INTERVAL = 60 * 60 * 1000;
      boolean cacheIsExpired = true;

      // the cache is expired if
      // a) the cache file does not exists, or
```

```
        // b) CACHE_INTERVAL has passed since last cache
        File cacheFile = new File( application.getRealPath("/xml_cache.xml") );
        cacheIsExpired = !cacheFile.exists() ||
              (System.currentTimeMillis() - cacheFile.lastModified()) >
              CACHE_INTERVAL;

        if ( !cacheIsExpired ) {
          // forward the request to the static file:
          application.getRequestDispatcher("/xml_cache.xml").forward(request,
                                                                     response );
          //response.sendRedirect("xml_cache.xml");
        } else {
          // build the XML document and then cache it

          // define the XML Document and the root element:
          Document doc = new Document();
          Element root = new Element("articles");

...
          // rest of else clause as before, until:

          // set the root element:
          doc.setRootElement( root );

          // output the XML to the cache file:
          FileOutputStream fos = new FileOutputStream(cacheFile);

          XMLOutputter outputter = new XMLOutputter();
          outputter.setEncoding("ISO-8859-1");
          outputter.output( doc, fos );

          fos.flush();
          fos.close();

          // and finally output the XML to the page:
          outputter.output( doc, out );
        }
      } catch ( Exception e ) {
              out.println("<error>" + e.getMessage() + "</error>");
      } finally {
        // close the connection
        if ( conn != null ) {
          conn.close();
        }
      }
%>
```

The Flash Animation

Now that the data has been prepared, we can start creating the Flash Animation. For this section you'll need to have Macromedia Flash installed. This product is not free, but a fully functional evaluation copy can be downloaded from *http://macromedia.com*.

> Note: This section assumes some knowledge of Flash. It focuses on the XML aspects of Flash – an alternative HTML version is discussed later.

We need to create the Flash project that will house the ticker, load the XML document, animate the content, and finally embed it in an HTML page. Let's now go through these steps.

Preparing the File

We create a new Flash file with the name `news_ticker.fla`.

> Note: The `news_ticker.fla` file is in the download package for this chapter. I used Flash MX when writing the chapter, and the movie file was exported for Flash version 5.

The news ticker will show the headlines, printing one character at a time. The ticker contains two lines, one for the current headline, and another for the previous headline. It loops through the headlines.

In the file we create three layers: `Scripts`, `Buttons`, and `Text-fields`. We set the height of the movie to 60 pixels (this can be done in the *Movie properties* window, which you get by pressing *CTRL-M*).

The Text-fields Layer

Prepare this layer as described below:

- Insert a regular frame at frame 25.
- Create a text field at the top of the movie, 520 px wide and 23 px high. It should be set to dynamic text, single line. Set the font to Arial, and the size to 12 points. Set the *Var:* value of this text field to `line0`.
- Create an identical text field below, and set its *Var:* value to `line1`.

The Buttons Layer

Prepare this layer as described below:

- Insert a regular frame at frame 25.

- Create a symbol of type button. The button should have the same dimensions as the text fields created in the `Text-fields` layer. Add this button twice to the `Buttons` layer, so that the two buttons exactly overlap the two text fields. Set the alpha effect to 0% on both buttons. These buttons will take the user to the full story.

- Add the following action to the upper button:

```
on (press) {
    if (currentHeadline == 0) {
        getURL (urls[0], "_self");
    } else {
        getURL (urls[currentHeadline-1], "_self");
    }
}
```

- Add the following action to the lower button:

```
on( press ) {
    if ( currentHeadline > 0 ) {
        getURL( urls[currentHeadline], "_self" );
    }
}
```

These variables will be defined in the `Scripts` layer below.

The Scripts Layer

Prepare this layer as described below:

- Insert blank keyframes at frames 1, 2, and 3

- Insert a blank keyframe at frame 25

First we'll be declaring some global variables that we'll use in functions created later on. The role of each variable is explained with a comment above the variable declaration. Add the following action to frame 1 of the `Scripts` layer (right-click the frame and select *'Actions'*):

```
// Maximum Number of Chars in one Line
var maxChars = 100;

// the current headline being displayed by the ticker
var currentHeadline = 0;

// number of headlines loaded from the XML file
var numberOfHeadlines = 0;

// maximum number of headlines
var maxNumberOfHeadlines = 10;
```

```
// Number of Lines
var numberOfLines = 2;

// the current line
var currentLine = 0;

// text that is displayed if no articles are found:
var noArticleText = "No articles found...";

// Initialize lines-array
var lines = new Array( numberOfLines );
for ( var i = 0; i < numberOfLines; i++ ) {
  lines[i] = "";
}
```

By now the Flash Timeline should look something like this:

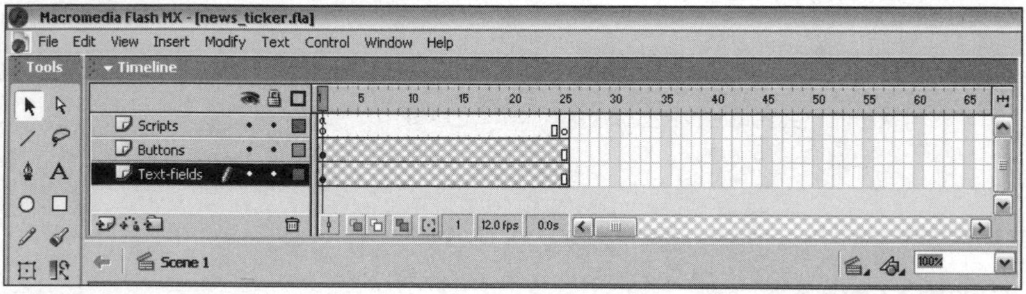

Loading the XML

To load the XML, we add the following action to frame 1 of the `Scripts` layer (below the actions previously added):

```
// Load the XML
var xmlURL = "news.jsp";
var doc = new XML();
doc.ignoreWhite = true;
doc.onLoad = processXMLData;
doc.load( xmlURL );
```

The `xmlURL` variable holds the URL to the JSP file, which produces the XML document that contains the articles to be read. We then create the variable `doc` as an `XML` object. We tell Flash to ignore all white space by setting `doc.ignoreWhite = true` (the default is `false`, meaning that if the Flash player finds any white space in the XML, it turns it into empty nodes, giving you a real problem – including a broken XML tree). We specify that when the document is loaded, the function `processXMLData()` should be called, and then we load the XML document from the URL. This causes the `processXMLData()` function to be called. That function is opposite (we add this function to the actions of frame 1):

```
// function that processes the data from the XML document
function processXMLData( success ) {

  if ( success ) {
    var root = this.firstChild;

    var articles = root.childNodes;
    var article;
    var str;

    var arraySize = Math.min( maxNumberOfHeadlines, articles.length );
    headlines = new Array( arraySize );
    urls = new Array( arraySize );

    // loop through the headlines
    for ( var i = 0; i < headlines.length; i++ ) {

      article = articles[i];
      headline = article.childNodes[0];
      if ( headline != null ) {
        str = headline.firstChild.nodeValue;
        if ( str.indexOf(" ",maxChars) == -1 ) {
        index = str.length;
        } else {
       index = str.indexOf(" ",maxChars);
        }
        // the headline length must not exceed maxChars
        if ( str.length > index ) {
          headlines[i] = str.substring(0,index) + "...";
        } else {
          headlines[i] = str + " ";
        }
        urls[i] = article.childNodes[2].firstChild.nodeValue;
      }
    }
    numberOfHeadlines = headlines.length;

  } else {
    // print the error message, indicating that no articles were found
    set ("line0.text",noArticleText);
  }
}
```

Flash calls this function after it has loaded the XML document, supplying the `success` argument. If the XML document is received successfully, the `success` argument is `true`. If the document was not received, or if an error occurred in receiving the response from the server, the `success` argument is `false` (in which case we print the message defined in the `noArticleText` global variable).

The newly loaded XML document can be referenced from within the `onLoad` function through the `this` variable.

We then loop through the <article> elements, and put all the headlines into the headlines array, and all the links into the urls array. We trim the headline if it is too long, according to the maxChars variable, which we defined globally. In the above code we are not using the category, but if we wanted to include the category name before the headline ("category: headline"), we could add the following line:

```
...
  }
  urls[i] = article.childNodes[2].firstChild.nodeValue;
  headlines[i] = article.childNodes[1].firstChild.nodeValue + ": " + headlines[i];
}
...
```

We're not using any attributes in our animation, but if we had an id attribute on the <article> element, we could retrieve it in the Flash ActionScript in the following way:

```
var id = article.attributes.id;
```

Creating the Animation

We've parsed the XML document, and now all we have to do is loop through the headlines, printing them out one character at a time. For this we add the following functions to the actions of frame 1 in the Scripts layer (below the actions previously added):

```
// function to copy the lines to the text fields:
function copyTextField( num ) {
  set( "line" + num +".text", lines[num] );
}

// function that prints the next chararcter in the headline
function printNextChar() {

  var wordChar = "";
  var sentence = "";
  var wordCharLen = 0;

  if ( currentHeadline < numberOfHeadlines ) {

    sentence = headlines[currentHeadline];

    // how long is the next sentence?
    while ( (charCount+wordCharLen) < sentence.length && wordChar != " " ) {

      wordCharLen++;
      wordChar = sentence.charAt( charCount+wordCharLen );
      if ( (charCount+wordCharLen) == sentence.length ) {
        gotoAndPlay( 10 );
      }
    }

    if ( (lines[currentLine].length+wordCharLen) < maxChars ) {
```

```
        // add next char
        lines[currentLine] += sentence.charAt(charCount);
        // copy text
        copyTextField( currentLine );
        // add to char counter
        charCount++;
      } else {
        // increase index count
        if ( currentLine + 1 < numberOfLines ) {
          currentLine++;
        } else {
          // copy lines
          for ( var i = 0; i < numberOfLines; i++ ) {
            lines[i] = lines[i+1].valueOf();
            copyTextField(i);
          }
          charCount++;
        }
      }

    } else {
      // start over
      charCount = 0;
      currentHeadline = 0;
    }
  }
```

The `copyTextField(num)` function simply copies the text at index `num` in the `lines` array to the text field in the `Text-fields` layer, using the set function. The `printNextChar()` function prints the headline char by char. When all the characters of the headline have been printed, we jump to frame 10:

```
if ( (charCount+wordCharLen) == sentence.length ) {
  gotoAndPlay( 10 );
}
```

As we will see in the next section, jumping to frame 10 just means that we break out of the printing loop and move on to print the next headline (the number 10 was arbitrarily chosen; you could also set this to 15 if you wanted a shorter pause between lines, or 5 if you wanted a longer one).

The variable `currentHeadline` holds the index of the headline currently being printed. And if we've reached the last headline, we set `currentHeadline = 0`, and start over.

Putting It All Together

We've now added all the actions for frame 1. We just need to add short actions to the other three keyframes in the Scripts layer (frames 2, 3, and 25) and then we're done. The actions in these frames will control the flow, which will be the following:

- Frame 1: Load the XML and initialize variables
- Frame 2: Print the next character of the current headline

- Frame 3: Go to frame 2
- Frame 25: Shift the current headline down, and start printing the next by going to frame 2

In frame 2 of the Scripts layer, we add the following action:

```
printNextChar();
```

And in frame 3 of the Scripts layer we add the following action:

```
gotoAndPlay( 2 );
```

We see that frames 2 and 3 loop until the whole headline has been printed. Then (as we saw earlier) we jump to frame 10, which eventually takes us to frame 25 which shifts the headline down, and then we are sent back to frame 2 to print the next headline. The actions in frame 25 are as follows:

```
// Are there any lines left?
if ( currentLine + 1 < numberOfLines ) {
  currentLine++;
} else {
  // shift rows
  for ( var i = 0; i < numberOfLines; i++ ) {
    lines[i] = lines[i+1].valueOf();
    copyTextField(i);
  }
}

// Increase index count
currentHeadline++;
charCount = 0;

gotoAndPlay (2);
```

The Flash timeline should now look something like this:

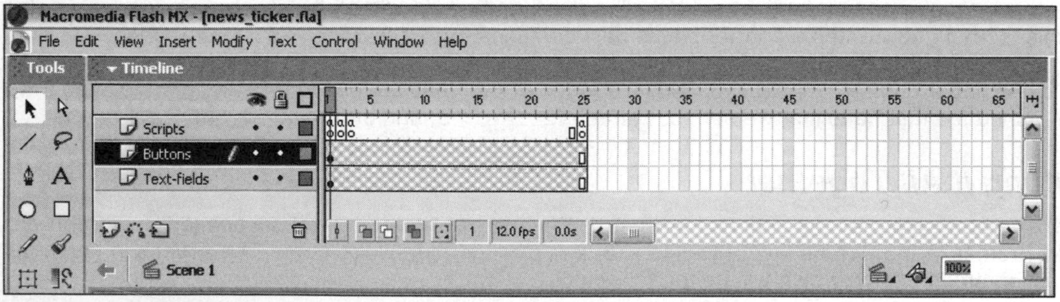

We've now finished the Flash movie, and can therefore export it to `news_ticker.swf`.

Embedding the File

The final stage of the process is to embed the movie file in an HTML page. Macromedia Flash automatically generates the embed code for us if we choose *'Publish'* from the *'File'* menu. The following code is a result of such generation:

```
<OBJECT classid="clsid:D27CDB6E-AE6D-11cf-96B8-444553540000"
codebase="http://download.macromedia.com/pub/shockwave/cabs/flash/swflash.cab#versi
on=5,0,0,0"
 WIDTH=550 HEIGHT=60>
 <PARAM NAME=movie VALUE="http://localhost:8080/news/news_ticker.swf">
 <PARAM NAME=quality VALUE=high>
 <PARAM NAME=bgcolor VALUE=#FFFFFF>
 <EMBED src="http://localhost:8080/news/news_ticker.swf"
  quality=high bgcolor=#FFFFFF
   WIDTH=550 HEIGHT=60
   TYPE="application/x-shockwave-flash"

PLUGINSPAGE="http://www.macromedia.com/shockwave/download/index.cgi?P1_Prod_Version
=ShockwaveFlash">
 </EMBED>
</OBJECT>
```

This code can then be inserted into any HTML page. For example, as in the following page (`news_ticker.html`). (Note the wrap in the `PLUGINSPAGE` attribute for ease of reading within the book.)

```
<HTML>
<HEAD>
<TITLE>news_ticker</TITLE>
</HEAD>
<BODY bgcolor="#FFFFFF">
<OBJECT classid="clsid:D27CDB6E-AE6D-11cf-96B8-444553540000"
codebase="http://download.macromedia.com/pub/shockwave/cabs/flash/swflash.cab#versi
on=5,0,0,0"
 WIDTH=550 HEIGHT=60>
 <PARAM NAME=movie VALUE="http://localhost:8080/news/news_ticker.swf">
 <PARAM NAME=quality VALUE=high>
 <PARAM NAME=bgcolor VALUE=#FFFFFF>
 <EMBED src="http://localhost:8080/news/news_ticker.swf"
  quality=high bgcolor=#FFFFFF
   WIDTH=550 HEIGHT=60
   TYPE="application/x-shockwave-flash"
   PLUGINSPAGE="http://www.macromedia.com/shockwave/download/index.cgi?
     P1_Prod_Version=ShockwaveFlash">
 </EMBED>
</OBJECT>
</BODY>
</HTML>
```

Viewing this page in a browser (using IE below) would result in something like this:

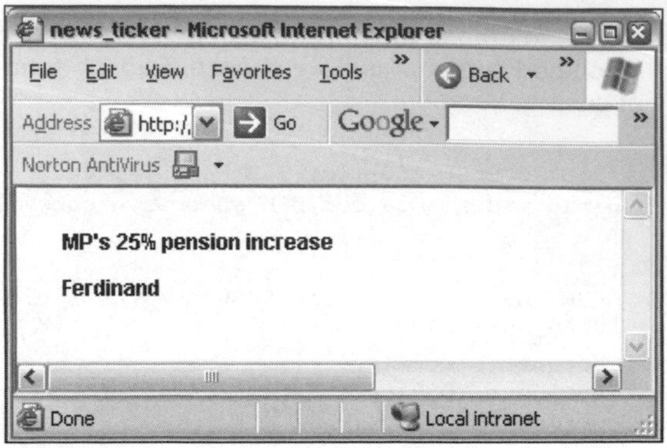

Plan B: Flash Not Supported

Believe it or not, there are still users out there who do not have the Flash player installed. And there are also those users who have Flash, but an old version. As much as we'd like to ignore that minority, we simply can't. We must check if the browser supports our Flash movie. If it does, then we display the Flash movie. If it doesn't we just display a link to a page that displays the news headlines. (We could also create a scrolling effect with JavaScript, but for simplicity's sake this is left up to the reader.)

The following client-side script checks whether Flash is installed (this script was taken from *http://www.xs4all.nl/~ppk/js/flash.html*: go there for more information). It performs the Flash detection, and stores the result in a variable called `flashinstalled`.

```
<script language="Javascript">
<!--

var flashinstalled = 0;
var flashversion = 0;
MSDetect = "false";
if (navigator.plugins && navigator.plugins.length)
{
  x = navigator.plugins["Shockwave Flash"];
  if (x)
  {
    flashinstalled = 2;
    if (x.description)
    {
      y = x.description;
      flashversion = y.charAt(y.indexOf('.')-1);
    }
  }
  else
    flashinstalled = 1;
  if (navigator.plugins["Shockwave Flash 2.0"])
```

```
    {
      flashinstalled = 2;
      flashversion = 2;
    }
  }
  else if (navigator.mimeTypes && navigator.mimeTypes.length)
  {
    x = navigator.mimeTypes['application/x-shockwave-flash'];
    if (x && x.enabledPlugin)
      flashinstalled = 2;
    else
      flashinstalled = 1;
  }
  else
    MSDetect = "true";

  // -->
  </script>

  <script language="VBScript">

  on error resume next

  If MSDetect = "true" Then
    For i = 2 to 6
      If Not(IsObject(CreateObject("ShockwaveFlash.ShockwaveFlash." & i))) Then

      Else
        flashinstalled = 2
        flashversion = i
      End If
    Next
  End If

  If flashinstalled = 0 Then
    flashinstalled = 1
  End If

  </script>
```

After the detection, the variable `flashinstalled` can have three values:

- `2`: Flash installed
- `1`: Flash not installed
- `0`: Unknown if Flash is installed

We can now modify the embed code to check whether Flash is installed (remember that the detect script above must also appear in the page). The page now looks like this (`news_ticker.html`):

```
<HTML>
<HEAD>
<TITLE>news_ticker</TITLE>
</HEAD>
<BODY bgcolor="#FFFFFF">
<SCRIPT language="JavaScript">
<!--
if ( flashinstalled == 2 )
{
  document.write('<OBJECT classid="clsid:D27CDB6E-AE6D-11cf-96B8-444553540000" '
   + 'codebase="http://download.macromedia.com/pub/shockwave/cabs/flash/'
   + 'swflash.cab#version=5,0,0,0" '
   + 'WIDTH=550 HEIGHT=60>'
   + '<PARAM NAME=movie VALUE="http://localhost:8080/news/news_ticker.swf">'
   + '<PARAM NAME=quality VALUE=high>'
   + '<PARAM NAME=bgcolor VALUE=#FFFFFF>'
   + '<EMBED src="http://localhost:8080/news/news_ticker.swf" '
   + 'quality=high bgcolor=#FFFFFF '
   + 'WIDTH=550 HEIGHT=60 '
   + 'TYPE="application/x-shockwave-flash" '
   + 'PLUGINSPAGE="http://www.macromedia.com/shockwave/download/'
   + 'index.cgi?P1_Prod_Version=ShockwaveFlash">'
   + '</EMBED>'
   + '</OBJECT>');
}
else
{
  // print a link to the news overview:
  document.write('<a href="http://localhost:8080/news/overview.jsp">'
   + 'Check out the latest news!</a>');
}
-->
</SCRIPT>
<NOSCRIPT>
  Your need Flash to view the news ticker.
  <a href="http://localhost:8080/news/overview.jsp">Click here</a>
  to view the non-Flash version.
</NOSCRIPT>
</BODY>
</HTML>
```

This code checks whether the Flash player is installed and, depending on the outcome, either displays the Flash news ticker, or a link to a news overview. Note that we also display a link to the news overview for those users with JavaScript disabled in their browsers (this is done with the `<NOSCRIPT>` tag). Since this overview does not exist, we'll have to create it. We'll create an XSLT stylesheet that transforms the news XML document to HTML, and then we'll create a JSP that displays the output of the transformation.

The XSLT Stylesheet

We begin by creating an XSLT stylesheet that transforms our news XML document to HTML. This is a very straightforward stylesheet which we create in the `$NEWS_HOME` directory and name `news_to_html.xsl`:

```
<?xml version="1.0" encoding="iso-8859-1"?>
<xsl:stylesheet xmlns:xsl="http://www.w3.org/1999/XSL/Transform" version="1.0">

  <xsl:output method="html" encoding="iso-8859-1"/>

  <xsl:template match="/articles">
    <html>
      <head>
      <title>News overview</title>
      <style>
        .headlines {
          color: #000000;
          font-size: 12px ;
          font-family: Arial, Helvetica, sans-serif;
          font-weight: bold;
        }
        a.headlines {
          color: #AAAAAA;
          font-size: 12px ;
          font-family: Arial, Helvetica, sans-serif;
          font-weight: bold;
        }
        a.headlines:hover {
          color: #000000;
          text-decoration: underline;
        }
      </style>
      </head>
      <body>
        <table cellpadding="2" cellspacing="0">
        <xsl:apply-templates select="article" />
        </table>
      </body>
    </html>
  </xsl:template>

  <xsl:template match="article">
    <tr>
      <td>
        <div class="headlines">
        <xsl:value-of select="category" />:
        </div>
      </td>
      <td>
      <div class="headlines">
        <a class="headlines">
          <xsl:attribute name="href">
            <xsl:value-of select="link" />
          </xsl:attribute>
          <xsl:value-of select="headline" /></a>
      </div>
      </td>
    </tr>
  </xsl:template>

</xsl:stylesheet>
```

We simply create a table that contains the headlines, and each headline is a link to the full story (using the value of the `<link>` element).

The Transformation

We need to create a JSP that transforms the XML document from `news.jsp` using the `news_to_html.xsl` stylesheet. We create this file in the `$NEWS_HOME` directory and name it `overview.jsp`:

```
<%@ page import="java.net.URL,
                 java.io.File,
                 javax.xml.transform.Transformer,
                 javax.xml.transform.TransformerFactory,
                 javax.xml.transform.stream.StreamSource,
                 org.jdom.Document,
                 org.jdom.input.SAXBuilder,
                 org.jdom.output.XMLOutputter,
                 org.jdom.transform.JDOMResult,
                 org.jdom.transform.JDOMSource" %>
<%
    // set the content type of the page to HTML:
    response.setContentType("text/html");

    try {

      // parse the XML:
      SAXBuilder sb = new SAXBuilder();
      URL url = new URL("http://localhost:8080/news/news.jsp");
      Document doc = sb.build( url );

      // transform:
      TransformerFactory tFactory = TransformerFactory.newInstance();
      StreamSource xsl = new StreamSource(
                          new File(application.getRealPath("/news_to_html.xsl")) );
      Transformer transformer = tFactory.newTransformer(xsl);

      JDOMResult output = new JDOMResult();
      transformer.transform(new JDOMSource(doc), output);

      // output the XML
      XMLOutputter outputter = new XMLOutputter();
      outputter.setEncoding("ISO-8859-1");
      outputter.output( output.getDocument(), out );

    } catch ( Exception e ) {
      out.println("Error occurred: " + e.getMessage());
    }
%>
```

Firstly we parse the `news.jsp` document and load it into a `Document` object, using the `SAXBuilder`. Then we create a `Transformer` instance using the `news_to_html.xsl` stylesheet. We use this transformer to transform the document using the XSLT stylesheet. The result of the transformation is stored in the `JDOMResult` object. Finally we output the result using the `XMLOutputter`, which we have seen before.

The Full Story

The last thing we have to do to meet the requirements is to create the page that displays the full story. Note that this page will only display the articles from the newspaper's local database, since the `<link>` element for the XML articles points to the *www.xml.com* web site.

We'll need three files: one to create an XML document containing the news article (`story.jsp`), one for the XSLT stylesheet that transforms the XML to HTML (`story_to_html.xsl`), and the third for transforming the XML using the stylesheet and outputting the result (`full_story.jsp`). We create these files in the `$NEWS_HOME` directory.

> Note: We might have gone for the easier solution and just created one page that retrieves the data and formats it directly to HTML. Instead, we've gone for the solution that provides a clear separation of content and presentation, making it easier to maintain and extend.

Let's start with the XML.

XML Interface To a Story

The XML format for the story should reflect the database structure. Following is an example XML instance document:

```
<article id="2">
  <headline>A headline</headline>
  <body-text>Some text</body-text>
  <author>Johnny Bop</author>
  <category>General</category>
  <creation-date>18.07.2002 13:00</creation-date>
</article>
```

We now create the `story.jsp`. This page is very similar to `news.jsp` which we created earlier, but somewhat simpler since we're just selecting one row from the database. You should therefore be familiar with the code:

```
<%@ page import="java.sql.Connection,
                 java.sql.PreparedStatement,
                 java.sql.ResultSet,
                 java.text.SimpleDateFormat,
                 javax.naming.Context,
```

```
                    javax.naming.InitialContext,
                    javax.sql.DataSource,
                    org.jdom.Document,
                    org.jdom.Element,
                    org.jdom.output.XMLOutputter" %>

<%  Connection conn = null;

    // get the ID from the query string:
    int articleID = 0;
    try {
      articleID = Integer.parseInt( request.getParameter("id") );
    } catch ( NumberFormatException ne ) {}

    // set the content type of the page to XML:
    response.setContentType("text/xml");

    try {

      // define the XML Document and the root element:
      Document doc = new Document();
      Element root = new Element("article");

      // look up the correct DataSource:
      Context initCtx = new InitialContext();
      Context envCtx = (Context) initCtx.lookup("java:comp/env");
      DataSource ds = (DataSource) envCtx.lookup("jdbc/NewsDB");

      // get a connection:
      conn = ds.getConnection();

      // select all the news articles:
      String sql = "SELECT a.*, c.name "
                 + "FROM articles a, categories c "
                 + "WHERE a.category_id = c.id "
                 + "AND a.id = ?";
      PreparedStatement ps = conn.prepareStatement(sql);
      ps.setInt( 1, articleID );
      ResultSet rs = ps.executeQuery();

      if ( rs.next() ) {
        root.setAttribute( "id", rs.getString("id") );
        root.addContent(
           (new Element("headline")).addContent(rs.getString("headline")));
        root.addContent(
           (new Element("body-text")).addContent(rs.getString("body_text")));
        root.addContent(
           (new Element("author")).addContent(rs.getString("author")));
        root.addContent(
           (new Element("category")).addContent(rs.getString("name")));

        // we need to format the creation date:
        SimpleDateFormat formatter = new SimpleDateFormat("dd.MM.yyyy HH:mm");
        String dateString = formatter.format(rs.getTimestamp("creation_date"));
        root.addContent((new Element("creation-date")).addContent(dateString));
      }
```

```
        // close the ResultSet and the statement:
        rs.close();
        ps.close();

        // set the root element:
        doc.setRootElement( root );

        // output the XML
        XMLOutputter outputter = new XMLOutputter();
        outputter.setEncoding("ISO-8859-1");
        outputter.output( doc, out );

      } catch ( Exception e ) {
        out.println("Error occurred: " + e.getMessage());
      } finally {
        // close the connection
        if ( conn != null ) {
            conn.close();
        }
      }
%>
```

Let's go quickly through the things that are new. Since we are displaying details for a single article, we need to have the ID of the article to display. We send the ID in the query string (remember the links, for example *http://localhost:8080/news/full_story.jsp?id=4*). The following code retrieves the ID from the query string:

```
      int articleID = 0;
      try {
        articleID = Integer.parseInt( request.getParameter("id") );
      } catch ( NumberFormatException ne ) {}
```

We've then added the following lines to the SQL statement to constrain the `ResultSet` to only one record (with the ID specified):

```
                    + "AND a.id = ?";
        PreparedStatement ps = conn.prepareStatement(sql);
        ps.setInt( 1, articleID );
```

Then we add elements to the root element, just as we did before. The last thing to mention is that we format the `creation_date` to a specific pattern. This is done in the following way:

```
          SimpleDateFormat formatter = new SimpleDateFormat("dd.MM.yyyy HH:mm");
          String dateString = formatter.format(rs.getTimestamp("creation_date"));
          root.addContent((new Element("creation-date")).addContent(dateString));
```

> Note: I have not included a caching mechanism for this page, but you can easily use the caching mechanism from `news.jsp` in this case also.

Now let's move on to the XSLT stylesheet.

The XSLT Stylesheet

We now need to create the XSLT stylesheet that transforms `story.jsp` to HTML. We name it `story_to_html.xsl`. This stylesheet is very simple and needs no further introduction:

```
<?xml version="1.0" encoding="iso-8859-1"?>
<xsl:stylesheet xmlns:xsl="http://www.w3.org/1999/XSL/Transform" version="1.0">

  <xsl:output method="html" encoding="iso-8859-1"/>

  <xsl:template match="/article">
    <html>
      <head>
      <title>The Full Story</title>
      <style>
        .headlines {
          color: #000000;
          font-size: 14px;
          font-family: Arial, Helvetica, sans-serif;
          font-weight: bold;
        }
        .bodyText {
          color: #000000;
          font-size: 12px;
          font-family: Arial, Helvetica, sans-serif;
        }
        .other {
          color: #000000;
          font-size: 10px;
          font-family: Arial, Helvetica, sans-serif;
          font-weight: bold;
        }
        table {
          width: 500px;
        }
      </style>
      </head>
      <body>
        <table cellpadding="2" cellspacing="0">
          <tr>
            <td>
              <div class="other">
              <xsl:value-of select="category" /> |
              <xsl:value-of select="creation-date" />
              </div>
            </td>
          </tr>

          <tr>
            <td>
```

```
            <div class="headlines">
            <xsl:value-of select="headline" />
            </div>
          </td>
        </tr>

        <tr>
          <td>
            <div class="bodyText">
            <xsl:value-of select="body-text" />
            </div>
          </td>
        </tr>

        <tr>
          <td>
            <div class="other">
            Author: <xsl:value-of select="author" />
            </div>
          </td>
        </tr>

        <tr>
          <td>
            <div class="other">
            <a href="javascript:history.back()">Back</a>
            </div>
          </td>
        </tr>
      </table>
    </body>
  </html>
</xsl:template>

</xsl:stylesheet>
```

The Transformation

And now for the final touch, we create the JSP that reads `story.jsp`, applies the `story_to_html.xsl` stylesheet, and outputs the results. This page is similar to `overview.jsp` that we created earlier, so there should be no big surprises in the following code (`full_story.jsp`):

```
<%@ page import="java.net.URL,
                 java.io.File,
                 javax.xml.transform.Transformer,
                 javax.xml.transform.TransformerFactory,
```

```
                javax.xml.transform.stream.StreamSource,
                org.jdom.Document,
                org.jdom.input.SAXBuilder,
                org.jdom.output.XMLOutputter,
                org.jdom.transform.JDOMResult,
                org.jdom.transform.JDOMSource" %>
<%
    // set the content type of the page to HTML:
    response.setContentType("text/html");

    // get the ID from the query string:
    int articleID = 0;
    try {
      articleID = Integer.parseInt( request.getParameter("id") );
    } catch ( NumberFormatException ne ) {}

    try {

      // parse the XML:
      SAXBuilder sb = new SAXBuilder();
      URL url = new URL("http://localhost:8080/news/story.jsp?id=" + articleID);
      Document doc = sb.build( url );

      // transform:
      TransformerFactory tFactory = TransformerFactory.newInstance();
      StreamSource xsl = new StreamSource(
          new File(application.getRealPath("/story_to_html.xsl")) );
      Transformer transformer = tFactory.newTransformer(xsl);

      JDOMResult output = new JDOMResult();
      transformer.transform(new JDOMSource(doc), output);

      // output the XML
      XMLOutputter outputter = new XMLOutputter();
      outputter.setEncoding("ISO-8859-1");
      outputter.output( output.getDocument(), out );

    } catch ( Exception e ) {
      out.println("Error occurred: " + e.getMessage());
    }
%>
```

We retrieve the article ID from the query string, parse `story.jsp`, transform it to HTML using `story_to_html.xsl`, and finally print the result to the output stream.

Summary

In this chapter, we created a JSP that retrieved data from a database and from an online XML feed, and merged the data into a single XML document. We provided a simple caching mechanism. We then created a Flash movie that read the XML document, and animated the news headlines. We provided a backup plan for those users not equipped with the Flash player. Finally, we created a page for viewing the full story.

One thing to note is that, in the JSP pages in this chapter, I've traded design principles for simplicity. As a rule of thumb we should never have business logic in the JSP pages. All business logic should be embedded in classes, or servlets. It would therefore be a good idea to move all the logic to classes, which would then be made available to the application by putting them into the `$NEWS_HOME/WEB-INF/classes` directory.

The Flash ticker can of course be used to display other information than news headlines. It could for example be used to display special offers, upcoming events, etc. You can extend this as you like.

Further Reading

Following is a list of technologies discussed in this chapter, with links to more information.

- **Macromedia Flash:** Macromedia Flash is a multimedia graphics program especially for use on the Web. Flash enables you to create interactive "movies" on the Web. Flash uses vector graphics, which means that the graphics can be scaled to any size without losing clarity/quality. Flash does not require programming skills (unless you wish to use ActionScript) and is easy to learn. See *http://www.macromedia.com/software/flash/* for more information.

- **JDBC:** JDBC Data Access API lets you access virtually any tabular data source from the Java programming language. It provides cross-DBMS connectivity to a wide range of SQL databases, and now, with the new JDBC API (version 3.0), it also provides access to other tabular data sources, such as spreadsheets or flat files. See *http://java.sun.com/products/jdbc/* for more information.

- **JDOM:** JDOM is, quite simply, a Java representation of an XML document. JDOM provides a way to represent that document for easy and efficient reading, manipulation, and writing. It has a straightforward API, is lightweight and fast, and is optimized for the Java programmer. It's an alternative to DOM and SAX, although it integrates well with both DOM and SAX. While JDOM interoperates well with existing standards such as the Simple API for XML (SAX) and the Document Object Model (DOM), it is not an abstraction layer or enhancement to those APIs. Rather, it seeks to provide a robust, lightweight means of reading and writing XML data without the complex and memory-consumptive options that current API offerings provide. See *http://www.jdom.org* for more information.

- **MySQL:** MySQL is a popular open source Database Management System (DBMS) that is known for its blistering performance. It runs on numerous operating systems, including most Linux variants. And best of all: it's free. See *http://www.mysql.com* for more information.

- **J2EE:** Java 2 Platform, Enterprise Edition. See *http://java.sun.com/j2ee/* for more information.

- **RSS:** Rich Site Summary (RSS) is a lightweight XML format designed for sharing headlines and other web content. RSS defines an XML grammar (a set of HTML-like tags) for sharing news. Each RSS text file contains static information about your site, plus dynamic information about your news stories, all surrounded by matching start and end tags. See *http://my.netscape.com/publish/formats/rss-spec-0.91.html* for more information.

- **Tomcat:** Tomcat is the servlet container that is used in the official Reference Implementation for the Java Servlet and JavaServer Pages technologies. It can run as a standalone web server, or integrate into Apache. Tomcat is developed in an open and participatory environment and released under the Apache Software License. Tomcat is intended to be a collaboration of the best-of-breed developers from around the world. See *http://jakarta.apache.org/tomcat* for more information.

11

- Advanced XML PHP case study (weather information portal)
- Generating XML from a MySQL database using PHP
- Transforming and styling the XML using CSS/XSLT on the server

Author: Allan Kent

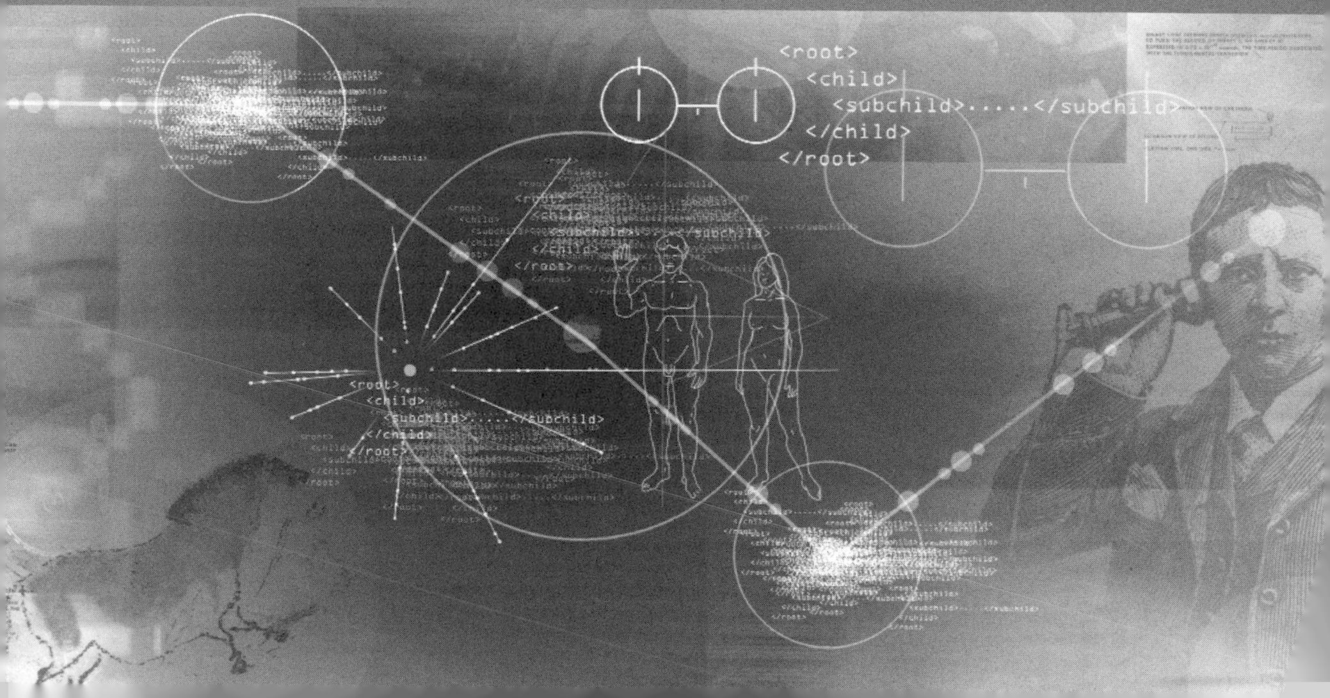

Case Study: Displaying XML from a MySQL Database Using PHP & XSLT

Last but by no means least, it's time to take a detailed look at using XML with PHP, in a real-world environment. We've seen how PHP can interact with XML and XSL documents in *Chapter 8* – in this chapter we will take it further, looking at how we can grab dynamic content from a database, turn the results into an XML document, and then use XSLT to provide XHTML content to the browser.

Sample Application – Community Weather Portal

In order to demonstrate these techniques we build up a fully operational sample web application – maintaining a database of the current weather conditions in every city around the world is not a task to be taken lightly, so we will draw on the power of the Internet community and develop a **Community Weather Portal**. This application will provide a hierarchical navigation to allow the user to navigate down to their city and, when the city of choice is found, the application will display the current weather conditions for that city. If a user navigates to a section of the web site where their country, area or city is not present, a form in the page will allow the user to add it. If the user is at city level, the form will allow them to enter the current weather conditions in their city.

General Requirements

In order to write our application we will need to have certain tools and services installed and available to us. Since we will be working with XML and XSLT we will need to have a PHP installation with XSLT support. Our data will be stored in a MySQL database.

XSLT

In older versions of PHP, XSLT support was achieved using the sablot extension that used Sablotron. As of version 4.1, the sablot extension has been renamed to XSLT, and although at the moment it uses Sablotron and Expat, in future it will also support alternative libraries such as Xalan and libxsl. Both Sablotron and Expat can be downloaded from *http://www.gingerall.com.*

The XSLT extension is not compiled into PHP by default, so you will need to either enable it, or compile it into PHP. For details on how to install PHP with XSLT support, refer back to the PHP sections of *Chapter 8*, and the `InstallPHP.txt` file that accompanies the code download for *Chapter 8*.

MySQL

Before we start looking at the scripts we will be using to build the application, let's take a look at the database structure that we will use. Because the number of possibile cities we could have in our database is quite large, I have decided to store the information in a database rather than in an XML file, because large XML files can become rather cumbersome to understand and process. We can be saved the hassle of having to work with the whole dataset all the time by using PHP to extract the XML we need from the database each time a call is made.

You are certainly not restricted to using MySQL as the database here, but since it is stable, cross-platform, enjoys great community support, and is free, it is a good choice. The table structure that we are creating is fairly simple and any database should be able to support it.

Our tables are joined in a hierarchical fashion, each containing the data for one level of the site's geographical hierarchy – the navigation for our main page will go down this hierarchy, being viewed in the following order (from biggest to smallest):

- Select Continent
- Select Country
- Select Area (these "areas" could be states, counties, or whatever, depending on where in the world you live)
- Select City

When you travel down the hierarchy, the places you came from will be added as links to the navigation bar of our main page. This is sometimes called a **breadcrumb** trail – a trail of links that you can follow to easily get back up the hierarchy, to whence you came. Now that you have a better idea how the site navigation will work in relation to the database, let's take a look at what the actual database structure will look like:

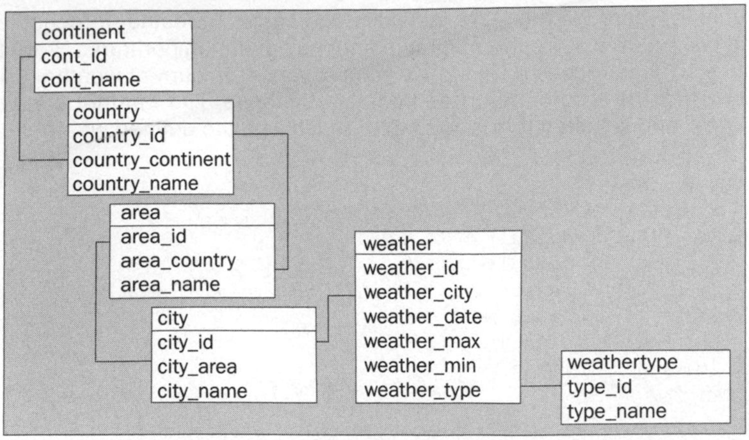

Let's go through the SQL script needed to create our database – you can find the full version in the code download, as `Weather.sql`. The `continent`, `country`, `area`, and `city` tables (below) are fairly self-explanatory – they contain the `id` and `name` of each geographical area. In addition, they also include a row detailing which area from the above hierarchy level these are contained in (for example, which continent each country is contained in) – it is through these rows that we will link each table back to its "parent", and build our hierarchy.

The name of the database that we are creating is `weather` – once you have created it, you can go ahead and create the tables that follow (see the `InstallMySQL.txt` file in the download for more details).

```
CREATE TABLE continent (
  cont_id int(11) NOT NULL auto_increment,
  cont_name varchar(20) default NULL,
  PRIMARY KEY (cont_id)
) TYPE=MyISAM;

CREATE TABLE country (
  country_id int(11) NOT NULL auto_increment,
  country_continent int(11) default NULL,
  country_name varchar(100) default NULL,
  PRIMARY KEY (country_id)
) TYPE=MyISAM;

CREATE TABLE area (
  area_id int(11) NOT NULL auto_increment,
  area_country int(11) default NULL,
  area_name varchar(100) default NULL,
  PRIMARY KEY (area_id)
) TYPE=MyISAM;

CREATE TABLE city (
  city_id int(11) NOT NULL auto_increment,
  city_area int(11) default NULL,
  city_name varchar(100) default NULL,
  PRIMARY KEY (city_id)
) TYPE=MyISAM;
```

The `weather` table is where we will store individual forecasts. A weather forecast is linked to a specific city, and will need to store the minimum and maximum temperatures, a weather condition, and the date that the entry was received. Since we want to report on current weather conditions, we will use this date to restrict the records returned from the database. The weather condition is stored in the `weather_type` field and is linked to a `type` table, which lists the defined weather conditions:

```
CREATE TABLE weather (
  weather_id int(11) NOT NULL auto_increment,
  weather_city int(11) default NULL,
  weather_date int(11) default NULL,
  weather_max int(4) default NULL,
  weather_min int(4) default NULL,
  weather_type int(11) default NULL,
PRIMARY KEY (weather_id)
) TYPE=MyISAM;
```

The `type` table lists the defined weather condition types that people can choose from in reporting on the weather:

```
CREATE TABLE weathertype (
  type_id int(11) NOT NULL auto_increment,
  type_name varchar(40) default NULL,
  PRIMARY KEY (type_id)
) TYPE=MyISAM;
```

Finally, we insert some weather conditions into our database to get started:

```
INSERT INTO weathertype VALUES (1,'sunny');
INSERT INTO weathertype VALUES (2,'windy');
INSERT INTO weathertype VALUES (3,'cloudy');
INSERT INTO weathertype VALUES (4,'rain');
INSERT INTO weathertype VALUES (6,'rainstorms');
INSERT INTO weathertype VALUES (7,'snow');
INSERT INTO weathertype VALUES (8,'snowstorms');
```

Components of the Weather Portal Application

Before we jump in and start looking at the code for the individual files, let's quickly look at how they interact, and summarize what each one does.

The main page (`index.php`) is made up of `sidebar.php` and `standard.php`; `standard.php` itself is also constructed from several components:

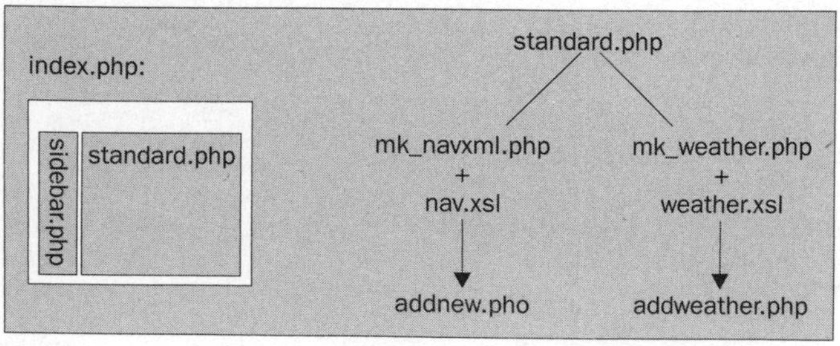

Second, here is a summary of the purpose of each file/path involved in the application:

`weather.php`	This file contains the database username and password, as well as the code for connecting to our database.
`index.php`	This is the home page of our application. All content will be built into this page.
`standard.css`	The stylesheet to provide our application's look and feel.
`sidebar.php`	Here we will build the sidebar for our application, providing a "breadcrumb trail" back to the home page.
`standard.php`	This script contains the logic for determining what content to display – navigation or content.
`mk_navxml.php`	This script queries the database and returns an XML document of the next level of navigation.
`nav.xsl`	The XSL file to transform our navigation XML into XHTML.
`addnew.php`	The script called by our form to add a new record into the database.
`mk_weather.php`	This script queries the database and returns the current weather conditions as saved in the database. The results are returned as an XML document.
`weather.xsl`	The XSL file to transform the weather conditions into XHTML for display on our page.
`Addweather.php`	The script called by the form to add a new weather record into the database.
`/images/`	A folder containing images for each of the defined weather conditions from the `type` table, as well as an image to use as a heading for our page.

Program Listing

Now we have seen what the overall application architecture looks like, and where its constituent components fit in, let's look at each component file in more detail.

weather.php

As we mentioned above, the `weather.php` script will simply contain some settings for our application. Along with the settings for our database connection, here we include the code to select and connect to our database. Wherever we need a database connection in our scripts we can include this file: this way we only have to store our connection details (database name, usernames, and passwords) once, and if we ever change these, they conveniently only need changing in a single location:

```
<?php
  $wdb_host = '';
  $wdb_user = 'user_weather';
  $wdb_pass = 'weatherpassword';
  $wdb_name = 'weather';
  mysql_connect($wdb_host, $wdb_user, $wdb_pass);
  mysql_select_db($wdb_name);
?>
```

index.php

The `index.php` script is the script that we will use to build all of our content into (the content will be dependent on the arguments passed to the script via the URL string in the address bar).

Since we have 4 possible areas of navigation (Continent, Country, Area, and City) we will use these as the arguments to the script wherever relevant (hence the four different variables seen below). The first thing we have to do then is determine which one has been passed, and grab that value from the superglobal `$_GET` array.

Here we need to remember that, as of PHP version 4.2.0, variables passed via the URL no longer have global scope. For example, in older versions of PHP you could provide a link or URL:

http://www.mywebsite.com/myscript.php?theoption=15

Inside the script `myscript.php` you would then have a variable `$theoption` with a value of 15. Similarly with forms, the values of all forms `<input>` elements would be available within the script as variables of the name of the `<input>` element, so:

```
<input type='text' name='criteria'>
```

would be available in the script called by the form as `$criteria`. This was bad, as this behavior allowed people to inject variables into your PHP code via the URL string. Now that variables are not global by default, you will have to access them via `$_GET` or `$_POST`, depending on whether your variables have been posted via `HTTP get` or `post`.

Therefore, variables passed via the query string can no longer taint variables that you have defined in your script. For example, we would now access those variables seen in the examples above as `$_GET['theoption']` in the case of the URL query string, and `$_POST['criteria']` in the case of the form.

Although you can override this in the `php.ini` file, we do not wish to promote such bad practices.

Before we look at the actual code for the page, let's take a look at what the page will look like when we are done, to aid understanding of the code itself:

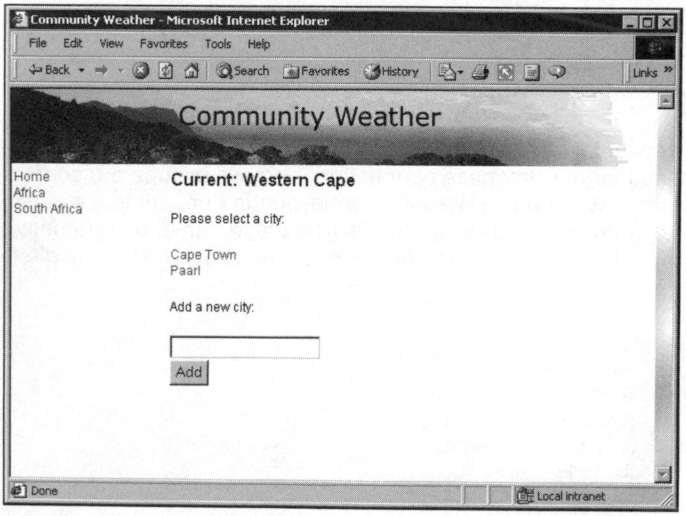

Now onto the code – the first section offers a choice of one of four possible variables, determined by what navigation level we are currently at – `$continent`, `$country`, `$area`, or `$city`. The variable chosen will later be used to determine what data to pull out and display from the database.

```
<?php
  if (isset($_GET['continent'])) {
    $continent = $_GET['continent'];
  }
  if (isset($_GET['country'])) {
    $country = $_GET['country'];
  }
  if (isset($_GET['area'])) {
    $area = $_GET['area'];
  }
  if (isset($_GET['city'])) {
    $city = $_GET['city'];
  }
?>
```

> At this point it is worth noting that if you are using PHP to output files with an XML header, and you have the `short_open_tag` directive turned on in your `php.ini`, you are likely to run into problems (this directive allows you to also use `<?` as the opening tag for a PHP code block). With this directive turned on,
>
> ```
> <?xml version="1.0" encoding="iso-8859-1"?>
> ```
>
> will be interpreted as PHP code, because it uses the same delimiters, and will return an error.

`index.php` continues:

```
<!DOCTYPE html PUBLIC "-//W3C//DTD XHTML 1.0 Strict//EN"
 "http://www.w3.org/TR/xhtml1/DTD/xhtml1-strict.dtd">
<html xmlns="http://www.w3.org/1999/xhtml">
  <head>
    <title>Community Weather</title>
    <meta http-equiv="Content-Type" content="text/html; charset=iso-8859-1" />
    <link href="standard.css" rel="stylesheet" type="text/css" />
  </head>
  <body>
    <div id="layHeading" style="position:absolute; left:0px; top:0px;
                               width:600px; height:70px; z-index:1">
      <img src="images/header.jpg" width="600" height="70"
           alt="Page Heading"/>
    </div>
```

The header image (`header.jpg`), and all the other images used in this sample application are available in the code download for this book at *http://www.glasshaus.com*.

The next piece of code in index.php (see below) is another <div> element, which will contain our application's navigation – the breadcrumb trail we described earlier. In the screenshot at the beginning of this section you could see that the current page was displaying the **Area** 'Western Cape' and provided links to the **Cities** Cape Town and Paarl. In the sidebar is navigation to the sections I browsed through to get to this area – the **Continent** Africa, and the **Country** South Africa. The navigation is generated by sidebar.php (which we will look at below), so it is a simple matter of including this file inside the <div>:

```
    <div id="layNavigation" style="position:absolute; left:2px;
                                top:75px; width:140px; z-index:2">
      <?php include('sidebar.php'); ?>
    </div>
```

Lastly, we have a third <div>, into which we include standard.php (see below for more explanation of this script). standard.php will contain the logic for determining whether we have to display further levels of navigation (countries, areas, or cities), or weather information if we are at City level in the hierarchy.

```
    <div id="layContent" style="position:absolute; left:150px; top:75px;
                             width:450px; z-index:3">
      <?php include_once ('standard.php'); ?>
    </div>
  </body>
</html>
```

That's it for index.php – by using the include() statement we've managed to keep all of our data out of this file, leaving us free to concentrate on the structure of our main screen.

standard.css

This stylesheet improves the look of our main page, index.php. You will notice that, in the index.php code above, there is a <link> to this stylesheet. There is nothing out of the ordinary here:

```
body {
  font-family: Geneva, Arial, Helvetica, sans-serif;
  font-size: 12px;
  font-style: normal;
  font-weight: normal;
  font-variant: normal;
  color: #000000;
}
strong {
  font-size: 12px;
  font-weight: bold;
}
a {
  color : #0066FF;
}
a:VISITED, a:LINK {
  text-decoration : none;
}
a:HOVER, a:ACTIVE {
  text-decoration : underline;
}
```

sidebar.php

As mentioned before, the `sidebar.php` script builds the breadcrumb trail for the user to navigate to previous levels of the hierarchy.

```
<a href='index.php'>Home</a><br />
<?php
```

Since we will be connecting to the database, we include our `weather.php` file here:

```
  include_once('weather.php');
```

What we have to do now is test to see which of the three variables (`$country`, `$area`, or `$city`) are set. We don't have to test for `$continent`, since the only navigation level above Continent level is the home page, and we always provide a link to that.

```
  if (isset($country)) {
```

If we are at Country level, then all we need to do is provide a link to the Continent that that Country is on:

```
    $sql = 'SELECT country.country_continent, continent.* FROM country, continent
            WHERE country_continent=cont_id AND country_id='.$country;
    $cRes = mysql_query($sql) or die(mysql_error());
    if (mysql_num_rows($cRes)==1) {
      $cRow = mysql_fetch_array($cRes);
?>
```

And provide a link back to it:

```
<a href='index.php?continent=<?php echo $cRow['cont_id']; ?>'>
  <?php echo $cRow['cont_name']; ?>
</a><br />

<?php
    }
  }
  if (isset($area)) {
```

If we are at an Area level, then we need to provide links back to the respective Country and Continent:

```
    $sql = 'SELECT area.area_country, country.*, continent.* FROM area, country,
            continent WHERE area_country=country_id AND country_continent=cont_id
            AND area_id='.$area;
    $aRes = mysql_query($sql) or die(mysql_error());
    if (mysql_num_rows($aRes)==1) {
      $aRow = mysql_fetch_array($aRes);
?>

<a href='index.php?continent=<?php echo $aRow['cont_id']; ?>'>
  <?php echo $aRow['cont_name']; ?>
</a><br />
```

```
<a href='index.php?country=<?php echo $aRow['country_id']; ?>'>
  <?php echo $aRow['country_name']; ?>
</a><br />

<?php
    }
  }
  if (isset($city)) {
```

When we are at a City level we need to be able to link back to Area, Country, and Continent. Since we know the structure of our hierarchy, we can get all the information in a single row from our database:

```
    $sql = 'SELECT city.city_area, area.*, country.*, continent.* FROM city, area,
            country, continent WHERE city_area=area_id AND area_country=country_id
            AND country_continent=cont_id AND city_id='.$city;
    $cRes = mysql_query($sql) or die(mysql_error());
    if (mysql_num_rows($cRes)==1) {
      $cRow = mysql_fetch_array($cRes);
?>

<a href='index.php?continent=<?php echo $cRow['cont_id']; ?>'>
  <?php echo $cRow['cont_name']; ?>
</a><br />
<a href='index.php?country=<?php echo $cRow['country_id']; ?>'>
  <?php echo $cRow['country_name']; ?>
</a><br />
<a href='index.php?area=<?php echo $cRow['area_id']; ?>'>
  <?php echo $cRow['area_name']; ?>
</a><br />

<?php
    }
  }
?>
```

That's the sidebar complete.

standard.php

As we mentioned before, this script contains the logic for determining what content to display in the page. The only thing we really need to test for is if the variable `$city` has been set. If it has, then we know that the person has navigated down to an individual city and we can display the weather for that city. Otherwise we have to display further navigation to reach the city level.

As we saw in *Chapter 8*, the first thing we have to do is create an XSLT processor:

```
<?php
  $xsltHnd = xslt_create();
```

We then set the base URI (make sure the path specified here points to where your XSLT is stored):

```
  xslt_set_base($xsltHnd,'file://c:/xml/');
```

If `$city` is set, then we include the script to build the XML document of the current weather, and set the `$xsl` variable to the name of the XSLT stylesheet used for displaying the weather:

```
if (isset($city)) {
  include('mk_weather.php');
  $xsl = 'weather.xsl';
}
```

Otherwise, we include the script to build the XML document of the navigation and set `$xsl` to the XSLT stylesheet for building the navigation:

```
else {
  include('mk_navxml.php');
  $xsl = 'nav.xsl';
}
```

We then set up the `$arguments` array. By creating an associative array, the XML document is identified by the key `/_xml`:

```
$arguments = array(
  '/_xml' => $xml,
);
```

The HTML is then built by applying our XSLT stylesheet to the XML document. Finally, we output the returned HTML. Because we are passing a fifth argument of our associative array, we need to provide a fourth argument. The fourth argument is the result string, but since we are returning the result to `$html`, we can set this argument to `NULL`. The second argument now tells the `xslt_process` function that "the XML document to process can be found in the array specified as the fifth argument, identified by the key `/_xml`".

```
$html = xslt_process ($xsltHnd, 'arg:/_xml', $xsl, NULL, $arguments);
echo $html;
?>
```

mk_navxml.php

The `mk_navxml.php` script is where we start getting into the meat of the application. This script is responsible for creating the XML document that will be the source of the information used to build the actual navigation for our site. Even though we have four possible scenarios in this script (`$area` set – so display cities, `$country` set – so display areas, `$continent` set – so display countries, and nothing set – so display continents) we will want the XML document to be standard across each of these possibilities. If we were building a different XML file for each of these options there would be no real point in using XML for this, other than separating the data and presentation layers of our application.

Before we start building the XML files, let's plan what the XML file will look like. This is a blank 'template' of the XML that we will build:

```
<?xml version="1.0" encoding="UTF-8"?>
<entries>
  <current type=""></current>
  <items>
    <linksto> </linksto>
    <entry id=""> </entry>
  </items>
</entries>
```

The root, or document element of our XML document is <entries>. The <current> element specifies where we currently are in the navigation. The <items> element will contain a <linksto> element to specify what we will link to from this level, and a list of <entry> elements, one for each navigation item at this level – the values specified in the <entry> elements will be used by the XSLT stylesheet later to create the links to the subsequent levels of navigation.

There are three possible scenarios that we need to take into account, so let's look at an example of the XML we will want to produce for each one.

First Scenario – No Sub-Navigation Items

The first scenario is where the user has reached a point in the navigation where there are no sub-navigation items:

```
<?xml version="1.0" encoding="UTF-8"?>
<entries>
  <current type="area" id="2">Natal</current>
  <items>
    <linksto>city</linksto>
  </items>
</entries>
```

Here we have navigated to Natal (a province within South Africa) – our <current> element specifies that we are in an area, the name of which is Natal. However, our <items> collection does not yet contain any <entry> tags, since we have not yet created any subnavigation (City) items.

Second Scenario – Manually Changing Variables in the URL

Another scenario might be where the user manually rewrites the URL in the address bar, perhaps changing one of the variables to see what happens. For example, the URL on my machine for generating the above XML file was *http://skumlet/index.php?continent=1*.

If I now go and change that to *http://skumlet/index.php?continent=7657657*, one of two things can happen. Either the value "7657657" is a valid id for a continent in our database (not very likely), in which case we can simply display the sub-navigation for that continent, or it is not a valid id – in this case we need to tell the user that. The XML document we need to produce should look like this:

```
<?xml version="1.0" encoding="UTF-8"?>
<entries>
  <current>Error</current>
  <error>You appear to have selected an invalid continent</error>
</entries>
```

Since there is no valid current value we put Error in there and leave out the <items> collection. We have also added an <error> tag with a descriptive error message for the user.

Third Scenario – Dealing with Subnavigation Items

Our third and most likely scenario is where there are subnavigation items. This XML document is very similar to our first one, except that the <items> collection will have a number of <entry> elements:

```
<?xml version="1.0" encoding="UTF-8"?>
<entries>
  <current type="continent" id="1">Africa</current>
  <items>
    <linksto>country</linksto>
    <entry id="4">Egypt</entry>
    <entry id="3">Namibia</entry>
    <entry id="2">Nigeria</entry>
    <entry id="1">South Africa</entry>
  </items>
</entries>
```

The `<entry>` tags have an `id`, which is that entrys `id` in the database, as well as the name of that navigation item (in this case country names).

Now let's take a look at the code for building these XML documents:

```
<?php
  include_once('weather.php');
```

As seen below, what we are going to do in this script is build a variable called `$xml`, which will contain the contents of the XML document. We start it off with our header and the document element:

```
  $xml .= '<?xml version="1.0" encoding="UTF-8"?>';
  $xml .= '<entries>';
```

We can then test to see which of our three variables – `$area`, `$country`, or `$continent` – are set. Remember that if `$city` has a value, the logic in `standard.php` will have branched to include the `mk_weather.php` script rather than this one.

```
  if (isset($area)) {
```

The first thing to do is get the current area information. This query has an added advantage of allowing us to test whether the area `id` that has been passed through in the URL is valid:

```
    $sql = 'SELECT * from area WHERE area_id='.$area;
    $tRes = mysql_query($sql) or die(mysql_error());
    if (mysql_num_rows($tRes)==0) {
```

If our query returned no rows, then we know that the area `id` was invalid and we can output an error:

```
      $xml .= ' <current>Error</current>';
      $xml .= ' <error>You appear to have selected an invalid
                area</error>';
    }
```

If the query was valid and we were returned a result, we grab the contents of the row and pop the area name into a variable for later use:

```
    else {
      $tRow = mysql_fetch_array($tRes);
      $area_name = $tRow['area_name'];
```

Then we need to select all of the subnavigation (in this case cities) under this area:

```
    $sql = 'SELECT * FROM city WHERE city_area='.$area.'
            ORDER BY  city_name';
    $cRes = mysql_query($sql) or die(mysql_error());
    $xml .= ' <current type="area" id="'.$area.'">'.$area_name.'</current>';
    $xml .= ' <items>';
    $xml .= ' <linksto>city</linksto>';
```

We can then loop through the result set. We don't need to test to see whether any results were actually returned (if there are results we can output them; if not, then there will be no <entry> tags); we will test for that in our XSLT stylesheet.

```
    while ($cRow = mysql_fetch_array($cRes)) {
      $xml .= ' <entry id="'.$cRow['city_id'].'">'.$cRow['city_name'].'</entry>';
    }
    $xml .= ' </items>';
  }
  $xml .= '</entries>';
}
```

We then do exactly the same for the country – this time we return Areas as <entry> elements:

```
elseif (isset($country)) {
  $sql = 'SELECT * from country WHERE country_id='.$country;
  $tRes = mysql_query($sql) or die(mysql_error());
  if (mysql_num_rows($tRes)==0) {
    $xml .= ' <current>Error</current>';
    $xml .= ' <error>You appear to have selected an invalid country</error>';
  }

  else {
    $tRow = mysql_fetch_array($tRes);
    $country_name = $tRow['country_name'];
    $sql = 'SELECT * FROM area WHERE area_country='.$country.'
            ORDER BY area_name';
    $cRes = mysql_query($sql) or die(mysql_error());
    $xml .= ' <current type="country"
                id="'.$country.'">'.$country_name.'</current>';
    $xml .= ' <items>';
    $xml .= ' <linksto>area</linksto>';
    while ($cRow = mysql_fetch_array($cRes)) {
      $xml .= ' <entry id="'.$cRow['area_id'].'">'.$cRow['area_name'].'</entry>';
    }
    $xml .= ' </items>';
  }
  $xml .= '</entries>';
}
```

And the same again for the continents:

```
    elseif (isset($continent)) {
      $sql = 'SELECT * from continent WHERE cont_id='.$continent;
      $tRes = mysql_query($sql) or die(mysql_error());
      if (mysql_num_rows($tRes)==0) {
        $xml .= ' <current>Error</current>';
        $xml .= ' <error>You appear to have selected an invalid continent</error>';
      }
      else {
        $tRow = mysql_fetch_array($tRes);
        $continent_name = $tRow['cont_name'];
        $sql = 'SELECT * FROM country WHERE country_continent='.$continent.'
                ORDER BY country_name';
        $cRes = mysql_query($sql) or die(mysql_error());
        $xml .= ' <current type="continent"
                 id="'.$continent.'">'.$continent_name.'</current>';
        $xml .= ' <items>';
        $xml .= ' <linksto>country</linksto>';
        while ($cRow = mysql_fetch_array($cRes)) {
         $xml .= ' <entry id="'.$cRow['country_id'].'">'.$cRow['country_name'].'</entry>';
        }
        $xml .= ' </items>';
      }
      $xml .= '</entries>';
    }
```

If neither `$continent`, `$country` nor `$area` have been set, we are at the top level, and will therefore display a list of continents:

```
    else {
      $sql = 'SELECT * FROM continent ORDER BY cont_name';
      $cRes = mysql_query($sql) or die(mysql_error());
      $xml .= ' <current type="home">Home</current>';
      $xml .= ' <items>';
      $xml .= ' <type>home</type>';
      $xml .= ' <linksto>continent</linksto>';
      while ($cRow = mysql_fetch_array($cRes)) {
        $xml .= ' <entry id="'.$cRow['cont_id'].'">'.$cRow['cont_name'].'</entry>';
      }
      $xml .= ' </items>';
      $xml .= '</entries>';
    }
  ?>
```

At the end of this script our `$xml` variable contains an XML document, which we then transform into XHTML – this happens in the `standard.php` script as we saw earlier:

```
  $html = xslt_process($xsltHnd, 'arg:/_xml', $xsl, NULL, $arguments);
```

nav.xsl

Now let's take a look at the XSLT stylesheet we'll use to transform the XML document we created in the previous script into the XHTML that we will display in the page. We start off with the XML declaration, and the opening `<xsl:stylesheet>` element, with relevant namespace, and versioning:

```
<?xml version="1.0"?>
<xsl:stylesheet version="1.0" xmlns:xsl="http://www.w3.org/1999/XSL/Transform">
 <xsl:output method="html"/>
```

Since we will be using the value of `entries/items/linksto`, we grab it and store it in a variable. Since we're dealing with an XSLT stylesheet here, the variables we'll talk about in this section are XSL variables:

```
  <xsl:variable name="linksto">
    <xsl:value-of select="entries/items/linksto"/>
  </xsl:variable>
```

We set another variable called `numLinks` that contains the number of subnavigation links that we have. We can use this value later to determine whether any links exist or not:

```
  <xsl:variable name="numLinks">
    <xsl:value-of select="count(entries/items/entry)" />
  </xsl:variable>
  <xsl:template match="/">
```

Unfortunately XSLT does not have an `If ... Else` language structure, so we have to use the `<xsl:choose>` element to simulate an `If ... Else`:

```
    <xsl:choose>
```

When we have an error, we output an error message:

```
      <xsl:when test="//entries/current='Error'">
        <h4>Error</h4>
        <xsl:value-of select="entries/error" />
      </xsl:when>
```

If there is not an error, then we can display the details:

```
      <xsl:otherwise>
        <h4>Current: <xsl:value-of select="entries/current" /></h4>
```

We use another `<xsl:choose>` element to determine whether we have any subnavigation or not. If not, rather than outputting nothing, we tell the browser that there are no links:

```
        <xsl:choose>
          <xsl:when test="$numLinks=0">
            There is currently no
            <xsl:value-of select="$linksto" />
            in the database under
            <xsl:value-of select="entries/current" />
          </xsl:when>
```

If we have links, let's display them. We'll use the value of the `$linksto` variable to create the URL that we are linking to:

```
          <xsl:otherwise>
            <p>Please select a <xsl:value-of select="$linksto" />:</p>
            <xsl:for-each select="entries/items/entry">
              <a>
                <xsl:attribute name="href">
                  index.php?
                  <xsl:value-of select="$linksto" />
                  =
                  <xsl:value-of select="@id" />
                </xsl:attribute>
                <xsl:value-of select="." />
              </a><br />
            </xsl:for-each>
          </xsl:otherwise>
        </xsl:choose>
```

An example of the XHTML that we will get from this is as follows:

```
<p>Please select a country:</p>
<a href='index.php?country=4'>Egypt</a><br />
<a href='index.php?country=3'>Namibia</a><br />
<a href='index.php?country=2'>Nigeria</a><br />
<a href='index.php?country=1'>South Africa</a><br />
```

Once we are done displaying all the links, we display a form to add a new entry at the current level:

```
        <p>
          Add a new <xsl:value-of select="$linksto" />:<br />
          <form action="addnew.php" method="POST">
```

In addition to the new entry itself, we also need to pass the level at which we are adding this entry, the `id` of the parent record, and the current level that we are at. The level that we are adding the entry into will determine which table we need to insert the record into; the parent `id` will then be inserted into the record and the current level that we are at will be used to redirect us back to our current page once the record has been inserted:

```
            <xsl:text disable-output-escaping="yes">
              &lt;input type="hidden" name="current" value="
            </xsl:text><xsl:value-of select="entries/current/@type" />
            <xsl:text disable-output-escaping="yes">
              " /&gt;
            </xsl:text>
            <xsl:text disable-output-escaping="yes">
              &lt;input type="hidden" name="parent" value="
            </xsl:text><xsl:value-of select="entries/current/@id" />
            <xsl:text disable-output-escaping="yes">
              " /&gt;
            </xsl:text>
            <xsl:text disable-output-escaping="yes">
```

```
            &lt;input type="hidden" name="into" value="
          </xsl:text>
          <xsl:value-of select="$linksto" />
          <xsl:text disable-output-escaping="yes">
            " /&gt;
          </xsl:text>
          <input type="text" name="entry" /> <br />
          <input type="submit" value="Add" />
        </form>
      </p>
```

The form slots into a position within the `<xsl:choose>` elements, so it is only displayed if we have a valid record.

```
        </xsl:otherwise>
      </xsl:choose>
    </xsl:template>
  </xsl:stylesheet>
```

addnew.php

Our form calls the `addnew.php` script when we want to insert a new navigation entry.

```
<?php
  include_once('weather.php');
```

The form that our data is coming from looks fairly simple:

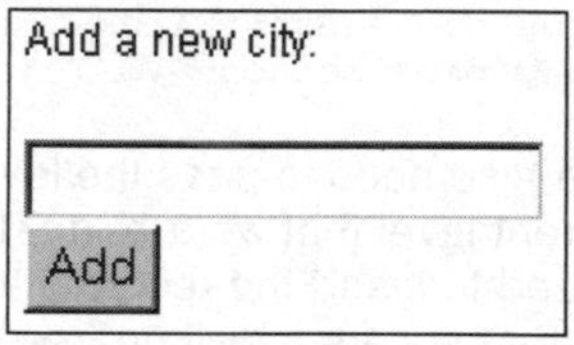

However, remember, it also includes hidden fields that contain the current navigation-level type (continent, country or area), it's `id`, and the type of navigation that we will add.

First we grab the values of the `<input>` elements from the `$_POST` global array. It's not necessary to do this – we could use the `$_POST` global array throughout our code – but this makes our code easier to understand.

```
  $into = $_POST['into'];
  $current = $_POST['current'];
  $parent = $_POST['parent'];
  $entry = $_POST['entry'];
```

Since we don't want to include any blank records, we first test to see whether the user has entered anything into the form, and then, depending on the value of `$into` (the variable containing the type of entry that we are adding), we set `$sql`:

```
    if (strlen(trim($entry)) > 0) {
      switch ($into) {
        case 'continent':
        $sql = 'INSERT into continent (cont_name) VALUES
                ("'.htmlspecialchars($entry,ENT_QUOTES).'")';
        break;
        case 'country':
        $sql = 'INSERT into country (country_name, country_continent) VALUES
                ("'.htmlspecialchars($entry,ENT_QUOTES).'",'.$parent.')';
        break;
        case 'area':
        $sql = 'INSERT into area (area_name, area_country) VALUES
                ("'.htmlspecialchars($entry,ENT_QUOTES).'",'.$parent.')';
        break;
        case 'city':
        $sql = 'INSERT into city (city_name, city_area) VALUES
                ("'.htmlspecialchars($entry,ENT_QUOTES).'",'.$parent.')';
        break;
```

If `$into` is not set for some reason, or the user has not entered a value in the form, we set `$sql` to a blank string. We can then use this as a test condition around the line that calls the SQL query:

```
        default:
        $sql = '';
        break;
      }
    }
    else {
      $sql ='';
    }
```

If `$sql` is not empty, we insert the record and then redirect to the page we were just on. `$current` contains the level that we were at, while `$parent` contains the `id` of that entry:

```
    if (strlen($sql) > 0) {
      mysql_query($sql) or die(mysql_error());
    }
    header('Location: index.php?'.$current.'='.$parent);
  ?>
```

At this point we have completed all of the code to build the navigation of the site. Test it out, and you should see something like this:

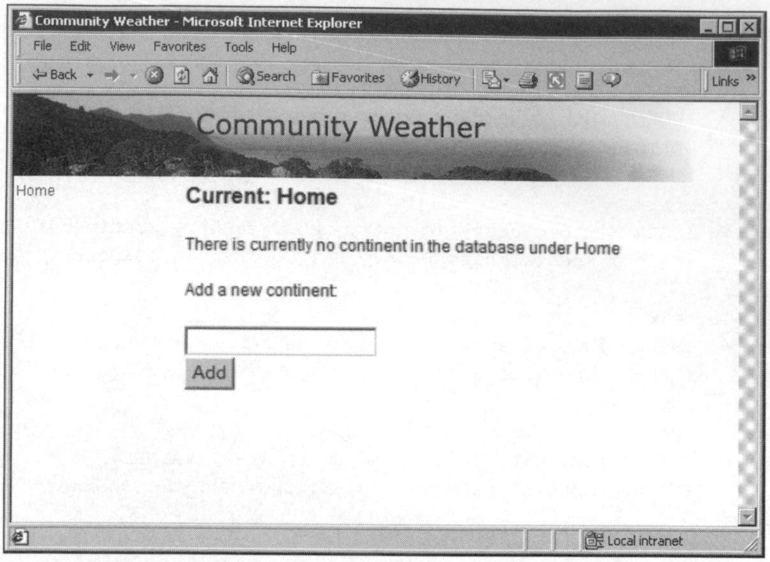

Once we add a continent (in this case, Africa), navigate to it, and add some country navigation elements, our page will look like this:

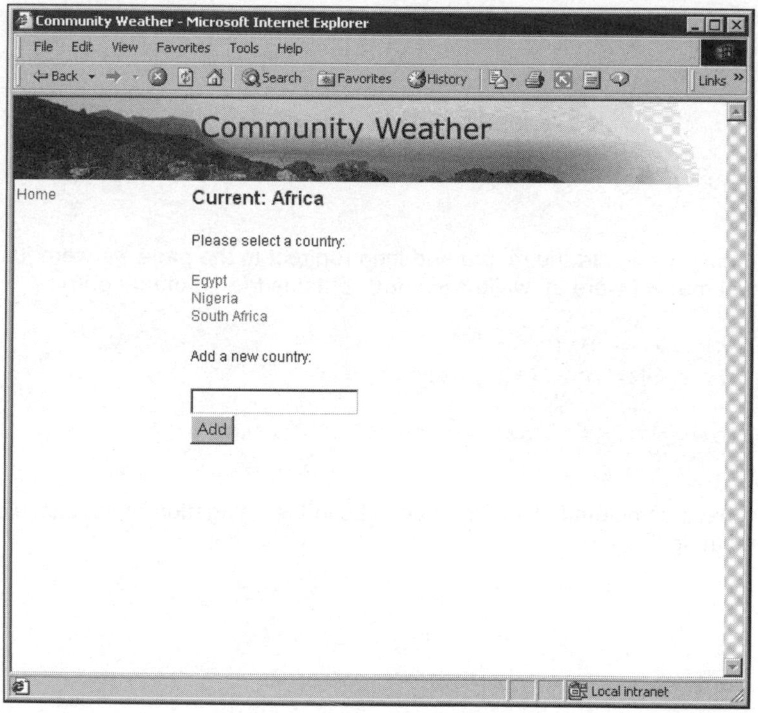

mk_weather.php

The last three scripts that we have to write handle the actual weather information. As we did for the navigation, we will have a script to generate the weather XML, an XSLT stylesheet to transform the XML, and a script to add a new weather report.

Once again we will have 3 possible scenarios.

First Scenario – No Current Weather Reports

The first is where we have no current weather reports for the selected city:

```
<?xml version="1.0" encoding="UTF-8"?>
<weather>
  <city id="1">Cape Town</city>
  <weathertypes>
    <type id="1">sunny</type>
    <type id="2">windy</type>
    <type id="3">cloudy</type>
    <type id="4">rain</type>
    <type id="6">rainstorms</type>
    <type id="7">snow</type>
    <type id="8">snowstorms</type>
  </weathertypes>
</weather>
```

The `<weather>` element is our document element. We need to specify the current city name and it's `id` in the database (the `id` will be used in the form we build later so that we know which city to link the report with).

Since we will be building a form in our page, we need to give the user a list of weather types to choose from. The `<weathertypes>` element contains a list of weather types from the database for us to use in building the form.

Second Scenario – User Enters an Invalid City id

The second scenario is where the user has edited the URL and the city is not valid:

```
<?xml version="1.0" encoding="UTF-8"?>
<weather>
  <city>Error</city>
  <error>You appear to have selected an invalid city</error>
</weather>
```

Again, in this scenario we provide the user with an informative error message.

Third Scenario – Current Weather Reports Available

The third scenario is where we have current weather reports for the city. In this case we want to include the weather conditions as well as the possible weather types:

```
<?xml version="1.0" encoding="UTF-8"?>
<weather>
  <city id="1">Cape Town</city>
```

```
    <temperature>
      <minimum>12</minimum>
      <maximum>22</maximum>
    </temperature>
    <outlook>sunny</outlook>
    <weathertypes>
      <type id="1">sunny</type>
      <type id="2">windy</type>
      <type id="3">cloudy</type>
      <type id="4">rain</type>
      <type id="6">rainstorms</type>
      <type id="7">snow</type>
      <type id="8">snowstorms</type>
    </weathertypes>
  </weather>
```

The <temperature> element gives us the minimum and maximum, and the <outlook> element is the current outlook for the city – therefore it contains one of the defined weather types. Now that you have seen examples of the XML our code will be creating, let's take a look at the code itself:

```
<?php
  include_once('weather.php');
  $xml = '<?xml version="1.0" encoding="UTF-8"?>';
  $xml .= '<weather>';
```

Our first query grabs the city name, as well as allowing us to test whether the city `id` is valid or not:

```
  $sql = 'SELECT * FROM city WHERE city_id='.$city;
  $cRes = mysql_query($sql) or die(mysql_error());
```

If the city `id` that we have been passed is not valid, we produce an error, as follows:

```
  if (mysql_num_rows($cRes)==0) {
    $xml .= '<city>Error</city>';
    $xml .= '<error>You appear to have selected an invalid city</error>';
  }
```

If, on the other hand, we have a valid city, we follow this code, and grab the current weather reports:

```
  else {
    $cRow = mysql_fetch_array($cRes);
    $cityname = $cRow['city_name'];
```

We only want current weather reports to be included in our report of the weather – entries that were added 3 days ago are hardly relevant now. We'll say that anything added in the last 8 hours is current and we can use those. We declare a variable – `$weatherWindow` – and set its value to the current time, less 8 hours:

```
    $weatherWindow = time() - 28800;
    $xml .= '<city id="'.$city.'">'.$cityname.'</city>';
```

We don't really need to keep old weather entries in the database, so instead of using the `$weatherWindow` variable in our `SELECT` statements, we can rather use it to delete all the old records and then just select all the records that are left.

```
$sql = 'DELETE FROM weather WHERE weather_city='.$city.' AND
        weather_date <   '.$weatherWindow;
mysql_query($sql) or die($sql);
```

Our next query is going to grab the number of times that each weather type occurs for the specified city. If 18 people say that it's sunny and 1 person reckons it's raining, we can safely assume it's sunny. We could get clever here and analyze the changes of weather type over the 8 hour period and make a decision based on that – it is quite feasible that the weather can change – but we are looking at how we can utilize XML, not developing algorithms for analyzing meteorological data!

```
$sql = 'SELECT count(weather.weather_type) AS tOrder, weathertype.type_name
        FROM weather, weathertype WHERE weather_type=type_id
        AND weather_city='.$city.' GROUP BY weather_type ORDER BY tOrder DESC';
$wRes = mysql_query($sql) or die(mysql_error());
```

If we get no records returned, there are obviously no current weather reports, so we don't add any weather-specific data. Just as we tested for this in the XSL file for the navigation, we will do the same here:

```
if (mysql_num_rows($wRes)>0) {
  $wRow = mysql_fetch_array($wRes);
```

If we have results, then we can grab the minimum and maximum values. We'll do that by getting the average temperature that people put in for each. The `AVG` function returns a floating-point number, so we'll need to round that off.

```
  $sql = 'SELECT ROUND(AVG(weather_max)) AS maxavg FROM weather
          WHERE weather_city='.$city;
  $wMaxRes = mysql_query($sql) or die($sql);
  $wMaxRow = mysql_fetch_array($wMaxRes);
  $sql = 'SELECT ROUND(AVG(weather_min)) AS minavg FROM weather
          WHERE weather_city='.$city;
  $wMinRes = mysql_query($sql) or die($sql);
  $wMinRow = mysql_fetch_array($wMinRes);
  $xml .= '<temperature>';
  $xml .= ' <minimum>'.$wMinRow['minavg'].'</minimum>';
  $xml .= ' <maximum>'.$wMaxRow['maxavg'].'</maximum>';
  $xml .= '</temperature>';
  $xml .= '<outlook>'.$wRow['type_name'].'</outlook>';
}
```

We're done with the city-specific weather, so we output the available weather types:

```
$xml .= '<weathertypes>';
$sql = 'SELECT type_id, type_name FROM weathertype';
$tRes = mysql_query($sql) or die($sql);
while ($tRow = mysql_fetch_array($tRes)) {
```

```
        $xml .= ' <type id="'.$tRow['type_id'].'">'.$tRow['type_name'].'</type>';
      }
      $xml .= '</weathertypes>';
    }
    $xml .= '</weather>';
?>
```

weather.xsl

As we did with the navigation, we need an XSLT stylesheet to transform our data:

```
<?xml version="1.0"?>
<xsl:stylesheet version="1.0" xmlns:xsl="http://www.w3.org/1999/XSL/Transform">
  <xsl:output method="html" />
```

We'll need to test to see whether we got any weather results back, so we grab the `count()` of weather/temperature and store that in a variable. The value would be 1 if we got results, or 0 if there were no results.

```
    <xsl:variable name="numTemp">
      <xsl:value-of select="count(weather/temperature)" />
    </xsl:variable>
    <xsl:template match="/">
    <xsl:choose>
```

We then test to see if there was an error:

```
      <xsl:when test="//weather/city='Error'">
        <h4>Error</h4>
        <xsl:value-of select="weather/error" />
      </xsl:when>
```

If not, we display the weather details:

```
      <xsl:otherwise>
        <h4>Weather for <xsl:value-of select="weather/city" /></h4>
        <xsl:choose>
```

If `$numTemp` is 0, then we didn't get any weather details and we display a message to that effect:

```
          <xsl:when test="$numTemp=0">
            There are currently no entries for
            <xsl:value-of select="weather/city" />
          </xsl:when>
          <xsl:otherwise>
```

Since we don't have a worldwide temperature to use, we'll be storing all of our temperatures in Celsius. On our page we'll want to display the temperature in both Celsius and Fahrenheit, so we'll need to convert the temperatures here:

```
<xsl:variable name="MinF">
  <xsl:value-of select="round(((weather/temperature/minimum * 9) div 5)
                        + 32)" />
</xsl:variable>
<xsl:variable name="MaxF">
  <xsl:value-of select="round(((weather/temperature/maximum * 9) div 5)
                        + 32)" />
</xsl:variable>
```

For the weather outlook, I made some images to put in the page and add some spice. However, since you should be rewarded for buying this book and not made to suffer what passes for artwork in my world, I got someone else to redesign them:

Thanks to Gavin Cromhaut for the images – for more information on books he has contributed to, go to http://www.friendsofed.com/photoshop/index.html.

The image selection is performed as follows:

```
<strong>Outlook:</strong><br />
<xsl:text disable-output-escaping="yes">
  &lt;img src="images/
</xsl:text>
<xsl:value-of select="weather/outlook" />
<xsl:text disable-output-escaping="yes">
  .jpg" width="100" height="80" alt="
</xsl:text>
<xsl:value-of select="weather/outlook" />
<xsl:text disable-output-escaping="yes">
  " /&gt;
</xsl:text><br />
```

We then put the minimum and maximum temperatures (in both Celsius and Fahrenheit) in a table:

```
        <table border="0">
          <tr>
            <td></td>
            <td><strong>Celsius</strong></td>
            <td><strong>Fahrenheit</strong></td>
          </tr>
          <tr>
            <td><strong>Minimum</strong></td>
            <td><xsl:value-of select="weather/temperature/minimum" /></td>
            <td><xsl:value-of select="$MinF" /></td>
          </tr>
          <tr>
            <td><strong>Maximum</strong></td>
            <td><xsl:value-of select="weather/temperature/maximum" /></td>
            <td><xsl:value-of select="$MaxF" /></td>
          </tr>
        </table>
      </xsl:otherwise>
    </xsl:choose>
```

and then include a form for the user to add a new weather report.

```
    <p>
      <hr />
      Add a new entry:<br />
      <form action="addweather.php" method="POST">
```

We need to include the current city `id`, so that we can link this weather report to the city in the database:

```
        <xsl:text disable-output-escaping="yes">
          &lt;input type="hidden" name="city" value="
        </xsl:text>
        <xsl:value-of select="weather/city/@id" />
        <xsl:text disable-output-escaping="yes">
          " /&gt;
        </xsl:text>
        Minimum: <input type="text" name="min" size="2" maxlength="3" /><br />
        Maximum: <input type="text" name="max" size="2" maxlength="3" /><br />
```

We also provide a way of letting the user specify what unit the temperature is in:

```
        Temperature is in:
        <select name="temptype">
          <option value="C">Celsius</option>
          <option value="F">Fahrenheit</option>
        </select><br />
```

And a list of the available weather types:

```
              Weather:
              <select name="weather">
                <xsl:for-each select="weather/weathertypes/type">
                  <xsl:text disable-output-escaping="yes">
                    &lt;option value="
                  </xsl:text>
                  <xsl:value-of select="@id"/>
                  <xsl:text disable-output-escaping="yes">
                    "&gt;
                  </xsl:text>
                  <xsl:value-of select="." />
                  <xsl:text disable-output-escaping="yes">
                    &lt;/option&gt;
                  </xsl:text>
                </xsl:for-each>
              </select><br />
              <input type="submit" value="Add" />
            </form>
          </p>
        </xsl:otherwise>
      </xsl:choose>
    </xsl:template>
  </xsl:stylesheet>
```

addweather.php

The last script that we need to write is for taking the contents of the form, and adding the data to the database:

```
  <?php
```

Since all the temperatures will be stored in Celsius, we will use a function to take the temperatures that were entered and convert them to Celsius. Rather than have the logic for determining whether a temperature is in Celsius or Fahrenheit in the code itself, we'll do that inside the function (`alterTemp()`):

```
  function alterTemp($temperature, $current) {
    if ($current=='C') {
```

If the current temperature is Celsius, then we don't need to do anything and can return the temperature as is:

```
      $newtemp = $temperature;
    }
```

If it's Fahrenheit, then we convert to Celsius and return that:

```
    else {
      $newtemp = ((($temperature -32) * 5) / 9);
    }
    return $newtemp;
  }
  include_once('weather.php');
```

```
    mysql_connect($wdb_host, $wdb_user, $wdb_pass);
    mysql_select_db($wdb_name);
    $city = $_POST['city'];
    $min = $_POST['min'];
    $max = $_POST['max'];
    $weather = $_POST['weather'];
    $temptype = $_POST['temptype'];
```

We want to make sure that the person has entered valid numeric values for the minimum and maximum temperatures – if they have then we can enter the information into the database.

```
    if (is_numeric($min) && is_numeric($max)) {
      $sql = 'INSERT INTO weather (weather_city, weather_date, weather_min,
                                   weather_max, weather_type)
              VALUES ('.$city.','.time().','.alterTemp($min,$temptype).',
                      '.alterTemp($max,$temptype).','.$weather.')';
    }
    else {
      $sql = 'SELECT (1+1)';
    }
    mysql_query($sql) or die(mysql_error());
    header('Location: index.php?city='.$city);
?>
```

And that's it – you can go ahead and test it out. Your page should look something like this:

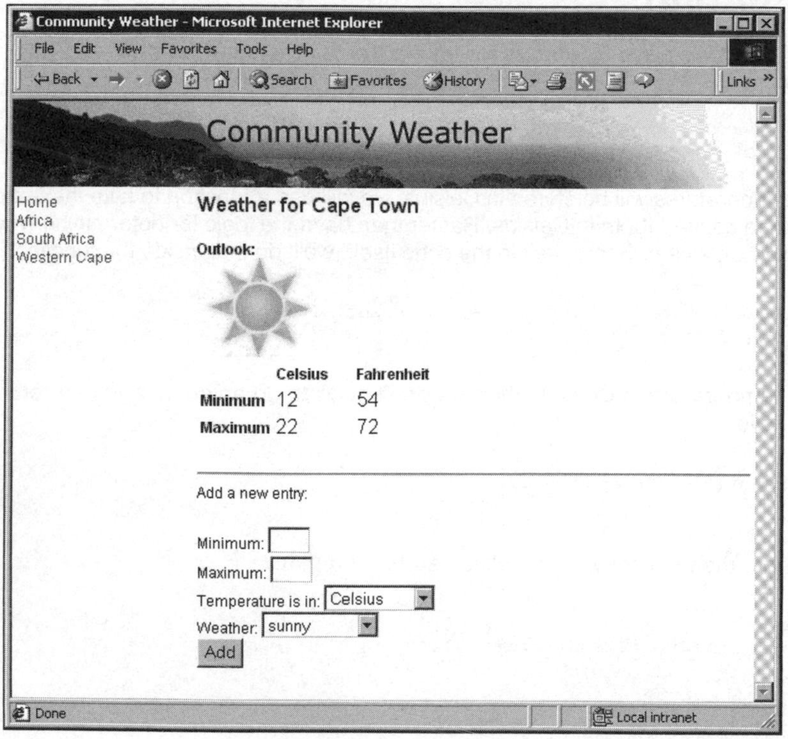

Summary

In this chapter we've looked at how we can use XML and XSLT within PHP to implement a fully operational weather portal application. Our application had two main areas that required XSL transformations – the navigation and the content of the page itself. We saw how we could take our data from the MySQL database and construct a standard XML file to cover every eventuality in the navigation and content, thereby minimizing the number of XSLT stylesheets we had to create.

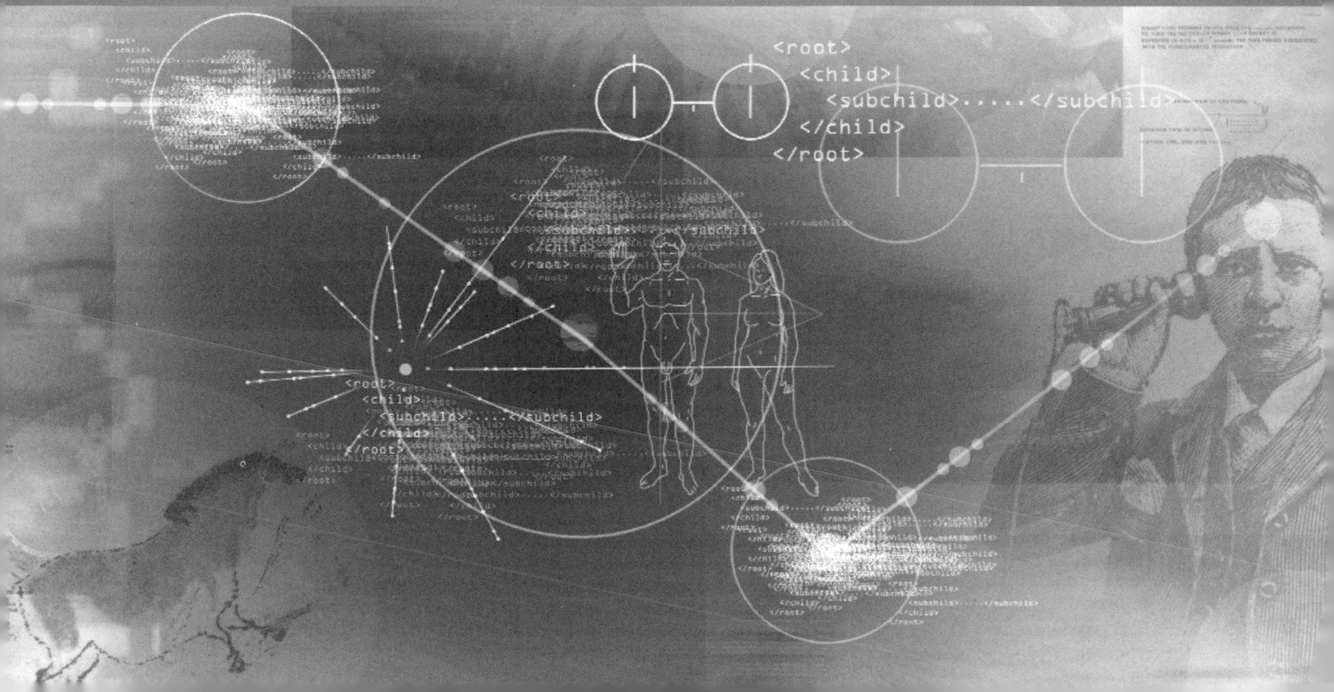
<root>
<child>
<subchild>.....</subchild>
</child>
</root>

Index

A Guide to the Index

The index is arranged alphabetically in word-by-word order (so that, for example, New York would appear before Newark), with any symbol prefixes ignored and asterisks used to represent variant endings. Acronyms have been preferred to their expansions as main entries as they are easier to recall. Unmodified entries generally represent the main treatment of a topic; sub-headings relate to particular aspects. Please send any comments or suggestions specifically about the index to *billj@glasshaus.com.*

A

D

E

F

G

H

I

M

N

O

P

Q

R

S

V

W

X

Z

Notes

Notes

glasshaus

web professional to web professional

glasshaus writes books for you. Any suggestions, or ideas about how you want information given in your ideal book will be studied by our team. Your comments are always valued at glasshaus.

Free phone in USA 800-873 9769
Fax (312) 893 8001

UK Tel.: (0121) 687 4100 Fax: (0121) 687 4101

Practical XML for the Web – Registration Card

Name ______

Address ______

______

______

______

City ______ State/Region ______

Country ______ Postcode/Zip ______

E-Mail ______

Occupation ______

How did you hear about this book?

- ❐ Book review (name) ______
- ❐ Advertisement (name) ______
- ❐ Recommendation ______
- ❐ Catalog ______
- ❐ Other ______

Where did you buy this book?

- ❐ Bookstore (name) ______ City ______
- ❐ Computer store (name) ______
- ❐ Mail order ______
- ❐ Other ______

What influenced you in the purchase of this book?

❐ Cover Design ❐ Contents ❐ Other (please specify):

______

How did you rate the overall content of this book?

❐ Excellent ❐ Good ❐ Average ❐ Poor

What did you find most useful about this book? ______

______

______

What did you find least useful about this book? ______

______

______

Please add any additional comments. ______

______

______

What other subjects will you buy a computer book on soon?

______

What is the best computer book you have used this year?

______

Note: This information will only be used to keep you updated about new glasshaus titles and will not be used for any other purpose or passed to any other third party.

Check here if you DO NOT want to receive support for this book ❐

1086

glasshaus

web professional to web professional

Note: If you post the bounce back card below in the UK, please send it to:

glasshaus, Arden House, 1102 Warwick Road,
Acocks Green, Birmingham B27 6HB. UK.

Computer Book Publishers

NO POSTAGE
NECESSARY
IF MAILED
IN THE
UNITED STATES

BUSINESS REPLY MAIL

FIRST CLASS MAIL PERMIT#64 CHICAGO, IL

POSTAGE WILL BE PAID BY ADDRESSEE

glasshaus
29 S. LA SALLE ST.,
SUITE 520
CHICAGO IL 60603-USA